PENGUIN CLASSICS

DEMOCRACY IN AMERICA

ALEXIS DE TOCQUEVILLE was born in 1805 into an aristocratic French family with connections to both the Church and the Bourbon monarchy. He acquired his liberal sympathies from intensive study of French and English Constitutional history, which was to prove formative to his lifelong concern with liberty and the availability of choice. Impressive academic achievements led to a legal career in government service in 1827. It was as a junior magistrate at Versailles that he met Gustave de Beaumont, the man with whom he would travel to America to prepare a study of their penal system for the French government.

After a lengthy journey around the United States with his companion, Tocqueville left the report on penal reform for Beaumont to complete, and turned his attention to other work. The result of this was his hugely influential two-volume *Democracy in America*, the first volume of which was published in 1835 (at which point he also married Mary Mottley, an Englishwoman) and the second in 1840. The book secured both his reputation as a writer and thinker, and his election to the prestigious Académie Française in 1841.

In 1839 Tocqueville was elected to the Chambre des Députés, a post he held until the 1848 revolution when he abandoned politics after a brief period as foreign minister to Louis Bonaparte.

His last, and arguably most significant, work, *L'Ancien Régime and the French Revolution*, was partially published in 1856. Tocqueville died in 1859 prior to its completion.

GERALD BEVAN was educated at King Edward's School, Five Ways, in Birmingham, St John's College, Cambridge, where he studied Modern and Medieval Languages, and Balliol College, Oxford. His career in the teaching of French, Latin and Religious Studies ended in 1993 at St Albans School, as Director of Studies and Head of Modern Languages. He specializes in French literature from the seventeenth, eighteenth, and nineteenth centuries. He collaborated in a translation of Cassiodorus' *De Anima* during the 1970s and retirement is now allowing him to expand his interest in translation.

ISAAC KRAMNICK is the Richard J. Schwartz Professor of Government and the Vice Provost for Undergraduate Education at Cornell University in Ithaca, New York. His writings in political theory include studies of Bolingbroke and Burke, and *Republicanism and Bourgeois Radicalism*. He is the co-author (with Barry Sheerman, MP) of a biography of Harold Laski and a co-author (with R. Laurence Moore) of a book on church and state in America, *The Godless Constitution*. He has also edited *The Federalist Papers* and Thomas Paine's *Common Sense* for Penguin Classics and the *Portable Enlightenment Reader* for Viking.

ALEXIS DE TOCQUEVILLE

Democracy in America

and Two Essays on America

Translated by GERALD E. BEVAN
with an Introduction and Notes by
ISAAC KRAMNICK

PENGUIN BOOKS

PENGUIN BOOKS

Published by the Penguin Group
Penguin Books Ltd, 80 Strand, London WC2R ORL, England
Penguin Putnam Inc., 375 Hudson Street, New York, New York 10014, USA
Penguin Books Australia Ltd, 250 Camberwell Road, Camberwell, Victoria 3124, Australia
Penguin Books Canada Ltd, 10 Alcorn Avenue, Toronto, Ontario, Canada M4V 3B2
Penguin Books India (P) Ltd, 11, Community Centre, Panchsheel Park, New Delhi – 110 017, India
Penguin Books (NZ) Ltd, Cnr Rosedale and Airborne Roads, Albany, Auckland, New Zealand
Penguin Books (South Africa) (Pty) Ltd, 24 Sturdee Avenue, Rosebank 2196, South Africa

Penguin Books Ltd, Registered Offices: 80 Strand, London WC2R ORL, England

www.penguin.com

These translations of *Democracy in America*, "Two Weeks in the Wilderness",
and "Excursion to Lake Oneida" first published in 2003.

14

Translations and Translator's Note copyright © Gerald Bevan, 2003
Introduction and Notes copyright © Isaac Kramnick, 2003
All rights reserved

The moral rights of the editors have been asserted

Set in 10.25/12.25 pt PostScript Adobe Sabon
Typeset by Rowland Phototypesetting Ltd, Bury St Edmunds, Suffolk
Printed in England by Clays Ltd, St Ives plc

ISBN-13: 978-0-140-44760-6

www.greenpenguin.co.uk

Penguin Books is committed to a sustainable future
for our business, our readers and our planet.
The book in your hands is made from paper
certified by the Forest Stewardship Council.

Mixed Sources
Product group from well-managed
forests and other controlled sources
www.fsc.org Cert no. SA-COC-1592
© 1996 Forest Stewardship Council
FSC

Contents

Democracy in America

Chronology

1805 Born in Paris, on 29 July to Hervé, Comte de Tocqueville, and Louise-Madeleine, Comtesse de Tocqueville, French Catholic aristocrats

1809 James Madison elected American President

1812 War of 1812 breaks out between Great Britain and the United States

1814 Napoleon falls and the Bourbon monarchy is restored under Louis XVIII

1817 James Munroe elected American President

1820–23 Tocqueville studies at the Collège Royal in Metz, where his father is Prefect

1823–7 Tocqueville studies law in Paris

1824 Charles X succeeds to the French throne

1825 John Quincy Adams elected American President

1827 Tocqueville granted an appointment as a minor judicial officer in the Versailles court of law

1829 Andrew Jackson elected American President

1830 Charles X's edicts restricting suffrage and censoring the press spark a revolution on 27 July which brings his reign to an end

1830 The 'July' Monarchy of Louis-Philippe begins on 7 August

1831 Tocqueville and his companion Gustave de Beaumont arrive in Newport, Rhode Island, on 9 May, for their nine-month visit to America

1832 President Andrew Jackson vetoes a bill on 10 July to extend the charter of the Bank of the United States

1833 Tocqueville publishes *Du Système pénitentiare aux États-Unis* with co-author Beaumont; first visit to England

1835 January. Publication of *Democracy in America* Part I
Second Visit to England

1835 Marriage to Mary Mottley, an Englishwoman

1836 Journey to Switzerland

1837 Martin van Buran elected American President

1839 Tocqueville elected to the French Chamber of Deputies;
writes 'Report on the Abolition of Slavery'

1840 Tocqueville publishes the two volumes of Part II of
Democracy in America

1841 Journey to Algeria

1841 Tocqueville elected to the Académie Française

1841 William Henry Harrison elected American President and
dies after one month of service

1841 John Tyler takes over the American Presidency

1845 James Polk elected American President

1846 Second journey to Algeria

1848 Revolution in Paris: Louis-Philippe abdicates the French
throne on 24 February amidst growing popular demands by
republican and socialist reformers for change

1848 Tocqueville elected in April to the Constituent Assembly
for the Second Republic; later appointed French Foreign Minister by Louis Napoleon

1848 Louis Napoleon Bonaparte, nephew of Napoleon, elected
President of the French Second Republic in December

1849 Zachery Taylor elected American President. He dies after
only sixteen months in office

1850–51 Stay in Italy: writes *Souvenirs*, his unfinished book on
the 1848 Revolution

1850 Millard Fillmore succeeds Taylor in American Presidency

1851 Louis Napoleon forcibly dissolves the Assembly

1851 Tocqueville resists the *coup d'état* of Louis Napoleon, is
arrested and briefly imprisoned

1852 Louis Napoleon declares himself Emperor, as Napoleon
III

1852 Tocqueville begins *L'Ancien Régime et la Révolution*

1853 Studies at the Tours Archives

1853 Franklin Pierce elected American President

1854 Journey to Germany

1856 Death of his father
1856 Publication of *L'Ancien Régime et la Révolution*
1857 James Buchanan elected American President
1859 Having moved to Cannes for health reasons, he dies there
of tuberculosis. He is buried three weeks later in his chateau
in Normandy

Introduction

I

If the number of times an individual is cited by politicians, journalists, and scholars is a measure of their influence, Alexis de Tocqueville—not Jefferson, Madison, or Lincoln—is America's public philosopher. Since the 1950s, Tocqueville has been a towering presence in American life. Every president since Dwight D. Eisenhower has quoted *Democracy in America*, which Tocqueville wrote after his nine-month visit to America in 1831. During the Cold War, while the Soviet Union had the German Karl Marx as its official philosopher, America had Tocqueville, the Frenchman who in the nineteenth century saw the democratic future in America.

Not that his influence and visibility have declined with the end of the Cold War. In summer 1996, both Bill Clinton and Newt Gingrich cited Tocqueville in speeches to their party conventions. Indeed, a year earlier, in his first address to the nation as Speaker of the House, Gingrich claimed Tocqueville's book as a prophetic anticipation of the Republican's "Contract with America". He put it on a list of "required reading" for the members of Congress. Not to be outdone, Hillary Clinton offered the same text in 1996 as the best place to find the caring civil society she envisioned in her book *It Takes a Village*.

Tocqueville is everywhere in the United States, pervading its public discourse. In 1978, Eugene McCarthy, the senator from Minnesota and former presidential candidate, wrote a book which explored contemporary American problems from the perspective of what Tocqueville had written about them in the nineteenth century. Three years later, on the 150th anniversary of his visit to America, the journalist Richard Reeves retraced Tocqueville's seven thousand mile journey across the country east of the Mississippi in search of the pulse of Ronald Reagan's America. His book, *American Journey: Traveling with Tocqueville in Search of Democracy in America*, found striking continuities in the intervening century and a half, even though for some unexplained reason his twentieth-century journey added up to eighteen thousand miles.

By the end of the twentieth century, by far the most ambitious tribute to Tocqueville was to be found on C-SPAN, the noncommercial public service established by America's cable television network industry and received by more than seventy million American households. For nine months in 1997–8, C-SPAN's high-tech TV truck followed Tocqueville's path and beamed live television shows from the towns, cities, farms, forests, and rivers that Tocqueville had visited. Timing their programs to correspond to the exact day Tocqueville had made his original stops, beginning as he did in May and ending the following February, the network's sixty-five hours of live programing were supported by annotated route maps, reading materials, an interactive web site, and local town hall discussions. The network offered teachers detailed lesson plans and copies of the series videos for classroom use. In 1998 it was all put together in a book and published as *Traveling Tocqueville's America*. The book's preface offered as the original inspiration for this mammoth enterprise the network's collective curiosity about Tocqueville which had been aroused by the hundreds of political speeches it had covered since its creation in 1979 in which "political figures, presidents and congressmen, liberals and conservatives" quote from Tocqueville's *Democracy in America*.[1]

No book, speech, or article on almost any American subject in recent decades is considered complete without some thoughtful words, not from Jefferson, but from Tocqueville. Reporters especially love to quote him, following the *New York Times'* James Reston's enthusiastic suggestion that "Tocqueville's observations are still as fresh as this morning's newspapers."[2]

Use of Tocqueville is so widespread that some journalists even
question the whole phenomenon. In 1984, the *Washington Post*,
for example, noted that "citing Tocqueville is a bit like citing
the Bible; you can find almost anything in it to support your
argument."[3] The humorist Russell Baker even went so far as to
suggest in his *New York Times* column, "Observer," that "of
all the great unread writers I believe Tocqueville to be the most
widely quoted."[4]

Some have sought to hold back the Tocqueville tide, none
more dramatically than the editor of the *New Republic*, who
for three years in the 1980s continued to alert contributors to
the magazine to avoid including quotes from Tocqueville, on
the grounds that such citations were the ultimate cliché in contemporary journalism. Nonetheless, Tocqueville was hot copy
in the presidential election year 2000. His thoughts on religion
in America were trumpeted in the press after Senator Joseph
Lieberman's vice-presidential nomination and two and a half
weeks after the election, with the outcome still in doubt, the
New York Times editorial page excerpted a passage from
Tocqueville on American politics being ultimately absorbed by
legal issues and presided over by lawyers.

Tocqueville is, indeed, ubiquitous in the United States and
not just in political speeches or in journalism for the chattering
classes. Some of his appearances are not surprising, of course.
His *Democracy in America* has, for example, flourished in the
college curriculum for the last fifty years, appearing on sylla-
buses in a wide array of disciplines. In addition, hardly a year
goes by without American professors, along with the occasional
French and English expert on Tocqueville, flying off to attend
conferences at Yale, Claremont, or Bellagio devoted to weighty
analysis of Tocqueville and America. But Tocqueville shows up
in less likely places as well. Anyone who gives $10,000 or more
to the charity giant United Way anywhere in the United States
is automatically made a member of the National Alexis de
Tocqueville Society, created by United Way in 1972 and so
named because, as the brochure puts it, "Tocqueville's most
important observation was that Americans helped each other in
time of need."[5] On the other hand, anyone wanting to help

themselves can click on to www.Tocqueville.com, an e-commerce company which specializes in financial planning.

Tocqueville's special hold over the American imagination is rooted in the enduring importance of his great work, *Democracy in America*, which the late scholar and journalist Max Lerner, on the left, described as "the greatest book ever written on America"[6] and the distinguished political scientist Edward Banfield, on the right, decreed "the greatest book ever written by anyone about America."[7] For over a century and a half Tocqueville's book has held up a mirror to Americans, allowing each generation to see themselves and their values in it.

II

The public philosopher for democratic and predominantly Protestant America was a Catholic aristocrat, to the manor born on 29 July 1805, who spent much of his youth in his family's ancestral chateau at Verneuil in Normandy, not far from the Channel coast. His parents were members of the lower nobility and loyal followers of three French kings. Their support of Louis XVI had led to their imprisonment during the Terror of 1793: they expected the guillotine but were spared. Other members of their family, such as Tocqueville's great-grandfather, Malesherbes, were less fortunate. The famous philosopher and reformer had criticized Louis XVI's despotism in the 1770s, but had nonetheless defended his monarch before the Revolutionary Convention in 1793 which sentenced the king to death. Malesherbes was guillotined by the Jacobins for his defense of Louis, as were Tocqueville's mother's older sister and brother-in-law.

Tocqueville's parents did not flee France during the revolutionary or Napoleonic years, as had many of their fellow aristocrats, and became quite wealthy through inheriting property left them by relations who had either emigrated or been executed. When the Bourbon monarchy was restored in 1814, Tocqueville's father was rewarded by Louis XVIII with important appointments in the royal civil service. He served as *préfet*, or chief royal administrator, in the capitals of various *départe-*

ments such as Dijon and Metz. Royal favor continued after 1824 when Charles X, the youngest brother of Louis XVI, succeeded his two older brothers to the throne, since Tocqueville's father staunchly supported Charles, a self-proclaimed reactionary who had himself crowned at Reims with all the pomp and pageantry of France's medieval monarchs.

As a boy, Tocqueville was tutored at home by an elderly priest, Abbé Leseur, who had also been his father's tutor. At fifteen he was enrolled at a lycée in Metz, and he did well at school, winning the first prize in rhetoric. Years later he would link his three years at school in Metz with the beginnings of his religious doubt. Reading the French philosophers of the enlightenment in his father's library ended once and for all any religious certainty he had, though he never went so far as disbelief. The erosion of his Catholic faith also heralded in his late teens what Tocqueville called "the blackest melancholy," which would plague him all his life.

Choosing a legal over a military career, Tocqueville studied law in Paris from 1823 to 1827. His father, who was by now very close to Charles X, having been promoted to service at the royal household in Versailles and elevated to the peerage in 1827, arranged a judicial appointment for his son in 1827. He became a *juge auditeur*, a kind of apprentice judge, at the Versailles court of law. In his rounds of hearing witnesses and assisting the public prosecutor, Tocqueville met Gustave de Beaumont, a deputy public prosecutor also working in the law courts at Versailles, who would become his lifelong friend and collaborator.

During his time in Paris, Tocqueville had numerous romantic liaisons, falling in love with a sprightly bourgeois girl with whom he carried on a five-year affair until his parents put an end to it. Soon afterwards, in 1826, he began a relationship with Mary Mottley, a middle-class Englishwoman, nine years older than Tocqueville and employed as a governess in Paris. Against the wishes of his parents (and perhaps spurred on by this) the couple became engaged in 1828 and were married in 1835. While they remained married until Tocqueville's death, it was never a close relationship; they had no children and Tocqueville was openly unfaithful.

While studying law in Paris and especially during his three years as a junior official at Versailles, Tocqueville embarked on a rigorous regime of study and reading, immersing himself in the works of Machiavelli, Montesquieu, Pascal, Rousseau, and Burke. He not only read the statesman and historian François Guizot's *History of Civilization* (1828) but faithfully attended his famous course of lectures on European history at the University of Paris. From Guizot's work and the writings of other French liberals of the period such as Benjamin Constant (*Principles and Politics*, 1815; *On Ancient and Modern Liberty*, 1817) and Pierre-Paul Royer-Collard, Tocqueville learned about the historical development of French and English political institutions, and the reasons behind the emergence of a more liberal polity in England. Some of their ideas would be absorbed by Tocqueville and become forever his own, such as Royer-Collard's belief in the inevitability of democratization, or the conviction shared by the Protestants Constant and Guizot that Christianity was itself involved in the progressive realization of democratic freedom, insisting as it did on the basic equality of all humans whatever their stations, with no one born to rule or obey.

Tocqueville's historical and political studies prompted the ambitious and thoughtful young man to try his own hand at writing. In 1826, at the age of twenty-one, he wrote more than 350 pages of observations on a trip to Sicily, all but seventeen pages of which have been lost. Two years later he wrote an essay on English history, to which he would return in later years. But most importantly, these years of study and historical reflection helped shape Tocqueville's political attitudes, freeing him from the unquestioning royalism of his father. In the writings of Guizot, Constant, and Royer-Collard, Tocqueville found a liberal alternative to the ultra-royalism of Charles X. In the five years of his reign, Charles and his chief minister Villere sought to restore the *ancien régime*, thereby returning to France the political and social system it had endured before the Revolution. Furthermore, they returned the clergy to their classrooms and revived primogeniture and entail (respectively the exclusive right of an eldest son to succeed to the estate of his ancestor, and the restriction of succession of a landed estate to a specified line of heirs). The vote was restricted to landowners of sizable estates, and offices in the army to aristocrats. Censorship returned, freedom of religion was in jeopardy, and equal access to careers blocked, as preference was once again given to children of the nobility.

Tocqueville was one child of the nobility who considered the turning back of the clock to be futile. Like his mentors, the opposition liberals, he saw the decline of the aristocracy as irreversible, a product of the inexorably wider distribution of property and the inevitable demise of a status-based hierarchical society. Like the liberals, he worried about the vulnerability of property and contractual rights and the threat to individual independence, to the rights to think, speak, and believe without restraint by priests or politicians. Like Royer-Collard, Tocqueville was concerned that the French revolutionaries, Napoleon, and the Bourbon restoration had centralized all power in the despotic state, eliminating the provincial and communal privileges and rights of local government that had once restrained and decentralized authority in the *ancien régime*. But like them he rejected the restoration of aristocratic and clerical privileges, and thought federalism a more promising antidote to centralization, with cities, towns, and provinces having real autonomy. Clearly, then, Tocqueville was wrestling with ideas about democracy, despotism, centralization, localism, freedom, and individualism in the European experience even before he went to America.

If Tocqueville found the reign of Charles X too reactionary, he was equally critical of what succeeded it in 1830, the year democratic revolution spread across Europe. On 29 July 1830 barricades were erected in Paris behind which mobs defied the army and the police, all in response to Charles' edicts of the previous day dissolving the Chamber of Deputies, implementing censorship of the press and changing the suffrage to reduce the voting power of bankers, merchants, and industrialists while limiting the vote to the aristocracy. Fearing the fate of his brother, Louis XVI, Charles abdicated and fled to Britain. While Parisian students and workers wanted to declare a democratic republic, the bourgeoisie insisted on retaining a constitutional monarchy, albeit one that was somewhat liberalized. The impasse was ended by the aging Marquis de Lafayette, who proposed as the new king the Duke of Orleans, Louis-Philippe, a relative of the Bourbons who as a young man in 1792 had fought in the Republican army. On 7 August the Chamber offered him the throne, all sides accepting what would be variously called for the next eighteen years the "Orleanist," the "July" or the "bourgeois" monarchy.

Louis-Philippe styled himself "the citizen king," calling himself not the "King of France" but the "King of the French" and flying not the Bourbon lily but the tricolor of the Revolution. He cultivated a popular bourgeois manner, wearing, for example, somber clothing and carrying an umbrella. His regime rested on the powerful support of the commercial classes and as the years went by it was opposed by radical democrats on the left and royalists on the right who saw his rule as beholden to an insurrection.

Nor did Tocqueville admire Louis-Philippe. He appreciated the continued commitment to representative government, even if the suffrage reached only two hundred thousand voters, and he wanted a larger role in the new order for remnants of the old aristocracy, who, unlike merchants, would, he assumed, place the national interest above self-interest. But what really turned Tocqueville against the "citizen king" was his retinue of bourgeois sponsors, upstart new men of commerce and money with their middle-class predilection for comfort and mediocrity.

Louis-Philippe's "July" monarchy set off a train of events that led ultimately to Tocqueville taking his monumental trip to America. It began with the crisis over whether Tocqueville would take the oath of allegiance to the "citizen king," required of all judicial officers in the state's service. Tocqueville was, as he wrote to Mary Mottley, at war with himself.[8] He knew that his parents, deeply allied to the Bourbon cause, had refused to take the oath, and would consider him a traitor to their class if he were to do so. On the other hand, his close friend Gustave de Beaumont, who was equally dismissive of Louis-Philippe, did swear the oath. To do otherwise, he argued, would be to close the door to any future advancement in government service. Tocqueville saw sense in his friend's argument and in August 1830 he reluctantly swore allegiance to Louis-Philippe's bourgeois monarchy, consoling himself that it was at least a constitutional regime pledged both to preserve order and to protect individual rights.

That same month Tocqueville and Beaumont developed their plan to visit America. Restless, ambitious, and deeply concerned that the regime's suspicions of them might forever condemn them to the role of minor functionaries, they hit upon the idea of asking the new minister of the interior to send them across the Atlantic to study America's unique invention, the penitentiary, which had aroused great interest in French prison reform circles. It was a natural link to their work as judicial magistrates, they argued, and the minister agreed to sponsor the study of American prisons, but provided no funding for the venture. The families of both young men put up the cash for that, and they did so willingly since each had unique ties to America. Beaumont was a young cousin of the great Marquis de Lafayette and Tocqueville was a relative of the French writer François René, Vicomte de Chateaubriand, who had not only been to America but had lived with a Native American tribe and written an idealized novel, *Atala*, about them.

Studying American prisons was merely an excuse to get the official leave of absence required for their trip. While visiting prisons would lend structure and legitimacy to their travels across America it was a minor motive for the journey. Frustrated in their administrative ambitions. Beaumont and Tocqueville saw the journey as a career-creating opportunity. Tocqueville, in particular, had begun to contemplate a political career, and he calculated, quite presciently, that becoming a specialist in American affairs would set him apart from and above his peers. He sensed that understanding America, the only country where the people governed, given the nearly total white male suffrage in 1830, would provide a useful edge for anyone involved in the politics of an evolving French democracy.

America spoke to the intellectual and political puzzles that roiled through Tocqueville's reading and studies in the 1820s.

He worried how the new ideals of democracy in France could ever put a brake on the power of the central government, as it came to be run more and more by the people themselves. The central power of the state in France had been historically checked by local authorities, like the aristocracy in their provincial *parlements*, but with the virtual destruction of the nobility what would now resist the potential for centralized despotism? America more than Britain seemed to hold the answer, since the local aristocracy still flourished in the latter, and America, with no aristocracy of its own, was closer to the French system. No wonder, then, that behind Tocqueville's desire to go to America, ostensibly to study prisons, was his concern with broader political issues such as centralization, localism, and, of course, federalism.

When Tocqueville, only twenty-five, and Beaumont, only twenty-eight, sailed from Le Havre on 2 April 1831 they had already told their friends of their plans to write an important book on "all the mechanisms of this vast American society,"[9] and not simply a study of the prison system. It would be a "great work which would make our reputation some day."[10] They had studied English that winter, which they both could read better than they could speak. Tocqueville brought with him a great-coat, some hats, including a silk one, boots, linen, and a leather trunk. They each brought a gun and Beaumont took some sketch books and a flute. Five and a half weeks later, on 9 May, they arrived in Newport, Rhode Island, and two days after that in New York City, where the newspapers had already announced the arrival of the two distinguished French visitors who would be studying American prisons.

They remained in North America for the next nine and a half months, a total of 271 days in the United States and fifteen in Canada. They had hoped to stay longer, but by November the French government sought to end the mission and pressed for their quick return. When they finally left to return to France on 20 February, 1832 they had traveled over seven thousand miles by stagecoach, horseback, steamer, and canoe. They had visited seventeen of the then existing twenty-four states, traveling from Boston in the east to Green Bay, Wisconsin, on the western frontier, from French Canada in the north to New Orleans in the south. Their route had taken them from New York to Philadelphia and Baltimore down the Ohio and Mississippi rivers and back through the south from Montgomery to Norfolk and Washington.

It was not an easy trip. After being tormented by mosquitoes all summer they encountered the coldest winter yet recorded in the new nation. They nearly drowned when their steamship hit a rock in the Ohio River and Tocqueville became gravely ill at one point, recovering only after extensive recuperation in a log cabin in Tennessee. They did, in fact, visit all the important prisons in America, beginning with a visit to Sing Sing in Ossining on the Hudson, where they were impressed by the unusual sight of nine hundred unchained convicts hard at work outdoors. Try as they might to elude their official mission, Beaumont wrote home, "everyone finds a way of introducing some amiable allusion to prisons."[11]

Wherever they went the two young Frenchmen were frequently received as celebrities in the cities they visited, welcomed with banquets and fashionable balls, at which they met mayors, governors, senators, professors, university presidents, and judges. They interviewed an ex-President, John Quincy Adams, and at the White House in January they met with President Andrew Jackson, whom Tocqueville did not like. They were presented to Salmon P. Chase, the Chief Justice of the United States Supreme Court, and met Sam Houston, future president of the republic of Texas, who happened to be on the same steamer as them going down the Mississippi. They also met ordinary Americans, especially when they left the cities and traveled where almost no one knew them. They asked questions of whomever they met and every night when they retired to their lodgings or their cabin, and sometimes even to their tent, they wrote up these conversations in great detail, meticulously filling up scores of diaries and notebooks, which they carried back to France. They also learned about America from books, pamphlets, and government documents, such as *The Federalist Papers* and Chancellor James Kent's *Commentaries on American Law*, which they accumulated and read on their travels.

Tocqueville was always observing and writing, seldom relaxing as Beaumont did with his sketching and flute playing. "Tocqueville, when traveling, never rested," Beaumont wrote. "Rest was foreign to his nature, and whether his body was actively employed or not, his mind was always at work . . . It never occurred to him to consider an excursion as an amusement, or conversation as relaxation . . . For Tocqueville, the most agreeable conversation was that which was the most useful. The bad day was the day lost or ill-spent. The smallest loss of time was unpleasant to him."[12]

That Tocqueville drove himself so hard was but one facet of his complex personality. A small, slight man with large sad eyes and a sallow complexion, he struck people as frail, highly-strung and nervous. Often sick, he complained frequently of stomach trouble and he eventually became tubercular. Constant rounds of meeting and interviewing Americans were painfully demanding for someone who described himself as stiff, cold, and not especially outgoing. His voice was soft and he was not particularly good at public speaking. He appeared remote and aloof to people, and generally lacking in warmth. The German poet Heine later described Tocqueville as "a man of head with little heart." What he "lacks in feeling," he wrote, "is possessed to a winning degree by his friend, M. de Beaumont."[13]

Tocqueville was driven by ambition and the desire for literary and political fame. Determined to make his mark in the world, Tocqueville himself recognized "every day that I have a need to be foremost which will be the cruel torment of my life."[14] He deserved to succeed because he was convinced of his own intellectual superiority. "All about one," he once wrote, "I see people who reason badly and who speak well; that continually throws me into despair. It seems to me that I am above them, but whenever I make an appearance, I feel beneath them."[15]

Like many ambitious people convinced of their own importance, Tocqueville at the same time had serious doubts about himself. He had long periods of deep melancholy (depression not yet having received its name), when he seemed detached, withdrawn, and shy, lost in silence and solitude. No surprise, then, that at some point during his visit he escaped the interviews and meetings for the quiet of what he described as the American "desert" or the American "wilderness." In a trip deep into the woods of the north-western frontier in Michigan, Wisconsin, and lower Canada, beyond the smallest European settlements, he sought the most "savage solitude" where only the occasional Native American was to be found. Guns at the ready, he and Beaumont went deep into the forest as they discovered in astonishment and awe that:

> In that spot, the wilderness was probably just as it appeared six thousand years before to our ancestors' eyes—a delightful and scented solitude festooned with flowers; a magnificent dwelling, a living palace constructed for man but into which the master had not yet made his way. The rowing boat slipped along effortlessly and silently. All around us reigned total serenity and peace. It was not long before we ourselves became, as it were, soothed at the sight of such a scene. Our conversation began to become more and more intermittent. Soon we were only whispering our thoughts. At length we fell silent altogether and, both putting up our oars, we descended into a quiet reverie filled with inexpressible magic.[16]

We know of Tocqueville's quest for solitude because, when he and Beaumont returned from this trip beyond the frontier in Michigan, Tocqueville wrote a short essay, *Quinze Jours dans le désert*, the one sustained piece of writing about America he actually produced while in the country. He finished his lyrical description of the forest solitude on 29 July, his twenty-sixth birthday and the first anniversary of the previous year's tumultuous events in France:

> It was in the heart of this profound solitude that we suddenly thought of the 1830 Revolution whose first anniversary we had just reached. I cannot say how impetuously the memories of 29 July took hold of our minds. The shouts and smoke of the conflict, the noise of the cannon, the rumble of the muskets, the even more horrific ringing of the alarm bell, this whole day with its heated atmosphere seemed suddenly to emerge from the past

xxii   INTRODUCTION

and to be reproduced like a living tableau in front of me. It was only a sudden illumination, a fleeting dream. When I looked up and glanced around me, the apparition had already vanished but never had the silence of the forest seemed to me more glacial, its shade more gloomy or its isolation more complete.[17]

The populated "civilized" America to which Tocqueville returned and which he explored for the next five and a half months was lightyears from the revolutionary turmoil of Europe. In 1831 America was five times the size of France and had thirteen million people inhabiting twenty-four states and three territories; Andrew Jackson was President and the country was restless with democratic energy. Jackson was a frontiersman, the first President not to come from the Virginia and Massachusetts elite. His rough country supporters tramped through the White House and he would employ many of them in government service, convinced that governing required no special skills. The United States was, meanwhile, being knit together by an ambitious policy of internal improvements, which saw an emergent network of roads and canals unleashing a torrent of commercial enterprise.

Other Europeans flocked to Jacksonian America to capture its democratic spirit as well, and to write books for their fellow countrymen. English writers Charles Dickens, Harriet Martineau, Frances Trollope, Germans Francis Grund, and Francis Lieber, and the Pole Adam G. de Gurowski all wrote about the striking social equality they found in America, the absence of differences in status. They all noted the American obsession with work and the restless quest for the "almighty dollar."[18] Noteworthy as they were, none of their books would be remotely as important as the monumental book Tocqueville wrote about America.

It took Tocqueville eight years finally to write up his thoughts on America, and he did it in two stages. Two volumes, comprising Part I of the Text, appeared in French in 1835, and were translated simultaneously into English by Henry Reeve, a twenty-two-year-old English friend of Tocqueville's. That translation was published in America in 1838 with a preface written by a New York state assemblyman. In 1840 two more volumes appeared, which constitute Part II of *Democracy in America*. Tocqueville decided not to include his *Quinze Jours dans le désert* with his book. He feared his description of the American treatment of its aboriginal peoples might undercut the appeal of his friend Beaumont's novel, *Marie, or Slavery in the United States*, which was about American slavery, and which was also set in the wilderness. Tocqueville's moving evocation of his July days in the wilderness was published only after his death and not until the twentieth century was it translated into English. We include this short text in this volume because it is rarely found in an English translation and it is an important and neglected expression of Tocqueville's immediate experience of America, unmediated by the years of his return to France. For the same reason we also include the much shorter *Excursion to Lake Oncida*, with its moving description of the search earlier in July for a French couple who had settled in America shortly after the French Revolution. Found in Tocqueville's collected works, it has, to our knowledge, never before been translated into English and completes his writings on America for this Penguin edition.

When he read the 1835 volumes, Royer-Collard, one of Tocqueville's intellectual mentors, wrote, "since Montesquieu there has been nothing like *Democracy in America*."[19] The French publisher, Gosselin, who had never actually read the manuscript, could not believe the extraordinary success of the first printing and wrote in awe to Tocqueville, "Well, it seems you've written a masterpiece."[20] But there was no greater contemporary praise for *Democracy in America* than that of the reviewer of the American edition, who in 1838 wrote in the *Knickerbocker* magazine that Americans "have hitherto been an enigma to the world; our author has at last partly solved it."[21]

III

Tocqueville's voice is strikingly personal in *Democracy in America*, addressing his readers directly as few canonical texts do. In one chapter he shares his concern about delving into excessive technical details, "without discouraging the reader's curiosity"; in another he observes that "such a method risks arousing the reader's objections, but the importance of the subject under scrutiny is my excuse." Unusually direct is his suggestion at one point that his reader "put down the book for a moment . . . to consider for himself the subjects I have attempted to explain to him." The tone of the text often shifts abruptly. Long, matter-of-fact descriptions of historical events or of American practices and institutions are interrupted by unannounced excursions into philosophical or spiritual speculation or into emotionally hyperbolic descriptions of nature. In his footnotes especially, but in the text as well, Tocqueville is a master of the quick move from authorial Olympian neutrality to biting and ironic first person asides.

Even more striking for some readers than the change in voice is an apparent change in Tocqueville's attitudes in the years between the publication of the first two and the last two volumes. Ever since John Stuart Mill, some have insisted that *Democracy in America*'s publication as two separate entities five years apart accounts for the reason it reads like two different texts. The first, full of detailed descriptions and assessments of America and American politics, is read as a practical and optimistic picture of democracy's promise. The second part, this reading holds, is less specific, more abstract and philosophical, more gloomily meditative and pessimistic with a picture of a homogeneous, conformist world of egalitarian mediocrity. Seeing its two parts as fundamentally different exaggerates discontinuities, however. A fundamental unity runs through both parts of the text: Tocqueville's insistence that America is the embodiment of a providentially sponsored evolution of the democratic spirit as it replaces, in some cases for better and others for worse, the aristocratic ideals that had flourished for centuries in England and France.

Everything Tocqueville wrote about America was informed by his conviction that America embodied the spirit of the age, the world-historic transformative process whereby hierarchical, deferential, and communal values were inexorably being supplanted by new ideals of individualism and equality. Tocqueville remains to this day the classic chronicler of this historical moment in the West, which he, in fact, labeled as the transition from the aristocratic era to the democratic, the former characterized by respect for rank, the latter by the end of privilege based on birth.

America was proof that the democratic spirit did not necessarily degenerate into anarchy and disorder as writers in the Western tradition ever since Plato had predicted. Europeans need not fear the future, for, as Tocqueville demonstrated, America was a democracy where liberty, property, and religion were all highly honored. Nor could Europeans stop the democratic tide; it was historically inevitable, indeed, divinely inspired. To resist democracy was, according to Tocqueville, to resist the will of God. For seven hundred years democratic revolutionary ideals had spread through Europe seeking to broaden the avenues of power, and behind it all Tocqueville saw the egalitarian ideals of Christ, the conviction that human beings were by nature equal and alike.

In America people were, in fact, equal and alike with "a blending of social ranks and the abolition of privileges" and "society one single mass." Tocqueville was struck by the absence of any social distinctions between public officials and ordinary citizens, who dressed the same and stayed at the same inns, he noted. Servants "did not have a pre-determined subordinate position," were not members of a separate caste; they could easily become masters. But as representative of the new democratic world spirit as America was, Tocqueville suggested it was also exceptional and unique.

The equality of conditions in America was in part a product of America's utter novelty, a political society born whole by people who came from someplace else, a society which Tocqueville described, in his first letter home, as one whose inhabitants had no common past, no shared "roots, no memories, no prejudices, no routine, no common ideas, no national character."²² Those who settled America were already social equals; low-born and noble were not found among them. These people of generally equal rank who colonized America found no ruling class there which possessed exclusive political privilege by title and, therefore, did not have to engage in a democratic revolution. Unlike Europeans, they were born equal instead of becoming so.

Tocqueville sometimes suggests that all Americans were social equals, that "in America paupers are not to be found; everyone has property of his own to defend." He suggests that Americans are politically equal, as well, there being "no class of persons who do not exercise the right to vote." His perception of Jacksonian America exaggerates both its social and its political equality, to be sure, but he was not blind to class, gender, and racial differentials in America, as we shall see. He understood that some Americans were richer than others and that conflict between rich and poor often fueled political strife, whether it was between the Federalist and Democratic parties, or Jacksonians and the Bank. Taking the exclusion of women from politics as given and justified, and acknowledging the anomaly of America's treatment of enslaved Africans, Tocqueville's point is that America's white male population did not assume that some among them were naturally superior and others naturally inferior, which made America much more democratic, more egalitarian, than Europe.

It was more democratic than Europe from the perspective of Tocqueville's second understanding of democracy as well. Alongside his social reading of democracy as a society of nearly equal men—a relatively new concept—is his political sense of democracy as the sovereignty of the people, the people ruling themselves, which was the original meaning of democracy in ancient Greece. In no other country had authority and power been so expanded from the one or the few to the many as in America, where, according to Tocqueville, the divine right of kings had been replaced by the divine right of the people. "The people reign in the American political world like God over the universe." Very few white men were barred from voting in Jacksonian America while in Europe very few men could vote to begin with. Sounding much like Rousseau, Tocqueville was convinced that because Americans took an active part in politics they respected the law. Since they participated in crafting legislation they regarded laws as their own, as self-imposed.

The people were able to govern in America because there was no real intervening state apparatus, no permanent officialdom, which in Europe claimed to direct and administer society. Coming from the Bourbon as well as the Napoleonic tradition of a highly centralized administrative system, Tocqueville was surprised to discover that American society got along by itself with the state and governing institutions playing a negligible role in people's lives. Public power was hard to find when there was no army, virtually no taxation and seemingly non-existent executive authorities. In America, Tocqueville wrote to his father less than a month after he had arrived, "there is no, or at least there doesn't appear to be, any government at all . . . no central idea whatsoever seems to regulate the movement of the machine."[23]

Tocqueville offered three reasons for this vacuum of public authority: historical, geographical, and ideological. The bearers of state power, armies, bureaucracies, public treasuries, and police, he argued, were created by the nationalizing monarchies of post-Reformation Europe in their power struggle with provincial notables, a struggle which never occurred in America, where everyone was born equal. Nor was there much need for centralized public power since America had no neighbors threatening invasion. With no enemies to worry about America could do without a standing army, the traditional embodiment of state power. Finally, the Americans' love of freedom and independence made them instinctively suspicious of being governed by anyone but themselves. They viewed all authority with a jaundiced eye.

The unprecedented political power of ordinary people in America had unfortunate side effects. The absolute sovereignty of the people seldom puts superior men, the ablest or the most talented, into office. It produced a less brilliant, less heroic public life with few noble deeds and high enterprises; more attention was paid to popular concerns like peace, comfort, and

prosperity. Mediocre and unlettered men governing, uninter-
ested in glory and memorable distinction, was probably inevitable in a democracy, but with a resulting general wellbeing,
according to Tocqueville. What deeply troubled him, however,
was the dangerous political potential of popular democracy, of
the unlimited power of the majority in the United States. He
worried that it might produce a new tyranny as bad as the
traditional misrule of kings, aristocrats, or priests, a tyranny of
the majority.

This concept, the most enduring contribution of *Democracy
in America*, is used by Tocqueville in two different senses. The
tyranny of the majority is the all too real unlimited political and
legislative authority of the people, on the one hand, and the less
tangible but irresistible pressures in a democracy forcing citizens
to conform to the opinions held by the majority, on the other.
His concern with the people's unfettered power to make the
laws is focussed more on the individual state legislatures, which
the majority controls at its pleasure, than with the federal
government, which, he suggests, is concerned less with law-
making than with managing foreign affairs. There should be
restraints on popular sovereignty, Tocqueville insists, limits to
the sway of the majority. He writes, "The maxim that in matters
of government the majority of a nation has the right to do
everything, I regard as unholy and detestable." Americans, he
laments, bow before the superior power of the people in the
way that courtiers do to monarchs. Unlimited power in human
affairs, he suggests, is always a bad and dangerous thing; only
God can be omnipotent. Better, what Tocqueville labels the
quiet rule of the majority, where the people rule but cannot pass
laws that violate higher moral ideals of justice and reason or
that threaten vested rights of the body politic, like the sanctity
of property.

The only examples of majority tyranny in the American states
that Tocqueville cites in the text surprisingly have nothing to do
with legislative actions: newspaper editors killed in Baltimore
for opposing the war of 1812 and massive prejudice against
African-Americans in Pennsylvania. Nor does the one time he
refers to majority tyranny on the federal level, the Bonapartist

potential he discerns in President Jackson's appeal, speak to an act of a legislature. His fear of majority despotism in America is based less on what he has found there, less on the reality of American politics, than on what he has read. It is rooted in the writings of the American founders and their insistence that limits be placed on the sovereign power of the people, on the need to check and restrain what they took to be the abuses of liberty. No matter that he actually describes no legislature in Jackson's America with despotic powers, Tocqueville has absorbed Madison and Hamilton's *Federalist Papers*, from which he constantly quotes, with their persistent attacks on all-powerful state legislatures during the period of the Articles of Confederation, a half-century earlier. Tocqueville repeats Jefferson's warning about the tyranny of legislatures, as well. In their Constitution the founders of America courageously resisted the despotism of the majority by dividing and dispersing sovereign power with a bicameral legislature, a veto wielding executive and an independent judiciary, institutional practices that Tocqueville felt state governments should more zealously copy. More profoundly, the founders had made the exercise of unlimited popular power impossible through crafting the federal system itself, further complicating its exercise by dividing power between the central government and the individual states.

If the founders' achievement calmed Tocqueville's fears of legislative tyranny, he was less sanguine about the subtler despotism of public opinion in America. His brooding misgivings about the conflict between mass opinion and the intellectual, moral, and spiritual independence of the individual in a democratic society, written decades before the similar fearful analysis in John Stuart Mill's *On Liberty*, constitute the most memorable and influential theme of *Democracy in America*. The individual is irresistibly pressured in America to accept the views of the multitude, Tocqueville observes, since public opinion surrounds, directs, and oppresses. Tocqueville knew "of no country where there is generally less independence of thought and real freedom of debate than in America." As proof of this tyranny of the majority he notes several times the difficulty of finding any public display of religious unbelief.

Much of Tocqueville's text is devoted to how American institutions and American character counteract the potential for the tyranny of the majority. He admires how the selection of United States senators is filtered through an already elected body of state officials as opposed to the totality of the citizenry choosing them. Convinced that such indirect elections produce men of elevated thoughts, he recommends its wider use so that legislatures will not run the risk of perishing wretchedly on the reefs of democracy.[24] In general, according to Tocqueville, there would be less chance of a tyranny of the majority if the states strengthened their executive branches and resolved to keep an independent judiciary. Judicial review, the uniquely American principle by which courts declare statutes unconstitutional, was yet another constitutional barrier to the tyranny of legislatures in the United States. The entire legal apparatus—courts, judges, and attorneys, in fact—served as a powerful break on democracy in America, slowing down rapid shifts of public opinion. Tocqueville is particularly cheered by the prominence of lawyers in American life, sensing in them a kind of aristocratic preference for formality, order, and historical continuity. Like the provincial legal nobility of pre-revolutionary France, American lawyers, Tocqueville believes, constitute a sort of privileged body with a similar contempt for the judgment of the many.

Tocqueville singles out two other features of American life—its "spirit of association" and its "spirit of locality"—as fundamental to its success in curbing the excesses of democracy. He is struck by how Americans love to form associations, to join voluntarily in varied private groups that promote public safety, religion, and morality, or encourage commerce, industry, science, and culture. This predisposition is an important and necessary guarantee against the tyranny of the majority. America's voluntary associations are people-made, democratic substitutes for the older organic bodies like the nobility and the clergy that mediated between individuals and the state in the *ancien régime*. Equally as important as these ubiquitous intermediate social associations in preventing tyranny is the American spirit of provincial liberty. Tocqueville describes an America where local liberties and local self-government are regarded more highly than identification with individual states or the nation writ large. Every village, he writes, forms a sort of Republic, accustomed to govern itself. Unlike his fellow Frenchmen, Tocqueville notes, Americans take care of themselves in their local townships. They police and fix their roads, repair their churches, never expecting strangers, officials from the central government, to do their work.

The enthusiastic involvement of Americans in private associations and local self-government not only checks abuse of power but also helps overcome the excessive individualism of Americans. Both activities take Americans outside of themselves, drawing them away from a preoccupation with private interests and turning them to shared common needs and sympathy for others. This transcendence of self is profoundly important for Tocqueville, who is fascinated by and worried about the individualism he sees rampant in America, an individualism at the core of all its attitudes, values, customs, manners, and fundamental feelings, all of which Tocqueville finds even more important than institutional arrangements in explaining America to his fellow Frenchmen.

One of the earliest usages of the word individualism in English was in the 1840 translation of Tocqueville's second volume of *Democracy in America*. He used the word in two different but related ways, as a political and as a social concept. It signifies a political shift from public and communal concerns to private and personal interests. Americans, Tocqueville concludes, are preoccupied with the narrow circle of self or family, worrying more about their own ambitions and personal rights than engaging in a quest for a common good. Foremost among these sacred rights is the universally held American belief in the right of individual judgment. Linked to their common Protestantism and unconscious acceptance of Cartesian modernism, Americans, according to Tocqueville, regard individual reason as the sole source of truth and thus each American is considered the best judge of what concerns themselves, society having no claims on the individual unless their private actions harm the common good.

Behind this non-civic or privatized tendency of American life,

Tocqueville discerns an even more profound social individualism. Americans see themselves as individuals in a Lockean state
of nature, as self-making, self-realizing, free and equal agents.
Free of Europe's feudal and corporate past in which each
person's status was determined by an inherited assignment to an
estate or class, Americans never consider themselves aristocrats,
peasants, or artisans for life, but rather self-creating individuals,
relying on their own industry and talent to define and make
themselves. Devoting so much energy to being author of self,
they have little left for public life. They are active and busy,
Tocqueville concludes, but as private, self-centered individuals
not as participatory citizens. "The passions which stir Americans most deeply are commercial not political ones," he writes.

A major theme in *Democracy in America* is Tocqueville's
recurring evocation of Americans as ceaselessly active and rest-
lessly striving. The American spirit is energetic and enterprising.
Like atomistic Hobbesean individuals, Americans are never at
rest or settled, but always in a hurry, in permanent agitation
and constant motion, incessantly jostling one another. Nothing
is fixed. Perpetually on the move, Americans change jobs and
homes whenever opportunity calls. Tocqueville marvels at meeting men who have successively been lawyers, farmers, merchants, ministers of the Gospel, and doctors.

Everywhere in America, except in the South with "its idle and
indolent" slave owners, men constantly exert themselves. Good
Lockeans and good Protestants, they march across the wilderness "draining swamps, turning the course of rivers, inhabiting
remote places and conquering nature." Adventurers and speculators all, they leave nothing as they found it. In love with
novelty and fired by ambition, the American sheds the past as
easily as he changes work. Nor does he respect or "care for
what occurred before his time."

Tocqueville appreciates that the desire to better one's position
in life fuels American restlessness. Since the privileges of birth are
absent and careers are open to talent and ambition, Americans
"have opened the door to universal competition." Few in
America, he observes, are content with their "present fortune;
all are constantly struggling, in a thousand ways, to improve

it." With no inherited, hierarchical ranking to distinguish them, Americans, Tocqueville suggests, turn to money to provide the status differences among themselves and to raise some above "the common herd."

With barely disguised disdain, the aristocrat Tocqueville returns repeatedly to the acquisitive and materialist core of American individualism, suggesting, in fact, that Americans' distinctive national trait is a love of money. No two chapters go by without a suggestion that Americans love only to get rich, or "spend every day in the week in making money." He constantly reminds his readers of Americans' "love of" and "passion for wealth," of their "unbounded desire for riches" and that "the love of wealth ... is at the bottom of all that the Americans do." Their obsession with money and the pleasure of material life explain for Tocqueville the avidity with which Americans rush to the frontier, braving Indians and disease to secure these abundant riches that the frontier offers.

The American "spirit of gain" also accounts for America having fewer great artists, distinguished scientists, and celebrated poets, according to Tocqueville. Their exclusively commercial habits divert the American mind from the pleasures of imagination and labors of the intellect to the pursuit of wealth. No other peoples in the world love property more, Tocqueville wrote, and he put this commercial reading of Americans to practical use. When he and Beaumont found themselves deep in the Michigan–Wisconsin wilderness, where no one knew them, they won the confidence of the few people they met by pretending to be land speculators, with conversation flourishing in the language of money-making.[25]

Rampant American individualism with its legions of fortune hunters, scurrying feverishly to better themselves, is more worrisome than merely the offense it gives to Tocqueville's anti-commercial sensitivities. His worst fear is that disconnected and docile individuals will apathetically succumb to a despotic, tutelary state. In love with property and "the enjoyment of the present moment," Americans turn from public life and "stand independently," creating the danger that individuals seeking only their own interest, existing for themselves alone, will leave all common concerns to the government, which if it offers them order and security will be granted more and more power unto omnipotence. Tocqueville conjures up a nightmarish democratic despotism, seemingly mild in its paternal control, but totalitarian in its reach. In this frightening fantasy the state takes over education, which the liberal Tocqueville, like Mill, opposed; it provides for economic wellbeing and manages most commercial affairs, virtually relieving individuals of the need to think for themselves. The horrible prospect comes full circle when self-centered individuals, whose initial abandonment of public affairs ultimately led to the state's despotism, find themselves isolated and alone, "lost in the crowd."

American democracy escapes this desperate fate because joined to the countervailing influence of localism and associationalism is religion, which provides another powerful brake to excessive individualism and self-absorption. This recognition of religion's significant role in American social life is yet another of Tocqueville's often cited insights. He is the first to suggest that the separation of Church and state is the basis of religion's singular importance in America. Removed from politics and respected all the more for not being entangled in factional struggle, religion has greater influence in America, by Tocqueville's reckoning, than it does in any country in the world, not on its laws, to be sure, but on its customs and habits. Most significantly, religion in the United States is credited with drawing the individual away from exclusive concern for self, providing cohesiveness and community in the face of the socially isolating impact of individualism. Religion, Tocqueville contends, also restrains the insatiable desire of Americans for material wellbeing, turning their thoughts "away from the pleasures of this earth." Religion curbs excess in general, calming "their restlessness" while teaching self-restraint as well as a love of order and peace. Women particularly are religion's moralizing agents in America, according to Tocqueville; in the homes over which they preside they encourage the moderation of opinion and taste.

Tocqueville gives much attention to women in the text, as he does to others left out of American democracy, Native Americans and African-American slaves. Though he never questions their exclusion from suffrage, like Rousseau he assigns women civil importance since morals are the work of women. He is struck by the independence and freedom of single women in America, one feature of which is their greater tendency to choose a loved husband than exists in more aristocratic societies. But since marriage in America is a more voluntary contract between loving equals, Tocqueville notes that chastity and fidelity are thereafter more strictly enforced than in Europe. While family life is fundamentally less hierarchical in America, the father having less authority and the abolition of primogeniture making children more equal to each other, married women, Tocqueville notes, still live lives of extreme dependence, living in their husbands' homes as if in a cloister. Having voluntarily chosen marriage, married American women, Tocqueville concludes, accept their duties with no lamentation over their loss of independence.

This is not the case with America's aboriginal peoples, with its "savages," as Tocqueville and others in the nineteenth century labeled the Native American. Their freedom was stolen from them by the "underhand dealings of American officials" and the "greed of the settlers." Tocqueville's recurring depiction of American acquisitiveness and "grasping search for gain" is rendered in its bitterest and most pathological terms in his evocations of the sufferings of the Native Americans. Their utter destruction was a result of the inexorable march of the white race to conquer "the untouched splendor of America," to transform its impenetrable forests to settled communities in the name of civilization and industry.

There is something awesome in this human urge, Tocqueville admits, but he also feels bitter regret at the power God has given us over nature. He assails the hypocrisy of Americans who proclaim all men brothers while brutalizing native peoples with liquor and wine. Even more to their shame, as Americans "exterminate the Indian race" they claim not to violate fundamental principles of morality. Yet, their fraudulent and unjust policies defy all notions of reason and natural right. Tocqueville bitterly and ironically suggests that "man could not be destroyed with more respect for the laws of humanity."

The same is true, of course, for slavery—a clear violation, Tocqueville holds, of natural law and a total perversion of the laws of humanity. Both Tocqueville and Beaumont, the latter in *Marie, or Slavery in the United States*, condemn the atrocities of slavery which left African-Americans of the South no better than brutes, doomed to a humiliation which went on for ever and wretched conditions which were part of their inheritance. In addition to its brutality, Tocqueville, like Lincoln some years later, was particularly struck by how slavery dishonored and degraded work, encouraging idleness and indolence among masters. The abolition of slavery would thus benefit the white as well as the black man, for the labor of free men was more productive as well as more virtuous, according to Tocqueville.

Nor was Tocqueville blind to the discrimination and injustice experienced by free African-Americans in the North, which he deplores almost as intensely as slavery itself. But whites and free African-Americans will never live on an equal footing in America, Tocqueville admits, quoting Jefferson as his authority on the inability of whites to rise above racial prejudices. As for the South, Tocqueville predicts the most horrible of civil wars between the races, with one or the other being eliminated.

That it was ultimately a different kind of civil war that ended slavery does not detract from Tocqueville's uncanny ability to foresee the American future, which in no small way helps to account for the timeless appeal of *Democracy in America*. His predictions were sometimes wrong. The federal government did not lose strength, nor did the presidency; states would never be allowed to leave the Union at will; wars would not become rarer as social conditions became more equal and Americans would tolerate compulsory conscription, just as they retained capital punishment in their criminal codes; nor would the state take over manufacturing and become the grand employer in America.

The accuracy of its predictions is a much more important legacy of Tocqueville's text than its mistakes. Men and women have become more equal, while not necessarily alike. Business-men would emerge as a new aristocracy in America. Journalists, less interested in the principles than in the character of poli-ticians, would track them into private life and disclose all their weaknesses and vices. The Supreme Court has evolved into an incredibly powerful institution. Globalism has homogenized national cultures and variety is disappearing from the human race; the same ways of acting, thinking, and feeling are to be met with all over the world. More and more aspects of American life are governed by a network of small complicated rules, minute and uniform. Texas has become a part of the United States and the Union does extend from the Atlantic to the Pacific. Tocqueville's speculation that one hundred years from 1835 America would have forty states and more than a hundred million people was not far off the mark. And, finally, there is Tocqueville's prescient sense that the destiny of half the globe would ultimately be in the hands of the Americans and the Russians, the one representing freedom, the other servitude.

IV

As he had intended, Tocqueville attracted notice as an expert on America soon after returning to France when both he and Beaumont left their state positions and turned to writing full time. Their *Du Système pénitentiaire aux Etats-Unis* won a coveted literary prize in 1833, worth 12,000 francs, which they used to pay off some of the debt incurred in the American trip. With the assistance of two young American researchers employed in Paris, Tocqueville was able to write the first volume of *Democracy in America* in fifteen months, which when published in 1835 saw him elected to the Academy of Moral and Political Science. Volume II would take five years to write but its publication in 1840 would the following year usher Tocqueville into the Académie Française; at the age of thirty-six he was one of the forty *immortels*, the highest honor France could bestow on an artist or intellectual.

Having achieved the fame he had sought, Tocqueville wanted influence as well, and turned to politics, which explains the five-year gap in publication. After his mother died in 1836 he inherited the family chateau in Normandy and from there ran for the Chamber of Deputies, into which he was eventually elected in 1839. He was re-elected in 1842 and 1846 as the delegate from Valognes, the small town fifteen miles south of Cherbourg, where the ancient Tocqueville family seat was located.

In the legislature Tocqueville quickly emerged as an authority on foreign affairs. Labeling slavery a moral abomination, he drafted a report urging its abolition in the French colonies. At the same time, however, he vociferously defended the French conquest of Algeria, asserting that it was a heroic mission to bring civilization and progress to a backward people. He also argued for prison reform and freedom of the press. His speeches, however, often too erudite and longwinded, lacked rhetorical flair and he was an ineffectual debater. Much too thoughtful and uncomfortable with political maneuvering, he lacked the political skills required to become a party leader. Tocqueville would nonetheless play an important role in the revolutionary upheavals that engulfed Paris in 1848.

Put down in 1830, republicanism had never really died and by the middle 1840s French radicals were demanding universal suffrage and a republic. Liberals like Tocqueville wanted to expand the suffrage but retain the constitutional monarchy. By 1848 republican agitation was augmented by socialists, like Louis Blanc, who wanted the creation of state-supported, collectivist manufacturing workshops. Fearful of the threat such working-class demands posed to liberal institutions in their call for an intrusive and supervisory state, Tocqueville bitterly attacked socialism in a January 1848 speech to the Chamber of Deputies. State provision of industrial jobs would lead, he predicted, to centralized, monolithic state control, and the ultimate erosion of private property, so fundamental and valuable an expression of individual independence.

A month later, when Louis-Philippe refused to allow meetings and demonstrations planned by radical and socialist reformers to take place, barricades went up in the streets of Paris and rioting ensued in which twenty people were killed. Three days later, the "bourgeois" king abdicated and, like Charles X before him, made for England. A provisional government proclaimed universal suffrage, and a constituent assembly elected in May,

which included Tocqueville, appointed a committee, with
Tocqueville as one of its members, to draft a new constitution.
He proposed a bicameral legislature and the indirect election of
the president as part of an elaborate system of checks and
balances on absolute power, patterned after the American Constitution. The committee was suspended a month and a half into
its work when three days of class warfare in Paris, "the bloody
June days," left more than ten thousand people dead or
wounded in the violent suppression of worker uprisings by
General Cavaignac, the head of the regular army.

Tocqueville applauded the quashing of the socialist threat and
even supported Cavaignac in the hastily called direct election of
a new president held under universal suffrage in December
1848. But Louis Napoleon, the nephew of Napoleon Bonaparte,
who had become the head of the family when Napoleon's only
son died in 1832, trounced Cavaignac by 5.4 to 1.5 million
votes. A new legislative assembly was elected in May 1849, also
under universal suffrage, and Tocqueville was elected once again
from his Normandy seat, winning 110,000 of the 120,000 votes
cast. Louis Napoleon, who admired Tocqueville, appointed him
foreign minister in the cabinet of Prime Minister Odilon Barrot,
in which post Tocqueville remained for five months until Barrot's ministry was dismissed. By 1852, Louis Napoleon had
replaced the republic with a revived empire and declared himself
emperor. Under the title Napoleon III, he set about crafting the
first modern dictatorship, rooted in popular support—just as
Tocqueville had foreseen in *Democracy in America*.

Meanwhile, Tocqueville's own fortunes had taken a decided
turn for the worse. In a letter to *The Times* in London he
denounced the so-called Second Empire, lamenting the destruction of freedom of the press and the loss of human liberty, and
insisting that the plebiscite which had brought Louis Napoleon
to power was but "military terrorism" used to get people to
vote for Louis, leaving France "torn from the alliance of free
nations."[26] Tocqueville was arrested and briefly imprisoned and
these travails, combined with early signs of tuberculosis in 1850,
led him to abandon public life in the 1850s.

Retreating to his chateau, and increasingly concerned about

the fate of individual rights and representative government
under Napoleon III, he felt totally estranged from the new order
and was horrified at how easily many of his contemporaries
accommodated themselves to Napoleon's illiberal regime. He
wrote to friends about his "moral and intellectual isolation"
and how his mind "no longer has . . . a country."[27] Much of
Tocqueville's time in Normandy was spent writing, first his
Souvenirs, his memoirs of the revolutionary events of 1848, not
published until after his death, and then his second great work,
The Ancien Regime and the Revolution, published in 1856.

Almost as successful as *Democracy in America*, *The Ancien
Regime* returned Tocqueville to the historical and political
themes that had preoccupied him since his studies of the 1820s
and his writing of *Democracy in America* in the 1830s. The
central argument of *The Ancien Regime*, in fact, expanded on
claims he had made in an 1836 article he published in John
Stuart Mill's *London and Westminster Review*. In a sweeping
historical survey exploring the centuries-old decline of feudalism
in France, Tocqueville indicts the modern absolutist state, whose
despotism he had so feared in *Democracy in America*. Napoleon
III's empire, the book argues, was only the latest example of the
centralizing tendencies in French politics, whose roots long
preceded the Jacobin revolution in the work of Richelieu, Louis
XIII, and Louis XIV as they disempowered the aristocratic and
provincial bodies that had for so long shared power with the
monarchy. The Jacobin revolutionaries, no less than Napoleon
I and Napoleon III, perfected the centralized functions of the
all-powerful administrative state, at the same time that the
English and the Americans worked on dividing and dispersing
state power. Sounding very much like Edmund Burke, Tocqueville singled out for blame the Enlightenment *philosophes*,
intellectuals like Voltaire and Rousseau, whose generalized principles, grounded in simple and abstract formulas rather than
the complex reality of natural tradition and customs, helped
legitimize the concentration of power at the center.

Despite his declining health, Tocqueville visited England in
1857 to accept the critical acclaim generated by *The Ancien
Regime*. He was royally feted, literally, for among his many

invitations was a summons to Buckingham Palace for conversation and dinner with Prince Albert. Escorted back to Cherbourg by a ship from the British fleet, it would be Tocqueville's
last public triumph. In 1858 he coughed up blood so violently
that his wife was moved to take him to winter in Cannes, but to
no avail. In his last months Tocqueville turned to Catholicism
for solace and he died on 16 April, 1859 in Cannes at the age
of fifty-three. He was buried at his chateau three weeks later in
a funeral attended by an immense crowd but with no representative of Napoleon III's government present. So was laid to rest
in Normandy the man who, one hundred years later, would
become America's public philosopher.

V

After Tocqueville's death, *Democracy in America* receded from
public attention in America. There were some, however, who
did not forget it. The historian Henry Adams wrote to his
brother in 1863 that Tocqueville was his model, whose writings
were the "gospel of my private religion," and whom Adams
praised again in his 1889 history of early nineteenth-century
America.[28] *Democracy in America* was used after the Civil War
as a school text, but by World War I it was out of print and
generally ignored by progressive historians such as Frederick
Jackson Turner and Charles A. Beard, whose emphasis on class
conflict and worker unrest was a distinctly non-Tocquevillian
take on Jacksonian America. Mill, who was dramatically influenced by Tocqueville's writings, was more likely to be cited
when writers worried about the "tyranny of the majority." Still,
Tocqueville was brought to the public's attention again in 1935,
the 100th anniversary of the publication of Part I of *Democracy
in America*. A young Henry Steele Commager wrote a piece in
the *New York Times Magazine* commemorating the event and
the French government gave President Franklin D. Roosevelt
the gift of a bust of Tocqueville.

The renaissance of *Democracy in America* that began in
the 1930s was sparked by the work of two scholars, one an

American, the other a European, both of whom wedded centen-
nial interest to what they took to be the relevance of the book's
argument for the politics of the period. George William Pearson's *Tocqueville and Beaumont in America*, published in 1938,
was a massive compendium of the young Frenchmen's travel
notes, diaries, and letters home (including *Quinze Jours dans le
désert*), which the young Yale professor had acquired from the
Tocqueville family. Two years later J. P. Mayer, a political
scholar in England who had edited Marx's *Eighteenth Bru-
maire*, published his *Alexis de Tocqueville* in London, labeling
Tocqueville "the prophet of the mass age." Thus began the
use of *Democracy in America* as a prescient text, relevant to
contemporary issues. Pearson, a critic of the New Deal and its
planned economy, saw Tocqueville's text as a warning against
an intrusive central state, while Mayer, worrying about the rise
of totalitarian regimes in Europe and sharing the general anxiety
over democracy in the interwar period, offered a re-examination
of Tocqueville's ideas as relevant and urgent for 1940.

What the Tocqueville renaissance needed was a new, easily
available edition of *Democracy in America* and in 1945 the
publisher Alfred Knopf provided it. The new edition, edited
by a Queens College (New York) professor, Phillips Bradley,
became the extremely popular text of choice until 1966, when
Harper & Row brought out a new edition, edited by J. P. Mayer,
with a new translation by Mayer's friend, George Lawrence. The
Tocqueville revival had succeeded so well that the publication of
this new translation was reviewed in the literary supplements of
the *New York Times*, the *Washington Post* and the *Chicago
Tribune*. *Book Week* devoted the entire front page and half an
inside page of its Christmas issue to the new *Democracy in
America*.

The fuss generated by the 1966 edition is testimony to the
explosion of interest in Tocqueville during the 1950s and 1960s,
especially on American college campuses, where *Democracy in
America* could be found at the center of two important intellectual developments, the rise of American studies and the emergence of Cold War social science. Scholars convinced that there
was a distinctive American way of thinking, a consistent Ameri-

can character, or mind, even a civilization, looked to Tocqueville for inspiration. David Riesman's immensely influential *Lonely Crowd: A Study in the Changing American Character* (1950), with its concern about the standardization of American life overtaking inner-driven individualism, is an extended conversation with Tocqueville's *Democracy in America*. Max Lerner's *America as a Civilization* cites Tocqueville forty times. Meanwhile, "consensus school" scholars never tired of quoting Tocqueville either. In their 1950s books they argued that conflicts of class and interest were insignificant beside the common ideals historically held by Americans, and Tocqueville was their guide as well. Had he not described Americans as united by common opinions sharing a uniformity of beliefs?

Tocqueville's *Democracy in America* was a staple reference in American social science during the Cold War. When scholars tried to distinguish the foundational differences between America's liberal democracy and the totalitarian regimes of Nazi Germany and the Soviet Union, they focussed on America's thriving civic culture, its rich non-governmental associational life which totalitarian regimes eliminated, and this always involved touching base with Tocqueville. Similarly, the pluralist political scientists who denied the existence of a power elite in America enthusiastically cited Tocqueville's hymns to the dispersal of power in America. Some scholars saw democracy itself as the precursor of totalitarianism and Tocqueville was credited as the first to argue this case. How appropriate, then, in 1965 that Raymond Aron included Tocqueville with Montesquieu, Comte, and Marx as a founder of sociological thought.

Democracy in America is a protean text, capable of being stretched and adapted to serve just about everyone. The political usefulness of Tocqueville is, in fact, an important component of his long-sustained revival from the 1930s to the present day. With the exception of Pearson, his early champions paraded him for the antifascist left. The English socialist Harold Laski wrote often about Tocqueville in the 1930s, claiming that one lesson of *Democracy in America* was that once a people started on the path to equality there was no logical end to the journey short of abolishing all significant material differences among people. Professor Bradley, the editor of the influential 1945 Knopf mass market edition, was a close friend of Laski's and, indeed, there was a Laski foreword in his 1945 edition (it was dropped from 1950 reprints). Max Lerner, the leftist journalist, was a friend of Laski's as well, and editor with J. P. Mayer of the 1966 edition. The introduction was Lerner's and the following year he turned it into a small book on Tocqueville with his reading from the left emphasizing, for example, a passage in which Tocqueville observes that an egalitarian society provides "not the particular prosperity of the few, but the greater wellbeing of all . . . Equality may be less elevated, but it is more just, and in its justice lies its greatness and beauty."[29]

Tocqueville's attack on the lack of independence of mind and freedom of discussion in America, his criticism of the majority's intolerance of unpopular ideas and its allowing only praise of America, never criticism, were wonderfully welcome to critics of McCarthyism (the politics of Senator Joseph McCarthy) and the conformist Cold War culture that had little respect for dissenters and intellectuals. Tocqueville was enlisted by critics of mass culture on the left (and right) who, like him, saw a market culture producing homogeneity and mediocrity, never beauty and individuality. The left also liked to quote his fear of manufacturers becoming the political elite, and, of course, his constant critique of American materialism and bourgeois avariciousness.

If the early Tocqueville revival was assisted by the left, the latest stages of his renaissance have been presided over by the right. Since the sesquicentennial celebration of *Democracy in America* in the 1980s and early 1990s the intellectual right has virtually owned Tocqueville. Under the conservative sponsorship of the Bradley, Earhart and Heritage Foundations, and the Claremont and American Enterprise Institutes, Tocqueville has emerged a neoconservative superhero, championing liberty over equality and warning about the need to set realistic limits to democratic faith. He is their cultural ideal, an aristocratic liberal who accepts the inevitability of democracy, but insists on spelling out its shortcomings. Conservatives like Allan Bloom enlisted Tocqueville in an elitist defense of intelligence and wisdom against the wild instincts of a democracy which in the name of relativism would deny the existence of absolute moral truths.

Neoconservative critics of socialism and the welfare state never tire of quoting Tocqueville's misgivings about the modern managerial state which provides for people's needs while sapping their individuality and robbing them of any semblance of self-reliance. Many conservatives who praise Tocqueville find much of Burke in him, including his recognition of the importance of religion in America and its capacity to free Americans from their materialist preoccupations with self-centered gratification. Conservatives even find antifeminist ammunition in Tocqueville with his suggestion that further equality of the sexes would degrade them both.

The widespread conservative takeover of Tocqueville's *Democracy in America* has merged in recent years with the communitarian embrace, making Tocqueville the official prophet of communitarianism and *Democracy in America* its sacred text. It stands to reason that a movement opposed to radical individualism and self-centeredness would see Tocqueville as its theoretical godfather. Today's communitarians have as their top priority maintaining the intricate web of nonpolitical social and civic associations of civil society, where individuals meet and learn to trust one another. They worry that television, the internet, and the general privatized nature of contemporary life have subverted the rich associational life that so impressed Tocqueville. Like him, most communitarians hope a renewed religious life can take Americans outside themselves and undermine hyperindividualism. Even the few communitarians on the left, like Robert Bellah, whose important 1987 book bears a title, *Habits of the Heart*, taken from a passage in *Democracy in America*, share this view, seeing religion as turning Americans from loneliness and materialistic isolation to community and sociability.

In spelling out the communitarian agenda in its 1998 *A Call to Civil Society: Why Democracy Needs Moral Truths*, the Council on Civil Society, a star-studded collection of communitarian scholars and political leaders, sponsored by the Institute for American Values and the University of Chicago Divinity School, lists what it labels the "seedbeds of civic virtue," whose renewal will halt America's "long-term decline." "First and most basic is the family," next, "the local community or neighborhood," third is "faith communities and religious institutions," and fourth is "voluntary civic organizations." Tocqueville is more than alive and well: he is flourishing in the civil society movement, and not just in Chicago. Tocqueville civil society conferences were held in Bulgaria, Czechoslovakia, Romania, and Yugoslavia in the 1990s. In Eastern Europe, then, Tocqueville has replaced Marx as the best nineteenth-century expert on how to run a twenty-first century society.

Not all the voluminous attention Tocqueville's *Democracy in America* receives today is praise. It has its critics, and they are mainly from the left. Some fault the book for an overly egalitarian reading of Jacksonian America. Critics claim that not only does it gloss over the subordinate status of women, African-Americans, and Native Americans, but it also misreads the proportion of "free" Americans who were middle class, or as he put it "comfortably off," while ignoring the riches of the wealthy and the misery of the poor. Others are bothered by what they take to be his false picture of Americans united in consensual agreement and his exaggerations about the tyranny of the majority. On this latter point, some agree with John Stuart Mill, who in his 1835 review made the more general point that Tocqueville mistook for democracy and its tendencies, the tendencies of modern commercial society.

That he is also criticized by contemporary scholars is further proof of Tocqueville's sway over the American imagination. To be attacked is to be noticed and Tocqueville is everywhere for everyone. He is even enlisted by postmodernist intellectuals, much to the horror of his conservative acolytes. Postmodernists applaud him for his Pascal-like rejection of certainty and his glorying in contradictions, the bipolarity of aristocracy and democracy, for example. Simultaneously embracing opposites, he is given credit for not seeing reality as uniform and orderly, but as complex and contradictory.

Tocqueville, America's public philosopher in spite of himself, is truly everywhere in American public life, even where he should not be. Thus in 1989, when the United States Library of Congress, than whom there is no more important intellectual and historic arbiter for Americans, commemorated the bicentennial of the French Revolution, it officially and ceremoniously marked the occasion with an exhibition devoted to Tocqueville, who, of course, had nothing to do with 1789. No matter. The exhibition was named "A Passion for Liberty," his words from *Democracy in America*: Tocqueville, he who must be quoted.

NOTES

1. Anne Bentzel, *Traveling Tocqueville's America: Retracing The 17-State Tour That Inspired Alexis de Tocqueville's Political Classic Democracy in America* (Baltimore, 1998), p. ix.
2. *New York Times*, 2 July 1986.
3. *Washington Post*, 6 November 1984.
4. *New York Times*, 23 November 1976.
5. United Way, National Alexis de Tocqueville Society Awards.
6. Max Lerner, *Tocqueville and American Civilization* (New York, 1969), p. 3.
7. Edward Banfield, in *Interpreting Tocqueville's Democracy in America* (Savage, Maryland, 1975), p. 239.
8. Matthew Mancini, *Alexis de Tocqueville* (New York, 1994), p. 5.
9. James T. Schleifer, *The Making of Tocqueville's Democracy in America* (Chapel Hill, 1980), p. 3.
10. Ibid.
11. Larry Siedentop, *Tocqueville* (New York, 1994), p. 11.
12. Mancini, p. 15.
13. J. P. Meyer, *Alexis de Tocqueville* (New York, 1940), p. 209.
14. Siedentop, p. 9.
15. Joseph Epstein, introduction to *Democracy in America* (New York, 2000), p. xxiv.
16. "Two Weeks in The Wilderness", see below, p. 922.
17. Ibid., p. 927.
18. Charles Dickens, cited in Marvin Meyers, *Jacksonian Persuasion* (New York, 1957), p. 125.
19. Epstein, p. xxvii.
20. André Jardin, *Tocqueville: A Biography* (Baltimore, 1998), p. 224.

21. Michael Kammen, *Alexis de Tocqueville and Democracy in America* (Washington, DC, 1998), p. 11.

22. Bruce James Smith, *Politics and Remembrance: Republican Themes in Machiavelli, Burke and Tocqueville* (Princeton, 1985), p. 168.

23. Schleifer, p. 122.

24. Until 1913, US senators were appointed by their state legislators. Since then, they have been elected by the eligible voters of the state they represent.

25. "Two Weeks in the Wilderness", see below, pp. 883–4, 890.

26. Mayer, p. 104.

27. Siedentop, p. 136.

28. Kammen, p. 10.

29. Lerner, p. 75.

I would like to thank Michael Millman of Penguin Putnam for his unfailing support. Marwan Hanania, Jeff Selinger, and, as always, Michael Busch have provided invaluable assistance.

Further Reading

Henry Steele Commager, *Commager on Tocqueville* (Columbia: University of Missouri Press, 1993).

Seymour Drescher, *Tocqueville and England* (Cambridge, Mass.: Harvard University Press, 1964).

Abraham S. Eisenstadt (ed.), *Reconsidering Tocqueville's Democracy in America* (New Brunswick, New Jersey: Rutgers University Press, 1988).

André Jardin, *Tocqueville: A Biography* (Baltimore: Johns Hopkins University Press, 1998).

Michael Kammen, *Alexis de Tocqueville and Democracy in America* (Washington, DC: Library of Congress, 1998).

John C. Koritansky, *Alexis de Tocqueville and the New Science of Politics: An Interpretation of Democracy in America* (Durham, North Carolina: Carolina Academic Press, 1986).

Max Lerner, *Tocqueville and American Civilization* (New York: Harper & Row, 1996).

Ken Masugi (ed.), *Interpreting Tocqueville's Democracy in America* (Savage, Maryland: Rowman and Littlefield, 1991).

J. P. Mayer, *Alexis de Tocqueville, A Biographical Study* (New York: Viking Press, 1940).

George Wilson Pierson, *Tocqueville in America* (Baltimore: Johns Hopkins University Press, 1996).

James T. Schleifer, *The Making of Tocqueville's Democracy in America* (Chapel Hill, North Carolina: University of North Carolina Press, 1980).

Larry Siedentop, *Tocqueville* (New York: Oxford University Press, 1994).

Translator's Note

This translation has used the 13th edition of Tocqueville's text, which can be taken as the most definitively reliable despite the calligraphic difficulties of his original manuscript. Any study of that Tocqueville manuscript will lead us to realize that endless amendments and additions are possible in arriving at an up-to-date text. While this translation has disregarded the decipherings of modern scholars, I can recommend the two-volume work by Eduardo Nolla, published by the Librarie Philosophique J. Vrin, Paris, 1990, for those who wish to follow this path.

Any translator will recall Tocqueville's rebuke to his first English translator, Henry Reeve, whose overly weighty version carried an interpretation which the author never intended. Certainly, the translator must be without bias and has to serve the meaning. Tocqueville's mastery of and enthusiasm for democracy and his balanced view of the political and social issues of early nineteenth-century America are such that the translation needs to convey these dimensions to the reader. Reeve's rendering is intellectually dense and elegantly inflated: the style of the original is neither and the translator must avoid any unnecessarily deferential respect for Tocqueville's influential and important work.

Tocqueville seems consciously to avoid a style which might, through excessive imagery or elaboration of language, divert the reader from the message which pervades the book. The very complication and variety of information which besieged Tocqueville on his travels could have sunk a lesser intelligence. He exercises a control and discipline which are remarkable, managing the impressions and opinions in modest and direct language, democratic in its appeal and contained in its authority. All this helps to deal with that inherent pitfall faced by any translator, namely, how to transport a two-hundred-year-old language into a modern idiom which, in itself, will not date over the ensuing decades; at least Tocqueville has managed that in his own text. Thus, this translation has aimed both to achieve an English version which respects the original style and language and to create a vehicle to convey Tocqueville's ideas. The style I have used is self-consciously easy to read yet aims at an available elegance. While the original displays the characteristic euphony of the French language, this version has not been afraid to convey the meaning using the broader dimension of English idiom.

The arrangement of Tocqueville's paragraphs has been almost entirely adopted, since it lightens the task of reading and avoids the heaviness which characterizes the Reeve translation.

The inclusion of Tocqueville's journey to the northern boundary of America—*Two Weeks in the Wilderness*—and another, shorter piece entitled *Excursion to Lake Oneida*, qualifies this edition as the only one available of all his writings on America. The new translation, we hope, will come to be seen as the definitive version for this new century and will be judged as the most accurate and attractive rendering of this seminal political authority.

The reader should be alerted that Tocqueville's references to race might not gain modern approval. The translation makes no concessions to modern susceptibilities but reflects the climate of the age in which the text was written. However, it is remarkable that Tocqueville displays a deep sympathy for the Negroes, the Indians and those of mixed race which allays any misgivings we might have.

I have had the good fortune to be joined by two collaborators of discernment and critical intelligence. Monique Meager—Maîtrise de la Sorbonne and lecturer in French—has brought the indispensable talents of her bilingual background and her residence in France and England. In these days of computerization, I would have been unable to undertake the lengthy task presented by Tocqueville's two-volume work without the support and encouragement of Gay Scase—currently Head of Languages at St Albans School, Hertfordshire—whose indefatigable enthusiasm, friendship and humor have sustained me through the meticulous process of the collation, interpretation, and accuracy that this monumental study demands. While I take responsibility for the final form of the text, we have both traveled along paths of variants and differing perspectives, attempting to divine what Tocqueville might truly have thought beneath this innocuously beguiling, unfussy, and whimsically down-to-earth view of American manners and preoccupations.

Above all, I was enthralled by this French aristocrat's lofty honesty and uncompromising integrity. It remains astonishing how broad was his viewpoint and how apt were his forecasts.

GEB
St Albans
April 2002

Democracy in America

Contents

VOLUME 1

VOLUME 2

THE AUTHOR'S NOTE TO THE SECOND VOLUME

PART 1

THE INFLUENCE OF DEMOCRACY UPON THE INTELLECTUAL MOVEMENT IN THE UNITED STATES

PART 2

INFLUENCE OF DEMOCRACY ON THE OPINIONS OF AMERICANS

PART 3

THE INFLUENCE OF DEMOCRACY ON CUSTOMS AS SUCH

PART 4

THE INFLUENCE EXERCISED BY DEMOCRATIC IDEAS AND OPINIONS ON POLITICAL SOCIETY

VOLUME 1

AUTHOR'S INTRODUCTION

Of all the novel things which attracted my attention during my stay in the United States, none struck me more forcibly than the equality of social conditions. I had no difficulty in discovering the extraordinary influence this fundamental fact exerts upon the progress of society; it sets up a particular direction to public attitudes, a certain style to the laws, fresh guidelines to governing authorities, and individual habits to those governed.

Soon I came to recognize that this very fact extends its influence well beyond political customs and laws; it exercises no less power over civil society than it does over the government. It forms opinion, creates feelings, proposes ways of acting, and transforms anything it does not directly instigate itself.

Consequently, as I studied American society, I increasingly viewed this equality of social conditions as the factor which generated all the others and I discovered that it represented a central focus in which all my observations constantly ended.

Then I turned my thoughts back to our own hemisphere and it seemed to me that I could see something similar there to the situation I observed in the New World. I saw that, while the equality of social conditions had not reached the extreme limits of the United States, it was growing closer to that level and that the democracy prevailing over American societies appeared to me to be advancing rapidly to power in Europe.

That was the moment I conceived the idea for the book that lies before the reader.

Everyone can see that a widespread revolution toward democracy is in full swing amongst us but it is not viewed by everyone in the same way. Some look upon it as something new and, taking it as an accident, are still hoping to be able to check its progress, whereas others consider it irresistible because they see it as the most sustained, longstanding, and permanent development ever found in history.

I turn my thoughts back for a moment to the France of seven hundred years ago which I discover was split between a small number of families who owned the land and ruled over the people living there; the right of governing at that time moved down the generations along with the family inheritance; men had only one method of acting against each other and that was force; only one source of power existed and that was landed property.

But along came the political power of the clergy which, from the outset, soon expanded. The clergy opened its ranks to all, rich and poor alike, commoner and lord alike; by means of the Church, equality began to permeate the government and the man who might have vegetated in eternal enslavement as a serf was elevated to the heart of the nobility when he became a priest, often taking his seat above kings.

As society became more civilized and stable over time, the different relationships between men became more complicated and numerous. The need of civil laws was sharply felt which gave rise to lawgivers emerging from the darkened precincts of the law courts or the dusty backwater of the clerks' offices to sit in the courts of monarchs alongside feudal barons wrapped in ermine and mail.

Kings suffered ruin from their great enterprises; nobles grew exhausted in their private feuds; commoners made money from trade. The influence of money began to assert itself in state affairs. Business opened a new pathway to power and the financier became a political influence both despised and flattered.

Gradually education expanded and a taste for literature and the arts was awakened; the mind then turned into an element of success; knowledge was a weapon of government and intelligence, a social force; men of letters entered public life.

Meanwhile, as new avenues to power were discovered, the value of high birth declined. In the eleventh century nobility was beyond all price; in the thirteenth, it could be purchased; 1270 saw the first appointment to the peerage and the principle of equality was at last introduced into government by the aristocracy itself.

Over the past seven hundred years it has sometimes happened that, in their struggle against the authority of the king or in their attempt to relieve their rivals of power, the nobles have given some political power to the people.

Still more frequently we have seen kings involving the lower classes of the state in government in order to reduce the power of the aristocracy.

French kings have shown themselves to be the most energetic and consistent of levelers. When they have been ambitious and strong, they have striven to raise the people to the same level as the nobles. When they have been mild-tempered and weak, they have allowed the people to rise under their own efforts. Some have supported democracy through their talents, others through their defects. Louis XI and Louis XIV took care to reduce everything below the throne to the same level, while Louis XV[a] ended up in the dust along with the whole of his court.

As soon as citizens began to own land on any other than a feudal tenure and when emergence of personal property could in its turn confer influence and power, all further discoveries in the arts and any improvement introduced into trade and industry could not fail to instigate just as many new features of equality among men. From that moment, every newly invented procedure, every newly found need, every desire craving fulfillment were steps to the leveling of all. The taste for luxury, the love of warfare, the power of fashion, the most superficial and the deepest passions of the human heart seemed to work together to impoverish the wealthy and to enrich the poor.

From the moment when the exercise of intelligence had become a source of strength and wealth, each step in the development of science, each new area of knowledge, each fresh idea had to be viewed as a seed of power placed within people's grasp. Poetry, eloquence, memory, the beauty of wit, the fires of imagination, the depth of thought, all these gifts which heaven shares out by chance turned to the advantage of democracy and, even when they belonged to the enemies of democracy, they still promoted its cause by highlighting the natural grandeur of man. Its victories spread, therefore, alongside those of civilization and education. Literature was an arsenal open to all, where the weak and the poor could always find arms.

Reading through the pages of our history, we shall scarcely find any great events which did not promote the cause of equality over the last seven hundred years.

The Crusades[b] and the English[c] wars decimated the nobles and divided up their lands; the setting up of municipal corporations introduced democratic freedom into the feudal monarchy; the invention of firearms reduced the serf and the nobleman to the same level on the field of battle; the printing press presented the same resources to the minds of everyone; the postal service deposited knowledge on the threshold of the poor man's cottage as much as at the gate of the palace; Protestantism maintained that all men are equally capable of finding the pathway to heaven. The discovery of America opened up a thousand new roads to fortune and delivered wealth and power to the most humble of adventurers.

If you look closely at what happened in France from the eleventh century, you will not fail to notice that, at the end of each fifty-year period, a twin revolution has affected the state of society. The nobleman has dropped down the social scale while the commoner has risen; the one moves down, the other climbs up. Each half-century brought them closer and they will soon meet.

Nor is this simply a feature peculiar to France. In whatever direction we glance, we perceive the same revolution in motion throughout the entire Christian world.

Everywhere we look, the various events of people's lives have turned to the advantage of democracy; all men have helped its progress with their efforts, both those who aimed to further its success and those who never dreamed of supporting it, both those who fought on its behalf and those who were its declared opponents; everyone has been driven willy-nilly along the same road and everyone has joined the common cause, some despite themselves, others unwittingly, like blind instruments in the hands of God.

The gradual unfurling of equality in social conditions is, therefore, a providential fact which reflects its principal characteristics; it is universal, it is lasting and it constantly eludes human interference; its development is served equally by every event and every human being.

Would it be wise to think that a social change which lies so far back in history could be halted by the efforts of a single generation? Can it be believed that democracy, which has destroyed feudalism and overcome kings, will retreat before the wealthy or the middle classes? Will it stop now that it has become so powerful and its adversaries so weak?

So where are we going? No one could possibly say, for we have already lost the terms of comparison: social conditions are currently more equal among Christians than they have ever been at any time in history or anywhere in the world; thus the extent of what has already been achieved prevents our seeing what may still be achieved.

The whole of the book in front of the reader has been written under the pressure of a kind of religious terror exercised upon the soul of the author by the sight of this irresistible revolution which has progressed over so many centuries, surmounting all obstacles, and which is still advancing today amid the ruins it has caused.

God does not need to speak for himself in order for us to discover the definitive signs of his will; it is enough to examine the normal course of nature and the consistent tendency of events. I know without needing to hear the voice of the Creator that the stars trace out in space the orbits which his hand has drawn.

If lengthy observation and sincere reflection brought contemporary man to recognize that the gradual and progressive development of equality constitutes both the past and the future of his history, that discovery alone would confer upon this development the sacred character of a decree from the ruler upon high. Any desire to halt democracy would then appear a struggle against God himself so that nations would merely have to fit in with that social state imposed upon them by Providence.

The Christian nations of our day appear to me to present a

frightening spectacle; the change carrying them along is already powerful enough for it to be impossible to stop yet not swift enough for us to despair of bringing it under control. Their destiny is in their own hands but it will soon slip from their grasp.

The first of the duties currently imposed upon the rulers of our society is to educate democracy, to reawaken, if possible, its beliefs, to purify its morals, to control its actions, gradually to substitute statecraft for its inexperience and awareness of its true interests for its blind instincts, to adapt its government to times and places, and to mold it according to circumstances and people.

A new political science is needed for a totally new world.

But that is something we scarcely consider. Positioned as we are in the middle of a rapid stream, we stare fixedly at a few ruins we can still see on the shore as the current drags us away backwards toward the abyss.

In no country in Europe has the great social revolution I have just described made more rapid advances than in France but this progress has always been haphazard.

Never have the heads of state made any advance preparations for it; it has occurred despite them or unknown to them. The most powerful, the most intelligent, and the most upright classes of the nation have not made any attempt to take it over so as to control it. Democracy has thus been abandoned to its primitive instincts; it has grown like those children who, deprived of a father's care, are left to fend for themselves in the streets of our towns and who come to learn only the vices and wretchedness of our society. We seem unaware of its arrival even when it has unexpectedly taken control of supreme power. Then each person has slavishly submitted to its slightest whim; it is worshipped as the symbol of force. When afterwards it was weakened by its own excesses, the legislators conceived the rash plan of destroying it instead of attempting to educate and amend it. Their only idea was to drive it out of government with no wish to teach it how to govern.

The result was that the democratic revolution has taken place in the fabric of society without anyone's effecting the changes in laws, ideas, customs, and manners necessary to make this revolution beneficial. Thus we have democracy minus anything to lessen its defects or to promote its natural advantages; already aware of the defects it entails we still remain ignorant of the benefits it can bring.

When the power of the crown, supported by the aristocracy, peacefully governed the nations of Europe, society, in the midst of its wretchedness, enjoyed several kinds of happiness which we have difficulty in imagining or appreciating at the present time.

The power of a few subjects erected insurmountable barriers against the tyranny of the king; and kings, moreover, feeling endowed with an almost divine character in the eyes of the populace, derived from the very respect they aroused the wish never to abuse their power.

The nobles, placed at a remote distance from the people, assumed meanwhile the kind of benevolent and quiet interest in their destiny that the shepherd grants to his flock and, far from seeing the poor as their equals, they watched over their fate as though it were a duty placed in their hands by Providence.

The people, never imagining a social state other than their own, nor thinking that they could ever become the equals of their leaders, welcomed any blessings coming their way without discussing their rights. They loved their leaders when they were kind and fair, while having no difficulty, nor feeling any humiliation, in tolerating their harshness, as they would the inevitable calamities which they received at the hands of God. Moreover, custom and habits had set limits to tyranny and had established a kind of law at the very heart of violence.

Since the nobleman did not entertain the thought that anyone might wish to snatch away his privileges, which he regarded as legitimate, and since the serf looked upon his inferior position as a result of the immutable natural order, we may imagine that a kind of mutual goodwill might be established between these two classes so differently endowed by fate. At that time, society beheld inequality and unhappiness but men's souls were not humiliated.

It is not the exercise of power nor the habit of obedience that degrade men but the exercise of a power which is regarded as unlawful, or obedience to a power seen as wrongly held and oppressive.

On the one side lay property, violence, and leisure along with the pursuit of luxury, refinements of taste, intellectual pleasures, and the cultivation of the arts; on the other, work, coarse living conditions, and ignorance.

But at the heart of this ignorant and coarse crowd you came across energetic passions, generous opinions, deep beliefs, and primitive virtues.

The body of society, organized in this way, was able to enjoy stability, strength, and, above all, a sense of honor.

But now the classes are muddled; those barriers raised between men are being lowered; estates are being split up and power shared; education is expanding and men's intelligence tends toward equality; the condition of society is becoming democratic and the authority of democracy is finally taking root peacefully in all institutions and all social customs.

So I can conceive of a society in which everyone would look upon the law as his own work, would become attached to it and obey it quite easily; a society in which the authority of the government would be respected as necessary, not divine, and in which the affection accorded to the head of state would not be a passion but a reasoned and peaceful feeling. Since each man would have his rights, the preservation of which would be guaranteed, a manly trust would be established between all classes along with a kind of mutual courtesy, removed alike from arrogance or servility.

The people, instructed as to their true interests, would realize that, in order to benefit from the advantages of society, they would have to bow to its requirements. The freedom to associate that citizens would enjoy could then replace the individual power of the nobles and the state would be protected from tyranny and license.

I realize that in a democratic state established in this way, society will not stand still, but the changes in the community can be ordered and progressive; if such a society displays less brilliance than an aristocracy, there will also be less wretchedness; pleasures will be less outrageous and wellbeing will be shared by all; the sciences will be on a smaller scale but ignorance will be less common; opinions will be less vigorous and habits gentler; you will notice more vices and fewer crimes.

In the absence of the enthusiasm and heat of religious beliefs, sometimes great sacrifices may be obtained from citizens as a result of their understanding and experience. Since every man is weak he feels the same needs as his fellows and, knowing that he can gain their support only if he offers them his help, he will quickly discover that his own private interest fuses with that of the whole community.

The nation, taken as a whole, will be less brilliant, less self-important, less sturdy perhaps but the majority of citizens will enjoy a greater degree of prosperity and the people will seem peaceful not because they have abandoned the hope of better things but because they know they are well off.

If everything failed to be good and useful in such a state of affairs, at least society would have taken hold of whatever good and useful elements it offered and men, having renounced forever the social advantages provided by aristocracy, would have grasped from democracy all the benefits it can present to them.

But as we have left behind the social conditions of our ancestors and have cast behind us their institutions, ideas, and customs in one confused heap, what have we put in their place?

The renown of royal authority has vanished away without being replaced by the majesty of laws; nowadays the people despise authority while fearing it, and fear now extorts from them more than respect and love achieved formerly.

I observe that we have destroyed those independent beings who were capable of fighting single-handed against tyranny but I perceive that government has inherited by itself all those powers it has wrenched from families, corporate bodies, or individuals. Thus, the power of a small number of citizens, sometimes oppressive and often conservative, has given way to the weakness of the whole community.

The dividing up of fortunes has reduced the distance separating rich from poor but as the gap has grown smaller they have discovered fresh reasons for mutual hatred; casting terrified and envious glances at one another, each seeks to deprive the other of power; for both of them equally, the concept of rights does not exist and power appears as the sole reason for action in the present and the only guarantee for the future.

The poor man has retained most of the prejudices of his forefathers without their beliefs, their ignorance without their virtues; he has entertained the dogma of self-interest as a guide for his actions without understanding how it works and his self-centeredness is no less blind than was formerly his devotion to others.

Society is peaceful not because it is aware of its own strength and wellbeing but because it believes itself to be weak and unsteady; it is frightened that any effort it makes may cost it its life. Everyone senses the malaise but no one has the necessary courage or energy to pursue any better course. People have desires, regrets, sorrows, and joys which produce nothing visible or lasting, like the passions of old men which end up as nothing but impotence.

Thus, we have abandoned whatever advantages the old regime possessed without grasping those gains offered by the present state of things; we have destroyed an aristocratic society and, as we complacently stand in the midst of the ruins of the old building, we seem to be willing to stay there forever.

What is occurring in the intellectual world is no less deplorable.

Since democracy in France has been hampered in its progress or abandoned, without support, to its lawless passions, it has overturned everything that has crossed its path and has shaken everything it has not completely destroyed. We have not seen it gradually taking over society in order to assert its power peacefully; it has not ceased to march forward through the confusion and agitation of a conflict. Flushed by the heat of the struggle and pushed beyond his natural boundaries by the opinions and excesses of his opponents, each person loses sight of the very object of his aims and expresses himself in a language which is alien to his real feelings and his innermost instincts.

As a consequence of that arises the strange and confused state of affairs we are forced to witness.

I waste my time in scouring through my recollections for I can find nothing more worthy of sorrow or pity than what is happening before our eyes. It is as if we have ruptured the natural link between a man's opinions and his tastes or his actions and his beliefs. The harmony which has always been observed between the feelings and the ideas of men appears in ruins and all the rules governing moral parallels have been abolished.

We still come across zealous Christians whose minds derive spiritual nourishment from the truths of the next world and who doubtless remain excited by human freedom as the source of all moral greatness. Christianity, which has made all men equal before God, will not flinch to see all citizens equal before the law. But by a strange combination of events, religion is temporarily involved with powers overturned by democracy and it often happens that it repels that equality it loves and curses freedom as an opponent would, whereas it could support freedom's struggles by taking it by the hand.

Alongside these religious men, I observe others whose sights are upon the earth rather than toward heaven. They are the followers of liberty not simply because they see it as the source of the noblest virtues but above all because they regard it as the spring of the greatest benefits. They sincerely wish to guarantee its authority and to enable men to taste its blessings. I realize that these people are about to call upon the help of religion, for they must know that the reign of liberty cannot be established without morality, nor morality without beliefs. It is enough for them to have seen religion on the side of their opponents; some attack it while others dare not defend it.

Past centuries have witnessed immoral and venal souls advocating slavery while some independent spirits and generous hearts were struggling in a hopeless fight for the preservation of human freedom. These days we often encounter a few men, noble and proud by nature, whose opinions are directly at variance with their inclinations and who praise a slavishness and degradation they have never personally experienced. Others, on the other hand, speak of freedom as if they were aware of its sanctity and majesty and noisily claim for humanity those rights which they have always refused to acknowledge.

I observe virtuous and peaceful men who have naturally been placed as leaders of the populace around them because of their pure morals, quiet habits, wealth, and education. Filled with a sincere affection for their country, they are ready to make great sacrifices for it. However, civilization often finds them to be its enemies; they confuse its abuses with its blessings and the idea of evil is, in their minds, inseparably linked with that which is new.

Alongside them, I see others who strive, in the name of progress, to turn men into materialistic beings and who want to discover the expedient while paying scant attention to fairness, knowledge far removed from beliefs, and prosperity which has nothing to do with virtue. These people are called the champions of modern civilization, insolently placing themselves at its head, usurping a position left open to them and one which highlights their unworthiness.

So where are we now?

Men of religion fight against freedom and the friends of freedom attack the religions; some noble and generous spirits praise slavery while some dishonorable and servile souls advocate independence; some honorable and enlightened citizens are opposed to all progress while some unpatriotic and immoral men become apostles of civilization and education!

Have all centuries resembled our own? Has man always looked out upon a world like our own, where nothing is consistent, where virtue is without genius, genius without honor, where the love of order is joined to an inclination for tyranny and the holy worship of liberty to a disdain for the law, where conscience casts a dim light upon human actions and where nothing any longer seems to be prohibited or permitted, honest or shameful, true or false?

Am I to believe that the Creator made man to leave him struggling endlessly with the intellectual wretchedness that surrounds us? I cannot think so. God is preparing a calmer and more stable future for European societies; I am unaware of his plans but I shall never stop believing in them because I cannot fathom them and I prefer to mistrust my own intellectual capacities than his justice.

There is one country in the world where the great social revolution I speak of seems to have gradually reached its natural limits; it has taken place there simply and easily, or rather it can be stated that this particular country is seeing the results of the democratic revolution which we are undergoing without having endured the revolution itself.

The immigrants settling in America at the start of the seventeenth century somehow unlocked the democratic from all those other principles it had to contend with in the old communities of Europe and they transplanted that alone to the New World, where it has been able to grow freely and develop its legislation peacefully by moving in harmony with the country's customs.

It seems beyond doubt that sooner or later we shall attain, like the Americans, an almost universal equality of social conditions. I am not concluding from this that we shall ever be necessarily led to draw the same political consequences which the Americans have derived from what is a similar state of society. I am far from supposing that they have found the only form of government available to a democracy but it is enough that in both countries the inspiration of laws and customs should be the same for us to take a great interest in finding out what it has produced in each of them.

It is not simply, therefore, to satisfy a curiosity, albeit justified, that I have examined America; my aim has been to discover lessons from which we may profit. It would be a bizarre mistake to think that I intended to write a hymn of praise; whoever reads this volume will be fully convinced that such was never my plan, any more than it has been my aim to advocate any form of government in particular; for I belong to those who believe that absolute perfection is almost never a feature of a system of laws. I have not even intended to judge whether this social revolution, which I believe to be irresistible, is advantageous or disastrous for mankind. I have acknowledged that this revolution is already accomplished or about to be so and I have chosen among those peoples who have experienced its effects the one in which its development has been the most comprehensive and peaceful, in order that I may make out clearly its natural consequences and the means of turning it to men's advantage. I confess that in

America I have seen more than America itself; I have looked there for an image of the essence of democracy, its inclinations, its personality, its prejudices, its passions; my wish has been to know it if only to realize at least what we have to fear or hope from it.

In the first part of this work I have, therefore, attempted to show the direction which democracy in America, left to its inclinations and abandoned almost without hindrance to its instincts, has naturally given to its laws, the course it has imprinted on the government and in general the control it has taken over public affairs. I set out to discover the advantages and drawbacks which it entails. I have sought out the safeguards Americans used to guide it and those others they omitted; I have undertaken to highlight the reasons which allow it to govern society.

In a second part, I aimed to portray the influence equality of social conditions and democratic government have exerted upon civil society, upon habits, ideas, and manners but I am beginning to feel less enthusiastic about achieving this plan. Before being able to fulfill the task I set for myself, my work will have become almost useless. Someone else is bound to reveal to readers the leading traits of the American character and, by concealing the seriousness of the description beneath a cloak of flippancy, to lend to the truth a charm with which I could not have adorned it.[1]

I do not know whether I have succeeded in revealing what I have seen in America but I am confident that I sincerely wished to do so and that, except unwittingly, I have never given

1. At the time I published the first edition of this work, Monsieur Gustave de Beaumont, my traveling companion in America, was still working on his book entitled *Marie, ou l'Esclavage aux Etats-Unis*, which has since appeared. M. de Beaumont's main aim was to let people know the position of Negroes in Anglo-American society. His work will cast a sharp and fresh light upon the question of slavery, one which is vital for the united republics. I do not know whether I am mistaken, but it seems to me that, having deeply interested those who will wish to satisfy their emotions and seek out the images in the volume, M. de Beaumont's book should gain a still more substantial and longer lasting success among those readers who, above everything else, long for real insights and profound truths.

way to the need to adapt facts to ideas, instead of ideas to facts.

Whenever a point could be supported by written documentary evidence, I took care to revert to the original texts and to the most authentic and valued works.[2] I have cited my sources in the notes and anyone can verify them. Whenever it was a matter of opinion, political practice, or remarks on manners, I sought to consult the most informed men. Whenever an issue was important or doubtful, I was not satisfied with one witness but formed my judgment on the evidence of many witnesses.

At this point, the reader must of necessity take my word. I could often have quoted in support of my assertions authoritative names which are well-known to him or which deserve to be, but I have refrained from doing so. A stranger can often learn important truths at a host's fireside which the latter would perhaps conceal from a friend. A host can find some relief from the silence he is forced to keep because he does not fear his indiscreet remarks to a stranger who will not stay long. Each of these confidential conversations were recorded as soon as they took place but they will never leave my writing-case; I prefer to do injury to my narrative than add my name to that list of those travelers who repay the generous hospitality they received by causing sorrow or awkwardness.

I realize that, despite my precautions, nothing is easier than to criticize this book should anyone ever think of doing so.

Those who wish to take a close look will, I think, discover a dominant thought which binds together, so to speak, the various sections of the whole book. But the range of the topics which I have had to deal with is very wide and anyone attempting to single out one fact to challenge the body of facts, to quote one

2. Legislative and administrative documents have been supplied to me with a kindness which I shall always remember with gratititude. Among those American civil servants who have thus supported my researches, I will mention particularly Mr Edward Livingston, then Secretary of State (now the Minister Plenipotentiary in Paris). During my stay with Congress, Mr Livingston was quite willing to forward most of the documents which I possess relating to the federal government. Mr Livingston is one of those few men one likes from reading their writings, whom one admires and respects even before knowing them and to whom one is happy to owe a debt of gratitude.

idea wrenched from the main body of ideas, will manage to do so with ease.

I should, therefore, like people to do me the favor of reading my work in the same spirit that has guided my efforts and to judge this book by the overall impression it leaves, just as I myself have come to my opinions not for a particular reason but through the mass of evidence.

Neither should it be overlooked that the author who wishes to be understood is obliged to push each one of his ideas to its utmost theoretical conclusion and often to the limits of what is false and impracticable, for it is sometimes necessary to depart from the rules of logic in the case of actions, which is not the case with the spoken word. Man finds it almost as difficult to be inconsistent while speaking, as to be consistent in his actions.

Finally, I point out myself what a great many readers will regard as the fundamental defect of the work. This book does not exactly follow any particular person; in writing it I did not set out to serve or oppose any party; I attempted not to view things differently from others but to look further; while they busy themselves with tomorrow, my wish was to contemplate the future.

PART 1

CHAPTER I

THE EXTERIOR CONFIGURATION OF NORTHERN AMERICA

North America divided into two vast regions, one inclining
toward the pole, the other toward the equator—
The Mississippi Valley—Traces found there of the upheavals
of the planet—Shore of the Atlantic Ocean upon which the
English colonies were founded—Different aspects of North
and South America at the time of their discovery—North
American forests—Prairies—Wandering tribes of natives—
Their physical appearance, customs, and languages—
Traces of an unknown people.

North America gives us, in its external contours, general features easily discernible at first glance.

A sort of orderly method has prevailed in the separation of land and water, mountain and valley. A simple and majestic organization becomes evident in the very midst of the confusion of features and amid the extreme variation of scene.

It is divided almost equally into two vast areas. The one is confined to the north by the Arctic circle and to the west and east by the two great oceans. It then makes its way south, forming a triangle whose irregularly drawn sides finally come together beneath the great lakes of Canada.

The second starts where the first ends, extending over the remainder of the continent.

The one leans slightly toward the pole, the other toward the equator.

The land included in the first area slopes so imperceptibly toward the north that one might even call it a plateau. In the middle of this huge raised plain one meets neither lofty mountain nor deep valley.

The waters wend their haphazard way; the rivers flow into each other, merge and part, meet up again, disappear into a thousand marshlands, lose their way constantly in an intricate maze of water which they have created and finally reach the polar seas only after countless meanderings. The great lakes which bring this first area to a close are not confined, as most lakes in the Old World, between hill and rocks; their banks are level and rise only a few feet above the level of the water, thus each of them forming, as it were, a huge cup filled to the brim. The slightest shifts in the structure of the globe would tip their waves in the direction of the pole or toward the tropics.

The second area has more features which better prepare it to become the permanent home of man; two long mountain chains bisect it throughout its length: one of which, called the Allegheny range, follows the Atlantic seaboard, the other running parallel to the sea in the south.

The region enclosed between the two mountain chains comprises 1,341,650 square miles.[1] The area is therefore roughly six times bigger than that of France.

However, this immense land mass forms just one single valley which slopes down from the rounded summit of the Alleghenies to rise again up to the peaks of the Rockies without meeting any obstacles.

In the bottom of the valley flows a huge river toward which all the water runs down from the mountains.

Previously the French had called the river the St Louis in memory of their absent homeland; the Indians, in their pretentious language, have named it the Father of the Waters, or the Mississippi.

The Mississippi has its source at the extremity of the two

1.   See Darby's *View of the United States*, p. 499.

great areas referred to above, near the highest point of the plateau which separates them.

Nearby, rises another river[2] which discharges its waters into the polar sea.

The Mississippi itself appears at certain moments doubtful about the path it should take; several times it retraces its steps and it is only after checking its course in the heart of lakes and mountains that finally it makes up its mind and slowly traces its path toward the south.

At times quietly flowing along the bottom of the bed of clay hollowed out by nature, sometimes swollen by storms, the Mississippi irrigates more than 2,500 square miles along its course.[3]

Thirteen hundred and sixty-four miles above its estuary,[4] the river is already 15 feet deep on average and vessels of 300 tons sail up its length for a distance of 450 miles.

Fifty-seven broad navigable rivers flow into it. Among the tributaries of the Mississippi are counted a river of 3,096 miles,[5] one of 2,125,[6] one of 1,449,[7] one of 1,187,[8] four of 485,[9] without mentioning a countless number of streams which appear from all directions to vanish into it.

The valley irrigated by the Mississippi seems to have been created for itself alone; it dispenses, as it pleases, both good and evil like a god. In the vicinity of the river, nature displays an inexhaustible fertility; gradually, as one moves away from its banks, the vegetation becomes poorer, the land impoverished, everything languishes or dies. Nowhere have the great upheavals of the planet left clearer traces than in the valley of the Mississippi. The entire appearance of the land bears witness to the effort of the water which brings sterility as much as abundance. The waves of the primeval ocean have piled up thick layers of

2. The Red River.
3. See *Warden's Description of the United States* vol. 1, p. 166.
4. Ibid., vol. 1, p. 169.
5. The Missouri, ibid., vol. 1, p. 132.
6. The Arkansas, ibid., vol. 1, p. 188.
7. The Red River, ibid., vol. 1, p. 190.
8. The Ohio, ibid., vol. 1, p. 192.
9. The Illinois, St Pierre, St Francis, Des Moines.

humus on the floor of the valley which have been worn down over the course of passing time. On the right bank of the river you encounter extensive plains, as even as the field flattened by the laborer's roller. On the other hand, as you approach the mountains, the land adopts an increasingly uneven and sterile look; the ground is, as it were, pierced in a thousand places and primitive rock formations appear here and there like the bones of a skeleton after time has eaten away the muscles and the flesh. A granite sand, and stones awkwardly hewn, cover the surface of the earth; some plants struggle to thrust their shoots past these obstructions; it is as if a fertile field were covered with the rubble of a vast building. By analyzing these stones and sand, it is, in fact, simple to note a direct parallel between their substance and that of the arid and broken peaks of the Rocky Mountains. Having deposited the earth upon the floor of the valley, there is no doubt that the waters carried on their work, dragging with them a part of the rocks themselves; they have tumbled down the nearby slopes and, after crushing each other, have peppered the foot of the mountains with debris wrenched from their peaks. (See Appendix A, p. 823.)

The Mississippi basin is, all in all, the most magnificent habitation that God ever prepared for man and yet you could still say that it is no more than a vast desert.

On the eastern slope of the Alleghenies, between the foot of these mountains and the Atlantic Ocean, unfurls a long stretch of rocks and sand forgotten by the receding sea. The land mass is only 116 miles wide on average but is 945 miles long. The ground in this section of the American continent lends itself reluctantly to the efforts of cultivation. The vegetation is thin and without variety.

It is along this inhospitable coastline that the first efforts of human endeavor concentrated. Along this tongue of arid land we see the birth and growth of the English colonies which were to become one day the United States of America. Still to this day the heart of power is concentrated there, whereas behind this are grouped, almost unseen, the real elements of the great people to which, doubtless, the future of the continent belongs.

When the Europeans landed upon the shores of the West

Indies and later upon the South American shores, they believed themselves to be transported to the lands of fable, celebrated by poets. The sea sparkled with the fires of the tropics. The extraordinary clarity of its waters revealed its depths to the sailor for the very first time.[10] Here and there appeared small scented islands seemingly floating like baskets of flowers upon the ocean's calm surface. In these magical places what lay before one's eyes seemed ready for the needs of man or measured for his pleasures. Most of the trees were laden with nourishing fruit and those least useful to man charmed his sight by the brilliance and variety of their colors. In a forest grove of sweet-scented lemon trees, wild fig trees, round-leaved maple, acacia, and oleander, all intertwined by flowering creepers, a host of birds unknown in Europe flashed their crimson and blue wings while mingling the chorus of their voices with the harmonies of nature, full of movement and life. (See Appendix B, p. 824.)

Death was concealed beneath this shining mantle; but it was not then obvious and, in addition, the atmosphere of these climatic conditions produced a kind of draining influence which riveted man to the present and rendered him indifferent to the future.

North America assumed a different appearance: there all was weighty, serious, solemn; it might be said that it had been created to become the realm of the mind just as the other was the home of the senses.

A turbulent ocean of mists surrounded its shore; granite rocks and sandy strands fenced it round, woods covering its banks displayed a somber and sad foliage; nothing much else could be seen growing there but the pine trees, the larch, the ilex, the wild olive, and laurel.

After forcing your way through this first barrier, you entered the shade of the central forest where the tallest trees in either hemisphere grew close together. The plane tree, the catalpa, the

10. Malte-Brun tells us (vol. 3, p. 726) that the Caribbean waters are so transparent that corals and fish are visible at a depth of sixty fathoms. The ship seemed to float on air, the navigator became giddy as his gaze penetrated through the crystal sea and beheld underwater gardens, beds of shells, gilded fishes gliding among the tufts and clumps of seaweed.

sugar maple, and the Virginia poplar linked their branches with those of the oak, beech, and lime.

As in the forests under man's control, death struck here relentlessly but no one took on the responsibility of removing the debris which it had caused. The layers of debris grew ever higher; there was not sufficient time to reduce them quickly enough to dust and to prepare fresh spaces. Yet, in the very midst of this debris, the work of reproduction never ceased. All species of climbing plants and grasses forced their way past the obstacles to the light; they crawled along fallen trees, crept into the wood dust, raising and cracking the dried bark which still covered them, and cleared a path for their young shoots. Thus death arrived in some way to aid life. Both were present, aiming seemingly to bind and meld their endeavors.

In the profound darkness of these forests a thousand streams, as yet outside the control of man, kept the air constantly damp. Hardly any flowers, any wild fruit, any birds were seen.

The fall of a tree overturned by age, a river's waterfall, the bellowing of buffalo, and the whistling of the winds were the only disturbances in the silence of nature.

To the east of the great river, the woods partly disappeared and, in their place, lay endless prairies. Had nature, in its infinite variety, blocked the cultivation of these trees in this fertile countryside or, rather, had the forest covering it been destroyed previously by the hand of man? This is something neither tradition nor the researches of science has succeeded in clarifying.

These huge deserts were not, however, wholly free of the presence of man; a few tribes had been moving about for centuries beneath the shades of the forest or on the pastures of the prairies. From the estuary of the St Lawrence as far as the delta of the Mississippi, from the Atlantic Ocean to the sea in the south, these natives resembled each other in ways which bore witness to their common origins. However, they differed from all other known races:[11] they were neither white like Europeans,

---

11. With the progress of discovery, it has been found that some resemblance exists between the physical appearance, the language, and the habits of North American Indians and those of the Tungus, Manchus, Mongols, Tartars, and other wandering tribes of Asia. The land occupied by these

nor yellow like the majority of Asiatics, nor black like Negroes; their skin had a reddish color, their hair long and gleaming, their lips thin and their cheekbones very prominent. The different languages spoken by the native races of America exhibited variations in vocabulary but they were all subject to the same rules of grammar. These rules deviated in several respects from those which, up to that point, had appeared to shape the formation of human language.

The idiom of the Americans seemed the result of a new combination of elements; it heralded, on the part of its inventors, an effort of intelligence of which present-day Indians appear incapable. (See Appendix C, p. 824.)

The social arrangements of these people also differed in several respects from what we saw in the Old World: one might have said that they had multiplied their numbers freely in the heart of their deserts, with no contact with races more civilized than their own. Thus with them one did not encounter those nebulous and incoherent ideas of good and evil, that deepest corruption, which is usually linked with ignorance and crude ways of life in civilized nations which have reverted to barbarity. The Indian owed a debt only to himself: his virtues, vices, and prejudices were his own achievement: he had grown up in the primitive independence of his nature.

The coarseness of the populace in civilized countries results not only from their ignorance and poverty but from the fact that, being coarse, they are in daily contact with enlightened and wealthy men.

The sight of their adversity and weakness, in contrast each day to the happiness and power of some of their compatriots, arouses, at the same time, anger and fear in their hearts; the feeling of their inferiority and dependence frustrates and humiliates them. This inner state of mind finds a parallel in their ways

---

tribes is not very far from Bering's Strait, which allows us to suppose that at a remote period people came across to inhabit the desert continent of America. But this is a point which has not yet been clarified by science. See Malte-Brun, vol. 5; the works of Humboldt; Fischer: *Conjecture sur l'origine des Américains*; Adair: *History of the American Indians*.

as it does in their language; they are simultaneously rude and vulgar.

The truth of this is easily proved by observation. The populace is coarser in aristocratic countries than anywhere else, in affluent towns more so than in the countryside.

In those places where one encounters very powerful and rich men, the weak and poor feel, as it were, burdened by their lowly status and, since they discover no means of being able to recover equality, they lose any sense of hope in themselves, drifting below any standards of human dignity.

The vexing effect of this contrast of human conditions is not to be found in the lives of the natives: the Indians, while they are all ignorant and poor, are all equal and free.

When the Europeans arrived, the native North Americans had no knowledge of the value of wealth and revealed an indifference toward the comforts which civilized man acquires with his means. However, nothing coarse could be perceived in them; rather there resided in their actions a characteristic reserve and a kind of noble politeness.

Gentle and hospitable in times of peace, pitiless in war, even beyond the known bounds of human ferocity, the Indian ran the risk of dying of hunger so as to help the stranger knocking upon his cabin door in the evening and yet would tear apart the quivering limbs of his prisoner with his own hands. The most notorious republics of ancient times had never admired courage more steadfast, souls more proud or a love of independence more uncompromising than that which was concealed by the wild woods of the New World at that time.[12] Europeans made but little impression when they landed upon the North American shores; their presence evoked neither envy nor fear. What hold could such men have over them? The Indian could live without

12. "One has seen among the Iroquois attacked by superior forces," says President Jefferson (*Notes on Virginia*, p. 148), "old men disdain to recur to flight or survive the destruction of their country, and brave death like the ancient Romans in the sack of Rome by the Gauls." Further, on p. 150: "There was never an instance known of an Indian begging his life when in the power of his enemies: on the contrary, he courts death by every possible insult and provocation."

necessities, suffer without complaint, die singing.[13] Like all the other members of the human family, these primitive men believed in the existence of a better world and worshipped, under different names, the Creator of the universe. Their ideas of the great intellectual truths were, in general, simple and philosophic. (See Appendix D, p. 826.)

However primitive appears the race whose character we are tracing, it could not be doubted that another, more civilized and more advanced in every way than this one, had preceded it in these same lands.

An obscure tradition, although one widely known to the majority of the Indian tribes of the Atlantic seaboard, informs us that, once upon a time, the settlement of these same races had been situated to the west of the Mississippi. Along the banks of the Ohio and in the central valley, we still find, every day, man-made tumuli. Digging to the very center of these monuments, one scarcely ever fails, so it is said, to come across human bones, strange instruments, weapons, metal utensils of all kinds, even some whose use is unknown to present-day races.

Present-day Indians are able to give no information on the history of this unknown people. Neither have those who lived three hundred years ago, at the time of the discovery of America, said anything from which one can draw even a theory. The traditional stories, these decaying monuments, cast no light. Yet, at that time, thousands of people lived who were similar to us; one cannot possibly doubt that. When did they arrive there, what was their origin, destiny, history? When and how did they perish? No one could say.

What a strange thing! There are races which have so utterly disappeared from the earth that even the memory of their name has been blotted out; their languages have gone, their reputation has faded away like a sound without an echo; but I know of not

13. See *Histoire de la Louisiane*, by Lepage Dupratz; Charlevoix: *Histoire de la Nouvelle France*; Letters of the Rev. G. Heckewelder, *Transactions of the American Philosophical Society*, vol. 1; Jefferson: *Notes on Virginia*, pp. 135–90. What is said by Jefferson is of special weight, given the personal merit of the writer, his especial position and the down-to-earth age in which he lived.

a single race which has not at least a grave to remind us of its passing. Thus of all the works of man, the most lasting is still the one which records his annihilation and wretchedness.

Although the vast country we have just described was inhabited by countless native tribes, it is justifiable to assert that, at the time of its discovery, it formed only a desert. The Indians took up residence there but did not possess it. It is through agriculture that man takes ownership over the soil and the first inhabitants of North America lived off the products of hunting. Their unforgiving prejudices, their indomitable passions, their vices and, still more perhaps, their savage virtues, exposed them to inevitable destruction. The ruin of these races began the day the Europeans landed on their shores; it has continued since then; it is reaching its completion at the present time. Providence, in placing them in the midst of the riches of the New World, seemed to have granted them only a short period of enjoyment; they had, in some sense, only a waiting brief. These shores so ready for commerce and industry, these deep rivers, this inexhaustible Mississippi Valley, this entire continent thus appeared like the still empty cradle of a great nation.

There it was that civilized men were to try to build society upon new foundations and that, applying for the first time theories unknown until then or considered inapplicable, they were about to give to the world a sight for which the history of the past had not prepared it.

CHAPTER 2

ON THE ORIGIN OF THE ANGLO-AMERICANS AND ON ITS IMPORTANCE FOR THEIR FUTURE

Usefulness of knowing the origin of the population in order to be able to understand their social condition and their laws—America is the only country where the origin of a

*great people can be clearly observed—In what respects all
those who came to live in English America resembled each
other—In what respects they differed—Remarks applicable
to all those Europeans who established themselves on the
shores of the New World—Colonization of Virginia—
Ditto New England—Original character of the first
inhabitants of New England—Their arrival—Their first
laws—Social Contract—Penal code borrowed from the
laws of Moses—Religious ardor—Republican spirit—
Intimate union of the spirit of religion and the spirit
of freedom.*

A man is born; his first years go by in obscurity amid the
pleasures or hardships of childhood. He grows up; then comes
the beginning of manhood; finally society's gates open to welcome him; he comes into contact with his fellows. For the first
time he is scrutinized and the seeds of the vices and virtues of
his maturity are thought to be observed forming in him.

This is, if I am not mistaken, a singular error.

Step back in time; look closely at the child in the very arms of
his mother; see the external world reflected for the first time in
the yet unclear mirror of his understanding; study the first
examples which strike his eyes; listen to the first words which
arouse within him the slumbering power of thought; watch the
first struggles which he has to undergo; only then will you
comprehend the source of the prejudices, the habits, and the
passions which are to rule his life. The entire man, so to speak,
comes fully formed in the wrappings of his cradle.

Something similar happens in the case of nations; they always
carry the marks of their beginnings. The circumstances which
accompanied their birth and contributed to their development
affect the remainder of their existence.

Were it possible to return to the very elements of social
groupings and to examine the first monuments of their history,
doubtless we could discover the source of the prejudices, habits,
and ruling passions, in fact of every ingredient of what we
call the national character. There we would light upon the
explanation for customs which nowadays are in apparent

contradiction to the prevailing manners; for laws which seem in opposition to accepted principles; for confused opinions encountered haphazardly in society, like those remnants of shattered chains sometimes still hanging from the vaulting of an ancient building, no longer supporting anything. In that way, an explanation would be forthcoming for the fate of certain nations which appear to be drawn by an unknown force toward a goal of which they are unaware. Until now such a study of the facts has been missing; the spirit of analysis has come to nations only in their mature years, and when, at last, they considered giving thought to the cradle of their life, time had already wrapped it in a cloud; ignorance and pride had surrounded it with legends which obscured the truth.

America is the only country in which we have been able to watch the natural and peaceful development of a society and define the influence exerted by the origins upon the future of the states.

At the time when the European nations landed on the shores of the New World, the features of their national characters were clearly set; each of them had a distinct appearance; and since they had already proceeded to that level of civilization which leads men to a study of themselves, they have conveyed to us a faithful portrait of their opinions, customs, and laws. Fifteenth-century man is almost as well known to us as we are to ourselves. Thus America highlights what the ignorance or the barbarity of early times has concealed from our gaze.

Since the men of our day are close enough to the period when American social groups were formed to know in detail their constituent parts, yet already far enough from that time to be able to judge what those earliest seeds have produced, they seem destined to see further than their predecessors into human events. Providence has placed within our grasp a torch our fathers lacked and has allowed us to discern in the destiny of nations the early inspirations which the opaque passage of time blocked from their view.

When, after giving close attention to the history of America, we examine carefully its political and social state, we can feel perfectly confident of this truth: that there is no opinion, habit, or law, maybe not even an event, I would venture to say, which is not easily explained by the point of departure. The readers of this book will therefore discover in this chapter the seed of what follows and the key to almost the whole work.

The immigrants who came at different times to dwell in the land which today covers the American Union differed from each other in many respects; their intentions were not similar and they governed themselves according to different principles.

However, these men shared common features and found themselves in a situation common to them all.

Language is possibly the strongest and most lasting link to bind men together. All the immigrants spoke the same language, all were children of the same people. Born into a country disturbed for centuries by struggles of different factions and where these factions were forced one by one to come beneath the protection of the law, their political education had been fashioned in this hard school and thus notions about rights and principles of real freedom were more widespread amongst them than among most other European peoples. At the time of the first wave of immigrants, government by common consent, that fertile propagator of free institutions, was already deeply rooted in the customs of the English and, with it, the doctrine of the sovereignty of the people had already been introduced into the very heart of the Tudor monarchy.[a]

We were at that time in the middle of the religious disputes which shook the Christian world. England had plunged, with a kind of madness, in this new direction. The character of the people, which had always been of a serious and reflective turn of mind, had become austere and argumentative. Knowledge had much increased by such intellectual contests and thus the mind became better developed. During this preoccupation with religion, morals became purer. All these general features of the nation could be more or less discerned in the faces of those of its sons who had sought a new life upon the other side of the Atlantic Ocean.

One observation, moreover, to which we shall have occasion to return later, applies not only to the English but also to the French and Spanish and to all the Europeans who came one after the other to settle upon the shores of the New World. Every new European colony contained, if not in a developed form, at least the seed of a fully grown democracy. There were two reasons for this: in general, it can be stated that when they left their mother country, the emigrants had no particular concept of any superiority one over the other. It is hardly the happy and the powerful who choose exile; poverty, along with wretchedness, offers the best guarantee of equal status known to man. However, it did happen, on several occasions, as a consequence of political or religious quarrels, that noblemen of high standing landed in America. Laws were established to form a hierarchy of position but it soon became evident that the soil of America rejected absolutely a landed aristocracy. To clear this unfriendly land, nothing short of the persistent and committed efforts of the owner himself was needed. Once the ground was prepared, it was found that its produce was not enough to support both an owner and a tenant farmer. The land was parceled up naturally, therefore, into smallholdings cultivated solely by the owner. Now, aristocracy takes root in the land, attaches itself to the soil from which it derives its power; it is not established by privileges alone, it is not founded on birth but upon the ownership of property handed down through the generations. A nation can offer huge fortunes and great misery; but if these fortunes are not attached to land ownership, true aristocracy does not exist, simply rich classes and poor ones.

All the English colonies, therefore, at the time of their inception, shared a great kindred spirit. From the start, they all seemed destined to promote the development of liberty, not the aristocratic liberty of their mother country, but middle-class, democratic liberty, a complete example of which had still not been encountered in the history of the world.

Within this general picture, however, marked divergences could be observed, as I must reveal.

We can distinguish two main branches in the great Anglo-American family which, so far, have grown without losing their distinct identity, the one in the south and the other in the north.

Virginia welcomed the first English colony. The immigrants[b] reached there in 1607. At that time, Europe was particularly taken with the idea that gold and silver mines are the source of national wealth: a fatal idea which has done more to impoverish those European nations who were enslaved by it and has destroyed more men in America than the united influence of war and bad laws. The men sent to Virginia[1] were, therefore, seekers of gold, adventurers without substance or character whose turbulent and restless outlook disturbed the early days of the colony,[2] making its progress uncertain. After them came men skilled in crafts and farming who, although more moral and less rowdy, were scarcely in any way superior to the lower classes in England.[3] No noble views, no spiritual thought presided over the foundation of these new settlements. Hardly had the colony been established than slavery[4] was introduced. This was the principal fact which was to exercise a huge influence over the characters, laws, and the entire future development of the South.

Slavery, as I shall explain later, brings dishonor to work; it introduces idleness into society together with ignorance and pride, poverty, and indulgence. It weakens the powers of the mind and dampens human effort. The influence of slavery, together with the English character, explains the customs and the social conditions of the South.

Upon the same English background were depicted quite

1. The charter granted by the Crown of England in 1609 stipulated, amongst other things, that the colonials should pay the crown a fifth of all that was produced from the gold and silver mines. See *Life of Washington*, by Marshall, vol. 1, pp. 18–66.

2. A large number of the colonizers, says Stith (*History of Virginia*), were undisciplined young men, shipped off by their families to save them from an ignominious fate; dismissed servants, fraudulent bankrupts, the debauched, and others of the same sort, those more likely to pillage and destroy than promote the establishment of the new settlements, made up the rest. Seditious leaders easily persuaded this band into all kinds of extravagances and excesses. See, relating to the history of Virginia, the following works: *History of Virginia from the First Settlements to the Year 1624*, by Smith; *History of Virginia*, by William Stith; *History of Virginia from the Earliest Period*, by Beverley, translated into French in 1807.

3. It was not until later that a certain number of rich English landowners came to settle in the colony.

4. Slavery was introduced around the year 1620 by a Dutch vessel which landed twenty Negroes on the banks of the James River. See Chalmer.

different features in the North. At this point I may be allowed
to go into some detail.

It is in these English colonies of the North, better known as
the New England states,[5] that were brought together the two or
three main ideas which today constitute the social theory of the
United States.

The New England principles spread first of all to neighboring
states; subsequently, they reached successively the more distant,
ending up, if I may put it this way, by *permeating* the entire
confederation. Now they exert their influence beyond its limits
to the whole American world. The civilization of New England
has been like a beacon lit upon mountain tops which, after
warming all in its vicinity, casts a glow over the distant horizon.

The founding of New England was a novel spectacle and
everything attending it was unusual and original; nearly all
the colonies were first inhabited by men without education
or means, driven from the land of their birth by poverty or
wrongdoing or by greedy speculators and adventurers. Some
settlements cannot even claim so honorable an origin. San Dom-
ingo was founded by brigands and currently the English law
courts are busy supplying Australia with its population.

The immigrants who settled on the New England shores all
belonged to the comfortably off classes of the mother country.
Their gathering on American soil exhibited from the outset
the peculiar situation of a society containing neither lords nor
common people, neither poor nor wealthy, so to speak. Relatively speaking, there was a greater number of intelligent men
than in any present-day European nation. Perhaps without
exception, all had received a quite advanced education and
several of them had established a reputation in Europe for their
talents and knowledge. The other colonies had been founded by
adventurers without family; the settlers of New England
brought with them laudable elements of order and morality;
they landed on the empty coastline together with their wives
and children. But what set them apart above all the others was

5.   The states of New England are those situated to the east of the Hudson;
      today they are six in number: i) Connecticut; ii) Rhode Island; iii) Massa-
      chusetts; iv) Vermont; v) New Hampshire; vi) Maine.

the very aim of their undertaking. They were not forced to abandon their native land by necessity; they left behind a social position they might well have regretted and an assured livelihood. Nor did they move to the New World in order to better their lives or to increase their wealth. They tore themselves away from the comforts of their native land to obey a purely intellectual need; by suffering the inevitable deprivations of exile, their object was the triumph of an *idea*.

The immigrants or, as they so aptly styled themselves, the *Pilgrims*, belonged to that English sect given the name of Puritan by the austerity of their principles. Puritanism was not only a religious doctrine; it linked itself in several respects to the most prominent democratic and republican theories. From that feature had emerged its most dangerous opponents. Persecuted by the rulers of their homeland, bruised because of their austere principles by the daily habits of the society in which they lived, the Puritans sought out a land so rough and so neglected that they might be allowed to live there as they wished and to worship God without restriction.

A few quotations will reveal a clearer picture of the outlook of these pious adventurers than all I could add myself. Nathaniel Morton, the historian of the first years of the New England settlements, makes the following comment.[6]

"I have for some length of time," he says, "looking upon it as duty incumbent, especially upon the immediate successors of those that have had so large experience of those many memorable and signal demonstrations of God's goodness, viz. the first beginners of this plantation in New England, to commit to writing his gracious dispensations on that behalf; so that, what we have seen, and what our fathers have told us, we may not hide from our children, showing to the generations to come the praises of the Lord (Psalms 78: 3, 4). That especially the seed of Abraham his servant, and the children of Jacob his chosen, may remember his marvelous works (Psalms 105: 5, 6) how that God brought a vine into this wilderness; that he cast out the

6. *New England's Memorial*, p. 14, Boston 1826. See also Hutchinson's *History*, vol. 2, p. 440.

heathen and planted it; and he also made room for it, and he caused it to take deep root, and it filled the land; so that it hath sent forth its boughs to the sea, and its branches to the river (Psalms 80: 13, 15). And not only so, but also that he hath guided his people by his strength to his holy habitation, and planted them in the mountain of his inheritance (Exodus 15: 13), that as especially God may have the glory of all, unto whom it is most due; so also some rays of glory may reach the names of those blessed saints that were the main instruments."

It is impossible to read this opening without, despite oneself, the feeling of religious awe; one seems to breathe an atmosphere of ancient thought, a flavor of the Bible.

The writer's beliefs and convictions heighten his language. In our eyes, as well as in his own, it is no longer a band of adventurers seeking their fortune beyond the seas; it is the germ of a great nation which God has placed upon a predestined shore.

The author continues and depicts thus the departure of the first emigrants.[7]

"So they left that goodly and pleasant city (Delft Haven), which had been their resting place; but they knew that they were pilgrims and strangers here below, and looked not much upon these things, but lifted up their eyes to heaven, their dearest country, where God hath prepared for them a city (Hebrews 11: 16). When they came to the place, they found the ship and all things ready; and such of their friends as could not come with them, followed after them. One night was spent with little sleep with the most, but with friendly entertainment, and Christian discourse, and other real expressions of true Christian love. The next day they went on board, and their friends with them, where truly doleful was the sight of that sad and mournful parting, to hear what sighs and sobs, and prayers did sound amongst them; what tears did gush from every eye, that sundry strangers could not refrain from tears. But the tide calling them away, their reverend pastor falling down on his knees, and they all with him, with watery cheeks commended them with most

7. *New England's Memorial*, p. 22.

fervent prayers unto the Lord and then they took leave one of another, which proved to be the last leave to many of them."

The emigrants numbered about one hundred and fifty—as many women and children as men. Their intention was to found a colony on the banks of the Hudson; but, after roaming a long time upon the ocean, they were finally forced to land on the arid shores of New England, at the spot where the town of Plymouth stands today. The rock where the pilgrims disembarked is still a landmark.[8]

"But before we pass on," says the historian I have already cited, "let the reader, with me, make a pause, and seriously consider this poor people's present condition, the more to be raised up for the admiration of God's goodness towards them in their preservation."[9]

"For being now passed the vast ocean, and the sea of troubles before in their preparations, they had now no friends to welcome them, no houses to repair unto to seek for succour: for the reason it was winter, and they that know the winters of the country, know them to be sharp and violent, subject to cruel and fierce storms, dangerous to travel to known places, much more to search unknown coasts.—Besides, what could they see but a hideous and desolate wilderness, full of wild beasts and wild men? And what multitudes of them were there, they then knew now; all things stand in appearance with a weather-beaten face, and the whole country full of woods and thickets, represented a wild and savage hue; if they looked behind them, there was the mighty ocean which they had passed, and was now as a main bar and gulf to separate them from all the civil parts of the world—which way soever they turned their eyes

8.   This rock has become the object of veneration in the United States. I have seen carefully preserved fragments of it in several towns in the Union. Does this not clearly show that the power and the greatness of man lie entirely in the soul? Here is a stone trodden by the feet of a few wretched people for but an instant, and it becomes famous; it is held in esteem by a great nation, every morsel is revered and its very dust is distributed far and wide. Yet what has become of the thresholds of palaces? and who cares?

9.   *New England's Memorial*, p. 35.

(save upward to heaven) they could have little solace or content."

We must not imagine that the piety of these Puritans was speculative nor that it demonstrated an ignorance of the progress of human affairs. Puritanism, as I have already remarked, was almost as much a political theory as a religious doctrine. No sooner had they landed on this inhospitable shore, described by Nathaniel Morton, than the immigrants turned their attention to the constitution of their society, by passing an immediate act, as follows:[10]

"We, the undersigned, who for the glory of God, the advancement of the Christian faith and the honor of our native land have undertaken to found the first colony upon these remote shores, do agree in this document, by solemn and mutual consent before God, to band together in a body politic in order to govern ourselves and to work toward the achievement of our plans. By virtue of this contract, we agree to frame laws, acts, and orders and to appoint, as the need arises, magistrates to whom we shall owe submission and obedience."

This took place in 1620. From that time on, immigration continued apace. The religious and political fanaticism which ravaged the British Empire throughout the reign of Charles I,[c] drove fresh swarms of sectarians to the shores of America every year. In England, the middle classes continued to provide the stronghold for Puritanism and it was from the heart of the middle classes that the majority of the emigrants came. The population of New England grew rapidly and, in contrast to the mother country where there was still an autocratic hierarchy of classes, the colony displayed, increasingly, the novel sight of a society equally ordered in all its parts. Democracy, such as antiquity had never dared to imagine, burst free from the old feudal society, fully grown and fully armed.

The English government, content to remove the seeds of

10. The emigrants who founded the state of Rhode Island in 1638, those
     who established themselves in New Haven in 1637, the first settlers in
     Connecticut in 1639 and the founders of Providence in 1640 began
     similarly by drawing up a social contract which was submitted for the
     approval of all interested parties. Pitkin's *History*, pp. 42 and 47.

disturbance and the sources of revolution, viewed with relief the extensive emigration. It even gave powerful support to the exodus and took very little interest in the fate of those who landed on American soil in search of a refuge from its harsh laws. The government could be said to have treated New England as a region given over to dreams of fancy and to the initiatives of innovators.

The English colonies, and this is one of the main causes of their prosperity, have always enjoyed greater personal freedom and political independence than the colonies of other nations; but nowhere was this principle of liberty more completely applied than in the states of New England.

At that time there was a general acceptance that the territories of the New World belonged to the European nation which had first discovered them.

Almost all the shoreline of Northern America became thus an English possession toward the end of the sixteenth century. There were various means used by the British government to populate these new domains: in certain instances, the king chose a governor for a section of the new territory to rule in the name and under the direct orders of the crown,[11] this being the colonial system adopted in the rest of Europe. At other times, he granted to one man or a company the ownership of certain tracts of the country.[12] The entire concentration of civil and political power was then in the hands of one or several individuals who, under the scrutiny and control of the crown, sold land and governed the inhabitants. Finally, a third system gave to a certain number of immigrants the right to form a political society and to govern themselves in all respects which were not contrary to the laws of the mother country under whose patronage the right was granted.

This method of colonization so conducive to freedom was enacted only in New England.[13]

11. This was the case in the state of New York.
12. Maryland, the Carolinas, Pennsylvania, and New Jersey were in this situation. See Pitkin's *History*, vol. 1, pp. 11–31.
13. See the work entitled *Historical Collection of State Papers and Other Authentic Documents Intended as Materials for a History of the United*

From 1628,[14] such a charter was granted by Charles I to emigrants who founded the colony of Massachusetts.

But in general, charters were accorded to the colonies of New England only years after their existence had become an established fact. Plymouth, Providence, New Haven, the states of Connecticut and Rhode Island[15] were founded without the help and, to some degree, without the knowledge of the mother country. The new inhabitants, without denying the supremacy of the homeland, did not set out to derive their powers from that source but set up their own institutions. Thirty or forty years passed before, in the reign of Charles II,[d] a royal charter legitimized their existence.

So, it is often difficult, when perusing the first historical and legislative records of New England, to perceive the ties which connected the immigrants to the land of their forefathers. We see them at all times exercising the rights of sovereignty, appointing magistrates, declaring peace or war, establishing law and order, enacting laws as if they owed allegiance to God alone.[16]

There is nothing more unusual or at the same time more enlightening than the laws passed during this period; it is there

---

States of America, by Ebeneser Hasard, printed at Philadelphia, 1792, for a great number of documents with important information valued for their content and authenticity relevant to the early years of the colonies; including the various charters granted by the English crown as well as the first acts of government.

See also the analysis of all these charters made by Mr Story, Supreme Court Judge of the United States, in the introduction to his *Commentaries on the Constitution of the United States.*

These documents show that the principles of representative government and the external forms of political liberty were introduced into all the colonies almost from the moment of their creation. These principles were more fully developed in the North than in the South, but they existed everywhere.

14. See Pitkin's *History*, vol. 1, p. 35. See Hutchinson's *The History of the Colony of Massachusetts*, vol. 1, p. 9.
15. Ibid., pp. 42–7.
16. The inhabitants of Massachusetts, in establishing criminal and civil law and law courts, had strayed from procedures followed in England: in 1650, the name of the king did not yet appear at the head of judicial mandates. See Hutchinson, vol. 1, p. 452.

that the key to the great social mystery which the United States now presents to the world is to be found.

Among these significant records, we shall particularly mark as one of the most characteristic, the code of laws which the small state of Connecticut enacted in 1650.[17]

The lawmakers of Connecticut[18] turned their attention initially to penal legislation for the composition of which they had the bizarre idea of using biblical texts.

"Whosoever shall worship a God other than the Lord shall be put to death." This was their opening statement. After that, ten or twelve similar measures taken verbatim from Deuteronomy, Exodus, and Leviticus.

Blasphemy, witchcraft, adultery,[19] rape were punished by death; grave offenses perpetrated by a son upon his parents were dealt the same penalty. Thus legislation belonging to a crude and half-civilized nation was transferred to the heart of a society endowed with enlightened minds and gentle ways. Never was the death penalty more frequently prescribed and never more rarely enforced.

The overriding concern of these legislators is the preservation of moral order and good practices in their society; thus they proceed continually to penetrate to the heart of man's conscience and not a single wrongdoing escapes the condemnation of the magistrate. The reader may have noticed the harshness of the law against adultery and rape. The simplest relations between unmarried people were strictly repressed. The judge was empowered to inflict one of the following three penalties upon the

---

17. *Code of 1650*, p. 28 (Hartford, 1830).
18. See also in Hutchinson's *History*, vol. 1, pp. 435–56, the analysis of the penal code adopted in 1648 by the colony of Massachusetts; this code is drawn up following the same principles as those of Connecticut.
19. Adultery was also punished by death by Massachusetts law and Hutchinson, vol. 1, p. 441, says that, in fact, several people suffered death for this crime. On this subject, he quotes a curious anecdote of an event which took place in the year 1663. A married woman had had intimate relations with a young man; she was widowed and she married him; several years passed. The public eventually began to suspect the extent of the intimacy that must have already existed between the two; they were pursued by the law; they were imprisoned and only narrowly escaped execution.

guilty: a fine, a lashing, or marriage,[20] and, if the records of the old courts of New Haven are to be believed, prosecutions of this kind were common enough. On 1 May 1660, we discover the decision to fine and punish a girl accused of having uttered a few immodest words and of having allowed herself to be kissed.[21]

The *Code of 1650* is peppered with warning measures. Laziness and drunkenness are harshly punished.[22] Innkeepers cannot serve more than a certain quantity of wine to each customer. Fines or a lashing are used to repress any lying considered harmful.[23] In other places the legislator, utterly oblivious of the great principles of religious freedom that he himself demanded in Europe, used the fear of fines to force attendance at church,[24] going so far as inflicting harsh punishments[25] and often death on Christians wishing to worship God in ways other than his own.[26] In fact, he is obsessed with such a zeal for rules that he is preoccupied with considerations quite unworthy of him. Thus we find, in this same code, a law forbidding the use of tobacco.[27]

---

20. *New Haven Antiquities*, p. 104. See also Hutchinson's *History*, vol. 1, p. 435, for other equally extraordinary judgments.

21. *Code of 1650*, p. 48. It seems that sometimes judges inflicted these punishments cumulatively, as can be seen in a sentence pronounced in 1643 (p. 114, *New Haven Antiquities*), by which Margaret Bedfort, convicted of reprehensible behavior, was condemned to be whipped and afterward was made to marry Nicolas Jemmings, her accomplice.

22. Ibid., *Code of 1650*, pp. 50, 57.

23. Ibid., p. 64

24. Ibid., p. 44.

25. This was not peculiar to Connecticut. See, amongst others, the law passed on 13 September 1644 in Massachusetts which condemned Anabaptists to exile from Massachusetts (*Historical Collection of State Papers*, vol. 1, p. 538). See also the law passed on 14 October 1656 against the Quakers: "Whereas," states this law, "an accursed sect of heretics called Quakers has sprung up . . ." There follow clauses which impose huge fines for ships' captains who bring Quakers to the country. Quakers who do manage to gain entry will be whipped and condemned to imprisonment with hard labor. Those who defend their opinions shall first be fined then imprisoned and finally driven out of the province. Same collection, vol. 1, p. 630.

26. By the penal code of Massachusetts, any Catholic priest who set foot in the colony after having once been driven out was condemned to death.

27. *Code of 1650*, p. 96.

Yet we must not lose sight of the fact that there was no imposition of these strange and despotic laws. They were freely voted
in by all the interested parties, whose customs were even more
austere and puritanical than the laws. In 1649, a solemn association was formed in Boston to issue warnings concerning the
worldly indulgence of long hair.[28] (See Appendix E, p. 827.)

Such aberrations no doubt bring discredit to human reason.
They witness to the inferiority of our nature which has a poor
grip on what is true and fair and more often than not simply
chooses between two excesses.

Alongside these penal laws, so redolent of the narrow bigotry
of sect and religious fanaticism exacerbated by persecution and
which fermented still deep in their souls, we find in place and
closely linked to them a body of political laws which, although
enacted two hundred years ago, seem still to anticipate the spirit
of freedom of our own times.

The general principles upon which modern constitutions are
founded were hardly grasped by the majority of seventeenth-
century Europeans; they were not completely established even
in Great Britain, yet were accepted and settled by the laws of
New England: the involvement of the people in public affairs,
the free vote on taxes, the personal responsibility of those in
power, individual freedom, and trial by jury were all actually
established without debate.

These influential principles enjoy an implementation and a
development which no European country has yet been brave
enough to grant.

In Connecticut, from the beginning, the electoral body consisted of all the citizens; an idea everyone easily understood.[29]
In this infant nation, there existed an almost perfect equality of
wealth and even more so of intelligence.[30]

28. *New England's Memorial*, p. 316.
29. *The Constitution of 1638*, p. 17.
30. In 1641, the General Assembly of Rhode Island unanimously declared
   that the government of the state consisted of a democracy and that the
   power lay with the body of free men who alone had the right to pass laws
   and to oversee their enforcement. *Code of 1650*, p. 70.

In Connecticut at that time all those entrusted with executive power were elected up to and including the state governor.[31]

Citizens of more than sixteen were obliged to bear arms. They formed a national militia which appointed officers and which was to hold itself in a state of constant readiness to defend the country.[32]

In the laws of Connecticut and those of New England generally, we see the origin and development of this communal independence which to this very day forms, as it were, the principle and vigor of American liberty.

In most European nations, the initial movements of power resided with the upper echelons of society and passed gradually and always in a partial manner to the other sections of society.

By contrast, in America we can state that the organization of the township preceded that of the county, the county that of the state, the state that of the Union.

In New England, townships were fully and definitively constituted from 1650.

The individual township was the place where local interests, passions, duties, and rights clung together and it fostered at its heart real political activity which was active, thoroughly democratic, and republican. The colonies still recognized the supremacy of the mother country; the monarchy was still the law of the state but the republic was already vigorous in every township.

The towns appointed every rank of magistrate; levied and apportioned their own taxes.[33] In the New England town, the law of representation had no place; the affairs which affected everyone were discussed, as in Athens, in the public squares or in the general assembly of the citizens.

What strikes us, when we peruse carefully the laws instituted during the initial period of American republics, is the legislator's knowledge of government and his advanced theories. The conception he has of the duties of society toward its members is loftier and more comprehensive than that of his European

31. Pitkin's *History*, p. 47.
32. Constitution of 1638, p. 12.
33. *Code of 1650*, p. 80.

counterparts. He also felt obligations still not observed elsewhere. In the states of New England, from the outset, the condition of the poor was safeguarded;[34] strict measures were taken to maintain roads with surveyors to oversee them;[35] the towns drew up public registers in which they entered notes of public debates, deaths, marriages, and births;[36] clerks were appointed to keep these registers;[37] officers were responsible for the administration of unclaimed property, others to determine the boundaries of inherited lands and there were several others whose main function was to maintain public order in the community.[38]

The law uses a thousand different details to anticipate and satisfy a mass of social needs only vaguely felt in France even now.

But it is in mandates relating to public education that, from the outset, the original character of American civilization is revealed in the clearest light.

"Granted," says the law, "that Satan, the enemy of mankind, locates his most powerful weapons in men's ignorance and that it matters that the wisdom of our fathers does not remain buried in their tombs; granted that the education of children is one of the first concerns of the state, with the aid of the Lord . . ."[39] Here follow clauses establishing schools in every township and obliging the inhabitants, under pain of heavy fines, to support them. High schools were founded in the same way in the more populated districts. Town magistrates had to make sure that

34. *Code of 1650*, p. 78.
35. Ibid., p. 49.
36. See Hutchinson's *History*, vol. 1, p. 455.
37. *Code of 1650*, p. 86.
38. Ibid., p. 40.
39. Ibid., p. 90. [Tocqueville's is a liberal translation of the text, which reads in the English as follows: "It being one cheife project of that old deluder, Sathan, to keepe men from the knowledge of the scriptures, as in former times, keeping them in an inknowne tongue, so in these latter times, by perswading them from the use of tongues, so that at least, the true sence and meaning of the original might bee clouded with false glosses of saint seeming deceivers; and what learning may not bee buried in the grave of our forefathers, in church and commonwealth, the Lord assisting our endeavors . . ."]

parents sent their children to school; they had the right to inflict fines against those who refused; if the refusal persisted, society, assuming the place of the family, took possession of the child, removing from the father those natural rights which he had so badly abused.[40] The reader will doubtless have noticed the preamble to these enactments: in America religion leads to wisdom; the observance of divine laws guides man to freedom.

If, after a rapid glance at American society in 1650, we examine the condition of Europe and, more especially, that of the Continent about this same time, we cannot help but feel profound astonishment. On the continent of Europe at the beginning of the seventeenth century, absolute monarchy every where stood triumphant on the ruins of the oligarchic and feudal liberty of the Middle Ages. At the heart of this splendor and literary excellence, the idea of rights had perhaps never been more entirely neglected. Never had nations enjoyed less political activity. Never had ideas of true liberty less preoccupied people's minds. It was at that very time that these same principles, unknown or neglected by European nations, were being proclaimed in the deserts of the New World to become the future symbol of a great nation. The boldest theories of the human mind were distilled into practice in this apparently humble society which probably no statesman would have been bothered to consider. Left to the original impulses of his own imaginative nature, man concocted by hit and miss an unprecedented legal system. In the heart of this unknown democracy, which had still not spawned either generals or philosophers or great writers, a man could stand before a free nation and give this fine definition of freedom to the applause of all around him:

"[N]or would I have you to mistake in the point of your own *liberty*. There is a *liberty* of corrupt nature, which is affected both by *men* and *beasts*, to do what they list; and this *liberty* is inconsistent with *authority*, impatient of all restraint; by this *liberty*, *Sumus Omnes Deteriores*; tis the grand enemy of *truth* and *peace*, and all the *ordinances* of God are bent against it. But there is a civil, a moral, a federal *liberty*, which is the proper

40. Ibid., p. 83.

end and object of *authority*; it is a *liberty* for that only which is *just* and *good*; for this *liberty* you are to stand with the hazard of your very lives."[41]

I have expressed enough to characterize Anglo-American civilization in its true colors. This civilization is the result (and this is something we must always bear in mind) of two quite distinct ingredients which anywhere else have often ended in war but which Americans have succeeded somehow to meld together in wondrous harmony; namely the *spirit of religion* and *the spirit of liberty*.

The founders of New England were both sectarian fanatics and noble innovators. Although held by the most restricting ties of certain religious beliefs, they were free of every political prejudice.

From that arose two inclinations which, though different, were not in opposition and we can easily discern their traces in the morals as well as the laws of the country.

Men sacrifice their friends, families, and country to a religious opinion. They are thought to be devoted to the pursuit of this intellectual goal which they have purchased so dearly. However, we see them seek with an almost matching zeal material wealth and moral pleasures: heaven in the other world, comfort and freedom in this.

In their hands, political principles, laws, and human institutions appear flexible and can be shaped at will into any combination.

Before their advance, the barriers which imprisoned the society into which they were born were lowered; old opinions which for centuries had governed the world, melted away. An almost limitless path, a field without horizon opened before them; the human spirit rushes forward to travel these places. But, it stops of itself at the limits of the political world and lays aside the use of its most awesome abilities. It renounces doubt,

41. Mather's *Magnalia Christi Americana*, vol. 2, p. 13. This speech was made by Winthrop; he was accused of having committed arbitrary acts while in office. After this speech, a fragment of which I have quoted above, he was acquitted with some acclaim and from that time onward was always re-elected governor of the state. See Marshall, vol. 1, p. 166.

abandons the need for innovation, and even refuses to lift the veil of the inner sanctum. It respectfully bows before truths it accepts without discussion.

Thus, in the moral world everything is classified, systematized, anticipated, and decided beforehand. In the political world everything is in a state of agitation, dispute, and uncertainty. In the one, a passive if voluntary obedience; in the other, an independence scornful of experience and eager in its pursuit of authority.

Far from harming each other, these two inclinations, despite their apparent opposition, seem to walk in mutual agreement and support.

Religion looks upon civil liberty as a noble exercise for man's faculties and upon the world of politics as a field prepared by the Creator for the efforts of man's intelligence. Religion, being free and powerful and content with the place reserved for it in its own sphere of influence, is fully aware that its rule is all the more unshaken because its domination over men's hearts is supported by its own strength alone.

Liberty looks upon religion as its companion in its struggles and triumphs, as the cradle of its young life, as the divine source of its claims. It considers religion as the guardian of morality, morality as the guarantee of law and the security that freedom will last. (See Appendix F, p. 831.)

REASONS FOR CERTAIN ANOMALIES PRESENTED BY THE LAWS AND CUSTOMS OF THE ANGLO-AMERICANS

Remains of aristocratic institutions at the heart of the most complete democracy—Why?—Careful distinction must be drawn between that which stems from the Puritan influence and that which is of English origin.

The reader should not draw, from the above, conclusions which are too general and final. The social condition, religion, and customs of the first immigrants have surely exercised a huge influence upon the fate of the new country. However, they did not found an entirely new society from their own totally original ideas because no one can possibly release himself from the past. They succeeded in mixing, either intentionally or unwittingly, their own ideas and practices with other practices and ideas derived from the education or traditions of their native country.

If we wish to understand and assess the Anglo-Americans of the present time, we must carefully tell the difference between that which stems from the Puritan influence and that which is of English origin.

In the United States we often meet laws and customs which are in direct contrast with their surroundings. They seem formulated in a spirit opposed to the predominant features of American legislation; these customs appear to conflict with the whole social setting. If the English colonies had been founded in an age of darkness or if their beginnings had already disappeared in the obscurity of time, there would be no solution to the problem.

One single example will clarify my thought.

American civil and criminal law recognizes only two courses of action: prison or bail. The first step in this procedure is to obtain bail money from the defendant or, on his refusal, to imprison him. After that, they examine the validity of the accusation and the seriousness of the charges.

Clearly such a legislative procedure disadvantages the poor and favors only the wealthy.

The poor man cannot always find the money for bail, even in a civil matter. If he is obliged to await justice from prison, his enforced constraint soon reduces him to a wretched state.

By contrast, the wealthy man always evades prison in civil matters. Furthermore, if he has committed an offense, he has no difficulty in wriggling out of the punishment which should come his way. After providing bail money, he vanishes. Therefore, it can be stated that the only penalty inflicted upon him by the law boils down to a fine.[42] Could there be any legislation more aristocratic than that?

42. Doubtless there are crimes for which bail is not appropriate, but they are few in number.

However, in America the poor create the law and it is their custom to reserve the greatest social advantages for themselves.

The explanation for this state of affairs is to be found in England, for the laws I speak of are English.[43] The Americans have not changed them, even though they offend the main body of their legislation and their ideas.

The thing a nation alters least in its practices is civil legislation. Civil laws are familiar territory only for legal experts who have a direct interest in maintaining them as they are, whether good laws or bad, simply because they know them well. The majority of the nation hardly knows them at all. It sees their implementation only in individual cases, has only a slight grasp of their drift and obeys them without much reflection.

I could have quoted many more than this one example.

The picture of American society is, if I may put it this way, overlaid with a democratic patina beneath which we see from time to time the former colors of the aristocracy showing through.

CHAPTER 3

THE SOCIAL CONDITION OF THE ANGLO-AMERICANS

The condition of society is normally the result of circumstances, sometimes of laws, more often than not a combination of these two causes; but, once it is established, we can consider it as the fundamental source of most of the laws, customs, and ideas which regulate the conduct of nations; whatever it does not produce, it modifies.

In order to become acquainted with the legislation and manners of a nation we must, therefore, start by studying the social condition.

---

43. See Blackstone and Delolme, bk 1, ch. 10.

THAT THE SALIENT FEATURE OF THE SOCIAL CONDITION OF THE ANGLO-AMERICANS IS ITS ESSENTIAL DEMOCRACY

The first immigrants of New England—The equality that existed between them—The aristocratic laws introduced into the South—Period of Revolution—Change in the laws of inheritance—Effects produced by this change—Equality pushed to its utmost limits in the new states of the West— Equality of minds.

We could offer several important observations on the social condition of the Anglo-Americans but there is one which dominates all the rest. The social condition of the Americans is eminently democratic—a characteristic it has possessed from the birth of the colonies and which it possesses even more today.

I stated in the preceding chapter that great equality was widely spread among the immigrants who settled upon the shores of New England. The seeds of aristocracy were never planted in that part of the Union. The only influence which obtained there was that of the intellect. The people became accustomed to revere certain names as emblems of wisdom and virtue. The voice of a few citizens acquired a power over the others which might rightly have been called aristocratic, if it had been transferable permanently from father to son.

This is what came to pass east of the Hudson; to the south-west of that river, and down as far as the Floridas, the case was different.

In the majority of the states to the south-west of the Hudson, some great English landowners had settled and had imported with them aristocratic principles together with English laws of succession. I have argued the reasons why the institution of a powerful aristocracy in America was impossible. These reasons, existing as they did south-west of the Hudson, had nonetheless less force than to the east of that river. In the South, one single man, with the help of slaves, could cultivate a large tract of land. Therefore in this part of the continent it was common to see wealthy landed proprietors. Yet, their influence was not altogether aristocratic, as the term is understood in Europe, since they possessed no privileges and slave labor denied them tenant farmers and thus they had no patronage. However, the greater landowners to the south of the Hudson constituted a superior class, having ideas and tastes of its own and, in general, encompassing all political action in its center. It was a sort of aristocracy hardly distinguishable from the mass of the people whose enthusiasms and interests it readily embraced, arousing neither love nor hatred: to sum up, a class which was weak and lacking in vigor. This was the class which headed the revolt in the South and which gave to the American revolution[a] its greatest men.

During that period, society was shaken to its core: the people in whose name the battle had been fought became powerful enough to wish to act independently. Democratic inclinations were awakened; having thrown off the yoke of the mother country, it coveted every kind of independent action. Individual influences gradually ceased to have effect; habits and laws advanced in harmony toward the same goals.

But it was the law of inheritance which was the last step on the way to equality.

I am astonished that commentators old and new have not attributed to the laws of inheritance a greater influence on the progress of human affairs.[1] These laws do belong, true enough, to the civil code but they ought to take their place at the head of every political institution since they have an unbelievable effect upon the social conditions of people, while political laws only mirror what the state actually is. They have, moreover, a reliable and consistent method of operating on society since they take a hold to some degree on all future generations yet unborn. Through the impact of these laws, man exerts an almost

---

1. I understand by the law of inheritance all the laws whose principal object is to regulate the distribution of property after the death of its owner. The law of entail is thus; it does indeed prevent the owner from disposing of his goods before his death but only with the view of preserving them intact for his heir. The main aim of the law of entail, therefore, is to regulate the final destiny of property after the death of the owner. The rest of it is the means which it employs to accomplish this.

godlike power over the future of his fellow men. The legislator can remain inactive for centuries once he has settled the inheritance laws. Once his work has been set in motion, he can withdraw his hand, for the machine acts under its own steam, moving as if self-directed toward a prescribed goal. When framed in a certain way, this law unites, draws together, and gathers property and, soon, real power into the hands of an individual. It causes the aristocracy, so to speak, to spring out of the ground. If directed, however, by opposite principles and launched along other paths, its effect is even more rapid; it divides, shares out, and disperses both property and power. Sometimes it can happen that people are scared by the speed of its progress so that they at least try, out of desperation at being unable to stem its action, to place difficulties and obstacles in its way. They vainly seek to offset its motion by efforts in the opposite direction. The law crushes and shatters all impediments as it moves forward. It ceaselessly rises and falls upon the ground until all you see is a fine and shifting dust which is the foundation of democracy.

When the law of inheritance allows and even more so when it decrees the equal division of the father's property between all his children, its effects are twofold; we must carefully distinguish these although they tend toward the same end.

By virtue of the law of inheritance, the death of each landowner entails a revolution in property ownership; not only do possessions change hands, but also, so to speak, their very nature changes. There is a fragmentation into ever decreasing parcels.

That is the direct and, to some degree, the physical effect of this law. In countries where legislation institutes equality of inheritance, possessions and landed wealth in particular have a permanent tendency to diminish. However, if the law was allowed to follow its own course, it would take some time for the effects of this legislation to be felt. For supposing that the family consists of not more than two children (and the average in a country like France is only three), these children, on sharing the wealth of both their parents, will not be poorer than their father or mother taken separately.

But the law of equal division exercises its influence not merely upon property itself, it also affects the minds of the owners, calling their emotions into play. Huge fortunes and above all huge estates are destroyed rapidly by the indirect effects of this law.

Among nations where the law of inheritance is based upon the rights of the eldest child, landed estates mostly pass from generation to generation without division. The result is that family feeling takes its strength from the land. The family represents the land, the land the family, perpetuating its name, history, glory, power, and virtues. It stands as an imperishable witness to the past, a priceless guarantee of its future.

When the law of inheritance institutes equal division, it destroys the close relationship between family feeling and the preservation of the land which ceases to represent the family. For the land must gradually diminish and ends up by disappearing entirely since it cannot avoid being parceled up after one or two generations. The sons of a wealthy landowner, provided they are few in number and fortune favors them, may entertain the hope of being no less wealthy than their father but not possessing the same property that he did. Their wealth will of necessity derive from sources different from his.

The instant you remove from a landowner that interest in the preservation of his land which is fueled by his family feeling, memories, pride, ambition, you can take it as certain that sooner or later he will sell up. He has a great incentive to sell up, for movable assets produce greater returns than other assets and more readily satisfy the passions of the moment.

Once shared out, great estates never come together again; for the small landowner earns proportionately a better return from his land than the large landowner does from his and sells it for a higher sum.[2] Thus the financial calculations which persuaded the wealthy owner to sell huge estates will even more so prevent his buying small estates in order to unite them into a large one.

This so-called family feeling is often based upon an illusion of selfishness when a man seeks to perpetuate and immortalize

2. I don't mean that the small landowner is the better farmer but that he farms with more enthusiasm and care and thus, by his hard work, makes up for any skill which he might lack.

himself as it were in his great-grandchildren. Where family feeling ends, self-centeredness directs a man's true inclinations. As the family becomes a vague, featureless, doubtful mental concept, each man focusses on the convenience of the present moment and, to the exclusion of all else besides, thinks only of the prosperity of the succeeding generation and no more. He does not aim to perpetuate his family or, at least, seeks to perpetuate it by other means than that of a landed estate.

Thus, not only does the law of inheritance cause difficulties for families to keep their estates intact but it also removes the incentive to bother and, to some degree, it compels them to cooperate with the law in their own ruin.

The law of equal division proceeds along two paths: by acting upon things, it acts upon persons; by acting upon persons, it affects things. In these two ways, it manages to strike at the root of landed property, achieving the rapid dispersal of both families and fortunes.[3]

It is not for us, Frenchmen of the nineteenth century, who witness daily the political and social changes produced by the law of inheritance, to doubt its power. Each day we see it visiting our lands again and again, overturning the walls of our dwellings as it advances and destroying the boundaries of our fields. But if the law of inheritance has achieved much already in French society, much remains to be done. Our memories, opinions, and customs place powerful obstacles in its path.

---

3. Land being the most stable kind of property, from time to time we come across rich men who are prepared to make great sacrifices to acquire it and who will willingly forfeit a considerable amount of their income to secure what is left, But those are isolated cases. The love of real estate is, generally, no longer found other than amongst the poor. The small landowner who has less understanding, less imagination, and fewer cravings than the large landowner, is, in general, preoccupied only with the desire to increase his property and it often happens that by inheritance, marriage, or business opportunities he is gradually able to accomplish this. Thus to balance the tendency which leads men to divide up the land, there exists another which urges them to add to it. This tendency, which is sufficient to prevent estates from being continually divided up, is not strong enough to create great territorial wealth and is certainly not strong enough to keep estates in the same family.

Its work of destruction is almost over in the United States where we can best study its results.

The English laws concerning the inheritance of property were abolished in almost all the states at the time of the Revolution. The law of entail was modified in such a way as to leave virtually unaffected the free circulation of possessions. (See Appendix G, p. 840.)

The first generation passed away; the estates began to be parceled up. This process increased in speed as time went by. Nowadays, after a lapse of little more than sixty years, society has already quite an altered appearance: the families of the great landowners have been swallowed up by the masses. In the state of New York, which had a goodly number of these, only two remain, swimming on the brink of the abyss which is poised to engulf them. The sons of these opulent citizens are merchants, lawyers, or doctors. The majority have fallen into complete obscurity. The last traces of hereditary rank and distinction have gone; the law of inheritance has reduced all men to one level.

There are just as many wealthy people in the United States as elsewhere; I am not even aware of a country where the love of money has a larger place in men's hearts or where they express a deeper scorn for the theory of a permanent equality of possessions. But wealth circulates with an astonishing speed and experience shows that rarely do two succeeding generations benefit from its favors.

This portrait, however biased you think it might be, still gives only half an idea of what is taking place in the new states of the West and Southwest.

At the end of the last century, bold pioneers began to penetrate the valleys of the Mississippi, which was akin to a new discovery of America. Soon the bulk of emigrants moved there and unknown societies rose from the desert. States whose names had not even existed a few years before lined up with the states of the American Union and, in the West, democracy reached the extremes of its development.

In these states, founded in a makeshift fashion, the inhabitants occupied the land as of yesterday, hardly knowing each other, unaware of the background of their neighbors. In this part of the American continent, the population is, therefore, free of the influence of great names and great wealth as well as that natural aristocracy of knowledge and virtue. No one there wields that respectable power which men grant to the memory of a person whose life was spent entirely doing the good deeds which come his way. The new states of the West already have inhabitants but society has no existence among them.

However, not only are fortunes equal in America, equality extends to some degree to intelligence itself.

I do not think that there is a single country in the world where, in proportion to the population, there are so few ignorant and, at the same time, so few educated individuals as in America.

Primary education is available to all; secondary is within the reach of no one, which can be explained quite easily as the inevitable result, so to speak, of my arguments above.

Almost all Americans enjoy a life of comfort and can, therefore, obtain the first elements of human knowledge.

In America there are few rich people; therefore, all Americans have to learn the skills of a profession which demands a period of apprenticeship. Thus America can devote to general learning only the early years of life. At fifteen, they begin a career; their education ends most often when ours begins. If education is pursued beyond that point, it is directed only toward specialist subjects with a profitable return in mind. Science is studied as if it were a job and only those branches are taken up which have a recognized and immediate usefulness.

In America, most wealthy people started from poverty; almost all those who now enjoy leisure were busy in their youth, the consequence of which is that when the taste for study might have existed, time was short, and when they had the time to devote to it, the taste had gone.

There is no class, then, in America which passes to its descendants the love of intellectual pleasures along with its wealth or which holds the labors of the intellect in high esteem.

Therefore, devotion to such work lacks not only the will but also the effort.

There is in America a certain common level of human

knowledge, which all citizens approach, some on their way upwards, some on their way downwards. Therefore a mass of individuals share roughly the same number of ideas in religion, history, science, political economy, legislation, and government.

Variations in intellect come directly from God and men cannot prevent this being so.

But it is at least a consequence of what I have just stated that, although the intelligence of men is different, as the Creator has willed it, there is at its disposal an equal means of development.

In present-day America, therefore, the aristocratic element has always been feeble from the beginning and it has been, if not totally destroyed, at least sufficiently weakened for us not to ascribe to it very much influence in the progress of human affairs.

On the other hand, time, events and laws have given the democratic element not only a dominant but also, so to speak, a unique role. We cannot perceive any corporate or family influence; we cannot even discover the lasting influence of any single individual.

Present-day America exhibits, therefore, in its social state, the strangest phenomenon: men enjoy greater equality of fortune and intelligence or, expressed another way, are as equally strong as in any other country in the world or in any other country in the annals of history.

POLITICAL CONSEQUENCES OF THE SOCIAL CONDITION OF THE ANGLO-AMERICANS

The political consequences of such a social condition are easy to work out.

One has to understand that equality ends up by infiltrating the world of politics as it does everywhere else. It would be impossible to imagine men forever unequal in one respect, yet equal in others; they must, in the end, come to be equal in all.

Now, I am aware of only two means of establishing equality in the world of politics: rights have to be granted to every citizen or to none. For nations who have attained the same social conditions as the Anglo-Americans, it is, therefore, very difficult to discover a mid-point between the supremacy of all and the absolute power of one.

We need not conceal the fact that the social condition I have just described could as easily support one or other of these two consequences.

In fact, a manly and lawful passion for equality arouses in men the desire to be strong and honored; this passion tends to raise the weak to the ranks of the strong. But also, we encounter in the hearts of men a degenerate taste for equality which inspires the weak to bring the strong down to their own level and reduces men to prefer equality in a state of slavery to inequality in a state of freedom. Not that nations with a democratic system have a natural scorn for freedom—rather they have an instinctive taste for it. But freedom is not the chief and constant aim of their desires; it is for equality that they reserve an everlasting love. With swift advances and sudden bursts of effort, they seek freedom; if they miss their aim, they fall back in resignation. But nothing can bring them satisfaction if they lose equality and they would prefer death to the loss of it.

On the other hand, when the citizens of a state are all almost equal, they find it difficult to defend their independence against the onslaughts of power. Since no one among them is strong enough to struggle alone and win, only the combined strength of all can guarantee freedom. Now such a combination is not always to be found.

Nations can, therefore, draw two great political consequences from an identical social condition; these consequences are amazingly different even though they proceed from the same source.

The Anglo-Americans, the first to be subject to this fearful choice which I have just described, have been lucky enough to escape absolute power. Their circumstances, origins, knowledge, and, above all, their customs, have given them the opportunity to establish and maintain the sovereignty of the people.

CHAPTER 4

THE PRINCIPLE OF THE SOVEREIGNTY OF THE PEOPLE IN AMERICA

It dominates all of American society—Implementation of this principle by the Americans even before their Revolution—Development given to it by the Revolution— Gradual and irresistible diminution of feudal systems.

If we wish to discuss the political laws of the United States, we must start with the doctrine of the sovereignty of the people.

The principle of the sovereignty of the people which we find more or less at the heart of almost all human institutions, generally stays, as it were, buried deep. It is obeyed without being recognized or, if for a moment it be brought to light, we hastily thrust it back down into the darkness of its sanctuary.

The will of the nation is one of those phrases most widely abused by schemers and tyrants of all ages. Some have seen it appear in votes bought by agents of power, others in the votes of a frightened or self-seeking minority. Some have even discovered it in the silence of a nation and have supposed that, from this apparent submission, they had a right to control.

In America the sovereignty of the people is not, as with certain nations, a hidden or barren notion; it is acknowledged in custom, celebrated by law. It expands with freedom and reaches its final aims without impediment. If there is a single country in the world where the doctrine of the sovereignty of the people can be properly appreciated, where it can be studied as it applies to the affairs of society and its advantages and risks be estimated, that country is undoubtedly America.

I have observed that, from the outset, the principle of the sovereignty of the people had been the driving force of the English colonies in America although its domination over the government of society was far less then than it is these days.

Two impediments, one external, one internal, checked its

pervasive progress. It could not disclose itself openly in the laws of the colonies since they still had to obey the mother country; it had to restrict itself to concealing its influence in the provincial assemblies and especially the townships where it expanded in secret.

American society was not yet prepared to accept it with all its consequences. The educated of New England and the wealthy south of the Hudson exerted for a long time, as I have shown in the last chapter, a kind of aristocratic influence which tended to retain the exercise of social power in the hands of a few.

The officers of state were far from being elected, nor was there universal suffrage. Everywhere the right to vote was restricted within specified limits and was dependent upon a property qualification which was low in the North and higher in the South.

The American Revolution broke out. The doctrine of the sovereignty of the people came out from the townships and took over the government. All classes of society committed themselves to its cause. Battles were fought and victories won in its name until it became the law of laws.

A transformation almost as rapid was completed in the heart of society: the law of inheritance finally broke down all local influences.

At the moment when everyone was beginning to perceive this result of the laws and the Revolution, victory had already pronounced for the democratic cause with no turning back. All power was, in fact, in its hands; no struggle against it was permitted. The upper classes surrendered without uttering a word, without raising a fist to an evil which was henceforth inevitable. What usually happens to fading powers happened to them: self-centeredness gripped their ranks. Since they could not wrench power from the hands of the people and since their hatred of the masses was not enough to derive any pleasure from confronting them, their only thought was to win their favors at any cost. The most obviously democratic laws were therefore supported by those very men whose interests were bruised by them. In this manner, the upper classes did not arouse the animosity of the people but did accelerate the triumph of the new order of things. Thus something very strange happened:

the thrust of democracy proved all the more irresistible in those states where aristocracy had been most deeply rooted.

The state of Maryland, which had been founded by men from the nobility, was the first to declare universal suffrage[1] and introduced the most democratic systems into the whole of its government.

When a nation starts to tamper with electoral qualifications, we can anticipate, sooner or later, their complete abolition. That is one of the most unchanging rules governing society: the further the limits of electoral rights are pushed back, the more we feel the need to push them back. For after each concession, the strength of democracy increases and its demands grow with every new power it gains. The ambition of those left below the level of qualification is frustrated in proportion to the great number of those above it. The exception in the end becomes the rule; concessions follow each other without respite and the process can be stopped only when universal suffrage is achieved.

At the present time, the principle of the sovereignty of the people has taken all the practical steps the imagination can possibly think of. It has released itself from all those fictions which surround it in other countries and it makes its appearance in all shapes and forms according to the demands of the circumstances. Sometimes the people make laws corporately, as in Athens; sometimes deputies, elected by the votes of all, act as the people's representatives under their watchful eye. There are countries where a power which, though to some degree foreign to the body of society, influences it and forces it to advance in a certain direction. There are others where power is divided, being both inside and outside the ranks of society.

Nothing like that can be seen in the United States where society acts independently for its own advantage. All power rests in its hands; almost no one would venture to imagine or, still less, voice the idea of seeking power elsewhere. The people share in the making of its laws through their choice of legislators and in the implementation of those laws by the election of the members of the executive. It may almost be said that the people

1. , Amendments made to the constitution of Maryland in 1801 and 1809.

are self-governing in so far as the share left to the administrators is so weak and so restricted and the latter feel such close ties with their popular origin and the power from which it emanates. The people reign in the American political world like God over the universe. It is the cause and aim of all things, everything comes from them and everything is absorbed in them. (See Appendix H, p. 842.)

CHAPTER 5

THE NECESSITY OF EXAMINING WHAT HAPPENS IN INDIVIDUAL STATES BEFORE CONSIDERING THE UNION AS A WHOLE

In the following chaper, I propose to examine the form of government in America which is founded on the principle of the sovereignty of the people, the ways in which it proceeds, the obstacles it meets, and its advantages and risks.

The first difficulty stems from the complexity of the United States' constitution, where two distinct social groups are locked and, as it were, fitted into each other. We observe two completely separate and almost independent governments, one which answers the ordinary daily needs of society without clear limitations, the other which acts in exceptional circumstances to meet certain general concerns with very clear limitations. In a word, there exist twenty-four small sovereign nation states which link together to form the body of the Union.

To examine the Union before the state is to follow a road strewn with obstacles. The federal government in the United States was the last to take shape, being a variation or summary of the political principles of the republic which was widespread in society and had an existence of its own before the federal government came into being. Moreover the federal government, as I have just said, is the exception whereas that of the state is the rule. The writer who would display the whole of such a picture before explaining the details would risk obscurity or repetition.

The mighty political principles which govern present-day American society undoubtedly began and developed in the state. Thus close scrutiny of the state holds the key to the rest. The states which today make up the American Union all present the same features as regards the outer appearance of their institutions. Their political or administrative existence is concentrated in three centers of action which we might compare to the various centers of the nervous system in the human body.

At the lowest level is the township followed by the county and ending with the state.

THE AMERICAN TOWNSHIP SYSTEM

Why the author chooses to begin his examination of political institutions with the township—The township is common to all the people—The difficulty of establishing and preserving independence in the townships—Its importance—Why the author has chosen the township system in New England as the principal focus of his study.

It is not without design that I look first at the township, which is the grouping so close to man's nature that wherever men gather together township automatically comes into being.

Municipal society exists in all nations whatever their customs or laws. Man it is that makes monarchies and founds republics; the township seems a direct gift from the hand of God. But if the town has existed as long as man has, its freedom is uncommon and easily broken. A nation can always establish great political assemblies because a certain number of men can usually be found in its midst whose knowledge will to some extent take over the practical handling of affairs. The township has coarse elements which often resist the regulations of the legislator. The difficulty of establishing the independence of townships, instead of decreasing as nations become more civilized, increases as their knowledge grows. A highly civilized society has little tolerance for the attempt at freedom at the town level and is disgusted at the sight of its countless mistakes. It also loses heart at the success of an experiment before the final results are reached.

Of all the types of freedom, that of the townships, established with so much difficulty, is the most susceptible to the onslaughts of power. Left to their own devices, municipal institutions can scarcely struggle against a strong or enterprising government. A successful defense depends upon the full development of these institutions and the matching of their own ideas and customs to national ones. Thus municipal freedom is easy to destroy if it does not blend with the customs of the people, which it cannot do until it has long been supported by their laws.

Municipal freedom is therefore, so to speak, outside man's creation and is only infrequently realized. Somehow it comes into being spontaneously, developing almost secretly in the heart of a semi-barbarous society. The constant influence of laws and customs, circumstances, and, above all, the passing of time aid its consolidation. Among all the nations of continental Europe, it can be stated that not a single one has any experience of it.

However, the strength of free nations resides in the township. Town institutions are to freedom what primary schools are to knowledge: they bring it within people's reach and give men the enjoyment and habit of using it for peaceful ends. Without town institutions a nation can establish a free government but has not the spirit of freedom itself. Brief enthusiasms, passing interests, the instability of circumstances may grant the external forms of independence but that despotism which has been forced back into the depths of the social fabric resurfaces sooner or later.

To explain in detail to the reader the general principles upon which resides the political organization of the township and county in the United States, I have thought it useful to use as a model one state in particular, to examine closely what happens there and to cast a brief glance over the rest of the country.

I have chosen one of the states of New England.

The township and the county have not the same method of organization in all areas of the Union; however, it is easily recognizable that throughout the Union almost the same principles have guided the formation of both.

Now, my perception has been that these principles have developed further in New England and attained more extensive results there than anywhere else. They stand out, as it were, in greater relief which exposes them more readily to the scrutiny of the foreigner.

The institutions of New England towns form a complete and regulated entity; they are very old; they gain strength from their laws and still more from their customs; their influence over the whole of society is prodigious.

On all these counts they deserve to attract our attention.

LIMITS OF THE TOWNSHIP

The township of New England stands between the French *canton* and the *commune*, containing, in general, between two and three thousand persons,[1] large enough for its inhabitants to share broadly the same interests and with enough people to ensure the elements of good administration.

POWERS OF THE TOWNSHIP IN NEW ENGLAND

The people, the source of all power in the township as elsewhere—Management of its own affairs—No town council—The greater part of authority concentrated in the hands of selectmen—How the selectmen operate—General assembly of townspeople (town meeting)—Listing of all the township officials—Obligatory and remunerated offices.

In the township, as everywhere else, the people are the only source of power but nowhere does it exert its influence with more immediate effect. In America, the people constitute a master whose pleasure has to be satisfied to the utmost limits.

In New England, the majority acts through its representatives when general state business is conducted. At that level, it had to be so but, in the township, where law and government are closer

1.   In 1830, there were 305 townships in Massachusetts; the population was 610, 014; that gives an average of about 2,000 for each township.

to those governed, the system of representation is not adopted. There is no town council. The body of voters, having appointed its magistrates, directs them in everything other than the pure and simple execution of the laws of the state.[2]

This order of doing things is so alien to our ideas and so contrary to our habits that I must supply some examples to illustrate it.

Public duties are extremely numerous and extensively divided up in the township, as we shall see further on. However, the majority of the administrative powers are vested in the hands of a small number of individuals elected each year called the "selectmen."[3]

The general laws of the state have laid a certain number of obligations upon these selectmen, who do not need any authorization from those they represent to fulfill them but they are personally responsible, if they evade them. State law, for example, gives them the duty of drawing up the lists of voters in their township which, if they fail to do so, makes them guilty of an offense. In all things governed by the township, the selectmen are the executives of the will of the people, as in France the mayor executes the proceedings of the municipal council. Usually they act upon their own responsibility and they put into practice the principles already adopted by the majority. Were they to introduce some change or other in the established order of things or to embark upon a new initiative, they would have to return to the source of their power.

2.   The same rules do not apply to the large townships. These generally have a mayor and a municipal body divided into two branches, but that is an exception which needs the authorization of a law. See the law of 23 February 1822, regulating the powers of the city of Boston. *Laws of Massachusetts*, vol. 2, p. 588. This applies to the large towns. Small towns also often have an individual administration. In 1832, 104 such municipal administrations were counted in the state of New York. (*William's Register.*)

3.   Three selectmen are elected in the smallest townships, nine in the biggest. See *The Town Officer*, p. 186. See also the principle laws of Massachusetts regarding selectmen: law of 20 February 1786, vol. 1, p. 219; 24 February 1796, vol. 1, p. 488; 7 March 1801, vol. 2, p. 45; 16 June 1795, vol. 1, p. 475; 12 March 1808, vol. 2, p. 186; 28 February 1787, vol. 1, p. 302; 22 June 1797, vol. 1, p. 539.

Suppose it is a matter of founding a school: the selectmen call the whole body of the electorate together on a certain day and at an appointed place; they explain the need for a school, the means of satisfying it, the money required and the most suitable site. When the gathering has been consulted on all these matters, the principle is adopted, the site fixed, the tax is agreed, and the execution of its resolution is entrusted to the selectmen.

Only the selectmen have the right to call the town meeting but they can be prompted into doing so. If ten landowners come up with a new project and wish to seek the agreement of the town, they demand a general gathering of the inhabitants. The selectmen have to comply and have only the right to preside over the meeting.[4]

These political customs and social practices are clearly far removed from our own. I do not presently wish either to assess them or to explain the hidden reasons which cause them to thrive. I merely describe them.

The selectmen are elected every year in the month of April or May. The town meeting chooses at the same time many other municipal magistrates,[5] entrusted with certain important administrative functions. Some as assessors must establish the rates of tax; others as collectors must raise money. One officer called a constable is in charge of law and order, the supervision of public places and assists in the day-to-day execution of the law. Another, the town clerk, records all the debates and notes all the decisions of the Civic Council. A treasurer keeps the communal funds. In addition to these civil servants, a superintendent for the poor has the very difficult task of fulfilling the law relating to the destitute; governors of schools control public education; road surveyors look after all the public highways. There you have the list of the principal officers of the municipal administration. But the division of duties does not end there. Among the officers of the town,[6] we also find parish com-

---

4.   See *Laws of Massachusetts*, vol. 1, p. 150; law of 25 March 1786.
5.   Ibid.
6.   All these officials really do exist. To learn the details of the functions of all these officials, see *The Town Officer* by Isaac Goodwin (Worcester, 1827); and the general laws of Massachusetts in three volumes (Boston, 1823).

missioners who audit the expenses of public worship and different classes of inspectors, some of whom direct fire fighting, others harvesting. Some supervise boundary disputes, others the measuring of timber, yet others, weights and measures.

In all, nineteen main offices exist in the township. Each citizen is obliged to accept these different offices under threat of a fine. Most of these jobs are paid, so that poor citizens can devote their time to them without loss. In general, it is not the American method to pay a fixed salary to civil servants. Every service has its price and payment is in proportion to what they have done.

LIFE IN THE TOWNSHIPS

Everyone is the best judge of what is in his own interest—Corollary of the principle of the sovereignty of the people—Application of these doctrines in American townships—The township of New England, sovereign in all that concerns it alone, subject to the state in all other areas—Duties of the township toward the state—In France, the government lends its officers to the township—In America, the township lends its officers to the government.

I have previously stated that the principle of the sovereignty of the people hovers over the whole political system of the Anglo-Americans. Every page of this book will reflect certain fresh instances of this doctrine. In nations where it exists, every individual takes an equal share in sovereign power and participates equally in the government of the state. Thus he is considered as enlightened, virtuous, strong as any of his fellow men.

Why then does he obey society and what are the normal limits of his obedience?

He obeys not because he holds an inferior position to those who run the administration or is less capable than his neighbor of self-government but because he recognizes the usefulness of his association with his fellow men and because he knows that this association cannot exist without a regulating power.

While he has become a subject in all the mutual duties of

citizens, he remains master in his own affairs where he is free and answerable only to God for his actions. Out of that grows the general truth that the individual is the sole and best placed judge of his own private concerns and society has the right to control his actions only when it feels such actions cause it damage or needs to seek the cooperation of the individual.

This doctrine has universal acceptance in the United States. Elsewhere, I shall examine the general influence it has over the day-to-day activities of life; here I am speaking about the townships.

The township as a whole in its relation to central government is a single entity like any other and is subject to the theory to which I have just alluded. Municipal freedom in the United States flows directly from the doctrine of the sovereignty of the people. All American republics have more or less accepted this independence but circumstances have particularly favored its development in New England.

In this part of the Union, political life took root at the very heart of the townships; one could almost say that they were, from the very beginning, independent nations.

When afterwards the kings of England demanded their share of sovereignty, they restricted themselves to the central power of the state, leaving the townships where they found them. At the present time, the New England townships owe allegiance to the state but, in the beginning, this was not so, or was scarcely so. Powers have not been granted to them; rather they seem to have relinquished a portion of their independence in favor of the state. The reader has to bear this important distinction in mind.

The townships submit to the rule of the state only in those matters I shall term *social*; that is those matters which are of common concern. They have remained independent bodies in everything which relates to them alone. Among the inhabitants of New England, I do not think a single person exists who grants the state authorities the right to interfere in their essentially local interests.

We see the townships of New England buying and selling,

prosecuting or defending in the courts, raising or lowering budgets without the slightest opposition of any state authority.[7]

They are bound to comply with the duties laid upon them by society. Thus, if the state needs money, the township has not the freedom either to grant or to withhold its agreement.[8] If the state proposes a road, the township does not have the power to refuse to allow it to cross its territory and, if any state edict on law and order is passed, the township must enforce it. If the state intends to organize education on a uniform basis throughout the country, the township is bound to create the schools ordained by law.[9] We shall see, when we speak of the administration of the United States, in what way and by whom the townships, in all these different instances, are still forced to obey. To establish this obligation is my only aim for, although strictly imposed by the central government, it is in principle only. The actual execution of the order relies, in general, upon the individual rights of the township; therefore taxes are, it is true, voted by the state laws but are levied and collected by the township; the school is established by edict but built, paid for, and administered by the township.

In France, the state collector receives the taxes of the township; in America, the township collector receives the taxes of the state. Thus, in France, central government lends its officers to the township; in America the township lends its civil servants to the central government, which alone shows how different these two societies are.

THE SPIRIT OF THE TOWNSHIP IN
NEW ENGLAND

Why the township in New England wins the affection of those who live there—The difficulty of creating a community spirit in Europe—The rights and duties in

7. See *Laws of Massachusetts*, law of 23 March 1786, vol. 1, p. 250.
8. Ibid., law of 20 February 1786, vol. 1, p. 217.
9. See same collection, law of 25 June 1789, vol. 1, p. 367, and 8 March 1827, vol. 3, p. 179.

America which contribute to the formation of this spirit—
There is a greater sense of the homeland in the United States
than elsewhere—How community spirit shows itself in
New England—The happy effects of this.

In America, not only do institutions belong to the community
but also they are kept alive and supported by a community
spirit.

The New England township possesses two advantages which
strongly arouse the interest of men, namely independence and
authority. Its sphere of action is indeed restricted but, within
that sphere, its movements are unlimited. This independence
alone guarantees it real importance even though its population
and size would not warrant it.

It is best to realize that men's affections, in general, come
down on the side of authority. Patriotism does not long prevail
in a conquered nation. The inhabitant of New England is
devoted to his township, not because he was born there as much
as because he views the township as a strong, free social body
of which he is part and which merits the care he devotes to its
management.

In Europe, governments often bewail the absence of this
community spirit, for everyone agrees that it is an ingredient in
public order and tranquillity, even though they do not know
how to create it. By making the township strong and independent, they are afraid they might disintegrate the social fabric and
expose the state to the forces of anarchy. Once you remove the
strength and independence of the township, you will reduce the
citizens to administrative units.

Note another important fact: the New England township is
so constituted as to give a place to the warmest affections
without arousing the ambitious passions of the human heart.

The officers of the county are not elected and their power is
circumscribed. The state itself has only a secondary importance
and its very being is obscure and tranquil. Few men would agree
to move away from the center of their own interests simply to
suffer the troublesome burden of state administration.

The federal government endows its administrators with

power and glory but those who thus influence its destinies are not numerous. The presidency is a high office reached only at an advanced time in a man's life and other high-ranking federal offices are attained through chance and after distinction has been achieved in some other career. Such posts cannot be a permanent aim for the ambitious. In the township, at the center of everyday affairs, we see concentrated the desire for reputation, the need of real involvement, the taste for power and popularity. These passions, which so often disturb society, change character when they find fulfillment near home and to some extent in the heart of the family circle.

Look at the skill with which the American township has taken care, so to speak, to scatter its power in order to involve more people in public affairs. Independently of the electors called from time to time to fulfill their public duties, a great number of tasks and many different officers within the sphere of their powers represent the powerful body in whose name they are acting. What a huge number of men thus find a source of profit in the local power system and become involved in it for themselves.

The American system, while sharing out the local authority among a large number of citizens, is not afraid to diversify the duties of the township. In the United States, one is correct in thinking that love of one's country is a brand of religion to which men become devoted through ritual observance.

In this way, the life of the township is constantly brought to people's notice and makes its presence felt through the fulfillment of a duty or by the exercise of a right. Such a political fact keeps society in a state of continuous yet calm activity which animates it without disturbing it.

Americans cling to the city for the same reason that mountain dwellers adore their hills because, for them, their country has more characteristic features and a more distinct appearance than anywhere else.

The life of New England townships is generally a happy one. The government they have chosen is very much to their taste. Within the peace and prosperity which prevail in America, municipal outbursts are rare. The management of local concerns is relaxed. In addition, the political education of the people has long been completed or rather the people arrived fully instructed into the land they now occupy. In New England, class divisions do not feature, even in their memory; thus no section of the township is tempted to dominate another, so that injustices strike only individuals, leaving the general population in a state of contentment. If the government makes mistakes, and it is easy enough to point them out, they are hardly noticed because the government emanates from those it governs and, as long as it acts as well as can be expected, it is protected by a sort of paternal pride. Besides, there is nothing to compare it with. England formerly had sovereignty over this collection of colonies but the people always directed the affairs of each township. This sovereignty is, therefore, not only an ancient but also a primitive state.

The native of New England is devoted to his township because of its strength and independence; he is involved because he helps to run it; he loves it, for he has nothing to complain about; his ambition and future rely upon it; he is engaged in all the happenings of local life; he is comfortable in this confined space; he is engaged in the government of society; he is accustomed to those procedures without which freedom runs the risk of revolution; he is imbued with their spirit; he acquires a taste for order; he understands the balance of powers and has clear, practical ideas on the nature of his duties and the extent of his rights.

THE COUNTIES OF NEW ENGLAND

The county in New England, similarity with the arrondissement *in France—Created purely for administrative purposes—No representation— Administered by non-elected officers.*

The American county has many points of similarity with the *arrondissements* of France. The latter have a similar arbitrary boundary and form an area the different parts of which have no necessary connection, no affection, no tradition or community feeling. Its formation has only an administrative objective.

The township covered too restricted an area for an effective administration of justice. The county therefore forms the primary center for justice with a county court,[10] a sheriff to execute its decrees, a prison for criminals.

There are needs which are perceived as similar by all the towns in a county; thus it was to be expected that a central authority should satisfy these needs. In Massachusetts, these powers rest in the hands of a certain number of magistrates appointed by the state governor with the advice[11] of his council.[12]

Those who administer the county possess only limited and extraordinary powers which are used in a very small number of predetermined cases. The state and the township are quite able to deal with normal public business. These administrators simply prepare the county budget for the legislature to vote upon.[13] No direct or indirect assembly represents the county which, as as result, has no real political existence.

In most American constitutions a twofold tendency can be observed which persuades the legislators to disseminate executive power while centralizing legislative power. The New England township has within itself an indestructible principle of existence. At a county level this would only ever be a fictional principle and the need for that has never been felt. All the townships together have only one representative, namely the state, where all the national authority is vested. Outside the activity at town and national levels, there are only the efforts of individuals.

ADMINISTRATION IN NEW ENGLAND

*In America, the administration is unnoticeable—Why—
Europeans believe that liberty is created when the social
authority is deprived of some of its rights: Americans by
dividing it up—Almost all the actual administration is*

10. See the law of 14 February 1821, *Laws of Massachusetts*, vol. 1, p. 551.
11. Ibid., 20 February 1819, vol. 2, p. 494.
12. The council of the governor is an elected body.
13. See the law of 2 November 1791, *Laws of Massachusetts*, vol. 1, p. 61.

*confined to the township and is divided up amongst the
town officers—No trace of an administrative hierarchy is
discernible, either in the township or above it—Why this is
so—How it happens that the state is administered in a
uniform manner—Who is empowered to see that the
township and the county obey the law—The introduction
of judicial power in the administration—Consequence of
the principle of election being extended to all
functionaries—The justices of the peace in New England—
By whom appointed—They administer the county and
ensure the administration of the townships—Court of
sessions—The way it acts—Who accesses it—Right of
inspection and complaint spread around like the other
administrative functions—Informers encouraged by the
sharing of fines.*

What strikes the European traveler in the United States is the
absence of what we call government or administration. In
America, written laws exist and one sees that they are executed
daily; although everything is in motion the engine behind it is
not visible. The hand which controls the social machine is
nowhere on view.

However, just as all nations, when expressing their thoughts,
have to use certain grammatical structures as part of human
language, so all societies are obliged, in order to secure their
existence, to submit to a certain amount of external authority
without which they fall into anarchy. Such authority can be
distributed in various ways but it must always exist somewhere.

Two methods exist to lessen the power of authority in a
nation.

The first is to weaken the very principle of this power by
removing from society the right or the opportunity to defend
itself in certain cases. Weakening the authority in this way is
what Europeans generally call the foundation of freedom.

The second way of lessening the action of this authority lies
not in stripping society of some of its rights or in paralyzing its
efforts but in distributing the exercise of its power in several
hands, in multiplying the number of civil servants to whom just

enough power is granted to perform what is asked of them. This division of social powers may lead some nations to anarchy but, in itself, it is not anarchic. Such a sharing out of authority does, I admit, make its action less irresistible and less dangerous but does not entirely destroy it.

Revolution in the United States was the result of a mature and thoughtful taste for freedom and not of a vague and ill-defined feeling for independence. It was not based upon the passions of disorder but on the contrary love of order and the law directed its course.

In the United States, therefore, it was never intended for a man in a free country to have the right to do anything he liked; rather, social duties were imposed upon him more various than anywhere else. It never occurred to the people to attack the principle of social authority or to contest its rights; they simply divided the exercise of power in order that the office should be strong and the officer weak and that society should be free and well governed.

There is no country in the world where the law has a more absolute voice than in America, nor where the right of applying it is shared among so many hands.

The administrative power in the United States offers in its constitution nothing centralized or hierarchical; that is why it remains unobtrusive. Power exists but its representative is nowhere to be seen.

Above, we have seen that the New England townships were not under protection; thus they themselves take care of their own interests.

Also the municipal magistrates carry out the execution of the general laws of the state or see most frequently that they are carried out. [14]

14. See *The Town Officer*, particularly under the words "Selectmen," "Assessors," "Collectors," "Schools," "Surveyors of Highways." One example in a thousand: the state forbids traveling on Sundays without a reason. The "tithingmen," municipal officials, are specially responsible for the obeying of this law. See law of 8 March 1792, *Laws of Massachusetts*, vol. 1, p. 410. The selectmen prepare the voting lists for the election of the governor and convey the result of the poll to the secretary of the republic. Law of 24 February 1796, ibid., p. 488.

Apart from general laws, the state sometimes enacts general police regulations but normally it is the townships and town officials who, joining forces with the justices of the peace and according to local needs, regulate the minor details of social life and promulgate rules that relate to public health, good order, and the moral welfare of their citizens. [15]

Finally, the town magistrates on their own initiative and without needing prompting from external agencies, provide for these unforeseen needs which societies often experience.[16]

The consequence of what I have just stated is that in Massachusetts the administrative power is almost wholly restricted to the township[17] but is distributed among many individuals.

In the French commune, there is really only one administrative officer, namely the mayor. We have seen that there were at least nineteen in New England and these are, in general, not dependent upon each other. The law has carefully drawn around each of these magistrates a sphere of action within which they enjoy all the power needed to fulfill the duties of their office independently of any other township authority.

Looking beyond the township, hardly any trace of an administrative hierarchy exists. Sometimes county officers amend the decision taken at township level or by their magistrates,[18] but in

---

15. Example: the selectmen authorize the construction of sewers, fix the
     location of slaughterhouses and other trades which may be a nuisance to
     their neighbors. See the law of 7 June 1785, ibid., p. 193.
16. Example: the selectmen supervise public health in cases of contagious
     diseases, and take the necessary measures in conjunction with the justices
     of the peace. Law of 22 June 1797, ibid., p. 539.
17. I say "almost" because there are several incidents of communal life regu-
     lated by the justices of the peace, either in their individual capacity or as
     a body meeting in the county town. Example: it is the justices of the peace
     who grant licenses. See law of 27 February, 1787, ibid., p. 297.
18. Example: licenses are granted only to people who can produce a certificate
     of good conduct from the selectmen. If the selectmen refuse to give this,
     the person can complain to the justices of the peace meeting in the court
     of sessions who may grant it. See law of 12 March 1808, ibid., vol. 2,
     p. 186. The townships have the right to make bylaws and enforce their
     observation by fines of fixed amounts. But these bylaws need to be
     approved by the court of sessions. See the law of 23 March 1786, ibid.,
     vol. 1, p. 254.

general one can say that the county authorities have no right to control the conduct of town authorities[19] except in matters concerning the county itself.

The magistrates of the township and county are bound to communicate the results of their actions to the officials of central government[20] in a very small number of predetermined cases. But no central government official has the duty to make general police regulations or edicts for the execution of laws; nor to maintain a regular communication with the county or town administrators; nor to supervise their conduct, control their actions or punish their mistakes. Nowhere does there exist a central point on which the radii of administrative power can converge.

How then can the affairs of society be managed upon a virtually uniform plan? How can the compliance of the counties and their officials or the township and theirs be enforced?

In the states of New England, the legislative power embraces more concerns than it does in France. The legislature extends to some degree to the very heart of the administration; the law descends to minute details and prescribes at the same time the principles and methods of applying them. Thus the secondary layers of the administration are restricted by a host of narrow and strictly defined duties. The result of this is that, provided that the secondary layers of administration obey the law, society moves in a uniform manner in all its branches. Yet, the question remains how this conformity to the law can be enforced upon these secondary layers of administration.

In general, one can say that society has at its disposal only two means of forcing administrators to obey the laws: one of them can be entrusted with the discretionary power of controlling all the others and of dismissing them, if they disobey; or courts can be instituted to impose penalties on offenders. But

19. In Massachusetts, the county officers are frequently called upon to assess the actions of the officials of the township, but we shall see later that they do this as a judicial authority not as an administrative one.

20. Example: the township educational committees are bound to send an annual report on the schools to the secretary of the republic. See the law of 10 March 1827, ibid., vol. 3, p. 183.

the freedom to adopt either of these methods is not always available.

The right to control a civil official presupposes the right to dismiss him, if he fails to follow orders given, or to promote him, if he fulfills all his duties conscientiously. But, it would be impossible to dismiss or promote an elected officer. The nature of elected officials is to remain untouched until the end of their term of duty. In reality, the elected magistrate has nothing to expect or fear except from his constituents, when all public offices come from an election. No real hierarchy between these officials could possibly exist since one and the same man cannot combine the right of commanding and effectively enforcing obedience and because the power of issuing an order cannot be joined to that of bestowing a reward or inflicting a punishment.

Therefore, peoples who make use of elections in the secondary layers of government have, of necessity, to employ judicial penalties as a means of administration.

This does not strike the observer at first sight; for those in power look upon the election of officials as a first concession and subjecting the elected magistrate to the jurisdiction of the law as a second. They are equally afraid of both these innovations; and since they are urged more to grant the first than the second, they accede to the election of the official while leaving him independent of the judge. However, the second of these two measures is the only counterweight to the other. But beware that an elected authority not subject to judicial power sooner or later eludes all control or is destroyed. Between the central power and the elected government bodies, only the law courts can act as an intermediary. They alone can force the elected officer to obey without violating the rights of the elector.

The extension of judicial power into the political domain should therefore be in direct ratio to the extension of the elected offices. If these two do not go hand in hand, the state ends up in anarchy or servitude.

Throughout time, it has been observed that familiarity with the law was a poor training for man's exercise of administrative authority.

The Americans have borrowed from their fathers, the English, the idea of an institution with no known parallel on the continent of Europe, namely justices of the peace.

The justice of the peace holds the middle ground between the man of the world and the magistrate, the administrator and the judge. The justice of the peace is an educated citizen, not necessarily trained in the knowledge of the law. His sole responsibility is the policing of society, a task which demands good sense and integrity more than legal knowledge. When a justice of the peace joins the administration, he brings with him a certain taste for formalities and openness which renders him of no use at all to the tyrant; furthermore, he is not the slave of those legal superstitions which make magistrates so ineligible for government.

The Americans have adopted the institution of justice of the peace while ridding it of the aristocratic character which was its distinctive feature in the mother country.

The governor of Massachusetts[21] appoints, in all the counties, a certain number of justices of the peace whose duties last seven years.[22] In addition, from these justices of the peace he designates three to form, in each county, what is called a court of sessions.

The justices of the peace take a personal share in the public administration. Sometimes they are entrusted with certain administrative functions conjointly with elected officers;[23] sometimes they constitute a tribunal before which the magistrates can summarily prosecute an obstructive citizen, or a citizen can expose the abuses of the magistrates. But it is in the court of sessions that the justices of the peace exert the most important of their administrative duties.

The court of sessions meets twice a year in the county town;

21. We shall see later what a governor is; here it is enough to note that he represents the executive power of the whole state.

22. See the Constitution of Massachusetts, chapter 2, section 1, para. 9, and chapter 2, para. 3.

23. One example among many: a stranger arrives in a township coming from a country where a contagious disease is raging. He falls ill. On the advice of the selectmen, two justices of the peace can order the county sheriff to have him sent away and to look after him. Law of 22 June 1797, vol. 1, p. 540. In general, justices of the peace intervene in all important acts of administrative life and so give them a semi-judicial character.

in Massachusetts, it is empowered to enforce the obedience of most[24] of the public officials.[25]

It must be noted that in Massachusetts the court of sessions is both an administrative body properly so called and a political tribunal.

I have stated that the county had only an administrative existence. It is the court of sessions which controls autonomously that small number of concerns which, because they are connected with several townships or all the townships of the county simultaneously, cannot be dealt with by any one of them in particular.

As far as county business is concerned, the duties of the court of sessions are therefore purely administrative and if the court often introduces judicial formalities into its procedures, that is simply a way of clarifying matters[26] and a guarantee it grants to the public. But whenever it upholds the administration of a township, it almost always acts as a judicial body and only in a few rare cases as an administrative one.[27]

The first obvious difficulty is to ensure that the township itself obeys the general laws of the state, since it enjoys an almost independent authority.

We have noted that the townships have to appoint annually a certain number of magistrates, called assessors, who levy

---

24. I say "most" because in fact certain administrative offenses are referred to ordinary courts. Example: when a township refuses to provide the funds necessary for its schools or to appoint the education committee, it is fined very heavily. That fine is imposed by a court called the *supreme judicial court*, or the court of *common pleas*. See law of 10 March 1827, ibid., vol. 3, p. 190. The same applies when a township fails to supply munitions of war. Law of 21 February 1822, ibid., vol. 2, p. 570.

25. In their individual capacity justices of the peace take part in the government of townships and counties. The most important acts of township life cannot be performed without the agreement of one of them.

26. The subjects concerning the county which come before the court of sessions may be listed as follows: 1) erection of prisons and courts of justice; 2) the preparation of the county budget (it is the state legislature which votes it); 3) the allocation of the taxes thus voted; 4) grants of certain patents; 5) the building and repair of county roads.

27. Thus, when a road is in question, the court of sessions, with the help of a jury, deals with almost all the practical difficulties.

taxes. If a township attempts to evade the duty of paying taxes by omitting to appoint assessors, the court of sessions condemns it to a heavy fine[28] which is levied individually on all the citizens. The county sheriff, an officer of justice, executes the decree. This is how, in the United States, the authorities appear keen to maintain a careful distance from public scrutiny. An administrative order almost always hides behind a judicial decree, whereby it is all the more powerful because it assumes that almost irresistible authority granted by men to legal processes.

This procedure is easy to follow and to understand. The demands upon the township are, in general, clear and precise; it turns upon a simple, not a complicated, fact; on a principle, not its detailed application.[29] The real difficulty begins when it is a matter of exacting obedience, not from the townships, but from their officials.

All the wrongdoings which a public official can commit must fall within one of these categories:

He may perform what the law commands without enthusiasm or zeal.

He may neglect to perform what the law commands.

Finally, he may do what the law prohibits.

It is only the last two categories which could possibly come under the jurisdiction of a tribunal since only established and substantive facts can serve as grounds for judicial action.

Thus, if selectmen omit the legal formalities prescribed for municipal elections, they can be made to pay a fine.[30]

But when the public official performs his duty stupidly and

28. See law of 20 February 1786, vol. 1, p. 217.
29. There is an indirect method of forcing a township to obey. The townships are obliged by law to keep their roads in good repair. If they fail to vote the funds necessary for their upkeep, the town surveyor is then authorized, in his official capacity, to levy the required sum. As he is himself responsible to individual citizens for the bad state of the roads and can be sued by them in the court of sessions, one can be sure that he will make use of the extraordinary power which the law has given him against the township. Accordingly, by threatening the official, the court of sessions enforces obedience from the township. See law of 5 March 1787, ibid., vol. 1, p. 305.
30. *Laws of Massachusetts*, vol. 2, p. 45.

obeys the dictates of the law without enthusiasm or zeal, he stands quite outside the reach of a court of law.

The court of sessions, although invested with its administrative powers, is impotent, in this case, to force him to fulfill his whole duty. Only the fear of dismissal can check these quasi offenses and, since the court of sessions has not set up the communal authorities, it cannot dismiss officials it does not appoint.

Besides, to establish negligence and lack of zeal, a subordinate official would have to be kept under constant supervision. Now, the court of sessions sits but twice a year, makes no inspections, and judges only those offenses which are placed before it.

An arbitrary power to dismiss public officials may be the only guarantee from them of that sort of active and educated obedience which cannot be imposed upon them by any court of law.

In France, we seek to ensure this final guarantee through the *hierarchy of the administration*; in America, it is sought through the principle of *election*.

Thus, to sum up in a few words what I have just shown:

If the public official of New England commits a *crime* in the exercise of his duties, the ordinary courts are *always* called upon to try him.

Should he commit a *misdemeanor in his administrative capacity*, a purely administrative court is responsible for setting his punishment and when the matter is serious or urgent, the judge acts as the official ought to have acted.[31]

Finally, were the same official guilty of one of those intangible offenses which human justice can neither define nor judge, he would appear annually before a court from which there is no appeal and which can at once reduce him to impotence; his power disappearing with his mandate.

---

31. Example: if a township persists in not appointing assessors, the court of sessions appoints them and the officials so chosen are endowed with the same powers as elected officials. See law already quoted of 20 February 1787.

This system undoubtedly possesses great advantages but, in its execution, it encounters one practical difficulty I must point out.

I have already noted that the administrative court, called the court of sessions, had no right to examine the town officers; it can act only when, to use the legal expression, it is *seised* of the matter. Now that is the subtle difficulty of the system.

The Americans of New England have never appointed a public prosecutor attached to the court of sessions[32] and one is forced to imagine that such an appointment was difficult. If they had merely placed a public prosecutor in each county town, without granting him assistants in the townships, how could he have gained any more knowledge about what was going on in the county than the members of the court of sessions themselves? But, had he been given assistants in every township, he would have enjoyed central control over that most formidable of powers, that of judicial administration. Besides, laws are the children of habit and nothing akin to this existed in the legislation of England.

The Americans, as with all other administrative functions, have thus separated the right of supervision from that of complaint.

Grand jurors are bound by the law to apprise the court to which they are attached of all offenses which may have been committed in their county.[33] Certain major administrative offenses are prosecuted automatically by the normal public prosecutor;[34] the duty of punishing delinquents falls mostly to the treasury official who has to collect the fine imposed. Thus, the town treasurer is responsible for the prosecution of most of the administrative offenses committed which come to his attention.

32. I say *attached to the court of sessions*. There is an officer who performs some of the functions of a public prosecutor attached to the ordinary courts.

33. For example, grand juries are obliged to warn the courts of the bad state of the roads. *Law of Massachusetts*, vol. 1, p. 308.

34. If, for example, the county treasurer does not supply his accounts. Ibid., p. 406.

But above all, American legislation appeals to the interests of each individual[35] which is the overriding principle constantly evident in any study of United States law.

American legislators display but little trust in human integrity, while assuming always that men are intelligent. Therefore, they mostly depend upon the self-interest of individuals to aid the execution of the law.

When an individual is actually positively harmed by an administrative mistake, it is understood, in effect, that his personal interest will persuade him to lodge a complaint.

But, it is simple to foresee that, in the case of some legal ruling which is useful to society as a whole but of no real value to the individual, no one will be keen to bring a complaint. In this way, through a kind of tacit consent, laws could well fall into disuse.

When Americans are thrust by their system into such extremes, they have to encourage informers by offering them, in certain cases, a share of the fines[36]—a dangerous expedient of ensuring the execution of the law by lowering moral standards.

Above and beyond county officials, it has to be said that no administrative power exists outside the power of the government.

35. This is an example among a thousand: a private individual damages his carriage or is injured on a badly maintained road; he can sue the township or the county responsible for damages before the court of sessions. Ibid. p. 309.

36. In the event of an invasion or a riot, if officials of a township fail to provide the militia with necessary supplies and munitions, the township may be fined from $200 to $500. One can easily suppose that in such a case no one would have any interest or desire to assume the role of prosecutor. So, the law adds: "All citizens shall have the right to prosecute for the punishment of such offenses, and half the fine shall belong to the prosecutor." See the law of 6 March 1810, ibid. vol. 2, p. 236. That same provision is very often repeated in the laws of Massachusetts. Sometimes it is not private individuals whom the law thus invites to prosecute public officials, but the public official is encouraged in this way to punish private individuals. Example: an inhabitant refuses to carry out the share of work on a main road assigned to him. The surveyor of highways should prosecute him; and if he manages to have him convicted, half the fine goes to him. See the law quoted above, vol. 1, p. 308.

GENERAL IDEAS CONCERNING ADMINISTRATION
IN THE UNITED STATES

Differences in the systems of administration in the states of the Union—Life in the township less vigorous and less active the further south one goes—The power of the magistrate increases, that of the voters diminishes—Administration passes from township to county—States of New York, Ohio, and Pennsylvania—Principles applicable to the administration of the whole Union—Election of public officials and the inalienability of their functions—Absence of hierarchy—Introduction of judicial procedures into the administration.

I have previously stated that, after a detailed examination of the constitution of township and county in New England, I would take a broad look at the rest of the Union.

There are townships and a community life in every state but nowhere in the confederation of states does one encounter a township exactly similar to those in New England.

As one moves gradually southwards, it is evident that township life becomes less active; the township has fewer magistrates, rights or duties; the population does not exert such an immediate influence on affairs. The township meetings happen less frequently and deal with fewer matters. The power of the elected magistrate is thus comparatively greater while that of the voter is smaller; local community spirit is less alive and less powerful.[37]

We begin to perceive these differences in the state of New York; they are very evident in Pennsylvania; but they become

---

37. For details see *The Revised Statutes of the State of New York*, pt 1, ch. 11, entitled *Of the Powers, Duties and Privileges of Towns*, vol. 1, pp. 336–4. In the *Digest of the Laws of Pennsylvania*, look under the words "Assessors," "Collectors," "Constables," "Overseers of the Poor," and "Supervisors of Highways." And in the *Acts of a General Nature of the State of Ohio*, law of 25 February 1834, concerning townships, p. 412. The particular provisions concerning various municipal officials, such as: "Township's clerks," "Trustees," "Overseers of the Poor," "Fence Viewers," "Appraisers of Property," "Township's Treasurer," "Constables," "Supervisors of Highways."

less striking as we advance toward the Northwest. The majority of the immigrants who were to found the states in the Northwest set out from New England and they brought the administrative customs of the mother country to their adopted homeland. A township in Ohio has much in common with one in Massachusetts.

We have seen that in Massachusetts the mainspring of public administration rests in the township, which is the central focus for men's interests and loyalties. But that ceases to be the case as we descend to those states where knowledge is not so widely experienced and where, consequently, the township offers fewer guarantees of a wise administration and a full complement of officials. Therefore, as we move away from New England, the county somehow takes over from the township in communal life and becomes the main administrative center as well as the intermediary between the government and ordinary citizens.

I have stated that in Massachusetts county business is controlled by the court of sessions, which is composed of a certain number of officials appointed by the governor and his council. The county has no representative assembly and its budget is voted by the state legislature.

On the other hand, in the great state of New York and in Ohio and Pennsylvania, the citizens of each county elect a certain number of representatives who meet to form a county assembly.[38]

The county assembly possesses, within certain limits, the right to tax its citizens; and in that respect, it is like a real legislature. At the same time it exercises an executive power in the county, directing in several instances the administration of the townships and restricting their powers within limits much narrower than those in Massachusetts.

---

38.   See *Revised Statutes of the State of New York*, pt 1, ch. 11, vol. 1, p. 340, and ch. 12, p. 366; also in *The Acts of the State of Ohio*, law of 25 February 1824, concerning county commissioners, p. 263. See the *Digest of the Laws of Pennsylvania* under the words "County Rates," and "Levies," p. 170. In the state of New York, each township elects a commissioner to take part in the administration of both county and township.

These are the main differences presented by the constitution of the township and county in the various states of the Union. Were I to wish to go into the detail of the means of execution, I would have many other differences to point out. But my aim is not to design a course on American administrative law.

I think I have said enough to reveal the general principles which uphold the United States administration. They are variously applied and provide outcomes which differ according to the place. At root, however, they share the same features. Laws vary, their form alters but the same spirit gives them all life.

Township and county may not everywhere be organized in the same manner but it is at least true that, in the United States, the county and township are founded upon the same idea, namely that each man is the best judge of his own interest and the best able to provide for his own private needs. Township and county are, therefore, responsible for guarding their own particular interests. The state governs but does not administer. Exceptions to this rule are encountered but not one contrary principle.

The first result of this doctrine has been the electing of all the township and county administrators by the citizens themselves or at least choosing the magistrates exclusively from among them.

As the administrators are everywhere elected or cannot be removed, it has been impossible to establish the rules of a hierarchy of authority anywhere. Thus, there are as many independent officials as there are offices and the administrative power has been shared by a multitude of hands.

Since there is no hierarchy anywhere and the administrators are elected and irremovable before the end of their contract, the obligation arose to introduce courts of law into the administration to a greater or lesser extent. Hence the system of fines, whereby the second layer of authority and its representatives are forced to obey the laws. This system exists from one end of the Union to the other.

However, the power to punish administrative offenses and to perform, where necessary, administrative acts has not been granted in all the states to the same judges.

Anglo-Americans have derived from the same source the institution of justices of the peace and this is found in all the states but they have not always made it work in the same way.

Universally, justices of the peace participate in the administration of towns and counties,[39] either directly as administrators or in the punishment of certain administrative offenses. But in the majority of states, the most serious offenses are dealt with by the ordinary courts.

Hence the election of administrative officers, the inalienability of their office, the absence of administrative hierarchy and the introduction of judicial control over the secondary layers of government are the principal characteristics of American administration from Maine to the Floridas.

In some states, there are the beginnings of a centralization of the administration. New York has advanced most along this path.

In the state of New York, in some cases the officials of central government exercise a kind of supervision and control over the conduct of secondary authorities.[40] In other cases, they act as a court of appeal in decisions made.[41] In the state of New York,

39. There are even states in the South where county court judges are responsible for all details of administration. See *The Statutes of the State of Tennessee*, under the headings "Judiciary," "Taxes," etc.

40. Example: control of public education is centralized in the hands of the government. The legislature appoints the regents of the university with the state governor and the lieutenant governor as *ex officio* members. (*Revised Statues*, vol. 1, p. 456.) The regents of the university visit all the colleges and academies every year and make an annual report to the legislature; their supervision is not theoretical for the following reasons: the colleges, in order to become *corporations* able to buy, sell, and own property, need charters; now a charter is granted by the legislature only on the advice of the regents. The state annually distributes the interest from a special fund created to encourage education to the colleges and academies. It is the regents who apportion that money. See ch. 15, "Public Education," in *Revised Statutes*, vol. 1, p. 455. Each year the commissioners of public schools must send in a report about them to the superintendent of the republic. Ibid., p. 488. A similar report must be sent to him annually concerning the number and condition of the poor. Ibid. p. 631.

41. If anyone feels himself injured by any act of the school commissioners (who are municipal officers), he can appeal to the superintendent of primary schools, whose decision is final. Ibid., p. 487.

judicial penalties are used less than elsewhere as an administrative tool and the right to prosecute administrative offenses is vested in fewer hands.[42]

The same tendency is faintly evident in certain other states[43] but, in general, one can say that the overwhelming characteristic of public administration in the United States is its extraordinary decentralization.

THE STATE

I have spoken of the townships and the administration; it now remains for me to speak of the state and the government.

This is ground I can cover rapidly without fear of being misunderstood, for all I have to say is found in the written constitutions easily available to anyone.[44] These constitutions rest upon one simple rational theory.

All constitutional nations have adopted most of their provisions and so have become familiar to us.

Therefore, at this point, I need give only a short analysis; later I shall attempt an assessment of what I am about to describe.

Here and there in the laws of the state of New York one finds provisions similar to those quoted above. But in general such attempts at centralization are weak and not very useful. While giving the chief officials in the state the right to supervise and control subordinate officials, they give them no right to reward or punish them. The same man is never responsible both for giving the order and for punishing disobedience; he, therefore, has the right to command but not the ability to demand obedience.

In 1830, the superintendent of schools complained in his annual report to the legislature that several school commissioners had not, in spite of reminders, sent him the due statements of account. "If this omission continues," he added, "I shall be reduced to prosecuting them, in the terms of the law, before the competent courts."

42. Example: the district attorney is responsible for recovering all fines above $50 unless the law has expressly made some other official responsible for them. *Revised Statutes*, pt 1, ch. 10, vol. 1, p. 383.

43. There are several signs of administrative centralization in Massachusetts. Example: the committees of municipal schools are responsible for sending an annual report to the secretary of state. *Laws of Massachusetts*, vol. 1, p. 367.

44. See the text of the constitution of New York.

LEGISLATIVE POWER OF THE STATE

Division of the legislature in two houses—Senate—
House of Representatives—Different functions of these
two bodies.

The legislative power of the state is entrusted to two assemblies, the first of which generally bears the name of the Senate.

The Senate is usually a law-making body but sometimes becomes an executive and judicial one. It takes part in government in several ways according to the constitution of the different states[45] but it is in the nomination of its officials that it normally assumes an executive power.

It has judicial power in judging certain political misdemeanors and occasionally in pronouncing on certain civil cases.[46]

The number of members is always small.

The other branch of the legislature, normally entitled the House of Representatives, has no power whatever in the administration and takes part in judicial power only in cases of impeaching public officials before the Senate.

Members of the two houses submit almost everywhere to the same conditions of election. Both are elected in the same way and by the same citizens.

The only difference between them stems from the longer term of office for senators than those belonging to the House of Representatives. The latter rarely remain in office for more than a year; the former sit normally for two or three years.

By granting senators the privilege of being appointed for several years and by re-electing them in succession, the law has taken steps to preserve, at the center of the legislative body, a nucleus of men already accustomed to public business and able to exercise a practical influence on newcomers.

By dividing the legislature into two, Americans have, therefore, intended not to create one hereditary house and another elected; they did not mean the one to be aristocratic, the other

45.   In Massachusetts, the Senate has no administrative function.
46.   As in the state of New York.

democratic; neither did they aim to make the first an adjunct of the establishment, while leaving to the other the concerns and passions of the people.

The only advantages to result from the present constitution of two houses in the United States are the division of legislative power, the consequent check upon the movement of political assemblies, and the creation of a court of appeal for the revision of the laws.

Time and experience have made Americans aware that, if these are its only advantages, the division of legislative powers is still a necessity of the first importance. Only Pennsylvania, of all the united republics, had initially attempted to establish a single assembly. Franklin[a] himself, attracted by the logical conclusions of the dogma of the sovereignty of the people, had agreed to this measure but they were soon forced to change the law and establish the two houses. Thus the principle of the division of the legislature received its final consecration. Henceforth, the necessity of dividing the legislative process between several bodies became regarded as a proven truth. This theory, almost unknown in classical republics, brought in almost by chance like most great truths, misjudged by several modern nations, has finally become an axiom of present-day political science.

THE EXECUTIVE POWER OF THE STATE

The office of governor in an American state—His position in relation to the legislature—His rights and his duties— His dependence upon the people.

The executive power of the state is represented by the governor. I do not use this word 'represented' casually, for the state governor does indeed represent the executive power but exercises only some of its rights.

This supreme magistrate, called the governor, is positioned alongside the legislature as a moderator and adviser. He is armed with a suspensive veto which allows him to stop or at least check its movements at will. He lays before the legislative body the needs of the country and points out the best ways of providing for them. He is the natural executor of its decrees in all matters which involve the whole nation.[47] In the absence of the legislature, he must take all appropriate measures to protect the state from violent upheavals and unexpected dangers.

The governor concentrates the entire military power of the state in his hands; he is the commander of the militia and the head of the armed forces.

When public authority, which men have agreed to grant to the law, is disregarded, the governor marches forward at the head of the physical power of the state; he breaks down resistance and restores accustomed order.

Besides, the governor plays no further part in the administration of the townships and counties, or at least only very indirectly by appointing justices of the peace whom he cannot subsequently dismiss.[48]

The governor is a magistrate, carefully elected in general, for only one or two years in such a way that he always remains closely dependent upon the majority who elected him.

POLITICAL EFFECTS OF ADMINISTRATIVE DECENTRALIZATION IN THE UNITED STATES

Clarification of the distinction between governmental and administrative centralization—In the United States, no administrative centralization but considerable governmental centralization—Some unfortunate effects caused in the United States by extreme administrative decentralization—Administrative advantage from this system—The power which runs society is less ordered, less enlightened, less educated, and much greater than in Europe—Political advantages of the same order of things— In the United States, the consciousness of the nation—

47. In practice, it is not always the governor who executes the plans of the legislature, for the latter often appoints special agents to supervise their execution at the same time as it votes the measure in principle.

48. In several states, the justices of the peace are not appointed by the governor.

Support which those governed give to the government—
Provincial institutions more necessary as the social
conditions become more democratic—Why?

Centralization is a word endlessly repeated nowadays whose meaning no one, in general, seeks to define.

However, two very distinct kinds of centralization exist which need to be recognized.

Certain concerns are shared by all national groups, such as the formation of general laws and relations with foreign nations.

Other concerns are of special interest to certain national groups such as, for example, business undertaken by the townships.

To concentrate in one place or in the same hand the power to control the former is to create what I shall call governmental centralization. To concentrate in the same way the power to control the latter is to create what I shall call administrative centralization.

There are some points where the two kinds of centralization happen to coalesce. Yet, by broadly classifying the objects which fall more particularly into the realm of each one of them, the distinction can easily be made.

It is realized that governmental centralization acquires immense power when joined to administrative centralization. In this way, it accustoms men completely and continuously to disregard their own wishes and to obey, not only for once and upon one point but in every respect and at all times. Thereupon, not only does this power tame them but it also affects their habits; it isolates them and then submerges them one by one into the mass of the community.

These two kinds of centralization give each other mutual support and have a mutual attraction but I could not possibly believe that they are inseparable.

Under Louis XIV, France saw the greatest centralization of government since the same man passed the general laws and held the power of their interpretation; he represented France abroad and acted in her name. "I am the State," he would say and he was right.

However, under Louis XIV, there was less administrative centralization than at the present time.

In our time, we see one power, England, where government centralization is carried to an extreme degree; the state seems to move as a single man; it shifts great hordes of people at will; it gathers and spreads its might wherever it wishes.

England, which has achieved such great things for fifty years, has no administrative centralization.

For my part, I cannot conceive that a nation can either exist, much less prosper, without a strong centralization of government.

But it is my opinion that administrative centralization only serves to weaken those nations who submit to it, because it has the constant effect of diminishing their sense of civic pride. It is true that administrative centralization succeeds in concentrating all the available resources of the nation at any given time and in a particular place but it militates against the increase of those resources. It brings victory on the day of battle but, in the long run, diminishes a nation's power. It can, therefore, contribute admirably to the passing greatness of one particular man while not at all to the lasting prosperity of a nation.

It must be borne in mind that whenever we say that a state cannot act because it has no centralization, what is almost always meant, albeit subconsciously, is the centralization of government. The German Empire, people keep saying, has never been able to take advantage of its strength. Agreed. But why? Because the strength of the nation has never been centralized; because the state has never been able to enforce obedience to its central laws; because the separate entities of the body politic have always had the right or the means to refuse cooperation to the guardians of the common authority even in the case of concerns shared by all the citizens; because, to put it another way, it possessed no centralization of government.

The same remark applies to the Middle Ages. The cause of all the wretchedness of feudal society is that the power, not only of administration, but of government was divided between a thousand hands and split in a thousand ways. Thus, the absence of any governmental centralization prevented the European nations from advancing energetically toward any goal.

We have seen that no administrative centralization existed in the United States, nor hardly any trace of a hierarchy. There, decentralization has been carried to a stage which no European nation could tolerate, I believe, without a deep sense of awkwardness and it has even produced some troublesome effects in America. But, there is a high level of government centralization in the United States. It would be simple to demonstrate that the power of the nation is more concentrated there than it was in any of the former European monarchies. Not only is there in each state only one single legislative body, not only is there one authority which creates political life around itself, but, in general, numerous district or county assemblies have been avoided for fear they might be tempted to exceed their administrative functions and to hamper the procedures of government. In America, the legislature of every state is not confronted by any power capable of standing in its way. Nothing could impede its progress, neither privileges, nor local immunities, nor personal influence, not even the power of reason, for it represents the majority voice which claims to be the sole organ of reason. It has, therefore, no other limitations to its actions than its own will. Alongside and in its control is the representative of executive power which, with the support of physical force, is bound to compel any malcontents to obey.

Only in certain details of governmental action do we see any weaknesses.

American republics have no permanent armed forces to restrain minorities but these minorities have so far never been reduced to declaring war and the need for an army has not yet been felt. Usually the state uses the township or county officials to deal with citizens. Thus, for example, in New England, it is the township assessor who fixes the taxes, the collector who raises them, the treasurer of the township forwards the receipts to the public treasury and any claims arising are submitted to the ordinary courts. Such a manner of collecting taxes is slow and awkward; it would constantly constrict the progress of any government with extensive financial requirements. In general, it is desirable that, in all matters essential for its existence, the government both has its own civil servants, whose appointment and dismissal are under its control and enjoys swift methods of proceeding. But it will always be simple for central government, such as it is organized in America, to introduce, when the need arises, more vigorous and effective methods of action.

The republics of the New World will not perish from the want of centralization in the United States, as has so often been asserted. So, far from being not sufficiently centralized, it can be said that American governments are too much so, as I will demonstrate later. Legislative assemblies daily encroach upon the powers of the government and their tendency is to appropriate them all entirely to themselves, just as happened in the French Convention.[b] Social power, centralized in this way, constantly changes hands because it is under the sway of popular power. It often lacks wisdom and foresight because it has total power, wherein lies its danger. It is, therefore, its very strength, not its weakness, that threatens its ultimate destruction.

Administrative decentralization gives rise to several differing consequences in America.

We have seen that America had almost entirely separated the administration from the government, a move which seems to me to have overstepped the boundaries of good sense; for order, even in subsidiary affairs, is still of national concern.[49]

As the state has no officials of its own stationed at different locations in its territory to whom it can issue a common directive, the consequence is that it rarely attempts to establish any general police regulations. Now, such a need is acutely felt and Europeans often note their absence. This apparent disorder on the surface convinces them, at first glance, of complete anarchy in society. Only an examination of the background makes them think again.

49. The authority which represents the state, even when it does not administer, should not, I think, surrender its right to inspect local administration. Suppose, for instance, that a government officer were posted at some fixed spot in every county and could bring before the courts offenses committed in the townships or the county, would that not ensure more uniform good order without compromising local independence? However, nothing like that exists in America. There is nothing above the county courts. And it is, in a sense, only by chance that those courts become aware of the administrative offenses which they ought to suppress.·

Certain enterprises involve the whole state but they cannot be carried out because there is no administration at a national level to manage them. Left to the care of the townships and counties, in the hands of elected and temporary officers, they come to nothing and produce no lasting result.

Those who support centralization in Europe maintain that the government is better able to administer localities than they can themselves. That may be true when central government is enlightened and local authorities are not, when it is energetic and they are slow, and when it is accustomed to command and they to obey. One can, moreover, appreciate that with the increase of centralization, this dual tendency increases so that the capacity of the one and the incapacity of the other become more striking.

But I cannot accept that it is so when a nation is as enlightened, as watchful over its own interests and as accustomed to reflect about them as the Americans are.

On the contrary, I am convinced that in such an instance, the united strength of the citizens will always be better placed to achieve social wellbeing than the authority of government.

I confess that it is difficult to highlight for certain a way of awakening a sleeping population and to stimulate the passion and enlightenment it lacks. I am quite aware that convincing men to look after their own affairs is a burdensome task. It would often be easier to involve them in the details of court etiquette than in the repair of their common dwelling. But I also think that when the administration at the center claims to replace completely the free assembly of those primarily concerned, it is either deceiving itself or you.

However enlightened and wise one imagines a central power to be, it cannot entirely on its own incorporate all the details of the life of a great nation, because such a task exceeds human strength. Whenever it aims, unaided, to create and operate so many different forces, it settles for a very imperfect result or exhausts itself in futile efforts.

It is true that centralization easily succeeds in imposing upon the external behavior of man a certain uniformity which comes to be loved for itself without reference to its objectives, just as the religious may adore a statue while forgetting the god it represents. Centralization has no difficulty in imposing an aspect of regularity upon day-to-day activities; in exercising a wise supervision of social control; in suppressing trivial disorders and petty offenses; in holding the status quo of a society which cannot be seen strictly as either decadence or progress; in maintaining in society a sort of administrative lethargy which administrators usually call good order and public tranquillity.[50] To sum up, its forte is obstruction, not action. When the issue is a profound shake-up of society or the imposition of swift progress, its strength evaporates. Whenever its measures require help from individuals, this huge machine is astonishingly weak and is suddenly reduced to impotence.

Then, it sometimes happens that centralization, out of desperation, attempts to summon the citizens to its aid but says the following to them: "You will act as I wish, to the extent that I wish and precisely in the direction I wish. You will be responsible for the following details without any design on directing the whole; you will toil in darkness and will judge my work later by its results." It is not under such conditions that one achieves the support of men's will. Men must walk in freedom, responsible for their own behaviour. Man is built in such a way that he prefers to stand still rather than march forward without independence toward an unknown goal.

I shall not deny that, in the United States, one frequently regrets the absence of these uniform rules which seem constantly to watch over our lives in France.

Occasionally, one encounters major instances of social indifference and neglect. Gross blemishes appear here and there at apparent variance with the surrounding civilization.

Useful undertakings which require sustained attention and

---

50. China seems to offer the perfect example of the sort of social prosperity which a very centralized administration can provide for a submissive people. Travelers tell us that the Chinese have peace without happiness, industry without progress, stability without strength, and material order without public morality. In their case, society always gets on fairly well, never very well. I imagine that when China is opened to Europeans, they will find it the finest model of administrative centralization in the world.

vigorous precision in order to succeed often end up by being abandoned, for, in America, as elsewhere, the people move forward by sudden impulses and short-lived efforts.

Europeans, used to the constant presence of a civil servant interfering in almost everything, find it difficult to get used to the different machinery of central administration. In general, one can say that those small details of social regulations which make life enjoyable and comfortable are neglected in America but the guarantees, essential to man's life in society, exist there as everywhere. For Americans, the force behind the state is much less regulated, enlightened, or prudent but a hundred times greater than in Europe. Without doubt there is no country in the world where men make as much effort to create social wellbeing. I know of no nation which has managed to establish as many efficient schools or churches, more in harmony with the religious needs of the inhabitants, or better maintained municipal roads. It is, therefore, no good looking in the United States for uniformity and permanence of attitude, minute attention to detail, or perfection of administrative procedures.[51] What one does find is the picture of power, somewhat wild perhaps, but

51. A talented writer who, in comparing the financial systems of France and the United States, has proved that intelligence cannot always substitute for knowledge of facts, correctly reproaches the Americans for the type of confusion prevailing in their municipal budgets, and after quoting the example of a departmental budget in France, adds: "Thanks to centralization, the wonderful creation of a great man, municipal budgets from one end of the kingdom to the other, in the smallest communes as well as in the great cities, are equally orderly and methodical." That is certainly an achievement I admire; but I see most of those French communes, whose accounting systems are so excellent, plunged in profound ignorance of their true interests and victims of such an invincible apathy that society there seems to vegetate rather than thrive; on the other hand, I observe in those American townships, with their untidy budgets lacking all uniformity, an enlightened, active, and enterprising population; there, I perceive a society always at work. This contrasting picture astonishes me, for in my view the principal objective of good government is to ensure the welfare of people and not to establish a certain order at the heart of their misery. I wonder if the same cause may not be responsible for the prosperity of the American township and for the apparent disorder of its finances, and conversely, for the distress of the French commune and for its immaculate budget. In any case, I distrust a good mingled with so many evils and gladly put up with an evil compensated by so many benefits.

full of strength; life liable to accidents but also full of striving and activity.

Moreover, I grant, if you like, that the villages and counties of the United States would be more conveniently administered by a central authority some distance away and unknown to them than by civil servants chosen from among them. If I have to, I will accept that America would enjoy greater security and that a wiser and more judicious use would be made of social resources, if the administration of the whole country were concentrated in the hands of one man. The political advantages which Americans derive from a system of decentralization would still make me opt for that rather than the opposite.

After all, what good is it to me to have an authority always ready to see to the tranquil enjoyment of my pleasures, to brush away all dangers from my path without my having to think about them, if such an authority, as well as removing thorns from under my feet, is also the absolute master of my freedom or if it so takes over all activity and life that around it all must languish when it languishes, sleep when it sleeps and perish when it perishes.

There are European nations where the inhabitant sees himself as a kind of settler, indifferent to the fate of the place he inhabits. Major changes happen there without his cooperation, he is even unaware of what precisely has happened; he is suspicious; he hears about events by chance. Worse still, the condition of his village, the policing of the roads, the fate of the churches and presbyteries scarcely bothers him; he thinks that everything is outside his concern and belongs to a powerful stranger called the government. He enjoys what he has as a tenant, without any feeling of ownership or thought of possible improvement. This detachment from his own fate becomes so extreme that, if his own safety or that of his children is threatened, instead of trying to ward off the danger, he folds his arms and waits for the entire nation to come to his rescue.

Furthermore, this man, although he has so comfortably sacrificed his own will, still does not like obeying any more than the next man. Granted he submits to the whim of a clerk but, as soon as force is withdrawn, he enjoys defying the law as if it were a conquered enemy. So we see him constantly wavering between slavishness and license.

When nations have reached this point, they have to modify their laws and customs or perish, for the spring of public virtue has, as it were, dried up. Subjects still exist but citizens are no more.

I maintain that such nations are ready for conquest. If they do not disappear from the world stage, it is only because they must be surrounded by nations either similar or inferior to them; or they must retain in their hearts a sort of indefinable intuition of patriotism, some unconscious pride in the name they bear, some indistinct memory of their past glory which, though unable to latch on to anything in particular, is enough, when pressed, to imprint upon them some impulse of self-preservation.

It would be a mistake to find reassurance by reflecting that certain nations have made extraordinary efforts to defend a country where they have lived as virtual strangers. Look more closely and you will see that religion was almost always their main motivation.

The permanence, reputation, or prosperity of the nation had become for them sacred dogmas and in defending their country, they were defending also that holy city where they were all citizens.

The Turkish people have never participated in the control of society's affairs; however, they have achieved huge undertakings as long as they saw the triumph of the religion of Mohammed[c] in the conquests of the sultans. Today, their religion is disappearing; despotism alone remains; and they are declining.

When Montesquieu[d] attributed a peculiar power to despotism, he paid it an honor, I think, which it did not deserve. Despotism, by itself, can maintain nothing of lasting value. Looking more closely, one perceives that it is religion, not fear, which has supported the prosperity of absolute governments.

Whatever happens, you will never come across true exercise of power among men, except by the free agreement of their wills; only patriotism or religion can carry, over a long period, the whole body of citizens toward the same goal.

Laws cannot restore fading beliefs, but can involve men in

the destiny of their own country. Laws can awaken and direct that indistinct feeling of patriotism which never leaves the human heart and creates a considered and lasting sentiment by linking it to everyday thoughts, passions, and customs. And let no one say that it is too late to attempt such a thing; nations age differently from men. Each fresh generation is like a new nation, ready to be molded by the legislator.

What I most admire in America are not the administrative results of decentralization but the political effects. In the United States, the motherland is felt everywhere and is a subject of concern from village to the whole Union. The inhabitants care about each of their country's interests as they would their own. They rejoice in the glory of the nation in whose successes they recognize their own contribution and are uplifted. They are elated by the all-round prosperity from which they benefit. They have for their homeland a feeling much the same as they have for their own families. It is from a sort of self-centeredness that they interest themselves in the welfare of their country.

To the European, a civil servant represents but a superior force, to an American, he represents the law. One can, therefore, state that in America one man never obeys another man, only justice or the law.

Thus, if he has an often exalted opinion of himself, it is at least salutary. He fearlessly trusts in his own powers which appear to be sufficient for every eventuality. Suppose an individual thinks of some enterprise which might have some direct connection with the welfare of society. It does not occur to him to seek support from public authority. He publishes a plan, offers to carry it out, summons the help of other individuals and struggles personally against all obstacles. Doubtless, he often has less success than the state would have enjoyed in his stead but, in the longer term, the combined result of all these individual enterprises exceeds greatly what government could achieve.

Administrative power arouses neither jealousy nor hatred because it is closely connected to those it governs and it represents, generally speaking, their interests. No one feels able to rely entirely upon it as its resources are limited.

Thus, when administrative power exercises its proper authority, it is not left to its own devices, as in Europe. No one considers that individual duties have ceased because a public representative happens to act. On the contrary, everyone guides, supports, and sustains him.

The efforts of individuals, combined with those of society, often achieve what the most intense and energetic administration would fail to achieve. (See Appendix J, p. 842.)

I could quote many facts to support my opinion but prefer to select only the one which I know best.

In America, the means available to the authorities to uncover crime and to arrest criminals are small in number.

There is no administrative police force; passports are unknown. The United States criminal police force cannot be compared with ours in France. The officers of the public prosecutor's office are few and they do not always enjoy independent powers of arrest; the examination of prisoners is swift and verbal. However, I doubt whether crime evades punishment less often in any other country. The reason for that is that everyone feels involved in providing evidence of the offense and in apprehending the offender.

During my stay in the United States, I saw the inhabitants of a county where a major crime had been perpetrated spontaneously form committees with the aim of arresting the guilty man and handing him over to the courts.

In Europe, the criminal is a luckless fellow, fighting to save his life from the authorities; the population, to some degree, watches as he struggles. In America, he is an enemy of the human race and has everyone entirely against him.

I think that provincial institutions are useful to all nations but they are never more needed than in a society which is democratic.

In an aristocracy, one can always be sure that a certain degree of order will be maintained in freedom.

The ruling class has much to lose and, therefore, order is a main concern for them.

Equally, one can say that, in an aristocracy, the nation is

sheltered from the excesses of tyranny because organized forces
exist ready to resist a despot.

A democracy without provincial institutions has no guarantee
against such ills.

How can liberty be upheld in great matters amongst a multitude which has not learned to make use of it in small ones?

How can tyranny be resisted in a country where each person
is weak and where individuals are not united by any shared
concerns?

Those who fear anarchy and those who are afraid of absolute
power should, therefore, share the desire for a gradual development of provincial liberties.

Moreover, I am convinced that no nations are more liable to
fall beneath the yoke of administrative centralization than those
with a democratic social order.

Several causes contribute to this outcome, among which are
the following:

The entrenched tendency of these nations is to concentrate all
government power in the hands of the one sole authority directly
representing the people because, outside the people, there is
nothing to be seen but a confused mass of equal individuals.

Now, when such an authority is endowed with all the attributes of government, it is very difficult for it not to try to
interfere in all the details of administration and, in the long run,
it hardly ever fails to find opportunities for doing so. We have
witnessed this happening in France.

In the French Revolution,ᵉ two opposing tendencies existed
which must not be confused: one favored freedom, the other
despotism.

In the former monarchy, the king alone made the law. Beneath
the power of the king were a few half-destroyed vestiges of
provincial institutions which lacked cohesion, order, or sanity.
In the hands of the aristocracy, they had sometimes been tools
of oppression.

The Revolution announced itself as opposed both to royalty
and to provincial institutions. It directed its hatred indiscriminately against all that had gone before, both absolute power

and those elements which could mitigate such power. It was simultaneously republican and centralizing.

This dual character of the French Revolution is a fact which the supporters of absolute power took great pains to exploit. When they are seen defending administrative centralization, do you suppose they were working in favor of despotism? In no way at all; they were defending one of the great victories of the Revolution. (See Appendix K, p. 843.) In this way, one can remain populist and opposed to the rights of the people, a closet servant of tyranny and an avowed lover of freedom.

I have visited the two nations which have developed provincial liberties to the highest degree and I have heeded the views of the parties dividing the nations.

In America, I met men whose secret aim was to destroy the democratic institutions in their country. In England, I met others who loudly attacked the aristocracy. I did not encounter a single person who did not consider provincial liberty a great blessing.

In both these countries, I have observed the ills of the state imputed to an infinite number of different reasons but never to freedom at a local level.

I have heard citizens attribute the greatness or the prosperity of their country to a multitude of reasons but they have all placed the advantages of provincial freedom first and foremost of all.

Am I to believe that men who are by nature so at odds that they agree neither about religious doctrine nor about political theory, will come to an agreement about one single fact which they are best able to assess since they see its daily operation and yet this one fact is wrong?

Only nations who have few or no provincial institutions deny their usefulness; that is to say, only those with no knowledge of them will slander them.

CHAPTER 6

JUDICIAL POWER IN THE UNITED STATES AND ITS EFFECTS UPON POLITICAL SOCIETY

Anglo-Americans have preserved all the properties of judicial power shared by other nations—However, they have made it a powerful political force—How—In what way the Anglo-American judicial system differs from all the others—Why American judges have the right to declare laws unconstitutional—How they use that right—Precautions taken by the legislature to prevent abuse of that right.

I have believed it necessary to devote a separate chapter to the power of the judges. Their political power is so extensive that to make only a passing reference to it would appear to lessen its importance in readers' eyes.

Confederations have existed in other countries besides America; republics are found elsewhere than on the shores of the New World. The representative system of government has been adopted in several European states but I do not think, up until now, any nation in the world has constructed judicial power in the same way as the Americans.

What a foreigner has the greatest difficulty in understanding in the United States is the way the judiciary is organized. He hears the authority of the judge invoked in every political event, from which he naturally concludes that the judge is one of the foremost political powers in the United States. When he then begins to scrutinize the constitution of the courts, he discovers, at first glance, only judicial attributes and procedures. In his view, the magistrate appears to intervene in public affairs only by chance, but by a chance which occurs every day.

When the parliament of Paris objected and refused to register an edict, or when it summoned a dishonest official to its bar, one could see an obvious instance of the political action of the judiciary. But nothing akin to that occurs in the United States. Americans have preserved all the usually accepted characteristics of judicial authority. They have limited its sphere of action precisely to within its usual cycle of functions.

In all nations, the first characteristic of judicial power is to act as arbitrator. For there to be court intervention, rights must be contested. For there to be a judge, an action must be brought to court. As long as a law does not challenge a right, judges have no occasion to consider the matter. The law exists but is not noticed. When a judge, in connection with a lawsuit, attacks a law relative to this case, he enlarges the sphere of his powers but does not exceed them, since he has had to judge the law in some way in order to settle the case. Whenever he pronounces upon a law without reference to a particular case, he steps right outside his sphere and invades that of the legislature.

The second characteristic of judicial power is to pronounce upon individual cases not upon general principles. If a judge, in deciding a particular question, destroys a general principle because he is quite certain that every consequence of that principle will be similarly undermined and thus will become barren, he remains within the accepted sphere of this authority. But were the judge to attack the general principle head on and to destroy it without having any particular case in view, he steps outside the sphere inside which all nations have agreed to restrict his authority. He becomes something more important and useful perhaps than a magistrate but he ceases to represent the judiciary.

The third characteristic of judicial power is that it can act only when summoned or, according to legal jargon, when it is seised of the matter. This characteristic is not as commonly found as the other two. However, despite the exceptions, I think one may consider it as essential. By its nature, judicial power is not active; it has to be triggered into action. Once a crime is denounced before it, the guilty party can be punished; called upon to redress an injustice, it does so; when an act needs interpretation, it interprets it; but it does not, on its own, prosecute criminals, seek out injustices, or investigate facts. Judicial authority would, in a sense, do violence to this natural passivity if it took the initiative and established itself as a judge of the laws.

Americans have preserved these three distinctive character-istics of judicial power. The American judge pronounces a decision only when he litigates. His concern is only a particular case and to act he must wait to be seised of the matter.

The American judge is, therefore, exactly like the magistrate of other nations. However, he is invested with immense political power.

How does this come about? He moves within the same sphere and uses the same procedures as other judges. Why does he enjoy a power the latter do not possess?

The reason lies in this one fact: Americans have granted their judges the right to base their decisions upon the consti-tution rather than upon the laws. In other words, they have allowed them not to apply laws which would appear to be unconstitutional.

I realize that a similar right has sometimes been claimed by the courts of other countries but it has never been granted them. In America, it is recognized by all the authorities and you will not meet a party nor even a single man to contest it.

The explanation for this must reside in the very basis of American constitutions.

In France, the constitution is, or is supposed to be, immutable. No authority could change it in any particular; such is the accepted theory. (See Appendix L, p. 844.)

In England, the right of altering the constitution rests with Parliament. There, the constitution can, therefore, sustain end-less changes or in reality it does not exist at all. Parliament, at the same time as being a legislative body, may also alter the constitution. (See Appendix M, p. 845.)

In America, political theories are simpler and more rational.

An American constitution is not supposed immutable, as in France, nor could it be altered by ordinary powers of society, as in England. It forms a separate entity which, since it represents the will of the people, places the same duties upon legislators as it does upon plain citizens but these can be changed by the will of the people according to established structures and already anticipated instances.

In America the constitution can thus vary, but during its existence it is the fount of all authority. The dominant power rests with it alone.

It is easy to see how these differences must affect the standing and rights of the judiciary in the three countries mentioned.

If, in France, courts of law were able to disobey laws on the basis that they considered them unconstitutional, the constituent power would be, in effect, in their hands since they alone would have the right to interpret a constitution whose provisions no one could change. Therefore, they would themselves take the place of the nation and would dominate society so far as the inherent weakness of the judiciary would allow them to do so.

I realize that this refusal to allow judges the right to declare laws unconstitutional gives indirect power to the legislature to alter the constitution, since it no longer encounters any legal obstacle in its way. Yet, it is still better to grant the power to alter the constitution of the nation to men who, however imperfectly, represent the will of the people than to others who represent only themselves.

It would be even more unreasonable to grant English judges the right to resist the will of the legislature since Parliament, which makes the laws, also shapes the constitution and consequently cannot, under any circumstance, call a law unconstitutional when it stems from the three authorities: King, Lords, and Commons.

Neither of these two arguments applies to America.

In the United States, the constitution rules both legislators and ordinary citizens. It is, therefore, the primary law and cannot be modified by a law. Hence, it is right that the courts obey the constitution rather than all the laws. This touches the very essence of judicial authority; it is, in a way, the natural duty of any judge to choose from legal provisions those which bind him most strictly.

In France, equally, the constitution is primary among the laws and judges have an equal duty to take it as a basis for their decisions. But, by exercising this duty, they could not fail to trample on a duty even more sacred than their own: namely that of society in whose name they are acting. In this case, ordinary reason has to yield to reasons of state.

In America, where the nation can always reduce the judges to obedience by changing the constitution, such a danger is not to be feared. On this point, politics and logic are thus in accord and the nation as well as the judges preserve their privileges.

When in the United States' courts a law is invoked which the judge considers contrary to the constitution, he can, therefore, refuse to apply it. This is the only power which is peculiar to the American judge but considerable political influence derives from it.

In practice, very few laws can long escape the searching analysis of the judges for there are very few which do not injure some private interest and which advocates cannot or should not bring before the courts.

Now, from the day when the judge refuses to apply a law in a case, it immediately loses a part of its moral force. Those harmed by it are thereupon alerted to a way of eluding the obligation to obey it: lawsuits multiply and that law becomes ineffective. Then, one of two things happens: either the people change the constitution or the legislature repeals the law.

Americans have, therefore, entrusted huge political power to their courts but, by obliging them to attack the law only by judicial means, they have greatly lessened the dangers of this power.

If a judge had had the power to attack the laws from a theoretical or general standpoint, to take the initiative or to censure the legislator, he would have erupted upon the political stage where, having become the champion or opponent of a party, he would have provoked all the emotions dividing the country to take sides in the contest. But when a judge attacks a law in an obscure argument in a particular case, the importance of the attack is partly concealed from the public gaze. His decision aims to affect only one private individual and only accidentally does the law find itself harmed.

Besides, the law censured in this way is not destroyed: its moral force is lessened but its physical effect is not suspended. In the end it surrenders only gradually and under repeated judicial onslaughts.

In addition, it is easily understood that, by placing the censure of a law squarely in the hands of an individual interest and by closely linking the proceedings against the law to those against a man, the legislation will certainly not be attacked lightly. In this system, the law is no longer exposed to the daily attacks of parties. By pointing out the mistakes of the legislator, a real need is met. To serve as a basis for a case, a fact must be clearcut and substantial.

I wonder whether the behavior of American courts, while being the most conducive to public order, is not also the best way of favoring liberty.

If a judge could attack the legislators only head on, there would be times when he would be frightened to do so and others when factional enthusiasms would drive him daily to dare to do so. Thus it would come about that laws would be attacked when the authority supporting them was weak and unquestioning obedience would ensue when it was strong; that is to say, attacks upon the laws would often take place when it would be more useful to respect them and they would be respected when it would be simple to be repressive in their name.

But, an American judge is dragged, despite himself, on to the political field. He judges the law only because he has to take on a case and he has no choice but to take on a case. The political question he has to resolve is linked to the interests of the litigants and he could not possibly refuse to deal with it without denying them justice. By fulfilling the strict duties imposed upon the position of judge, he acts as a citizen. It is true that under this system, judicial censure of the laws exercised by the courts cannot extend without exception to all the laws, for some exist which could never give rise to that clearly formulated kind of argument we call a lawsuit. And when such an argument is possible, there may conceivably be no one who would wish to involve the courts.

Americans have often felt this disadvantage but have left the remedy incomplete, thus avoiding the risk of making it, in every case, effective to a dangerous degree.

Within its restricted limits, the power granted to American courts to pronounce on the constitutionality of laws remains still one of the most powerful barriers ever erected against the tyranny of political assemblies.

OTHER POWERS GRANTED TO AMERICAN JUDGES

In the United States, all citizens have the right to prosecute public officials before the ordinary courts—How they avail themselves of this right—Article 75 of the French constitution in year VIII—The Americans and English cannot understand the meaning of this article.

The matter is so natural that I do not know whether it is necessary to say that, with a free nation like America, all citizens have the right to prosecute public officials before ordinary judges and that all judges have the right to condemn public officials.

Allowing them to punish the agents of the executive when they violate the law is not a special privilege granted to the courts. To forbid them to do so would be to deprive them of a natural right.

It has never seemed to me that the competence of the government was weakened by making all officials answerable to the courts.

On the contrary, it has seemed to me that, by acting in this fashion, Americans have increased the respect owed to government officers who take much more care to avoid criticism.

Nor have I noticed in the United States the instigation of many political trials and I can easily explain this. A lawsuit, whatever its nature, is always a difficult and costly matter. It is easy to accuse a public figure in the newspapers but only serious reasons persuade anyone to prosecute him in court. To take legal proceedings against a public official one must, therefore, have a just cause of complaint and public officials scarcely ever provide such a cause, if they fear prosecution.

This does not depend on the republican form of government adopted by the Americans, for the same phenomenon takes place every day in England.

These two nations have never thought they strengthened their independence by allowing the main agents of the executive to be brought to trial. They have felt that their liberty was more successfully ensured by small everyday lawsuits being available to the least of their citizens than through pretentious procedures which are never used until it is too late.

In the Middle Ages when it was difficult to catch criminals, whenever judges did seize a few, they often inflicted awful punishments on these wretched people, which did not reduce the number of the guilty. It has since been discovered that by making justice both more certain and milder, it becomes at the same time more effective.

The Americans and English think that oppression and tyranny should be treated like theft: make prosecution easier and punishment lighter.

In year VIII of the French Republic, article 75 of the constitution appeared drawn up in the following terms: "Government agents below the rank of minister cannot be prosecuted for matters in relation to their duties except by virtue of a decision of the council of state, in which case, the prosecution takes place before the ordinary courts."

The constitution of year VIII passed away but not this article, which survived and is still used every day as an obstruction to citizens' just complaints.

I have often attempted to convey the sense of this article 75 to the Americans and the English; it has always proved very difficult to do so.

The first thing they noticed was that the council of state[a] in France was a powerful court set at the center of the kingdom. It was a kind of tyranny to send all plaintiffs before this court as a preliminary step.

But, whenever I sought to convey to them that the council of state in France was not a judicial body in the ordinary sense of the term but an administrative body whose members depended on the king, so that the king, after regally commanding one of his servants, called the prefect, to commit a wrongdoing, could regally command another of his servants, called the council of state, to prevent the former from being punished; and whenever I explained how the citizen, injured by the prince's order, was reduced to asking that very prince permission to seek for justice, they refused to believe such monstrosities and accused me of lies and ignorance.

It often happened, under the old monarchy, that parliament decreed the arrest of a public official who was committing an offense. Sometimes the royal authority intervened to annul the proceedings. Tyranny at that moment revealed itself openly and, by obeying, men bowed to a superior force.

We have thus stepped back from the position our ancestors occupied; for we allow under the flag of justice, and consecrate in the name of the law, what was imposed on them by violence alone.

CHAPTER 7

POLITICAL JURISDICTION IN THE UNITED STATES

What the author means by political jurisdiction—How political jurisdiction is understood in France, in England, in the United States—In America, the political judge is concerned with public officials alone—He pronounces on dismissals rather than penalties—Political jurisdiction a usual means of government—Political jurisdiction as understood in the United States is, despite its leniency, or perhaps because of it, a very potent weapon in the hands of the majority.

By political jurisdiction I mean the decisions pronounced by a political body temporarily endowed with the right to judge.

In absolute governments, it is useless to introduce extraordinary procedures into judicial matters; the prince, in whose name the accused is prosecuted, is master of the courts, as everything else, and has no need to seek any guarantee outside the power everyone knows he possesses. The only conceivable fear he might have is that even the external appearance of justice will not be observed and that his authority will be dishonored by those whose desire is to affirm it.

But, in most free countries, where the majority can never influence the courts as an absolute prince would do, it has sometimes happened that judicial power has been placed temporarily in the hand of the representatives of the people. It has been thought better to merge these powers for a moment than to damage the vital principle of government unity. England, France, and the United States have introduced political jurisdiction into their laws: it is curious to examine the way in which these three great nations have exploited it.

In England and in France, the House of Peers constitutes the highest criminal court of the land.[1] It does not pass judgment on all political offenses but it can do so.

Alongside the House of Peers stands another political body endowed with the right of prosecution. The only difference between the two countries in this respect is the following: in England, the Commons can impeach anyone they like before the Lords, whereas, in France, they can use this method to prosecute only ministers of the crown.

In both countries, however, the House of Peers has available all the provisions of the penal law to punish offenders.

In the United States, as in Europe, one of the two branches of the legislature is endowed with the right to prosecute, while the other has the right to pronounce judgment. The House of Representatives denounces the offender, the Senate punishes him.

But the Senate cannot be seised of the matter unless prompted by the House of Representatives, which can only prosecute public officials. Thus, the Senate has more restricted powers

---

1. The House of Lords in England constitutes the final court of appeal in certain civil cases. See Blackstone, bk 3, ch. 4.

than the court of peers in France while the Representatives have a greater power of impeachment than French deputies.

But the greatest difference between America and Europe lies in this: in Europe, political courts can apply all the provisions of the penal code; in America, when they have deprived an offender of his public status and have declared him unworthy of holding any public office in the future, their powers are at an end and the work of the ordinary courts begins.

Suppose the President of the United States has committed high treason.

The House of Representatives impeaches him, the Senate pronounces his dismissal. Then he appears before a jury which alone can remove his freedom or his life. This accurately illustrates the matter with which we are dealing.

In introducing political jurisdiction into their laws, the Europeans' intention has been to reach great criminals whatever their birth, rank, or authority in the state. To succeed, they have combined, at any given time, all the rights of the courts into a great political assembly.

The legislator then becomes a magistrate; he has the power to establish, classify, and punish the crime. By granting him the powers of a judge, the law has also imposed upon him all the duties of justice and has bound him to observe all its formalities.

When a political court, French or English, tries a public official and condemns him, as a result of that alone it deprives him of his office and may declare him unworthy of holding any other in the future. But in this case, the dismissal and bar on political office are a consequence of the sentence, not the sentence itself.

In Europe, political judgment is, therefore, more of a judicial act than an administrative measure.

The opposite is the case in the United States, where it is easy to be convinced that the political judgment is very much more an administrative measure than a judicial act.

It is true that the Senate's decision is judicial in form because, in delivering it, senators are duty bound to conform to the solemn formalities of procedure. Yet again, it is judicial in the motives upon which it is based because the Senate is generally duty bound to pivot its decisions upon a common law offense. Nevertheless, its objective is administrative.

If the main aim of the American legislator had essentially been to arm a political body with great judicial power, he would not have restricted its sphere of action to public officials for the most dangerous enemies of the state may not hold any office at all. This is especially true in republics where party influence is the foremost of powers and where a leader can possess all the more authority when he has no legal power.

If the American legislator had wished to grant society itself the power to ward off greater crimes, like a judge, by means of the fear of punishment, he would have put all the resources of the penal code at the disposal of the political courts. However, he provided them with only an incomplete weapon and the most dangerous of criminals could not possibly be reached. For the bar on political office hardly matters to the man who wishes to overturn the laws themselves.

The main aim of political jurisdiction in the United States is then to withdraw power from the man who wishes to misuse it and to prevent this same citizen from acquiring it in the future. As can be seen, it is an administrative act which has been granted the solemn gloss of a judgment.

In this matter, Americans have thus created something ambiguous. Dismissal from administrative office has been granted all the guarantees of political jurisdiction, while removing from this jurisdiction its severest sanctions.

Everything follows from this fixed point; then we discover why the American constitutions subject all civil officials to the jurisdiction of the Senate and exempt soldiers, even though their crimes are more to be dreaded. In the civil administration, Americans have, so to speak, no officials who can be dismissed; some are irremovable, while others hold their authority by a mandate which cannot be revoked. To rid them of their power, they all have to be brought to trial. But the military depends upon the head of state, who himself is a civil official. By condemning the head of state, the same blow strikes them all.[2]

2.   An officer may not be deprived of his rank but can lose his command.

Now, if we can go on to compare the European with the American systems with regard to the effects each one does or can produce, we discover differences no less marked.

In France and England, political jurisdiction is regarded as an extraordinary weapon which society should use only for self-preservation in times of danger.

One has to say that political jurisdiction, as understood in Europe, violates the conservative principle of the balance of powers and constantly threatens the life and liberty of men.

Political jurisdiction in the United States only indirectly threatens the principle of the balance of power; it does not threaten citizens' existence; it does not hover, as in Europe, over everyone's heads since it strikes only those who accept public office and consequently subject themselves, in advance, to its sanctions. It is both less to be feared and less effective.

So, legislators in the United States have not regarded it as an extreme remedy for the great ills of society but an ordinary means of government.

From this viewpoint, it possibly exercises more real influence on society in America than in Europe. One should not, in fact, be duped by the apparent leniency of American legislation where political jurisdiction is concerned. In the first place, it is to be observed that, in the United States, the court which passes these judgments is made up of the same elements and subjected to the same influences as the body responsible for the impeachment. That gives an almost irresistible drive to the vindictiveness of both parties.

While political judges in the United States are unable to impose as severe penalties as those in Europe can, there are, nevertheless, fewer chances of being acquitted by them. Condemnation is less to be feared and more certain.

In establishing political courts, Europeans had, as their main aim, the *punishment* of the guilty; the Americans, the *removal of their authority*. In the United States, political jurisdiction is, in a sense, a preventative measure. The judge should not be tied down to precise definitions of criminal law.

Nothing could be more alarming than the vagueness of American laws when they are defining political crimes properly so called. Article 1, section IV of the Constitution of the United States avers: "The crimes which will involve the impeachment of the president are treason, bribery or other serious crimes and offenses." Most of the state constitutions are even more obscure.

"The senate shall [. . .] hear and determine all impeachments made [. . .] against any officer or officers of the commonwealth," says the constitution of Massachusetts, "for misconduct and maladministration in their offices."[3]

"All [. . .] offending against the State, either by maladministration, corruption, neglect of duty, or any other high crime or misdemeanor," says the constitution of Virginia, "shall be impeachable by the house of delegates." There are constitutions which do not specify any crime in order to subject public officials to a limitless sense of responsibility.[4]

But the feature which, in this whole matter, makes American laws so formidable is, I dare assert, their very leniency.

We have seen that, in Europe, the removal of an official and the barring him from office, is one of the consequences of the punishment but that, in America, it is the punishment itself. Consequently, it follows that, in Europe, political courts are endowed with terrible powers which they sometimes do not know how to use so that they fail to punish, for fear of punishing too severely. But, in America, there is not that reluctance to step back from a penalty which does not make people groan. To condemn a political opponent to death, in order to rid him of his authority, seems an horrific assassination in everyone's eyes. Declaring one's adversary unworthy to possess that power and to deprive him of it, while leaving him life and liberty, can seem the honorable result of the struggle.

Now that judgment, so easy to pronounce, is nonetheless the height of misfortune for the general run of those to whom it applies. Great criminals will doubtless risk its empty severity; ordinary citizens will view it as a decree which destroys their status, stains their honor and condemns them to a shameful idleness, worse than death.

3.   Ch. 1, section 2, para. 8.
4.   See the constitution of Illinois, Maine, Connecticut, and Georgia.

Hence, political jurisdiction in the United States exercises upon the progress of society an influence all the more extensive as it seems less formidable. It has no direct effect on the governed but it does make the majority wholly masters of those who govern. It does not grant the legislature some immense power to use only at a time of crisis; rather, it allows it to claim a moderate and steady power to use every day. While the force of it is smaller, it is more convenient to use and easier to abuse.

By preventing political courts from pronouncing judicial penalties, Americans seem to me to have thus provided against the most terrible consequences of legal tyranny, rather than tyranny itself. Everything considered, I wonder whether political jurisdiction as understood in the United States, is not the most fearsome weapon ever lodged in the hands of the majority. Once the American republics begin to degenerate, I believe we shall easily recognize that to be so; it will be enough to notice whether the number of political judgments increases. (See Appendix N, p. 846.)

CHAPTER 8

THE FEDERAL CONSTITUTION

Up to this point, I have examined each state as if it were a complete whole and have demonstrated the various forces the nation sets in motion along with the methods it employs. But all these states I have considered as independent are nevertheless obliged, in certain cases, to obey a superior authority, that of the Union. Now is the time to scrutinize that part of sovereign power which has been granted to the Union and to take a swift look over the federal constitution.[1]

---

1.   See the text of the federal constitution.

HISTORICAL REVIEW OF THE FEDERAL CONSTITUTION

Origin of the first Union—Its weakness—Congress appeals to the constituent power—Space of two years between this time and the promulgation of the new constitution.

The thirteen colonies[a] which simultaneously sloughed off the yoke of England at the close of the last century had, as I have already stated, the same religion, language, customs, and near enough the same laws; they battled against a common enemy; they must, therefore, have had strong reasons for uniting closely with each other and for merging into one and the same nation.

But each of them, having enjoyed a separate existence and a government to suit its size, had formed its own peculiar concerns and ways of operating. Each of them revolted against a solid and complete union which would have submerged its individual importance beneath a federal importance. As a result, two tendencies followed: one which induced the Anglo-Americans to unite, the other to separate.

As long as the war with the mother country lasted, necessity prolonged the principle of union. And, although the laws constituting this union[b] were defective, the link continued in spite of them.[2]

But from the moment peace was declared, the defects of the legislation stood revealed: the state seemed to dissolve all at once. Each colony became an independent republic and assumed its own absolute sovereignty. The federal government, condemned to weakness by its very constitution, and no longer sustained by the feeling of public danger, witnessed the outrages done to its flag by the great nations of Europe while it was unable to drum up sufficient resources to confront the Indian tribes or to pay the interest on debts incurred during the War of

2.   See the articles of the first confederation formed in 1778. This federal constitution was not adopted by all the states until 1781. See also the analysis of this constitution in numbers 15–22 inclusive of *The Federalist* and that of Mr Story in his *Commentaries on the Constitution of the United States*, pp. 85–115.

Independence. On the verge of disintegration, it chose officially to declare its weakness and to appeal to the constituent authority.[3]

If ever America showed itself capable of rising for a few moments to that lofty degree of renown which the proud imagination of its inhabitants would constantly wish to reveal to us, it was at that supreme time when the national authority had just in some way abdicated its dominion.

The spectacle of a nation battling vigorously to achieve its independence is one which every century has displayed to our eyes. Moreover, the descriptions of Americans' efforts to slip from under the English yoke have been greatly exaggerated. Separated by 2,800 miles of sea from their enemies, aided by a powerful ally, the United States owed victory more to their geographical position than to the courage of their armies or to the patriotism of their citizens. Whoever would dare to compare the American war to the wars of the French Revolution or the efforts of the Americans to ours when France, exposed to attacks from the whole of Europe, penniless, without credit or allies, hurled a twentieth of her population before her advancing enemies, snuffing out with one hand the fire which gnawed at her innards while with the other brandishing the torch around her? But what is new in the history of societies is the sight of a great nation, warned by its legislators that the workings of government are grinding to a halt, turning its attention, without haste or fear, upon itself, sounding out the depths of the ill, standing still for two whole years in order to uncover the remedy at leisure and, on discovery of the remedy, submitting to it voluntarily without its costing humanity a single tear or a drop of blood.

When the inadequacy of the first federal constitution was perceived, the outburst of political passion prompted by the Revolution was somewhat calmed down and all the great men it had created were still alive. That proved a twin blessing for America. The assembly which was responsible for the drafting

3.   Congress made this declaration on 21 February 1787.

of the second constitution, though small in number,[4] contained the finest minds and the noblest characters that had ever emerged in the New World. George Washington[c] presided over it.

This national commission, after long and mature deliberation, offered for the people's acceptance the body of organic laws which currently governs the Union. All the states adopted it in turn.[5] The new federal government took up office in 1789 after an interregnum of two years. The American Revolution ended, therefore, exactly when ours was beginning.

BRIEF DESCRIPTION OF THE FEDERAL CONSTITUTION

Division of powers between the federal government and the states—State government remains the general rule, the federal government is the exception.

A primary difficulty the Americans had to confront was how to share out sovereignty so that the various states forming the Union continued to govern themselves in everything to do with their internal prosperity without the whole nation, represented by the Union, losing its corporate entity or ceasing to supply the general needs of all. This was a complex question which was hard to resolve.

It was impossible to fix in advance, precisely and completely, the share of authority which was to go to each of the governments dividing the sovereignty.

Who could foresee every detail of a nation's life?

The duties and rights of the federal government were simple and relatively easy to define because the Union had been created with a view to responding to certain great general needs. The duties and rights of the state governments, on the other hand,

---

4.   It had only fifty-five members, including Washington, Madison, Hamilton, and the Morrises.
5.   It was not the legislators who adopted it. The people appointed deputies for this sole purpose. There were searching debates about the new constitution in each of these assemblies.

were many and complicated because these governments were involved in every detail of social life.

Therefore, a careful definition of the attributes of the federal government was drawn up along with a declaration that whatever was not included within it returned to the jurisdiction of the state governments. Thus, the state government remained the general rule and the federal government the exception.[6]

But since it was anticipated that in practical terms questions could arise relating to the precise limits of this exceptional authority and that it would have been risky to leave the resolution of such questions to ordinary courts instituted in the various states by the states themselves, a Federal Supreme Court[7] was created to be a unique tribunal, one of whose prerogatives was to maintain the division of power between the two governments exactly as the constitution had established it.[8]

6.   See amendments to the federal constitution; *The Federalist*, no. 32; Story, p. 711; Kent's *Commentaries on American Law*, vol. 1, p. 364. Note, too, that every time the constitution has not reserved for Congress the *exclusive* right to regulate certain matters, the states may do so before Congress sees fit to begin. Example: Congress has the right to make a general law about bankruptcy but does not do so; each state drafts one of its own. Moreover, that point was established only after argument before the courts. It is simply a legal decision.

7.   The action of this court is indirect, as we shall see later.

8.   This is how no. 45 of *The Federalist* explains the division of sovereignty between the Union and each individual state: "The powers delegated by the proposed constitution to the federal government," it says, "are few and defined. Those which are to remain in the state governments are numerous and indefinite. The former will be exercised principally on external objects, as war, peace, negotiation, and foreign commerce; [. . .] The powers reserved to the several States will extend to all the objects which, in the ordinary course of affairs, concern the lives, liberties [. . .] and prosperity of the State." I shall often have occasion to quote *The Federalist* in this work. When the draft law, which has since become the constitution of the United States, was still before the people and submitted for their adoption, three men, already famous and later to become even more so— John Jay, Hamilton, and Madison—associated together with the object of pointing out to the nation the advantages of the plan submitted to it. With this intention they published in the form of a journal a series of articles which together represent a complete treatise. They gave their journal the name of *The Federalist*, and that name is used for the book.

      The Federalist is a fine book which, although it particularly concerns America, should be familiar to statesmen of all countries.

POWERS OF THE FEDERAL GOVERNMENT

*Power granted to federal government to make war
and peace and to levy general taxes—Internal political
strategies within its sphere of action—The government
of the Union more centralized in certain respects
than the royal government under the old
French monarchy.*

Nations in relation to each other are but single units. A nation needs a single government above all to give it the advantage when dealing with foreigners.

Therefore, the right to declare peace and war was granted exclusively to the Union along with the concluding of commercial treaties, levying of armies, and equipping of fleets.[9]

The necessity of having a national government does not become such an imperative when it comes to the management of the internal affairs of society.

However, certain general concerns can only be dealt with under a general authority.

The right to regulate everything relating to the value of money was left to the Union; it was responsible for the postal service, it was given the right to open the main lines of communication which were to unite the various areas of the country.[10]

In general, the authority in the different states was considered free within its own sphere; however, it could abuse this independence and take unwise measures which could damage the security of the Union as a whole. In such rare cases, well-defined in advance, the federal government was allowed to intervene in the internal affairs of the states.[11] In this way, while appreciating that all federated republics might modify or alter their

9.   See section 8 of the constitution; nos 41 and 42 of *The Federalist*; Kent's *Commentaries*, vol. 1, p. 207ff; and Story, pp. 358–82, 409–26.
10. There are several other rights of this kind such as bankruptcy legislation and the granting of patents. It is easy to see what made it necessary for the Union as a whole to intervene in these matters.
11. Even in this case, its intervention is indirect. The Union intervenes through the courts, as we shall see later.

legislation, they were prohibited from making their laws retroactive or from creating a body of nobles inside the state.[12]

Finally, as the federal government had to be capable of fulfilling the obligations imposed upon it, it was given the unlimited right to levy taxes.[13]

When we look closely at the division of powers settled by the federal constitution, noting on the one hand the share of sovereignty reserved for the individual states and on the other the portion of power assumed by the Union, it is easy to see that the federal legislators had grasped very clearly and appropriately those notions of governmental centralization which I have previously outlined.

Not only do the United States form a republic but also a confederation. However, national authority is in certain respects more centralized there than it was in several of the European absolute monarchies in the same period. I will quote but two examples.

France could count thirteen sovereign courts which, more often than not, had the right to interpret the law without appeal. In addition, it possessed certain provinces, styled *pays d'Etat*, which, when the sovereign authority responsible for representing the nation had commanded the levy of a tax, could refuse their agreement.

The Union has only one tribunal to interpret the law as it has but one legislature to make it; the tax voted by the representatives of the nation is obligatory for all citizens. The Union is, therefore, more centralized in these two essential respects than was the monarchy in France. However, the Union is only a gathering together of confederated republics.

In Spain, certain provinces had the power to establish a customs system of their own which, by its very essence, is part of the national sovereignty.

In America, Congress alone has the right to regulate the commercial relations of the states among themselves. The

12. Federal constitution, article 1, section 10.
13. Constitution, sections 8, 9 and 10; *The Federalist*, nos 30–36 inclusive; *ibid.*, nos 41, 42, 43, 44; Kent's *Commentaries*, vol. 1, pp. 207, 381; Story, pp. 329, 514.

government of the federation is thus more centralized in this respect than the kingdom of Spain.

It is true that in France and Spain the power of the king always found itself in a position to carry out, by force if necessary, what the constitution of the kingdom refused him the right to do; so eventually the same point was reached. But here I am discussing the theory.

FEDERAL POWERS

After enclosing the federal government in a sharply drawn sphere of action, the main concern was how to set it into motion.

LEGISLATIVE POWERS

*Division of the legislative body into two branches—
Differences in the way the two houses are formed—The
principle of independence of the states wins in the
formation of the Senate—The dogma of the sovereignty of
the nation in the composition of the House of
Representatives—Unusual effects resulting from the fact
that constitutions are logical only in the early life of
a nation.*

The organization of the Union's powers in many respects followed the plans previously drawn up by the individual constitutions of each state.

The federal legislative body of the Union was composed of a Senate and a House of Representatives.

A spirit of conciliation brought in various rules in the formation of each of these assemblies.

I have voiced the opinion already that in the establishment of the federal constitution two opposed interests came face to face. These two interests had given rise to two opinions.

Some wished to make the Union a league of independent states, a sort of congress where the representatives of distinct peoples would assemble to discuss certain points of common interest.

Others wished to unite all the inhabitants of the former colonies into a single nation giving it a government which, though its sphere of action should be limited, might act within this sphere as the one sole representative of the nation. The practical consequences of these two theories were very different.

As a result, if a league was to be organized and not a national government, it was up to the majority of the states to make the law, not the majority of the inhabitants of the Union. For then every state, great or small, would preserve its character as an independent power and would enter the Union on a perfectly equal footing.

On the other hand, the moment the inhabitants of the United States were considered a single nation, it would be natural for a simple majority of all the citizens of the Union to make the law.

One appreciates that the small states could not consent to the application of this doctrine without a complete abdication of their existence in everything connected with federal sovereignty; for they would pass from being a coequal authority to an insignificant fraction of a great nation. The first system would have granted them an excessive power; the second would cancel it completely.

In this state of affairs there occurred what usually occurs when interests are in opposition to arguments: the rules of logic were massaged. The legislators adopted a middle course which reconciled forcibly two systems theoretically irreconcilable.

The principle of the independence of the states prevailed in the formation of the Senate; the dogma of the sovereignty of the nation in the composition of the House of Representatives.

Each state was to send two senators to Congress and a number of representatives in proportion of its population.[14]

14. Every ten years, Congress settles once again the number of deputies each state should send to the House of Representatives. In 1789, the total was 69; in 1833, it was 240. (*American Almanac*, 1834, p. 194.)

   The constitution provided that there should not be more than one representative for every 30,000 people but no minimum was fixed. Congress has not thought it necessary to increase the number of representatives in proportion to increased population. By the first law passed on this subject, that of 14 April 1792 (see Story's *Laws of the United States*, vol. 1, p. 235), it was decided that there should be one representative for

At the present time, following these arrangements, the state of New York has forty representatives in Congress and only two senators; the state of Delaware has two senators and only one representative. The state of Delaware is, therefore, in the Senate the equal of the state of New York, while the latter enjoys, in the House of Representatives, forty times more influence than the former. Thus it can happen that the minority of a nation dominating the Senate could entirely paralyze the will of the majority represented by the other house, which would be contrary to the spirit of constitutional governments.

All this demonstrates how rare and difficult it is to unite in a logical and rational manner all the several parts of legislation.

Time, in the long term and within the same nation, always gives rise to different interests and sanctions various rights. Thereafter, when a general constitution has to be established, each of these interests and rights constitutes a goodly number of natural obstacles to prevent any particular political principle from being implemented with all its consequences. It is, therefore, only in the first stages of societies that logic can completely govern law-making. When you see a nation profiting from this advantage, do not hasten to conclude that it is wise; think rather that it is young.

At the time when the federal constitution was shaped, the only two directly opposed interests still to exist for the Anglo-Americans were the interest of individuality for separate states and the interest of union for the whole nation. A compromise had to be found.

It has to be appreciated, however, that this aspect of the constitution has not so far produced the evil consequences which might have been feared.

All the states are young; they are close to one another; their customs, ideas, and needs are the same; differences stemming from their greater or smaller size are not significant enough to

---

every 33,000 inhabitants. The final law, passed in 1832, fixed the number of one representative for 48,000 inhabitants. The population, for this purpose, was calculated as all free men and three-fifths of the number of slaves.

result in strongly opposed interests. As a result, the smaller states have never been seen joining forces in the Senate against the plans of the bigger states. Besides, there is such an irresistible power in the legal expression of the will of the whole nation that the Senate is very weak when faced by the House of Representatives expressing its majority vote.

In addition, it should not be forgotten that it was not the task of the American legislators to reduce to one single nation the people for whom they wished to make laws. The aim of the federal constitution was not to destroy the existence of the states, rather to restrain them. As soon, therefore, as real power was left in the hands of these secondary bodies (and it could not be wrenched from them), one abandoned in advance the use of restraint to bend them to the will of the majority. This granted, the introduction of the power of the individual states into the mechanism of federal government had nothing unusual about it, since it attested to the existence of an acknowledged power which had to be handled without forcible constraint.

ANOTHER DIFFERENCE BETWEEN THE SENATE AND THE HOUSE OF REPRESENTATIVES

The Senate appointed by provincial legislators—The representatives by the people—Two elections for the former—Single election for the latter—Term of different offices—Functions.

The Senate differs from the other house not only in the principle of representation but also by the type of election, the length of the term of office and by the differences in its functions.

The House of Representatives is appointed by the people, the Senate by the legislators of each state. The one results from direct election, the other from a two-stage election. The term of office for representatives lasts only two years; that of senators six.

The House of Representatives has only legislative functions; it participates in judicial power only in the impeachment of public officials. The Senate cooperates in the making of laws; it judges those political offenses which the House of Representatives brings before its scrutiny; in addition, it is the great executive council of the nation. Treaties concluded by the President must be ratified by the Senate; his appointments are not final until they have been approved by the same body.[15]

THE EXECUTIVE POWER[16]

Dependence of the President—Elective and responsible—Free in his own sphere to act under the supervision but not direction of the Senate—Salary of the President fixed at his entry into office—Suspensive veto.

The American legislators had a difficult task to fulfill in wishing to create an executive authority dependent upon the majority yet strong enough to act independently and without restraint within its own sphere.

It was essential to the maintenance of the republican form of government that the representative of executive power should be subject to the will of the nation.

The President is an elective magistrate. His honor, his property, his freedom, his life are a permanent pledge to the people of the good use he will make of his power. In exercising this power, he is, moreover, not completely independent: the Senate supervises him in his foreign policy and also in his appointments to office. As a consequence of this, he can neither corrupt nor be corrupted.

The legislators of the Union acknowledged that the executive power could not worthily or usefully accomplish its task unless they managed to give it more stability and strength than had been granted in the separate states.

The President was appointed for four years and could be re-elected. With time before him, he had the courage to work for the public good and the means to do so.

15. See *The Federalist*, nos 52–6, inclusive; Story, pp. 199–314; constitution, sections 2 and 3.
16. *The Federalist*, nos 67–77, inclusive; constitution, article 2; Story, pp. 315, 515–780; Kent's *Commentaries*, p. 255.

The President became the sole representative of executive power in the Union. Care was taken not to subject his will to that of a council, a dangerous measure which weakens the actions of the government and diminishes its responsibilities. The Senate has the right to annul certain of the President's acts but it cannot in any way force him to act nor can it share the executive power with him.

The action of the legislature over the executive power can be direct and I have just shown that Americans had taken measures to prevent that; but it can also be indirect.

The power of the two houses to deprive any public official of his salary takes away some of that official's independence. Since they have control over all law-making, the fear exists that they can gradually remove that share of power which the constitution had vested in his hands.

This dependency of the executive power remains one of the inherent defects of republican constitutions. Americans have been unable to eliminate the tendency legislative assemblies have to take possession of government but they have reduced its irresistibility.

The President's salary is fixed on his assumption of office for the whole duration of his tenure. In addition, the President has a suspensive veto which enables him to halt the passage of laws which might destroy that share of independence granted to him by the constitution. However, there could only be an unequal contest between the President and the legislature since the latter can always, by persisting with its plans, overcome the resistance facing it. But at least the suspensive veto forces it to retreat and to reconsider the question at hand. At which point, it can settle the matter only by a two-thirds majority. Moreover, the veto is a sort of appeal to the people. The executive power which, without such a guarantee, could have been secretly oppressed, can plead its case and convey its arguments. But if the legislature persists with its plans, surely it can always overcome the resistance it confronts? To which I reply that there is in the constitution of all nations, whatever its complexion, a point at which the legislator is bound to have recourse to the good sense and virtue of the citizens. This point is nearer and more obvious in republics, more remote and more carefully concealed in monarchies; but it is always there somewhere. No country exists where the law can anticipate everything or institutions take the place of reason and custom.

HOW THE POSITION OF PRESIDENT OF THE UNITED STATES DIFFERS FROM THAT OF A CONSTITUTIONAL KING OF FRANCE

Executive power in the United States is limited and exceptional like the sovereign power it represents—In France the executive power extends to everything—The king one of the instigators of law—The President is only the executor of the law—Other differences which stem from the length of term of office—The President is hampered in the exercise of executive power—The king is free—France, notwithstanding its differences, more like a republic than the Union is like a monarchy—Comparison of the number of officials who depend upon the executive power in the two countries.

The executive power plays such a considerable role in the destiny of nations that I wish to pause for a moment at this point so as to explain better the place it holds in the American system.

In order to form a clear and accurate idea of the position held by the President of the United States, it is useful to compare him to the king in one of the constitutional monarchies of Europe.

In making such a comparison, I shall give little importance to the external trappings of power, which deceive rather than guide the observer.

When a monarchy gradually develops into a republic, the executive power retains titles, honors, respect, and even money long after the reality of power has disappeared. The English, having beheaded one of their kings and dismissed another, still dropped to their knees before the successors of those princes.

On the other hand, when republics fall beneath the yoke of one man, his power continues to appear simple, plain, and modest as if he had not yet become superior to everyone. When emperors exercised despotic control over the lives and fortunes of their fellow citizens, they were still addressed as Caesar and they were in the habit of dining without formality with their friends.

Thus a surface assessment has to be abandoned for a deeper examination.

Sovereignty in the United States is shared by the Union and the states, whereas with us it is undivided and compact. That produces the first great difference I perceive between the President of the United States and the king of France.

In the United States, the executive authority is limited and exceptional, like the very sovereignty in whose name it acts; in France, like sovereignty, it extends to everything.

Americans have a federal government; we have a national one.

Therein lies the first cause of inferiority arising from the very nature of things, but not the only cause. The second in importance is that one can, properly speaking, define sovereignty as the right to make laws.

The king of France is a constituent part of sovereign power because without his agreement the laws cannot exist; in addition he executes the laws.

The President is also the executor of the laws but he does not really take a part in the making of them because even by withholding his assent, he cannot prevent their coming into being. He is not, therefore, a constituent part of sovereign power, only its agent.

Not only is the French king one constituent part of the sovereign power but he also takes his part in the nomination of the legislature, which is the other part. He participates by appointing the members of one chamber and by dissolving the other's mandate whenever it pleases him. The President of the United States has no say in the make-up of the legislative body and could not dissolve it.

The king takes his share along with the chambers in the right to introduce laws; the President has no such initiative.

The king is represented in each chamber by a certain number

of agents who explain his views, support his opinions, and maintain his principles of government.

The President is excluded from Congress as are his ministers and he makes his influence and opinions known to that great body by indirect means only.

The king of France advances shoulder to shoulder with the legislature which cannot act without him, as he cannot act without it.

The President exercises an inferior and dependent power in relation to the legislature.

In the exercise of the executive power properly so-called, a function which seems most closely allied to that of the French king, the President still suffers from several very considerable causes of inferiority.

In France, the authority of the king has, in the first place, the advantage of his length of tenure of office. Length of tenure is one of the first ingredients of power. Only long-lasting power engenders affection or fear.

The President of the United States is an official elected for four years. The king of France is an hereditary leader.

In the exercise of executive power the President of the United States is constantly subject to a jealous scrutiny. He prepares treaties but does not conclude them; he puts forward names for appointment to office but cannot confirm them.[17]

The king of France is absolute master in the realm of executive power.

The President of the United States is responsible for his actions. French law declares the person of the king inviolable.

However, above both hovers a commanding power, namely, public opinion, which is less clearly defined, less acknowledged, less encapsulated in law in France than in the United States but

17. The constitution had left it doubtful whether the President was bound to take the advice of the Senate concerning the dismissal as well as the appointment of a federal officer. *The Federalist*, in no. 77, seemed to establish that he was; but in 1789, Congress formally decided that, as the President was responsible, he ought not to be forced to employ agents who did not have his confidence. See Kent's *Commentaries*, vol. 1, p. 289.

which exists nonetheless. In America, it works through elections and decrees; in France, through revolutions. France and the United States have thus, despite the differences in their constitutions, this shared feature: that public opinion ends up being the commanding power. The main generating principle of laws is, therefore, if truth be told, the same in both nations even though it enjoys more or less free development and the resulting consequences may often be different. This principle is essentially republican by nature. Thus it is my opinion that France, with its king, is more like a republic than the Union, with its President, is like a monarchy.

In all the above remarks, I have been careful to highlight only the main points of difference. Had I wished to go into details, the description would have been all the more striking. But having so much to say, I wished to be brief.

I have observed that the power of the President of the United States is exercised within the limits of a restricted sovereignty, whereas that of the king of France is undivided.

I could have demonstrated that the governmental power of the king of France exceeds even its natural limits, however extensive they may be, and infiltrates the administration of individual interests in a thousand ways.

Added to this source of influence is the power which ensues from the great number of public officials who almost all owe their appointment to the executive authority. This number in France has exceeded all known bounds and stands at 138,000,[18] each of which must be considered as an element of power. The President has no absolute right to appoint public officials and these hardly amount to twelve thousand.[19]

---

18.   The sums paid by the state to these various officials total two hundred million francs a year.

19.   An almanac called *The National Calendar* is published annually in America; in it are found the names of all federal officials. It is *The National Calendar* for 1833 which provided the figure I quote here.

It would result from what I have just said that the king of France disposes of eleven times as many appointments as the President of the United States, although the population of France is only one and a half times as great as that of the Union.

ACCIDENTAL CAUSES WHICH CAN INCREASE
THE INFLUENCE OF EXECUTIVE POWER

External security enjoyed by the Union—Waiting policy—
Army of 6,000 soldiers—Only a few ships—
President possesses great prerogatives, but no chance of
using them—In those he has the chance to use,
he is weak.

If the executive power is weaker in America than in France, the reason must be attributed perhaps more to the circumstances than to the laws.

It is mainly in its relations with foreign countries that the executive power of a nation has the chance to display its skill and strength.

If the life of the Union was constantly under threat, if its major interests were daily intertwined with those of other powerful nations, you would see the prestige of the executive increase in public opinion because of what was expected of it and what it did.

The President of the United States is, it is true, head of the army which, however, only has six thousand men; he commands the fleet of only a few vessels; he controls the affairs of the Union in relation to foreign nations but the United States has no neighbors. Separated from the rest of the world by the ocean, still too weak to have any designs on marine supremacy, it has no enemies and its concerns rarely come into contact with those of the other nations of the Earth.

This reveals very clearly that the practice of government must not be judged by theory.

The President of the United States enjoys almost royal prerogatives which he has no chance of exercising and those rights which he can at present use are very circumscribed. The laws enable him to be strong; circumstances keep him weak.

On the other hand, it is circumstances which, much more than laws, endow the royal authority of France with its greatest power.

In France, the executive power battles ceaselessly against

prodigious obstacles and displays immense resources in order to overcome them. It increases in power as a result of the size of the things it does and the importance of the events it controls without the need to alter its constitution.

Had the laws made it as weak and circumscribed as that of the Union, its influence would soon increase even more so.

WHY THE PRESIDENT OF THE UNITED STATES HAS NO NEED TO HAVE A MAJORITY IN THE TWO HOUSES IN ORDER TO CONDUCT BUSINESS

It is an accepted maxim in Europe that a constitutional king is unable to govern when opinion in the legislative chambers is not in accord with his.

We have seen several Presidents of the United States lose the support of the majority of the legislative body without being forced to relinquish power and without any resulting damage being inflicted upon society.

I have heard this quoted as proof of the independence and strength of the executive power in America. Only a few moments suffice to convince us that it is, on the contrary, proof of its impotence.

A European king needs to engage the support of the legislative body to fulfill the task imposed by the constitution because such a task is considerable. A constitutional king in Europe is not simply the executor of the law; the duty of the execution falls so utterly upon his shoulders that he would be able to paralyze the power of a law which was opposed to him. He needs the chambers to enact the law; the chambers need him for its execution. These two authorities are interdependent and the workings of the government grind to a halt, if they are at variance.

In America, the President cannot block the making of laws and could not evade the duty of executing them. His enthusiastic and sincere agreement, while doubtless useful, is not necessary to the function of government. In all essential respects, he is directly or indirectly subject to the legislature. Where he is wholly independent, he has little or no power. Thus it is his weakness and not his strength which allows him to carry on opposed to the legislative power.

In Europe, agreement between the king and the chambers is vital because there is always the potential for serious conflict. In America, such agreement is not indispensable because conflict is impossible.

THE ELECTION OF THE PRESIDENT

The danger of the system of election increases in proportion to the extent of the prerogative of executive power— Americans are able to adopt this system because they can manage without a strong executive power—How circumstances favor the establishment of the elective system—Why the election of the President does not alter the principles of government—Influence of the election of the President upon subordinate officials.

The system of election applied to the head of the executive power of a great nation presents dangers which experience and historians have amply indicated.

I only wish to speak about this in relation to America.

The dangers of the system of election may be more or less formidable according to the place and importance of the executive power in the state as well as the type of election and the circumstances of the electorate.

The criticism rightly directed at the elective system applied to the head of state is that it offers so splendid a lure to individual ambitions and so inflames them in their pursuit of power that often legal means no longer satisfy them so that they appeal to force when right lets them down.

Clearly the greater the prerogatives of the executive power, the stronger is the lure; the more aroused the ambitions of candidates, the more they derive support from a host of partisans who hope to share power after their man has won.

The dangers of the system of election increase, therefore, in direct proportion to the influence exercised by the executive power on state affairs.

The revolutions in Poland should not simply be attributed to the elective system as such but to the fact that the election was for the head of a great monarchy.

Before discussing the essential advantage of the elective system, a preliminary question remains to be answered as to whether the geographical location, laws, habits, customs, or opinions of a nation into which such a system is to be introduced will admit the establishment of a weak and dependent executive power. For to wish the representative to be armed with excessive power and, at the same time, elected, is, in my opinion, to express two contradictory aims. I know of only one means of moving from an hereditary monarchy to the condition of an elective authority: that is to restrict beforehand its sphere of action, gradually to reduce its prerogative, and to accustom the people by degrees to live without its protection. But European republicans have scarcely any interest in such a course. Since many of them hate tyranny only because they suffer from its severities, they are not chafed by the extent of executive power. They only attack the source of power with no perception of the close link between these two things.

No one has yet come forward willing to expose his honor and his life to become President of the United States, because the President enjoys only a temporary, limited, dependent power. The prize of fortune must be great to attract desperate players into the lists.

So far, no candidate has managed to arouse the enthusiastic sympathies or the dangerous passions of the people in his favor, for the very simple reason that, having reached the position of head of government, he is not able to share out among his friends either much power, or wealth, or glory and his influence in the state is too weak for any faction to feel that its success or downfall depends upon his elevation to power.

Hereditary monarchies possess one great advantage: the private interest of a family is permanently and intimately bound up with the interests of the state and, therefore, never a moment passes by when the state interest is abandoned to its own devices. I do not know whether business is better managed in monarchies than elsewhere but at least someone is always at hand to concern himself with such things, well or ill, according to his capability.

In elective states, on the other hand, the machinery of government, to some extent, ceases to function of its own accord as an election approaches and even for some time prior. Doubtless laws could be devised to speed up the election so as never to leave the seat of government empty. But whatever was done, the void would exist in men's minds in spite of the legislator's efforts.

As the election draws near, the head of the executive powers thinks only of the ensuing battle; his future has gone; he can undertake nothing and only feebly prosecutes what someone else will possibly complete. "I am so near the moment of retiring," wrote President Jefferson[d] on 21 January 1809 (six weeks before the election), "that I take no part in affairs beyond the expression of an opinion. I think it is fair that my successor should now originate those measures of which he will be charged with execution and responsibility . . ."

As for the nation, it turns its attention to one place and concerns itself with watching the gradual birth in progress.

The broader the place the executive holds in the management of affairs, the wider and more necessary its habitual activity, the greater the danger from such a state of things. Among a people which is used to the government and even more so to the administrative protection of a powerful executive authority, the election could not fail to cause a profound disturbance.

In the United States, the activity of the executive power can slow without risk because such an activity is weak and circumscribed. When the head of government is elected, the one surefire consequence is instability in internal and external politics. That is one of the principal defects of this system.

But this defect is more or less noticeable according to the power granted to the elected magistrate. In Rome, the principles of government never varied even though the consuls were changed every year, because the Senate, which was an hereditary body, was the authority controlling everything. In most European monarchies, were one to elect the king, the kingdom would change complexion at every new choice.

In America, the President exercises quite an influence upon

state affairs but he does not direct them; the preponderant power resides in the representatives of the nation as a whole. You have, therefore, to change the people en masse, not simply the President, if you wish to alter the guiding political principles. So, in America, the system of elections applied to the head of the executive power does not harm in any very perceptible way the stability of the government.

Moreover, the lack of stability is so fundamental a weakness in the elective system that it does not make itself felt acutely in the sphere of activity of the President, restricted though that is.

The Americans have been correct in thinking that the head of the executive power, since he has to bear wholly the responsibility for the duties he is called to fulfill, ought to remain as free as possible to choose his own agents and to remove them at will; the legislative body supervises rather than directs the President. The consequence of this arrangement is that at each new election the fate of every federal employee is virtually hanging in the air.

In the constitutional monarchies of Europe, the complaint is that the fate of all the humbler servants of the administration often depends on that of the ministers. It is worse still in those states where the head of government is elected. The reason for this is simple: in constitutional monarchies, ministers rise and fall in rapid succession but the principal representative of executive power remains the same, which restricts the spirit of innovation within definite limits. In such regimes, administrative systems vary in the details rather than in the principles; sudden alterations of principle could not take place without triggering a sort of revolution. In America, such a revolution occurs every four years in the name of the law.

As for the sufferings of individuals which follow naturally from such a legislative system, one must confess that the want of stability in the fate of public officials does not produce in America the ill effects one might anticipate anywhere else. In the United States, it is so easy to acquire an independent position that the public official who loses his job may sometimes be deprived of the comforts of life but never of the means of subsistence.

I stated at the beginning of this chapter that the dangers from this type of election, applied to the head of the executive power, were more or less extensive according to the circumstances of the nation which elects him.

It would be an empty exercise to attempt to weaken the role of the executive power because there is one area over which this power has great influence whatever its legal position, namely foreign affairs, where a negotiation can scarcely be instigated or pursued with success except by one person.

The more a nation is in a precarious and perilous position and the need for continuity and stability is felt in the management of foreign affairs, the more dangerous the system of election of the head of state becomes.

The policy of the Americans toward the world at large is simple; it might almost be said that no one needs them and they need no one. Their independence is never threatened.

With them, therefore, the role of the executive power is as constrained by circumstances as by law. The President can frequently change his views without involving the state in damage or destruction.

Whatever prerogatives are possessed by the executive power, the period immediately before and during an election must always be seen as a time of national crisis, which is all the more dangerous whenever the internal position of a country is embarrassed and foreign threats are magnified. There are very few nations in Europe which would not fear invasion or anarchy whenever they elected a new leader.

In America, society is so formed that it can carry on independently; foreign dangers never threaten. The election of the President is a source of agitation not disaster.

METHOD OF ELECTION

Skill of American legislators in their choice of method of election—Formation of special electoral body—Separate vote of these electors—In what circumstances the House of Representatives is called upon to choose the President— Results of the twelve elections which have taken place since the constitution has been in force.

Independently of those dangers inherent in the system, many others arise from the actual methods of election and these can be avoided by care on the legislator's part.

Whenever a nation gathers in arms in the public square to choose a leader, it runs risks not only from that very method of election but also from the dangers of a civil war which such an election entails.

When Polish laws made the choice of king turn upon the veto of one man alone, they became an invitation to murder that man or prepared the way for anarchy.

In the course of an examination of the institutions of the United States and a careful scrutiny of the political and social situation of the country, there is evidence of an admirable congruency between fortune's favors and man's efforts. There were two great causes of internal peace: America was a brand-new country and the inhabitants had long been accustomed to freedom. Moreover, America feared no conquest. American legislators exploited these favorable circumstances and had no difficulty in establishing a weak and dependent executive power, which could, without risk, be made elective.

The only remaining task was to choose the least risky of the different systems of election; the rules they laid down in this respect amplify excellently the guarantees already supplied by the physical and political constitution of the country.

The problem was to find that method of election which expressed the genuine will of the people, while least arousing their passions, and which left as little as possible in suspense. The first step agreed was that a simple majority was enough to decide the matter. But the principal difficulty was to obtain this majority without those fearful intervals of delay which they wished most to avoid.

In practice, it is rare to see one man unite the majority of votes in a great nation at the first attempt. This is an even greater difficulty in a republic of confederated states where local influences are much more developed and powerful.

To get round this second obstacle, they decided to delegate the electoral powers of the nation to a body of representatives. Such a method of election made a majority more likely because the smaller number of voters stood a greater chance of reaching an agreement. It also offered more safeguards for a judicious choice.

But should the right of election be conferred upon the legislative body itself, which was the normal representative of the nation, or should they rather form an electoral college whose sole function would be to proceed to the nomination of a President?

The Americans took the latter view. They thought that those men they sent forward to enact ordinary laws would only partially be able to represent the wishes of the people in relation to the election of their chief magistrate. Besides, being elected for more than a year, the wishes of their electorate could already have changed. They judged that by making the legislature responsible for the election of the chief of the executive power, its members would become the subject of corrupt manipulation and the plaything of intrigues long before the election, whereas special electors would, like juries, remain unknown in a crowd and would, right up to the day when they had to act, appear for an instant only to announce their decision.

It was settled, therefore, that each state would appoint a certain number of electors[20] who, in turn, would elect the President. As it had been noticed that those assemblies responsible for the choosing of heads of government in elective countries never failed to become centers of passion and intrigue and that, occasionally, they usurped powers which did not belong to them and that often their proceedings and the resulting uncertainty lasted long enough to threaten the stability of the state, it was settled that the electors would vote on the same day but without assembling together in the same place.[21]

This two-tier method of election made a majority more likely though not certain, for the electors could differ among themselves as much as their constituents.

In that eventuality, a choice had to be made between three

20. Equal to the number of members it sent to Congress. There were 288 electors in the election of 1833. (*The National Calendar*).
21. The electors from each state assemble, but they send into the central government the list of individual votes, not the total of the votes.

possible measures: either to appoint new electors, or to consult once more those already appointed, or, finally, to defer the election to a new authority.

The first two methods, apart from their uncertainty, entailed delays and prolonged an agitation which is always twinned with danger.

The third was, therefore, chosen and it was agreed that the votes of the electors would be sent sealed to the president of the Senate who, on the appointed day and in the presence of the two houses, would count the votes. If none of the candidates had gathered a majority, the House of Representatives would proceed immediately to conduct an election. Its rights were carefully restricted and the Representatives could elect only the one of the three candidates who had obtained the most votes.[22]

As we can see, only in a rare eventuality, and one difficult to anticipate, is the election entrusted to the normal representatives of the nation; moreover, they can choose only a citizen already named by a powerful minority of the special electors. That is a fortunate combination which reconciles respect for the will of the people with the speed of execution and those precautions demanded by the interests of the state. However, allowing the question to be decided by the House of Representatives in the case of a split vote does not succeed in reaching a complete solution of all the difficulties, for there may be no decisive vote in the House of Representatives. In which case, the constitution offers no remedy. But by restricting the number of candidates to three and entrusting the choice to a few enlightened men, it has smoothed out all the obstacles[23] over which it could have some control. The rest are inherent in the election system itself.

Throughout the forty-four years of the federal constitution,

22. In this context it was the majority of states, not the majority of members, which was decisive. As a result, New York has no more influence in the matter than Rhode Island. Thus the citizens of the Union are first consulted as members of one united nation; when they cannot agree, the division into states is brought back into play and each of the latter is given a separate and individual vote.

    This is just one more of the oddities found in the federal constitution, which can only be explained by the clash of interests.

23. However, in 1801 Jefferson was not elected until the thirty-sixth ballot.

the United States has chosen a President twelve times, ten of which took place instantly by the simultaneous votes of the special electors at different points around the country.

The House of Representatives has only twice used the exceptional powers granted to it in the case of a split vote; the first in 1801 for the election of Mr Jefferson; the second in 1825 when Mr Quincy Adams was appointed.

CRISIS OF THE ELECTION

The presidential election may be considered a national crisis—Why?—Passions of the people—Preoccupation of the President—Calm which follows the turmoil of the election.

I have often spoken of the conditions favorable to the adoption of the elective system in the United States and I have shown the precautions taken by the legislators to lessen the dangers of it. Americans are accustomed to all kinds of elections. Experience has taught them what degree of turmoil is tolerable and where they should stop. The vast extent of the land mass over which their inhabitants are scattered ensures that any clash between different parties is less probable and less dangerous than elsewhere. The political conditions of the nation at the times of elections have so far presented no real danger.

Nevertheless, the presidential election may be considered as a time of national crisis.

The President's influence over the conduct of affairs is doubtless weak and indirect but it extends over the whole nation. The choice of a President impinges only slightly upon each individual citizen but it does concern them all. Now a single concern, however small, assumes a great degree of importance the moment it becomes a concern of everyone.

In comparison with a European king, no doubt the President has few opportunities of enlisting followers; however, the positions at his disposal are sufficiently numerous for several thousand electors to be directly or indirectly involved in his cause.

In addition, in the United States as elsewhere, parties feel the need to rally round one man so as to make themselves more easily known to the crowd. Therefore, they exploit the name of the candidate for the presidency as a symbol and personify their own theories in him. Thus, parties are strongly involved in tipping the election in their favor, not so much to promote the triumph of their own ideas with the help of a President-elect as to prove by his election that these ideas have gained a majority.

Long before the appointed day arrives, the election becomes the greatest and, as it were, the only matter which occupies people's minds. Then political factions redouble their enthusiasm; every possible phoney passion that the imagination can conceive in a contented and peaceful country comes out into the light of day.

The President, for his part, is absorbed in the task of defending himself. He governs no longer in the interests of the state but out of concern for his re-election. He bows before the majority and often, instead of checking their passions as his duty requires, he hastens to anticipate their whims.

As the election draws near, intrigues multiply and turmoil spreads. Citizens divide up between several camps each of which adopts the name of its candidate. The whole nation descends into a feverish state; the election becomes the daily theme of newspapers, the subject of private conversations, the object of every maneuver and every thought, the only concern of the present moment.

It is true that as soon as the result has been announced, this passion is dispelled, all returns to calm, and the river which momentarily overflowed its banks returns peacefully to its bed. But should we not find it astonishing that such a storm should have arisen in the first place?

RE-ELECTION OF THE PRESIDENT

When the head of the executive power comes up for re-election it is the state itself which becomes locked into intrigue and corruption—Desire to be re-elected dominates all the thoughts of a President of the United States—

*Disadvantages of re-election peculiar to America—Natural
weakness of democracies is the gradual subordination of all
the state powers to the slightest wishes of the majority—
Re-election of the President fosters this weakness.*

Have the legislators of the United States been wrong or right to
allow the re-election of the President?

To prevent the head of the executive power from being re-
elected seems at first sight contrary to reason. The influence
exerted by the talents or character of a single man upon the
destiny of a whole nation, especially in difficult circumstances
and in times of crisis, is well known. Laws which forbade the
citizens from re-electing their first magistrate would deprive
them of the best means of bringing prosperity to the state or of
saving it. Besides, what a peculiar outcome it would be if a man
were excluded from government at the very moment he had
finally proved his competence to govern well.

Doubtless, these are strong arguments; yet cannot equally
powerful reasons be advanced against them?

Intrigue and corruption are natural weaknesses of elective
governments. But when the head of state can be re-elected, these
weaknesses stretch out endlessly and threaten the very existence
of the country. When an ordinary candidate seeks success
through intrigue, his maneuvrings can only take place within
a restricted sphere, but when the head of state puts himself
forward he borrows the power of government for his private
use.

In the first example, we see a man with modest resources; in
the second case, the state itself with its huge resources is involved
in intrigue and corruption.

The ordinary citizen who uses disreputable practices to gain
power brings harm only indirectly to the prosperity of the public;
but whenever the man who represents the executive power
enters the fray, the cares of government move into a secondary
place because his principal concern is his election. For him,
all negotiations, like laws, are only electoral schemings; jobs
become the reward for services rendered, not to the nation but
to its head. Even if the action of the government is not always

opposed to the interests of the country, at the very least it no longer serves it, even though it was created for that purpose.

It is impossible to observe the normal course of affairs in the United States without realizing that the wish to be re-elected dominates the President's thoughts and that all the policies of his administration are geared to this objective. His slightest actions are secondary to this aim and, as the moment of crisis draws near, his private interest takes the place of the general interests in his mind.

The principle of re-election makes the corrupting influence of elective governments still more widespread and more dangerous, while leading to a decline in the political morality of the nation and the substitution of craft for patriotism.

In America, it attacks at still closer range the sources of national existence.

Every government bears within itself a natural weakness which seems inherent in the very nature of its being; to spot that clearly is the genius of the legislator. A state can survive the effect of many bad laws and the ill they cause can often be exaggerated. But any law which encourages this deadly seed cannot fail, in the long term, to prove fatal, even though its bad consequences may not be immediately evident.

In absolute monarchies, the source of destruction is the unlimited and unreasonable extent of royal authority. Any measure which removed the powers the constitution put in place to counterbalance the royal authority would, therefore, be radically evil, even though its effects would for a long time appear insubstantial.

Similarly, in countries governed by a democracy in which the people attract everything to themselves, the laws which accelerate this action until it becomes irresistible inflict a direct attack on the existence of the government.

The greatest merit of the American lawgivers is their clear realization of this truth and their courage to act accordingly. They had the idea that a certain number of authorities would stand above the people and would, without being completely independent, nevertheless enjoy quite a considerable degree of freedom in their own sphere of influence. The result was that, while remaining obliged to follow the general direction of the majority, they could still combat its whims and refuse any dangerous demands.

To achieve this, they combined all the executive power of the nation in the hands of one man; they gave extensive prerogatives to the President and armed him with the veto to stand against the encroachments of the legislature.

But when they introduced the principle of re-election, they in part destroyed their work. They granted the President a considerable power, while depriving him of the will to exploit it.

If the President were ineligible for re-election, he would not be independent of the people for he is still responsible to them; but the support of the people would not be so necessary as to force him to bend to their will in everything.

Once the President of the United States can stand for re-election (and this is true especially these days when political morality is lax and great men are rare), he is but a docile tool in the hands of the majority. He likes what they like, hates what they hate; he hastens to anticipate their wishes, to forestall their complaints and to bend to their every desire. The legislators intended him to guide them, whereas he follows them.

Thus, in their desire not to deprive the state of the talents of one man, they have rendered those talents almost useless. In order to preserve a resource for extraordinary circumstances, they have exposed the country to everyday dangers.

THE FEDERAL COURTS OF JUSTICE[24]

Political importance of judicial power in the United States—Difficulty of dealing with this subject—Usefulness of justice in the confederations—What courts could be used

24. See chapter 6, entitled "Judicial Power in the United States." This chapter states the general principles of the Americans in the matter of justice. See also Article 3 of the federal constitution. See The *Federalist*, nos 78–83, inclusive; *Constitutional Law, Being a View of the Practice and Jurisdiction of the Courts of the United States*, by Thomas Sergeant. See Story, pp. 134–62, 489–511, 581, 668. See the organic law of 24 September 1789 in the collection entitled *Laws of the United States*, by Story, vol. 1, p. 53.

by the Union—Need to establish federal courts—
Organization of federal justice—The Supreme Court—
How it differs from all courts of justice known to us.

I have looked at the legislative and executive power of the Union. It remains to consider the power of the judiciary.

Here I must be frank to the readers about my fears.

Judicial institutions exercise a great influence upon the destiny of the Anglo-Americans and hold a very important place in the political institutions properly so called. From that point of view, they are particularly deserving of our attention.

But how can one explain the political activity of the American courts without embarking upon certain technical details about their constitution and procedures? And how can I plunge into these details without discouraging the reader's curiosity by the natural aridity of such a subject? How can one remain clear while continuing to be brief?

I do not flatter myself that I have avoided these different perils. Ordinary men will still find me too long-winded, lawyers will consider me too brief. But that is a general disadvantage of my subject and the particular part of it I am dealing with at this moment.

The greatest difficulty was, not to know how the federal government would be constituted, but how one would ensure obedience to its laws.

Governments in general have only two methods of overcoming the resistance of the people they govern, namely, the physical force at their own disposal and the moral force which they derive from the decisions of the courts.

A government which had only war as its means of enforcing obedience to its laws would be well on its way to ruin. One of two things would probably befall it: if it was weak and moderate, it would use force only as a last resort and would overlook many minor acts of insubordination. Then the state would gradually fall into anarchy.

If it was bold and powerful, it would have daily recourse to violence and soon you would see it decline into a purely military despotism. Both its activity and its inactivity would be equally fatal for the people it governed.

The major objective of justice is to substitute the concept of law for that of violence and to position intermediate authorities between the government and the use of physical force.

The authority granted to the intervention of the courts by the general opinion of men is so surprisingly great that it clings to the outer form of justice even when the substance no longer exists and gives a bodily reality to a shadow.

The moral force which courts of law enjoy makes the use of physical force infinitely less frequent for, in most cases, it takes its place; and when physical force has to be used, it doubles its authority by linking up with this moral force.

A federal government, more than any other, should aspire to obtain the support of justice because, being weaker by nature, resistance against it is easier to organize.[25] If it had to use force in every case and as its first move, it would be inadequate to its task.

The Union, therefore, had a special need of the courts in order to force citizens to obey the laws and to rebuff any attacks against them.

But what courts should the Union use? Each state already possessed a judiciary organized at its center. Should it turn to these courts or should it organize a federal judiciary? It is easy to demonstrate that the Union was unable to adapt the established state courts to its wants.

Doubtless it matters for the judicial authority to be independent of all others to ensure the security of each citizen and the freedom of all of them. But it is no less necessary to the existence of the nation that the different authorities of the state have the same origin, follow the same principles and act in the same sphere. In a word, they should be *in tune with each other* and

25. Federal laws need tribunals most and yet they have made least use of them. The reason for this is that most confederations have been formed by independent states who had no real intention of obeying the central government and who, while giving it the right to command, carefully observed the capacity to disobey.

homogeneous. No one, I presume, has ever thought of trying in foreign courts offenses committed in France, so as to be able to ensure the impartiality of the magistrates.

Americans form a single nation in relation to their federal government but, at the center of this nation, political bodies have been allowed which are dependent upon the national government in a few respects and independent in all the rest. These all have a distinct origin, their own maxims, and their special methods of conducting affairs. Entrusting the execution of the laws of the Union to courts instituted by these political bodies was to deliver the nation into the hands of foreign judges.

Furthermore, each state is not only foreign to the Union but is also a perpetual opponent since, when the sovereignty of the Union loses ground, the states gain advantage.

Thus, to entrust the enforcement of the laws of the Union to the courts of individual states would be to deliver the nation not merely to foreign but also to biased judges.

Besides, it was not simply their character alone which made the state courts unfit to serve the national end but their number above all.

When the federal constitution was formed, thirteen courts of justice already existed in the United States, judging cases without appeal. Today, there are twenty-four. To suppose that a state can carry on when its fundamental laws may be interpreted and applied in twenty-four different ways at the same time, is to impose a system which is equally opposed to reason and to the lessons of experience.

The American legislators, therefore, agreed to institute a federal judiciary to apply the laws of the Union and to settle certain questions of general concern which were carefully defined in advance.

All the judicial power of the Union was concentrated in one single court called the Supreme Court of the United States. But in order to facilitate the dispatch of business, lower courts were added to it, empowered to decide cases of small importance without appeal or to give a preliminary ruling in more serious disputes. The members of the Supreme Court were not elected by the people or the legislature; the President of the United

States had to choose them after taking the advice of the Senate.

In order to guarantee their independence of the other authorities, they were made irremovable and the decision was taken that their salaries, once fixed, would move beyond the control of the legislature.[26]

It was relatively easy to proclaim in principle the establishment of a federal judiciary but difficulties arose in abundance when it was a question of determining its powers.

MEANS OF DETERMINING THE JURISDICTION OF THE FEDERAL COURTS

Difficulty of determining the jurisdiction of the different courts in the confederations—The courts of the Union obtained the right to determine their own jurisdiction—Why this ruling challenges the share of sovereignty which individual states had reserved for themselves—The sovereignty of these states constrained by the laws and the interpretation of the laws—Thus, the risk to individual states is more apparent than real.

26. The Union was divided into districts, each with a resident federal judge. The court presided over by this judge was called a district court.

In addition, each judge of the Supreme Court had to tour a certain part of the territory of the republic annually in order to try the most important cases on the spot; the court over which he presided was called the circuit court.

Finally, the most serious cases had to be brought, either directly or on appeal, before the Supreme Court. For this purpose all the circuit judges assembled annually to hold a solemn session.

The jury system was introduced into the federal courts in the same way as in the state courts and for similar cases.

Obviously there is hardly any analogy between the Supreme Court of the United States and our *Cour de Cassation*. A case can be brought before the Supreme Court in the first instance, but before the *Cour de Cassation* only at a second or third stage. The Supreme Court does indeed, like the *Cour de Cassation*, form a unique tribunal responsible for establishing a uniform legal system; but the Supreme Court judges fact as well as law, and *itself* pronounces, without sending the case back before another tribunal—two things which the *Cour de Cassation* cannot do.

See the organic law of 24 September 1789, *Laws of the United States*, by Story, vol. 1, p. 53.

An initial question arises: as the constitution of the United States recognized two separate sovereign powers in the presence of each other, represented in the legal realm by two different types of courts, frequent collisions between the two could not have been prevented, whatever care was taken to lay down the jurisdiction of each of them. Now, if that arose, who had the right to judge the competence of each court?

In nations that form one and the same political body, when a question of jurisdiction arises between two courts, the dispute is generally brought before a third court, which acts as arbitrator.

This is easily done because in such nations the questions of legal jurisdiction have no connection with questions of national sovereignty.

But above and beyond the high court of an individual state and the high court of the United States, it was impossible to establish any court at all which did not belong to one or the other.

It proved therefore necessary to grant one of these two courts the right to judge its own case and to accept or refuse competence in the matter disputed. Such a privilege could not be granted to the different courts of the states; that would have been to destroy the sovereignty of the Union *in fact*, after having established it *in law*. For the interpretation of the constitution would soon have returned to the individual states that share of independence which the terms of the constitution took from them.

By instituting a federal court, the intention had been to relieve the states of the right to decide, each in its own way, questions of national interest and thus to create a uniform legal body to interpret the laws of the Union. Such an intention would have been missed if the courts of the individual states, by refraining from judging cases as federal, had been able to judge them by claiming that they were not in fact federal.

The Supreme Court of the United States was therefore entrusted with the right to decide all questions of jurisdiction.[27]

27. Furthermore, to make these lawsuits of competence less frequent, it was decided that in a very large number of federal cases the tribunals of the particular states would have the right to pronounce concurrently with the tribunals of the Union; but then the unsuccessful party always had the right to appeal to the Supreme Court of the United States. The Supreme

This was the most serious blow against the sovereignty of the states, which was thus restricted not only by the laws but also by the interpretation of the laws, by a known boundary and by another that was not known, by a fixed rule and by one which was arbitrary. The constitution had truly placed precise limitations upon federal sovereignty but, whenever the latter came into direct conflict with state supremacy, a federal court was to pronounce judgment.

However, the dangers threatened by these procedures against the sovereignty of the states were not as serious in real terms as they appeared to be.

We shall see further on that in America real power resides in provincial government rather more than in federal government. Federal judges are aware of the relative weakness of the power in whose name they act and are more inclined to give up a right of jurisdiction in cases where the law has given it them than to claim one illegally.

DIFFERENT CASES OF JURISDICTION

*Subject matter and litigant, bases of federal jurisdiction—
Lawsuits involving ambassadors, the Union, an individual
state—Who judges them—Lawsuits arising from the laws
of the Union—Why judged by federal courts—Lawsuit
relating to the non-performance of contracts tried by the
federal courts—Consequence of this.*

When they had established the way of settling federal competence, the legislators of the Union defined the cases which should come within its jurisdiction.

It was agreed that certain litigants could be judged only by the federal courts whatever the subject of the lawsuit.

Then it was fixed that certain lawsuits could be judged only by these same courts whatever the status of the litigants.

Court of Virginia disputed the right of the Supreme Court of the United States to judge an appeal against its decisions, but in vain. See Kent's *Commentaries*, vol. 1, pp. 300, 370ff; Story's *Commentaries*, p. 646; the organic law of 1789, *Laws of the United States*, vol. 1, p. 53.

Thus these two issues of litigant and subject matter became the bases of federal competence.

Ambassadors represent nations friendly to the Union; all that involves ambassadors in some way involves the whole Union. When an ambassador is a party to a lawsuit, that suit becomes an affair affecting the wellbeing of the nation and it is natural for a federal court to pronounce judgment.

The Union itself may be involved in a case; in that event it would have been contrary to common sense as well as to the customs of nations for courts other than its own to be called upon to pass judgment. Alone, federal courts could do so.

When two individuals from two different states are involved in a case, it would be unsuitable to have the matter judged by courts from only one of the states. It offers more confidence, if a court is chosen which can evoke the suspicions of neither party; the court which quite naturally fits that bill is that of the Union.

When the two litigants are not private individuals but states, the same consideration of equity combines with a political concern of the first importance. At this point the status of the litigants endows all disputes with a national importance. Even the smallest litigation between states involves the peace of the whole Union.[28]

Often the very nature of the lawsuits was to prescribe the rule of competence. Thus it was that all issues connected with maritime trade were to be settled by federal courts.[29]

The reason for this is simple to illustrate: almost all these

28. The constitution also stated that cases between a state and the citizens of another state should be tried before the federal courts. The question was soon raised whether the constitution had intended to cover all cases that might arise between a state and the citizens of another state, regardless of which of the two was the *plaintiff*. The Supreme Court decided that it did, but this decision alarmed the individual states, who were afraid of being dragged against their will into the federal courts at every turn. An amendment to the constitution was therefore introduced, by virtue of which the judicial power of the Union could not extend to trying cases *brought against* one of the states by the citizens of another. See Story's *Commentaries*, p. 624.

29. Example: all acts of piracy.

questions turn upon the interpretation of international law. In this connection they essentially involve the Union in relation to foreign nations. Moreover, because the sea is not included in one judicial sphere more than another, only national courts can claim the right to judge in cases which originate in maritime affairs.

The constitution has included within one category almost all the lawsuits which should by their nature come before the federal courts.

The guidelines it lays down in this connection are simple but draw together a vast system of ideas and a multitude of facts.

The federal courts, it states, will be obliged to pronounce judgments in all the lawsuits *arising under the laws of the United States*.

Two examples will illustrate perfectly the legislator's thought.

The constitution prohibits the states from making laws concerning the circulation of money; despite such a prohibition, one state enacts such a law. The interested parties refuse to obey it, seeing that it is contrary to the constitution. They have recourse to a federal court because the basis of complaint is laid down in the laws of the United States.

Congress imposes an import duty; difficulties arise in the collection of this tax. It is still before the federal courts that the case has to be presented because the reason for the case lies in the interpretation of a law of the United States.

These guidelines are in precise agreement with the fundamental principles of the federal constitution.

It is true that the Union, as established in 1789, possesses only a limited sovereignty but the intention was that, within this sphere, it should form one and the same people.[30] Within that sphere it is sovereign. Once this point has been made and accepted, the rest becomes simple. For once you acknowledge that the United States, within the limits imposed by the

30. Some restrictions to this principle were certainly introduced by treating each state as an independent power in the Senate and making them vote separately in the House of Representatives for the election of the President; but those are exceptions. The opposite principle is the dominant one.

constitution, forms a single nation, you must grant it the rights that belong to all nations.

Now, from the beginnings of society it has been agreed that each nation has the right to employ its courts to rule upon all questions which concern the execution of its own laws. It is said in response that the Union is in the unusual position of forming a nation only in respect of certain matters without being one for all other purposes. What is the result? At least for all laws which connect to these matters it enjoys the rights of absolute sovereignty. The essence of the difficulty is knowing what these matters are. When that is settled (and we have seen above how it was resolved in dealing with the question of competence), there is in truth no further question. For once it had been established that a lawsuit was federal, that is to say, belonged to the sphere of sovereignty reserved for the Union by the constitution, it followed naturally that a federal court alone had to pronounce judgment.

Every time therefore that a man wished to attack the laws of the United States or invoke them in his defense, he had to apply to the federal courts.

Thus the jurisdiction of the courts of the Union expands or contracts according to the expansion or contraction of the sovereignty of the Union itself.

We have observed that the main aim of the legislators in 1789 had been to separate sovereignty into two distinct parts. Into one they placed the control of all the general concerns of the Union; into the other, the control of all the concerns special to its constituent parts.

Their main care was to arm the federal government with sufficient powers for it to be able, in its own sphere of influence, to withstand the encroachments of individual states.

As for the states, the general principle was to leave them independent in their own sphere. The central government cannot control them nor even inspect their conduct.

I have shown in the chapter about the separation of powers that this latter principle had not always been respected. There are certain laws that an individual state cannot enact, even though they apparently belong to its own sphere of interest.

When one state of the Union passes a law of this kind, citizens who are damaged by the execution of this law can appeal to the federal courts.

Thus the jurisdiction of the federal courts extends, not only to the cases which arise under the laws of the Union but also to all those which arise under laws enacted by individual states in opposition to the constitution.

States are prohibited from promulgating retroactive laws in criminal matters; the man condemned under such a law can appeal to federal justice.

Likewise, the constitution has prohibited the states from enacting laws which might destroy or impair the obligations of contracts.[31]

As soon as an individual thinks that a right of that sort has been impaired by a law passed in his state, he may refuse to obey and may appeal to federal justice.[32]

31. It is perfectly clear, says Story, p. 503, that any law which extends, restricts, or in any way changes the intention of the parties, resulting from the stipulations in the contract, necessarily damages it. In the same place the author carefully defines what federal jurisprudence means by a contract. The definition is very broad. A concession made by the state to an individual and accepted by him is a contract, and cannot be removed by the terms of a new law. A charter granted by the state to a company is a contract and is law to the state as well as to the person to whom the charter has been granted. This article of the constitution, therefore, guarantees the position of a large proportion of *acquired rights*, but not of all of them. I may legitimately possess a property without its having passed into my hands through a contract. For me its possession is an acquired right, but that right is not guaranteed by the federal constitution.

32. Here is a remarkable example quoted by Story, p. 508. Dartmouth College, in New Hampshire, had been founded by virtue of a charter granted to certain individuals before the American Revolution. By virtue of this charter its administrators formed a constituted body, or using the American expression, a corporation. The legislature of New Hampshire thought it should change the terms of the original charter and transferred to new administrators all the rights, privileges, and franchises derived from this charter. The former administrators resisted and appealed to the federal court, which found in their favor since the original charter was an authentic contract between the state and those to whom the charter had been granted. The new law could not change the provisions of this charter without violating the rights acquired by virtue of a contract and consequently violating article 1, section 10 of the constitution of the United States.

This provision appears to me to attack more profoundly than any other the sovereignty of the states.

The rights accorded to the federal government for national purposes are clearly set down and are easy to understand. Those rights granted indirectly by the article I have just quoted are not easily grasped by common sense nor are their limits clearly drawn. In fact, a host of political laws exercise an influence upon the existence of contracts and could thus supply pretexts for encroachment by the central authority.

PROCEDURE OF THE FEDERAL COURTS

Natural weakness of justice in the confederations—Efforts legislators must make so as to bring, as far as possible, only isolated individuals and not states before the federal courts—How the Americans have succeeded in this— Direct action by federal courts against single individuals— Indirect attack against those states which violate the laws of the Union—Decision of federal justice weakens but does not destroy provincial laws.

I have described the rights of the federal courts; it is just as important to know how they exercise them.

The irresistible force of justice in countries where sovereignty is undivided is derived from the fact that the courts of those countries represent the whole nation in a struggle with the single individual affected by the judicial decision. To the idea of right is added that of the force which supports that right.

But in countries where sovereignty is divided, it is not always like that. Justice in such countries is most often confronted, not by an isolated individual but by a fraction of the nation and thus its moral authority and physical strength are diminished.

In federal states, justice is therefore naturally weaker and the victim stronger.

The legislator in the confederate states must strive persistently to give to the courts a standing analogous to that enjoyed by those in nations where sovereignty has not been divided. In other words, his constant efforts must support the idea that federal justice should represent the nation and the victim should represent an individual interest.

A government, whatever other functions it has, needs to constrain its subjects in order to force them to discharge their obligations; it needs to act against them to defend itself against their attacks.

As for the direct action of the government against its subjects, to force them to obey the law, the constitution of the United States so arranged things (and this was its master stroke) that the federal courts, acting in the name of these laws, never had to deal with other than individuals. In fact, since it had been declared that the confederate states formed one and the same people within the limits drawn by the constitution, the result was that the government created by this constitution, and acting within its limits, was endowed with all the rights of a national government whose main function was to transmit its injunctions directly to the private citizen. Thus, when the Union voted a tax, for example, it did not apply to the states for the levying of it, but to every American citizen according to his assessment. Federal justice, in its turn, being responsible for the execution of this Union law, had to condemn not the recalcitrant state but the taxpayer. Like the justice of other nations, it was confronted by an individual.

Observe that, in this instance, the Union has picked out its own opponent who is weak; quite naturally, this opponent comes off worse.

But when the Union, instead of attacking, is itself reduced to self-defense, the difficulty increases. The constitution recognizes the states' authority to enact laws. Those laws may impair the privileges of the Union. At such a point, a collision with the sovereignty of the state making the law is inevitable. It only remains to choose the least dangerous remedy which is clearly indicated in the general principles which I have previously stated.[33]

It might be thought that in this hypothetical case, the Union could have summoned the state before a federal court, which

33. See the chapter entitled "Judicial Power in the United States."

would have declared the law void; that would have been to follow the most natural logic. But, in this way, the federal courts would have been in direct opposition to the state, something they wanted to avoid as much as possible.

The Americans thought it almost impossible for the execution of a new law not to harm some private interest.

It is upon such private interests that the authors of the federal constitution rely to attack the legislative measure that the Union complains about. Protection is offered to just that interest.

A state sells some land to a company. A year later a new law disposes of that same land in some other way, thus violating that section of the constitution which prohibits the alteration of rights acquired by a contract. When the buyer under the new law appears to take possession, the owner under the first law takes him before the courts of the Union to have his title declared void.[34] Thus in real terms, federal justice is tussling with the sovereignty of a state but attacks it only indirectly and upon the grounds of an application of detail. Thus it strikes at the consequences of the law, not its principles; it weakens but does not destroy it.

A last hypothesis remained.

Each state formed a corporation with a separate existence and civil rights; consequently, it could sue and be sued before the courts. One state could, for example, prosecute another state.

In such a case, the Union was no longer contesting a provincial law but judging a lawsuit in which one of the parties was a state. It was a lawsuit like any other; only the standing of the parties was different. In this instance, the danger highlighted at the beginning of this chapter still exists, with no chance of being avoided. Inherent in the very essence of federal constitutions will always be the creation within the bosom of the nation of bodies sufficiently powerful for justice to have difficulty in controlling them.

34. See Kent's *Commentaries*, vol. 1, p. 387.

HIGH STANDING OF THE SUPREME COURT
AMONG THE GREAT POWERS OF THE STATE

*No nation has established a more powerful judiciary than
the Americans—Extent of its powers—Its political
influence—Peace and the very existence of the Union
depend upon the wisdom of the seven federal judges.*

When, after scrutinizing the organization of the Supreme Court,
we come to consider the whole body of powers granted to it,
we easily discover that never has a more powerful judiciary been
established in any nation.

The Supreme Court's position is higher than any known court
both by the nature of its rights and by the categories subject to
its jurisdiction.

In all the civilized countries of Europe, the government has
always displayed a great reluctance to leave the ordinary judge
to settle questions which concerned itself. This reluctance is
naturally greater when the government is absolute. On the other
hand, as freedom increases, the prerogatives of the courts are
continually extended; but not a single European nation has yet
held that every legal question, whatever its origin, could be left
to judges of common law.

In America this theory has been put into practice. The
Supreme Court is the one and only national court, responsible
for the interpretation of laws and treaties. Questions of overseas
trade and all those relating to international rights reside within
its exclusive competence. One might even say that its prerogatives are almost entirely political even though its constitution is
wholly judicial. Its sole object is to see to the execution of the
laws of the Union, and the Union regulates only the relations
between the government and its subjects, and between the nation
and foreigners; relations between citizens themselves are almost
all regulated by the sovereignty of the states.

To this reason of primary importance we must add a still
greater. Among the European nations, courts see before them
only private individuals; but one might say that the Supreme
Court of the United States summons sovereign powers to its

bar. When the court usher, at the head of the steps of the court, pronounces these few words: "The state of New York versus the state of Ohio," one does not feel part of an ordinary court of justice. And when one realizes that one of these litigants represents a million people and the other two million, one is struck by the responsibility which must weigh upon the seven judges, whose decision will please or disappoint such a great number of their fellow citizens.

The peace, prosperity and very existence of the Union lie continually in the hands of the seven federal judges. Without them the constitution would be a dead letter; it is to them that the executive authority appeals against the encroachments of the legislature; the legislature, to defend itself against the assaults of the executive; the Union, to enforce obedience from the states; the states, to rebuff the impertinent onslaughts of the Union; public interest against private interest; the spirit of conservation against the destabilizing effects of democracy. Their power is immense but rests upon public opinion. They are all-powerful as long as the people agree to obey the law; they are powerless when the people have contempt for it. Now, of all powers, that of public opinion is the hardest to exploit because its limits are impossible to define with any precision. It is often just as dangerous to lag behind as it is to outpace it.

The federal judges must not only be upright citizens, learned men of integrity, and possess the qualities necessary for all magistrates, but they must also display statesmanship. They must be able to perceive the spirit of their age, to confront obstacles that need to be overcome, steer out of the current whenever the wave threatens to carry them away, and with them the sovereignty of the Union and the obedience to its laws.

The President may lose his footing without any damage to the state because his duties are limited. Congress may make errors without destroying the Union because above Congress stands the electoral body which is able to change its ethos by changing its members.

But if the Supreme Court ever happened to be composed of reckless or corrupt men, the confederation would have to dread anarchy or civil war.

However, let us not make any mistake; the original source of this danger lies not in the constitution of the court but in the very nature of federal governments. We have seen that nowhere is it more necessary for a strong judicial authority than in confederated nations, because nowhere else are there individual persons able to struggle against society who are greater and more capable of resisting the use of physical force by the government.

Now the more an authority has to be powerful, the more scope and independence it has to be given. The more scope and independence it has, the more dangerous is the possible abuse of its power. The origin of the abuse is not, therefore, in the constitution of this authority but in the very constitution of the state which makes the existence of such an authority necessary.

HOW THE FEDERAL CONSTITUTION IS SUPERIOR TO THAT OF THE STATES

How the Constitution of the Union can be compared to that of the individual states—The superiority of the Constitution of the Union must be attributed particularly to the wisdom of the federal legislators—The legislature of the Union less dependent upon the people than that of the states—The executive power freer in its sphere—The judicial power less subject to the will of the majority— Practical consequences of this—The federal legislators have lessened the dangers inherent in government by democracy; the legislators of the states have increased these dangers.

The federal constitution differs fundamentally from that of the states in its intended aims but it is much closer in the means of reaching those aims. The government's objective is different but the forms of government are the same. From this particular point of view it might be profitable to compare them.

I think that the federal constitution is superior to all the state constitutions and that superiority stems from several causes.

The present Constitution of the Union was drafted later than those of most of the states and thus could profit from all the experience acquired.

However, we shall be led to the conviction that this is but a subsidiary cause when we recollect that eleven new states have been added to the American confederation since the adoption of the federal constitution and that these have almost always exaggerated rather than diminished the weakness of earlier constitutions.

The major reason for the superiority of the federal constitution is the very character of the legislators.

At the time of the formation of the confederation, its ruin seemed imminent and was, so to speak, obvious for all to see. In such extreme circumstances the people chose, not perhaps men they loved most but those that they held in the highest esteem.

I have already observed that the legislators of the Union had almost all been remarkable for their intelligence and even more so for their patriotism.

They had all received their upbringing amid a crisis in society during which the spirit of liberty had been constantly locked in a struggle against a powerfully tyrannical authority. Once the struggle was over, these men called a halt even though, as is usual, the passions aroused in the crowd still persisted in their fight against dangers long since gone. They had taken a quieter and more penetrating look at their native land and had realized that a final revolution was over; henceforth, the perils which threatened the nation could arise only from abuses of liberty. They were courageous enough to speak their minds because they profoundly felt a sincere and warm affection for this very liberty; they dared to voice their desire to restrain it because they certainly did not wish to destroy it.[35]

35. At this time the famous Alexander Hamilton, one of the most influential draftsmen of the Constitution, was not afraid to publish the following in no. 71 of *The Federalist*: "There are some who would be inclined to regard the servile pliancy of the executive to a prevailing current, either in the community or in the legislature, as its best recommendation. But such men enterain very crude notions, as well of the purposes for which government was instituted as of the true means by which the public happiness may be promoted.

   The republican principle demands that the deliberate sense of the community should govern the conduct of those to whom they entrust the

Most of the state constitutions grant only a one year term to the mandate of the House of Representatives and two to the Senate. The result is that members of the legislature are permanently and closely tied to the slightest wishes of their constituents.

The Union legislators considered that this extreme dependence of the legislature distorted the main results of the representative system by placing in the people themselves not only the source of power but also the government itself.

They increased the term of the electoral mandate to allow the deputy a greater scope for the exercise of his own judgment.

Like the various state constitutions, the federal constitution divided the legislative body into two branches.

But in the states, these two parts of the legislature were composed of the same elements elected in the same manner. The result was that the passions and wishes of the majority came into the open with equal ease and found tools as readily available in both houses. All this gave a violent and precipitate character to the drafting of laws.

---

management of their affairs; but it does not require an unqualified complaisance to every sudden breeze of passion, or to every transient impulse which the people may receive from the arts of men, who flatter their prejudices to betray their interests.

It is a just observation that the people commonly *intend* the PUBLIC GOOD. This often applies to their very efforts. But their good sense would despise the adulator who should pretend that they [always] *reason right* about the *means* of promoting it. They know from experience that they sometimes err, and the wonder is that they so seldom err as they do, beset as they continually are by the wiles of parasites and sycophants; by the snares of the ambitious, the avaricious, the desperate, by the artifices of men who possess their confidence more than they deserve it, and of those who seek to possess rather than to deserve it.

When occasions present themselves in which the interests of the people are at variance with their inclinations, it is the duty of the persons whom they have appointed to be the guardians of those interests to withstand the temporary delusion in order to give them time and opportunity for more cool and sedate reflection. Instances might be cited in which a conduct of this kind has saved the people from very fatal consequences of their own mistakes, and has procured lasting monuments of their gratitude to the men who [had] courage and magnanimity enough to serve at the peril of their displeasure."

In the federal constitution, the two houses also depended upon the votes of the people but it varied the conditions of eligibility along with the method of election in order that if, as with certain nations, one of the two branches of the legislature did not represent interests different from the other, it should at least represent a superior wisdom.

A man had to reach a mature age to be chosen Senator and the assembly charged with his election was itself elected and of limited numbers.

Democracies are naturally inclined to concentrate all the power of society in the hands of the legislature; for this is the authority which stems most directly from the people and thus has the greater part of the people's all-embracing power. We notice that its usual tendency is therefore to unite every kind of authority into its own hands.

This concentration of powers, as well as damaging significantly the proper conduct of business, establishes the tyranny of the majority.

The state legislators have frequently yielded to these democratic instincts while the Union legislators always courageously resisted them.

In the states, the executive authority is vested in the hands of a magistrate who is apparently placed on a level with the legislature but who, in reality, is only a blind agent and passive tool of its will. From where might he draw his strength? From the term of his office? Generally he is appointed for only one year. From his powers? He has, so to speak, none. The legislature can reduce him to impotence by entrusting the execution of its laws to special commissions chosen from its own members. Were it to wish to do so, it could to some extent negate his powers by cutting off his salary.

The federal constitution has concentrated all the rights and responsibility of the executive power in a single individual. It has granted four years of office to the President and has guaranteed the enjoyment of his salary throughout his tenure of office; it has provided him with a body of officials and armed him with a suspensive veto. In short, after carefully defining the scope of executive power, it has sought to give him as strong and independent a position as possible within that sphere.

In the constitutions of the states, the judicial power has remained the least dependent of all the powers upon the legislature.

However, in all the states the legislature has retained its control over the fixing of judges' fees, a fact which of course subjects the latter to its immediate influence.

In certain states, judges have only a short-term appointment which, once more, deprives them of a great part of their power and freedom.

In other states, the legislative and judicial powers are wholly linked together. Thus the Senate of New York constitutes in certain lawsuits the upper tribunal of the state.

The federal constitution, on the other hand, has taken care to separate the judiciary from all the others. Moreover, it has made the judges independent by declaring their salary fixed and the office irrevocable.

The practical consequences of these differences are easy to discern. The business of the Union is, for any attentive observer, infinitely better managed than the business of any individual state.

The federal government is more equitable and temperate in its proceedings than that of the states. There is more wisdom in its outlook; its projects are planned further ahead and more skillfully; its measures are executed with more aptitude, consistency, and firmness.

A few words will suffice to sum up this chapter.

Two main dangers threaten the existence of democracies: namely, the entire subservience of the legislature to the will of the electorate and the concentration of all the other powers of government in the legislature.

The legislators of the states have encouraged the development of these dangers. Those of the Union have done their utmost to make them less of a threat.

WHAT DISTINGUISHES THE FEDERAL CONSTITUTION OF THE UNITED STATES FROM ALL OTHER FEDERAL CONSTITUTIONS

The American confederation appears similar to all others—However its effects are different—Reason for this—How this confederation is distinct from all the others—The American government is not a federal but an incomplete national government.

The United States of America does not represent the first and only example of a confederation. Leaving aside ancient history, modern Europe has provided several. Switzerland, the German Empire, the Dutch Republic have been or still remain confederations.

A study of the constitutions of these different countries allows us to observe with astonishment that the powers they confer on the federal government are more or less the same as the American Constitution confers upon the government of the United States. As with the latter, they grant to the central authority the right to make peace or war, to raise money or troops, to provide for the general needs, and to regulate the common interests of the nation.

However, among these different nations, the federal government has always remained weak and powerless, whereas that of the Union conducts its business with vigor and ease.

Furthermore, the first American Union was not able to survive because of the excessive weakness of its government, which had nevertheless been granted as extensive a series of rights as the present federal government. One might even say that in certain respects its privileges were greater.

There are therefore, in the present Constitution of the United States, a few new principles which exercise a profound influence, although they fail to strike us initially.

This constitution, which at first sight we are tempted to confuse with the federal constitutions preceding it, rests in fact upon an entirely new theory which may be hailed as a great discovery in modern political science.

In all the confederations previous to that of 1789 in America, the peoples who combined for a common purpose agreed to obey the injunctions of a federal government while retaining the right to direct and supervise the execution of the Union laws within their own territories.

The American states which united in 1789 agreed not only that the federal government dictated laws but also that it executed those laws itself.

In both cases, the right is the same, simply the application of it is different. But this single difference gives rise to momentous consequences.

In all the confederations preceding the present American Union, the federal government appealed to the individual governments to provide for its needs. Whenever one of the latter disliked the measure prescribed, it could always evade the necessity to comply. If strong enough, it had recourse to arms; if weak, it could tolerate resistance to the laws of the Union, though they were its own, by pretending it was helpless and by relying upon doing nothing.

Consequently one of two things has always happened: either the most powerful of the allied peoples has assumed the rights of the federal authority and dominated all the others in its name;[36] or the federal government has been left to its own resources, anarchy has reigned among the confederacy, and the Union has lost its powers to act.[37]

In America, the Union's subjects are single individuals, not states. When it wishes to levy a tax, it appeals not to the government of Massachusetts but to each of its citizens. The former federal governments presided over peoples but that of the Union over individuals. Its force is not borrowed but self-

---

36. This is what happened in Greece, under Philip, when that prince was responsible for executing the decrees of the Amphictyonic League. It is what happened in the Dutch Republic where the province of Holland has always made the law. The same thing is now taking place within the Germanic confederation. Austria and Prussia make themselves the agents of the Diet and dominate the whole confederation in its name.

37. It has always been like this in the Swiss confederation. Switzerland would have ceased to exist centuries ago were it not for the jealousies of her neighbors.

derived. It has its own administrators, courts, judicial officials, and army.

Doubtless the spirit of the nation, the passions of the masses and the provincial bias of every state still tend strangely to reduce the scope of federal power as it is laid down and to create pockets of resistance to its wishes. Because it has a restricted sovereignty, it cannot enjoy the same power as an authority with unlimited sovereignty. But that is an inherent defect of any federal system.

In America, each state has many fewer opportunities and temptations to offer resistance; if such a thought occurs, it can only put it into action by openly violating the laws of the Union, thwarting the usual course of justice, raising the flag of revolution; in a word, it has to adopt all of a sudden an extreme strategy and men hesitate long and hard before doing that.

In former confederations, the rights granted to the Union were sources of wars not power because they multiplied the nation's demands without increasing its means of exacting obedience. Thus we have almost always seen the actual weakness of federal governments increases in proportion to their nominal powers.

This is not the case in the American Union. Similarly to most ordinary governments, the federal government can do everything it has the right to do.

The invention of things comes more easily to the human mind than words, which accounts for the use of so many unsuitable terms and half-baked expressions.

When several nations form a permanent league and establish a supreme authority which, without acting directly upon single citizens as would be the case with a national government, nevertheless acts upon each one of the confederated peoples taken as a body, such a government is called federal even though different from all the others.

A form of society is then discovered in which several peoples are fused into one nation with regard to certain shared interests, while remaining as separate confederates for all else.

In such a case the central power acts without intermediary upon its subjects, administers and judges them itself, as do national governments, but acts in this manner only within strict limits. Clearly this is not a federal but an incomplete national government. Thus a form of government was found which was strictly neither national nor federal. Things have halted there but the new word needed to describe this new state of affairs does not yet exist.

It is because no Unions have understood this new style of confederation that they have come to civil war, enslavement, or inaction. The peoples who formed these leagues have all lacked the intelligence to perceive the remedy for their failures or the courage to apply such a remedy. The same defects were the downfall of the first American Union also.

But in America the confederated states, before gaining independence, had long been part of the same empire; therefore, they had not yet formed the habit of complete self-government and national prejudices had not yet put down deep roots. Being more enlightened than the rest of the world, they were all of equal intelligence and experienced only mildly those passions which normally make peoples oppose any extension of federal power. In addition, these passions were kept in check by the leading citizens. As soon as the Americans realized the failure, they firmly thought out the remedy. They adjusted their laws and saved their country.

ADVANTAGES OF THE FEDERAL SYSTEM IN GENERAL AND ITS SPECIAL USEFULNESS IN AMERICA

Happiness and freedom enjoyed by small nations—Power of great nations—Great empires favor advances in civilization—Force is often the first element in the prosperity of nations—The federal system has the aim of linking together the advantages of a large and a small territory—Advantages enjoyed by the United States from this system—The law adapts itself to the people's needs while the people do not adapt to the necessities of the law— Activity, progress, the love and habit of freedom among the American peoples—Public spirit in the Union is simply the aggregate of provincial patriotism—Things and ideas freely circulate throughout the United States—The Union is free and happy as a small nation and respected like a great one.

Among small nations, the eye of society sees everywhere; the spirit of improvement reaches the smallest details; national ambition is much affected by weakness; the efforts and the resources of the people turn almost entirely toward their inner prosperity and they are not prone to waste their labors upon the empty dreams of reputation. Moreover, each man's abilities being generally limited, his desires are equally so. The modest level of personal fortunes guarantees more or less equal conditions of life; social customs are simple and peaceful. Thus, all things considered, and noting the differing degrees of morality and education, one normally encounters more people in comfortable circumstances, a greater population and more contentment in small nations than in large.

When tyranny takes root in a small nation, it is more awkward than anywhere else because its influence spreads to everything within a circle which is much smaller in extent. Being unable to entertain any grand design, it concentrates upon a host of minute details. It displays both a violent and fretful character. It abandons the political domain which is properly its own to meddle in people's private lives. After actions, it aims to govern taste; after the state, it wishes to rule families. But that happens rarely because liberty represents in truth that natural condition of small societies in which government offers too few attractions to ambition and the resources of individuals are too limited for the sovereign power to be concentrated easily in the hands of one man. Should that happen, it is not difficult for citizens to combine in a common effort to dislodge both tyrant and tyranny.

Small nations have ever been, therefore, the cradle of political liberty. Most of them happen to have lost this liberty as they increased in size, which demonstrates that this was due to the small size of the population and not to the nation itself.

The history of the world affords no example of a great nation which has remained for a long time a republic.[38] This has suggested that such a thing was impracticable. My own opinion is that man, who daily has such a slender grasp of present reality and who realizes his constant astonishment at the unexpected in the most familiar things, should not set out to put limits on what is possible or to judge what is to come. What can be stated with certainty is that the existence of a great republic will always be much more vulnerable than that of a small one.

All the passions which threaten the life of republics spread with the increase of their territories, whereas the qualities which support them do not grow at the same rate.

The ambitions of individual citizens grow with the power of the state; the strength of parties increases with the importance of the ends they have in view; but the love of one's country which should withstand these destructive passions is no stronger in a large than in a small republic. It might even be easy to demonstrate that it is less developed and less powerful. Great wealth, abject poverty, big cities, lax morality, personal egotism, and the confusion of interests are dangers just as likely to arise from the size of states. Several of these features do not harm the existence of monarchies; some may even help them to last longer. Besides, monarchies have a government with autonomous strength; it uses the people without depending upon them. The bigger a nation, the stronger the prince; but a republican government has only the support of the majority to combat these destructive elements. Now the strength of this support is not proportionately more powerful in a big republic than in a small one. Thus, while the means of attack continues to increase in number and influence, the strength of the resistance remains constant. It may even be possible to say that it grows less because, as the population increases and the attitudes and interests become more diverse, it is consequently more difficult to form a unified majority.

We have also been able to observe that human passions gain

---

38. I am not speaking here of a confederation of small republics, but of a great consolidated republic.

intensity not only from the importance of the aim they have in view but also from the numbers of individuals who feel these emotions at one and the same time. Everybody has noticed that they are more stirred in the middle of an agitated crowd which shares their emotion than if they had been experiencing it by themselves. In a great republic, political passions become irresistible, not only because the aims they pursue are immense but also because millions feel them in the same way at the same time.

It is, therefore, permissible to say that in general terms nothing opposes the prosperity and freedom of men as much as great empires.

Great states enjoy advantages, however, which are peculiar to them and which have to be acknowledged.

Just as the desire for power in men of common stock is more intense in such states than elsewhere, so the love of reputation is more developed in certain souls who discover from the plaudits of a great nation an ambition worth their efforts and capable of raising them to some degree above their class. There, thought about everything receives swifter and more powerful support; ideas have a freer circulation; great cities resemble vast intellectual centers which radiate with the dazzling rays of the human mind. All this explains why great nations contribute more rapidly to knowledge and the general progress of civilization than do smaller ones. It must be added that important discoveries often require a concentration of national resources beyond the capacities of a small nation. In great nations the government has broader ideas and can free itself completely from the routine of precedent and from provincial self-centeredness. More genius shines from its designs, more boldness from its approach.

The inner wellbeing of small nations is more general and widespread provided they remain at peace; but a state of war harms them more than great nations whose distant frontiers may sometimes allow the mass of the people to remain clear of danger for centuries on end. For such people war is more a matter of discomfort than of ruin.

One consideration dominates all the rest in this matter as in many others, namely that of necessity.

If there were only small nations and no large ones, humanity would quite certainly be more happy and free but large nations cannot be avoided.

This introduces into the world physical strength as a new condition of national prosperity. How do comfort and freedom profit a nation, if it feels exposed every day to pillage and conquest? What good are its industries and trade, if another nation rules the seas and lays down the law in all the markets? Small nations are often wretched, not from their size but because they are weak; large nations prosper, not because of their size but because they are strong. Therefore, physical strength for nations is often one of the first conditions of happiness and even of existence. As a result of this, except in peculiar circumstances, small nations always end up by being united to great nations either by force or by joining voluntarily. I know of nothing more pathetic than the sight of a nation which can neither defend itself nor provide for itself.

The federal system was created in order to combine the several advantages which stem from the large or small size of nations. To observe all the benefits flowing from the adoption of this system, you only have to glance at the United States of America.

In great centralized nations, the legislator has to give to laws a uniform character which disregards the variations of place and customs. Since he has not studied individual cases, he can only proceed by general rules. So, men are obliged to bow before the needs of legislation, which is in no position to adapt itself to the needs and ways of man; and from this stems much trouble and wretchedness.

This obstacle does not exist in confederations: Congress regulates the main features of social behavior; all the details are delegated to provincial legislatures.

It would be difficult to imagine to what extent this separation of sovereignty contributes to the wellbeing of each of the states of the Union. In these small societies free from the cares of self-defense or territorial expansion, all public effort and individual energy are directed toward internal improvements. Since the central government of each state is placed alongside its citizens, it has daily notice of the needs that arise; so every year new plans are presented which, having been debated in the municipal assemblies or before the state legislature and published thereafter in the press, stimulate the interest and enthusiasm of all the citizens. This drive for improvement constantly stirs American republics without troubling them; there, ambition for power allows room for the love of prosperity which, though more vulgar, is less dangerous. An opinion with general currency in America holds that the existence and survival of republican types of government in the New World depend upon the existence and survival of the federal system. A great amount of wretchedness inundating the new states of South America is attributed to their desire to establish great republics there instead of breaking sovereignty up.

In fact, it is incontrovertible that in the United States the taste and support for republican government took root in the townships and at the heart of provincial assemblies. For instance, in a small state like Connecticut, where the cutting of a canal or the opening of a road represent great political business, where the state has neither army to pay nor war to support and where its rulers cannot be richly rewarded either financially or in terms of personal glory, it would be difficult to imagine anything more natural or befitting the nature of things than a republic. Now, this same republican spirit, these ways and customs of a free people, produced and developed in the various states, can then be applied quite easily to the nation as a whole. The public spirit of the Union is not itself anything other than a summing up of provincial patriotism. Each citizen of the United States transfers, as it were, the concern inspired in him by his little republic to the love of his shared homeland. By defending the Union, he is defending the growing prosperity of his district, the right to control its affairs, and the hope of establishing plans for improvement which are to bring him wealth; all those things, in fact, which in the normal run affect men more than the general concerns of the country and national glory.

Equally, if the spirit and customs of the inhabitants make them more fitted than others to bring prosperity to a great republic, the federal system has eased the task considerably. The confederation of the American states does not suffer from the

normal disadvantages found in large numbers of men. The Union is a great republic in area but to some degree it can be likened to a small republic because so few matters concern its government. Its acts are important but rare. Since the sovereignty of the Union is restricted and incomplete, its use is not at all dangerous to its freedom. Neither does it arouse that excessive craving for power and reputation so fatal to great republics. Since nothing needs to gather at a common center, there are neither great capital cities, nor inordinate wealth, nor extreme poverty, nor sudden revolutions. Political passions, instead of spreading instantly like wildfire over the whole country, crash against the individual concerns and passions of each state.

However, things and ideas enjoy a free circulation in the Union as with one and the same nation. Nothing stands in the way of the surging spirit of enterprise. Its government attracts men of talent and intelligence. Within the frontiers of the Union reigns a profound peace as within the heart of a nation ruled by a single government; outside its boundaries it ranks among the most powerful nations of the earth; two thousand miles of coastline are open to foreign trade; holding the keys to a whole world, its flag commands respect to the farthest seas.

The Union is as free and happy as a small nation, as glorious and strong as a great one.

WHY THE FEDERAL SYSTEM IS NOT WITHIN THE GRASP OF ALL NATIONS AND WHAT HAS ALLOWED THE ANGLO-AMERICANS TO ADOPT IT

In every federal system there are inherent defects beyond the powers of the legislator to overcome—Complexity of any federal system—It demands a daily exercise of intelligence from its citizens—The Americans' practical knowledge of government—Relative weakness of government of the Union, yet another defect of the federal system—The Americans have limited its seriousness without eliminating it—The sovereignty of individual states is apparently weaker but in reality stronger than that of the

*Union—Why—Apart from the laws, natural reasons for
unifying must exist among confederated people—What
these reasons are among Anglo-Americans—Maine and
Georgia, one thousand miles apart, are more naturally
united than Normandy and Brittany*—War is the main
danger for confederations—This is proved by the example
of the United States—The union has no great wars to
fear—Why—Dangers which the nations of Europe would
risk, if they adopted the American federal system.*

Occasionally the legislator succeeds, after a thousand efforts,
in having an indirect influence upon the fate of nations and
thereupon his genius is praised, whereas often the geographical
location of the country which he cannot alter, a state of society
created without his help, customs and ideas whose origins he
has no knowledge of, and a point of departure he does not
recognize, imprint on society an impetus of irresistible force
against which he struggles unsuccessfully and which sweeps him
along in his turn.

The legislator is like the man who steers his route upon the
ocean. He is able to guide the ship he is on but cannot change
its structure, create winds, or stop the ocean from heaving
beneath his feet.

I have demonstrated what advantages Americans derive from
the federal system. It remains for me to explain what allowed
them to adopt this system, for not all nations are granted its
advantages.

In the federal system we come across accidental defects which
stem from the laws; these can be corrected by the legislators.
Others, which are unavoidable in this system, cannot be eliminated by those nations adopting it. Therefore, such nations have
to find within themselves the strength needed to endure the
natural defects of their government.

Among the weaknesses inherent in all federal systems, the
most obvious of all is the complexity of the means it employs.
This system necessarily brings two sovereignties into confrontation. The legislator manages to make the operation of these
two sovereignties as simple and equal as possible and is able to

enclose both of them into their own carefully defined spheres of action. But he cannot meld them into one single entity or prevent their bumping into each other at some point.

The federal system rests therefore, whatever one does, upon a complicated theory which, in application, demands a daily exercise of rationality from its citizens.

In general, only simple ideas take hold of the minds of a people. A false yet clear and precise idea will always have more potency in society at large than a true but complex one. That is why parties, which are like small nations in the body of a large nation, are always swift to adopt as a symbol a name or principle which often only half represents the aim they have in mind and the means they are using but without which they could neither survive nor move. Those governments which rely upon only one single idea or upon one single easily definable feeling are perhaps not the best but undoubtedly they are the strongest and longest lasting.

However, on scrutinizing the Constitution of the United States, the most complete of all known federal constitutions, it is frightening to note how many differences of knowledge and discernment it assumes in those governed. The government of the Union rests almost entirely upon legal fictions. The Union is an idealized nation which exists, as it were, only in men's imagination and whose scope and limitations are revealed by understanding alone.

Once the general theory is well understood, the difficulties of applying it remain; these are countless because the sovereignty of the Union is so entwined in that of the states that it is impossible at first glance to see its limits. Everything in such a government is arbitrary and contrived and it can only suit a nation long accustomed to self-government and where political science reaches right down to the lowest rungs of society. Nothing has made me admire the good sense and practical intelligence of the Americans more than the way they evade the countless difficulties which derive from their federal constitution. I have scarcely ever encountered a single man of the common people in America who did not perceive with surprising ease the obligations entailed in the laws of Congress and those which owe their beginnings to the laws of his own state, nor who could not separate the matters belonging to the general prerogatives of the Union from those regulated by his local legislature and who could not point to where the competence of the federal courts begins and the limitation of the state tribunals ends.

The Constitution of the United States is akin to those fine creations of human endeavor which crown their inventors with renown and wealth but remain sterile in other hands.

Contemporary Mexico has illustrated this very thing.

The Mexicans, aiming for a federal system, took the federal constitution of their neighbors, the Anglo-Americans, as their model and copied it almost exactly.[39] But although they transported the letter of the law, they failed to transfer at the same time the spirit which gave it life. As a result, they became tangled endlessly in the machinery of their double system of government. The sovereignty of states and Union entered into a collision course as they exceeded the sphere of influence assigned to them by the constitution. Even today Mexico veers constantly from anarchy to military despotism and back again.

The second and most fatal of all the defects inherent in my opinion to the federal system itself is the relative weakness of the government of the Union.

The principle which upholds all the confederations is the fragmentation of sovereignty. Legislators may make this fragmentation less obvious, they may even conceal it for a short while from view but they cannot pretend that it does not exist. Now a fragmented sovereignty will always be weaker than one which is complete.

We have seen in the description of the Constitution of the United States the skillful way the Americans have both restricted the power of the Union within the tight sphere of federal governments and have succeeded in giving it the appearance and to some degree the force of a national government. By this means the legislators of the Union have reduced the normal danger of confederations without being able to eliminate it entirely.

The American government, so it is said, does not address itself

39. See the Mexico Constitution of 1824.

to the states but transmits its injunctions directly to its citizens and forces them individually to comply with the common will.

But were the federal law to clash violently with the interests and prejudices of a state, are there not reasons to fear that every single citizen of that state would consider himself involved in the cause of any man refusing to obey it? Since all citizens might feel damaged in the same way and at the same time by the authority of the Union, the federal government would be wasting its time if it were to fight them by attempting to isolate them all. They would instinctively realize that they had to unite to defend themselves and would discover an organization already prepared for that purpose in that area of sovereignty which their state was allowed to enjoy. Fiction would then give way to reality and one would be able to observe the power of one part of the country in an organized conflict with the central authority.

I would say as much for federal justice. If, in an individual trial, the Union courts violated an important state law, the conflict, in reality, whether or not in appearance, would be between the damaged state represented by one citizen and the Union represented by its courts.[40]

One would have to be very inexperienced in the ways of the world to think that man's passions, once given a means of obtaining satisfaction, could ever be prevented by legal fictions from seeing and exploiting such means.

American legislators have not destroyed the causes of conflict between these two sovereignties by reducing the likelihood of such a conflict.

It is even possible to go further and state that, in the event of

40. Example: the constitution has given the Union power to sell unoccupied land for its own profit. Suppose that Ohio claims the same right over lands within its territory, on the pretext that the Constitution refers only to lands which do not come under the jurisdiction of any particular state, and consequently wishes to sell them itself. It is true that the question at issue in the courts would be between purchasers holding their title from the Union and those holding theirs from the state, and not between the Union and Ohio. But what would become of this legal fiction, if the courts of the United States ordered the federal purchaser to be put in possession, while the courts of Ohio supported his rival's claim to the land?

such a conflict, they have failed to guarantee a power advantage to the federal government.

They have given money and soldiers to the Union but the states retained the affections and prejudices of the people.

The sovereignty of the Union is an abstract entity connected to a small number of external objects. The sovereignty of the states strikes every sense; it is easily understood and is seen constantly in action. The former is recent; the latter was born with the people themselves.

The sovereignty of the Union is a work of art. The sovereignty of the states is natural, autonomous, effortless like a father's control over his family.

The sovereignty of the Union affects men only where a few major interests are concerned; it represents an immense and distant country and a vague, ill-defined sentiment. The sovereignty of the states enfolds every citizen to some extent and affects every detail of daily life; it is responsible for protection of property, freedom, and life; it has a constant influence on his wellbeing or the opposite. The sovereignty of the states relies on memory, habits, local prejudices, the self-interest of district and family, on everything, to sum up, which promotes that powerful inner feeling of patriotism in men's hearts. How can one question its advantages?

Since legislators are unable to avoid dangerous collisions between the two sovereignties which the federal system brings face to face, their efforts to divert confederated peoples from war must be supplemented with special arrangements for promoting peace.

It results from this that the federal agreement cannot last long unless, in the peoples to which it applies, certain conditions of union guarantee a measure of comfort in their common life as well as smoothing out the task of government.

Thus the federal system not only needs sound laws to achieve success but also favorable circumstances.

All those nations which have joined in a confederation have shared a certain number of interests which created the intellectual ties of association.

But apart from material concerns, men have also ideas and

feelings. To ensure the long life of a confederation, a uniformity of civilization is no less necessary than a uniformity of needs in the diverse peoples forming it. The difference between the canton of Vaud and that of Uri[f] resembles the difference between the nineteenth and fifteenth centuries because Switzerland has never truly had a federal government. The union of the different cantons exists only on a map and you would clearly see this once a central authority attempted to prescribe the same laws throughout the whole territory.

In the United States, one fact which admirably supports the existence of the federal government is that the different states have roughly similar interests, common origins and language as well as the same level of civilization, all of which almost always produce an easy mutual agreement. I do not know of any European nation, however small, that presents more homogeneity in its different parts than the American nation whose size is half the area of Europe.

From the state of Maine to that of Georgia is a distance of some one thousand miles. However, there is less difference between the civilization of Maine and that of Georgia than between that of Normandy and that of Brittany. Consequently, Maine and Georgia, at the distant ends of a vast empire, have by nature more real opportunities to forge a confederation than Normandy and Brittany, separated by only a stream.

The geographical position of the country added further opportunities to the American legislators to those derived from the customs and practices of the people. The adoption and maintenance of the federal system must be attributed mainly to these factors.

The most significant of all the events which mark the life of a nation is the act of war when a people struggles against foreign countries like a single individual. It fights for its very existence.

As long as the only concern of a nation is to maintain internal order and to increase its prosperity, then skill in government, good sense in its citizens, and a certain natural affection men almost always feel for their homeland can easily be enough to achieve these things. However, for a nation to be in a position to wage a great war, its citizens must endure many painful sacrifices. To suppose a large number of men capable of submitting themselves to such social deprivations is to have a poor grasp of human nature.

Consequently, all nations which have had to wage mighty wars have been forced, almost despite themselves, to increase the powers of their government. Those unsuccessful in this have been conquered. A lengthy war almost always confronts nations with this sad choice: either defeat involves destruction or victory brings tyranny. It is, therefore, generally during a war that we see the most obvious and dangerous signs of a government's weakness; I have demonstrated that the inherent defect of federal governments was to be very weak.

In the federal system, not only is there no administrative centralization nor anything approaching it, but even governmental centralization is incomplete. This is always a great source of weakness when it comes to defending oneself against nations controlled by a completely centralized system.

In the federal constitution of the United States where the central government especially is invested with more real power than any other, this defect is still sharply felt.

A single example will allow the reader to judge.

The constitution grants Congress the right to call up the militia of the different states to active service whenever it is a question of suppressing an insurrection or repelling an invasion; another article states that, under such conditions, the President becomes the commander-in-chief of the militia.

In the war of 1812,[g] the President issued the order to the Northern militias to move toward the frontiers; Connecticut and Massachusetts, whose interests were harmed by the war, refused to send their contingents.

The constitution, they declared, gives the federal government authority to use militias in time of *insurrection* and *invasion* but at that time there was neither. They added that the same constitution which granted the Union the right of calling up militias for active service reserved to the states the right of appointing officers. It followed, in their view, that, even in time of war, no officer of the Union had the right to command the militias except the President in person. But this was a case of serving in an army commanded by some other person.

These absurd and pernicious doctrines were supported not only by the governors and the legislature but also by the courts of these two states; the federal government had to seek elsewhere those troops it lacked.[41]

How does it come about that the American Union, protected as it is by the comparative perfection of its laws, does not collapse in the middle of a great war? It is simply that it has no great wars to fear.

Situated at the center of a huge continent in which human industry can enjoy limitless expansion, the Union is almost as isolated from the world as if it were surrounded on all sides by the ocean.

Canada has only a million inhabitants and is divided into two hostile nations. The severity of its climate restricts the extension of its territory and keeps its harbors closed for six months of the year.

From Canada to the Gulf of Mexico some half-destroyed savage tribes retreat before the advance of six thousand soldiers.

To the south, the Union has one point of contact with the Mexican Empire, where one day serious wars may well develop. But for a long time to come the backward state of civilization, the degeneration of its morals, and its extreme poverty will stand in the way of any hope of achieving high status among nations. As for the European powers, distance reduces any threat they represent. (See Appendix O, p. 847.)

The great good fortune of the United States is not, therefore,

---

41. Kent's *Commentaries*, vol. 1, p. 244. Note that I have chosen this example cited above from a date after the establishment of the existing Constitution. Had I chosen to go back to the time of the first confederation, I would have quoted even more conclusive facts. Then real enthusiasm prevailed in the nation; the Revolution was led by an eminently popular man, but, nevertheless, at that time, Congress had, strictly speaking, no resources at its disposal. It lacked both men and money the whole time; the best laid plans failed in execution, and the Union, always on the verge of ruin, was saved much more by the weakness of its enemies than by its own strength.

to have created a federal constitution which allows them to withstand serious wars but to profit from such a geographical position that they have none to fear.

No one can appreciate more than myself the advantages of the federal system which I hold to be one of the most powerful devices to promote human prosperity and freedom. I envy the lot of nations which have been allowed to adopt it. But I am reluctant to believe that confederated nations could fight for a long time on equal footing against a nation with a centralized government.

The nation which, faced by the great military monarchies of Europe, divided its sovereignty, would appear, in my opinion, to be forsaking by this very act its power and possibly its life and reputation.

What an admirable position the New World enjoys that man has yet no other enemies than himself. To be happy and free, he has only to will it so.

PART 2

So far I have examined the institutions, perused the written laws, and described the present-day form of the political society of the United States.

Yet above all the institutions and beyond all the forms, there exists the sovereign power of the people which destroys or modifies them at will.

It remains for me to show along which paths this power which regulates the laws proceeds; what inner feelings and passions it possesses; what hidden springs drive it on or hold it back or direct its irresistible progress; what are the results of its unbounded force; and what destiny lies in store for it.

CHAPTER I

WHY IT CAN BE FIRMLY STATED THAT IN THE UNITED STATES IT IS THE PEOPLE WHO GOVERN

In America the people appoint the lawmakers and the executive; they form the jury which punishes breaches of the law. Not only are institutions democratic in principle but also in their consequences; thus the people *directly* nominate their representatives and, as a general rule, choose them *annually* so as to hold them more completely dependent. Therefore, in reality it is the people who rule. Although they have a representative government, it is quite clear that the opinions, bias, concerns,

and even the passions of the people can encounter no lasting
obstacles preventing them from exercising a day-to-day influence upon the conduct of society.

In the United States, as in any country ruled by the people,
the majority governs in the name of the people.

The majority is chiefly made up of peaceable citizens who,
out of inclination or self-interest, sincerely seek the good of the
country. They are surrounded by the constant agitation of those
parties which attempt to draw them in and enlist their support.

CHAPTER 2

PARTIES IN THE UNITED STATES

*An important distinction to be made between parties—
Parties which behave to each other like rival nations—
Parties properly so-called—Difference between large and
small parties—Their origins—Their diverse
characteristics—America has had great parties—It no
longer has any—Federalists[a]—Republicans[b]—Defeat of the
Federalists—Difficulty of forming parties in the United
States—How they manage to do so—Aristocratic or
democratic features found in all parties—Struggle of
General Jackson[c] against the bank.*

I should first establish an important division between parties.

Some countries are so large that the different populations
living there have conflicting interests although they unite under
the same sovereign government. This produces a perpetual state
of opposition. The several sections of the nation therefore constitute, strictly speaking, distinct nations rather than political parties and, if civil war were to break out, the conflict is between
rival nations rather than a struggle between sections of the
community.

But whenever citizens have conflicting opinions on issues
which interest all areas of the country alike, such as, for instance,

the general principles of government, then you will see the appearance of what I may correctly term parties.

Parties are a fundamental defect of free governments but they do not at all times share the same character or the same instincts.

At certain periods, nations may feel oppressed by such intolerable evils that the idea of totally altering their political constitution comes into their minds. At other periods the disease is deeper still and the whole social fabric itself is endangered. Such is a period of widespread revolution and of great parties.

Between the centuries of misery and disorder there are others when societies come to rest and the human race seems to draw breath. In actual fact, such times are more apparent than real. Time does not arrest its course for nations any more than for men; both move forward daily toward an unknown future. When we think things are stationary, it is because we fail to see their movements. Men who move at a walking pace appear stationary to those who are running.

However that may be, some periods occur when the changes taking place in the political constitution and the social structure of nations appear so slow and imperceptible that men think they have reached a final state. The human mind, believing itself to be firmly based upon sure foundations, does not seek to look beyond its set horizon.

This is a time of intrigues and small parties.

What I term great political parties are those committed to principles rather than their consequences, to general considerations rather than to individual cases, to ideas and not to men. These parties generally have more noble characteristics, more generous enthusiasms, more genuine convictions, a more open and bold approach than the others. In such parties, private interest, which always plays the most significant part in political passions, is concealed more skillfully beneath the veil of public interest. It sometimes manages to remain unobserved by those very people it inspires into action.

On the other hand, small parties generally lack any political credo. Since they do not feel elevated or sustained by lofty purposes, their character is imbued with a selfishness which obviously colors each of their actions. They always flare up without warning; their language is violent, but their progress is timid and over-cautious. The means they employ are as despicable as the very aim they have in view. That is why, when a violent revolution gives way to a time of calm, great men appear to vanish suddenly and minds withdraw into themselves.

Great parties overturn society; small ones agitate it; some tear it apart, others corrupt it; the former sometimes rescue it by shaking it to its core, the latter disturb it, invariably to no purpose.

America has today lost the great parties it once had; it has gained, as a consequence, much happiness but lost much moral purpose.

When the War of Independence came to an end and the foundations of the new government had to be established, the nation was divided between two opinions. These opinions were as old as the world and all free societies display them under different names and forms. The first aimed to restrict popular power, the second to extend it indefinitely.

Among Americans, the conflict between these two opinions never assumed that violent character which has often marked it elsewhere. In America, the two parties were in agreement on the most essential points. Neither of them had to destroy a former constitution nor to overturn an entire social order so as to triumph. As a consequence, neither of them affected the existence of a great number of individuals in asserting its principles. But they did entertain abstract ideals of the greatest importance such as their love of equality and independence, which were sufficient to rouse violent passions.

The party wishing to restrict popular power sought above all to apply its doctrines to the Constitution of the Union which earned it the name *federal*.

The other party, claiming to be the exclusive champion of liberty, took the title *republican*.

America is the land of democracy. Federalists were therefore always in the minority but they numbered in their ranks almost all the great men produced by the War of Independence. Their moral impact was far-reaching. Circumstances were also favorable to their cause. The ruin of the first confederation persuaded the people to dread anarchy and the Federalists made the most of this passing attitude. For ten or twelve years, they controlled affairs and succeeded in applying some, though not all, of their principles, for the current of opposition was daily growing too strong for them to fight against it.

In 1801, the Republicans finally took the reins of government. Thomas Jefferson was elected President and brought them the support of a famous name, a great talent, and his tremendous popularity.

The Federalists had only ever maintained their position through artificial means and with the aid of temporary resources; they had risen to power because of the virtues and talents of their leaders combined with fortunate circumstances. When the Republicans took their turn in government, the opposing party was as if swept away in the sudden flood. An overwhelming majority voted against it and it suddenly saw itself in such a small minority, that it fell into utter despair. Thereafter, the Republican or the Democratic party has marched from victory to victory, acquiring power right across society.

The Federalists, after the experience of defeat and seeing themselves without resources and isolated within the nation, split into groups. Some joined the victorious party; others lowered their flag and altered their name. For many years now they have entirely ceased to exist as a party.

The accession of the Federalists to power was, in my opinion, one of the most fortunate events to have accompanied the birth of the great American Union. The Federalists were struggling against the inevitable tendency of their age and country. Whatever the virtues or defects of their theories, they suffered the weakness of being inappropriate to the society they wished to rule. What happened under Jefferson would have happened sooner or later. But their government at least allowed the new republic time to settle and to foster without hindrance the swift development of those very doctrines they had opposed. Moreover, in the end a great number of their principles became incorporated in the political trappings of their opponents and the federal constitution which still exists today is a lasting monument to their patriotism and wisdom.

Thus, at the present time, no great political parties are to be seen in the United States. One comes across many parties which threaten the future of the Union but none appears to attack the present form of government nor the general progress of society. The parties threatening the Union rely not on principles but on material interests which represent, in the different provinces of such a vast empire, not so much parties as rival nations. Thus, we have recently seen the North supporting a system of commercial tariffs and the South taking up arms in favor of free trade simply because the North is an industrial zone and the South an agricultural one and that the system of restrictions profits the former and damages the latter.

Lacking large parties, the United States abounds in small ones and public opinion splinters endlessly on questions of detail. It is difficult to imagine the pains taken to create parties; it is no easy matter at the present time. In the United States no religious hatred exists because religion is universally respected and no individual sect is predominant. There is no class hatred because the nation is everything and no one dares to contest its authority. There is no public distress to exploit because the physical position of the country offers such a wide scope for industry that it is enough to leave a man to his own initiative to produce marvels. However ambitious, men have to move toward creating parties for it is difficult to topple the person with the power simply because you would wish to take his place. The skill of politicians lies therefore in the art of creating parties. A politician in the United States first seeks to work out his own interest by trying to discern those interests which are similar to his and could be linked to his own. He then contrives to discover whether by chance there might be somewhere in the world a doctrine or principle which could suit the purposes of this new association, allowing it the right to promote its own interests and giving it a wide circulation. It is very like the printing of the royal seal of approval on the title page of works published by our ancestors which, although included in the book, was no real part of it. Once all that is accomplished, the new political force is ushered on to the political stage.

For an outsider, almost all the domestic disputes of America appear at first sight incomprehensible or childish and one does not know whether to pity a nation so seriously concerned with such trifling issues or to envy the happiness it has of being able to discuss such things.

But when one happens to pay careful attention to the inner feelings which control groups in America, it is easy to discover that most of these groups are connected to one or other of the two great parties which have divided men from the onset of free societies. Gradually, as one investigates more deeply the innermost thoughts of these parties, some are seen to be pursuing the restriction of public power, others to widen it.

I am not saying that American parties always aim either overtly or covertly for the predominance of aristocracy or democracy in their country; I am saying that aristocratic or democratic passions can easily be found at the heart of all parties. Although not obvious to the gaze, they are virtually the main issue and the very soul of parties.

I shall quote a recent example: the President attacked the Bank;[d] the country was roused and formed parties; the educated classes generally rallied round the Bank, the common people round the President. Do you think that the common people could distinguish the reasons for their opinion amid the ins and outs of such a difficult issue which caused experienced men to hesitate? Not at all.

But the Bank is an important institution with an independent existence; the common people who make or break all authorities were surprised that they could do nothing in this case. Amid the fluctuation of all the rest of society, this immovable object offended the people's eye so that they wished to see whether they could successfully shake it as they do everything else.

REMAINS OF THE ARISTOCRATIC PARTY IN THE UNITED STATES

Secret opposition of the wealthy to democracy—They withdraw into private life—The taste they display for exclusive pleasures and luxury in the confines of their own homes—Their outward simplicity—Their affected condescension toward the people.

Sometimes, in a nation where opinions are divided, the balance between parties happens to break down and one of them acquires an irresistible advantage. It smashes all obstacles, overwhelms its opponents and exploits the whole of society for its own benefit. Then the losing party abandons all hope of success, goes into hiding or keeps quiet. All around is stillness and silence. The nation appears united in one thought. The victorious party stands up to say, "I have brought peace to this land and deserve to be thanked."

But beneath this apparent unanimity deep divisions and real opposition still lie hidden.

That is what happened in America. When the Democratic party had acquired the advantage, it was seen to have taken exclusive control of affairs. Since then, it has never ceased to mold customs and laws to its own desires.

Nowadays, one can say that the wealthy classes of United States society stand entirely outside politics and that wealth, far from being an advantage, has become a real source of unpopularity and an obstacle to the achievement of power.

The wealthy thus prefer to abandon the contest rather than tolerate the often unequal struggle against the poorest of their fellow citizens. Since they are unable to occupy a position in public life similar to the one they enjoy in their private life, they renounce the former to concentrate upon the latter. They represent a private society at the heart of the state with its own tastes and pleasures.

The wealthy man bows to this state of affairs as an evil beyond remedy. He even takes great care to conceal that he is hurt by this; he is heard in public praising the blessings of republican government and the advantages of democratic institutions. For what is more natural for men, next to hating their enemies, than to praise them?

Just look at this opulent citizen. Wouldn't you say he is like a medieval Jew who dreads that his wealth might be discovered? His clothes are simple and his demeanor is modest. Within the four walls of his house he adores luxury; he allows only a few chosen guests, whom he insolently calls his equals, to penetrate this sanctuary. No European aristocrat shows himself more exclusive in his pleasures, more jealous of the slightest advantages of his privileged position than he is. Yet here he emerges from home to make his way to work in a dusty den in the center of a busy town where everyone is free to accost him. On his way, his shoemaker might pass by and they stop; both then begin to chat. What can they say? These two citizens are concerned with affairs of state and will not part without shaking hands.

But beneath this conventional enthusiasm and amid this ingratiating ritual toward the dominant power, you can easily perceive in the wealthy a deep distaste for the democratic institutions of their country. The people are a power they both fear and despise. If one day the bad government of democracy prompted a political crisis, if ever monarchy appeared as a practical possibility, the truth of what I am putting forward would soon become patently obvious.

The two chief weapons employed by parties to ensure success are newspapers and associations.

CHAPTER 3

THE FREEDOM OF THE PRESS IN THE UNITED STATES

Difficulty of restricting the freedom of the press—Special reasons certain nations have for holding on to this freedom—The freedom of the press is a necessary consequence of the sovereignty of the people as understood in America—Violent language of the periodical press in the United States—The periodical press has instincts peculiar to itself; the example of the United States proves this to be so—America's opinion of judicial repression of offenses by the press—Why the press is less powerful in the United States than in France.

The freedom of the press makes its influence felt not only upon political opinions but also on all men's opinions. It modifies customs as well as laws. In another part of this work, I shall attempt to estimate the extent of the influence of freedom of the press on civil society in the United States. I shall try to point out the direction it has given to ideas as well as the habits it has inculcated in the minds and attitudes of Americans. But at present I intend to examine only the effects produced by press freedom in the political domain.

I confess that I do not accord to press freedom that entire and instantaneous affection which one grants to things which are supremely good by their very nature. My affection for it stems from my regard for the evils it prevents rather than for the benefits it produces.

Were anyone to show me an intermediate position which I could hope to take up between complete independence or entire enslavement of thought, I should perhaps adopt that position. But who will discover that intermediate position? Starting from unrestricted freedom of the press you aim to establish some order; what do you do? First you try the writers by jury; but if the juries acquit them, what was one single man's opinion becomes the opinion of the whole country. Thus you have tried too much and too little has been achieved and you must proceed further. You hand the authors over to permanent magistrates; however, the judges are obliged to hear the evidence before they can condemn. What people were terrified to confess in book form was blazoned forth in the plea for the defense; an obscure reference in one account is thus repeated in a thousand others. The written words are the external form and, if I can put it in this way, the body of the thought but not the thought itself. Tribunals arrest the body but the spirit eludes them and slips between their fingers. Thus you have tried too much and achieved too little and must continue to proceed. Finally, you hand over the writers to the censors; fine! We are getting close. But are not the political hustings free? Therefore you still have achieved nothing; no, I am wrong, you have increased the damage. Would you, perhaps, consider thought to be one of those physical forces which increase with the number of agents? Do you reckon writers are like soldiers in an army? The power of thought, in direct contrast to all physical forces, often increases with the very small numbers of those expressing it. The word of a powerful man which by itself reaches the passions of a silent gathering, has more strength than the muddled shouts of a thousand speakers. Free speech in one single public place becomes virtually a public utterance in every village in the land. Therefore you must destroy freedom of speech along with freedom to write; this time you are home and dry; everyone is reduced to silence. But what point have you reached? You had set out to repress the abuses of freedom and I discover you beneath the boots of a tyrant.

You have gone from extreme independence to extreme servitude without encountering a single place to rest on that long journey.

There are nations which, apart from the general motives I have just stated, have special reasons for their commitment to freedom of the press.

In certain nations who claim to be free, any of the agents of government may violate the laws with impunity and the constitution of the country gives no power of judicial redress to the victims. In such nations the independence of the press must not be considered one of the guarantees but the only guarantee remaining for the freedom and safety of their citizens.

Thus, if the governors of such nations spoke of removing independence from the press, the whole nation could reply: "Allow us to prosecute your crimes before the ordinary courts and perhaps then we will agree not to appeal to the tribunal of public opinion."

In a country where the doctrine of the sovereignty of the people obviously holds sway, censorship is not simply a danger; even more than that, it is an enormous absurdity.

Whenever each citizen is granted the right to govern society, recognition has to be given to his capacity to choose between the different viewpoints which trouble his fellow citizens and to appreciate the different facts which may guide his judgment.

The sovereignty of the people and the freedom of the press are, therefore, two entirely related concepts, whereas censorship and universal suffrage are in contradiction and cannot for long coexist in the political institutions of the same nation. Among the twelve million people living in the territory of the United States, not *one single person* has yet dared to suggest any restrictions on press freedom.

The first newspaper I saw on arriving in the United States contained the following article, which I translate faithfully:

> In this whole affair the language used by Jackson (the President) was that of a heartless despot, concerned only to preserve his own power. Ambition is his crime and it will be his punishment, too. Intrigue is his vocation; that will be the downfall of his plans and will deprive him of his power. He governs by corruption and his guilty maneuvers will result in his shame and confusion. He has acted in the political arena like a shameless and unbridled gambler. He has had some success but the hour of his reckoning draws near. Soon he will have to return his winnings, throw his false dice away and end up in some backwater where he can freely curse his stupidity. For repentance is not a virtue with which his heart has ever been acquainted. (Vincenne's *Gazette*)

Many people in France suppose that the violence of our press is due to the unstable state of our society, to our political passions and to the general feeling of uneasiness which is the consequence of that. Thus they endlessly await a time when society recovers its equilibrium and the press in its turn becomes calm. For my part, I am inclined to attribute its extraordinary ascendancy over us to the causes mentioned above; but I do not think that these causes have had much influence on the language it has used. The periodical press seems to have its own particular instincts and passions, independent of the circumstances in which it operates. What happens in America has wholly proved that to me.

At this time, America is possibly the country which harbors the fewest seeds of revolution in the world. In America, however, the press has the same destructive inclinations as in France and the same violence but lacks the same reasons for anger. In America, as in France, the press has the same extraordinary power, such a strange mixture of good and evil that, without its presence, freedom could not thrive and with its presence good order could hardly survive.

What needs saying is that the press has much less power in the United States than in France. Yet, nothing is rarer in this country than a legal prosecution against it. The reason for this is simple: the Americans, by accepting the doctrine of the sovereignty of the people, have applied it sincerely. They did not intend founding, from ingredients which change daily, a long-lasting constitution. Attacking existing laws is, therefore, not criminal provided that one has no intention of violently removing their power.

Besides, they believe that the courts are powerless to moderate the press, that the flexibility of human language perpetually eludes legal analysis and that such offenses somehow slip through the hands about to grasp them. They think that, in order to be able to act effectively against the press, one would need to find a court which was not only devoted to the existing order but which also could stand above the ferment of public opinion around it; a court which might judge without allowing publicity, pronounce its decrees without justifying them and punish the underlying intention more than the actual words.

Whoever had the power to establish and maintain such a court would waste his time prosecuting press freedom for he would then be absolute master of society itself and would be able to rid himself of the writers along with their writings. So where the press is concerned, no middle way exists between servitude and license. In order to enjoy the priceless advantages guaranteed by press freedom, one must submit to the unavoidable evils it produces. The wish to achieve the former while escaping the latter means submission to one of those illusions which normally sick nations use to soothe themselves when, tired of struggling and exhausted by their efforts, they seek the means of combining hostile opinions and opposing principles at the same time, in the same land.

The weakness of American newspapers is due to several causes, of which these are the chief:

The freedom to write, like any other freedom, is all the more formidable the newer it is, for a nation which has never heard state affairs discussed in its presence places its trust in the first tribune who comes forward. Among Anglo-Americans this freedom is as old as the foundation of the colonies; moreover, the press which can kindle human passions so effectively cannot yet create them all on its own. Now American political life is energetic, varied, even agitated, but rarely disturbed by deep passions which are not commonly aroused unless material interests are attacked. In the United States, these interests prosper. A glance at our newspapers and theirs is sufficient to show the difference between the Anglo-Americans and the French in this matter. In France, the trade advertisements take up a very limited space; the news items themselves are few; the essential part of a newspaper is that devoted to political discussion. In America, three-quarters of the bulky newspaper set before the reader's eyes is filled with advertisements; the rest is most frequently full of political news or just anecdotes. Only occasionally and in some obscure corner will you spot one of those burning discussions which are the daily nourishment of French readers.

The effective force of any power is increased in direct proportion to the centralization of its control. That is a general law of nature confirmed by observation and always known instinctively by even tin-pot despots.

The French press combines two distinct types of centralization.

Almost all its power is concentrated in the same place and, so to speak, in the same hands, for its outlets are few in number.

Thus the power of the press should be almost boundless, constituted as it is in a skeptical nation. It represents an enemy with which a government may conclude a truce of more or less long duration but which, in the long term, it resists with difficulty.

Neither of the types of centralization I have just mentioned exists in America.

The United States has no capital; both intelligence and power are spread throughout every part of this vast country; the rays of human ability do not radiate from one central point but cross each other in every direction. Americans have not situated the general regulation of thought in any particular place any more than the conduct of business.

All this depends upon local conditions which are not influenced by man. This, however, is how laws affect matters: in the United States there are no licenses for printers, no stamps or registration for newspapers and the system of guarantees is unknown.

The setting up of a newspaper is consequently an easy and simple enterprise; only a few subscribers are needed for an editor to cover his expenses. Therefore, the number of periodicals and occasional publications in the United States exceeds all belief. The most enlightened of Americans attribute the modest power of the press to this astonishing dispersal; it is an axiom of political science in the United States that the only means of neutralizing the effect of newspapers is to multiply their numbers. I cannot imagine why such a self-evident truth should not have become more commonly held in Europe. I have no difficulty in understanding that men who plan revolutions with the help of the press should attempt to confine its action to a few powerful outlets. On the other hand, I cannot remotely conceive why the official supporters of the establishment and the traditional upholders of existing laws should believe that they can weaken the activity of the press by concentrating it. European governments seem to act in relation to the press in a manner similar to the reaction of knights to their adversaries in times gone by. Their own practice has led them to observe that centralization was a powerful weapon and they wish to provide their enemies with the same central power so as to enhance their reputation in resisting their attacks.

In the United States, scarcely a hamlet lacks its newspaper. You can easily imagine that, among so many antagonists, neither discipline nor unified action is likely; each paper, therefore, fights beneath its own banner. Not that all political newspapers in the Union are lined up for or against the administration but they employ a hundred different means to attack or defend it. In the United States, therefore, newspapers are unable to form those great waves of opinion which undermine or sweep over the most powerful of barriers. This division of the influences of the press also produces other effects no less startling. Since a newspaper can be founded quite easily, everyone can take to it; alternatively competition reduces any hope of great profits, which dissuades the most able of industrialists from involvement in such enterprises. Moreover, even though newspapers could be a source of wealth, their excessive numbers prevent enough talented writers coming forward to edit them all.

So, generally, journalists in the United States have a lowly status, their education is rudimentary and the expression of their ideas is frequently coarse. Now in everything the majority holds sway; it lays down certain styles to which each person then conforms. The sum total of these shared customs is called their spirit: there is a spirit of the courts, the spirit of royalty. The spirit of the journalist in France is to discuss the great concerns of state in a manner which is violent but frequently dignified and eloquent; that may not always be so but there are always exceptions to the rule. The spirit of the journalist in America consists in a crude, unvarnished, and unsubtle attack on the passions of his readers; he leaves principles aside to seize hold of men whom he pursues into their private lives exposing their weaknesses and defects.

Such an abuse of the powers of thought has to be deplored. Later, I shall have the chance of analyzing the influence of newspapers upon the tastes and morality of the American people. But, to repeat myself, at this moment I am concerned with the world of politics alone. One cannot close one's eyes to the truth that the political effects of this press license contribute indirectly to the maintenance of public order. Consequently, those men already enjoying a superior status in the opinions of their fellow citizens dare not write in newspapers and thus lose the most formidable weapon at their disposal to stir popular passions for their own ends.[1] Above all, the result is that the personal opinions of journalists carry virtually no weight in readers' eyes. What the latter look for in newspapers is know-

1.   They write in the papers only on those rare occasions when they want to address the people and speak in their own name: when, for example, slanderous imputations have been spread around against them and they wish to re-establish the true facts.

ledge of facts; only by altering or distorting these facts can a journalist gain some influence for his views.

Although restricted to these resources, the press still exerts an immense power in America. It makes political life circulate in every corner of this vast land. The press it is whose ever watchful eye exposes the secret motivations of politics and forces men in public life to appear one by one before the court of popular opinion. The press it is which gathers the interest of the community around certain doctrines and formulates the slogans of the parties. The press it is which enables these parties to speak to each other without seeing each other, to come to understandings without actually meeting. When a great number of the press outlets manages to move along the same path, in the long run their influence becomes almost irresistible and public opinion ends up by giving way beneath blows which strike unrelentingly in the same spot.

In the United States, each individual newspaper has little power but, after the people, the periodical press nonetheless is the most powerful of social forces. (See Appendix A, p. 848.)

The opinions established under the sway of press liberty in the United States are often more deeply rooted than those formed elsewhere under the influence of censorship.

In the United States, democracy promotes an endless supply of new men to government which, as a result, introduces little consistency or orderliness into its measures. But the general principles of government are more secure there than in many other countries and the main opinions governing society have proved more lasting there. When an idea has seized the mind of the American people, be it correct or unreasonable, nothing is harder than to rid them of it.

The same phenomenon has been observed in England, the European country in which we have seen for a century the greatest freedom of thought and the most entrenched prejudices.

This is due to the very cause which, at first sight, would appear to be bound to prevent its happening, namely, the freedom of the press. Nations where this freedom prevails are attached to their opinions through pride as much as conviction. They love them because of their fairness and also because they have chosen them; they remain loyal to them, not only as something true but as something of their own.

There are several other reasons as well.

A great man[a] has said that *ignorance lies at both ends of knowledge*. Perhaps it would have been truer to state that deep convictions lie at the two ends, with doubt in the middle. In fact, human understanding may be considered as having three distinct states which frequently follow one another.

Man has strong beliefs because he adopts them without looking deeply into them. Doubt arises when he is faced with objections. He often succeeds in resolving these doubts and thereupon he believes once again. This time he no longer seizes truth by accident or in the dark; he sees it face to face and walks straight toward the light.[2]

When freedom of the press finds men in the first of these states, it leaves intact this habit of strong beliefs without reflection but it does change daily the subject of these intuitive convictions. Therefore, over the whole of the intellectual horizon, man's mind continues to see only one point at a time but that point does vary constantly. That is the time for sudden revolutions. Woe to those generations which first abruptly adopt the freedom of the press.

But soon the range of new ideas is almost universal. Experience comes upon them and man plunges into widespread doubt and mistrust.

It may be guaranteed that most men will halt in one or other of these two states, either believing without knowing why or ignorant of what precisely they ought to believe.

Only a very small number of men will ever be blessed with the attainment of this other kind of deliberate and self-confident conviction born of knowledge and arising from the very heart of agitation and doubt.

Now, it has been noted that in centuries of religious fervor,

2.   However, I do not know whether this well-considered and self-justified conviction ever raises man to the same degree of fervor or devotion as do dogmatic beliefs.

men sometimes changed beliefs, whereas in centuries of skepticism, each man hung on to his own. This happens in politics when the freedom of the press prevails. All social theories having been challenged and defeated in their turn, all those who had adopted one of them stick to it, not so much because they are convinced of its excellence but because they are unsure that a better one exists.

At the present time, men are not so ready to die for their opinions but they do not change them; at the same time, fewer martyrs or apostates appear.

To this reason we might add a still more powerful reason. When abstract opinions are in doubt, men end up by hanging on to their instincts and material interests alone which are much more obvious, tangible and permanent than opinions.

Whether democracy or aristocracy is the better form of government constitutes a very difficult question. But, clearly, democracy inconveniences one person while aristocracy oppresses another.

That is a truth which establishes itself and precludes any discussion: you are rich and I am poor.

CHAPTER 4

POLITICAL ASSOCIATIONS IN THE UNITED STATES

Daily use the Anglo-Americans make of the right of association—Three types of political association—How the Americans apply the representative system to associations—Dangers which the state incurs—Great Convention of 1831 concerned with tariffs—Legislative character of this Convention—Why the unrestricted exercise of the right of association is not as dangerous in the United States as elsewhere—Why, there, it may be considered necessary—Usefulness of associations in democratic nations.

In no country in the world has greater advantage been derived from association nor has this powerful instrument of action been applied to a wider variety of objectives than in America.

Apart from those permanent associations created by the law under the title of townships, cities, and counties, there are a great many others which owe their origins and growth solely to the initiatives of individuals.

Anyone living in the United States learns from birth that he must rely upon himself to combat the ills and obstacles of life; he looks across at the authority of society with mistrust and anxiety, calling upon such authority only when he cannot do without it. This begins to become apparent when school starts and children, even in their games, submit to rules they have established and punish offenses following their own definitions. The same spirit prevails in all the affairs of social life. Should an obstacle appear on the public highway and the passage of traffic is halted, neighbors at once form a group to consider the matter; from this improvised assembly an executive authority appears to remedy the inconvenience before anyone has thought of the possibility of some other authority already in existence before the one they have just formed. Where public pleasure is concerned, people will join together to make festivities grander and more orderly. Finally, associations are born to resist enemies of an entirely ideological nature and to share the fight against social excesses. In the United States, associations aim to promote public safety, business, industry, morality, and religion. There is nothing the human will despairs of attaining through the free action of the combined power of individuals.

Later I shall have the chance to mention the results produced by association in civil life but now I must confine my comments to the world of politics.

Once the right of association has been acknowledged, citizens may use it in different ways.

An association consists simply in the public assent which a number of individuals give to such and such a doctrine and their commitment to help in a specific way to make it prevail. Thus the right to associate almost merges with the freedom to write but already associations wield more power than the press. When an opinion is represented by an association, it has to assume a sharper and more accurate expression. It counts up its supporters and involves them in its cause; these supporters learn to know each other and their enthusiasm is increased by their numbers. Association binds the efforts of disparate minds and energetically drives them toward one single goal which it has clearly marked out.

The second stage in the exercise of the right of association is the power of assembly. When an association is allowed to set up centers of action in certain important places in the country, its activities become greater and its influence more widespread. There men see each other; executive measures are planned; opinions spread with a force and zeal which the written word can never achieve.

Lastly, there is in the exercise of the right of political association a final stage. The supporters of an opinion may unite in electoral colleges and appoint delegates to represent them in a central assembly. This is properly speaking the representative system applied to one party.

Thus, in the first case, men who profess the same opinion feel a purely intellectual bond between themselves; in the second, they gather in small assemblies which represent only a fraction of the party; finally, in the third, they form something like a separate nation within a nation, a government within a government. Their delegates, like those of the majority, represent by themselves all the collective power of their supporters and, like the latter, they appear as national representatives, enjoying all the moral authority which ensues. They do not possess, it is true, the right to enact laws as the others do, but they do have the power to attack existing laws and to draw up beforehand laws which should exist.

Let us imagine a nation not perfectly used to freedom or one in which deep-seated political passions are seething. Suppose that, alongside the law-making majority, a small minority is responsible solely for the *deliberation* of legislation, but stopping short of enactment, in such instances I have to believe that public order is under considerable threat.

There is, of course, a great gap between proving that a law is in itself better than another and proving that the former ought to be substituted for the latter. But this great gap, clearly visible to the minds of enlightened men, is already invisible to the imagination of the crowd. Besides, there are times when the nation is divided almost equally between two parties, each of which claims to represent the majority. If, alongside the ruling powers, a power happens to be established whose moral authority is almost as great, can one believe that in the long run it will merely speak without acting?

Will it always come to a halt before the abstract consideration that the aim of associations is to direct but not to force opinions, to recommend but not enact the law?

The more I observe the main effects of the independence of the press, the more I am convinced that this independence, in the modern world, is the principal and, as it were, the governing element of freedom. A nation, therefore, which intends to remain free is entitled to demand respect for this freedom at whatever cost. But *unrestricted* freedom of association in the political sphere cannot be entirely confused with the freedom to write. The former is both less necessary and more dangerous. A nation may set bounds upon it without losing control over its own affairs; it must sometimes do so in order to maintain this control.

In America, the freedom of association for political ends is unrestricted.

One example will illustrate better than all I could say just how far this freedom is tolerated.

We recall how much the question of tariffs or free trade has excited minds in America. Tariffs supported or undermined not merely opinion but very powerful material interests. The North accounted for its prosperity through tariffs; the South blamed them for almost all its sufferings. For a long time the tariff can be said to have been the sole source of political passions to agitate the Union.

In 1831, when the dispute was at its most poisonous, an unknown citizen of Massachusetts thought of suggesting through the newspapers that all the opponents of tariffs should send deputies to Philadelphia so as to consult together as to the means of making trade free. This suggestion, thanks to the invention of the printing press, took only a few days to circulate from Maine to New Orleans. The opponents of tariffs took it up with enthusiasm. They came together from everywhere and appointed deputies, most of whom were well known, while some had become famous. South Carolina, which subsequently took up arms in this same cause, sent sixty-three delegates. On 1 October 1831 the assembly which, following the American custom, had styled itself a convention, was constituted in Philadelphia and had more than two hundred members. Discussions were public and assumed, from the first day, a legislative tone. They debated the extent of congressional powers, theories of free trade and, finally, the various provisions of the tariff. After ten days, the assembly dispersed after publishing an address to the American people, in which they declared first that Congress had no right to impose a tariff and that the existing tariff was unconstitutional; secondly, that it was not in the interest of any nation, and especially the American nation, to have restricted trade.

We have to acknowledge that the unrestricted freedom of association in the political sphere has not so far produced the fatal results in the United States that perhaps we would anticipate elsewhere. The right of association was imported from England and it has always existed in America. The use of this right has now become part of habit and custom.

Nowadays the freedom of association is a vital safeguard against the tyranny of the majority. In the United States, all public power passes into the hands of a party once it has achieved a dominant position; its close friends occupy all the offices and control the organization of all its administration. The most eminent men in the opposing party are unable to cross the barrier which keeps them from power and, therefore, must establish themselves outside. The minority must bring to bear its entire moral strength against an oppressive physical power. Thus one dangerous expedient is used to oppose a still more fearful one.

The omnipotence of the majority appears to me such a considerable threat for American republics that the dangerous expedient used to restrict it seems actually something beneficial.

At this point I will express a thought which will recall what I said elsewhere when talking about municipal freedoms: there are no countries where associations are more necessary to prevent the tyranny of parties or the whims of princes than those whose social state is democratic. In aristocracies, secondary bodies form natural associations which check abuses of power. In countries where such associations do not exist and individuals are unable to create something like them artificially or temporarily, there is, as far as I can see, no longer a barrier holding back any sort of tyranny and a great nation may be oppressed with impunity by a fistful of rebels or even a single man.

The gathering of a great political convention (for all kinds exist) which may often become a necessary expedient is always, even in America, a serious event viewed with trepidation by the friends of their country.

This was clearly evident in the 1831 Convention at which the efforts of all the distinguished men of the assembly tried to moderate its language and limit its objectives.

In fact, the 1831 Convention probably had a considerable influence upon the minds of the discontented and prepared them for the open rebellion of 1832 against the commercial laws of the Union.

It cannot be concealed that unrestricted freedom of association in the political sphere is, of all freedoms, the last that a nation can tolerate. If such a freedom does not lead to actual anarchy, it does ever bring it, so to speak, close to that brink. But such a freedom, though dangerous, offers guarantees in one direction: in countries where associations are free, secret societies are unknown. In America, there are factions but no conspiracies.

Different ways in which the right of association is
understood in Europe and in the United States
—The different uses made of it.

The most natural freedom open to man after that of acting on his own is that of joining forces with his fellows and acting in common. The right of association appears to me, by nature, almost as inalienable as individual liberty. The legislator could not possibly intend its destruction without attacking society itself. However, if the freedom to unite is beneficial and a source of prosperity for some nations, there are other nations which disfigure it through excess and turn an ingredient of life into a cause of destruction. I have thought that the comparison of the various routes followed by associations in those countries where freedom is understood and in those where this freedom degenerates into license would be equally valuable to governments and to political parties.

Most Europeans still see in associations a weapon of war hastily created and immediately tested on the field of battle.

An association may be formed for the purpose of discussion but the idea of impending action preoccupies the minds of everyone. An association constitutes an army; talk is needed to count numbers and build courage; after that comes the march on the enemy. In the eyes of the members, legal measures may be viewed as means of success but they are never the only means.

This is not how Americans understand the right of association. In America, the citizens who form the minority unite firstly to show their numerical strength and thus weaken the moral ascendancy of the majority; secondly, to stimulate competition and accordingly to discover the arguments best placed to make an impression upon the majority. For they always hope to draw the latter over to their side and thereafter to exercise power in its name.

Political associations in the United States are therefore peaceful in their aims and legal in their methods. When they claim that they are aiming to win their case legally, in general they are stating the truth.

The difference between the Americans and ourselves in this matter has several causes.

In Europe some political parties differ so much from the majority that they cannot hope to win its support and they believe they are strong enough by themselves to struggle against it. When such a party forms an association, its aim is not to convince but to fight. In America, men widely divided from the majority by their opinions are helpless to oppose its power; all others hope to win it over.

So the exercise of the right of association becomes dangerous when great parties see no chance of becoming the majority. In a country like the United States where differences of opinion are quite subtle, the right of association can remain, so to speak, unrestricted.

The thing which persuades Europeans to see in the freedom of association nothing but the right to wage war on the government is our lack of experience when it concerns freedom. The first notion which occurs to the mind of a political party as to a man, when it becomes more powerful, is the idea of violence; the notion of using persuasion comes only later on, for that is born of experience.

The English, whose internal divisions are so deep set, rarely abuse the right of association because they have had long experience of it.

The French, in addition, have such a passionate taste for war that there is no enterprise so reckless or so threatening to the safety of the state that a man does not consider himself honored to die for it, arms in hand.

But, in the United States, of all the reasons which help moderate the violent aspects of political association, the most powerful is perhaps universal suffrage. In countries with universal suffrage, the majority is never in doubt because no party can reasonably set itself up as the representative of those who have not voted. Thus associations know, and everyone knows, that they do not represent the majority; their very existence proves this to be so, for, if they did represent the majority, they themselves would change the law instead of demanding its reform.

The moral authority of the government they attack is thereby increased while their own is considerably weakened.

In Europe, almost all associations claim or believe that they represent the wishes of the majority. This claim or belief increases their authority amazingly and serves wonderfully to legalize their acts. For what could be more excusable than violence to bring about the triumph of the cause of oppressed right?

Thus it is that in the vast complexity of human laws, sometimes liberty carried to extremes corrects the abuses of liberty and extreme democracy anticipates the threats to democracy.

In Europe, associations see themselves to some degree as the legislative and executive council of the nation which cannot make its own voice heard; they set out from this concept to act and rule. In America, where they can only represent a minority of the nation as everyone can see, they argue and petition.

The methods used by European associations are in harmony with their proposed aims.

Since the major aim of these associations is to act rather than argue, to fight rather than convince, they are naturally led to adopt an organization which has nothing civil about it and to introduce military ways and language. Thus we see them centralize the management of their forces as much as they can and entrust the power of all the members to a small number of leaders.

The members of these associations respond to a word of command like soldiers on active service; they profess the doctrine of passive obedience or rather, by uniting, they have entirely sacrificed their judgment and their free will in one fell swoop. As a result, there often reigns at the heart of these associations a tyranny as unbearable as that exercised in society by the government they are attacking.

Such tyranny lessens their moral authority considerably. They thus forfeit the sacred character which belongs to the struggle of the oppressed against the oppressors. For how can a man claim to want to be free when in certain instances he agrees slavishly to obey some of his fellow men, yielding up his will and his very thoughts to them?

The Americans too have introduced a form of government within associations which is, if I may put it so, a civil administration. Individual independence is recognized in it; as in society, all men are progressing simultaneously toward the same end but none of them is bound to move along exactly the same track. No one has sacrificed his will or his reason but they exert them for the success of a common enterprise.

CHAPTER 5

GOVERNMENT BY DEMOCRACY IN AMERICA

I realize that I am treading on live cinders. Every single word in this chapter is bound to bruise at some point the different parties which divide my country. Nonetheless I shall speak my thoughts.

In Europe we find it difficult to assess the true character and the permanent instincts of democracy because in Europe two opposed principles are in conflict; it is not precisely known how far this is due to the principles themselves or to the passions aroused by the conflict.

This is not the case in America where the people are in an unimpeded dominance with no dangers to fear nor wrongs to avenge.

Therefore, in America, democracy follows its own inclinations. Its behavior is natural and its movements are free. That is where it must be judged. And who would find such a study more useful and interesting than ourselves since we are daily carried along by an irresistible movement, walking like blind men toward what may prove to be a tyranny perhaps or a republic, but surely toward a democratic social state?

UNIVERSAL SUFFRAGE

I have previously mentioned that all the states of the Union had adopted universal suffrage. It is found in populations at different stages on the social ladder. I have had the chance to observe its effects in various places and among races of men whom language, religion, or customs turn into virtual strangers to each other, in Louisiana as well as in New England, in Georgia as in Canada. I have noted that universal suffrage was far from producing in America all the benefits or all the ills expected from it in Europe and that its results were in general other than is supposed.

THE PEOPLE'S CHOICE AND THE INSTINCTS OF AMERICAN DEMOCRACY IN ITS CHOICES

In the United States the most outstanding men are rarely called upon to direct public affairs—Reasons for this—The envy which, in France, drives the lower classes against the upper classes is not a French instinct but a democratic one—Why, in America, eminent men often keep away from a political career of their own volition.

Many people in Europe believe without saying so, or say so without believing it, that one of the great advantages of universal suffrage is to summon men worthy of public trust to the direction of public affairs. The people could not possibly govern on their own, so it is said, but they do always sincerely support the welfare of the state and their instinct unfailingly tells them which men are fired by a similar desire and thus are the most competent to wield power.

For my part, I am bound to say, what I have seen in America does not give me any reason to think that this is the case. When I stepped ashore in the United States, I discovered with amazement to what extent merit was common among the governed but rare among the rulers. It is a permanent feature of the present day that the most outstanding men in the United States are rarely summoned to public office and one is forced to acknowledge that things have been like that as democracy has gone beyond its previous limits. The race of American statesmen has strangely shrunk in size over the last half-century.

One can point out several reasons for this phenomenon.

Whatever one does, it is impossible to raise the intelligence of a nation above a certain level. It will be quite useless to ease the access to human knowledge, improve teaching methods, or reduce the cost of education, for men will never become educated nor develop their intelligence without devoting time to the matter.

Therefore the inevitable limitations upon a nation's intellectual progress are governed by how great or small is the ease with which it can live without working. This limitation is further off in certain countries and nearer in others; for it not to exist at all, however, the people would need to be free of the physical cares of life. It would have to cease to be the people. Thus it is as difficult to imagine a society where all men are enlightened as a state where all the citizens are wealthy; those are two related difficulties. I willingly accept that the bulk of the population very sincerely supports the welfare of the country; I might go even further to state that in general the lower social classes seem to be less likely to confuse their personal interests with this support than the upper classes. But what they always lack, more or less, is the skill to judge the means to achieve this sincerely desired end. A long study and many different ideas indeed are needed to reach a precise picture of the character of one single individual! Would the masses succeed where greatest geniuses go astray? The people never find the time or the means to devote to this work. They have always to come to hasty judgments and to latch on to the most obvious of features. As a result, charlatans of all kinds know full well the secret of pleasing the people whereas more often than not their real friends fail to do so.

Moreover, it is not always the ability to choose men of merit which democracy lacks but the desire and inclination to do so.

One must not blind oneself to the fact that democratic institutions promote to a very high degree the feeling of envy in the human heart, not so much because they offer each citizen ways of being equal to each other but because these ways continuously prove inadequate for those who use them. Democratic institutions awaken and flatter the passion of equality without ever being able to satisfy it entirely. This complete equality every day slips through the people's fingers at the moment when they think they have a hold on it; it flees, as Pascal says, in an eternal flight. The people become excited by the pursuit of this blessing, all the more priceless because it is near enough to be recognized but too far away to be tasted. The chance of success enthuses them; the uncertainty of success frustrates them. Their excitement is followed by weariness and bitterness. So anything which exceeds their limitations in any way appears to them as an obstacle to their desires and all superiority, however legitimate, is irksome to their eyes.

Many people suppose that this secret instinct which persuades the lower classes to remove the upper classes as far as they can from the direction of affairs is found only in France; that is wrong. The instinct I am mentioning is not French, it is democratic; political circumstances may have given it a particularly bitter taste, but they do not bring it into being.

In the United States, the people have no especial hatred for the upper classes of society; but they feel little goodwill for them and exclude them from power; they do not fear great talents but have little liking for them. Generally speaking, it is noticeable that anything which thrives without their support has trouble in winning their favor.

While the natural instincts of democracy persuade the people to remove distinguished men from power, the latter are guided by no less an instinct to distance themselves from a political career, where it is so difficult for them to retain their complete autonomy or to make any progress without cheapening themselves. This thought is very naively expressed by Chancellor Kent.[a] This celebrated author I speak of, having sung the praises of that part of the constitution which grants the appointment of judges to the executive power, adds: "It is probable, in fact, that the most appropriate men to fill these places would have too much reserve in their manners and too much severity in their principles ever to be able to gather the majority of votes at an election that rested on universal suffrage." (Kent's *Commentaries on American Law*, vol. 1, p. 273.)

That was what was being printed without contradiction in America in the year 1830.

I hold it proved that those who consider universal suffrage as a guarantee of the excellence of the choice made are under a complete delusion. Universal suffrage has other advantages but not that one.

CAUSES WHICH ARE ABLE PARTLY TO CORRECT
THESE INSTINCTS OF DEMOCRACY

*Contrary effects on nations as on men of great dangers—
Why America saw so many men at the head of affairs fifty
years ago—Influence of intelligence and customs upon the
people's choices—Example of New England—States of the
Southwest—Influence of certain laws upon the people's
choices—Election by two stages—Its effect on the
composition of the Senate.*

When great dangers threaten the state, the people often make a
happy choice of those citizens best suited to save them.

It has been noticed that, in the face of imminent danger, a
man rarely remains at his normal level; he either rises well
above himself or dips well below. The same happens to nations.
Extreme dangers, instead of lifting a nation, sometimes end by
bringing it low; they arouse its passions without giving them
direction and confuse its perceptions without clarification. The
Jews were still slitting each other's throats even in the midst of
the smoking ruins of the Temple. But more commonly, with
nations as with men, extraordinary courage arises from the very
imminence of the dangers. Then great characters stand out like
those monuments hidden by the darkness of the night and
seen suddenly in the glare of a conflagration. Genius no longer
disdains to appear on the stage and the people, alarmed by the
dangers facing them, momentarily forget their envious passions.
At such a time, it is not rare for famous names to emerge from
the ballot box. I have said above that statesmen of modern
America seem greatly inferior to those who appeared at the head
of affairs fifty years ago. Circumstances, as well as laws, were
responsible for that. When America was fighting the most just
of causes, that of one nation escaping from another's yoke;
when it was a question of introducing a new nation into the
world, the spirits of all rose to reach the height of the goal to
which their efforts aspired. In this general commotion, outstanding men anticipated the nation's call and the people embraced
them and adopted them as their leaders. But such events take

place at rare intervals and one must judge by the commonplace aspect of things.

If fleeting events sometimes succeed in checking the passions aroused by democracy, the intelligence and customs of the community exercise a no less powerful but more lasting influence upon its inclinations. This is very obvious in the United States.

In New England, where education and freedom are the daughters of morality and religion, and where an already ancient and long-settled society has managed to shape its own maxims and customs, the people, while they have avoided all the superiorities which wealth and birth have ever created among men, have become used to respecting intellectual and moral superiorities and to submit to them willingly. Therefore, New England democracy makes better choices than elsewhere.

On the other hand, as one goes further south to those states where social ties are less ancient or less secure, where education is not so widespread and where the principles of morality, religion and freedom are less happily combined, one observes that the aptitudes and virtues of government leaders are increasingly rare.

Lastly, when we get right down to the new states of the Southwest where the body of society, formed yesterday, is still no more than a mass of adventurers and speculators, the observer is dismayed to see into what hands public authority has been entrusted and he wonders what force, independent of legislation and of men, will enable the state to grow and society to prosper.

Certain laws have a democratic character, yet succeed in correcting partially democracy's dangerous instincts.

When you enter the House of Representatives in Washington, you are struck by the coarse appearance of this great assembly. Your eye often seeks in vain a single famous man. Almost all its members are unknown people whose names fail to stimulate any mental picture. For the most part, they are village lawyers, businessmen or even men from the lowest classes. In a country where education is almost universal, it is claimed that the representatives of the people cannot always write correctly.

A couple of paces away lies the Senate whose narrow precincts contain a large proportion of America's famous men. There is hardly a single man who does not recall some recent claim to fame. They are eloquent lawyers, distinguished generals, able magistrates, well-known politicians. All the speeches which emanate from this assembly would bring glory to the greatest parliamentary debates of Europe.

How does this curious contradiction come about? Why does the nation's elite gather in this house rather than the other? Why does the first assembly attract so many coarse elements whereas the latter has a monopoly of talents and intelligence? Yet both spring from the people, both are the product of universal suffrage and no voice has so far been raised in America to maintain that the Senate might be antagonistic to popular interests. So how does such a wide difference arise? I know of only one explanation: the election for the House of Representatives is direct; the one for the Senate is in two stages. The whole citizen body appoints the legislature of each state and the federal constitution converts one by one these legislatures into electoral colleges, which return members to the Senate. Thus the senators represent, albeit indirectly, the result of universal suffrage, for the legislature which appoints senators is not an aristocratic or privileged body deriving its electoral right from itself; it fundamentally depends upon the totality of citizens; it is generally elected by them every year and they are always able to control its choices by adding new members to its ranks. But it is enough that the will of the people has passed through this elected assembly for it to have become refined in some sense and to have emerged clad in a nobler and more beautiful form. Men thus elected, therefore, represent exactly the ruling majority of the nation but they represent only the highest concepts current in the community, the generous instincts which fire its imagination and not the petty emotions which trouble or the vices which disgrace it.

It is easy to see in the future a moment when American republics will be forced to extend the two tiers in their electoral system for fear of perishing wretchedly on the reefs of democracy.

I have no scruple in confessing that I see in the two-stage

electoral system the only means of placing the advantage of political liberty within the reach of all classes of society. Anyone hoping to turn this means into the exclusive weapon of one party, or anyone fearing such an outcome, seems to me to be making an equal mistake.

INFLUENCE WHICH AMERICAN DEMOCRACY HAS EXERCISED ON ELECTORAL LAWS

Elections at long intervals expose the state to violent crises—Frequency of elections keeps up a feverish agitation—Americans have opted for the latter of these disadvantages—Versatility of the law—Opinions of Hamilton,[b] Madison,[c] and Jefferson on this topic.

When elections occur at long intervals, the state runs the risk of being overthrown each time. Then the parties make the utmost efforts to seize a prize which comes so rarely within their grasp and, since the outcome is almost beyond remedy for those candidates who lose, their ambition, pushed to the point of desperation, must be a source of fear. If, by contrast, the equal struggle is soon to be repeated, the losers retain their patience.

When elections follow in rapid succession, their frequency keeps society in a feverish excitement and public affairs in a continuous state of change.

Thus, on one side, the state risks the onset of unease or, on the other, revolution; the former system damages the quality of government, the latter threatens its existence.

Americans have preferred to risk the first of these evils to the second. In this choice they have been guided more by instinct than reason, since democracy pushes its inclination for variety to the edge of passion and the consequence is a strange changeability of legislation.

Many Americans consider the instability of their laws as a necessary result of a system whose general effects are useful. Yet there is no one in the United States, I believe, who wishes to deny this instability or who does not regard it as a great weakness.

Hamilton, having demonstrated the usefulness of a power which has been able to prevent or, at least, to impede the promulgation of bad laws, adds: "It may perhaps be said, that the power of preventing bad laws includes that of preventing good ones, and may be used to the one purpose as well as the other. But this objection will have little weight with those who can properly estimate the mischiefs of that inconstancy and mutability in the laws which form the greatest blemish in the character and genius of our governments." *Form the greatest blemish in the character and genius of our government* (*The Federalist*, no. 73).

"The facility," says Madison, "and excess of law-making seem to be the diseases to which our governments are most liable." (*The Federalist*, no. 62).

Jefferson himself, the greatest democrat to emerge from American democracy, has highlighted the same dangers.

"The instability of our laws is really an immense evil, he says. I think it would be well to provide in our constitution that there shall always be a twelve-month between the engrossing a bill and passing it: that it should then be offered its passage without changing a word: and that if its circumstances should be thought to require a speedier passage, it should take two thirds of both houses instead of a bare majority."[1]

CIVIL SERVANTS UNDER THE CONTROL OF AMERICAN DEMOCRACY

Simplicity of American civil servants—Absence of uniforms—All officials are salaried—Political consequences of this fact—No public career in America—Results of this.

American civil servants remain indistinguishable from the mass of the citizens; they have neither palaces nor guards, nor ceremonial uniforms. This simple government attire does not stem simply from a peculiar twist of the American character but from the basic principles of their society.

1.   Letter to Madison of 20 December 1787, M. Conseil's translation.

In the eyes of democracy, the government is not a blessing but a necessary evil. Some powers must be granted to civil servants for, without such power, what use would they be? But the external appearance of power is not vital for the conduct of affairs and is unnecessarily offensive to the public.

The civil servants themselves are perfectly aware that they have gained the right to hold a superior position in relation to others, which they derive from their authority only if they place themselves on a level with the whole community through their way of life.

I can imagine no one plainer in his behavior, more approachable, more sensitive to requests than an American civil servant.

I like this unselfconscious approach of democratic government and I perceive something admirably manly in this inner strength which characterizes the office rather than the official, the man rather than the external symbols of power.

As for the influence that uniforms exert, I believe that the importance they have to carry in a century like ours is much exaggerated. I have not noticed American officials in the exercise of their authority greeted with any less respect or regard because they have nothing but their own merit to recommend them.

On the other hand, I very much doubt whether a special garment induces men in public life to respect themselves if they are not naturally disposed to do so, for I cannot believe that they have more regard for their clothes than their person.

When I see some of our magistrates harassing or indulging their wit against litigants or shrugging their shoulders at the defense pleas or smiling smugly as the charges are listed, I should like to try to take their robes from them so as to find out whether, clothed as ordinary citizens, they might recall the natural dignity of the human race.

Not one American public official wears uniform but they all receive a salary. This flows even more naturally than the preceding example from democratic principles. A democracy may surround its magistrates with pomp and cover them with gold and silk without directly compromising the principle of its existence. Such privileges are transitory and belong to the place not the man. But the creation of unpaid offices is to form a class of wealthy and independent officials; that is the core of an aristocracy. If the people still retain the right to choose, the exercise of that right has inevitable limitations.

Whenever a democratic republic converts salaried offices to unpaid ones, I think one may conclude that it is veering toward monarchy. And whenever a monarchy begins to remunerate unpaid offices, it is a sure sign of progression toward a despotism or a republic.

I, therefore, think that to change from salaried to unpaid offices is by itself the instigation of a real revolution.

The complete absence of unpaid offices is for me one of the most obvious indications of the absolute sway American democracy holds. Services of whatever kind rendered to the public are rewarded so that everyone has not only the right but also the means of performing such services.

If all the citizens of democratic states are able to take up office, all are not tempted to canvass for them. The choice of the electorate is limited not by the qualifications for candidature but by the number and capability of the candidates.

In nations where the principle of election is universally applied, properly speaking no public career exists. Men reach office to some degree by accident and have no guarantee of staying there. This is especially true with annual elections. The result is that in times of calm, public office offers little attraction to ambition. In the United States, men of moderate desires commit themselves to the twists and turns of politics. Men of great talent and passion in general avoid power to pursue wealth; it often comes about that only those who feel inadequate in the conduct of their own business undertake to direct the fortunes of the state.

These reasons, quite as much as any poor decisions of democracy, have to account for the great number of coarse men holding public office. I do not know whether the people of the United States would choose men of superior qualities who might canvass their votes but it is certain that such men do not bid for office.

THE ARBITRARY POWER OF MAGISTRATES[2]
UNDER THE SWAY OF AMERICAN DEMOCRACY

Why the arbitrary power of magistrates is greater under
absolute monarchies and democratic republics than in
limited monarchies—Arbitrary power of magistrates in
New England.

Under two types of government, magistrates exercise considerable arbitrary power, namely, under the absolute government
of a single individual and under that of democracy.

This same effect issues from almost analogous causes.

In despotisms, no one's fate is secure, whether they be public
officials or ordinary individuals. The ruler, holding in his hand
the lives, fortunes, and sometimes the honor of those he employs,
believes he has nothing to fear from them and allows them great
freedom of action because he feels sure they will never use it
against him.

In despotisms, the ruler is so enamored of his power that he
fears the restrictions of his own regulations; he likes to see his
agents acting in an almost random manner so as to be assured
that he will never observe in them any inclination which runs
against his wishes.

In democracies, since the majority is able to remove power
annually from the hands of those entrusted with it, it has no
fear of any abuse against itself. Since the majority has the power
to indicate its wishes to its rulers from moment to moment, it
prefers to leave them to their own efforts rather than bind them
to inflexible rules which, by fettering them, would, to some
extent, fetter the majority itself.

Looking quite closely, one actually discovers that the arbitrary power of democratic magistrates is even greater than it
would be in despotic states, where the ruler can punish at any
time all the mistakes he perceives. But he could not possibly
flatter himself that he has spotted every mistake he ought to

2.   Here I mean the word *magistrate* in its widest sense: I apply it to all
       entrusted with the execution of the law.

punish. On the other hand, in democracies, the sovereign power is both all-powerful and present everywhere. Thus we see that American officials are much freer in the sphere of action allotted to them by law than any European counterpart. Often they are merely shown the goal to be reached while being left free to choose their own means.

In New England for example, the formation of the jury list is left to the selectmen of each township; the only rule imposed on them is as follows: they should choose juries from citizens who enjoy electoral rights and whose reputation is excellent.[3]

In France, we would consider the life and liberty of men to be in danger, if we entrusted the exercise of such a formidable right to an official, whoever he was.

In New England, these same magistrates are able to have the names of drunkards posted in taverns and to prevent the inhabitants of the town from supplying them with wine.[4]

Such a moralistic power would appall people in the most absolute of monarchies; here, however, people have no difficulty in obeying.

Nowhere has the law left greater scope to arbitrary power than in democratic republics because such power appears not to scare them. It may even be said that magistrates become freer as voting rights are wider spread and the duration of the magistracy is shortened.

That is why it is so difficult to convert a democratic republic into a monarchy. Though they are not elected, magistrates

---

3.   See the law of 27 February 1813 in the *General Collection of the Laws of Massachusetts*, vol. 2, p. 331. It must be added that the jurors are subsequently drawn by lot from the lists.

4.   Law of 28 February 1787, ibid., vol. 1, p. 302. Here is the text: "The selectmen in each town shall cause to be posted up in the houses and shops of all taverners, innholders and retailers, within such towns, a list of the names of all persons reputed common drunkards, common tipplers, or common gamesters, misspending their time and estate in such houses. And every keeper of such house or shop, after notice given him, that shall be convicted before one or more Justices of the Peace, of entertaining or suffering any of the persons in such list, to drink or tipple, or game, in his or her house, or any of the dependencies thereof, or of selling them spiritous liquor, shall forfeit and pay the sum of thirty shillings."

normally retain the rights and the habits of elected magistrates. That leads to despotism.

Only in limited monarchies does the law define the sphere of action around public officials while at the same time taking care to guide their every step. This fact is easily explained.

In limited monarchies, power is divided between the people and the prince. Both have a vested interest in the stability of magistrates.

The prince is unwilling to entrust the fate of public officials to the hands of the people for fear that they betray his authority; the people, from their point of view, are afraid that magistrates, being absolutely dependent upon the prince, might serve to oppress their liberty; thus they are, in a sense, left dependent upon no one.

The same reason which persuades prince and people to make officials independent induces them to seek guarantees against the abuse of that independence so that they do not turn it against the authority of the former or the liberty of the latter. Both agree, therefore, upon the necessity of marking out, in advance, a line of conduct for public officials and find it in both their interests to impose upon these officials rules they cannot possibly disregard.

ADMINISTRATIVE INSTABILITY IN THE UNITED STATES

American society often leaves behind fewer records of its proceedings than a family does—Newspapers are the only historical monuments—How extreme administrative instability injures the art of government.

Men reach power for one brief moment before disappearing in a crowd, which changes its appearance daily; the result is that the proceedings of American society often leave behind fewer records than a private family does. In a sense, public administration hands down its records via an oral tradition. Nothing is written or, if it is, it flies off in the slightest gust of wind like Sibylline leaves, to vanish without recall.

The sole historical monuments in the United States are newspapers. If one number is missing, the chain of events is, as it were, broken; the present and the past are no longer connected. I am quite certain that in fifty years time it will be more difficult to gather together authentic documents about the details of American social life than about the administration of medieval France. And if a barbarian invasion happened to take the United States by surprise, in order to find out anything about the people who lived there one would have to turn to the history of other nations.

Administrative instability has begun to permeate our thinking; I might almost say that today everyone has ended up with a taste for it. No one has any concern for what happened before his time. No methodical system is in force; no collecting of material takes place; no documents are gathered together when it would be easy to do so. When by chance they are in someone's possession, little care is taken of them. Among my papers I have original documents given to me by public administrators to answer some of my inquiries. American society seems to live from hand to mouth like an army in the field. However, the skill of administration is assuredly a science and all sciences, in order to improve, need to group together the discoveries of the different generations as they follow each other. One man, in the brief span of his life, notes one fact, another conceives an idea; one man invents a method, another finds a formula; the human race collects en route these various fruits of individual experiments and formulates the sciences. It is difficult for American administrators to learn anything from each other. Thus they bring to the conduct of society the enlightenment which they discover widespread in that society and not the knowledge which should be their own. So democracy, pushed to the limits, damages the art of government. In this context, it is better suited to a nation whose administrative education is already complete than to a nation uninitiated in public affairs.

Moreover, this does not apply solely to the science of administration. Democratic government, founded upon such a simple and natural idea, nevertheless always implies the existence of a very civilized and educated society.[5] At first sight, it may be imagined as belonging to the earliest ages of the world; a closer examination allows us to discover that it had to come about last.

PUBLIC EXPENSES UNDER THE RULE OF
AMERICAN DEMOCRACY

In all societies citizens divide into a certain number of classes—The instinct of each of these classes in the organization of state finances—Why public expenses must tend to increase when the people govern—What makes the extravagancies of democracy less of a fear in America— Use of public funds under a democracy.

Is democratic government economical? First we must know with what we are comparing it.

The question would be easy to solve if we set out to draw a parallel between a democratic republic and an absolute monarchy. Public expenses would be much higher in the former than in the latter. But such is the case for all free states compared with those which are not so. Despotism certainly brings ruin to men, more by preventing them from producing than by taking away the fruits of their labors; it dries up the source of wealth while it often respects wealth once acquired. On the other hand, freedom spawns a thousand times more goods than it destroys and, in nations where this is understood, the people's resources always grow more quickly than taxes.

At present, I am concerned to compare nations which are free and to establish the influence of democracy upon state finances in such nations.

Societies, like other organized bodies, are shaped by certain fixed rules which they cannot sidestep and are made up of certain elements found in all places at all times.

It will always be simple to divide each nation theoretically into three classes.

5. I do not need to say that I am referring here to the democratic government which applies to a nation and not that which applies to a small tribe.

The first is composed of the wealthy. The second will include those who are, in all respects, comfortably off without being wealthy. In the third are locked those who have only little or no property and who live primarily on the work provided by the first two.

The individuals in these various categories may be more or less numerous according to the state of society, but it is impossible for these categories not to exist.

Each one of these classes will bring to the handling of state finances certain instincts peculiar to itself.

Let us suppose that the first alone makes the laws; it will probably concern itself but little with saving public money because a tax on a substantial fortune removes only part of the surplus without affecting it very much.

On the other hand, let us grant that the middle classes alone make the law. You can count on it that they will not raise extravagant taxes because nothing is more disastrous than a heavy tax on a slight fortune.

Government by the middle classes has to be, I do not say the most enlightened of free governments, nor especially the most generous, but the most economical.

Now, let me suppose that the lowest class is exclusively responsible for making the law; I see clearly opportunities for an increase rather than a decrease in public expenditure for two reasons:

As most of the voters then have no taxable property, all the money expended in the interests of society can only profit them without ever harming them; those who do have a little property easily find means of fixing taxes so as to fall upon the wealthy and to profit the poor; this is something the wealthy could not possibly pursue were they to be in charge of the government.

Countries where the poor[6] were exclusively responsible for

---

6.   It should be understood that the word *poor* has here, as in the rest of the chapter, a relative meaning, not an absolute one. Poor men in America might often appear rich compared with their European counterparts; nevertheless one would be right to call them poor in comparison with those of their fellow citizens who are richer than they are.

law-making could not therefore expect much economy in public expenses, which will always be extensive, either because taxes cannot touch those who vote for them or because they are assessed so as not to touch them. In other words, democratic government is the only one where those who vote for the tax can evade the obligation to pay it.

It is an empty objection to say that the interest of the people properly understood is to be careful with the fortunes of the wealthy because it would soon feel an ensuing constriction itself. Is it not also to the advantage of kings to make their subjects happy and of the nobility to know when it is appropriate to open their ranks? If a distant advantage could prevail over the passions and needs of the passing moment, neither tyrannical rules nor exclusive aristocracies would ever have come into being.

Again, someone may stop me and say: Who has ever thought of making the poor solely responsible for law-making? Who? Those who introduced universal suffrage. Does the majority or the minority make the law? The majority, of course; and if I demonstrate that the poor always make up the majority, am I not right to add that in countries where they have the vote, they alone make the law?

Now, certainly up to this time, in every nation of the world, those with no property or those whose property was too modest to allow them to live comfortably without working always comprised the greatest number. Therefore, universal suffrage really does entrust the government of society to the poor.

The vexing influence occasionally exercised by the power of the people on state finances was very evident in certain democratic republics of the ancient world in which the public treasury was drained away to help the poorest citizens or to provide the people with games and public spectacles. It is true that the representative system was almost unknown in the ancient world. Nowadays, popular passions find it more difficult to thrive in public affairs; however, you can guarantee that in the long run, the delegate will always in the end conform to the opinions of his constituents and support their inclinations as well as their interests.

However, the extravagancies of democracies are less a source of dread as the people become increasingly property-owning because then, on the one hand, the people need the money of the wealthy less, on the other, they will experience more difficulty in contriving a tax which will not touch the people themselves. In this respect, universal suffrage should be less dangerous in France than in England, where almost all taxable property is concentrated in a few hands. America enjoys a situation more favorable than France because the great majority of citizens own something.

Still more reasons exist for the possible increase of the financial budget in democracies.

Under an aristocratic regime, those men who rule the affairs of state are free from all need because of their own position in society; satisfied with their lot, they look to society for power and reputation; placed, as they are, above the dim mass of citizens, they do not always understand clearly how the general wellbeing must contribute to their own greatness. Not that they view the sufferings of the poor without pity; but they cannot feel their wretchedness as if they shared it themselves. Provided that the people appear to tolerate their lot, they themselves are satisfied and expect nothing more from the government. Aristocracy thinks more about preservation than improvement.

On the contrary, when public authority is in the hands of the people, they, as the sovereign power, seek out improvements in every quarter because of their own discontent.

The spirit of improvement then infiltrates a thousand different areas; it delves into endless detail and above all advocates those sorts of improvements which cannot be achieved without payment; for its concern is to better the condition of the poor who cannot help themselves.

Furthermore, an aimless restlessness permeates democratic societies where a kind of everlasting excitement stimulates all sorts of innovations which almost always involve expense.

In monarchies and aristocracies, the men of ambition flatter the sovereign's normal taste for renown and power and thereby often drive him to spend a great deal of money.

In democracies where the sovereign power is always in need

of funds, its favors can hardly be won except by increasing its prosperity and that can almost never be achieved without money.

In addition, when the people start to reflect upon their own position, a host of needs arise which they had not felt at first and which cannot be satisfied except by having recourse to state assets. The result is that public expenditure seems to increase with the growth of civilization and that taxes rise as knowledge spreads.

There is one final reason which often makes democratic government more expensive than any other. Sometimes democracy aims to economize in its expenditure but fails to succeed because it has no skill in managing money. As it frequently changes its mind and still more frequently its agents, its enterprises are badly conducted or remain incomplete. Firstly, the state expends more than is warranted by the scope of the intended aim; secondly, its expenditure is unprofitable.

INSTINCTS OF AMERICAN DEMOCRACY IN THE FIXING OF THE SALARIES OF CIVIL SERVANTS

In democracies, those who authorize high salaries have no opportunity of profiting from them—Tendency of American democracy to raise the salaries of secondary officials and to lower those of principal ones—Why this is so—Comparative table of the salaries of civil servants in the United States and France.

There is one major reason which, in general, persuades democracies to economize on the salaries of public officials.

Since, in democracies, those who authorize salaries are very numerous, they have little opportunity of ever benefitting themselves.

On the contrary, in aristocracies, those who authorize high salaries almost always entertain a vague hope of profiting from them. They are creating capital assets for themselves or are at least preparing resources for their children.

However, one must admit that democracies display a meanness only toward their principal agents.

In America, public officials of secondary rank are better paid than elsewhere but top-ranking officials are much less well paid.

The same reason governs both these contradictory effects. In both cases, the people authorize the salaries of public officials; they consider what needs they have and this governs their decisions. As they realize their own prosperity, it seems natural that their servants should share in it.[7] But when it comes to settling the salaries allotted to high-state officers, this rule fails and things are decided at random.

The poor have no clear idea of the needs of the upper classes of society. What seems a meager sum to a rich man is enormous to the man limited to the necessities of life and he reckons that the state governor with his 6,000 francs must still feel himself fortunate and the object of envy.[8]

If you undertake to make him understand that the representative of a great nation has to appear decked out with a certain splendor in the eyes of foreigners, at first he will see the point, but when he thinks of his simple dwelling and the modest fruits of his hard work, he will dream of all he could achieve with this same supposedly inadequate salary and will be astounded and almost dismayed at the sight of so much wealth.

Remember also that the second-rank official is down almost to the level of the people while the higher man dominates them. The former can therefore still arouse their sense of involvement whereas the latter begins to evoke their envy.

The United States illustrates this very clearly for salaries seem to decrease as the power of the civil servants increases.[9]

7.   The comfortable circumstances in which the lower ranks of civil servant live in the United States result from yet another cause, which is foreign to the general instincts of democracy. Every kind of private business is very lucrative; the state would not find any lower-rank civil servants if it did not agree to pay them well. Thus it finds itself in the position of a commercial concern which is forced to bear burdensome competition, whatever its economic inclinations might be.

8.   The state of Ohio, which has a million inhabitants, pays its governor a salary of $1,200 or 6,504 francs.

9.   To convey how obvious this truth is, all we have to do is to examine the salaries of a few of the agents of the federal government. I thought it necessary to indicate the salaries of the corresponding officers in France in order to clarify the comparison for the reader.

On the other hand, under aristocratic rule, high-ranking officials receive very large salaries whereas minor officers often have hardly enough to live on. The reason for this is easy to find in causes analogous to those I have mentioned above.

If democracies have no conception of the pleasures of the rich or envy them, aristocracy conversely has no understanding of the sufferings of the poor or is unaware of them. The poor man is not, accurately speaking, the fellow of the rich man; he belongs to another species. Aristocracy therefore shows little concern for the lot of its subordinate agents. It fails to raise their salaries unless they refuse to perform their services at too low a return.

It is the niggardly tendency of democracy toward its principal officers which persuades it to claim a marked leaning to frugality which it does not possess.

It is true that democracy hardly provides its government officials with a decent living but it spends huge sums to satisfy the people's needs or to facilitate their enjoyments.[10] That is a better use of taxes, not an economy.

UNITED STATES Treasury Department		FRANCE Ministère des Finances	
Messenger	3,734 francs	Messenger	1,500 francs
Lowest paid clerk	5,420	Lowest paid clerk	1,000–1,800
Highest paid clerk	8,672	Highest paid clerk	3,200–3,600
Chief clerk	10,840	Secrétaire Général	20,000
Secretary of State	32,520	Minister	80,000
President	135,000	King	12,000,000

Perhaps I have made a mistake in selecting France as my standard of comparison. In France, where democratic tendencies are increasingly infiltrating the government, it is already obvious that the Assemblies are strongly influenced to raise low salaries and above all to lower high ones. Thus, the Finance Minister who in 1834 is paid 80,000 francs received 160,000 francs under the Empire; the Directors-General of Finance who now receive 20,000 francs, then received 50,000 francs.

10. Among the various American budgets, consider the cost for the support of the poor and for public education. In 1831 the state of New York spent the sum of 1,200,000 francs for the maintenance of the poor. The sum devoted to public education is thought to have risen to at least 5,420,000 francs (William's *New York Annual Register*, 1832, pp. 205, 243). The state of New York, in 1830, had only 1,900,000 inhabitants, which is not more than double the population in the Département du Nord.

Democracies generally give little to their rulers and much to their citizens. The reverse is true for aristocracies where state money benefits especially the class which conducts affairs.

DIFFICULTY OF DISCERNING THE REASONS WHICH PERSUADE THE AMERICAN GOVERNMENT TOWARD ECONOMY

Anyone attempting to discover the facts which show the actual influence of laws on the lot of human beings is liable to make great mistakes, for there is nothing more difficult to appreciate than a fact.

One nation is shallow and enthusiastic by nature while another is thoughtful and calculating. This is due to its own physical constitution or to causes far removed of which I know nothing.

You observe nations which enjoy entertainments, bustle, and jollity without a regret for the millions vanished in smoke. You observe others which value only solitary pleasures and seem ashamed of appearing content.

In certain countries great store is placed upon the beauty of architecture; in others works of art are not prized at all and scorn is poured upon anything which does not brings profit. In some, reputation is all; in others, money is the ruling passion.

Apart from the laws, all these causes have a very powerful influence upon the management of state finances.

If the Americans have never spent the people's money on public festivities, it is not simply because, there, the people control the taxes but because they do not care for public displays of enjoyment.

If they reject excessive ornament in their architecture and value only its positive and material advantages, it is not only because they are a democratic nation but also a commercial one.

The habits of private life spill over into public life; with the Americans it is vital to distinguish between savings which are due to their institutions and those which derive from their habits and customs.

CAN THE PUBLIC EXPENDITURE OF THE UNITED STATES BE COMPARED WITH THAT OF FRANCE?

Two points to establish in order to appreciate the extent of public expenses, i.e. national wealth and taxation—Neither the precise wealth of France nor its expenses is known—Why one cannot hope to know the wealth and expenses of the Union—The author's researches to discover the total amount of taxes in Pennsylvania—General indications by which one can estimate the extent of a nation's expenses—The result of this investigation for the Union.

In recent times, there has been much preoccupation with the comparison between public expenditure in the United States and that in France. All these efforts have proved fruitless and few words suffice, I believe, to prove that this was bound to be so.

In order to appreciate the extent of public expenditure in a nation, two procedures are necessary: firstly, one must discover the amount of national wealth and then what proportion of that wealth is devoted to state expenditure. Anyone trying to ascertain the total of taxes without revealing the extent of resources available to provide for them would be wasting his efforts, for it is not interesting to know the amount of expenditure but the connection of such expenditure to the total revenue.

The same tax which can be borne easily by a wealthy taxpayer will end up by reducing a poor man to penury.

The wealth of nations is composed of several components: real estate is the first, goods and chattels the second.

It is hard to know the extent of land under cultivation in a nation, or its valuation, natural or acquired. It is even harder to calculate the value of a nation's personal property. It eludes almost every effort of analysis because of its diversity and quantity.

Thus, we observe that the most ancient of civilized nations in Europe, including even those whose administration is centralized, have not yet established exactly the state of their wealth.

In America, the idea of doing such a calculation has not even occurred to them. How could one be confident of succeeding in doing so in this new country where society has not yet reached a settled or definite state, where the national government does not have at its disposal, as ours does, a crowd of agents whose efforts can be controlled and directed simultaneously and where, finally, statistical records are not kept because no one is able to collect the documents or find the time to peruse them?

Therefore, the elements which could contribute to our calculations are unavailable. We are unaware of the comparative wealth of France and the Union. The wealth of the former is not yet known and the means of establishing that of the latter do not exist.

But I am willing to agree for a moment to forgo this vital ingredient in the comparison; I will abandon the investigation of the connection between tax and income and will confine my ambition to establishing the amount of tax.

The reader will acknowledge that this narrowing of the scope of my researches does not ease my task.

I am certain that the central French administration could, with the help of all the civil servants at its disposal, discover the exact total of direct or indirect taxes imposed on its citizens. But these efforts, which no one individual can undertake, have not yet been completed by the French government itself or at least their results have not been published. We are aware of state expenses and we know the total of departmental expenditure; what is happening in the communes is not known. Thus no one could yet say what is the level of public expenditure in France.

If I now turn to America, the difficulties before me are increasingly numerous and insurmountable. The Union publishes the exact total of its expenditure; I am able to obtain the individual budgets of the twenty-four constituent states; but who will inform me what the citizens spend upon the county and township administrations?[11]

11. The Americans, as we can see, have four types of budgets: the Union has its own; the states, the counties and the townships equally have their own. During my stay in America I conducted extensive research in order to discover the amount of public expenditure in the townships and in the counties of the principal states of the Union. I easily managed to obtain the budget of the largest townships but found it impossible to lay my

The federal authority cannot go so far as to force the provincial governments to enlighten us on this point. Even if these governments wished themselves to help us simultaneously, I doubt they could satisfy us. Apart from the natural difficulty of the undertaking, the political organization of the country would still be an obstacle to the success of their efforts. The magistrates in the townships or county are neither appointed by, nor dependent upon, state administrators. We are, therefore, justified in thinking that, if the state sets out to obtain the necessary information, it would encounter great obstacles from the negligence of the subordinate officials it would be forced to employ.[12]

---

hands on that of the smallest. As a result I can form no precise notion of municipal expenditure. As far as county expenditure is concerned, I have in my possession a few documents which, although incomplete, may still be of interest to the reader. I owe a debt to Mr Richard, former Mayor of Philadelphia, for the budgets of thirteen of the counties of Pennsylvania for the year 1830: Lebanon, Center, Franklin, Fayette, Montgomery, Luzerne, Dauphin, Butler, Allegheny, Columbia, Northumberland, Northampton, and Philadelphia. Their population in 1830 consisted of 495,207 inhabitants. Glancing at a map of Pennsylvania, you will see that these thirteen counties are scattered in every direction and affected by all the normal causes which may influence the condition of a country; consequently it is highly likely that they would represent the precise picture of the financial state of the counties of Pennsylvania. Now, the same counties spent 1,800,221 francs in 1830, or 3 francs 64 centimes for each inhabitant. I have calculated that during 1830 each of these inhabitants devoted 12 francs 70 centimes to the federal Union and 3 francs 80 centimes to Pennsylvania. The result is that in 1830 these same citizens donated to society as their contribution to overall expenditure (leaving aside municipal expenditure), the sum of 20 francs 14 centimes. This calculation is incomplete on two counts, as we can see, since it applies to only one single year and to one part of public expenditure; but at least it has the merit of being definite.

12. Those who have wished to establish a parallel between the expenses of France and America have been fully aware that it was impossible to compare the total public expenditures of France with those of the Union; but they have attempted to compare separate portions from among these expenditures. It is easy to show that this second method of proceeding is no less defective than the first.

For example, with what shall I compare the French national budget? With that of the Union? But the Union embraces far fewer objects than the French central government and its expenses must, of course, be much smaller. Shall I contrast the departmental budgets in France with those of

Besides, it is useless to inquire what Americans could manage in such a matter since it is certain that they have done nothing up until now.

So, today in America or in France, no single man can inform us what is contributed annually by each citizen of the Union to the expenditure of society.[13]

---

the individual states which compose the Union? But in general terms, the individual states are involved with more important and more numerous concerns than the administration of a French *département*; their expenditure is, therefore, naturally more extensive. As for the budgets of the counties, nothing in our system of finances resembles them. Would it be appropriate to see a correspondence of French expenditure with the budget at state or township level? Municipal expenditure exists in both countries but is not always similar. In America, the township takes responsibility for several offices which in France are left to the *département* or to the state. Besides, what should we understand by municipal expenditure in America? The organization of the township is different from state to state. Are we to take as the rule what is happening in New England or in Georgia, in Pennsylvania or the state of Illinois?

A kind of analogy may readily be perceived between certain budgets in both countries; but, since the elements in their composition are always more or less different, no serious comparison can be drawn between them.

13. Even if we knew the exact sum contributed by every American or French citizen to the public purse, we should only arrive at a part of the truth.

Governments demand not only supplies of money but also personal services which have a monetary value. When the state raises an army, besides the pay of the troops, furnished by the entire nation, it is still necessary for the soldier to give his time, which has a greater or lesser value according to the occupation which he could follow if he remained a free man. The same remark applies to the militia. The man who is in the militia devotes over a short period valuable time to the maintenance of public security and, in reality, surrenders to the state those earnings he is prevented from acquiring. I have quoted these examples but I could have quoted a lot more. The governments of France and America both levy taxes of this kind and these taxes weigh upon the citizens. However, who would be able to estimate exactly the relative amount in both countries?

This is not the last difficulty which obstructs a comparison of the public expenditure of the Union with that of France. The French state takes on certain obligations which are not assumed by the American state and vice versa. The French government pays the clergy, the American government leaves this problem to the faithful. In America, the state takes responsibility for the poor; in France they are abandoned to public charity. All French civil servants receive a fixed salary; Americans allow them to claim certain rights. In France, benefits in kind are encountered on only a small number of roads; in the United States, you meet them on almost all roads. Our

We must conclude that it is as difficult to compare usefully the social expenditure of Americans with that of the French as to compare the wealth of the Union with that of France. I would add that it would even be dangerous to try. When statistical method is not based upon rigorously accurate calculations, it leads to error rather than to guidance. The mind easily allows itself to be deluded by the deceptive appearance of precision which statistics retain even when wrong and it relies confidently upon mistakes apparently clothed in the forms of mathematical truth.

Let us give up figures, therefore, and attempt to find proofs elsewhere.

A country reveals its material prosperity thus: after paying his dues to the state, the poor man is left with some resources and the wealthy man with a surplus. Both of them appear content with their lot and seek daily to improve it further so that capital is always available to industry which is thus never short of investment. These are the telltale signs by which, since positive documentation is missing, it is possible to ascertain whether the public expenses borne by a nation are in proportion to its wealth.

The observer relying upon this evidence would doubtless estimate that the American gives to the United States a significantly smaller part of his income than does the Frenchman to France.

But how would one suppose it could be otherwise?

Part of the French debt is the result of two invasions; the Union has nothing like that to fear. Our position forces us to maintain a large army ready for war as a normal course. The Union's isolated position allows it to have no more than 6,000 soldiers. We maintain almost three hundred ships; the

---

thoroughfares are open to travelers without any payment at all; in the United States, a great number of toll roads abound. All these differences in the way in which taxes are levied in the two countries increase the difficulty of comparing the expenditure in both countries; for there are certain expenses which the citizens would not be responsible for or which would be smaller if the state did not undertake to act in their name.

Americans have only fifty-two.[14] How would it be possible for the American to pay the state as much as a Frenchman?

No parallel can therefore be established between the finances of two countries so differently situated.

An examination of events inside the Union, not a comparison of the Union with France, provides us with a possible assessment of whether democracy is genuinely economical.

I glance at each of the divergent republics of the confederation and discover that their government often lacks persistence in its planning and that it fails to impose a constant supervision of its employees. Naturally I draw from that, that it must often spend taxpayers' money to no effect or allocate more than is necessary to its undertakings.

I realize that, in its loyalty to its popular origins, the government goes to extraordinary lengths to satisfy the needs of the lower classes of society, to open the way to power for them and to spread prosperity and education among them. It looks after the poor, annually allocating millions to schools; it pays for all the services and rewards generously its humblest agents. Although I accept that such a method of government is useful and reasonable, I have to acknowledge that it is expensive.

I observe the poor man directing public affairs and controlling national resources; I am forced to think that, profiting from state expenditure, he will often entail the state in new expenses.

Thus my conclusion is that, without relying upon incomplete figures and without wishing to establish rash comparisons, the democratic government of Americans is not, as is sometimes claimed, cheap. I am not afraid to predict that, if the people of the United States were ever one day to be threatened with serious difficulties, taxes would be seen to rise as high as in most European aristocracies or monarchies.

14. See the detailed budgets of the French Naval Ministry and, for America, the *National Calendar* for 1833, p. 228.

CORRUPTION AND VICES OF THE RULERS IN A DEMOCRACY; THE RESULTING EFFECTS ON PUBLIC MORALITY

In aristocracies, the rulers sometimes seek to corrupt— Often in democracies they are themselves corrupt—In the former, their vices directly attack the morality of the people—In the latter, their influence is indirect but all the more fearsome.

Aristocracies and democracies accuse each other of facilitating corruption; a distinction must be made:

In aristocratic governments, men who head affairs are wealthy people whose desire is power only. In democracies, statesmen are poor and seek to make their fortune.

The result is that the rulers of aristocracies are less tempted by corruption and have a very modest liking for money, whereas the opposite occurs in democracies.

But in aristocracies, those whose ambition is to lead affairs have great wealth at their disposal and since the number of those who can assist them to reach that position is often severely limited, the government is to some degree up for auction. On the other hand, the aspirants to power in democracies are hardly ever rich and the number of those who confer power is very great. In democracies, there are possibly no fewer men to be bought but there are hardly any purchasers. Besides, too many people would have to be bought at the same moment to achieve one's aim.

Among those who have held power in France during the last forty years, several have been accused of having made their fortune at the state's and its allies' expense—a reproach seldom made against public officials in the former monarchy. But in France there is hardly an instance of votes bought at an election, whereas that is notoriously and publicly done in England.

I have never heard it said that in the United States wealth was ever used to bribe the populace; but I have often seen doubt cast upon the integrity of public officials. More frequently still, I have heard their success attributed to underhand intrigues or criminal practices.

If, therefore, the rulers in aristocracies sometimes seek to corrupt, democratic leaders prove to be corrupt. In the former case, the morality of the people is under direct attack; in the latter, the influence upon the public conscience is indirect, which is even more fearsome.

The state leaders of democratic nations are almost always subject to unfortunate suspicions and therefore to some extent they lend government support to the crimes of which they are accused. Thus they provide dangerous examples of the valiant struggles of virtue and afford glorious parallels for the hidden tricks of vice.

It is useless to say that dishonest passions reside in every rank of society, that they often ascend the throne by hereditary right, or that as a result one can encounter despicable men at the head of aristocratic nations as well as in democracies.

This answer does not satisfy me. At the heart of the corruption of those who acquire power by accident, there is something coarse and vulgar which makes it contagious to the crowd; on the other hand at the very center of the depravity of the nobility there prevails a certain aristocratic refinement and an air of grandeur which often prevents it from spreading elsewhere.

The people will never penetrate the hidden labyrinth of court life and will always have difficulty in discerning the corruption lurking beneath elegant manners, refined tastes, and graceful language. But stealing the public purse or selling the favors of the state for money are matters well understood by the first wretch who comes along and who is able to hope that his turn will arrive to do the same.

Moreover, it is much less frightening to witness the immorality of the great than to witness that immorality which leads to greatness. In democracies, ordinary citizens see a man emerging from their ranks and possessing, after a few years, wealth and power; the sight of this arouses their astonishment and envy; they wonder how their equal of yesterday is today invested with the right to be their ruler. It is inconvenient to attribute his rise to his talents or to his virtues because that would mean the admission to themselves that they are less virtuous or less capable than he was. Therefore, they ascribe, often rightly, the principal reason for his success to some of his vices. Thus, there is at work some odious muddle in our ideas of corruption and power, unworthiness and success, usefulness and dishonor.

THE EFFORTS OF WHICH DEMOCRACY IS CAPABLE

The Union has fought only once for its existence—The enthusiasm at the beginning of the war—Coolness at the end—Difficulty of establishing conscription or impressment of seamen in America—Why a democratic nation is less capable of sustained effort than any other.

I warn the reader that I am talking at this point about a government which pursues the actual wishes of the people and not one which merely rules in the name of the people.

There is nothing more irresistible than a tyranny which rules in the name of the people because, although it is invested with the moral power which belongs to the will of the majority, at the same time it acts with the decisiveness, alacrity, and persistence of a single man.

It is quite hard to say what degree of effort a democratic government can sustain in times of national crisis.

Until now, a great democratic republic has never existed. It would be insulting to republics to call the oligarchy which ruled in France in 1793 by that name. The United States is the first example of such a phenomenon.

Now, in the half century since the formation of the Union, its existence has been challenged only once, during the War of Independence. At the start of that long war, there were extraordinary signs of enthusiasm for the country's service.[15] But as the struggle was prolonged, the usual selfishness reappeared:

15. One of the most unusual, in my opinion, was the resolution that the Americans took for temporarily abandoning the use of tea. Those who know that men usually cling more to their habits than to their life will doubtless be surprised at this great and modest sacrifice from a whole nation.

money no longer reached the public treasury; men stopped volunteering for the army; the people pressed for independence but stepped back from the means of obtaining it. "Tax laws," says Hamilton, in *The Federalist* (no. 12), "have in vain been multiplied; new methods to enforce the collection have in vain been tried; the public expectation has been uniformly disappointed; and the treasuries of the States have remained empty. The popular system of administration inherent in the nature of popular government, coinciding with the real scarcity of money incident to a languid and mutilated state of trade, has hitherto defeated every experiment for extensive collections, and has at length taught the different legislatures the folly of attempting them."

Since that period, the United States has not had to sustain a single serious war.

To assess what sacrifices democracies are capable of imposing upon themselves, we must await the time when the American nation is forced to place in the hands of its government half of its income, as England has done, or has to throw a twentieth of its population on to the battlefield, as France has done.

In America, conscription is unknown; men are enlisted for payment. Compulsory recruitment is so alien to the ideas and so foreign to the customs of the people of the United States that I doubt whether they would ever dare to introduce it into their law. What we call conscription in France certainly constitutes the most burdensome of our taxes but, without conscription, how could we maintain a great continental war?

The Americans have not adopted the English system of pressing seamen. They have nothing corresponding to the French registration of seamen. The state navy, like the merchant service, is recruited from volunteers.

Now it is not easy to imagine a nation sustaining a great sea war without recourse to one of the measures mentioned above; thus the Union, although it has fought at sea with success, has never had many ships and the equipment of its small number of vessels has always cost it very dear.

I have heard American statesmen confess that the Union will scarcely maintain its rank on the seas unless it adopts impressment or registration of seamen but the difficulty is to force the people, who exercise the supreme authority, to tolerate either system.

It is beyond argument that, in times of danger, nations which are free generally display infinitely more energy than nations which are not but I am inclined to think that this is especially true of free nations where the aristocratic element is dominant. Democracy appears to me much more suitable for governing a society in times of peace, or for making a sudden, vigorous effort when such is needed than for braving the greats storms of political life over a long period. The reason for this is simple: enthusiasm induces men to expose themselves to danger and privations but only reflection will keep them there exposed for long periods. There is more calculation than one supposes in what we call impulsive courage and, although passion alone generally instigates the initial efforts, the sight of the end result allows them to continue. One risks a part of what one holds dear in order to save the rest. Now, it is this clear perception of the future based on enlightened experience which is bound to be absent in democracies. The people feel much more than they reason; and if current evils are great, it is to be feared that they might forget the greater evils which await perhaps a possible defeat.

Not only do the people see less clearly than the upper classes what they can hope or fear for the future, but also they suffer in a quite different manner the evils of the present. The noble who risks his life has an equal chance of attracting either glory or harm. When he hands over to the state the greater part of his income, he makes a brief sacrifice of some of the pleasures of wealth, whereas the poor man gains no prestige from death and the taxes which inconvenience the rich man often attack, in his case, the very source of his livelihood.

This relative weakness of democratic republics in times of crisis is perhaps the greatest obstacle to the foundation of a similar republic in Europe. For a democratic republic to survive without pitfalls in Europe, similar republics would have to be established simultaneously in all the other countries of that continent.

I believe that a democratic government should, in the long run, increase the real strength of society, but it cannot gather at one point and in a given time as many forces as an aristocratic government or an absolute monarchy. If a democratic country remained subject to a century of republican government, it is likely that at the end of the century it would be richer, more populated and more prosperous than neighboring despotic states. But in the course of that century, it would, on several occasions, run the risk of being conquered by them.

THE POWER WHICH AMERICAN DEMOCRACY EXERCISES OVER ITSELF

The American people take time to accept what is useful to their wellbeing, sometimes even refusing to do so— The American capacity for making mistakes which can be repaired.

The difficulty experienced by democracy in conquering the passions and silencing the desires of the passing moment in the interest of the future can be observed in the United States in the most trivial of things.

The people, surrounded by flatterers, find it difficult to master themselves. Every time they are asked to impose some privation or discomfort even for an aim their reason approves, they almost always start by refusing. The obedience of Americans to the laws has been justly praised. One must add that American legislation is made by and for the people. Therefore, the law in the United States patently favors those who, everywhere else, have the greatest interest in violating it. Thus, it is fair to think that an irksome law, whose real value was not observed by the majority, would neither be passed nor obeyed.

In the United States, no legislation relating to fraudulent bankruptcies exists. Would that be because there are none? No, it is because, on the contrary, there are many. The fear of prosecution as a bankrupt exceeds, in the minds of the majority, the fear of being ruined by other bankrupts. A kind of guilty tolerance exists, in the conscience of the public, toward an offense which is condemned by everyone.

In the new states of the Southwest,[d] the citizens almost always take justice into their own hands and an endless series of murders ensues. That is the result of the excessively rough habits of the people and the poor spread of education in those wild areas. Thus, they do not feel the advantage of giving strength to the law; duels are still preferred to lawsuits.

One day, in Philadelphia, someone was telling me that almost all the crimes in America were caused by the abuse of strong drink which the lowest classes could consume when they liked because they were sold it cheaply. "How is it," I asked, "that you do not place a duty on brandy?" "Our legislators," he replied, "have often considered it but it is a difficult undertaking. There is fear of revolt and besides, the members who voted for such a law would be certain to lose their seats." "So, therefore," I continued, "in your country drunkards are in the majority and temperance is unpopular."

When such things are brought to the notice of politicians, they merely reply: "Let time take care of that; the sense of evil will enlighten people and show them what they need." Often that is true. If democracy has more opportunities for making mistakes than a king or an oligarchy, it also has a better chance of returning to the truth when the light dawns because, in general, it harbors no interests which oppose the majority or challenge reason. But democracy cannot lay hold upon the truth except by experience and many nations might perish while they are waiting to discover their mistakes.

The great privilege enjoyed by Americans is, therefore, not only to be more enlightened than other peoples but also to have the capacity to repair their mistakes.

It must be added that, in order to profit from past experiences, democracy must already have reached a certain level of civilization and knowledge.

There are nations whose early education has been so defective and whose character displays such a weird confusion of passions, of ignorance, and of all kinds of false ideas that they could not by themselves perceive the reason for their sufferings; they sink beneath unrecognized evils.

I have traveled vast lands formerly inhabited by powerful Indian nations who now no longer exist; I have lived with tribes already disabled who watch their number decline and the luster of their primitive glories disappear; I have heard Indians themselves predict the final destiny of their race. However, every European can see what would be necessary to save these luckless peoples from inevitable collapse. They, of course, cannot see it and experience, year in year out, the woes which heap upon their heads; they will perish to the last man as they reject the remedy. Force would have to be used to compel them to live.

We see in astonishment the new nations of South America being torn asunder for a quarter of a century by an endless succession of revolutions and we expect to see their return to what may be called their natural state. But who can say for sure that revolutions are not these days the most natural state for the Spanish of South America? In that country, society is struggling in the depths of an abyss from which its own efforts cannot extricate it.

The people dwelling in this beautiful half of the Western hemisphere appear stubbornly determined to tear out each other's entrails; nothing can divert them from such an end. Exhaustion drives them to take a moment's rest which becomes the impetus for a fresh bout of frenzy. When I turn to consider them in this state, alternating between misery and crime, I am tempted to think that despotism would be a blessing for them.

But these two words will never be linked in my mind.

THE MANNER IN WHICH AMERICAN DEMOCRACY CONDUCTS FOREIGN AFFAIRS

Direction given to American foreign policy by Washington and Jefferson—Almost all the natural shortcomings of democracy are revealed in its conduct of foreign affairs while its good qualities are almost imperceptible.

We have seen that the federal constitution placed the control of the nation's foreign interests permanently in the hands of the

President and Senate,[16] which to a certain extent puts the general policy of the Union outside the direct daily influence of the people. One is not able to say, therefore, without qualification, that American democracy controls the state's external affairs.

Two men have set a direction for American policy which is still followed today; the first is Washington and Jefferson is the second.

Washington said in that admirable letter addressed to his fellow citizens and which was that great man's political testament:

The Great rule of conduct for us, in regard to foreign Nations, is in extending our commercial relations to have with them as little political connection as possible. So far as we have already formed engagements let them be fulfilled, with perfect good faith. Here let us stop.

Europe has a set of primary interests, which to us have none, or a very remote relation. Hence she must be engaged in frequent controversies, the causes of which are essentially foreign to our concerns. Hence therefore it must be unwise in us to implicate ourselves, by artificial ties, in the ordinary vicissitudes of her politics, or the ordinary combinations and collisions of her friendships or enmities:

Our detachment and distant situation invites and enables us to pursue a different course. If we remain one People, under an efficient government, the period is not far off, when we may defy material injury from external annoyance; when we may take such an attitude as will cause the neutrality we may at any time resolve upon to be scrupulously respected; when belligerent nations, under the impossibility of making acquisitions upon us, will not lightly hazard the giving us provocation; when we may choose peace or war, as our interests guided by our justice shall Counsel.

16. "The President," says the Constitution, article 2, section 2, no. 2, "shall have power, by and with the advice and consent of the Senate, to make treaties." The reader should remember that Senators are returned for a term of six years and that, being chosen by the legislature of each state, they are the result of a two-stage election.

Why forego the advantages of so peculiar a situation? Why quit our own to stand upon foreign ground? Why, by interweaving our destiny with that of any part of Europe, entangle our peace and prosperity in the toils of European ambition, rivalship, interest, humor or caprice?

'Tis our true policy to steer clear of permanent alliances, with any portion of the foreign world. So far, I mean, as we are now at liberty to do it, for let me not be understood as capable of patronizing infidelity to existing engagements (I hold the maxim no less applicable to public than to private affairs, that honesty is always the best policy). I repeat it therefore, let those engagements be observed in their genuine sense. But in my opinion, it is unnecessary and would be unwise to extend them.

Taking care always to keep ourselves, by suitable establishments, on a respectably defensive posture, we may safely trust to temporary alliances for extraordinary emergencies.

Earlier, Washington had expressed this fine and apposite idea: "The nation that delivers itself to habitual sentiments of love or of hatred toward another becomes a sort of slave to them. It is a slave to its hatred or to its love."

Washington's political career was always guided by these maxims. He succeeded in maintaining his country in peace when the rest of the globe was at war and he laid down as a point of doctrine that the true interest of the Americans lay in never participating in the internal dissensions of Europe.

Jefferson went even further and introduced this other maxim into the policy of the Union: "that Americans ought never to demand privileges from foreign nations in order not to be obliged to accord them themselves."

These two principles, whose evident truth brought them within the grasp of popular understanding, have greatly simplified the foreign policy of the United States.

Since the Union does not meddle in the affairs of Europe, it has, so to speak, virtually no external concerns at stake, for, as yet, it has no powerful neighbors in America. Being beyond the passions of the Old World by geography as much as by preference, it has no need to protect itself from them any more than to espouse them. As far as the passions of the New World are concerned, they are still hidden in the future.

The Union is free from pre-existing commitment and can take advantage of the experience of the old European nations without being obliged, as they are, to take the past into account and to adapt it to the present. The Union is not forced, as they are, to accept a mighty inheritance of mixed glory and wretchedness, national friendships and hatreds bequeathed by their ancestors. The foreign policy of the United States is to wait and see; it consists in keeping away from things much more than in interfering.

At the moment, therefore, it is very difficult to know what skills American democracy will develop in conducting the state's foreign affairs. Both its enemies and its friends must suspend judgment on this point.

For my part, I am not loath to express the view that it is in the conduct of foreign affairs that democratic governments appear to be decidedly inferior to others. Experience, customs, and education in the end almost always engender, in a democracy, that sort of everyday practical wisdom and that knowledge of the small business of life which we call common sense. Common sense is enough for society's normal dealings and in a nation whose education is complete, democratic freedom, when applied to the state's internal affairs, produces more than enough benefits to offset the disasters resulting from the mistakes of the government. Such is not always the case in the external relations of nation to nation.

Foreign policy demands the use of scarcely any of the qualities characteristic of a democracy and requires, on the contrary, the cultivation of almost all those it lacks. Democracy supports the increase of the state's internal resources, furthers comfort, develops public spirit, and strengthens respect for the law in the different social classes, all of which have only an indirect effect upon the standing of one nation in relation to another. But democracy cannot, without difficulty, coordinate the details of a great enterprise, fix on one plan and follow it through with persistence, whatever the obstacles. It is not capable of devising secret measures or waiting patiently for the result. Those are qualities which characterize more especially one single man or an aristocracy. Now these are the precise qualities which ensure that in the end a nation, like a single individual, wins through.

If, on the other hand, you concentrate on the natural failings of aristocracies, you will discover that their possible effects are hardly discernible in the management of the state's foreign affairs. The principal defect leveled at aristocracies is that of working for themselves alone and not for the population as a whole. In foreign policy, it is rare for aristocracies to have an interest distinct from that of the people.

The tendency of a democracy to obey, in politics, feelings rather than rational arguments and to abandon a mature plan for the enjoyment of a momentary passion, was clearly displayed in America at the time of the outbreak of the French Revolution. The most obvious insights of reason were sufficient as much then as they are today to convince Americans that their self-interest dissuaded them from becoming embroiled in a European conflict which would shed so much blood but from which the United States could not suffer any damage.

However, the people's sympathies for France declared themselves so violently that nothing less than the unbending character of Washington and his immense popularity were needed to prevent a declaration of war against England. Moreover, this great man's austere arguments directed against the generous but ill-considered passions of his fellow citizens almost deprived him of the only reward he had ever sought, namely, the love of his country. The majority pronounced itself against his policy; now the whole nation gives it approval.[17]

17. See the fifth volume of Marshall's *Life of Washington*. "In a government constituted like that of the United States," he says, page 314, "the first magistrate cannot, whatever his firmness may be, long hold a dike against the torrent of popular opinion; and the one that prevailed then seemed to lead to war." In fact, in the session of Congress held at that time it was frequently evident that Washington had lost his majority in the House of Representatives. The violence of the language used against him outside the house was extreme and in a political meeting they did not scruple to compare him indirectly with the traitor Arnold (page 265). "Those who held the party of the opposition," says Marshall (page 355), "claimed that the partisans of the administration composed an aristocratic faction that

If the constitution and public support had not given to Washington the control of the state's foreign affairs, the nation would certainly have done at that time precisely what it condemns today.

Almost all the nations which have had a strong effect upon the world by conceiving, pursuing, and carrying out great designs, from the Romans to the English, were ruled by aristocracies. How is that surprising?

Nothing is so fixed in its views as an aristocracy. The population at large may be led astray by its ignorance or its passions; a king's mind can be taken off its guard and persuaded to waver in its plans; besides, a king is not immortal. But an aristocratic body is too numerous to be caught, too small to yield facilely to the intoxication of ill-considered passions. An aristocratic body is a firm and enlightened individual who never dies.

CHAPTER 6

WHAT ARE THE REAL ADVANTAGES DERIVED BY AMERICAN SOCIETY FROM DEMOCRATIC GOVERNMENT

Before beginning the present chapter, I need to remind the reader of what I have already mentioned several times in the course of this work.

The political constitution of the United States seems to me to be one of the forms of government which a democracy can assume but it is not my view that American institutions are either the only or the best ones that a democratic nation might adopt.

So, by pointing out the benefits derived by Americans from

---

had submitted to England and that, wanting to establish a monarchy, was consequently the enemy of France; a faction whose members constituted a sort of nobility that had the stock of the Bank as securities and that so feared every measure that could influence its funds that it was insensitive to the affronts that the honor and the interest of the nation commanded it equally to repel."

democratic government, I am far from claiming or thinking that similar advantages can be obtained only from the same laws.

THE GENERAL TENDENCY OF LAWS UNDER THE CONTROL OF AMERICAN DEMOCRACY AND THE INSTINCTS OF THOSE WHO APPLY THEM

The vices of democracy are immediately obvious—Its advantages become clear only in the long term—American democracy is often clumsy but the general tendency of its laws is beneficial—Under American democracy public officials have no entrenched interests which conflict with those of the majority—Results of this.

The vices and weaknesses of democratic government are easy to see; they can be proved by obvious facts whereas its beneficial influence works in an imperceptible and almost hidden way. A single glance allows us to detect its faults whereas its qualities are revealed only in the long term.

The laws of American democracy are often defective or incomplete; they sometimes violate acquired rights or give a sanction to others which are dangerous. Even if they were good, their frequent changes would still be a great evil. All this becomes clear at a first glance.

So how is it that American republics sustain themselves and prosper?

In laws, one should make a careful distinction between their aim and the means adopted to achieve that aim, as between their absolute and their relative excellence.

I am supposing that the legislator must aim to support the interests of the few at the expense of the many; his measures are executed so as to achieve his proposed aim in the shortest time and with the least effort. The law will be well drafted but its aim bad; its very effectiveness will make it the more dangerous.

Democratic laws generally tend toward the good of the greatest possible number for they stem from the majority of all the citizens, a majority which may be in error but which could not follow a path contrary to its own interests.

Aristocratic laws tend, by contrast, toward concentrating wealth and power solely in the hands of a small number, because aristocracy consists of a minority by its very nature.

So, in general terms, it may be stated that the purpose of a democracy, in its legislation, is beneficial to a greater number of people than that of an aristocracy. But that is the sum total of its advantages.

Aristocracy is infinitely more skillful in the science of legislation than democracy could ever be. Being master of itself, passing impulses do not affect it; its plans ripen over the long term until favorable conditions occur. Aristocracy moves forward cannily, knowing the art of bringing together the collective force of all its laws at the same time to the same point.

Democracy is not like that; its laws are almost always defective or untimely.

The means adopted by a democracy are therefore more imperfect than those used by an aristocracy; often it works, unintentionally, against itself but its aim is more beneficial.

If you imagine a society so organized by nature or its constitution that it can bear the passing effects of bad laws or can avoid disaster as it awaits the consequences of the general tendency of those laws, you will appreciate that democratic government, despite its defects, is still the best suited to the prosperity of that society.

That is exactly what happens in the United States. I repeat here what I have described elsewhere: the great privilege enjoyed by Americans is to be able to retrieve the mistakes they make.

I shall say something similar about public officials.

It is easy to see that American democracy often makes mistakes in the choice of its politicians but it is not so simple to say why the state prospers in their hands.

Notice, first of all, that although the rulers of a democracy are less honest and competent, the electorate is more enlightened and more alert.

The people in democracies, constantly busy as they are with their affairs and jealous of their rights, stop their representatives straying from a certain general line prescribed by their self-interest.

Notice too, that, although a democratic magistrate may abuse his power more than another, in general he holds office for less time.

But there is another more general and more satisfactory reason than any of these.

No doubt it is important to the welfare of nations that their rulers possess virtues and talents but what possibly matters even more is that their rulers do not have interests in opposition to the mass of constituents for, in such a case, those virtues could become almost useless and those talents harmful.

I have underlined that it is important for governments not to have interests opposed to or different from the mass of their constituents; I have not said that they should have interests in line with those of all their constituents for I do not know whether such a thing has ever happened.

Up to the present time, no one has discovered a political system which equally favors the development and prosperity of all classes in society. These classes have continued to form something like distinct nations within the same nation and experience has shown that it was almost as dangerous to place the fate of all these classes in the hands of any one of them as it is to make one nation the judge of any other nation's destiny. When the rich alone rule, the interests of the poor are always in danger; and when the poor make laws, the rich see their interests in great jeopardy. What, then, is the advantage offered by democracy? The real advantage is not, as is claimed, to favor the prosperity of all, but only to serve the wellbeing of the greatest number.

In the United States, those responsible for public affairs are often inferior in capability and in moral standards to those men aristocracy would bring to power, but their interests are mingled and identified with those of the majority of their fellow citizens. They may, therefore, frequently commit faithless acts and serious errors but they will never systematically pursue a line of conduct antagonistic to that majority; and they could not ever impose an exclusive or dangerous character on the government.

The bad administration of one magistrate in a democracy is, moreover, an isolated fact which has an influence for only the short period of his administration. Corruption and incompetence are not common interests capable of connecting men in any permanent fashion.

A corrupt or incompetent magistrate will not join his efforts to another magistrate's, simply because the latter is as incompetent or corrupt as he is, nor will these two men ever work together to promote corruption or incompetence in their distant descendants. The ambition and intrigues of the one will help, on the contrary, to unmask the other. The vices of a democratic magistrate are, generally speaking, altogether personal.

In aristocratic governments, men in public positions have class interests which occasionally coincide with those of the majority but more often than not remain quite separate. These interests form a shared and lasting bond between them which invites them to unite and combine their efforts toward an end which does not always promote the happiness of the greatest number. Not only do they tie the rulers to each other but also unite the latter to a large proportion of the governed, for many citizens make up part of the aristocracy even if they have no official office.

The aristocratic magistrate, therefore, finds a reliable support within society just as he finds the same within the government.

This common objective which unites the magistrates of aristocracies to the interests of one section of their contemporaries, also identifies them with those of future generations, in, so to speak, an act of submission. They work for the future as much as for the present. The aristocratic magistrate is, therefore, propelled in the same direction both by the passions of those governed and by his own, as well as, I may almost add, by those of posterity.

How can we be surprised, if he puts up no resistance? So we often see, in aristocracies, class spirit influencing even those who are not corrupted by it; and they shape society unconsciously to their own ends and prepare it for their own descendants.

I cannot say whether another aristocracy as liberal as that of England has ever existed or one which has, uninterruptibly, furnished the government of a country with men so worthy and intelligent.

Yet, it is easy to observe that in the legislation of England, the welfare of the poor has often ended up by being sacrificed to that of the wealthy and the rights of the greatest number to the privileges of the few. Thus, the England of the present time combines at its center all the extremes of human fate and you encounter sufferings there almost as great as its power and glory.

In the United States, where public officials promote no class interests, the general and continuous course of government is beneficial even though the rulers are often incompetent and sometimes despicable.

There is a hidden tendency at the heart of democratic institutions which often makes men support the prosperity of all, in spite of their mistakes or vices, whereas in aristocratic institutions a secret bias sometimes emerges, in spite of talents and virtues, to lead men to contribute to the sufferings of their fellows. In this way, it can happen that, in aristocratic governments, public officers commit evil acts without wishing to do so and in democracies bring about good results without having intended them.

PUBLIC SPIRIT IN THE UNITED STATES

Instinctive patriotism—Well-considered patriotism—Their different characters—Nations should strive toward the second when the first disappears—The efforts of Americans to achieve this—The interests of the individual closely linked to those of the country.

There exists a patriotism which springs mainly from that instinctive, disinterested, and indefinable feeling which binds a man's heart to his birthplace. This unreflecting love blends with the liking for ancient customs, respect for ancestors, and the memories of the past. Those who experience it cherish their homeland as they love their father's house. They love the peace they find there; they are attached to the quiet habits they have formed there; they are tied to the memories it recalls, even feel a tenderness in their life of obedience. Often this patriotism is also intensified by religious fervor which then works wonders. It is itself a sort of religion; it does not reason, it believes, feels, and acts. Some nations have in a sense personified their country and have seen this personification in the prince himself. They have thus transferred to him some of the feelings which compose patriotism; they feel pride in his triumphs and have boasted of his power. Time was, under the old monarchy, when the French experienced a kind of joy in surrendering themselves irrevocably to the arbitrary will of the monarch and were wont to say proudly: "We live under the most powerful king in the world."

Like all instinctive passions, patriotism drives men to temporary efforts rather than sustained endeavors. Having saved the state in time of crisis, it often allows it to languish in peace time.

When nations are still simple in their manners and fervent in their beliefs, when society rests gently upon an ancient order of things whose legitimacy goes uncontested, this instinctive love for one's country reigns supreme.

There exists yet another patriotism more rational than that: it is less generous, less passionate perhaps but more creative and lasting; it springs from education, develops with the help of laws, increases with the exercise of rights and in the end blends in a sense with personal interest. A man understands the influence which the wellbeing of his country has upon his own; he knows that the law allows him to contribute to the production of his own wellbeing and he is involved in the prosperity of his country, in the first place as something useful to him and then as work he should do.

But sometimes in the life of nations there occurs a moment when ancient customs are changed, behavior patterns destroyed, beliefs upturned, the value of memories has vanished and where, nonetheless, education has remained in an imperfect state and political rights are ill-founded and restricted. At such a time, men no longer perceive their native land except in a feeble and ambiguous light; their patriotism is centered neither on the land which they see as just inanimate earth nor on the customs of their ancestors which they have been taught to view as a yoke, nor on religion which they doubt, nor on laws which they do not enact, nor on the legislator whom they fear and despise. So, they can no longer see their country portrayed either under its own or borrowed features and men retreat into a narrow and unenlightened egoism. These men escape from prejudices without recognizing the power of reason; they have neither the instinctive patriotism of a monarchy nor the reflective patriotism of a republic; but they have come to a halt between the two in the midst of confusion and wretchedness.

What's to be done in such a predicament? Retreat. But nations do not return to youthful opinions any more than men return to the first tastes of their infancy; they may regret them but not rekindle them. So one must move forward and hurry to unite, in people's eyes, the interest of the individual with that of the country, for disinterested patriotism escapes never to return.

Certainly, I am far from claiming that to achieve this result the exercise of political rights should be granted all at once to every man; but I do say that the most potent, and possibly the only remaining weapon to involve men in the destiny of their country is to make them take a share in its government. In our day, civic spirit seems to me inseparable from the exercise of political rights and I believe that henceforth the increase or decrease of the number of citizens will be in proportion to the extension of those rights.

How is it that in the United States, where the inhabitants arrived but yesterday on the land they occupy, where they have brought with them neither customs nor memories, where they have met each other for the first time without prior acquaintance or where, to sum up, the feeling for one's country can hardly exist, each person gets as involved in the affairs of his township, canton, and the whole state as he does in his own business? It is because each person in his own sphere takes an active part in the government of society.

The common man in the United States perceives the influence of public prosperity upon his own happiness, an idea so simple and yet so little understood by the people. Moreover, he has grown used to regarding this prosperity as his own work. Thus he sees in public fortune his own and he works for the welfare of the state, not simply from duty or from pride, but, I would venture to say, from greed.

There is no need to study the institutions or history of the Americans to recognize the truth of the above, for their customs are sufficient evidence. Since an American takes part in everything that goes on in this country, he believes it his duty to defend it against any criticism for not merely is his country being attacked but he himself: thus, we see that the pride he has in his nation exploits every trick and stoops to all the childishness of personal vanity.

There is nothing more irksome in the conduct of life than the irritable patriotism Americans have. The foreigner would be very willing to praise much in their country but would like to be allowed a few criticisms; that is exactly what he is refused.

So, America is a land of freedom where the foreigner, to avoid offending anyone, must not speak freely about either individuals, or the state, or the governed, or the government, or public and private undertakings, indeed about anything he encounters except perhaps climate and the soil both of which, however, some Americans are ready to defend as if they had helped to create them.

In our day, we must make up our minds and dare to choose between the patriotism of all and the government of the few, for the social strength and the involvement of the first cannot be combined at the same time with the guarantees of peace sometimes provided by the second.

THE IDEA OF RIGHTS IN THE UNITED STATES

No great nation is without some idea of rights—How such an idea can be imparted to a nation—Respect for rights in the United States—Source of that respect.

Next to the general conception of virtue, I know of none finer than that of rights, or rather these two ideas are inseparable. The idea of rights is no more than the concept of virtue applied to the world of politics.

Men clarified the definition of license and tyranny by means of the idea of rights. By the light of this idea, each man has achieved an independence without arrogance and an obedience which avoids humiliation. The man who submits to violence bends beneath the degradation; but when he obeys the right to give orders which he acknowledges in his fellow man, to some degree he rises above the very person giving him commands. No great man can exist without virtue; no great nation can exist without respect for rights; one might almost say that there is no society without such respect. For what sort of gathering of rational and intelligent beings have you got where force is the sole bond between them?

I am wondering how, in our time, the idea of rights can be taught to men in order to insert it, so to speak, into their sensual experience. I see only one way and that is to give them the peaceful use of certain rights. That indeed happens with children who are men except in strength and experience. When the child begins to move in the world of external objects, instinct leads him to make use of everything which falls into his grasp. He has no idea of other people's property nor of existence itself; but as he grows aware of the value of things and realizes that he too can be deprived of them, he becomes more circumspect and in the end respects in his fellows what he wants them to respect in him.

What a child does with his toys, later a man does with his belongings. Why in America, this land of democracy par excellence, does no one raise that outcry against property in general which often echoes throughout Europe? Do I need to explain? In America, the proletariat does not exist. Since each man has some private possessions to protect, he acknowledges the right, in principle, to own property.

It is the same in the world of politics. In America, the common man has a lofty conception of political rights because he has such rights himself; he does not attack those of others so as to avoid having his own violated. And whereas in Europe this same man would be reluctant to obey even a sovereign authority, the American obeys without a murmur the authority of the lowest magistrate.

This truth is displayed right down to the smallest details of a nation's life. In France, there are few pleasures exclusively reserved for the upper classes of society; the poor man is admitted almost everywhere the rich are; thus he behaves in a seemly way and respects everything which contributes to the enjoyment he is sharing. In England, where the wealthy have the privilege of enjoying themselves as well as the monopoly of power, the complaint is that when the poor man manages to steal furtively into the exclusive haunts of the rich, he likes to cause pointless damage there. Why be surprised at that? Trouble has been taken to see that he has nothing to lose.

Democratic government allows the idea of political rights to filter down to the least of its citizens, just as the division of possessions places the idea of the right to property within the general grasp of all men. That, in my view, is one of its greatest merits.

I am not saying that teaching all men to avail themselves of their political rights is an easy task; I simply say that, when that aim is achieved, the results are great.

And I would add that if ever there was a century when such an undertaking might be attempted, that century is ours.

Do you not see the decline of religions and the disappearance of the divine conception of rights? Do you not realize that morals are changing and with them the moral notion of rights is being removed?

Do you not notice how, on all sides, beliefs are ceding place to rationality and feelings to calculations? If, amid this general upheaval, you fail to link the idea of rights to individual self-interest, which is the only fixed point in the human heart, what else have you got to rule the world except fear?

So, when I am told that laws are weak and the governed are in revolt, that passions are strong, that virtue is powerless and that in this situation one must not even contemplate increasing democratic rights, my reply is that these are the very things one must contemplate. And, in truth, I think that governments have an even greater incentive to do so than society, for governments perish but society cannot die. However, I have no wish to exploit the example of America too far.

In America, the people have been endowed with political rights at a time when it was difficult for them to abuse them because citizens were few and their customs simple. As they have grown, Americans have not really increased democratic powers, merely extended their domain.

There can be no doubt that the moment of granting political rights to a nation hitherto deprived of them is a time of crisis, one that is often necessary but always perilous.

The child kills when unaware of the value of life; he carries off another's property before realizing that his own may be snatched away. The common man, from the moment that he is granted political rights, stands, in relation to those rights, in the same position as a child faced with the whole of nature. It is then that the famous phrase can be applied to him: *Homo puer robustus.*[a]

The truth is evident in America itself. Those states where citizens have enjoyed their rights for the longest time are the ones who still know how best to use them.

It cannot be repeated too often: nothing is more fertile in wondrous effects than the art of being free but nothing is harder than freedom's apprenticeship. The same is not true of tyranny, which often advertises itself as the cure of all sufferings, the supporter of just rights, the upholder of the oppressed and the founder of order. Nations are lulled to sleep amid the brief period of prosperity it produces and when they do wake up, wretched they are indeed. On the other hand, freedom is usually born in stormy weather, growing with great difficulty amid civil disturbances. Only when it is already old can one recognize its advantages.

RESPECT FOR THE LAW IN THE UNITED STATES

Americans' respect for the law—Paternal affection they feel for it—Individual interest everyone has in increasing the power of the law.

It is not always feasible to summon an entire nation either directly or indirectly to make laws but it is undeniable that, when that is a practical possibility, the law acquires a greater authority thereby. This popular beginning confers an unusual strength upon the legislation even though it often damages its wisdom and quality.

An exceptional strength follows the expression of will of a

whole nation. Once it emerges into the light of day, even the imagination of those contesting it is somehow overwhelmed.

Political parties know this well enough.

Therefore, they challenge the validity of the majority whenever possible. When they fail to gain a majority of those who voted, they claim it among those who abstained from voting; when that fails, they seek a majority among those who have no right to vote.

In the United States, except for slaves, servants, and the destitute fed by the townships, everyone has the vote and this is an indirect contributor to law-making. Anyone wishing to attack the law is thus reduced to adopting one of two obvious courses: they must either change the nation's opinion or trample its wishes under foot.

To this first reason may be added one more directly powerful, namely that every American discovers a kind of personal interest in obeying the laws because the man who today does not belong to the majority may tomorrow be among its ranks. That respect for the will of the lawgiver which he now has, he will soon require the same for his own laws. However vexing the law, the American has no difficulty submitting to it, not simply as the work of the majority but as his very own. He regards it as a contract to which he is one of the parties.

Therefore, you never see in the United States an ever-increasing and agitated crowd which regards the law as hostile or which looks upon it with fear and suspicion. On the other hand, one cannot fail to observe that all classes of society demonstrate a great trust in the legislation of the country and feel a sort of paternal affection for it.

I am wrong in saying all classes. Since the European ladder of power has been overturned in America, the wealthy hold a position parallel to that of the poor in Europe; they are the ones who distrust the law. I have said elsewhere that the real advantage of democratic government is not to guarantee the interests of all, as has sometimes been the claim, but simply to protect those of the greatest number. In the United States, where the poor man rules, the wealthy must always be apprehensive that he may abuse his power against them.

This attitude of mind among the wealthy may produce a muffled discontent which, however, does not violently disturb society, since that very reason which stops the rich from trusting the lawmaker also prevents him defying his orders. He does not make the law because he is rich and because of his wealth he does not violate it. In civilized nations, it is generally only those with nothing to lose who revolt. Hence, though democratic laws are not always worthy of respect, they are almost always given respect. For those who generally break laws cannot fail to obey those they have made themselves and from which they profit and citizens who might be tempted to infringe them are inclined by disposition and circumstance to obey the lawgiver's will. Moreover, in America, people obey the law not merely because they made it but also because they can alter it, if it ever happens to harm them. They obey what they see firstly as a self-imposed evil and secondly as an evil which is always temporary.

ACTIVITY REIGNING IN EVERY PART OF THE BODY POLITIC IN THE UNITED STATES AND ITS INFLUENCE ON SOCIETY

It is harder to imagine the political activity reigning in the United States than the freedom or equality prevailing there—The continuous feverish activity of the legislatures is only one episode and an extension of this general activity—The difficulty the American has of minding only his own business—Political agitation spreads to civil society—American industrial activity stems in part from this cause—Indirect advantages derived by society from democratic government.

When one moves from a free country into one that is not so, one is struck by a most extraordinary sight: there all is activity and bustle, here all is calm and stillness. In the former, improvement and progress are all that matter; in the latter, society appears to have obtained every blessing and simply longs for the leisure to enjoy them. However, the country which suffers so much turmoil to be happy is usually wealthier and more prosperous than the one that appears satisfied with its lot. And considering them one by one, it is hard to imagine how so many fresh needs are daily discovered in the one, while so few are experienced in the other.

If this observation applies to free countries which have preserved a monarchy or an aristocratic dominance, it is even more true of democratic republics, where no longer a section of the people undertakes to improve the state of society but the whole nation. Not only is it a matter of satisfying the needs and comforts of one class but of all classes simultaneously.

It is not impossible to imagine the great freedom enjoyed by Americans and one can also form an idea of their extreme equality but it would not be possible to understand the political activity prevailing in the United States without having been a direct witness of it.

No sooner do you set foot in America than you find yourself in a sort of tumult; a confused clamor rises on every side; a thousand voices reach your ears at once, each expressing some social need. Everything stirs about you; on this side, the inhabitants of one district have met to decide on the building of a church; on the other, they are working to choose a representative; further on, the delegates of a canton are hurrying to town so as to consult over certain local improvements; at another spot, village farmers leave ploughing furrows to discuss the plan for a road or a school; a few citizens gather simply to declare their disapproval of the government's course, while others join together to proclaim that the men in office are the fathers of their country. And yet another group, which regards drunkenness as the main source of ills in the state, has come to enter into a solemn commitment to give an example of temperance.[1]

The great political activity which constantly stirs the American legislature and which alone is noticed from outside, is only

1. Temperance societies are organizations whose members undertake to abstain from strong liquor.

At the time of my travels in the United States, temperance societies had already more than 270,000 members and their effect had been to reduce, in the state of Pennsylvania alone, the consumption of strong liquor by 500,000 gallons per annum.

an episode, and an extension of this general activity which begins in the lowest ranks of society and gradually reaches all classes of citizens. It would be impossible to work harder for happiness.

It is difficult to describe the place political concerns occupy in the life of an American. To have a hand in the government of society, and to talk about it, is the most important business and, so to speak, the only pleasure an American knows. Such is evident in the slightest habits of his life: even the women often go to public meetings to relax from domestic chores by listening to political speeches. For them, clubs replace theaters to a certain extent. An American does not know how to converse but he argues; he does not speak but he holds forth. He addresses you as he would a meeting and, if he happens to get excited, he will say: "Gentlemen," when addressing his audience of one.

In certain countries, the inhabitant shows a sort of distaste in accepting the political rights granted by the law; he regards communal concerns as a waste of his time and he prefers to enfold himself in a narrow selfishness staked out precisely by four ditches bounded by hedges.

In contrast, if an American were to be reduced to minding only his own business, he would be deprived of half his existence; he would experience it as a gaping void in his life and would become unbelievably unhappy.[2]

I am convinced that, if ever tyranny succeeds in getting a foothold in America, it will have even more difficulties in overcoming the habits formed by freedom than in conquering the love of freedom itself.

This constantly renewed agitation introduced by democratic government into the political domain subsequently passes into civil society. Perhaps, all in all, that is the greatest advantage of democratic government which I praise much more for what it causes to be done than for what it actually does.

It is beyond dispute that the people often manage public

2.   The same remark was made in Rome under the first Caesars.
      Montesquieu somewhere notes that nothing equaled the despair of certain Roman citizens who, after the excitement of political life, suddenly returned to the doldrums of private life.

affairs very badly but they would be unable to mind public affairs at all if the scope of their ideas did not develop more broadly and their minds did not escape their ordinary routine. The common man summoned to the task of governing society acquires a certain self-esteem. Since he then has the authority, men of enlightened education are placed at his disposal. He is constantly approached for his support and he learns a lot from the thousand different attempts at deceiving him. In politics, he takes part in enterprises which he has never imagined but which give him a general taste for such undertakings. Each day, people point out to him fresh improvements to the property of the community and he feels a new desire to improve his own. He is, perhaps, neither more virtuous nor happier than his forebears but he is more enlightened and active than they were. I am quite clear that democratic institutions, combined with the geography of the country, are the indirect reason, and not the direct one as so many say, for the remarkable industrial activity seen in the United States. This is not created by the laws but by the people who have learned to exploit the law in order to achieve it.

When those hostile to democracy claim that one man fulfills his duties more effectively than when all are involved in government, I think they are correct. Government by one man alone is more consistent in his rule than a crowd would be, supposing equal enlightenment in both these parties. He displays more persistence, more overall vision, more attention to detail, a better judgment of men. Anyone who refutes these things has either never seen a democratic republic at work or bases his assessment on very few examples. It is true that democracy, even when local conditions and popular attitudes foster its progress, does not display method and order in its government. Democratic freedom does not carry through each of its undertakings with the same perfect execution as intelligent tyranny; it often abandons them before reaping the profit, or embarks on dangerous ones; but, in the long term, it achieves more than tyranny; each task is less well done but more tasks are completed. Under its authority, it is not especially what public administration does which is great but what is done beyond and without its help. Democracy does not give its nation the most skillful administration but it ensures what the most skillful administration is often too powerless to create, namely to spread through the whole social community a restless activity, an over-abundant force, an energy which never exists without it and which, however unfavorable the circumstances, can perform wonders. Therein lie its real advantages.

In this century, when the fate of the Christian world appears to hang in the balance, some hasten to attack democracy as a hostile power as it is still growing; others already worship it as a new god emerging from the void. But both know the object of their hatred or desire only imperfectly; they fight in the dark and strike out at random.

What are you requiring of society and its government? One must be clear about that.

Do you wish to raise the human mind to a certain lofty and generous manner of viewing the things of this world? Do you wish to inspire in men a kind of scorn for material possessions?

Is it your desire to engender or foster deep convictions and to prepare the way for acts of deep devotion?

Is your main concern to refine manners, to raise behavior, to cause the arts to blossom? Do you crave poetry, reputation, glory?

Are you intending to organize a nation so that it will exercise strength of purpose over all others? Are you giving it the aim of undertaking mighty projects and leaving an impressive mark upon history, however its efforts turn out?

If, in your estimation, that should be the main objective of social man, do not choose a democratic government because it would not steer you to that goal with any certainty.

But, if it seems useful to you to divert man's intellectual and moral activity upon the necessities of physical life and use it to foster prosperity; if you think that reason is more use to men than genius; if you aim to create not heroic virtues but peaceful habits; if you prefer to witness vice rather than crime and to find fewer splendid deeds provided you have fewer transgressions; if, instead of moving through a brilliant society, you are satisfied to live in a prosperous one; if, finally, in your view, the main objective for a government is not to give the whole nation as much strength or glory as possible but to obtain for each of the individuals who make it up as much wellbeing as possible, while avoiding as much suffering as one can, then make social conditions equal and set up a democratic government.

If, however, there is not enough time to make a choice and a force beyond man's control is already carrying you along, regardless of your wishes, toward one of these two governments, at least seek to derive from it all the good it can do. And, aware of its good instincts as well as its unfortunate leanings, make every effort to restrict the consequences of the latter while promoting the former.

CHAPTER 7

THE MAJORITY IN THE UNITED STATES IS ALL-POWERFUL AND THE CONSEQUENCES OF THAT

Natural strength of the majority in democracies—Most American constitutions have artificially increased this natural strength—How—Pledged delegates—Moral power of the majority—View of its infallibility—Respect for its rights—What increases it in the United States.

It is the very essence of democratic government that the power of the majority should be absolute, for in democracies nothing outside the majority can keep it in check.

Most American constitutions have further sought to increase this natural strength of the majority by artificial means.[1]

Of all political powers, the legislature obeys most readily the will of the majority. Americans have decided that members of

1.   We saw, when we were looking at the federal constitution, that the Union legislators had made great efforts to counteract this. The result of these efforts has been to make the federal government more independent in its own sphere than that of the states. But the federal government scarcely ever concerns itself with anything but foreign affairs; it is the state governments that are in real control of American society.

the legislature should be appointed *directly* by the people and for a *very brief* term of office, so as to force them to bow not only to general public opinion but also to the passing passions of their constituents.

The members of both houses have been chosen from the same class and appointed in the same way; the consequence of this is that the deliberations of the legislative body are almost as swift as and no less irresistible than those of a single assembly.

Having constituted the legislature in this way, almost all the powers of government have been concentrated in its hands.

At the same time as the law increased the strength of naturally powerful authorities, it increasingly weakened those that were by nature weak. It granted the representatives of the executive neither stability nor independence and, by subordinating them completely to the whims of the legislature, it deprived them of what little influence democratic government might have allowed them to exert.

In several states, the majority elected the judicial authorities and in all states the latter depended in a way upon the power of the legislature whose representatives annually settled the judges' salaries.

Custom has furthered this process beyond what the law demanded.

Increasingly in the United States one habit is gaining ground which will, in the end, nullify the guarantees of representative government: very frequently the electors, having elected their delegate, will lay down a plan of behavior and will impose upon him a certain number of positive commitments he could in no way avoid. It is as if the majority itself, quite near to breaking into a rabble, were arguing its case in the marketplace.

In America, several special circumstances still tend to make the power of the majority not merely all-powerful but also irresistible.

The moral ascendancy of the majority is partly founded upon the idea that more enlightenment and wisdom are found in a group of men than in one man alone and that the number of legislators counts for more than who is elected. This is the theory of equality applied to intelligence and is a doctrine which attacks man's pride in its final hiding place; for that reason, the minority admits it reluctantly but gets used to it only after a long while. Like all powers, and possibly more than any other, that of the majority needs, therefore, to last a long time to appear legitimate. In the early stages, it commands obedience by constraint; only after living under the law for a long period of time do people begin to respect it.

The concept of the right of the majority to govern society, based on enlightenment, was brought to the United States by its first inhabitants. This idea, which alone would be enough to create a free nation, has today passed into common usage and appears even in the slightest habits of life.

The French, under the old monarchy, took it as read that the king could do no wrong and that whenever he acted badly, the blame should be laid at the door of his advisers. This made obedience wonderfully simple. One could grumble against the law while continuing to love and respect the legislator. Americans hold the same opinion of the majority.

The moral authority of the majority is also founded upon the principle that the interests of the greatest number must take precedence over those of the smallest. Now, it is readily understood that the respect professed for the right of the greatest number naturally grows or shrinks according to the state of the parties. When a nation is divided between several great irreconcilable interests, the privilege of the majority is often disregarded because it becomes too burdensome to submit to it.

If there existed a class of American citizens which the legislator was striving to strip of certain exclusive advantages which they had enjoyed for centuries, and wanted to bring them down from their elevated station to join the ranks of the crowd, this minority would probably not submit easily to his laws.

But, since the United States is peopled by men equal to each other, there is still no natural or permanent antagonism between the interests of the different inhabitants.

There is a state of society in which the members of a minority can never hope to win over the majority because, to do so, would entail the abandonment of the very object of the struggle they are waging against it. For example, an aristocracy could never become a majority as well as preserve its exclusive privileges and it could never let go of its privileges without ceasing to be an aristocracy.

In the United States political questions cannot be framed in such a general or absolute fashion and all parties are ready to acknowledge the rights of the majority because they are all hoping to be able one day to exercise them to their own advantage.

Hence the majority in the United States possesses immense actual power and a power of opinion almost as great; and when it has once made up its mind over a question, there are, so to speak, no obstacles which might, I will not say halt, but even retard its onward course long enough to allow it time to heed the complaints of those it crushes as it goes by.

The consequences of this state of affairs are dire and dangerous for the future.

HOW IN AMERICA THE OMNIPOTENCE OF THE MAJORITY INCREASES THE LEGISLATIVE AND ADMINISTRATIVE INSTABILITY NATURAL TO DEMOCRACIES

How the Americans increase the instability of the legislature which is natural to democracies by changing their legislators annually and by arming them with almost limitless power—The same effect felt in the administration—In America social improvements are promoted by an infinitely greater yet less consistent drive than in Europe.

I have previously mentioned the defects natural to democratic government and not a single one of them fails to increase along with the growing power of the majority.

To begin with the most powerful of all: the instability of the legislature is an inbuilt weakness of democratic government because it is in the nature of democracies to bring fresh faces to power. But this weakness is greater or less according to the power and means of action granted to the legislator.

In America, sovereign power is invested in the legislative

authority, which can then carry out any of its wishes swiftly and without opposition; every year it is given new representatives. This means that precisely that combination has been adopted which most favors democratic instability and allows democracy to apply to the most important issues its ever changing wishes.

Thus America is today the one country in the world where laws last for the least time. Almost all American constitutions have been amended over the last thirty years. Every American state has, therefore, altered the basis of its laws during that period.

As for the laws themselves, a glance over the various state archives is all you need to be convinced that the activities of the American legislator never slow down. Not that American democracy is of its nature more unstable than any other but it has, in the making of its laws, been allowed to follow the natural instability of its inclinations.[2]

The omnipotence of the majority and the swift and absolute manner of the execution of its will in the United States not only increase the instability of the law but also have the same effect on the enactment of the law and the activity of public administration.

Since the only authority one wishes to please is the majority, all its projects are supported with enthusiasm; but as soon as its attention is drawn elsewhere, all effort comes to an end, whereas, in all the free states of Europe where administrative authority enjoys an independent existence and a stable position, the wishes of the legislator continue to be executed even when he is otherwise occupied.

In America, a great deal more enthusiasm and energy are spent on certain improvements than would be spent elsewhere.

In Europe, an infinitely smaller but more consistent force is used on these same matters.

2.   The legislative acts passed by the state of Massachusetts alone from the year 1780 to the present time already fill three huge volumes. We have also to note that the collection to which I allude was revised in 1823 when many old laws which had fallen into disuse were set aside. Now the state of Massachusetts, which has a population no bigger than a French *département*, may be considered as the most stable in the entire Union and the one which shows the most prudence and wisdom in its undertakings.

Several years ago, several religious men undertook to improve the state of the prisons. The public was roused by their opinions and the rehabilitation of criminals became a popular cause.

New prisons were then built. For the first time, the idea of reforming the criminal crept into the prison cell alongside that of punishing him. But this fortunate revolution, which was carried along with such public zeal and which became irresistible through the combined efforts of the citizens, could not be accomplished in an instant.

Alongside the new penitentiaries built quickly, prompted by the desire of the majority, the old prisons still remained and continued to house a large number of the guilty. These seemed to turn more unsavory and more corrupting as the new ones became more reforming and more healthy. Such a twin effect is easy to understand: preoccupied with the idea of founding a new establishment, the majority had forgotten the already existing one. Then everyone averted their eyes from the object which had ceased to attract their masters' gaze and supervision stopped. The salutary bonds of discipline first relaxed and soon afterwards broke asunder. And by the side of the prison which was the lasting monument of gentleness and enlightenment in our time stood a cell which recalled the barbarity of the Middle Ages.

TYRANNY OF THE MAJORITY

How the principle of the sovereignty of the people should be understood—Impossibility of imagining a mixed government—Sovereign power must be placed somewhere—Precautions necessary for moderating its influence—These precautions have not been taken in the United States—The result of that.

The maxim that in matters of government the majority of a nation has the right to do everything I regard as unholy and detestable; yet, I place the origin of all powers in the will of the majority. Am I contradicting myself?

One universal law has been made, or at least accepted, not

only by the majority of such and such a nation but by the majority of all men: that is the law of justice.

Justice, therefore, forms the boundary stone of the right of each nation.

A nation resembles a jury entrusted with the task of representing universal society and of applying justice which is its law. Should the jury representing society have more power than society itself whose laws it administers?

When, therefore, I refuse to obey an unjust law, I am not denying the majority's right to give orders; I simply appeal to the sovereignty of the human race over that of the people.

Some people have not been frightened to state that a nation could not entirely exceed the limits of justice and reason in those things which involved only itself and that there is, therefore, no necessity to fear giving complete power to the majority representing it. But that is the language of a slave.

So, what is a majority taken as a collective whole, if not an individual with opinions and quite often interests, in opposition to another individual whom we call a minority? Now, if you admit that an all-powerful man can abuse his power against his opponents, why not admit the same thing for a majority? Have men, united together, changed their character? Have they become more patient of obstacles by becoming stronger?[3] For my part, I cannot think so and I shall never grant to several the power to do anything they like which I refuse to grant to a single one of my fellows.

It is not that I think, in order to preserve liberty, that several principles are best combined in the same government so as to place one in real opposition to another.

A so-called mixed government is an illusion. There is no truly mixed government (in the sense given to this word) because, in every society, one discovers in the end one principle of action which dominates all the others.

3.   No one would wish to assert that a nation cannot abuse its strength against another nation. Now the parties are virtually a set of small nations within a great one; they are like foreigners in relation to each other.

If we agree that one nation can be despotic toward another, how can we deny that one party may be the same toward another party?

England, in the eighteenth century, quoted particularly as an example of such types of government, was an essentially aristocratic state even though considerable democratic elements existed within it, for laws and customs were so set up that the aristocracy was always going to predominate in the end and to govern public matters along its own lines.

The error stemmed from the fact that people saw the interests of the great in constant conflict with those of the common people and thus thought only about this struggle instead of paying attention to the outcome of this struggle, which was the more important issue. When a society really does have a mixed government, that is to say, one equally divided between opposing principles, it embarks upon revolution or it breaks apart.

I, therefore, think that one social authority, superior to all the others, should be placed somewhere, but I believe freedom to be under threat when that authority sees no barrier in its way which can hinder its course and give it the time to restrain itself.

Omnipotence seems self-evidently a bad and dangerous thing. Its exercise appears to be beyond man's powers, whoever he might be, and I see that only God can be omnipotent without danger because his wisdom and justice are always equal to his power. There is, therefore, no earthly authority so worthy of respect or vested with so sacred a right that I would wish to allow it unlimited action and unrestricted dominance. When, therefore, I see the right and capacity to enact everything given to any authority whatsoever, whether it be called people or king, democracy or aristocracy, whether exercised in a monarchy or a republic, I say: the seed of tyranny lies there and I seek to live under different laws.

My main complaint against a democratic government as organized in the United States is not its weakness, as many Europeans claim, but rather its irresistible strength. And what I find most repulsive in America is not the extreme freedom that prevails there but the shortage of any guarantee against tyranny.

When a man or a party suffers from an injustice in the United States, to whom can he turn? To public opinion? That is what forms the majority. To the legislative body? That represents the majority and obeys it blindly. To the executive power? That is appointed by the majority and serves as its passive instrument. To the public police force? They are nothing but the majority under arms. To the jury? That is the majority invested with the right to pronounce judgments; the very judges in certain states are elected by the majority. So, however unfair or unreasonable the measure which damages you, you must submit.[4]

But, suppose you had a legislative body composed in such a way that it represented the majority without necessarily being the slave of its passions, or an executive authority with its own

4.   A striking example of the excesses which the despotism of the majority may occasion was seen in Baltimore during the war of 1812. At that time the war was very popular in Baltimore. A newspaper opposed to it aroused the indignation of the inhabitants by taking that line. The people came together, destroyed the printing presses and attacked the journalists' premises. The call went out to summon the militia which, however, did not respond to the call. In order to save these wretched fellows threatened by the public frenzy the decision was taken to put them in prison like criminals. This precaution was useless. During the night the people gathered once again; when the magistrates failed to summon the militia, the prison was forced, one of the journalists was killed on the spot and the others were left for dead. The guilty parties, when standing before a jury, were acquitted.

I said one day to someone who lived in Pennsylvania: "Kindly explain to me how, in a state founded by Quakers and celebrated for its tolerance, free Negroes are not allowed to exercise their civil rights. They pay their taxes; is it not fair that they should have the vote?"

"You insult us," he replied, "if you imagine that our legislators committed such a gross act of injustice and intolerance."

"Thus the blacks possess the right to vote in this country?"

"Without any doubt."

"So, how does it come about that at the polling-booth this morning I did not notice a single Negro in the crowd?"

"That is not the fault of the law," said the American to me. "It is true that the Negroes have the right to participate in the elections but they voluntarily abstain from making an appearance."

"That is indeed very modest of them."

"It is not that they are refusing to attend, but they are afraid of being mistreated. In this country it sometimes happens that the law lacks any force when the majority does not support it. Now, the majority is imbued with the strongest of prejudices against the blacks and the magistrates do not feel that they have enough strength to guarantee the rights which the legislator has conferred upon them."

"So you mean that the majority, which has the privilege of enacting the laws, also wishes to enjoy the privilege of disobeying them?"

independent strength, or a judiciary independent of the other two, you would still have a democratic government but with hardly any risk of tyranny.

I am not suggesting that, at the present time in America, there are frequent instances of tyranny. I am saying that no guarantee against tyranny is evident and that the causes for the mildness of the government should be sought more in circumstances and habits than in laws.

EFFECTS OF THE OMNIPOTENCE OF THE MAJORITY ON THE ARBITRARY POWER OF AMERICAN PUBLIC OFFICIALS

The freedom which American law allows to public officials within the sphere of office drawn for them—Their power.

A distinction must be made between arbitrary power and tyranny. Tyranny may thrive by means of the law itself and then it is no longer arbitrary; arbitrary power may thrive in the interests of the governed and then it is not tyranny.

Tyranny usually makes use of arbitrary power but can do without it when needs be.

In the United States the omnipotence of the majority, while supporting the legal despotism of the legislator, also supports the arbitrary power of the magistrate. Since the majority has absolute control over making the law and supervising its execution, and since it has equal control over rulers and ruled, it considers its public officials as its passive agents and is glad to leave to them the care of serving its strategies. It, therefore, does not itemize in advance the details of their duties and scarcely bothers to define their rights. It treats them as a master would his servants if, seeing their every action, he was always able to direct or correct their conduct at any moment.

Within the sphere of office drawn for them, the law generally leaves American officials a freer rein than ours. Sometimes the majority even allows them to stray from those rules. They then dare to do things which a European, accustomed to the spectacle of arbitrary power, finds astonishing; this is because they are assured of the views of the greatest number and gain strength from its support. Thus habits are forming at the heart of freedom which one day could be fatal to its liberties.

THE POWER EXERCISED BY THE MAJORITY IN AMERICA OVER THOUGHT

In the United States, when the majority has irrevocably decided any question, discussion ceases—Why?—The moral power exerted by the majority over thought—Democratic republics render despotism immaterial.

When one happens to examine how thought is exercised in the United States, one sees very clearly how far the power of the majority exceeds all the powers known to us in Europe.

Thought is an invisible power which cannot be bound and which makes fun of tyrannies. In our day, the most absolute sovereigns in Europe cannot prevent certain thoughts hostile to their authority from circulating secretly in their states or even in the heart of their courts. The same is not true of America; as long as the majority cannot make up its mind, speech is allowed; as soon as it has pronounced its irrevocable decision, speech is silenced. Friends along with enemies seem to hitch themselves to its wagon. The reason for that is simple: no monarch is so absolute that he can gather all the forces of society into his own hands and overcome resistance as can a majority endowed with the right of enacting laws and executing them.

Moreover, a king has a power which is only physical, affecting people's actions and unable to influence their wills. But the majority is endowed with a force both physical and moral which affects people's will as much as their actions and which at the same time stands in the way of any act and the desire to do it.

I know of no country where there is generally less independence of thought and real freedom of debate than in America.

Every possible religious or political theory may be preached freely in the constitutional states of Europe and may spread into all the others; for no European country is so subject to a single power that a man wishing to express the truth there cannot find support enough to protect him against the consequences of his independence. If he has the misfortune to live under an absolute government, he often enjoys the support of the people; if he lives in a free country, he may, if the need arises, shelter behind the authority of the monarch. The aristocratic part of society may support him in democratic countries, while democracy will do so in others. But within a democracy organized like that of the United States, only one power is encountered, only one source of strength and success, with nothing outside them.

In America, the majority has staked out a formidable fence around thought. Inside those limits a writer is free but woe betide him if he dares to stray beyond them. Not that he need fear an auto-da-fé[a] but he is the victim of all kinds of unpleasantness and everyday persecutions. A political career is closed to him for he has offended the only power with the capacity to give him an opening. He is denied everything, including renown. Before publishing his views, he thought he had supporters; it seems he has lost them once he has declared himself publicly; for his detractors speak out loudly and those who think as he does, but without his courage, keep silent and slink away. He gives in and finally bends beneath the effort of each passing day, withdrawing into silence as if he felt ashamed at having spoken the truth.

Formerly tyranny employed chains and executioners as its crude weapons; but nowadays civilization has civilized despotism itself even though it appeared to have nothing else to learn.

Princes had, so to speak, turned violence into a physical thing but our democratic republics have made it into something as intellectual as the human will it intends to restrict. Under the absolute government of one man, despotism, in order to attack the spirit, crudely struck the body and the spirit escaped free of its blows, rising gloriously above it. But in democratic republics, tyranny does not behave in that manner; it leaves the body alone and goes straight to the spirit. No longer does the master say: "You will think as I do or you will die"; he says: "You are free not to think like me, your life, property, everything will be untouched but from today you are a pariah among us. You will retain your civic privileges but they will be useless to you, for if you seek the votes of your fellow citizens, they will not grant you them and if you simply seek their esteem, they will pretend to refuse you that too. You will retain your place amongst men but you will lose the rights of mankind. When you approach your fellows, they will shun you like an impure creature; and those who believe in your innocence will be the very people to abandon you lest they be shunned in their turn. Go in peace; I grant you your life but it is a life worse than death."

Absolute monarchies had brought despotism into dishonor; let us guard against democratic republics reinstating it and rendering it less odious and degrading in the eyes of the many by making it more burdensome for the few.

Among the proudest nations of the Old World works were published which aimed to portray faithfully the defects and absurdities of their contemporaries; La Bruyère[b] was living in Louis XIV's palace when he wrote his chapter on great men and Molière[c] was criticizing the court in plays he was acting in front of the courtiers. But the dominating power in the United States does not understand being mocked like that. The slightest reproach offends it, the smallest sharp truth stimulates its angry response and it must be praised from the style of its language to its more solid virtues. No writer, however famous, can escape from this obligation to praise his fellow citizens. The majority lives therefore in an everlasting self-adoration. Only foreigners or experience might be able to bring certain truths to the ears of Americans.

If America has not yet found any great writers, we should not look elsewhere for reasons; literary genius does not thrive without freedom of thought and there is no freedom of thought in America.

The Inquisition[d] was never able to stop the circulation in Spain of books hostile to the religion of the majority. The power of the majority in the United States has had greater success than that by removing even the thought of publishing such books. You come across skeptics in America but skepticism cannot find an outlet for its views.

One finds governments that strive to protect public morals by condemning the authors of licentious books. In the United

States, no one is condemned for these types of work; there again no one is tempted to write them. However, it is not that all citizens have pure morals but that those of the majority are well regulated.

Here no doubt the use of this power is good; thus I speak only of power in itself. This irresistible power is a continuous fact and its good use only an accident.

EFFECTS OF THE TYRANNY OF THE MAJORITY ON AMERICAN NATIONAL CHARACTER; THE COURTIER SPIRIT IN THE UNITED STATES

The effects of the tyranny of the majority make themselves felt up until now more upon the morality than the behavior of society—They halt the development of great characters—Democratic republics organized on American lines place the courtier spirit within the reach of great numbers of citizens—Evidence of this spirit in the United States—Why more patriotism is present in the people than in those who rule in their name.

The influence of what I have been talking about makes itself felt only weakly in political society but already some vexing effects are evident in the American national character. I think that the presence of the small number of remarkable men upon the political scene has to be due to the ever-increasing despotism of the American majority.

When the American revolution broke out, such men emerged in great numbers; at that time, public opinion directed men's wills without tyrannizing them. The famous men of that period, in free association with the intellectual movement of that age, had a greatness all their own and spread their brilliance on the nation, not vice versa.

In absolute governments, great men surrounding the throne flatter the passions of the master and readily bow to his whims. But the mass of the nation does not take kindly to servitude, submitting to it often from weakness, habit, ignorance, or sometimes from its affection for royalty or for the king himself.

Nations have been known to derive a sort of pleasure or pride from sacrificing their will to that of the prince and thus inserting a kind of independence of mind into the very heart of their obedience. In such nations one encounters much less degradation than misery. Besides, there is a considerable difference between doing what you do not approve and pretending to approve what you are doing; the first is the act of a weak man but the second simply befits the ways of a valet.

In free countries, where everyone is more or less called upon to give an opinion of state affairs, and in democratic republics, where public and private life is constantly muddled together, where the sovereign is approachable from every side and where simply by raising one's voice one can attract his attention, you find many more people seeking to speculate on his weakness and to live off his passions than in absolute monarchies. It is not that men are naturally worse there than elsewhere, but that the temptation there is stronger and is available to more people at the same time. The consequence is a much more universal lowering of spiritual standards.

Democratic republics place the spirit of a court within the reach of a great number of citizens and allow it to spread through all social classes at once. That is one of the most serious criticisms that can be made against them.

That is especially true of democratic states organized on the lines of American republics in which the majority possesses such an absolute and irresistible power that a citizen has to abandon to some extent his rights and, so to speak, his very qualities as a man, if he wishes to diverge from the path marked out by the majority. Among the huge throng of those pursuing a political career in the United States, I saw very few men who displayed that manly openness, that male independence of thought, which has often distinguished Americans in previous times and which, wherever it is found, is virtually the most marked characteristic of great men. At first glance, one might suppose that all American minds had been fashioned on the same model because they so closely follow the same paths. It is true that sometimes foreigners meet Americans who deviate from the straitjacket of formulas; such men may deplore the defects of the law, the instability of democracies, and the lack of enlightenment. They often go so far as noting the defects which are changing the national character and outline the means for correcting them. But you are the only one to listen to them and you, the confidant of these secret thoughts, are nothing more than a foreigner passing through. They are quite ready to release useless truths to you and use quite another language once down in the market square.

If these lines ever reach the American public, I am convinced of two things: firstly, that readers will all raise their voices in condemnation; secondly many of them will forgive me from the depths of their conscience.

I have heard the motherland spoken of in the United States. I have encountered a sincere patriotism in the people. I have often looked in vain for any such thing in their rulers. An analogy makes this easily understandable: despotism corrupts the man who submits to it much more than the man who imposes it. In absolute monarchies the king often has great virtues but the courtiers are always the lowest of the low.

It is true that American courtiers never say: "Sire," or "Your Majesty," as if this difference was of great importance, but they do constantly speak of the natural enlightenment of their master. They do not seek to question which is the most admirable of the prince's virtues for they convince him that he has every virtue without his having acquired them and without, so to speak, desiring them. They do not give him their wives or daughters for him kindly to raise them to the position of his mistresses but, in sacrificing their opinions to him, they prostitute themselves.

American moralists and philosophers are not forced to wrap their opinions in veils of allegory but, before risking an inconvenient truth, they say: "We know we speak to a nation too far above human weaknesses for them to remain other than masters of themselves. We would not use such language unless we were addressing men whose virtues and education make them alone among all others worthy to remain free."

How could the flatterers of Louis XIV better that?

For my part, I believe that in all governments of whatever sort meanness will attach itself to force and flattery to power. I know of only one method of preventing men from being debased and that is to grant to no one who has omnipotence the sovereign power to demean them.

THE GREATEST DANGER FOR AMERICAN REPUBLICS COMES FROM THE OMNIPOTENCE OF THE MAJORITY

Democratic republics are exposed to collapse through the poor use of their power, not through their lack of it—The government of American republics more centralized and more energetic than that of European monarchies—Resulting danger—Madison's and Jefferson's opinion on this subject.

Governments usually collapse through lack of power or through tyranny. In the former case, power slips from their hands; in the latter, it is snatched away.

Many people, on seeing democratic states succumb to anarchy, have supposed that the government of these states was fundamentally weak and powerless. The truth is that the government loses all influence over society once war has broken out among the parties. But I think it is not the fundamental nature of democratic power to lack strength or resources; rather, it is the abuse of its strength and the poor use of its resources that bring about its downfall. Almost always anarchy grows out of tyranny or the incompetence of democracy but not its powerlessness.

Stability must not be confused with strength, nor the greatness of anything with its duration. In democratic republics, the authority directing society[5] is not stable for it often changes personnel and its aims. But wherever it is exercised, its strength cannot be resisted.

The government of American republics appears to me as centralized and more energetic than that of the absolute

5. This power may be centralized in an assembly when it is strong without being stable; or it may be centralized in one individual when it is less strong but more stable.

monarchies of Europe. So I do not suppose that weakness will cause its downfall.[6]

If ever freedom is lost in America, blame will have to be laid at the door of the omnipotence of the majority, which will have driven minorities to despair and will have forced them to appeal to physical force. Then one will see anarchy which will come as a consequence of despotism.

President James Madison has expressed these same thoughts. (See *The Federalist*, no. 51.)

"It is of great importance in a republic, not only to guard the society against the oppression of its rulers, but to guard one part of the society against the injustice of the other part. Justice is the end of government. It is the end of civil society. It ever has been, and ever will be, pursued until it be obtained, or until liberty be lost in the pursuit. In a society, under the forms of which the stronger faction can readily unite and oppress the weaker, anarchy may as truly be said to reign as in a state of nature, where the weaker individual is not secured against the violence of the stronger: and as, in the latter state, even the stronger individuals are prompted by the uncertainty of their condition to submit to a government which may protect the weak as well as themselves, so, in the former state, will the more powerful factions be gradually induced by a like motive to wish for a government which will protect all parties, the weaker as well as the more powerful. It can be little doubted, that, if the state of Rhode Island was separated from the Confederacy and left to itself, the insecurity of rights under the popular form of government within such narrow limits would be displayed by such reiterated oppressions of factious majorities, that some power altogether independent of the people would soon be called for by the voice of the very factions whose misrule had proved the necessity of it."

Jefferson also said: "The executive in our government is not the sole, it is scarcely the principal object of my jealousy. The

---

6.   I am supposing that is unnecessary to warn the reader that, in this instance, as in the rest of the chapter, I am speaking not of the federal government but of the individual governments of each state which are directed tyrannically by the majority.

tyranny of the legislators is the most formidable dread at present, and will be for long years. That of the executive will come in its turn, but it will be at a remote period."[7]

In this matter I prefer to quote Jefferson to anyone else because I regard him as the most powerful apostle democracy has ever had.

CHAPTER 8

WHAT MODERATES THE TYRANNY OF THE MAJORITY IN THE UNITED STATES

ABSENCE OF ADMINISTRATIVE CENTRALIZATION

The majority does not intend to do everything—It is obliged to use the magistrates of the townships and counties to execute its sovereign wishes.

I have previously made a distinction between two types of centralization; the one called governmental, the other administrative.

The first exists solely in America; the second is almost unknown.

If the directing authority in American societies had both these means of government available and combined the right of total command with the capacity and habit of total execution; if, after establishing the principles of government on a general level, it descended to the very details of application, and, after regulating the country's affairs on a grand scale, it could extend even to the affairs of individuals, freedom would soon be obliterated from the New World.

But, in the United States, the majority, which often has

---

7.   Letter from Jefferson to Madison, 15 March 1789.

despotic tastes and instincts, still lacks the most developed tools of tyranny.

In none of the American republics has the central government ever been occupied with anything but a small number of matters whose importance attracts its attention. It has not undertaken the regulation of society's secondary affairs. There is nothing to indicate it has even conceived the wish to do so. As the majority has become increasingly absolute, it has not enlarged the powers of the central authority; it has only made it omnipotent in its own sphere of action. Thus tyranny can be a burden at one point but could not extend to all points of influence.

Besides, however much the national majority may be driven by its passions, however enthusiastically it pursues its plans, it could not, in the same way, in every location, make all the citizens bow to its wishes at the same moment. When the central government which represents it issues a sovereign command, it has to rely for the execution of its orders upon agents who often do not depend upon it and who cannot be given minute by minute directions. As a result, municipal bodies and county administrations form so many hidden reefs which hold back or separate the flood of the people's will. Were the law to be oppressive, freedom would soon discover a means of protection in its method of executing this law. The majority could not possibly go into every detail nor, dare I say, into the trivialities of administrative tyranny. Indeed it does not imagine it could do so, for it does not possess total awareness of its own power. It still knows only its own natural forces and is unaware how far skill could extend its scope.

It is worth thinking about this point. If a democratic republic, similar to that of the United States, ever came to be founded in a country where the power of one man had already established a central administration and made it accepted by habit and law, I have no hesitation in saying that, in such a republic, tyranny would be less tolerable than in any of the absolute monarchies of Europe. You would need to go to Asia to find anything with which to compare it.

THE ATTITUDE OF THE AMERICAN LEGAL PROFESSION AND HOW IT ACTS AS A COUNTERBALANCE TO DEMOCRACY

The usefulness of examining what are the natural tendencies of the legal mind—The lawyers summoned to play an important role in a society struggling into existence—How the type of work undertaken by lawyers gives an aristocratic turn to their ideas—Chance circumstances which may block the development of these ideas—The ease with which the aristocracy unites with the lawyers—The use a despot could make of lawyers—How lawyers are the only aristocratic element which is naturally able to combine with elements natural to democracy— Particular causes which tend to give an aristocratic turn to the English and American legal mind—American aristocracy sits at the bar and on the bench—Lawyers' influence on American society—How their attitudes penetrate the legislature and administration ending up by giving the nation itself something of the instincts of magistrates.

On visiting Americans and studying their laws, one realizes that the power given to lawyers and the influence permitted to them in government today form the most potent barrier against the excesses of democracy. This result seems to stem from a general cause which it is worth examining for it may recur elsewhere.

Lawyers have been involved in all the movements in European society for five hundred years, now as tools of the political authorities, now using the political authorities as tools. In the Middle Ages, lawyers offered wonderful cooperation to kings in the development of their authority which, since that time, they have worked powerfully to restrict. In England they were seen in close union with the aristocracy; in France, they have proved its most dangerous enemies. Do lawyers, therefore, yield only to sudden and temporary impulses or do they obey, more or less according to circumstances, constantly recurring instincts which are natural to them? I should like to clarify this issue for perhaps lawyers are called upon to play the leading part in a political society struggling into existence.

Men who have made the law their special study have learned habits of orderliness from this legal work, a certain taste for formalities, a sort of instinctive love for a logical sequence of ideas, all of which make them naturally opposed to the revolutionary turn of mind and the ill-considered passions of democracy.

The specialized knowledge and study of the law acquired by lawyers guarantee them a position apart in society and make them into a sort of privileged intellectual class. In the exercise of their profession, they daily encounter the idea of superiority; they are experts in a vital area of knowledge which is not widely available; they arbitrate between citizens and the habit of guiding the blind passions of litigants toward an outcome gives them a certain scorn for the judgment of the crowd. In addition to that, they make up a natural professional body. Not that they all agree with each other or direct their combined energies toward the same point but that their shared studies and like methods link their minds together as their common interests link their desires.

Thus, in the depths of lawyers' souls a part of the tastes and practices of the aristocracy is found and they share the latter's instinctive liking for order, its natural love of formality and similarly conceive a deep distaste for the activities of the crowd and secretly despise the government of the people.

I do not imply that these natural tendencies of lawyers are strong enough to bind them in any irresistible fashion. What dominates lawyers, as all men, is individual self-interest and, above all, the concerns of the passing moment.

There are societies where lawyers cannot hold in the political world the same rank they occupy in their private life; in a society so ordered you may be certain that lawyers will be very active agents of revolution. But we must inquire whether it is a permanent feature of their character or accidental circumstances which lead them to destroy or to change. It is true that lawyers contributed to an unusual degree to the overthrow of the French monarchy in 1789. It remains to be seen whether they acted because they had studied law or because they could not share in making it.

Five hundred years ago, the English aristocracy placed itself at the head of the people and spoke in its name; today it supports the throne and stands as the champion of royal authority. But aristocracy has instincts and leanings which are peculiar to itself.

It is also necessary to be careful not to confuse isolated members of that body with the body itself.

In all free governments, whatever their make-up, lawyers will appear in the leading ranks of all parties. This same observation is true of the aristocracy. Almost all democratic movements which have troubled the world have been led by the nobility.

An elite body can never satisfy the ambitions of all its members; there are always more talents and passions than tasks to deploy and there are bound to be a great number of men who, being unable to rise quickly enough by exploiting the privileges of the group, seek fast promotion by attacking those very privileges.

Therefore I am not claiming that *all* lawyers will ever, or that most of them will *always*, prove supporters of order and enemies of change.

I am saying that in a society where lawyers unquestionably hold the high rank which naturally belongs to them, their attitude will be dominantly conservative and will prove anti-democratic.

When the aristocrats close their ranks to lawyers, they find the latter to be all the more dangerous as enemies because, although inferior to them in wealth and power, they are independent of them through their work and feel on a similar level through their intelligence.

But whenever the nobility has decided to share some of their privileges with the lawyers, these two classes have found many things which make it easy for them to join forces and have found that they belong to the same family, as it were.

Equally, I am inclined to believe that it will always be easy for a king to turn lawyers into the most useful instruments of his power.

There is immeasurably more natural sympathy between men

of the law and the executive officials than between the former and the people, even though lawyers often have to topple the executive; similarly, more natural sympathy exists between the nobility and the king than between the former and the people even though the upper social classes have been known to unite with others to fight against the power of the king.

What lawyers love above all is order and the greatest safeguard of order is authority. However, we must not forget that, valuing liberty as they might, they generally rate legality as much more precious. They fear tyranny less than arbitrary power and they are more or less content provided that it is the legislator himself who is responsible for removing men's independence.

I therefore think that the prince who sought, in the face of an encroaching democracy, to destroy the power of the judges in his states and to lessen the political influence of lawyers would be committing a great mistake. He would let go the substance of power to lay his hands on merely its shadow.

I am quite clear that he would find it better to bring the lawyers into the government. Having entrusted to them a violently achieved despotism, he might have received it back from them looking like justice and law.

Democratic government favors the political power of lawyers. When the wealthy, the nobles, and the prince are excluded from government, the lawyers come, as it were, into their own for they alone become the only enlightened and skilled men for a nation to choose outside its own ranks.

If lawyers are naturally drawn by their inclinations toward the aristocracy and the prince, their self-interest draws them just as naturally toward the people.

Thus lawyers like democratic government without sharing its inclinations or imitating its weaknesses; thus they derive a twin power from it and over it.

The people in a democracy are not suspicious of lawyers because they know that it is in their interest to serve the democratic cause; they listen to them without getting angry for they do not imagine that they have any ulterior motive. In fact, lawyers have no wish to overturn democracy's given government but they do strive endlessly to guide it along paths and by methods which are alien to its own. The lawyer belongs to the people out of self-interest and birth but to the aristocracy by customs and tastes; he is virtually the natural liaison officer between these two and the link which unites them.

The legal body represents the sole aristocratic element to mix effortlessly with the natural features of democracy and to combine with them in a happy and lasting way. I am aware of the inherent defects in the attitude of lawyers; nevertheless, without this combination of the legal with the democratic mind, I doubt whether democracy could govern society for long and I hardly believe that nowadays a republic could hope to survive, if the influence of lawyers in its affairs did not grow in proportion to the power of the people.

The aristocratic character which I detect in the legal mind is much more pronounced still in the United States and England than in any other country. This is due not only to English and American legal studies but to the very nature of the legislation and the position of lawyers as its interpreters in these two nations.

Both English and Americans have kept the law of precedent which means that they still draw their opinions in legal matters and the decisions they have to pronounce from the legal opinions and decisions of their fathers.

An English or American lawyer almost always, therefore, combines his taste and respect for what is old with his love for regularity and legality.

This has yet another influence over the way lawyers think and consequently over the course of society.

The English or American lawyer seeks out what has been done before, whereas the French lawyer inquires what he ought to do; the former looks for judgments, the latter, reasons.

Listening to an English or American lawyer, you are surprised to hear him citing so often others' opinions and talking so little of his own, while the opposite subsists in France.

The French lawyer will introduce his own system of ideas in however small a case he agrees to conduct and he will take the discussion back to the constituent principles of the law with a view to persuading the court to move the boundary of the contested inheritance back by a couple of yards.

This sort of denial of their own opinion in favor of the opinions of their fathers and this type of forced subjugation of their own thought must give the English and American legal minds more timid habits and cause them to adopt more static attitudes in their country than their colleagues in France.

Our written laws are often difficult to understand but everyone can read them, whereas nothing could be more obscure and less within the reach of the common man than legislation based on precedents. The necessity for lawyers in England and the United States and the elevated opinion one has for their learning separate them increasingly from the people and end up by placing them in a class apart. The French lawyer is only a man of learning but the English or American lawyers resemble somewhat Egyptian priests and are, like them, the sole interpreters of an obscure science.

The social position of English and American lawyers exerts no less great an influence on their habits and opinions. The English aristocracy which took care to draw into itself everything bearing any likeness to itself afforded lawyers a very large share of consideration and power. In English society, lawyers do not occupy the top position but are content with the one they have. They form, as it were, the younger branch of the English aristocracy and love and respect their elder counterparts without sharing their privileges. English lawyers, therefore, unite the aristocratic interests of their profession with the aristocratic ideas and tastes of the society in which they live.

Thus it is in England, above all, that we see the most striking portrait of the type of lawyer I am attempting to depict; the English lawyer values the laws not so much because they are good but because they are old; if he is reduced to modifying them in some particular to adapt them to the changes wrought by time on society, he has recourse to the most incredible subtleties in order to be persuaded that any addition to the work of his fathers has only developed and amplified their efforts. Do not hope to make him acknowledge that he is an innovator; he will consent to go to absurd lengths before confessing to such an enormous crime. It is in England that was born this legal attitude, which seems indifferent to the essence of things, paying attention only to the letter of the law and preferring to part company with reason and humanity rather than with the law.

English legislation is like an ancient tree on to which lawyers have grafted an endless series of the oddest shoots in the hope that, though the fruits are different, the leaves at least will match those of the venerable stem which supports them.

In America, there are neither nobles nor men of letters and the people distrust the wealthy. Lawyers, therefore, form the political upper class and the most intellectual section of society. Thus innovation can only damage them, which adds an interest in conservation to the natural liking for order.

If you ask me where American aristocracy is found, my reply would be that it would not be among the wealthy who have no common link uniting them. American aristocracy is found at the bar and on the bench.

The more one reflects on what is happening in the United States, the more one feels convinced that the legal body in this country forms the most power and, so to say, the only counterbalance to democracy.

In the United States, one has no difficulty in discovering the degree to which the legal mind is, both by its qualities and, I would even say, its defects, adapted to neutralize the inherent deficiencies in popular government.

When the American people become intoxicated by their enthusiasms or carried away by their ideas, lawyers apply an almost invisible brake to slow down and halt them. Their aristocratic leanings are secretly opposed to the instincts of democracy; their superstitious respect for what is old, to its love of novelty; their narrow views, to its grandiose plans; their taste for formality, to its scorn for rules; their habit of proceeding slowly, to its impetuosity.

The law courts are the most obvious institutions used by the legal fraternity to influence democracy.

The judge is a lawyer who, apart from his liking for order and rules learned from his legal studies, also imbibes a love of stability from the permanence of his office. His legal knowledge had already guaranteed him a high rank among his equals; his political power completes the task of placing him in a rank apart and of giving him the instincts of the privileged classes.

Armed with the right of declaring laws unconstitutional, the American magistrate intrudes constantly upon political matters.[1] He cannot compel the people to make laws but, at least, he puts pressure upon them not to be unfaithful to their own laws and to remain in harmony with themselves.

I am aware that in the United States a tendency exists which leads the people to reduce the power of the judiciary; in most individual state constitutions, the government can remove judges from office at the request of both houses. Certain constitutions have the court judges *elected* and subject to frequent re-election. I venture to predict that these innovations will have, sooner or later, disastrous results and it will be seen that an attack has been directed against not only the power of judges but against the democratic republic itself.

Besides, one should not think that in the United States the legalistic attitude stays solely within the enclosed world of the courts; it stretches well beyond that.

Since lawyers form the only enlightened class not distrusted by the people, they are naturally summoned to hold most public offices. They fill the ranks of the legislature and head the administrations; they exercise, therefore, a great influence over the shaping of the law and its execution. Although lawyers are obliged to yield to the public opinion which draws them along, it is easy to see signs of what they would do, if they were free. Americans who have introduced so many innovations in their political laws have made only slight changes, and those with some reluctance, in their civil laws, although several of these laws are flagrantly repugnant to their social state. That is because the majority always has to turn to lawyers in matters of civil law and American lawyers do not introduce innovation, if the choice is left to them.

For a Frenchman, it is very strange to hear the complaint among Americans against the obstructive spirit and prejudices of lawyers in favor of everything established.

1.   See what I have to say about judicial power in the first volume.

The influence of the legalistic attitude spreads yet further than the exact boundaries just indicated.

There is hardly a political question in the United States which does not sooner or later turn into a judicial one. From that comes the consequence that parties feel obliged to borrow legal ideas and language when conducting their own daily controversies. Since most men in public life are, or have been, lawyers, they apply their own habits and turn of mind to the handling of affairs. Jury service familiarizes all classes with this. Judicial language thus becomes pretty well the language of common speech; the spirit of the law starts its life inside schools and courtrooms only to spread gradually beyond their narrow confines; it insinuates itself, so to speak, into the whole of society right down to the lowest ranks until, finally, the entire nation has caught some of the ways and tastes of the magistrate.

Lawyers in the United States constitute a power which is little feared and hardly noticed; it carries no banner of its own and adapts flexibly to the demands of the time, flowing along unresistingly with all the movements of society. Nevertheless it wraps itself around society as a whole, is felt in all social classes, constantly continues to work in secret upon them without their knowing until it has shaped them to its own desires.

THE JURY IN THE UNITED STATES SEEN AS A POLITICAL INSTITUTION

The jury being one of the instruments of the sovereignty of the people must be closely related to the other laws which establish this sovereignty—Composition of American juries—Effects of juries on the national character— Education it gives to the people—How it tends to establish magistrates' influence and to spread legalistic attitudes.

Since my subject has naturally led me to talk of American justice, I shall not leave it without considering the jury.

One must make a distinction between the jury as a judicial institution and as a political one.

If it were a question of knowing how far the jury, especially in civil cases, serves the good administration of justice, I would admit that its usefulness could be challenged.

The jury system began in the early stages of society when only a few simple questions of fact were submitted to the courts; it is no easy task to adapt it to the needs of a very civilized nation when the relations between men have multiplied to an unusual extent and have assumed an intellectual and expert character.[2]

My main aim, at the moment, is to concern myself with the political aspect of juries; any other course would divert me from my theme. Seeing the jury as a judicial instrument, I will say a couple of words. When the English adopted the jury system, they were a semi-barbarian nation; since then, they have turned into one of the most enlightened nations on earth and their attachment to the jury system has appeared to grow along with their enlightenment. They have left their own country, some to found colonies, others independent states. The main body of the nation has retained a king; several groups of settlers have founded powerful republics; but, everywhere, the English have uniformly advocated the jury system.[3] They set it up everywhere

2.   Already it would be a useful and curious thing to consider trial by jury as a judicial institution, to weigh up the effects it produces in the United States and to inquire into the way in which the Americans have made use of it. The examination of this question alone could well furnish the subject of a whole book and one that was interesting for the French. For example, we might research what share of American institutions relating to trial by jury could be introduced into France and the steps we would need to take. The American state which would throw the most light upon the subject would be the state of Louisiana which has a population of both French and English. The two systems of law as well as the two nations are there found side by side, gradually combining with each other. The most useful books to consult would be the two-volume collection of the laws of Louisiana, entitled: *Digeste des Lois de la Louisiane*; and perhaps even more so a treatise of civil procedure written in both languages and entitled: *Traité sur les Règles des Actions civiles*, printed in 1830 in New Orleans by Buisson. This work has a special advantage: it supplies the French with an exact and authentic explanation of English legal terms. Legal language is almost a separate language among all nations and among the English more than anyone else.

3.   All the English and American legal minds agree on this point. Mr Story, Justice of the Supreme Court of the United States, speaks, in his *Commentaries on the Constitution*, on the excellence of the institution of trial by

or have hastened to re-establish it. A judicial institution which has thus commanded the approval of a great nation over centuries and has been copied enthusiastically in every stage of civilization, in every climate and under every form of government, cannot possibly be contrary to the spirit of justice.[4]

But let us leave that subject. Merely to see the jury as a judicial institution would be to narrow my viewpoint to an unusual degree, for, if it is very influential in the outcome of lawsuits, it is all the more so on the very destinies of society. The jury is, therefore, first and foremost, a political institution and must always be judged from that point of view.

By "jury" I mean a certain number of citizens chosen randomly and entrusted temporarily with the right to judge.

Using juries for the suppression of crime appears to me the

---

jury in civil cases. "The inestimable privilege of a trial by jury in civil cases," he says, "a privilege scarcely inferior to that in criminal cases, which is counted by all persons to be essential to political and civil liberty" (Story, bk 3, ch. 38).

4. If we intended to establish the usefulness of jury service as a judicial institution, many other arguments might be presented and among others the following:

As you gradually introduce the jury into public business, you are able with some ease to cut down the number of judges, which is a great advantage. When judges are very numerous, death takes a daily toll of the ranks of judicial officers and leaves vacant places for those still alive. The ambition of magistrates is, therefore, constantly captivated and they are naturally made dependent upon the majority or upon the man who fills vacant posts; advancement in the courts, therefore, is similar to promotion in the army. This state of things is entirely contrary to the sound administration of justice and to the intentions of the legislator. The intention behind making judges inalienable is for them to remain free; but how can it matter that no one can remove their independence, if they themselves sacrifice it of their own accord?

When judges are very numerous, it is impossible for you not to find many who are incompetent; for a great magistrate is not an ordinary man. Now, I do not know whether a half-enlightened court of law is not the worst of all combinations for attaining those ends which underlie the establishment of courts of justice.

As for me, I would prefer to hand over the decision of a case to ignorant jurors directed by a skillful magistrate than to entrust it to judges, the majority of whom have only an imperfect knowledge of jurisprudence and law.

introduction of a predominantly republican institution into government. Let me explain.

The jury system may be aristocratic or democratic according to the class which supplies the juries; but it always retains a republican character in that it entrusts the actual control of society into the hands of the ruled, or some of them, rather than into those of the rulers.

Force is only ever a passing element in success; immediately in its wake comes the idea of right. A government reduced to reaching its enemies only on the battlefield would soon be destroyed. The real sanction of political laws is placed, therefore, in the penal code and where this sanction fails to exist the law loses its power sooner or later. Thus the man who judges in a *criminal* trial is the real master of society. Now, the jury puts the people themselves, or at least one class of citizens, upon the judge's bench. The jury system, therefore, places the actual control of society in the hands of the people or of that class.[5]

In England, the jury is recruited from the aristocratic section of the nation. The aristocracy makes the laws, applies them and judges breaches of them. (See Appendix B, p. 848.) All is agreed: thus England is, in reality, an aristocratic republic. In the United States, the same system is associated with the nation as a whole. Each citizen is a voter, can be voted for and may be a juror. (See Appendix C, p. 849.) The jury system, as understood in America, seems to me as direct and as extreme a consequence of the doctrine of the sovereignty of the people as universal suffrage. They are both equally potent means of preserving the power of the majority.

All sovereigns who have wished to draw the sources of their power from themselves and to control society instead of letting

---

5. An important note must, however, be made.

Trial by jury certainly does give to the people a general control over the actions of citizens, but it does not grant the means of exercising this control in all cases or with an absolute authority.

When an absolute monarch has the right of trying crimes by his own representatives, the destiny of the accused is, so to speak, decided beforehand. But if the people were set upon conviction, the composition and non-accountability of the jury would still afford opportunities which are favorable to the innocent.

it control them, have destroyed or weakened the jury system. The Tudors used to imprison jurors who decided not to convict and Napoleon[a] had them chosen by his agents.

However obvious the majority of the above truths may be, the point of them does not strike everyone's mind and often the French still seem to have only a muddled idea of the jury system. If one wishes to know what elements should make up the list of jurors, discussion is limited to the education and competence of those called to be members of it as if it were a question of forming purely a judicial institution. In actual fact that would mean to be concerned with the least important aspect of the matter; the jury is above all a political institution; it must be considered as one form of the sovereignty of the people; it has to be entirely rejected were the sovereignty of the people to be discarded; otherwise it should be made to harmonize with those other laws which establish that sovereignty. The jury is the section of the nation responsible for the execution of the laws, just as the legislative assemblies are the section responsible for making them. For society to be governed in a settled and uniform way, the list of jurors must expand or contract with the lists of voters. My view is that the major preoccupation of the legislator should always be centered on this aspect of the matter. The rest is, so to speak, a side issue.

I am so convinced that the jury is primarily a political institution that I still see it as such when it is used in civil cases.

Laws are always unsteady when unsupported by custom which is the only tough and lasting power in a nation.

When juries are restricted to criminal cases, people see them in action only now and again and in special cases; they become accustomed to do without them in the ordinary course of events and look upon them as just a means, although not the only means, of obtaining justice.[6]

On the other hand, when the jury is extended to civil cases, this usage attracts everyone's attention all the time; it then impinges on the interests of all; everyone comes to help in its

6.   This is all the more true since the jury is used only in certain criminal cases.

work. In this way, it enters the very business of life; it molds the human mind to its procedures and becomes bound up, as it were, with the very conception of justice.

The jury system, if limited to criminal cases, is therefore always under threat; once introduced into civil cases, it can face up to the passing of time and the assaults of men. If juries could have been removed from the customs of the English as easily as from their laws, they would have collapsed altogether under the Tudors. It is, therefore, civil juries which really did save the liberties of England.

However the jury system is adopted, it cannot fail to exert a great influence upon the character of a nation but such an influence increases immeasurably the more it is used in civil cases.

Juries, especially civil juries, help to instill into the minds of all the citizens something of the mental habits of judges, which are exactly those which best prepare the people to be free.

They spread respect for the courts' decisions and the concept of right throughout all classes. Remove these two ideas and the love of independence will merely be a destructive passion.

They teach men the practice of equity. Each man, in judging his neighbor, believes he may be judged in his turn. That is especially true of juries in civil cases: almost no one fears that one day he will be the subject of a criminal hearing but everyone might suffer a lawsuit.

Juries teach all men not to shirk responsibility for their own actions; without that manly attitude no political virtue can exist.

They invest each citizen with a sort of magistracy; they make all men feel that they have duties toward society and that they are part of their government. By forcing men to concern themselves with something outside their own affairs, they challenge that personal selfishness which rusts the workings of societies.

Juries have an exceptional success in shaping people's judgment and improving their natural wisdom. That, in my view, is their main advantage. They must be looked upon as a free and ever-open classroom in which each juror learns his rights, enters into daily communication with the most learned and enlightened members of the upper classes and is taught the law in a manner both practical and within his intellectual grasp by the efforts of advocates, the opinions of judges and the very passions of the litigants. I believe one must attribute the practical intelligence and good political sense of Americans primarily to their long experience of jury service in civil cases.

I do not know whether juries are much use to litigants but I am sure that they are of great use to those who judge the case. They are, in my view, one of the most effective means available to society for educating the people.

The above applies to all nations; but what follows is of special concern to Americans and to democratic nations in general.

I have said above that, in democracies, lawyers, and among them magistrates, constitute the only aristocratic body capable of moderating the people's emotions. This aristocracy is not invested with any physical power but exerts its conservative influence on men's minds. Now, it is in the institution of civil juries that it finds the main sources of its power.

In criminal trials, when society is in conflict with one man, juries are inclined to look upon the judge as a passive instrument of society's power and they distrust his opinions. In addition, criminal cases rest entirely upon simple facts easily appreciated by common sense. On such ground, judge and juries are equal.

Such is not at all the case in civil suits; then the judge appears like an impartial arbitrator of the passions of the litigants. The jurors regard him with confidence and listen to him with respect, for this is a place where his intelligence is wholly superior to theirs. He is the one to unravel for them the various arguments which they find difficult to recall; he is the one to take them by the hand to direct them through the twists and turns of the hearing; he is the one to limit them to questions of fact and to tell them the response they should make to any question of law. His influence over them is almost boundless.

Finally, is it necessary to explain why I feel unmoved by the arguments based on the incompetence of juries in civil suits?

In civil cases, at least when questions of fact are not at issue, the jury only looks like a judicial body.

Juries pronounce the decision given by the judge. They invest this decision with the stamp of the society they represent, while he adds the stamp of reason and the law. (See Appendix D, p. 851.)

In England and America judges exercise an influence over the outcome in criminal trials which the French judge has never known. The reason for this difference is easy to understand: the English or American magistrate, having established his authority in civil courts, simply transfers it after that to tribunals of another kind, where it was not first acquired.

There are cases, and often they are the most important, when the American judge has the right to pronounce alone.[7] He then finds himself by chance in the position normal for a French judge but with much greater moral authority: memories of the jury still follow him around and his voice assumes almost as much force as that of the society represented by those juries.

His influence spreads even well beyond the enclosed world of the courts—whether in the relaxed atmosphere of private life or in the work of political life, whether in the marketplace or in one of the legislatures, the American judge constantly sees around him men who are accustomed to view his intelligence as something superior to their own. And well after his power has been exercised in deciding cases, it influences the habits of mind and even the very soul of all those who have cooperated with him in judging them.

Thus the jury, which seems to be reducing the rights of the magistracy, in effect is founding its sway and there is not a single country where judges are as powerful as in those where the people take a share in their privileges.

It is especially with the help of juries in civil cases that American judges promote what I have called the legalistic attitude, even down to the lowest of the social classes.

Thus the jury, the most energetic method of asserting the people's rule, is also the most effective method of teaching them how to rule.

---

7.   Federal judges almost always decide upon only those questions which touch closely upon the government of the country.

CHAPTER 9

THE MAIN CAUSES WHICH TEND TO MAINTAIN A DEMOCRATIC REPUBLIC IN THE UNITED STATES

A democratic republic continues in the United States. The main aim of this book has been to elucidate the causes of this state of affairs.

Among the reasons for this, there are several I have mentioned only in passing, or which the tenor of my subject has drawn me to touch upon unintentionally. Others I have been unable to discuss, while those I have been allowed to deal with at length have been left behind me, as it were buried in the detail of the book.

I have, therefore, thought that, before moving on to speak of the future, I should gather together in a short summary all the reasons which explain the present.

In this sort of synopsis I shall be brief for I shall take care to remind the reader only very cursorily of what he already knows; among the facts I have not yet had the opportunity to point out, I shall choose only the most important.

In my opinion, all the reasons which tend to maintain a democratic republic in the United States fall into three categories.

The first is the peculiar and accidental position in which Providence has placed the Americans; the second comes from their laws; the third derives from their usages and customs.

ACCIDENTAL OR PROVIDENTIAL CAUSES HELPING TO MAINTAIN A DEMOCRATIC REPUBLIC IN THE UNITED STATES

The Union has no neighbors—No great capital—The Americans have had the chances of birth in their favor—America is an empty country—How these circumstances are a powerful influence upon the maintenance of a democratic republic—How the wildernesses of America

are peopled—The eagerness of Anglo-Americans to
take possession of the uninhabited wilds of the New
World—Influence of physical prosperity on American
political opinions.

Apart from the will of men, a thousand other circumstances favor a democratic republic in the United States. Some are well known; others easy to reveal. I shall confine myself to the most prominent.

The Americans have no neighbors and thus no great wars, financial crises, devastations, or conquests to dread. They need neither heavy taxes, nor a large army, nor great generals; they have almost nothing to fear from that scourge which is more terrible for democratic republics than all these put together, namely, military glory.

How can we deny the incredible influence of military glory on the opinion of a nation? General Jackson, chosen by the Americans twice as head of their government, is a man of a violent disposition and mediocre ability; nothing in the course of his career has ever proved that he had the necessary qualities to govern a free nation. In addition, the majority of the enlightened classes in the Union has always been against him. So, who has placed him upon the President's chair and still keeps him there? The recollection of a victory he won twenty years ago beneath the walls of New Orleans; now, that New Orleans victory[a] was a very commonplace feat of arms which no one would consider for long except in a country of no battles at all. And the nation which is easily carried away by the prestige of military glory has assuredly to be the coldest, the most calculating, the least militaristic and, if one may put it so, the most prosaic in all the world.

America has no great capital city[1] whose direct or indirect

1.   America still has no capital city but already contains very large cities. In the year 1830, Philadelphia reckoned 161,000 inhabitants and New York 202,000. The ordinary people who dwell in these huge towns form a populace even more dangerous than that of European towns. In the first instance they are made up of freed Blacks condemned by the law and public opinion to an hereditary state of misery and degradation. In its midst you also meet

influence is felt throughout the length and breadth of the land, a fact I regard as one of the foremost reasons why republican institutions are maintained in the United States. In towns men can hardly be prevented from assembling, getting overexcited together, and adopting sudden passionate resolutions. Towns virtually constitute great assemblies with all the inhabitants as members. In them, the people wield astonishing influence over their magistrates and often carry their desires into execution without the latter's intervention.

Once the provinces are subject to the capital, the destiny of the whole empire is placed not only in the hands of a section of the nation, which is unfair, but also into the hands of a nation acting unilaterally, which is most dangerous. The supremacy of capital cities represents a great threat to the representative system. It submits modern republics to the same defects as those of ancient times which have all perished from their ignorance of this system of government.

It would be simple for me to list a great number of other secondary reasons which have supported and confirmed the establishment and continuance of the democratic republic in the United States. But in the midst of this host of favorable circumstances I observe two main ones which I am anxious to point out.

---

a crowd of Europeans forced by misfortune or misconduct to sail for the shores of the New World; these men bring to the United States our most serious vices and they possess none of those interests which might counteract that influence. Since they inhabit the country without being citizens of it, they are ready to turn all the passions which agitate the community to their own advantage. Thus, for some time we have seen serious riots breaking out in Philadelphia and in New York. Such disturbances are unknown in the rest of the country which is not alarmed by them because the population in the cities has not exercised up until now any power or any influence over the inhabitants of the countryside.

Nevertheless, I look upon the size of certain American cities and above all the nature of their inhabitants as a genuine danger threatening the future of the democratic republics of the New World and I do not hesitate to predict that that will be the source of their downfall unless their government succeeds in creating an armed force which will remain under the control of the majority of the nation, but which will be independent of the town population and thus able to repress its excesses.

I have already stated that I looked upon the origins of the Americans—what I have called their point of departure—as the first and most effective reason for the present-day prosperity of the United States. Americans have had the chances of birth in their favor: their forefathers imported to the land they now inhabit that equality of social conditions and intelligence from which the democratic republic was one day to emerge as from its natural source. That is still not all; besides this republican state of society, they bequeathed to their descendants the habits, ideas and customs which would be the best fitted to nurture a republic. When I think of what this original circumstance has achieved, I seem to see the whole destiny of America encapsulated in the first Puritan to land upon its shores, just as the first man led to the whole human race.

In the lucky circumstances which have supported and confirmed the establishment and continuance of the democratic republic in the United States, the most important is the choice of the country itself which Americans inhabit. Their fathers have given them the love of equality and freedom but it was God himself who granted them the means of long remaining equal and free by his gift of this boundless continent.

General prosperity supports the stability of all governments, but especially democratic governments which depend upon the attitudes of the greatest number and primarily upon the attitudes of those most exposed to privations. When the people rule, it is vital that they are happy, to avoid any threat to the stability of the state. Wretchedness has the same effect upon them as ambition does upon kings. Now, those physical causes, unconnected with laws, which can lead to prosperity are more numerous in America than in any other country at any time in history.

In the United States, not only is legislation democratic, but nature itself works on behalf of the people.

Where, within the memory of man, would we find anything akin to what is happening before our very eyes in North America?

The renowned societies of the ancient world were all founded in the midst of hostile nations which had to be conquered in order to take their place. Modern nations have themselves come across immense lands in some parts of South America inhabited by peoples less educated than themselves but who had already taken possession of the land and were cultivating it. To found their estates, they had to destroy or enslave numerous populations and have brought shame on civilized behavior through their triumphs.

But North America was populated only by nomadic tribes who had no thought of exploiting the natural richness of the soil. Strictly speaking, it was still an empty continent, a deserted land waiting to be inhabited.

Everything about Americans is unusual from their social condition to their laws; but what is more unusual still is the land that supports them.

When the earth was handed over to men by their Creator, it was young and inexhaustible, while they were weak and ignorant; by the time they had learned to take advantage of the treasure it contained, they already lived everywhere on its surface so that they had to fight for possession of some small refuge where they could reside in freedom.

Then North America was discovered, as if God had held it in reserve and it had only just emerged from the waters of the Flood.

In this land we see, as on the first days of creation, rivers which never dry up, green and moist solitudes, boundless fields as yet untouched by the plowshare. In this condition, it is offered to man, no longer isolated, ignorant or barbarous as in early history but to the man who has already gained mastery of the most important secrets of nature and who has combined with his fellows to learn from the experience of fifty centuries.

At this time of writing, thirteen million civilized Europeans are quietly spreading over this fertile wilderness unaware as yet of the exact extent of the resources before them. Three or four thousand soldiers drive before them the nomadic native tribes; behind these armed forces woodcutters stride out into the depths of the forests, removing wild animals, exploring the course of rivers and preparing for the triumphal progress of civilization across the wilderness.

Often in the course of this work, I have alluded to the physical prosperity enjoyed by Americans, which I have pointed out as one of the great reasons for the success of their laws. This reason had already been forwarded by a thousand others before me; it is the only one which has partially struck the attention of Europeans and become familiar to us. I shall, therefore, not enlarge upon a theme so often dealt with and understood; I shall simply add a few new facts.

It is generally supposed that the wildernesses of America are populated with the help of European immigrants disembarking annually on the shores of the New World, while the American population grows and multiplies on the soil occupied by their fathers. That is a mistaken view. The European arriving in the United States comes without friends and often without resources; he is forced to hire out his services in order to live and he seldom goes beyond the broad industrial zone stretching along the ocean. A wilderness cannot be cleared without capital or credit; before facing the risks of forest clearance, the body has to acclimatize itself to the rigors of this new climate. There are, therefore, Americans who abandon the place of their birth to create for themselves remote and extensive estates. Thus, the European quits his cottage to go and dwell on transatlantic shores and the American, born on these very shores, disappears in his turn into the central solitudes of America. This twin movement of immigration never halts; it starts in the heart of Europe, continues across the great ocean and then progresses across the solitudes of the New World. Millions of men are all marching together toward the same point on the horizon; they have different languages, religions, customs, but a common aim. They have been told that wealth was to be found somewhere toward the West and they rush to catch up with it.

Nothing is comparable to this continuous shift of mankind with the possible exception of what happened at the fall of the Roman Empire. Then, as now, men crowded together at the same point and formed a disorderly congregation in the same locations; but the plans of Providence were not the same. Then every newcomer brought death and destruction in his train, whereas today each of them carries with him the seeds of prosperity and life.

The distant consequences of this migration of Americans to the West still lie hidden in the future but the immediate results are easy to recognize: since a few of the former inhabitants move away each year from the states of their birth, the populations of these states grow very slowly although they are well established. Thus, in Connecticut, which still has only fifty-nine people to the square mile, the population has grown by only a quarter over the last forty years, whereas in England it has increased by a third over the same period. Hence the European immigrant always lands in a country half full where industry is short of manpower; he becomes a comfortably-off worker; his son moves off to seek his fortune in an empty land and turns into a wealthy landowner. The former amasses the capital which the latter puts to good use; neither foreigner nor native suffers poverty.

American legislation supports the division of property as much as possible; but there is one reason more powerful than legislation which stops the excessive division of this property.[2] This is very evident in those states which are at last beginning to be filled. Massachusetts is the most populated area of the Union with eighty inhabitants to the square mile, which is much less than in France with its one hundred and sixty-two.

In Massachusetts, meanwhile, it is already a rare occurrence for small estates to be divided up; generally the eldest retains the land while the younger sons seek their fortune in the wilds.

The law has established inheritance by the firstborn but one can state that Providence has re-established it without anyone's having cause to complain and, for once, at least without offending justice.

One single fact will allow us to judge the incredible number of individuals who leave New England in this way to settle themselves in the wilds. I have been told that in 1830 thirty-six members of Congress had been born in the small state of Connecticut whose population forms only one forty-third of that of the United States, while supplying one eighth of the representatives.

2.   In New England the land is split up into very small estates but it is rarely divided further.

But Connecticut itself sends only five members to Congress; the other thirty-one appear as representatives of the new states of the West. If these thirty-one individuals had stayed in Connecticut, they would probably have remained humble laborers instead of being wealthy landowners; they would have lived obscure lives with no hope of engaging in a political career and would have been unruly members of society rather than useful legislators.

The Americans are as aware of this point as we are.

In his *Commentaries on American Law* (vol. 4, p. 380), Chancellor Kent says: "It would be very unfounded to suppose that the evils of the equal partition of estates have been seriously felt in the United States, or that they have borne any proportion to the advantages of the policy, or that such evils are to be anticipated for generations to come. The extraordinary extent of our unsettled territories, the abundance of uncultivated land in the market, and the constant stream of emigration from the Atlantic to the interior states, operates sufficiently to keep paternal inheritances unbroken."

It would be difficult to depict the eagerness with which an American launches himself at this huge booty offered him by fortune. In order to pursue it, he fearlessly braves the Indian arrow and the diseases of the wilds; the silence of the woods holds no surprises for him, nor is he disturbed by the presence of wild beasts; he is constantly spurred on by a passion stronger than the love of life. Before him stretches an almost boundless continent and it is as though, already afraid of losing his place, he is in such a hurry not to arrive too late. I have mentioned the emigration from the old states but what shall I say of that from the new? Ohio was founded not fifty years ago; most of its population were not born there; its capital is not yet thirty years old and a huge stretch of unclaimed land still covers its territory; yet already the inhabitants of Ohio have started their march to the West. Most of those moving down into the fertile meadows of Illinois once lived in Ohio. These men left their first homeland to better themselves; they abandon their second to do better still. Almost everywhere they find wealth but not happiness. With them the desire for prosperity has become a restless and burning passion which increases each time it is satisfied. Long ago they broke the ties of attachment to their native soil and they have not forged new ones since. Emigration for them began as a need and has, today, become a sort of gamble which rouses emotions which they like as much as the profit.

Sometimes man advances so quickly that the wilderness closes in again behind him. The forest has only bent beneath his feet and springs up again once he has passed by. As one travels through the new states of the West, buildings are not infrequently found abandoned in the depth of the woods. Often the ruins of a cabin turn up in the remotest solitude and, to one's astonishment, half-finished clearances witness to both the power and waywardness of human beings. Amid these abandoned fields, on these day-old ruins, the ancient forest soon pushes out new shoots. Animals recover their hold over their domain, smiling nature covers up the traces of man with green branches and flowers and hurries to conceal his transient footsteps.

I recall, when crossing one of the still wild districts in the state of New York, that I reached the edge of a lake completely surrounded by forests as at the beginning of the world. A small island rose from the water. The trees covering it spread their foliage all round to conceal the edges entirely. Along the banks of the lake, nothing betrayed the presence of man; only a column of smoke could be seen on the horizon, rising directly upwards from the tree tops to the clouds, appearing to hang down from the sky rather than rising toward it.

An Indian canoe was drawn up on the sand; I took advantage of it to visit the island which had first attracted my attention and soon after I had reached its shore. The whole island was one of those exquisite New World solitudes which almost make civilized man regret the life in the wild. The marvels of healthy vegetation heralded the incomparable richness of the soil. As in all the wilds of North America a deep silence reigned, interrupted only by the monotonal cooing of wood pigeons or by the tapping of the green woodpecker against the bark of the trees. It was far from my thoughts that this place had ever been inhabited before, so completely did nature seem left alone; but, once I had reached the center of the island, I suddenly thought I could discern human traces. Then I carefully scrutinized everything in the vicinity and soon was able to see that a European had undoubtedly sought a refuge in this place. But how his labors had been altered! The wood he had once cut down in his haste to construct a shelter had since sprouted; his fences had become live hedges and his cabin was transformed into a copse. In the midst of these bushes, a few blackened stones could still be seen scattered around a small heap of ashes. This place was without doubt his hearth, covered with the ruins of a fallen chimney. For some moments I wondered in silence at the resources of nature and the weakness of man; when I finally had to retreat from this magic spot, I kept saying sadly: "What! Ruins so soon!"

We Europeans are accustomed to look upon a restless spirit, an inordinate desire for wealth and an extreme passion for independence as grave social dangers. Yet precisely all these things guarantee a long and peaceful future for the republics of America. Without those disquieting passions, the population would be concentrated around certain places and would soon experience, as we do, needs which are difficult to satisfy. What a fortunate country the New World is, where man's vices are almost as valuable to society as his virtues!

This exerts a great influence upon the way human behavior is judged in the two hemispheres. What we call the love of gain is often laudable hard work for the Americans who see a certain faintheartedness in what we consider to be moderation of one's desires.

In France simple tastes, quiet manners, family spirit, and love of one's birthplace are considered as powerful guarantees of the tranquillity and happiness of the state but in America, nothing appears more damaging to society than virtues of that sort. French Canadians who have faithfully preserved the tradition of their former customs already find it hard to live off their land and this small nation, which was born so recently, will soon fall prey to the afflictions of the older nations. In Canada the most enlightened, patriotic, and humane men go to extraordinary lengths to put the people off that simple happiness which still satisfies them. They extol the advantages of wealth in the same way that we would perhaps praise the attractions of a middle-of-the-road integrity and they spend more care on stimulating human passions than people elsewhere employ to calm them. To exchange the pure and peaceful pleasures even a poor man enjoys in his homeland for the sterile enjoyments of prosperity under a foreign sky, to flee the paternal hearth and the fields where his ancestors lie in peace, to abandon both living and dead in order to chase a fortune, are all things most praiseworthy in their eyes.

In our day America offers men a storehouse more extensive than human industry could ever exploit.

In America, therefore, there cannot be enough knowledge; for while all knowledge is useful to those who have it, it also turns to the advantage of those without it. New needs should not be a source of fear for there they are all easily satisfied. One should not dread the growth of too many passions since they can all find available and healthy sustenance. Men cannot have too much freedom because they are not ever tempted to misuse their liberty.

American republics of the present time resemble companies of merchants formed to exploit the empty lands of the New World and dedicated to the prosperity of their business ventures.

The passions which stir Americans most deeply are commercial not political ones or more accurately they transfer into politics the methods of business. They like orderliness without which business cannot hope to prosper and they value particularly the regularity of conduct which is the basis for solid businesses. They prefer good sense which creates vast fortunes rather than the genius which often fritters them away. Generalities terrify their minds, accustomed as they are to tangible calculations and for them practicality is more honored than theoretical concepts.

One must go to America to understand the power of material prosperity over political actions and even over those opinions which ought to be governed by reason alone. The truth of this is best illustrated if we look at foreigners. Most European emigrants carry with them to the New World this fierce love of independence and change which comes into being so frequently amid our calamities. In the United States, I occasionally met some of those Europeans who had been forced to flee their country because of their political opinions. They all surprised me by what they said, but one impressed me most of all. As I was passing through one of the most remote districts of Pennsylvania, I was overtaken by nightfall and I sought shelter at the door of a rich planter who was French. He sat me down near his fire and we started talking with the freedom typical of people who meet in a wood five thousand miles from their native land. I was aware that my host had been a great leveler and an ardent demagogue forty years before. His name had imprinted itself on history.

I was, therefore, singularly surprised to hear him discuss the rights of property as an economist, I almost said a landowner, might have done. He spoke of the necessary hierarchy which wealth establishes among men, of obedience to the established law, of the influence of good habits in republics, and of the help given by religions to orderliness and freedom. He even quoted the authority of Jesus Christ in support of one of his political opinions.

As I listened to him, I marveled at the stupidity of human reason. A thing is either true or false but how can one discover which amid the uncertainties of knowledge and the conflicting lessons drawn from experience? A new fact may emerge to remove all my doubts. I was poor and now, look, I am rich: if only prosperity, while affecting my behavior, left my judgment free! But no, my opinions are in fact altered by my fortune and the happy circumstance which I turn to my advantage in reality unearths the decisive argument which I had lacked before.

Prosperity influences Americans even more freely than foreigners. The American has always seen orderliness and public prosperity linked together and marching in step; he cannot imagine their existing apart. He has, therefore, nothing to forget, nor does he need to unlearn, as so many Europeans have to, the lessons of his early education.

THE INFLUENCE OF LAWS ON THE MAINTENANCE OF A DEMOCRATIC REPUBLIC IN THE UNITED STATES

Three main factors which maintain a democratic republic— Federal system—Municipal institutions—Judicial power.

The main aim of this book was to reveal American laws. If this aim has been achieved, the reader has already been able to judge for himself which laws genuinely foster the maintenance of a democratic republic and which threaten its existence. If I have failed to achieve this in the course of a whole book, I shall still less manage it in one chapter.

I do not wish, therefore, to pursue a route I have already traveled and a few lines of repetition must be enough.

Three factors seem to contribute more than all the others to the maintenance of a democratic republic in the New World.

The first is the federal system adopted by the Americans which allows the Union to profit from the strength of a large republic and the security of a small one.

The second is to be found in the municipal institutions which temper the tyranny of the majority while giving the people both the taste for freedom and the skill to achieve it.

The constitution of judicial power offers us the third. I have demonstrated how much the courts help to correct the excesses of democracy and how they manage to slow down and control the movements of the majority without ever being able to stop them altogether.

THE INFLUENCE OF CUSTOMS ON THE MAINTENANCE OF A DEMOCRATIC REPUBLIC IN THE UNITED STATES

I have said earlier that I considered customs to be one of the important general factors responsible for the maintenance of a democratic republic in the United States.

By *customs* I mean the term used by classical writers when they use the word *mores*; for I apply it not only to customs in the strict sense of what might be called the habits of the heart but also to the different concepts men adopt, the various opinions which prevail among them and to the whole collection of ideas which shape mental habits.

Thus, I include in the use of this word the entire moral and intellectual state of a nation. My aim is not to paint a portrait of American customs but for the moment merely to seek those which help to support political institutions.

RELIGION CONSIDERED AS A POLITICAL INSTITUTION WHICH POWERFULLY SUPPORTS THE MAINTENANCE OF A DEMOCRATIC REPUBLIC AMONG AMERICANS

North America populated by men professing a democratic and republican Christianity—Arrival of the Catholics— Why present-day Catholics form the most democratic and republican class.

Alongside every religion lies some political opinion which is linked to it by affinity.

If the human mind is allowed to follow its own bent, it will regulate political society and the City of God in the same uniform manner and will, I dare say, seek to *harmonize* earth and heaven.

Most of English America has been peopled by men who, having shaken off the authority of the Pope, acknowledged no other religious supremacy; they brought, therefore, into the New World a form of Christianity which I can only describe as democratic and republican. This fact will be exceptionally favorable to the establishment of a democracy and a republic in governing public affairs. From the start, politics and religion were in agreement and they have continued to be so ever since.

About fifty years ago Ireland began to pour a Catholic population into the United States. Also American Catholicism made converts. Today the Union has more than a million Christians professing the truths of the Church of Rome.

These Catholics display a firm loyalty to their religious worship and are full of fervent zeal for their beliefs. However, they are the most republican and democratic class in the United States. This fact is a surprise at first sight but further reflection easily reveals the hidden reasons.

In my opinion, it would be wrong to see the Catholic religion as a natural opponent of democracy. Among the different Christian doctrines, Catholicism seems to me, on the contrary, to be one of the most supportive of the equality of social conditions. For Catholics, religious society is composed of two elements: the priest and the laity. The priest rises alone above the faithful: beneath him all are equal.

On doctrinal matters, Catholicism places all human intellects on the same level; it compels both the learned and the ignorant, the man of genius and the common herd, to accept the same details of dogma; it imposes the same practices upon both rich and poor; it inflicts the same austerities upon both the powerful and the weak. It makes no compromise with anyone and applies the same standard to each person; it likes to blend all social classes at the foot of the same altar just as they are blended in the sight of God.

If Catholicism disposes the faithful toward obedience, it does not prepare them for inequality. I say quite the opposite for Protestantism which, generally speaking, leads men much less toward equality than toward independence.

Catholicism resembles absolute monarchy. Remove the prince and the conditions are more equal than in republics.

It has often happened that the Catholic priest has left his sanctuary to exercise a power in society and has taken his place in the social hierarchy; sometimes he has used his religious influence to ensure the continuation of a political regime of which he was part. Then, too, you may have seen Catholics supporting the aristocracy out of religious zeal.

But once priests are removed or remove themselves from government, as happens in the United States, no group of men is more led by their beliefs than Catholics to transfer the concept of equality of social conditions into the world of politics.

If, therefore, American Catholics are not strenuously attracted by their beliefs to democratic and republican opinions, at least they are not by nature opposed to them and their social position as well as their small numbers obliges them to adopt these opinions.

Most Catholics are poor and need government to be open to all citizens to attain government themselves. They constitute a minority and need to see respect for the rights of all in order to be guaranteed the free enjoyment of their own. These twin reasons urge them, maybe unknowingly, toward political doctrines which they would adopt with possibly less enthusiasm were they rich and in a superior position.

The Catholic clergy in the United States has not attempted to oppose this political tendency; rather it seeks to justify it. American Catholic priests have divided the intellectual world into two parts: in one they have placed revealed dogma which they obey without argument; in the other they have put political truth which they think God has abandoned to man's free inquiry. Thus American Catholics are both the most obedient believers and the most independent citizens.

Therefore, it can be said that in the United States there is no single religious doctrine which is hostile to democratic and republican institutions. All the clergy there speak the same language; opinions there coincide with the laws and, to express it this way, the human mind flows in only one direction.

I was living for a short while in one of the great cities of the Union when I was invited to a political meeting designed to help the Poles by sending them supplies of arms and money.

I found two or three thousand people gathered in a large hall prepared for them. Soon afterwards a priest, dressed in his ecclesiastical habit, came forward on to the platform intended for the speakers. The audience took their hats off and stood in silence as he said the following:

"Almighty God! Lord of Hosts! who hast upheld the courage and guided the arms of our fathers when they defended the sacred rights of their national independence; Thou who hast promoted their victories over a hateful oppression and hast granted the blessings of peace and freedom to our nation;

turn, O Lord, a favorable eye toward the other hemisphere; look with compassion upon an heroic nation which is fighting today as we have done in the past and in defense of the same rights! Lord, who hast created all men in the same image, do not allow tyranny to deform Thy work and maintain inequality upon the face of the earth. Almighty God! Watch over the destinies of the Poles, make them worthy to be free; may Thy wisdom reign in their councils and Thy strength in their arms; spread terror among their enemies; divide the powers which plot their ruin and do not allow the injustice which the world has witnessed for fifty years to be fulfilled in our time. Lord, who dost hold alike the hearts of nations and of men in Thy powerful hand, raise up allies for the sacred cause of true right; arouse the French nation at last from the apathy in which its leaders hold it, to fight once more for the freedom of the world.

"O Lord! Turn not Thy face from us; grant that we may always be the most religious and the most free nation of the earth.

"Almighty God, grant this day our prayer; save the Poles. We ask this in the name of Thy beloved son our Lord Jesus Christ who died on the cross for the salvation of all men. *Amen.*"

The whole assembly echoed *Amen* with reverence.

INDIRECT INFLUENCE OF RELIGIOUS BELIEFS UPON AMERICAN POLITICAL SOCIETY

Christian morality common to all sects—Influence of religion on American customs—Respect for the vows of marriage—How religion keeps the American imagination within certain limits and tempers its passion for innovation—Americans' opinion of the political usefulness of religion—Their efforts to extend and secure its power.

I have just demonstrated the direct action of religion on politics in the United States. Its indirect action seems to me even more powerful still and it is just when it is not speaking of freedom that it most effectively instructs Americans how to be free.

A countless number of sects in the United States all have differing forms of worship they offer to the Creator but they all agree about the duties that men owe to each other. Each sect adores God in its own particular way but all sects preach the same morality in the name of God. If it matters a lot to the individual that his religion is true, that is not the case for society as a whole. Society has nothing to fear or hope for from the afterlife; what matters is not so much that all citizens profess the true religion but that they profess one religion. Moreover, all the sects in the United States unite in the body of Christendom whose morality is everywhere the same.

One may suppose that a certain number of Americans follow their habits rather than their firm beliefs when they worship God. Besides, in the United States, the sovereign authority is religious and consequently hypocrisy must be common. Nonetheless, America is still the country in the world where the Christian religion has retained the greatest real power over people's souls and nothing shows better how useful and natural religion is to man, since the country where it exerts the greatest sway is also the most enlightened and free.

I have said that American priests proclaim their general support for civil liberties, including those who do not admit any religious freedom. However, they do not lend their support to any particular political system. They take pains to stand aside from public affairs and keep aloof from political parties. It cannot, therefore, be said that religion exercises any influence on the laws and on the details of political opinions in the United States but it does control behavior and strives to regulate the state by regulating the family.

I do not doubt for a moment that the great severity of behavior seen in the United States has its primary origin in religious belief. Religion is often powerless to restrain man in the face of the countless temptations offered by wealth and cannot moderate his eagerness to become rich, which everything around him helps to stimulate; but it reigns supreme in the souls of women, and they are the protectors of morals. America is certainly the country where the bonds of marriage are most respected and where the concept of conjugal bliss has its highest and truest expression.

In Europe almost all social disorder stems from disturbances at home and not far removed from the marriage bed. There men come to feel scorn for natural ties and legitimate pleasures; there they develop a liking for disorder, a restless spirit, and fluctuating desires. Shaken by the tempestuous emotions which often trouble his own home, the European finds it difficult to submit to the authority of the state's legislators. When the American returns from the turmoil of politics to the bosom of his family, he immediately finds a perfect picture of orderliness and peace. There, all his pleasures are simple and natural, his joys innocent and quiet; and since he reaches happiness through the regularity of his life, he has no difficulty in regulating his opinions as well as his tastes.

Whereas the European seeks to escape from his domestic troubles by disturbing society, the American draws the love of order from his home which he then carries over into his affairs of state.

In the United States, religion governs not only behavior but extends its influence to men's minds.

Among Anglo-Americans there are some who profess Christian dogmas out of belief, others because they are afraid they might appear to lack belief. So Christianity reigns without obstacles by universal consent; so, as I have already said elsewhere, the result is that in the world of morality everything is definite and settled, although the world of politics is given over to debate and human experiment. Thus, the mind of man never beholds an unlimited field in front of itself; however bold he might be, man senses from time to time that he must halt before insurmountable barriers and test his most audacious ideas against certain formalities, which either hold him back or stop him altogether.

The imagination of Americans, even in its greatest flights of fancy, is circumspect and cautious. Its impulses are restricted and its achievements unfinished. These habits of restraint are found in political society and to an unusual degree favor the tranquillity of the people and the stability of the institutions they have adopted. Nature and circumstance have turned the inhabitant of the United States into a bold man; this is easily proved by the manner in which he seeks his fortune. If the mind of the Americans were free of all shackles, one would soon encounter among them the boldest innovators and the most relentless logicians in the world. But American revolutionaries are forced publicly to profess a certain respect for Christian morality and equity, which does not allow them easily to violate the laws even when the latter are opposed to the execution of their plans; and were they to manage to rise above their scruples themselves, they would still feel hindered by those of their supporters. Up until now, no one in the United States has dared to promote the maxim that everything is legitimized in the interests of society, an impious maxim which seems to have been invented in an age of liberty simply to justify every future tyrant.

Thus, while the law allows the American people to do everything, religion prevents their imagining everything and forbids them from daring to do everything.

Religion, which never interferes directly in the government of Americans, should therefore be regarded as the first of their political institutions, for, if it does not give them the taste for liberty, it enables them to take unusual advantage of it.

This is also how the inhabitants of the United States themselves see their religious beliefs. I do not know whether all Americans put faith in their religion, for who can read into men's hearts? But I am sure that they believe it necessary for the maintenance of republican institutions. This is not an opinion peculiar to one class of citizens or to one party, but to a whole nation; it is found in every rank of society.

In the United States, if a politician attacks one sect, that is no reason for the very supporters of that sect not to vote for him, but if he attacks all the sects together, he is totally shunned and remains isolated.

While I was in America, a witness attended a court in the county of Chester (state of New York) and declared his disbelief in the existence of God and the immortality of the soul. The judge refused to accept his oath given that the witness had destroyed in advance any confidence in his testimony.[3] Newspapers reported the fact without comment.

Americans so completely identify the spirit of Christianity with freedom in their minds that it is almost impossible to get them to conceive the one without the other; and this is not one of those sterile ideas bequeathed by the past to the present nor one which seems to vegetate in the soul rather than to live.

I have seen Americans coming together to dispatch priests to the new states in the West in order to found schools and churches. Their fear is that religion might disappear in the depths of the forest and that the people growing up there might be less fitted for freedom than the society they had left. I have met wealthy New Englanders who left their native land in order to establish the fundamentals of Christianity and freedom on the banks of the Missouri or in the prairies of Illinois. In this way, in the United States, religious zeal constantly gains vitality from the fires of patriotism.

You will be mistaken if you think that these men are acting solely with an eye for the afterlife; eternity is only one of their concerns. Were you to question these missionaries of Christian civilization, you would be surprised to hear them speak so frequently of prosperity in this world and to discover a politician where you believed you would expect to find a priest. They will say: "All the American republics are interdependent; if the republics in the West succumbed to anarchy or suffered the yoke of tyranny, the republican institutions now flourishing on the shores of the Atlantic Ocean would be in great danger; we have an interest, therefore, in seeing that the new states are religious so that they allow us to remain free."

Such are the opinions of Americans, but their error is obvious

3. The *New York Spectator* of 23 August 1831 reports the fact in the following terms: "The Court of Common Pleas of Chester county (New York) a few days since rejected a witness who declared his disbelief in the existence of God. The presiding judge remarked that he had not before been aware that there was a man living who did not believe in the existence of God; that this belief constituted the sanction of all testimony in a court of justice and that he knew of no cause in a Christian country where a witness had been permitted to testify without such a belief."

because everyday some learned commentator proves to me that everything in America is fine except this religious spirit which I admire; and I am taught that human freedom and happiness on the other side of the ocean lack only Spinoza's[b] contention that the world is eternal and Cabanis's[c] belief that thought is a secretion of the brain. The only reply I can give to that in truth is that those who talk like that have not been to America and have no more seen a religious nation than a free one. I shall await their return.

There are some people in France who regard republican institutions as the fleeting means to achieve greatness. They scrutinize the immense gap separating their defects and sufferings from power and wealth and they would like to pile ruins into this abyss in an attempt to fill it. Such people stand in relation to freedom much as the medieval professional soldiers stood to kings: they wage war for their own profit whatever colors they wear; they estimate that the republic will last long enough to raise them from their present degradation. I am not addressing myself to those people; but there are others who see in a republican government a permanent and tranquil state, a vital goal toward which ideas and customs daily steer modern societies and they would sincerely like to prepare men to be free. When these men attack religious beliefs, they are following their emotions not their interests. Tyranny may be able to do without faith but freedom cannot. Religion is much more vital in the republic which they advocate than in the monarchy which they are attacking and in democratic republics most of all. How could society avoid destruction if, when political ties are relaxed, moral ties are not tightened? And what can be done with a nation in control of itself, if it is not subject to God?

MAIN CAUSES FOR THE POWERFUL POSITION OF RELIGION IN AMERICA

Care taken by Americans to separate Church and state—
The laws, public opinion, the clergy's own endeavors all
work toward this end—This separation accounts for
religion's power over Americans' souls—Why?—What is

*the natural state of contemporary man in relation to
religion?—What peculiar and accidental reasons in some
countries prevent men from achieving this state?*

The eighteenth-century philosophers had a quite simple explanation for the gradual weakening of beliefs. They would say that religious zeal had to burn itself out as freedom and education increased. How vexing that the facts are in conflict with this theory.

There are certain European populations whose unbelief is matched only by their brutishness and ignorance, whereas in America you see one of the most free and enlightened nations in the world fulfilling all their public religious duties with enthusiasm.

On my arrival in the United States, it was the religious atmosphere which first struck me. As I extended my stay, I could observe the political consequences which flowed from this novel situation.

In France I had seen the spirit of religion moving in the opposite direction to that of the spirit of freedom. In America, I found them intimately linked together in joint reign over the same land.

I felt my longing to know the reason for this phenomenon grow daily.

To find this out, I questioned the faithful of all communions; above all, I sought the company of priests who are the depositaries of the various beliefs and have a personal interest in their survival. My own religious affiliation brought me particularly into contact with Catholic priests with several of whom I soon established a certain closeness. To each of them I expressed my astonishment and revealed my doubts: my view was that all these men agreed with each other except over details; but they all attributed the peaceful influence exercised by religion over their country principally to the separation of Church and state. I assert confidently that, during my stay in America, I did not meet a single man, priest or layman, who did not agree about that.

This leads me to pay closer attention than I had before to the position of American priests in political society. I was surprised to discover that they held no public appointments.[4] I did not see one in the administration and I discovered that they were not even represented in the assemblies.

In several states, a political career was denied them by law[5] and in all the others by public opinion.

When I finally came to inquire into the attitude of the clergy themselves, I saw that most of them seemed to keep their distance voluntarily from power and to derive some sort of professional pride in remaining aloof.

I heard them pronouncing a curse on ambition and insincerity under whatever political opinions these vices were attempting to lurk. But I learned from them that men cannot be guilty in the eyes of God for opinions such as these, provided they are sincere, and that it is no more of a sin to make a mistake in some question of government than it is to go wrong in the building of one's house or plowing a furrow.

I observed them as they carefully distanced themselves from all parties, avoiding all contact with them with all the intensity of a personal involvement.

These facts finally convinced me that I had been told the truth. I then wanted to trace the reasons for such facts. I wondered how the real power of a religion came to be increased by reducing its apparent strength and I thought that it was not impossible to uncover the reason.

Never will the short span of sixty years close down a man's imagination; the imperfect joys of this world will never satisfy

4.   Unless this term is applied to the functions which many of them fill in the schools. The greater part of education is entrusted to the clergy.

5.   See the Constitution of New York, article 7, section 4. Also that of North Carolina, article 31; that of Virginia; that of South Carolina, article 1 section 23; that of Kentucky, article 2, section 26; that of Tennessee, article 8, section 1; that of Louisiana, article 2, section 2.

The article in the Constitution of New York is worded as follows:

"And whereas the ministers of the Gospel are, by their profession, dedicated to the service of God and the care of souls, and ought not to be diverted from the great duties of their functions; therefore no minister of the Gospel, or priest of any denomination whatsoever, shall at any time hereafter, under any pretext or description whatever, be eligible to, or capable of, holding any civil or military office or place within this State."

his heart. Man alone of all created beings shows a natural disgust for existence and an immense longing to exist; he despises life and fears annihilation. These different feelings constantly drive his soul toward the contemplation of another world and religion it is which directs him there. Religion is thus one particular form of hope as natural to the human heart as hope itself. Men cannot detach themselves from religious beliefs except by some wrong-headed thinking and by a sort of moral violence inflicted upon their true nature; they are drawn back by an irresistible inclination. Unbelief is an accident; faith is the only permanent state of mankind.

Considering religions simply from a purely human point of view, one can therefore say that all religions derive from man himself an unfailing element of strength which is one of the constituent principles of human nature.

I realize that there are occasions when religion can add to its own influence the artificial strength of laws and the support of the material powers which control society. We have seen religions closely linked to earthly governments, dominating men's souls by both terror and by faith. But when a religion contracts such an alliance, I am not afraid to say that it acts as would a man by sacrificing the future for the present and risks its legitimate authority by gaining a power to which it has no right.

When a religion seeks to base its empire only upon the desire for immortality which torments every human heart equally, it can aspire to universality but, when it happens to combine with a government, it has to adopt maxims which only apply to certain nations. Therefore, by allying itself to a political power, religion increases its authority over some but loses the hope of reigning over all.

As long as religion relies upon feelings which are the consolation of every suffering, it may attract the human heart to itself. When it is mixed up with the bitter passions of this world, it is sometimes forced to defend allies who have joined it through self-interest and not through love; it has to repel as enemies men who, while fighting against those allies of religion, still love religion itself. Thus, religion cannot share the material strengths of the rulers without suffering some of those animosities which the latter arouse.

Even the most firmly established of political powers have no other guarantee for their permanence beyond the opinions of one generation, the concerns of one century or often the lifetime of one man. A law may modify the social state which appears to be most fixed and settled; then everything changes.

Society's powers, just like our years upon the earth, are all more or less fleeting; they follow each other quickly like the various cares of life and no government has ever been able to rely upon some unchanging disposition of the human heart or to base itself upon some immortal principle.

As long as a religion derives its strength from opinions, feelings, and emotions which are found to recur in the same form at every period of history, it can brave the assaults of time, or, at least, it can be destroyed only by some other religion. But when religion aims to depend upon the principles of this world, it becomes almost as vulnerable as all other powers on this earth. By itself, it may aspire to immortality but, linked to fleeting powers, it follows their fortunes and often collapses together with those passions which sustain them for a day.

Religion, by uniting with different political powers, can therefore form only burdensome alliances. It has no need of their help to survive and may die, if it serves them.

The danger I have just pointed out exists at all times but is not always equally obvious.

There are centuries when governments appear to be imperishable and other times when society's existence seems frailer than that of a man.

Some constitutions keep their citizens in a sort of lazy slumber and others submit them to a feverish excitement.

When governments seem so strong and laws so stable, men do not perceive the danger that ensues from the union of religion with the state.

When governments seem so weak and laws so changeable, the danger is there for all to see but there is often no longer enough time to avoid it. One must, therefore, learn to see it coming from afar.

As a nation assumes a democratic social state and communities lean toward a republic, it becomes increasingly dangerous to unite religion with political institutions; for the time is coming when power will pass from hand to hand, when one political theory will replace another, when men, laws, and constitutions themselves will vanish or alter daily, and that not for a limited time but continuously. Agitation and instability cling naturally to democratic republics just as immobility and somnolence are the rule in absolute monarchies.

If Americans, who change their head of state every four years, choose new legislators every two years, replace provincial administrators annually, and if Americans, who have handed over the realm of politics to the experiments of innovators, had not placed their religion somewhere beyond their reach, what could it hold on to in the ebb and flow of human opinions? Amid the struggles of parties, where would it find its due respect? What would become of its immortality when all around it would be perishing?

American priests have realized this truth before everyone else and they allow it to guide their conduct. They saw that they had to forgo religious influence if they wished to win political power and they preferred to lose the support of authority rather than share its changing fortunes.

In America, religion is possibly less powerful than it has been at certain times and among certain nations, but its influence is more lasting. It restricts itself to its own resources of which no one can deprive it; it operates within a unique sphere which it occupies entirely and rules effortlessly.

I hear voices in all parts of Europe deploring the absence of belief and people are wondering how to restore to religion some vestige of its former power.

I think that we should carefully consider what ought to be *the natural state* of present-day man with regard to religion. Then, knowing what we can hope for and what we have to dread, we will have a clear picture of the aim toward which all our efforts should be directed.

Two great dangers threaten the existence of religions: schisms and indifference.

In centuries of fervent devotion, sometimes men happen to abandon their religion but they escape from its yoke only to submit to that of another. Faith changes its allegiance but does not die. Then the former religion rouses burning love or implacable hatred in all hearts; some leave it with anger, others cling to it with a fresh fanaticism; beliefs differ but irreligion is unknown.

But this is not the case when a religious belief is silently undermined by doctrines which I shall call negative since they promote the falsity of one religion without establishing the truth of any other.

Then amazing revolutions take place in the human mind without the apparent cooperation of man's passions and almost without his awareness. One observes men losing the object of their most cherished hopes through forgetfulness. As they are swept along by an unseen current against which they have not the courage to struggle but to which they submit with regret, they abandon the faith they love to pursue a doubt which leads to despair.

During the centuries I have just described, beliefs are forsaken through indifference rather than hatred; it is not a question of men's rejecting them; rather they abandon men. While no longer believing religion to be true, the unbeliever continues to consider it useful. Looking at religious beliefs from a human point of view, he recognizes their sway over moral behavior and their influence in legislation. He realizes their power to inspire men to live in peace and to prepare them to die gently. He is, therefore, full of regret for the faith he has lost, and now that he is deprived of a blessing whose value he fully appreciates, he is afraid to remove it from those who still possess it.

On the other hand, the man who still believes is not afraid to display his faith for all to see. He looks on those who do not share his hopes as unfortunate rather than hostile; he knows he can win their respect without following their example. He is, therefore, in conflict with no one; since he does not view the society in which he lives as an arena where religion has to struggle constantly against a thousand relentless enemies, he is attached to his fellow men while he condemns their weaknesses and sorrows over their mistakes.

With unbelievers hiding their incredulity and believers parading their faith, public opinion pronounces its support for religion, which is loved, upheld, and respected. Only by looking into the depths of men's souls will one see the wounds it has suffered.

The mass of mankind, never deprived of religious feelings, sees nothing to drive them away from established beliefs. The instinctive sense of another life leads them without difficulty to the foot of the altar and releases their hearts to the precepts and consolations of faith.

Why does this picture not apply to us? For there are men amongst the French who have ceased to believe in Christianity without adopting any other religion.

I see others who have come to a halt in a state of doubt, already pretending to believe in nothing.

Yet others are still believing Christians but dare not say so.

Among these lukewarm friends and ardent adversaries, there is finally a small number of believers ready to confront all obstacles and to despise all dangers on behalf of their beliefs. These people have triumphed over human weakness to rise above common opinion. Swept along by these very efforts, they no longer know precisely where to stop. As the French have seen in their homeland, that the first use that men have made of their independence has been to attack religion, they dread their contemporaries and recoil in alarm from the freedom these people are seeking. Unbelief to them looks like a novelty; thus they treat everything that is novel with a uniform hatred. They are, therefore, at war with their times and country and they view every one of these expressions of opinion as an inevitable enemy of faith.

At the present time, that ought not to be men's normal state in relation to religion.

Therefore, in France we come across an extraordinary incidental cause which prevents the human mind from following its own inclination and drives it beyond the limits within which it should naturally remain.

I am profoundly convinced that this extraordinary and incidental cause is the close union of politics and religion.

Unbelievers in Europe attack Christians more as political enemies than as religious opponents; they detest faith more as a party opinion than as a mistaken doctrine; when they reject the priest, it is less as a representative of God than as a friend of authority.

In Europe, Christianity has allowed itself to be closely linked with the powers of this world. Today these powers are collapsing and it is virtually buried beneath their ruins. It has become a living body tied to the dead; if the bonds holding it were cut, it would rise again.

I do not know what would have to be done to restore youthful energy to European Christianity. God alone could do this; but at least it depends upon men to leave to faith the deployment of all the strength it still has.

HOW THE EDUCATION, HABITS AND PRACTICAL EXPERIENCE OF AMERICANS CONTRIBUTE TO THE SUCCESS OF DEMOCRATIC INSTITUTIONS

What must be understood by the education of the American people—In the United States the human mind has received a training much less extensive than in Europe—No one has remained uneducated—Why—The speed at which opinions circulate in the half-populated states of the West—How practical experience is of more use to Americans than book-learning.

Throughout this book I have reminded readers of the influence which the education and habits of the Americans have had upon the maintenance of their political institutions. Therefore, it now remains for me to add little new to that.

Up until now America has had only a small number of noteworthy authors, no great historians, and not a single poet. Its inhabitants look upon real literature with disapproval and any third-rank European town publishes annually more literary works that the twenty-four states of the Union put together.

The American mind keeps its distance from general ideas and does not direct its attention to theoretical discoveries. Neither politics nor industry inspires such a course. In the United States new laws constantly appear on the statute books but no great writers have yet inquired into the general principles of these laws.

Americans have legal experts and commentators but no publicists and in politics they give examples for the world to follow without teaching it anything.

The same is true for the mechanical arts.

In America, European inventions are shrewdly adopted and, when they have been perfected, they are adapted with admirable skill to the country's needs. Men are industrious but they do not foster the science of industry. Good workmen exist but few inventors. Fulton[d] hawked his genius around for many years among foreign nations before he could devote himself to his own country.

Anyone wishing to ascertain the state of education among the Anglo-Americans has to view the same facts from two different angles. If he concentrates upon the learned, he will be surprised at how few there are; if he counts up the uneducated, the Americans will strike him as the most enlightened nation in the world.

The entire population falls between these two extremes, as I have already noted elsewhere.

In New England, each citizen learns the elementary concepts of human knowledge; beyond that he is taught the doctrines and evidence of his religion. He undergoes instruction on the history of his country and the principal features of its constitution. In Connecticut and Massachusetts you will seldom find a man who has only an inadequate knowledge of these things and anyone completely unaware of them is quite an oddity.

When I compare the Greek and Roman republics with that of America and the former's libraries full of manuscripts and their rude population with the latter's thousand newspapers and its educated people, when I think of all the efforts made to judge the latter in the light of the former and to anticipate what will happen today by studying what happened two thousand years ago, I am tempted to burn my books in order to apply only brand new ideas in such a newly formed society.

However, what I am saying about New England should not be applied in some vague sense to the Union as a whole. The further west or south one goes, the less extensive are the educational opportunities. In those states bordering the Gulf of Mexico,ᵉ just as in our countries, there are a certain number of individuals to be found who are uninstructed in the rudiments of human knowledge but you would be hard pressed to find a single district in the United States which was sunk in complete ignorance. The reason for this is simple: European nations emerged from the Dark Ages and barbarism to move toward civilization and education. Their progress has been uneven: some have run ahead, others have done no more than walk; several have plowed to a halt and still sleep upon the way.

ʹ   This has not happened in the United States.

The Anglo-Americans settled upon the land their descendants now occupy in a completely civilized state; they did not need to be educated; it was enough that they should not forget. Now, it is the sons of these very same Americans who annually transport their homes into the wilds and take with them the knowledge they have already acquired and a respect for learning.

Education has made them realize the usefulness of instruction and has persuaded them to pass on this same instruction to their children. In the United States, society had no infancy; it was born a fully grown man.

Americans never use the word "peasant" because they have no concept for the word to express; the ignorance of primitive times, rural simplicity, and rustic village life have not been preserved with them and they are unacquainted with the virtues, the vices, the crude manners, and the naive charms of a civilization in its earliest stages.

At the extreme borders of the confederated states, where the edges of society and the wilds meet, a population of bold adventurers who have fled from the poverty threatening them beneath their fathers' roofs have not been afraid to plunge into the deserted areas of America in order to seek a new homeland. As soon as the pioneer arrives in his place of refuge, he hurriedly cuts down trees and erects a cabin in the forest. There is no more wretched sight than these remote homesteads. The evening traveler approaches from far off to see the gleam of a hearth fire through the chinks in the walls and at night, if the wind rises, he hears the noise of the branches moving on the roof amid the forest trees. Who would not suppose that this poor cottage sheltered some coarse and uneducated people? However, one should not assume a connection between the pioneer and his place of refuge. All about him is primitive and wild, whereas he is the result, so to speak, of eighteen centuries of work and experience. He wears the clothes and speaks the language of towns; he is aware of the past, is curious about the future, and is ready to argue about the present. He is a very civilized man prepared to take up a temporary home in the woods, plunging into the wilderness of the New World with his Bible, axe, and newspapers.

It is difficult to imagine the incredible speed with which ideas circulate in these empty spaces.[6]

I do not believe that such a great intellectual activity takes place in the most educated and populated districts of France.[7]

It cannot be doubted that, in the United States, the education of the people powerfully contributes to the maintenance of

6. I have traveled a certain distance of the frontiers of the United States in a sort of open cart called the mail coach. Day and night we made our way at speed along roads not very well marked through huge forests of green trees; when the gloom became impenetrable my driver lighted branches of larch and, illuminated by them, we continued on our way. From time to time we came across a cottage in the woods which was the post office. The postman dropped an enormous bundle of letters at the door of this isolated dwelling and continued on our journey at full gallop, leaving with the inhabitants of that neighborhood the responsibility of fetching their part of the treasure.

7. In 1832 each inhabitant of Michigan gave 1 france 22 centimes to the post office revenue and each inhabitant of the Floridas 1 france 5 centimes (see *National Calendar*, 1833, p. 244.) In the same year each inhabitant of the Département du Nord paid 1 franc 4 centimes to the state for the same purpose. (See the *Compte général de l'administration des finances*, 1833, p. 623.) Now, Michigan at this time still had no more than seven inhabitants per square league and Florida, five. Education was less widespread and commercial activity less extensive in those two districts than in most of the states of the Union, whereas the Département du Nord, with 3,400 individuals per square league, is one of the most educated and most industrialized parts of France.

the democratic republic. That will always be so, in my view, wherever education to enlighten the mind is not separated from that responsible for teaching morality.

However, I exaggerate in no way this advantage and I am still more reluctant to believe, unlike many Europeans, that teaching men to read and write is enough to turn them immediately into citizens.

True wisdom is mainly born of experience and, if Americans had not gradually become used to self-government, the literary knowledge they possess would not presently be any help at all in bringing success.

I have lived for some time among the people in the United States and I cannot express how much I admire their experience and common sense.

Do not invite an American to speak about Europe; he will usually display great presumption and a rather ridiculous arrogance. He will merely express those vague and general ideas which, in all countries, are such a comfort to the uneducated. But ask him about his own country and you will see the mist clouding his mind melt away at once; his language and his thought will become lucid, sharp, and precise, he will inform you of his rights and how he has to exercise them; he will know the principles which govern the world of politics. You will see that he knows about administrative regulations and that he has familiarized himself with the workings of the law. The citizen of the United States has not drawn this useful knowledge and positive ideas from books: his literary education may have prepared him to receive them but it has not provided them.

An American gains his knowledge of the laws from his participation in legislation: he becomes educated about the formalities of government from governing. The great work of society is performed daily beneath his gaze and, so to speak, in his grasp.

In the United States, the general thrust of education is directed toward political life; in Europe, its main aim is to fit men for private life, as the citizens' involvement in public affairs is too rare an event for anything to be done about it in advance.

As soon as you glance at these two social systems, these differences are obvious even from the outside.

In Europe we often introduce ideas and behavior from our private life into our public life and as our experience is to move quickly from the family circle to the government of the state, we are often observed discussing the great concerns of society in the same way that we talk to our friends.

In contrast, Americans almost always carry the habits of public life over into their private lives. With them, the idea of a jury surfaces in playground games and parliamentary rituals are observed even in the organization of a banquet.

LAWS CONTRIBUTE MORE TO THE MAINTENANCE OF THE DEMOCRATIC REPUBLIC IN THE UNITED STATES THAN PHYSICAL CONDITIONS OF THE COUNTRY AND CUSTOMS EVEN MORE THAN LAWS

All the peoples of America enjoy a democratic state of society—Yet democratic institutions only exist among Anglo-Americans—The Spaniards of South America equally favored by geography as the Anglo-Americans are not able to sustain a democratic republic—Mexico, which has adopted the constitution of the United States cannot do so—The Anglo-Americans in the West find greater difficulty in maintaining it than those in the East—Reasons for these differences.

I have said that the maintenance of democratic institutions in the United States must be attributed to circumstances, laws, and customs.

Most Europeans know only the first of these three causes and give it an undue weight of importance.[8]

It is true that Anglo-Americans have brought equality of social conditions into the New World. You will never come across either commoners or nobles in their ranks; professional prejudices have always been as unknown as prejudices of birth.

8.   At this point I remind the reader of the general meaning which I give to the word *customs*: namely that collection of intellectual and moral characteristics which men bring to the social condition.

The state of society being thus democratic, democracy had no difficulty in establishing its authority.

But this fact is not peculiar to the United States; almost all American colonies were founded by men equal amongst themselves or who became so when they settled there. Not a single part of the New World exists where Europeans have been able to create an aristocracy.

Nevertheless, democratic institutions prosper only in the United States.

The American Union has no enemies to fight. It is as solitary in the wilderness as an island in the ocean.

Yet, to the Spaniards of South America, nature gave a similar isolation which did not prevent them from maintaining armies. They have waged war between themselves when foreign enemies did not exist. Only the Anglo-American democracy has so far been able to remain peaceful.

The territory of the Union provides limitless scope to human activity: it offers inexhaustible supplies for industry and labor. The love of wealth, therefore, replaces ambition and prosperity quenches the fires of party disputes.

But where in the world do you come across more fertile wildernesses, broader rivers, and more untouched and inexhaustible wealth than in South America? Yet, South America is unable to sustain a democracy. If all that was needed for nations to be happy was to be placed in a corner of the universe where they could spread out at will over unpopulated areas, then the Spaniards of South America would have no need to complain about their lot. And even if they were not enjoying the same happiness as the inhabitants of the United States, they ought at least to arouse the envy of European nations. However, there are no nations on the earth as wretched as those in South America.

Thus, physical causes not only fail to bring similar results in South and North America but, in the case of the former, they cannot even achieve anything which is superior to what we see in Europe, where geography works against them.

Physical causes, therefore, do not influence the destiny of nations as extensively as is supposed.

I have met men in New England prepared to abandon their homeland, where they might have gained a comfortable living, to seek their fortune in the wilderness. Nearby I saw the French Canadians crowded in an area too narrow for them when the same wilderness lay close at hand; the Canadian paid as high a price for land as he would have done in France, whereas the United States immigrant obtained a whole estate for the price of a few days' work.

Thus nature, in presenting Europeans with the empty lands of the New World, offers them something they do not always know how to use.

I see other peoples of America enjoying the same physical conditions of prosperity as the Anglo-Americans but without their laws and customs, and these nations are miserable. Anglo-American laws and customs represent, therefore, the particular and predominant reason, which I have been seeking, for their greatness.

I am far from claiming that American laws possess an absolute excellence, nor do I believe that they are applicable to all democratic nations and there are several of them, even in the United States, which seem dangerous.

Nevertheless, it cannot be denied that American legislation, all in all, is well adapted to the genius of the nation which it is intended to govern and to the nature of the country.

American laws are, therefore, good and must account for a great part of the success of the democratic government in America but I do not believe they are the principal cause. If they seem to me to have more influence over the social happiness of Americans than the geography of the country, I still have reasons to think that they have less influence than customs.

Federal laws make up, of course, the most important part of United States legislation.

Mexico, which is as fortunately situated as the Anglo-American Union, has adopted these same laws but cannot get used to a democratic form of government.

There is, therefore, another reason, apart from geography and laws, which enables democracy to rule in the United States.

But this is where another more powerful proof emerges.

Almost all the inhabitants of the Union have sprung from the same stock, speak the same language, pray to God in the same way, experience the same physical conditions, and obey the same laws.

So where must the observable differences come from?

Why, in the East of the Union, does the republican government appear strong and orderly, proceeding with mature deliberation? What imprints a character of wisdom and durability upon all its acts?

On the other hand, why, in the states of the West, do social authorities proceed so haphazardly?

Why, in the activity of public affairs, is there something disorderly, passionate, and, one might almost say, feverish, which does not augur well for a long future?

I am no longer comparing Anglo-Americans with foreign nations but am contrasting them with each other, as I seek to understand why they are not alike. At this point, all arguments drawn from the nature of the country and the difference in legal systems are irrelevant. Some other reason must be sought and where shall I find it, if not in a nation's customs?

It is in the East that the Anglo-Americans have been longest accustomed to democratic government and that they have shaped the habits and conceived the ideas which most favor its maintenance. Democracy has gradually permeated their customs, opinions, and social habits; it is to be found in every aspect of social life as much as in the laws. It is in the East that the literary study and practical education of the nation have reached the height of perfection and that religion has joined forces most closely with liberty. What are all these usages, opinions, habits, beliefs, if they are not what I have named "customs"?

But in the West, some of these advantages are still absent. Many Americans of the western states were born in the woods and they mix the ideas and customs of primitive life with the civilization of their fathers. Among them passions are more violent, religious morality has less authority, ideas are less formed. There men have less control over each other for they scarcely know each other. To a certain degree, therefore, the people of the West exhibit the inexperience and disorderly habits of emerging nations. Even though these western societies are formed from old elements, their arrangement is new.

Thus, of all Americans, it is especially the customs of Americans of the United States which make them capable of supporting a democratic government; and it is customs again that cause the various Anglo-American democracies to be more or less orderly and prosperous.

Europeans, therefore, exaggerate the influence of geography on the duration of democratic institutions. Too much importance is attributed to legislation and too little to customs. These three major causes serve unquestionably to regulate and control American democracy; but if I had to range them in order, I would say that physical causes contribute less than legislation and legislation less than customs.

I am convinced that the luckiest of geographical conditions and the best laws are unable to uphold a constitution in the face of poor customs, whereas the latter can still turn even the most unfavorable conditions and the worst laws to advantage.

The importance of customs is a commonly held truth and we are constantly brought back to it through study and experience. I find that it occupies a central position in my thoughts and all my ideas lead me to it.

I have only one more comment to add on this subject.

If, in the course of this book, I have not succeeded in convincing the reader of the importance I attach to the practical experience, behavior, opinions, and, in a word, the customs of Americans in maintaining their laws, I have failed in the main objective I set myself in writing it.

WHETHER LAWS AND CUSTOMS WOULD BE ENOUGH TO MAINTAIN DEMOCRATIC INSTITUTIONS IN ANY OTHER COUNTRY THAN AMERICA

Anglo-Americans, if transported to Europe, would have to modify their laws—A distinction has to be made between democratic institutions and American institutions—One can imagine democratic laws better than, or at least

different from, those adopted by American democracy—
The example of America simply proves that one need
not despair of regulating democracy with the help of
laws and customs.

I have stated that the success of democratic institutions in the United States was due more to laws and customs than geography.

But does it follow that these same causes transposed elsewhere would, by themselves, have the same power and if geography cannot replace laws and customs, can the latter in their turn replace geography?

It will be readily understood that the evidence for this is not at hand: there are peoples other than the Anglo-Americans in the New World and these I have been able to compare as they are subjected to the same physical conditions.

But outside America there are no nations which, while they are deprived of the physical advantages of the Anglo-Americans, have nevertheless adopted their laws and customs.

Thus we have no point of comparison in the matter and can only hazard conjectures.

In the first place, I think we should make a careful distinction between the institutions of the United States and democratic institutions in general.

When I reflect on the state of Europe, its great nations, its crowded cities, its powerful armies, the complexities of its political systems, I cannot believe that the Anglo-Americans themselves, if transported to our soil with their ideas, religion, and customs could live there without considerably altering their laws.

But it is possible to imagine a democratic nation organized in a way different from the American nation.

Is it, therefore, impossible to conceive a government founded on the actual will of the majority but in which the majority, repressing its natural feeling for equality for the sake of the order and stability of the state, should consent to invest one single family or one single man with all the attributes of executive power? Can one not imagine a democratic society in which national forces might be more centralized than in the United States, in which the people would exert a less direct and irresistible authority over public affairs and in which every citizen, endowed with certain rights, would take part within his own sphere in the proceedings of the government?

What I have seen among Anglo-Americans leads me to believe that democratic institutions of this nature, carefully introduced into society so that they might gradually mix with the habits and little by little be interfused with the very opinions of the people, could take hold elsewhere than in America.

If American laws were the only democratic laws one could imagine or the most perfect which it is possible to find, I accept that one might conclude that the success of United States legislation is no proof at all of the success of democratic legislation in general in a country less favored by nature.

But if American laws seem to me to be defective in many respects and if I find it easy to imagine different ones, the special nature of the country does not prove to me that democratic institutions could not succeed among a people who, although their physical circumstances might be less favorable, had better laws.

If men turned out differently in America from what they are elsewhere, if their social state gave rise to habits and opinions differing from those which originate in the same social state in Europe, what happens in American democracies would have nothing to say about what should happen in other democracies.

If Americans displayed the same inclinations as all democratic nations and their legislators had relied upon the nature of the country and the advantages of circumstances to restrain these inclinations within proper limits, the prosperity of the United States would have to be attributed to purely material causes and it would not offer any definitive proof to those nations who might want to follow their example but who did not enjoy their natural advantages.

But neither of these suppositions is supported by the facts.

In America I have encountered passions similar to those we find in Europe: some stemmed from the nature of the human heart itself, others from the democratic state of society.

That is how I discovered in the United States a restlessness of heart which is natural to men who live at a time when all social conditions are roughly equal and who see that they all have identical opportunities to better themselves. There I discovered the democratic sentiment of envy was expressed in a thousand different ways. I noticed that in the conduct of public affairs the people often displayed a wide mixture of presumption and ignorance and I concluded that, both in America and in Europe, men were prey to the same imperfections and liable to the same sufferings.

But when I happened to analyze the state of society closely, I had no difficulty in discovering that Americans had expended great and successful efforts to counteract these weaknesses of human nature and to correct the natural defects of democracy.

The various municipal laws they had in place seemed to me to be so many restraints in order to contain within a narrow sphere the citizens' restless ambitions and to turn to the township's profit the very democratic passions which might have overthrown the state. American legislators seemed to have had some success in opposing the notion of rights to the feelings of envy, the stability of religious morality to the constant flux of politics, the experience of people to their ignorance of theory and their day-to-day knowledge of business to the impetuosity of their desires.

Americans have not, therefore, relied upon the nature of their country to counteract the dangers emanating from their constitution or from their laws. They have applied remedies, which none but themselves had thought of before, to those evils they share with all democratic nations and, although they were the first to try them out, they have succeeded.

American customs and laws are not the only ones to suit democratic nations, but Americans have demonstrated that we should not lose heart in our attempts to regulate democracy by means of laws and customs.

If other nations, borrowing this general and creative idea from America but without wishing to imitate its inhabitants in the particular way in which they have applied it, attempted to adapt themselves to the social state imposed upon the men of our time and sought in this way to avoid the tyranny and anarchy which threaten them, what reasons have we to believe that they are bound to fail in their endeavors?

The organization and establishment of democracy among Christian nations is the great political problem of our time. Americans unquestionably have not resolved this problem but they have provided some useful lessons for those wishing to resolve it.

IMPORTANCE OF THE ABOVE IN RELATION TO EUROPE

It is easy to see why I have devoted such efforts to the above investigations. The question I have unearthed involves not only the United States but the whole world; not one nation but all mankind.

If nations with a democratic social state could remain free only as long as they live in a wilderness, we would have to despair of the future destiny of the human race; for men are rushing toward democracy and the available wildernesses are filling up.

If it were true that laws and customs were inadequate to maintain democratic institutions, what recourse would be available to nations other than the despotism of one man?

I realize that nowadays there are many honest people who are hardly alarmed by this picture of the future and who are so tired of freedom as to long for repose at last, far from the storms that attend it.

But such people have a poor understanding of the haven toward which they are steering. Hypnotized by their memories, they are judging absolute power by what used to be and not by what it might become today.

If absolute power were to be re-established among the democratic nations of Europe, I am quite certain that it would assume a new form and would take on features unknown to our forefathers.

Once upon a time in Europe, the law and the consent of the people invested kings with an almost unlimited power, although they hardly ever used it.

I shall not mention the prerogatives of the nobility, the authority of sovereign courts, the rights of corporations, provincial privileges, which deadened the onslaughts of the king's authority and sustained a spirit of resistance in the nation.

Apart from these political institutions which, even though they were often opposed to personal freedom, helped to maintain the love of freedom in men's hearts and whose usefulness was easy to see in this connection, public opinion and customs raised less conspicuous but no less powerful barriers around the king's authority.

Religion, the affection of his subjects, the goodness of the prince, honor, family spirit, provincial prejudices, custom, and public opinion hemmed in the power of kings, enclosing their authority within an invisible circle.

Then, nations' constitutions were despotic but their customs free. Princes had the right to do anything but lacked either the capacity or the desire.

What remains today of those barriers which once held tyranny in check?

Since religion has lost its sway over men's souls, the most obvious boundary between good and evil has been overthrown; in the realm of morality, everything seems doubtful and uncertain: kings and nations go forward at random and no one can say where the natural limits of despotism and the boundaries of license are to be found.

Prolonged revolutions have destroyed forever the respect which surrounded heads of state. Released from the burden of public esteem, princes may henceforth abandon themselves without fear to the intoxication of power.

When kings look into the hearts of the people who come into their presence, they are merciful because they feel strong; they cultivate the love of their subjects because it props up their throne. Then the reciprocal feelings of prince and people recall that tenderness at the heart of social family life. Subjects, while they murmur against the ruler, are still grieved to displease him and the ruler strikes his subjects with a light hand as a father chastises his children.

But once the prestige of royalty has faded away amid the

tumult of revolutions and kings, in succession upon the throne, have displayed by turns the weakness of *right* and the harshness of *fact*, no one any longer sees the sovereign as father of the state but each man sees him as its master. He is despised, if he shows weakness, and hated, if he shows strength. The king himself is filled with anger and fear, finding himself as a result a foreigner in his own land and treating his subjects as conquered enemies.

When provinces and towns formed so many different nations in the midst of a common country, each of them had a distinct individual character which stood in opposition to the general spirit of subjection; but today, when all sections of the same empire have lost their franchises, their customs, their prejudices, and even their memories and names and have grown used to obeying the same laws, it is no longer more difficult to repress them all together than it was formerly to repress them singly.

While the nobility enjoyed its power and indeed for a long time after it had lost it, aristocratic honor gave extraordinary strength to individual resistance.

Then you saw men who, in spite of their powerlessness, still entertained an inflated idea of their individual worth and dared to resist by themselves the pressure of public authority.

But nowadays, when all classes in the end meld together, when the individual increasingly disappears within the crowd and is readily lost in the obscurity of society, and these days when the honor of kings has almost lost its authority without being replaced by virtue and there is nothing to raise a man above himself, who can say where the demands of power and the servility of weakness will stop?

As long as family feeling was kept alive, the man who fought against tyranny was never alone; he found all round him clients, hereditary friends, and his relations. And had this support been lacking, he would still have felt upheld by his ancestors and his descendants. But, when family estates are divided up and when races are mixed together after so few years, what place is there for family spirit?

What power will customs retain in a nation which has completely changed in character and continues to change, in which there is a precedent for every act of tyranny and an example for every crime and in which nothing is so ancient that people are afraid of destroying it and nothing is so new that they have not the nerve to try it?

What resistance do customs offer when they have already proved so yielding?

What power has public opinion itself retained when not even twenty people are held together by any common bond, when there is no man, no family, no group, no class, no free association which could represent public opinion or set it in motion and when each citizen, equally powerless, poor and isolated, has only his personal weakness to fight against the organized force of the government?

To imagine some parallel to what would then happen among us, we would not have recourse to the history of France. We would need perhaps to question the memorials of the ancient world and to return to those awful centuries of Roman tyranny when habits were corrupt, memories blotted out, customs destroyed, opinions wavering, when freedom, banished from the laws, no longer knew where to flee for safety and when nothing any longer protected the citizens who, in their turn, no longer protected themselves. Men could be seen scoffing at human nature and princes exhausting the mercy of heaven before the patience of their subjects.

Those who think to rediscover the monarchy of Henry IV[f] or Louis XIV seem to me quite blind. For my part, when I consider the state already reached by several European nations and the one toward which all the others are striving, I am inclined to believe that soon there will only be room among them for either the freedom of democracy or the tyranny of the Caesars.

Is this not worth considering? In fact, if men were to reach the point of having to choose between total freedom or total slavery, total equality or total denial of rights, and if the rulers of society were reduced to the alternative, either gradually to raise the masses up to their position or to reduce all citizens below the level of common humanity, would that not be enough to overcome many doubts, to reassure many consciences and to prepare each man readily to make great sacrifices?

Should we not, therefore, consider the gradual development of democratic institutions and customs not as the best but as the only means left to us of being free? And, without loving democratic government, would we not be inclined to adopt it as the most suitable and most honorable remedy against the present ills of society?

It is hard to involve the people in government; it is harder still to provide them with the experience or to inspire them with the opinions which they need to govern well.

I grant that the will of a democracy is unstable, its agents crude, and its laws incomplete. But, if it were true that soon no intermediate state existed between the power of democracy and the yoke of a single man, should we not steer toward the former rather than bow voluntarily to the latter? And if we had to reach complete equality in the end, would it not be better to be leveled down by freedom than by a tyrant?

Those who, having read this book, should imagine that in writing it I wished to recommend that all nations with a democratic social system should imitate the laws and customs of the Anglo-Americans would be making a great mistake; they would have concentrated on the form of my thinking and abandoned the substance itself. My aim has been to demonstrate, using America as my model, that laws and, above all, customs enabled a democratic nation to remain free. Moreover, I am very far from thinking that we should follow the example represented by American democracy or imitate the means she has used to achieve this aim for I am well aware of the influence of the nature of the country and of previous history upon political constitutions and I would regard it as a great misfortune for mankind, if freedom should assume the same features in all places.

But I think that if we fail to introduce and gradually set up democratic institutions in France, and that if we abandon the attempt to inspire all citizens with the ideas and feelings which first of all prepare them for freedom and consequently allow them to enjoy it, there will be no independence for anyone, neither for the middle classes, nor the nobility, nor the poor, nor the wealthy, but only an equal tyranny for all; and I foresee that if we fail to establish among us the peaceful authority of the majority in time, sooner or later we shall arrive at the *boundless* power of one man.

CHAPTER 10

A FEW REMARKS ON THE PRESENT-DAY STATE AND THE PROBABLE FUTURE OF THE THREE RACES WHICH LIVE IN THE TERRITORY OF THE UNITED STATES

The main task I set myself is now performed and I have described, at least to the best of my ability, the laws of American democracy and I have revealed what its customs are. At this point I could stop but the reader would perhaps feel that I had not satisfied his expectations.

There is yet something else in America besides an immense and complete democracy and one can view the inhabitants of the New World from more than one point of view.

In the course of this work, my theme has often led me to mention the Indians and Negroes but I have never had the time to stop and describe the position these two races occupy in the democratic nation I was busily depicting. I indicated what spirit and which laws helped the formation of the Anglo-American confederation; I have been able to point out only cursorily and very incompletely the dangers threatening this confederation; I have found it impossible to reveal in detail its chances of survival, independently of laws and customs. When speaking of the united republics, I have not ventured to guess at how permanent the republican systems in the New World might be and, while alluding to the business activity in the Union, I have not been able to concentrate upon the future of the Americans as a trading nation.

These topics are like tangents to my subjects but do not occupy a central position because they concern America at large not democracy itself which I have above all wished to describe. So, at first I had to put them to one side but I must now return to them as I approach my conclusion.

The land now occupied or claimed by the American Union stretches from the Atlantic Ocean to the shores of the sea in the south. In the east and west its boundaries coincide with those of the continent. In the south it extends to the edge of the tropics and then, in the north, it rises to the regions of ice.

The men scattered over this area do not constitute, as in Europe, shoots of the same stock. They reveal, from the first viewing, three naturally distinct, I might almost say hostile, races. Their education, their law, their origins, even their external features had raised an almost insurmountable barrier between them; chance has brought them together on the same soil but has joined them together with no genuine contact so that each race pursues its destiny separately.

Among these very different men, the first to attract attention, the best educated, the most powerful, the happiest, is the white man, the European, the epitome of man; in a position inferior to him appear the Negro and the Indian.

These two unfortunate races have nothing in common, neither birth, nor facial features, nor language, nor customs; their misfortunes alone are similar. Both occupy an equally inferior position in the country they inhabit; both experience the effects of tyranny; and, if their sufferings are different, they are able to blame the same people.

Would you not accept, after seeing what happens in the world, that the European is to other races what man himself is to the animals? He uses them for his own convenience and destroys them when he fails to bend them to his will.

In one fell swoop, oppression has deprived the descendants of the Africans of almost all the privileges due to human beings! The American Negro has lost even the recollection of his homeland; he no longer hears the language of his fathers; he has renounced their religion and forgotten their ways. Ceasing, in this way, to belong to Africa, he still has not acquired any rights to the good things of Europe; but he is left suspended between the two societies; he has remained cut off from the two nations, sold by the one and rejected by the other; in the whole universe, his master's hearth affords him the only semblance of a home.

The Negro has no family; in a woman he can see only a passing companion of his pleasures and, from their birth, his sons are his equals.

Should I call it a blessing from God or the final curse of his anger, this disposition of the soul which makes a man insensitive to extreme suffering, often even giving him a sort of depraved taste for the cause of his own misfortunes?

The Negro, plunged in this abyss of suffering, scarcely feels his ill fortune; violence had enslaved him, habituation to slavery has given him a slave's thoughts and ambitions; his admiration for his tyrannical masters is even greater than his hatred and his joy and pride reside in his imitation of those who oppress him. His intelligence has sunk to the level of his soul.

For the Negro, slavery coincides with birth. What am I saying? Often he is bought in his mother's womb and he begins his life of slavery, so to speak, before he is born.

Equally devoid of needs and pleasures, he realizes from the first ideas he has of existence that he belongs to someone else whose interest is to watch over his days. He realizes that his own destiny is not in his own hands; even the power of thought appears to him a useless gift of Providence and he quietly enjoys all the privileges of his humiliation.

If he gains his freedom, he often feels independence as a shackle heavier than slavery itself for, throughout his life, he has learned submission to everything except reason and, when reason becomes his only guide, he cannot recognize its voice. A thousand new needs crowd round him and he lacks the necessary knowledge and energy to resist them. Such needs are masters to be opposed, whereas he has learned nothing but obedient submission. Thus, he has reached such depths of wretchedness that slavery brutalizes him and freedom destroys him.

Oppression has exerted very similar influences on the Indian races but with different results.

Before the white man's arrival in the New World, the inhabitants of North America lived quietly in the forests, exposed to the normal ups and downs of primitive life, with the vices and virtues of uncivilized peoples. Europeans, having scattered the Indian tribes into the wilderness, condemned them to a wandering vagabond life, full of indescribable suffering.

Primitive nations are ruled by opinions and customs alone.

By weakening the patriotism of the North American Indians, by dispersing their families, by obscuring their traditions, by disrupting their chain of memories, by changing all their habits, and by increasing their needs beyond measure, European tyranny has made them more unruly and less civilized than they were before. Their moral and physical state has never stopped deteriorating and as their unhappiness intensified, the more barbarous they have become. However, Europeans have been unable to alter entirely the Indian character and, although they have the power to destroy them, they do not possess the power to civilize or to reduce them to submission.

The Negro stands at the extreme limits of slavery; the Indian at the furthest boundary of freedom. Slavery produces in the former just as fatal results as independence does in the latter.

The Negro has lost even the ownership of his own body and cannot have any control over his own existence without committing a kind of theft.

The savage is left to his own devices as soon as he is capable of action. He has hardly any experience of family authority; he has never bowed his will to that of his fellow men; no one has ever taught him to distinguish between voluntary obedience and shameful submission, and the very name of the law is unknown to him. Freedom, in his view, signifies the escape from almost all the ties of society. He delights in this uncivilized independence and would prefer to die rather than give up any part of it. Civilization has little hold on such a man.

The Negro makes a thousand fruitless efforts to find a place in a society which drives him out; he bows to the tastes of his oppressors, adopts their opinions and, by imitation, aims to unite with them. He has been told from birth that his race is naturally inferior to the white man and, almost believing that to be true, he is, therefore, ashamed of himself. In every feature he sees traces of slavery and, if he could, he would willingly rid himself of all he has become.

The Indian, by contrast, has an imagination completely overtaken by the so-called nobility of his origin. He lives and dies
amid these proud dreams. Far from wishing to mold his customs
to ours, he is attached to barbarity as a distinctive emblem of
his race and he rejects civilization less perhaps from a hatred for
it than from a fear of ever being like Europeans.[1]

He has only the resources of his wild surroundings to challenge our well-developed arts, his unruly courage against our
tactical skills, and the instinctive spontaneity of his barbaric
nature against our elaborate designs. In such an uneven struggle,
he gives in.

The Negro, who would like to join the European, is unable
to do so. The Indian might succeed to some degree but it is
beneath him to try. The slavishness of the one delivers him up
to servitude; the pride of the other leads him to death.

1.   The native of North America retains his opinions and the slightest of his
     habits with a tenacity which has no parallel in history. For more than two
     hundred years the wandering tribes of North America have had daily
     connection with white men and they have never, so to speak, appropriated
     a single idea or custom. Yet Europeans have exercised a very great influ-
     ence over the Indians, whose character they have made more undisciplined
     without making them more European.
         In the summer of 1831, finding myself beyond Lake Michigan at a place
     called Green Bay, which serves as the extreme frontier between the United
     States and the Indians of the Northwest, I became acquainted with an
     American officer, Major H., who, one day, spoke to me about the inflexi-
     bility of the Indian character and recounted the following fact: "I knew
     once," he said to me, "a young Indian who had been educated in a New
     England school. There, he had achieved great success and had assumed
     the outward appearance of a civilized man. When the war broke out
     between ourselves and the English in 1810, I saw this young man again;
     at that time he was serving in our army at the head of the warriors of his
     own tribe. The Americans had admitted the Indians into their ranks only
     on condition that they abstained from the horrible custom of scalping
     their victims. On the evening of the battle of —, C. came and sat down by
     the fire of our bivouac. I asked what had happened to him that day. He
     answered me and, growing more and more animated by the recollection
     of his exploits, he ended up by opening his coat with the words: 'Do not
     betray me but just take a look at this!' I actually saw," said Major H.,
     "between his body and his shirt the scalp of an Englishman still dripping
     with blood."

I recall that one day as I was passing through the forests of the state of Alabama, I reached the log cabin of a pioneer. I had no wish to enter the American's dwelling but I went and rested for a little while on the edge of a spring not far off in the woods. As I was there, an Indian woman came up (we were then in the territory of the Creek nation) holding by the hand a small white girl of five or six whom I supposed to be the pioneer's daughter. A Negro woman was following her. The Indian woman's dress had a sort of wild luxury; metal rings hung down from her nostrils and ears; her hair fell freely upon her shoulders and was dotted with glass beads and I saw that she was not married because she was still wearing the shell necklace which it is the custom for a bride to lay upon the marriage bed; the Negro woman was dressed in tattered European clothes.

All three came and sat on the edge of the spring and the young Indian, taking the child into her arms, lavished upon her such fond caresses as mothers give, or so you might have thought; the Negro woman, too, sought to attract the young Creole's attention with a thousand innocent tricks, while the latter displayed, in the slightest of her movements, a sense of superiority, which contrasted strangely with her youthful weakness, as if she were deploying a kind of condescension on receiving the attentions of her companions.

Squatting in front of her mistress and watching for her smallest desires, the Negro woman seemed equally divided between an almost motherly attachment and a slavish fear, whereas you could see in the Indian woman, even in the outpouring of her tenderness, the presence of a free, proud, and almost fierce attitude.

I had drawn near and was silently observing this scene. My curiosity doubtless irritated the Indian woman for she suddenly stood up, pushed the child from her somewhat roughly and plunged into the forest, giving me an angry look.

I had often seen members of the three races of North America together in the same place; I had already recognized the thousand different signs of white supremacy: but something particularly moving took place in the picture I have just drawn; a bond of affection linked in this case the oppressed and the oppressors, and nature's efforts to draw them close made even more striking the wide gap between them caused by prejudice and law.

THE PRESENT STATE AND THE PROBABLE FUTURE OF THE INDIAN TRIBES WHICH POPULATE THE TERRITORY OF THE UNION

Gradual disappearance of the native races—How this comes about—Sufferings accompanying the forced migrations of the Indians—The primitive races of North America had only two means of escaping destruction: war or civilization—They are no longer able to make war— Why they did not wish to become civilized when they might have done so and no longer can now that they wish it— Example of the Creeks and Cherokees—Policy of individual states toward the Indians—Policy of the federal government.

All the Indian tribes[a] formerly living in the territory of New England, the Narragansetts, the Mohicans, the Pequots, now live only in men's memories; the Lenapes, who received Penn[b] one hundred and fifty years ago on the banks of the Delaware, have now vanished. I met the last of the Iroquois; they were begging for alms. All the nations I have just named once stretched to the shores of the ocean; now a journey of more than two hundred miles into the interior of the continent is necessary to come across an Indian. Not only have these wild tribes receded, they have been destroyed.[2] As the native peoples move away and die, an immense and growing population is taking their place. Never among nations had such an enormous development happened before, nor so swift a destruction.

It is easy to show how this destruction took effect.

When the Indians lived alone in the wilderness from which they are shut off today, their needs were few; they made their

2.   In the thirteen original states there are only 6,373 Indians remaining. (See *Legislative Documents*, 20th Congress, no. 117, p. 20.)

own weapons; their only drink was supplied by the waters of the rivers and their clothes came from the skins of those animals whose flesh provided their food.

The Europeans introduced firearms, iron, and whiskey to the indigenous tribes of North America; they taught them to substitute our cloth for the barbaric clothes with which the simple Indians had been previously satisfied. Although acquiring new tastes, the Indians did not learn the skills necessary to satisfy them and they had to have recourse to the industry of the whites. In return for these goods, which they could not make for themselves, these wild tribes had nothing to offer but the rich furs still found in their forests. From that moment hunting had to supply not only their own needs but also the frivolous enthusiasms of Europeans. They hunted animals no longer simply for food but in order to obtain the only objects they could barter with us.[3]

While the needs of the native peoples increased in this way, their resources were ever diminishing.

From the day when a European settlement rises in the neigh-

3.   Messrs Clarke and Cass, in their report to Congress, 4 February 1829, p. 23, stated: "The time when the Indians generally could supply themselves with food and clothing, without any of the articles of civilized life, has long since passed away. The more remote tribes, beyond the Mississippi, who live where immense herds of buffalo are yet to be found, and who follow these animals in their periodical migrations, could more easily than any others recur to the habits of their ancestors, and live without the white man or any of his manufactures. But the buffalo is constantly receding. The smaller animals, the bear, the deer, the beaver, the otter, the musk-rat, etc., principally minister to the comfort and support of the Indians; and these cannot be taken without guns, ammunition, and traps. Among the north-western Indians, particularly, the labor of supplying a family with food is excessive. Day after day is spent by the hunter without success, and during this interval his family must exist upon bark or roots, or perish. Want and misery are around them and among them. Many die every winter from actual starvation."

The Indians have no wish to live like Europeans and yet they cannot do without them nor are they able to live exactly as their fathers did. This fact alone is sufficient proof, although official sources bear equal witness to it. Some Indian tribesmen on the banks of Lake Superior had killed a European; the American government prohibited all communication with the tribe to whom the guilty parties belonged until the latter had been handed over. That is what happened.

borhood of territory occupied by the Indians, the wild game
takes fright.[4] Thousands of primitive men wandering in the
forests with no fixed dwelling did not threaten it; the moment
the endless noises of European industrial activity are heard in
any place, the animals begin to flee and withdraw to the West
where they instinctively learn that they will still come across
boundless open areas. In their report to Congress of 4 February
1829, Messrs Cass and Clark say: "The buffalo is constantly
receding. A few years since, they approached the base of the
Allegheny; and a few years hence they may even be rare upon
the immense plains which extend to the base of the Rocky
Mountains." I have been assured that this effect of the approach
of the white man was often felt up to five hundred miles from
their frontier. Their influence is thus exerted over tribes whose
names they hardly know and who suffer from the evils of
invasion long before they know the perpetrators.[5]

Bold adventurers soon penetrate into the Indian lands; they
advance forty or fifty miles beyond the whites' furthest frontier
and there build a dwelling for a civilized man amid barbarity
itself. It is easy for them to do so; a hunting people's territorial
boundaries are ill-defined. Moreover, this land belongs to the
nation as a whole and is not exactly the property of anyone.
Therefore, no area of it is defended by one person's interest.

A few European families, by settling in widely separated
locations, finally drive away the wild animals from all the
intervening land for ever. The Indians who had lived there up
to that time in some sort of abundance find it difficult to survive

4.   "Five years ago," says Volney in his *Tableau des Etats-Unis*, p. 370, "in
     going from Vincennes to Kaskaskia, a territory which today belongs to
     the state of Illinois, but which was entirely wild at that time (1797), you
     could not cross a prairie without seeing herds of four to five hundred
     buffaloes. Today there is not a single one left. They swam across the
     Mississippi, harried by the hunters and, above all, disturbed by the bells
     on the American cows."

5.   The truth of what I am presenting here can easily be proved by consulting
     the general picture of Indian tribes dwelling within the territories claimed
     by the United States. (*Legislative Documents*, 20th Congress, no. 117,
     pp. 90–105.) It will be seen that the tribes in the center of America are
     rapidly decreasing even though Europeans are still a good distance away
     from them.

and more difficult still to acquire the necessary articles of barter. Driving away their game is the equivalent of turning our farmers' fields into barren wastes. Soon they lose, almost entirely, the means of subsistence. Then, these doomed people are seen roaming like hungry wolves through their deserted forests. A deep-seated patriotism ties them to the soil which witnessed their birth[6] and they are left with nothing but suffering and death. Finally they reach a decision; they depart to follow the disappearing tracks of the elk, buffalo, and beaver and leave to these wild animals the choice of their new homeland. Strictly speaking, it is not the Europeans who drive away the native races of America, but famine: a lucky distinction which had escaped the casuists of former times but which has been discovered by modern scholars.

The fearful evils that attended these forced migrations are impossible to imagine. By the time the Indians leave their ancestral lands, they are already exhausted and worn down. The country where they are about to settle is already occupied by tribes who view the incomers with jealousy. At their backs lies hunger, before them war and everywhere suffering. To avoid so many enemies, they divide up and each man in isolation furtively seeks the means of survival; he exists in the vast tracts of desert like some outcast in civilized society. The long-weakened social bonds then burst. Already their homeland has disappeared; soon they will have no people; families will scarcely survive; their common name is lost, their language is forgotten, and the traces of their origins vanish. The nation has ceased to exist. It hardly features in the memories of American antiquaries and is known only to a few European scholars.

I should not like the reader to think this picture too highly colored. I have seen with my own eyes several of the cases of

6.   "The Indians," say Messrs Clarke and Cass, in their report to Congress, p. 15, "are attached to their country by the same feelings which bind us to ours; and, besides, there are certain superstitious notions connected with the alienation of what the Great Spirit gave to their ancestors, which operate strongly upon the tribes which have made few or no cessions, but which are gradually weakened as our intercourse with them is extended. 'We will not sell the spot which contains the bones of our fathers,' is almost always the first answer to a proposal to buy their land."

suffering I have just described. I have witnessed evils I would find it impossible to relate.

At the end of 1831, I stood on the left bank of the Mississippi at a spot the Europeans called Memphis. While I was there a numerous band of Choctaws[c] (or Chactas as the French in Louisiana call them) arrived; these savages were leaving their lands and seeking to reach the right bank of the Mississippi where they cherished the forlorn hope of finding a retreat which the American government had promised them. It was then the depths of winter and the cold was exceptionally severe that year; the snow had frozen hard on the ground; the river was drifting with huge ice-floes.

The Indians had brought their families with them and hauled along the wounded, the sick, newborn babies, and old men on the verge of death. They had neither tents nor wagons, simply a few provisions and arms. I saw them embark to cross the wide river and that solemn spectacle will never be erased from my memory. Not a sob or complaint could be heard from this assembled crowd; they stood silent. Their afflictions were of long standing and they considered them beyond remedy. Already the Indians had all embarked upon the boat which was to carry them; their dogs still remained upon the bank. When these animals finally saw that they were being left behind forever, they raised all together a terrible howl and plunged into the icy Mississippi waters to swim after their masters.

Nowadays the dispossession of the Indians is effected in a regular and, as it were, quite legal manner.

When the European population begins to approach the wild places occupied by a savage nation, the United States government usually sends a solemn embassy to the latter. The whites gather the Indians in a great plain and. after eating and drinking with them, address them as follows: "What are you doing in the land of your fathers? Soon you will have to dig up their bones in order to live. How is the country where you live worth more than any other? Are there woods, marshes, and prairies only where you are living now and can you live nowhere but under your own sun? Beyond these mountains which you see on the horizon and on the other side of the lake skirting the land to the west, there are vast countries where wild animals still roam in abundance; sell us your lands and go and live happily in those places." After delivering this speech, they display before the Indians firearms, woolen clothes, barrels of brandy, glass necklaces, pewter bracelets, earrings, and mirrors.[7] If, on seeing all these riches, they remain hesitant, it is suggested that they cannot refuse to agree to what is asked of them and that soon the government itself will be powerless to guarantee them the enjoyment of their rights. What can they do? Half convinced and half compelled, the Indians move away to dwell in new deserts where the whites will not allow them to live ten years in peace. Thus it is that Americans acquired for next to nothing whole provinces, which the richest monarchs of Europe could not afford to buy.[8]

7.   See in the *Legislative Documents*, 20th Congress, doc. 117, the account of what takes place upon these occasions. This curious extract can be found in the report which I have already quoted, made to Congress on 4 February 1829 by Messrs Clarke and Cass. Mr Cass is currently the Secretary of State for War.

"The Indians," says the report, "reach the treaty-ground poor, and almost naked. Large quantities of goods are taken there by the traders, and are seen and examined by the Indians. The women and children become importunate to have their wants supplied, and their influence is soon exerted to induce a sale. Their improvidence is habitual and unconquerable. The gratification of his immediate wants and desires is the ruling passion of an Indian. The expectation of future advantages seldom produces much effect. The experience of the past is lost, and the prospects of the future disregarded. It would be utterly hopeless to demand a cession of land, unless the means were at hand of gratifying their immediate wants; and when their condition and circumstances are fairly considered, it ought not to surprise us that they are so anxious to relieve themselves."

8.   On 19 May 1830, Mr Edward Everett declared before the House of Representatives that the Americans had already acquired by *treaty* 230,000,000 acres to the east and west of the Mississippi.

In 1808, the Osages gave up 48,000,000 acres for a rental of $1,000.

In 1818, the Quapaws gave up 20,000,000 acres for $4,000; they kept a territory of 1,000,000 acres for themselves as a hunting ground. It had been solemnly sworn that this would be respected; but it was soon invaded, just like the rest.

Mr Bell, reporting to Congress for the Committee on Indian Affairs, 24 February 1830, said: "To pay an Indian tribe what their ancient hunting grounds are worth to them after the game is fled or destroyed, as a mode of appropriating wild lands claimed by the Indians, has been found more convenient, and certainly it is more agreeable to the forms of justice, as

I have just described great evils; I add that they appear to me to be beyond repair. I believe that the Indian race of North America is doomed to perish and I cannot help thinking that the day the Europeans settle on the shores of the Pacific Ocean, it will have ceased to exist.[9]

The Indians of North America had only two paths to safety: war or civilization; in other words, they had to destroy the Europeans or become their equals.

When the colonies first came into existence, they could have combined their forces and freed themselves of the small number of foreigners who had just landed on the shores of the continent.[10] More than once they tried to achieve that and were on the point of succeeding. Today, the imbalance of resources is too great for them to be able to contemplate such an undertaking. Meanwhile, among the Indian nations arise men of genius who foresee the final destiny awaiting the native populations and strive to unite all the tribes in their common hatred of the Europeans; but their efforts are powerless. The tribes which live next to the whites are already too weakened to offer effective

---

well as more merciful, than to assert the possession of them by the sword. Thus the practice of buying Indian titles is only the substitute which humanity and expediency have imposed, in place of the sword, in arriving at the actual enjoyment of property claimed by the right of discovery, and sanctioned by the natural superiority allowed to the claims of civilized communities over those of savage tribes. Up to the present time, so invariable has been the operation of certain causes, first in diminishing the value of forest lands to the Indians, and secondly, in disposing them to sell readily, that the plan of buying their right of occupancy has never threatened to retard, in any perceptible degree, the prosperity of any of the states." (*Legislative Documents*, 21st Congress, no. 227, p. 6.)

9.   Indeed, this opinion seemed to be that of almost all American statesmen.
     "Judging of the future by the past," said Mr Cass to Congress, "we cannot err in anticipating a progressive diminution of their numbers, and their eventual extinction, unless our border should become stationary, and they be removed beyond it, or unless some radical change should take place in the principles of our intercourse with them, which it is easier to hope for than to expect."

10. Among other wars, look at the one conducted in 1675 by the Wampanoags and the other allied tribes, under the leadership of Metacom, against the colonies of New England and the one which the English had to undertake in Virginia in 1622.

resistance; the others, victims to that infantile indifference to the morrow, characteristic of the primitive's personality, wait for the danger to reach them before bothering about it. The former cannot, the latter will not, take action.

It is easy to predict that the Indians will never wish to be civilized or that, when they do so wish, their attempt will be too late.

Civilization is the result of a long social process which develops in one place and which each succeeding generation bequeaths to the next. Civilization has the most difficulty in establishing its power in those nations which live by hunting. Pastoral tribes shift from place to place but always follow a regular pattern in their migrations and constantly retrace their steps. The dwelling place of the hunter alters with that of the very animals he is chasing.

Several attempts have been made to introduce education to the Indians while leaving their wandering ways alone. The Jesuits had tried this in Canada and the Puritans in New England.[11] Neither achieved anything lasting. Civilization was born in the hut and met its death in the forest. The great mistake of these legislators for the Indians was not to realize that a nation, above all, has to take root in order to be ready for civilization and this cannot be done without introducing cultivation of the land. Therefore, the first action was to turn the Indians into farmers.

Not only do the Indians not possess this vital preliminary for civilization, but they find it very difficult to acquire.

Once men have indulged in the lazy and adventurous life of hunting, they feel an almost insurmountable distaste for the constant and regular work demanded by agriculture. This can be observed even within our societies; but that is even more evident in nations where hunting has become part of the national way of life.

Apart from this general cause, there is another no less powerful one applicable to the Indians alone. I have already mentioned it but I must return to it.

11. See the different historians of New England. See also the *Histoire de la Nouvelle-France*, by Charlevoix, and the *Lettres édifiantes*.

The native races of North America not only regard work as an evil but as a disgrace and their pride battles against civilization almost as stubbornly as their indolence.[12]

No Indian in his bark hut is so wretched that he does not preserve a proud idea of his own worth; he regards the concerns of industry as demeaning occupations; he compares the farmer to the ox plowing a furrow and in each of our crafts he sees only the labor of slaves. Not that he has conceived a very low idea of the power of the whites and of the scope of their intelligence but, although admiring the results of our efforts, he despises the means of achieving them and, while suffering our ascendancy, he still believes himself superior to us. Hunting and war seem to him the only occupations worthy of a man.[13] The Indian, in the miserable depths of his woods, cherishes the same ideas, the same opinions as the medieval nobleman in his castle and all he needs to complete the resemblance is to become a conqueror. Thus, however strange this may appear, it is in the forests of the New World and not among Europeans inhabiting its coasts that we find today the old prejudices of Europe.

More than once in the course of this work I have sought to explain the extraordinary influence which the state of society

12. "In all the tribes," says Volney in his *Tableau des Etats-Unis*, p. 423, "there still exists a generation of old warriors who, when they see the hoe being wielded, cannot stop themselves from bewailing the abandonment of the old ways and who maintain that savages owe their decadence to nothing more than innovations such as these and that, to recover their glory and power, all they have to do is to revert to their primitive ways."

13. The following description is to be found in an official document:

"Until a young man has been in an engagement with the enemy and can boast of several feats, he is not held in any esteem: he is regarded almost as a woman.

During their great war-dances, warriors, one after the other, come forward to strike the *post*, as they call it, and relate their exploits: on these occasions, their audience consists of the relatives, friends, and companions of the narrator. The deep impression which their words create is demonstrated by the silence in which the stories are heard and the noisy applause which greets their end. The young man who has nothing to relate at such gatherings considers himself most unfortunate and there have been instances of young warriors who, passions aroused, have left the dancing and set off alone to seek trophies which they might show and adventures which would allow them to vaunt themselves."

exercises, in my view, upon the laws and customs of men. I beg leave to add one more word on this subject.

When I note the parallel between the political institutions of our German ancestors and the wandering tribes of North America, between the customs described by Tacitus[d] and those I have witnessed from time to time, I cannot help thinking that the same cause produced the same effects in both hemispheres and that, within the apparent diversity of human affairs, it is more than likely that there is a small number of causatory facts from which all others derive. In all that we call Germanic institutions, I am, therefore, tempted to see merely barbaric habits and savage opinions in what we term feudal ideas.

Whatever the defects and prejudices preventing the North American Indians from becoming farmers and civilized, occasionally necessity forces them into it.

Several important nations in the south, including the Cherokees and the Creeks,[14] found themselves virtually surrounded by Europeans who disembarked on the shores of the Atlantic coast and arrived simultaneously down the Ohio and up the Mississippi at their borders. These Indians were not driven from place to place, as were the northern tribes, but have gradually been entrapped within overly narrow boundaries, just as hunters encircle a copse before simultaneously breaking into it. The Indians, standing between civilization and death, saw themselves reduced to a shameful existence, living by their labor like the whites; they thus became farmers and, without giving up entirely either their habits or customs, sacrificed only what was absolutely necessary for their existence.

14. These nations are now swallowed up into the states of Georgia, Tennessee, Alabama, and Mississippi. Formerly, in the South (where the remnants can still be found), there were four great nations: the Choctaws, the Chickasaws, the Creeks, and the Cherokees.

In 1830, the remnants of these four nations still amounted to about 75,000 individuals. It is thought that, at present, in the land occupied or reclaimed by the Anglo-American Union, there are about 300,000 Indians. (See *Proceedings of the Indian Board in the City of New York*.) The official documents supplied to Congress give the number as 313,130. The reader who is curious to know the name and strength of the tribes who inhabit the Anglo-American territory should consult the documents to which I have just referred. (*Legislative Documents*, 20th Congress, no. 117, p. 90–105.)

The Cherokees went further: they created a written language, set up a fairly stable form of government and, since everything in the New World proceeds at a giddy speed, they founded a newspaper before they all had clothes.[15]

In particular, the presence of half-castes has promoted the rapid development of European ways among the Indians.[16] The half-caste, sharing his father's education without entirely abandoning the primitive customs of his mother's race, represents the natural link between civilization and barbarity. Wherever the half-castes have multiplied, the primitive races have gradually modified their social condition and their way of life.[17]

15. I have brought back to France one or two copies of this extraordinary publication.

16. See in the report of the Committee on Indian Affairs, 21st Congress, no. 227, p. 23, the reasons for the increase of mixed races among the Cherokees; the principal cause goes back to the War of Independence. Many Anglo-Americans from Georgia, having taken the side of the English, were forced to retreat among the Indians, where they married.

17. Unfortunately, people of mixed race have been fewer in numbers in North America than elsewhere and have exercised less influence.

The population of this part of the American continent came from two great nations: the French and the English.

The former were not slow in forming unions with the daughters of the native peoples; but, by misfortune, a secret affinity existed between the Indian character and their own. Instead of giving the Indians the tastes and habits of civilized living, they it was who often became passionately attached to a barbarous way of life. They became the most dangerous inhabitants of the wilderness and won the friendship of the Indian by exaggerating his vices and virtues. M. de Sénonville, the Governor of Canada, wrote to Louis XIV in 1685: "For a long time we have believed that the Indians should be drawn nearer to us in order to make them more like the French; however, we have every reason to recognize that this was a mistake. Those who have been drawn to us have not become French and the French who lived amongst them have become barbarous. They dress as they do and live as they do." (*Histoire de la Nouvelle-France*, by Charlevoix, vol. 2, p. 345.)

The Englishman, on the other hand, remaining obstinately attached to the opinions, customs, and most insignificant habits of his forefathers, lived in the middle of the American wilds as if he were in the heart of European cities; he did not want to establish any contact with the Indians whom he mistrusted and took care to avoid mixing his blood with that of the barbarian.

Thus, while the French exercised no salutary influence upon the Indians, the English always treated them as foreigners.

The success of the Cherokees proves, therefore, that Indians have the capacity for civilized living but it offers no proof that they can fully achieve it.

The difficulty that the Indians experience in submitting to civilization stems from a general cause almost impossible for them to avoid.

A careful study of history reveals that, in general, barbaric nations have reached civilization by small degrees and by their own efforts.

Whenever they happened to derive education from a foreign nation, they held a position of conquerors not conquered.

When the conquered nation is educated and the conquerors half savage, as happened when the Roman Empire was invaded by the nations of the North or when the Mongols invaded China, the power afforded to the barbarian through his victory enables him to stay on a level with the civilized man and allows him to go forward as his equal until he becomes his rival; the one has the advantage of strength, the other intelligence; the former admires the knowledge and arts of the vanquished, the latter envies the power of the victors. The barbarians end up by inviting the civilized man into their palaces and the latter, in turn, open their schools to the former. But, whenever the nation with the physical power also enjoys an intellectual superiority, the conquered rarely pursues civilization; rather they withdraw or are destroyed.

Thus one can draw the general conclusion that savages seek out enlightenment with weapons in their hands but they do not receive it as a gift.

If the Indian tribes now living in the center of the continent could find enough energy to try to civilize themselves, perhaps they would succeed. For then, superior to the barbarous nations in their vicinity, they would gradually gain strength and experience and, whenever the Europeans finally appeared on their borders, they would be in a state, if not to maintain their independence, at least to have their rights to the land recognized and to become an integral partner of their conquerors. But the misfortune of the Indians has been to come into contact with the most civilized and, I may add, the most avaricious people on the earth at a time when they themselves are still half-barbarian and to discover that their teachers were masters from whom they received both tyranny and education.

Living freely in the depths of the forests, the North American Indian was wretched but felt himself inferior to no man; the instant he wishes to enter the social hierarchy of the whites, he can only occupy the lowest rank for he arrives uneducated and poor into a society endowed with knowledge and wealth. After leading a life of turmoil, beset with evils and dangers, but at the same time full of emotions and pride,[18] he has to submit to a

18.   There is in the adventurous life of these hunting peoples a certain irresist-
      ible charm which takes hold of a man's heart and carries him away despite
      all reason and experience. We can be sure of the truth of this by reading
      Tanner's *Memoirs*.
         Tanner was a European who was carried off at the age of six by the
      Indians and who spent thirty years with them in the woods. It is impossible
      to conceive of anything more terrible than the miseries he describes. He
      tells us of tribes without a chief, of families without a nation, of isolated
      men, the ravaged ruins of once powerful tribes wandering aimlessly
      through the icy wastes and desolate wilderness of Canada. Hunger and
      cold pursue them; each day life seems on the point of deserting them.
      Among these people, their way of life has lost its dominion and their
      traditions are powerless. These men become more and more savage.
      Tanner shared all these miseries; he was aware of his European origin; he
      was not kept away from the white man by force; on the contrary each year
      he came to trade with them, visited their houses, and saw how comfortable
      they were; he knew that whenever he wanted to return to the bosom of
      civilized society he could manage it easily and he remained thirty years in
      the wilderness. When, at length, he did return to the heart of civilization,
      he confessed that the existence whose miseries he had described held a
      secret attraction for him which he could not define; he frequently returned
      after he had left it and tore himself away from so much wretchedness with
      the most profound regret; and when at length he settled permanently
      amongst the whites, several of his children refused to come and share with
      him his tranquillity and comfort.
         I met Tanner myself on the shore of Lake Superior. He seemed to me to
      resemble more a savage than a civilized man.
         In Tanner's work you will find neither order nor taste; but the author,
      even without realizing it maybe, paints a vibrant picture of the prejudices,
      the passions, the vices, and, above all, the miseries of those amongst whom
      he lived.
         Viscount Ernest de Blosseville, author of an excellent work on English
      penal colonies, has translated Tanner's *Memoirs*. M. de Blosseville has
      included with his translation some notes which are of great interest and

boring, obscure, and humiliating existence. In his eyes the only result of this vaunted civilization is that he must earn his bread by demeaning hard labor.

And even that result he cannot always be sure to obtain.

When the Indians undertake to imitate their European neighbors and to cultivate the land as they do, they immediately expose themselves to the effects of disastrous competition. The white man has mastered the secrets of agriculture. The Indian is a crude beginner in a skill of which he has no knowledge. The former effortlessly grows his abundant harvests while the latter snatches at the fruits of the earth with an interminable struggle.

The European lives among a population whose needs he knows and shares.

The savage is isolated among a hostile people whose ways, language, and laws he does not completely grasp but whom he cannot do without. Only by exchanging his goods with those of the whites can he gain material comfort, for the members of his own race are of little help to him.

Thus, whenever the Indian wishes to sell the fruits of his labors, he cannot always find a buyer, while the European farmer discovers a market with ease and the Indian produces only at considerable expense what the European can sell very cheaply.

Therefore, the Indian has escaped the evils to which barbarous nations are exposed, only to suffer the still greater miseries of civilized nations and he encounters almost as many hardships living amid our abundance as in the depths of his forests.

In his heart, however, the habits of the wandering life are still not eradicated. Those traditions have lost none of their power; his passion for hunting has not been snuffed out. The savage joys he once experienced in the depths of the woods are then etched in his disturbed imagination in sharper colors; his former

---

which will allow the reader to compare the facts related by Tanner with those already related by a great number of observers, both past and present.

All those who want to know the current state of the North American Indians and wish to predict their future should consult M. de Blosseville's work.

privations seem to him by contrast less awful and the dangers faced at that time less intimidating. The independence he enjoyed with his equals contrasts with his servile position in a civilized society.

On the other hand, the empty spaces where he lived for so long are still near at hand; only a few hours' march will bring him back to them. His white neighbors offer him what he thinks is a large sum of money for the half-cleared field from which he hardly extracts enough to keep himself alive. Perhaps this money from the Europeans would enable him to live a quiet and happy life far away from them. He abandons the plow, takes up his weapons again and returns to the wilds forever.[19]

19. This destructive influence which highly civilized nations exert upon others less civilized can be observed among Europeans themselves.

Nearly a century ago, some French people had founded the town of Vincennes, on the Wabash river, in the middle of the wilderness. They prospered there until the American settlers arrived. Immediately, these settlers began to ruin the original inhabitants through competition; then they bought up their lands for a derisory amount. At the time when M. de Volney, from whom I borrow these details, passed through Vincennes, the French population had been reduced to about one hundred individuals of whom the majority were ready to move to Louisiana or Canada. The French were honorable men but uneducated and idle; they had adopted many of the habits of the tribesmen. The Americans, who were perhaps morally inferior to them, were intellectually vastly superior: they were industrious, educated, rich, and used to governing themselves.

In Canada, where the intellectual difference between the two peoples is much less pronounced, I myself saw the English, masters of commerce and industry, expanding on all sides and constraining the French within over-restricted boundaries.

Similarly, in Louisiana, almost all the commercial and industrial activity is concentrated in the hands of the Anglo-Americans.

Something even more striking is happening in Texas; the state of Texas is, as we know, part of Mexico and serves as a frontier with the United States. For several years, the Anglo-Americans have penetrated independently into that province which is still sparsely populated, buying lands and taking over industry, rapidly supplanting the original population. One can see that if Mexico does not hasten to put a stop to this development, Texas will soon be lost to them.

If a few differences, comparatively less noticeable in European civilization, lead to such results, it is easy to understand what must happen when the most complete European civilization comes into contact with the barbarous Indian civilization.

The accuracy of this sorry picture can be estimated from what is happening with the Creeks and Cherokees to whom I have already alluded.

These Indians, in the little they have achieved, have indubitably demonstrated as much natural genius as the peoples of Europe have in their greatest enterprises; but nations, like men, need time to learn, however intelligent or hardworking they may be.

While these Indian tribes were working to civilize themselves, the Europeans continued to surround them on all sides and to hem them in more and more. Today the two races have finally met and come into contact. The Indian is already superior to his savage father but still greatly inferior to his white neighbor. The Europeans, with the help of their resources and knowledge, have lost no time in acquiring most of the benefits which the ownership of land might have conferred on the native inhabitants; they have settled among them, seized their land, or bought it on the cheap, and have ruined the Indians by a competition which the latter had no means of tolerating. Isolated in their own land, the Indians now formed only a small colony of unwelcome foreigners in the midst of a numerous and imperious people.[20]

20. See, in *Legislative documents*, 21st Congress, no. 89, the excesses of all kinds committed by the white population upon Indian lands. Sometimes the Anglo-Americans established themselves on part of the territory, as if there were no land to be had anywhere else and federal troops had to come and evict them; sometimes, they carried off the livestock, burned the dwellings, destroyed the crops of the native population, or did violence to their persons.

From all these activities comes the proof that the Indians were daily subjected to violent abuse. The Union continually employed an agent among the Indians as its representative; the report of the Cherokee agent can be found amongst those documents which I quote: the words of this employee are almost always on the side of the Indians. "The intrusion of whites upon the lands of the Cherokees," he says, p. 12, "will cause ruin to the poor, helpless, and inoffensive inhabitants." Further on in the document it is seen that the state of Georgia, seeking to reduce the lands of the Cherokees, has created boundary markers; the federal agent remarks that, since this boundary was devised by the whites alone and without debate, it is absolutely without value.

Washington said in one of his messages to Congress: "We are more enlightened and more powerful than the Indian nations; we are therefore bound in honor to treat them with kindness, and even with generosity."

This noble and moral policy has not been pursued.

Normally the tyranny of the government joins forces with the greed of the colonists. Although the Cherokees and Creeks were settled on the land where they were living before the arrival of the Europeans, although the Americans have treated them as if they were foreign nations, those states in which they are found have been unwilling to acknowledge them as independent and have attempted to force these men, who had only recently emerged from the forests, to obey their magistrates, customs, and laws.[21] Wretched conditions had driven these unfortunate Indians toward civilization; oppression now drives them back to savagery. Many of them leave their half-cleared fields and renew their barbaric way of life.

If we consider the tyrannical measures adopted by the legislators of the southern states, the behavior of their governors, and the decrees of their courts, we shall readily be convinced that the complete expulsion of the Indians is the final objective of all their combined efforts. Americans in this part of the Union look enviously upon the lands occupied by the natives[22] who, they feel, have not entirely lost the traditions

---

21. In 1829, the state of Alabama divided the territory of the Creeks into counties and subjected the Indian population to European magistrates.

   In 1830, the state of Mississippi assimilated the Choctaws and the Chickasaws into the white population and declared that any among them who assumed the title of chief would be punished by a fine of $1,000 and a year's imprisonment.

   When the state of Mississippi extended these laws to cover the Chactas who lived within its boundaries, the tribe assembled; their chief let the intentions of the whites be known and read out to them some of the laws to which they would have to submit: the Indians unanimously declared that it would be preferable to go back into the wilderness. (*Mississippi Papers.*)

22. The people of Georgia, who find themselves so inconvenienced by the proximity of the Indians, occupy a territory which, as yet, does not contain more than seven inhabitants per square mile. In France, there are 162 individuals in the same amount of space.

of the life of a savage and, before civilization has finally attached them to the soil, they want to reduce them to despair and force them to move away.

The Creeks and Cherokees, under the oppression of individual states, appealed to central government which, not insensitive to their difficulties, would wish to preserve the remaining natives and to guarantee the free ownership of the territory which it has itself pledged to safeguard.[23] But when it seeks to execute this plan, the individual states oppose it strongly and, as a result, without much effort, it takes the decision to allow a few already half-destroyed savage tribes to perish so as not to place the American Union in danger.

The federal government, unable to protect the Indians, would at least wish to mitigate their fate and, to that end, it undertook to move them elsewhere at its own expense.

Between the thirty-third and thirty-seventh degrees of latitude north, stretches a vast territory which has adopted the name of Arkansas after the main river which irrigates it. It borders on one side the Mexican frontier and on the other the banks of the Mississippi. A great network of streams and rivers flows through it in all directions; its climate is temperate and its soil fertile. Only a few wandering bands of savages are to be seen there. The government of the Union wished to transport the remnants of the native populations in the south to the part of the territory nearest Mexico and at a considerable distance from the American settlements.

At the end of 1831 we were assured that ten thousand had already moved down to the banks of the Arkansas and others were arriving daily. But Congress has as yet been unable to make those whose fate it wishes to control come to a unanimous decision: some joyfully consent to move away from the home of tyranny; the more enlightened refuse to abandon their newly

23. In 1818, Congress gave orders that the territory of Arkansas should be visited by American commissioners, accompanied by a deputation of Creeks, Choctaws, and Chickasaws. This expedition was led by Messrs Kennerly, McCoy, Wash Hood, and John Bell. See the various reports of the commissioners and their journal in the Congressional Documents, no. 87, *House of Representatives*.

growing crops and their newly built dwellings, for they think that if the process of civilization is once interrupted, it will not be resumed. They are afraid that those sedentary habits only just set in motion will be permanently lost in a country which is still savage, where nothing has been prepared for the subsistence of an agricultural people. They know that they will encounter enemy hordes in these new wild areas and that to resist them they have lost the energy that barbarism gave them without having yet acquired the strength of civilization. The Indians readily discover, moreover, how temporary is the settlement proposed for them. Who will guarantee that they will be able at last to remain in peace in their new refuge? The United States commits itself to maintaining them there but the land they are presently occupying had been previously guaranteed by the most solemn of oaths.[24] Today the American government, it is true, does not remove their land from them but it tolerates encroachments. No doubt, in not many years' time, the same white population which is now pressing around them will once again be on their tracks in the wild deserts of Arkansas; then they will encounter again the same evils without the same remedies and once, sooner or later, land is no longer there for them, they will forever have to resign themselves to the grave.

There is less greed and violence in the treatment of the Indians by the Union than in the policy pursued by the states, but both governments are equally lacking in good faith.

The states, by extending what they call the advantages of their laws to the Indians, calculate that the latter will prefer to move away rather than to submit and central government, by promising these luckless people a permanent refuge in the

24. In the treaty made with the Creeks in 1790 can be found this sentence: "The United States solemnly guarantees to the nation of the Creeks all the lands that it possesses in the territory of the Union."

The treaty concluded in July 1791 with the Cherokees contains the following: "The United States solemnly guarantees to the nation of the Cherokees all the lands that it has not previously ceded. If a citizen of the US or anyone other than an Indian comes to settle on the territory of the Cherokees, the US declares that it withdraws its protection from this citizen and delivers him to the nation of the Cherokees to punish him as it seems good to them." Article 8.

West, is perfectly aware that it can offer no guarantee to them.[25]

Thus the states' tyranny forces the Indian tribes to flee; the Union's promises and offer of resources make this flight easy. These very different measures tend to the same end.[26]

In their petition to Congress, the Cherokees declared:[27] "By the will of our heavenly Father who rules the universe, the race of red men in America has become small; the white race has become large and renowned.

"When your ancestors arrived on our shores, the red man was strong and, although he was ignorant and wild, he welcomed them with kindness and allowed them to rest their swollen feet upon dry land. Both our fathers shook hands in sign of friendship and lived in peace. The Indian hastened to grant to the white man everything he demanded to satisfy his needs. Then the Indian was the master and the white man was the suppliant. Today, the position has changed: the strength of the red man has weakened. As his neighbors were growing in

25. This does not prevent them from making promises in the most formal manner. See the letter from the President addressed to the Creeks on 23 March 1829. (*Proceedings of the Indian Board in the City of New York*, p. 5): "Beyond the great river Mississippi, where a part of your nation has gone, your father has provided a country large enough for all of you, and he advises you to remove to it. There your white brothers will not trouble you; they will have no claim to the land, and you can live upon it, you and all your children, as long as the grass grows, or the water runs, in peace and plenty. *It will be yours forever.*"

In a letter written to the Cherokees by the Secretary of the War Department on 18 April 1829, he declares that they should not count on preserving possession of the lands which they occupy at the present but he gives them a most positive assurance for the time when they would be on the other side of the Mississippi (ibid., p. 6): as if he would not lack in the future the power which he lacks now!

26. To get an exact idea of the policies followed by the individual states and by the Union as far as the Indians were concerned, one should consult: 1) the laws of the individual states relating to the Indians (this collection can be found in the *Legislative Documents*, 21st Congress, no. 319); 2) the laws of the Union relating to the same subject, and in particular that of 30 March 1802 (these laws are found in Mr Story's work entitled: *Laws of the United States*); 3) finally, to understand the current state of relations between the Union and all the Indian tribes, see the report of the Secretary of War, Mr Cass, 29 November 1823.

27. 19 November 1829. This extract is literally translated.

number, his power was gradually diminishing; and now, of so many powerful tribes covering the surface of what you have called the United States, there barely remain a few who have been spared this universal disaster. The tribes of the north, once so famous among us for their power, have already almost disappeared. Such has been the fate of the red man of America. Here we are, the last members of our race; must we also die?

"From time immemorial, our common Father, who is in heaven, has given our ancestors the land we occupy; our ancestors have handed it down to us as their heritage. We have preserved it with respect, for it contains their ashes. Have we ever ceded or lost this inheritance? Allow us to ask you humbly what better right a nation can have to a country than the right of inheritance and immemorial ownership? We know that today the state of Georgia and the President of the United States claim that we have forfeited this right. But this seems to us a gratuitous allegation. At what time have we forfeited it? What crime have we committed which could deprive us of our country? Is it held against us that we fought under the banner of the king of Great Britain in the War of Independence? If that is the crime in question, why did you not declare, in the first treaty which followed this war, that we had forfeited the ownership of our lands? Why did you not insert at that time an article in the following terms: 'The United States wishes to grant peace to the Cherokee nation, but to punish them for having taken part in the war, we declare that they will no longer be considered farmers of the soil and that they will be forced to move away when required by those states bordering their territory'? That was the time to speak in those terms but no one thought of it and our fathers would never have agreed to a treaty, the result of which was to deprive them of their most sacred rights and to steal their country from them."

Such is the Indians' language; what they say is true and what they foresee seems to me inevitable.

From whatever angle one regards the fate of the native tribes of North America, one sees nothing but calamities without remedy: if they stay in their savage state, they are driven back by the march of progress; if they opt for civilization, their contact with men more civilized than they are exposes them to oppression and wretchedness. If they continue to wander among these wide open spaces, they perish; if they attempt to settle, they perish just the same. Education can come to them only with the help of Europeans but the approach of Europeans corrupts them and drives them back into barbarism. As long as they are left in these open spaces, they refuse to change their ways; when they are finally forced to change, there is no time left to do so.

The Spanish let their dogs loose on the Indians as if they were wild animals; they pillaged the New World as they would a town taken by storm, without discrimination or compassion. But it is impossible to destroy everything; unrestrained frenzy must come to an end. The remnant of the Indian populations who escaped these massacres ended up by mixing with their conquerors and by adopting their religion and customs.[28]

On the other hand, the conduct of the Americans of the United States toward the native races is characterized by a most singular affection for legal formalities. Provided that the Indians remain in their savage condition, the Americans in no way interfere with their business and treat them as independent peoples; they do not take over their lands without having acquired them through an appropriately drawn-up contract. If by chance an Indian nation is no longer able to live on its territory, they take them by hand as brothers and lead them away to die far from the land of their forefathers.

The Spanish, using unparalleled atrocities which bring an indelible shame upon themselves, have not succeeded in exterminating the Indian race, nor even in preventing them from sharing their rights; the Americans of the United States have attained both these results with amazing ease, quietly, legally, and generously, with no spilling of blood, with no violation to the great moral principles[29] in the eyes of the world. Men could not be destroyed with more respect for the laws of humanity.

28. We must not, however, honor the Spanish with this result. If the Indian tribes had not been tied to the land through agriculture at the time of the arrival of the Europeans, they would doubtless have been destroyed in South America, just as they were in North America.
29. Amongst other reports, see the one written by Mr Bell in the name of the

THE POSITION OF THE BLACK RACE IN THE
UNITED STATES;[30] DANGERS TO THE WHITES
FROM ITS PRESENCE

*Why it is more difficult to abolish slavery and obliterate its
traces in modern times than it was in ancient times—In the
United States white prejudice against the blacks seems to
grow stronger as slavery is removed—Position of the
Negroes in northern and southern states—Why Americans
are abolishing slavery—Slavery which brutalizes the
slave impoverishes the master—Differences between
the right and left bank of the Ohio—Reasons for this—
The black race, along with slavery, recedes toward the
South—How this is explained—Difficulties in abolishing
slavery encountered in the southern states—
Future dangers—General concerns—Foundation of a
black colony in Africa—Why the Americans of the South
increase the hardships of slavery while being
disgusted by it.*

The Indian tribes will die in the same state of isolation in which
they have lived, whereas the fate of the Negroes is, in a sense,
intertwined with that of the Europeans. The two races are bound

---

Committee for Indian Affairs, 24 February 1830, it which it is logically
established, p. 5, and learnedly proved that: "The fundamental principle,
that the Indians had no right, by virtue of their ancient possession, either
of soil or sovereignty, has never been abandoned either expressly or by
implication."

On reading this report, edited by a skillful hand, we are surprised by
the ease with which, from the very first words, the author dispenses with
arguments based on natural right and reason which he calls abstract and
theoretical principles. The more I think about it, the more I believe
that the only difference which exists between the civilized man and the
uncivilized, as far as justice is concerned, is this: the one contests the
justice of the rights which the other is content to violate.

30.   Before dealing with this matter, I must advise the reader as follows: in a
book which I mentioned at the beginning of this work and which is about
to be published, M. Gustave de Beaumont, my traveling companion, had
as his principal aim the enlightenment of the French as to the position of

together without thereby being united; it is as difficult for them to separate completely as to combine.

The most fearsome of all the ills threatening the future of the United States stems from the presence of the blacks on their soil. From whatever angle one sets out to seek the cause of the present embarrassments or of the future dangers of the Union, one is almost invariably brought up against this primary fact.

In general, men need to make great and consistent efforts to create lasting evils but there is one evil which has crept secretly into the world: at first its presence scarcely makes itself felt amid the usual abuses of power; it begins with one individual whose name history does not record; it is cast like an accursed seed somewhere in the soil; it then feeds itself, grows without effort, and spreads naturally inside the society which has accepted it: that evil is slavery.

Christianity had destroyed slavery; the Christians of the sixteenth century restored it even though they only ever acknowledged it as an exception to their social system and carefully restricted it to one single human race. Thus they inflicted a wound on humanity which was smaller but infinitely more difficult to cure.

Two things must be carefully distinguished: slavery in itself and its consequences.

The immediate evils caused by slavery were virtually the same in the ancient as in the modern world but the consequences of these evils were different. In antiquity, the slave belonged to the same race as his master and was often superior to him in

---

the Negroes in the midst of the white population of the United States. M. de Beaumont has treated in depth a question which my theme has only allowed me to touch upon.

His book, the notes to which contain a very great number of legislative and historical documents which are extremely valuable and hitherto unknown, presents, in addition, pictures whose vividness is equaled only by their authenticity. Those who want to understand to what excesses of tyranny men are steadily driven, once they begin to abandon nature and humanity, should read M. de Beaumont's work.

education and knowledge.[31] Freedom alone separated them; once freedom was granted, their differences easily melted away.

The ancients had, therefore, a simple means of ridding themselves of slavery and its consequences, which was to free their slaves. As soon as they adopted this measure generally, they succeeded.

Admittedly in the ancient world, the traces of slavery still persisted for some while after its abolition.

A natural prejudice leads a man to despise anyone who has been inferior to him a long time after he has become his equal; an imaginary inequality, rooted in custom, always follows the real inequality produced by wealth or the law. But, in antiquity, this secondary effect of slavery had a time limit, for the freedman was so like those who were born free that it soon became impossible to distinguish between the two.

In antiquity, the most difficult thing was to change the law; in modern times, the alteration of custom is the hard task and our real problems start where the ancients saw them end.

This is because, in modern times, the insubstantial and temporary fact of slavery is most fatally combined with the substantial and permanent difference of race. The memory of having been slaves disgraces a race and the race perpetuates the memories of slavery.

No African ever landed freely upon the shores of the New World; consequently, all those found there now are slaves or freedmen. Thus, the Negro transmits to all his descendants at birth the external mark of his shame. The law may abolish slavery but God alone can remove its traces.

The modern slave is different from his master, not only in lacking freedom but also by his origins. You may grant the Negro freedom but you will never manage to remove his position as an alien to a European.

That is still not the whole story: this man, born in degrading circumstances, this foreigner brought by slavery into our midst,

31. It is known that several of the most celebrated authors of antiquity were or had been slaves: Aesop and Terence, for example. Slaves were not always taken from uncivilized nations; war brought highly civilized men into servitude.

is hardly recognized as possessing the common features of humanity. His face seems hideous to us, his intelligence limited, and his tastes debased. We are very close to regarding him as being half-way between beast and man.[32]

Man in modern times, after the abolition of slavery, must, therefore, eradicate three much more intangible and tenacious prejudices: the prejudice of the master, the prejudice of race, and, finally, the prejudice of the whites.

For those of us who have been fortunate enough to be born among men similar by nature and equal before the law, it is very difficult to comprehend the insurmountable gap separating the American Negro from the European. But we are able to form some remote idea by analogy.

In France, we have seen in the past great inequalities which were based only upon legislation. What could be more fictitious than inferiority purely legal in origin! What more contrary to man's instinctive feelings than permanent differences established between people quite obviously similar! Yet, these differences have lasted for centuries and still remain in a thousand places. They have left traces everywhere which, although imaginary, time has scarcely been able to efface. If the inequality created solely by laws is hard to uproot, how can we destroy those distinctions which in addition seem to be founded immutably in nature itself?

For my part, when I observe the extreme difficulty aristocratic bodies of whatever nature experience in mingling with the mass of the people and the excessive care they take to preserve for centuries the ideological boundaries separating them, I despair of seeing the end of an aristocracy founded on obvious and indelible signs.

Those who hope that Europeans will one day mingle with Negroes, therefore, seem to me to be fostering a delusion. My reason does not lead me to believe that possibility, nor do I see anything in the facts to support that idea.

Until now, wherever the whites have been the more powerful,

32. To persuade whites to abandon the opinion that they hold about the moral and intellectual inferiority of their former slaves, the Negroes must change but they cannot as long as this opinion persists.

they have kept the Negroes in a state of degradation or slavery. Wherever the Negroes have been the stronger, they have destroyed the whites. Such has been the only reckoning to have existed between the two races.

If I observe present-day America, I can certainly see that, in some parts of the country, the legal barrier separating the two races is tending to come down but not that of custom. I see slavery in retreat but the prejudice which arises from it has not moved at all.

In that part of the Union where Negroes are no longer slaves, have they drawn nearer to the whites? Any inhabitant of the United States will have noticed just the opposite.

Racial prejudice seems to me stronger in those states which have abolished slavery than in those where slavery still exists and nowhere is it as intolerant as in those states where slavery has never been known.

It is true that in the North of the Union the law permits Negroes and whites to contract legal marriages but public opinion regards any white man united with a Negress as disgraced and it would be difficult to quote an example of such an event.

In almost all the states where slavery has been abolished, voting rights have been granted to the Negro but, if he comes forward to vote, he risks his life. He is able to complain of oppression but he will find only whites among the judges. Although the law makes him eligible for jury service, prejudice wards him off from applying. His son is excluded from the school where the sons of Europeans come to be educated. At the theatre, any amount of gold could not buy him the right to take his seat beside his former master; in hospitals, he lies apart. The black is allowed to pray to the same God as the whites but not at the same altars. He has his own priests and churches. Heaven's gates are not blocked against him. However, inequality hardly stops at the threshold of the next world. When the Negro passes on, his bones are cast aside and the differences of social conditions are found even in the leveling of death.

Thus, the Negro is free but is able to share neither the rights, pleasures, work, pains, nor even the grave with the man to whom he has been declared equal; he cannot be seen alongside this man either in life or death.

In the South, where slavery still exists, less care is taken to keep Negroes at a distance; they sometimes share the work and pleasures of the whites. To a certain extent people agree to mix with them and, although legislation is harsher toward them, habits are more tolerant and kindly.

In the South, the master has no fear of raising his slave to his level because he knows he will be able to cast him down at will into the dust. In the North, the white man fails to see sharply the barrier which separates him from a degraded race and he keeps his distance from the Negro with all the greater care since he is afraid that one day he might be confused for one of them.

Among southern Americans, nature sometimes reasserts her rights and does, for a moment, restore equality between whites and blacks. In the North, pride silences even the most commanding of man's passions. Perhaps the northern American would allow the Negress to become the passing companion of his pleasures, if the legislators had declared that she was not to hope to share his marriage bed but, when she is able to become his wife, he recoils from her in horror.

This is the way in the United States that the prejudice rejecting the Negro appears to increase in proportion to their emancipation and that inequality cuts deep into social customs, as it is effaced from the law.

But if the relative position of the two races inhabiting the United States is as I have just described it, why have Americans abolished slavery in the North of the Union, why do they retain it in the South and why is it that they have aggravated its hardships there?

The answer is easy. Slavery in the United States is destroyed in the interest, not of the Negroes, but of the whites.

The first Negroes were imported into Virginia about 1621.[33] In America, as everywhere else in the world, slavery, therefore, originated in the South. From there it spread from place to place;

---

33. See Beverley's *History of Virginia*. See also in Jefferson's *Memoirs* some curious details regarding the introduction of Negroes into Virginia and the first Act which prohibited their importation in 1778.

but as slavery moved northwards, the number of slaves grew less[34] and very few Negroes were ever seen in New England.

A century had already passed since the founding of the colonies and an extraordinary fact began to strike the attention of everyone. The population of those provinces which had virtually no slaves increased in numbers, wealth, and prosperity more rapidly than those which did have them.

In the former, however, the inhabitants were forced to cultivate the ground themselves or to hire someone else to do it; in the latter, they had laborers at their disposal whom they did not need to pay. With labor and expense on one side and leisure and savings on the other, nevertheless the advantage lay with the former.

This outcome seemed all the more difficult to explain since the immigrants all belonged to the same European race with the same habits, the same civilization, the same laws, and there were only barely perceptible shades of difference between them.

As time went on, the Anglo-Americans left the shores of the Atlantic Ocean to plunge day by day ever further into the abandoned spaces of the West, where they encountered new land and climates and had to overcome various obstacles. Races mingled; men from the South moved North; men from the North moved South. Amid all these circumstances, the same fact repeated itself at every step and, in general, the colony without slaves became more populous and prosperous than the one in which slavery flourished.

As further advances were made, people began, therefore to

34. There were fewer slaves in the North but the advantages of slavery were not contested more there than in the South. In 1740, the New York state legislature declared that one should encourage the direct importation of slaves as much as possible and that smuggling should be severely punished in order not to discourage the honest trader. (Kent's *Commentaries*, vol. 2, p. 206.)

In the *Historical Collections of Massachusetts*, vol. 4, p. 193, there is some curious research into slavery in New England carried out by Belknap. It seems that Negroes were introduced there in 1630 but that from the first the legislation and the way of the people opposed slavery.

See also, in the same work, the way that public opinion and then the law came to destroy slavery.

perceive that slavery, as cruel as it was for the slave, was fatal to the master.

But the truth of this provided its final proof when civilization reached the banks of the Ohio.

The stream named by the Indians as the Ohio, or the Beautiful River, irrigates one of the most magnificent valleys in which man has ever made his home. On both banks of the Ohio stretches undulating land whose soil lavishes upon the plowman inexhaustible riches. On both banks, the air is equally healthy and the climate temperate; each bank forms the frontier of a vast state: the one to the left tracing the many windings of the Ohio is called Kentucky, the other takes its name from the river itself. The two states differ in only one respect: Kentucky has accepted slaves but Ohio has rejected them from its lands.[35]

The traveler who, positioned at the center of the Ohio River, drifts downstream to its junction with the Mississippi is, therefore, steering a path between freedom and slavery, so to speak, and he only has to look about him to judge immediately which is the more beneficial for mankind.

On the left bank of the river the population is sparse; occasionally a troop of slaves can be seen loitering in half-deserted fields; the primeval forest grows back again everywhere; society seems to be asleep; man looks idle while nature looks active and alive.

On the right bank, by contrast, a confused hum announces from a long way off the presence of industrial activity; the fields are covered by abundant harvests; elegant dwellings proclaim the taste and industry of the workers; in every direction there is evidence of comfort; men appear wealthy and content: they are at work.[36]

The state of Kentucky was founded in 1775, Ohio just twelve

35. Not only does Ohio not allow slavery but it also refuses to allow freed slaves to enter its territory and forbids them to acquire land. See the statutes of Ohio.

36. Endeavor in Ohio is not limited to individuals; the state itself runs huge businesses; the state of Ohio has established a canal between lake Erie and the Ohio so that the valley of the Mississippi can link up with the river in the north. Thanks to this canal, goods which arrive in New York from Europe can be shipped as far as New Orleans across more than twelve hundred miles of the continent.

years later: twelve years in America is more than half a century in Europe. Today the population of Ohio is already more than 250,000 greater than that of Kentucky.[37]

The contrasting effects of slavery and freedom are easily understood and are enough to explain many of the differences between ancient and contemporary civilization.

On the left bank of the Ohio, work is connected with the idea of slavery, on the right bank with the idea of prosperity and progress; on the one side, it is a source of humiliation, on the other, of honor; on the left bank of the river no white laborers are to be found as they would dread to look like slaves; they have to look to Negroes for such work. On the right bank it would be a waste of time to look for an idle man, as the whites extend their energy and intelligence to every sort of work.

Thus, the men in Kentucky who are responsible for exploiting the natural abundance of the soil lack both enthusiasm and knowledge, whereas those who might possess these qualities either do nothing or cross over into Ohio in order to be able to profit by their efforts and do so without dishonor.

It is true that, in Kentucky, masters work their slaves without needing to pay them but they gain little profit from their efforts, whereas the money paid to free workers would be recouped with interest from the proceeds of their work.

The free worker receives wages but works more quickly than the slave and speed of execution is a major element in the economy. The white man sells his services but these are purchased only when they are useful; the black man can claim nothing as reward for his services but he must be fed at all times; he must be supported in his old age as in his prime, in his profitless childhood as in his productive adolescent years, in sickness as in health. Thus, the work of both these men is obtained only through an outlay of money. The free worker receives a wage; the slave receives education, food, care, clothing; the money expended by the master for the slave's maintenance slips away gradually in small sums so that it is hardly

37. The exact figures according to the census of 1830 are: Kentucky, 688,844;
      Ohio, 937,669.

noticed but in real terms the slave has cost more than the free man and his work has been less productive.[38]

The influence of slavery extends still further to make its way into the very soul of the master and to set a particular direction to his ideas and tastes.

On both banks of the Ohio, nature has endowed man with an enterprising and energetic character but on each side of the river men use this shared quality in quite different ways.

The white man on the right bank, being forced to live by his own efforts, has made material prosperity his life's main aim. Since he lives in a country offering inexhaustible resources to his hard work and continuous inducements to his activity, his enthusiasm for possessing things has passed the normal bounds of human greed. Driven on by his longing for wealth, he boldly embarks upon all the paths which fortune opens before him. He does not mind whether he becomes a sailor, a pioneer, a factory worker, a farmer, enduring with an even constancy the labors or dangers associated with these various professions. There is something wonderful in the ingenuity of his talent and a kind of heroism in his desire for profit.

The American on the left bank not only looks down upon work but also upon those undertakings which succeed through work. Living in a relaxed idleness, he has the tastes of idle men; money has lost a part of its value in his eyes; he is less interested in wealth than excitement and pleasure and he deploys in this direction

38. Independently of these causes which, wherever free workmen abound, make work more productive and more economical than that done by slaves, another cause peculiar to the United States should be pointed out: across the whole of the Union, cultivation of sugarcane has been successful only on the banks of the Mississippi, near the mouth of that river in the Gulf of Mexico. In Louisiana, the cultivation of sugarcane is extremely lucrative: nowhere does the laborer earn so much for his work; and, as there is always a certain relationship between the costs of production and the product itself, the price of slaves in Louisiana is very high. However, since Louisiana is one of the federal states, one can transport slaves there from all over the Union; therefore, the price paid for a slave in New Orleans raises the price of slaves in all the other markets. Thus it is that, in a region where the land is less productive, the cost of cultivation by slaves continues to be considerable; this gives a great advantage to the competition of free labor.

all the energy his neighbor devotes to other things; he is passionately fond of hunting and war; he enjoys the most vigorous of physical exercise; he is well versed in the use of weapons and from childhood he has learned to risk his life in single combat. Slavery, therefore, not merely prevents the whites from making money but even diverts them from any desire to do so.

The same reasons which have for two centuries worked in opposition to each other in the English colonies of the northern part of America have in the end created an amazing difference between the commercial capabilities of men from the South and those from the North. Today, only the North has ships, factories, railroads, and canals.

This difference is revealed not only between the North and the South but also between different people living in the South. Almost all the men in the most southerly states of the Union who have engaged in commercial enterprises and have sought to exploit slavery have come down from the North; people from the North spread daily over that part of the American territory where they have less fear of competition; there they discover resources which the inhabitants have not noticed; they comply with a system of which they disapprove and succeed in turning it to better advantage than those people who first founded and who still maintain it.

Were I inclined to pursue this parallel, I could easily demonstrate that almost all the observable differences in character between northerners and southerners have their roots in slavery; but that would divert me from my subject. At this moment I am seeking, not the sum of all the effects of slavery, but only those which it has produced upon the material prosperity of those who have adopted it.

The influence of slavery over the generation of wealth can only have been partially known amongst the ancients, where it existed in the whole civilized world, with only barbarous nations having no experience of it.

Indeed, Christianity destroyed slavery only by insisting on the rights of the slave; nowadays, it can be attacked in the name of the master; in this respect, self-interest and the morality of the case are reconciled.

Gradually, as the truth of this became evident in the United States, slavery retreated little by little in the face of the knowledge gained by experience.

Slavery had begun in the South and had then spread toward the North; at the present time, it is receding. Freedom, starting from the North, is moving without interruption toward the South. Among the major states, Pennsylvania stands today at the northern boundary of slavery but, even on these boundaries, the system is under attack. Maryland, immediately below Pennsylvania, is preparing imminently for its removal and Virginia, which comes next to Maryland, is already debating its usefulness and dangers.[39]

No great change in human institutions ever takes place without involving, among its causes, the law of inheritance by the firstborn son.

When, in the South, estates were inherited by this unequal method, each family was represented by one single wealthy man who had neither need nor liking for work. Around him, like so many parasitic plants, sharing the same way of life, lived the members of his family excluded from the common inheritance by law. Then, families in the South exhibited the same conditions as those still found in the noble families of certain European countries in which younger sons, deprived of the elder son's wealth, remain as idle as he does. This same effect was produced in both America and Europe by entirely similar causes. In the South of the United States, the whole of the white race formed an aristocratic body headed by a certain number of privileged individuals whose wealth was permanent and leisure inherited. These leaders of the American nobility maintained, in the body

39. There is one particular reason which removes the two states which I have just mentioned from the cause of slavery. The former wealth of this part of the Union was founded principally upon the cultivation of tobacco. Slaves are particularly suited to this cultivation: now, the commercial value of tobacco has been falling for many years; however, the value of the slaves remains the same. Thus the relationship between the production costs and the product itself has changed. The inhabitants of Maryland and Virginia are more disposed than they were thirty years ago to give up the use of slaves in the cultivation of tobacco or to give up both tobacco and slavery.

they represented, the traditional prejudices of the white race, holding idleness as honorable. At the heart of this aristocracy existed men who were poor but who never worked; poverty seemed preferable to effort. Negro workers and slaves thus had no competitors and, whatever one's opinion on the usefulness of their labors, one was obliged to employ them as the only men available.

As soon as this law of inheritance was abolished, fortunes began to diminish and all the families were simultaneously reduced to the state where work was necessary for survival; many of these families completely disappeared; all of them became half-aware of the time when each man would have to provide for his own needs. Today, wealthy men still exist but they do not form part of a consolidated hereditary body; they are unable to invent a shared spirit which they could maintain and infuse into all the ranks of society. By agreement, therefore, they began to abandon the prejudice which stigmatized work. There has been an increase of poor people but they have been enabled to set about earning their living without blushing about it. Thus, one of the most immediate results of equal inheritance has been to create a class of free workers. As soon as the free worker begins to compete with the slave, the latter feels his inferiority and the very basis of slavery, namely the master's self-interest, has been attacked.

As slavery recedes, the black race follows the same regression and returns to the tropics from where it originally came.

At first sight, this may appear extraordinary but one can soon see why.

The abolition of the principle of slavery does not enable the Americans to obtain freedom for their slaves.

Perhaps what follows would be hard to comprehend unless I quote an example and I will choose that of the state of New York. In 1788, the state of New York forbade the sale of slaves within its boundaries. In a roundabout way this prohibited importation. From then on, the number of Negroes increased only through the natural growth of the black population. Eight years later, a more decisive measure was taken: a declaration was issued to say that, from 4 July 1799, all children of slave parents should be free. That closed all means of increase; slaves are still there but slavery may be said not to exist.

From the time when a northern state prohibits the importation of slaves, no more blacks are brought there from the South.

As soon as a northern state forbids the sale of Negroes, the [...] he possession since his owner cannot get [...] to transporting him to the South.

[...] ern state declares that the son of a slave [...] ave loses much of his market value for [...] ger be included in the transaction and [...] ntage to transport him to the South.

[...] t stops southern slaves moving north- [...] laves southward.

[...] r cause more powerful than all those I

[...] es diminishes in a state, the need for [...] ee workers take over all the work, the [...] productive, becomes a possession of [...] e is still a great incentive to export him [...] etition does not present a threat.

[...] ery, therefore, does not succeed in [...] st changes his master; from the North,

[...] nd those born after the abolition of [...] y do not leave the North to go South [...] a similar position to the native races [...] peans; they stay half-civilized and [...] middle of a population infinitely [...] and knowledge; they are victims of [...] lerant customs. More wretched in [...] ndians, they carry the burden of the [...] e not able to claim possession of a

[...] s been abolished usually endeavor to make [...] greeable to freed Negroes; and as the different [...] as this is concerned, the unfortunate Negroes [...] ils.

single stretch of land; many collapse in misery;[41] the others gather together in towns where they take on the roughest work and lead a precarious and wretched existence.

Moreover, even if the number of Negroes were to continue to grow to the same extent as when they still did not enjoy freedom, with the number of whites increasing twice as fast after the abolition of slavery, the blacks would soon be, as it were, swallowed up in the sea of an alien population.

Generally speaking, land cultivated by slaves is less densely populated than land cultivated by free men; moreover, America is a new country so that, at the time when slavery is abolished by a state, it is still only half full. As soon as slavery is destroyed, the need for free workers is felt and a crowd of bold adventurers pours in from every direction to take advantage of the new opportunities opening up for industry. The land is divided up between them and a white family takes possession of each share. Thus, European immigration is directed toward the free states. What would the poor European do if, coming to seek comfort and happiness in the New World, he was about to live in a country where work is stained with ignominy?

Thus, the white population grows both by its natural increase and by an immense influx of immigrants, whereas the black population is in decline and receives no immigrants. Soon the ratio of the two races to each other is reversed. The Negroes only constitute an unhappy remnant, a poor little wandering tribe, lost in the midst of an immense nation which owns all the land. Their presence is marked only by the injustices and hardships to which they are subjected.

In many of the western states, the Negro race has never made its appearance; in all the northern states, it is vanishing. The important question for the future is, therefore, concentrated

41. A great difference exists between the death rate of the whites and that of the blacks in the states where slavery has been abolished: from 1820 to 1831, only one white person out of forty-two died in Philadelphia, while amongst the blacks the toll was one out of twenty-one. Mortality is not so great amongst the Negroes who are still slaves. (See Emmerson's *Medical Statistics*, p. 28.)

within a narrow circle which makes it less fearful but no easier to resolve.

As one progresses further to the South, it is harder to abolish slavery with advantage and this arises from several physical causes which I must explain.

The first is the climate; the closer Europeans move to the tropics, the more difficult work certainly becomes for them; many Americans even claim that below a certain latitude work becomes fatal for them, whereas the Negro runs no risk from working there.[42] But I cannot think that this notion, which brings support for the southerners' indolence, is based upon experience. It is no hotter in the South of the Union than in the south of Spain or Italy.[43] Why would the European be unable to perform the same work there? And if slavery has been abolished in Italy and Spain without damage to masters, why would not the same happen in the Union? So I do not believe that nature has forbidden the Europeans of Georgia or the Floridas, on pain of death, to gain their livelihood from the soil themselves, but this work would, of course, be more of a burden and less productive[44] to them than to New Englanders. Since the free worker in the South loses some of his edge over the slave, there is less of an advantage to abolish slavery.

All the plants known in Europe are grown in the North of the Union but the South has its own specialties.

It has been noticed that slavery is an expensive way of growing cereals. The farmer harvesting corn in a region where slavery is

42. This is true in places where rice is cultivated. Paddyfields, which are unhealthy places in any country, are particularly hazardous in those regions exposed to the burning tropical sun. Europeans would find it difficult to cultivate the land in this part of the New World, if they persisted in making it produce rice. But can they not get by without paddyfields?

43. These states are nearer the equator than Italy and Spain but the continent of America is infinitely colder than Europe.

44. Spain has already transported a certain number of peasants from the Azores to a district of Louisiana called Attakapas. As an experiment, slavery was not introduced among them. Today these men still cultivate the land without slaves; but there industry is so sluggish that it barely fulfills their needs.

unknown usually retains in his employment only a small number of workmen; when the harvest comes or during the sowing season, it is true that he hires many others but these stay only temporarily in his house.

To fill his barns or plant his fields, the farmer in a slave state is forced to support a great number of servants, who are needed for only a few days, for the whole of the year. For slaves, differently from free workers, cannot work for themselves while they wait until they have to be hired. To use them, the farmer has to buy them.

Apart from its general inconveniences, slavery is thus naturally less suited to areas of cereal cultivation than to those where other crops are grown.

On the other hand, the growing of tobacco, cotton, and, above all, sugarcane demands continuous attention. Women and children who could not be used in the growing of corn may be employed for these crops. Thus, slavery is, of course, more suited in the regions growing the produce I have just quoted.

Tobacco, cotton, sugarcane grow only in the South and represent the major sources of that region's wealth. In destroying slavery, southerners would be faced with one of the following alternatives: either they would be forced to change their system of cultivation and, thereby, would be in competition with the more energetic and more experienced northerners, or they would grow the same produce without slaves and, thereby, would have to endure the competition of those other states which had retained them.

Thus, the South has special reasons for preserving slavery which the North has not.

But there is another motive more compelling than all the others. If it had to, the South could indeed abolish slavery but how would it free itself of the blacks? In the North, the slaves are banished at the same time as slavery. In the South, such a twin result cannot be expected in one move.

By demonstrating that slavery is more natural and advantageous in the South than in the North, I have given sufficient indication that the number of slaves had to be greater there. The first Africans were brought to the South and ever since then the greater numbers have been imported there. The further south one goes, the stronger the prejudice which glorifies idleness. Those states nearest the tropics have no working whites; the Negroes are, therefore, naturally found in greater numbers in the South than in the North. As I have said above, these numbers increase daily, for as slavery is abolished at one end of the Union, so the Negroes accumulate at the other. Thus, the number of blacks increases in the South not simply by the natural increase in populations but also by the forced emigration of the Negroes from the North. The African race grows in this region of the Union for much the same reasons as those which promote such rapid growth of the Europeans in the North.

In the state of Maine, there is one Negro for every three hundred of the population; in Massachusetts, one in a hundred; in the state of New York, two in a hundred; in Pennsylvania, three; in Maryland, thirty-four; forty-two in Virginia and, finally, fifty-five in South Carolina.[45] Such was the proportion of the blacks to the whites in 1830. But this proportion continues to change, each day becoming smaller in the North and greater in the South.

It is obvious that in the most southerly states of the Union, slavery could not be abolished, as has happened in the northern states, without incurring very great risks which have not troubled the latter.

We have seen how the northern states handled the transition from slave-owning to freedom. They keep the present generation in irons while freeing their descendants; in that way, Negroes

45. In an American work entitled *Letters on the Colonization Society*, by Carey, 1833, the following is stated: "In South Carolina for the past forty years, the black race has increased more rapidly than the white." Mr Carey continues, "Taking the average population of the five southern states which first had slaves, Maryland, Virginia, North Carolina, South Carolina, and Georgia, we shall find that, from 1790 to 1830, the whites increased by a ratio of 80 per 100 in these states and the blacks increased by a ratio of 112 per 100."

In the United States, in 1830, the population of the two races was as follows: states where slavery is abolished, 6,565,434 whites, 120,520 Negroes. States where slavery still exists, 3,960,814 whites, 2,208,102 Negroes.

are gradually introduced into society. While the man who might make poor use of his independence is kept in a state of servitude, the man who still has time to learn the art of being free is given his freedom before he has reached the stage of becoming his own master.

It is difficult to apply this method in the South. On declaring that, from a specified time, the son of a Negro is free, the principle and concept of freedom are introduced into the very heart of slavery. The blacks kept in slavery by the legislator, seeing their sons escape from it, wonder at this unfair distribution of fate; they grow restless and irritated. From that moment slavery has lost, in their eyes, the kind of moral authority derived from custom and the passage of time; it is reduced to no more than an obvious abuse of power. The North had nothing to fear from this comparison because, there, the blacks were few and the whites very many in number. But if this first dawning of liberty happened to enlighten two million men at the same moment, the oppressors would have reason to tremble.

Having freed the sons of their slaves, the Europeans in the South would soon be forced to extend the same benefit to the whole black race.

In the North, as mentioned above, as soon as slavery is abolished and even as it becomes likely that its abolition is drawing near, a twofold migration ensues: slaves leave the area to be transported to the South; whites from the North and immigrants from Europe flow in to replace them.

These two causes cannot operate in the same way in the states furthest south. On the one hand, the mass of slaves is too large for there to be any hope of driving them from the area; on the other hand, Europeans and Anglo-Americans from the North are fearful of living in a country where respect for work has not yet been reinstated. Besides, they are right to consider those states where the Negro numbers equal or surpass the whites as threatened by great misfortunes and they refrain from turning their activity in that direction.

Thus, by abolishing slavery, southerners would not succeed, unlike their brothers in the North, in achieving freedom for the Negroes by gradual stages; they would not appreciably reduce the numbers of blacks and would be on their own keeping them in check. Not many years would pass, therefore, before we would see a large population of free Negroes situated at the heart of an almost equal nation of whites.

The same abuses of power which today support slavery would then become the source of the greatest dangers the southern whites would have to fear.

Today, only the descendants of Europeans own the land and are the absolute masters of industry; they alone are wealthy, educated, and armed. The black has none of these advantages; but, being a slave, he can do without them. Once free and responsible for his own fate, can he be deprived of all these things and not die? What gave the whites their power when slavery existed exposes them to a thousand dangers after it is abolished.

As long as the Negro stays a slave, he can be held in a state bordering on that of a beast; once free, there is nothing to stop him from learning enough to realize the extent of his ills and to catch a glimpse of the solution. There is, moreover, a curious principle of relative justice very deeply rooted in the heart of mankind. Men are much more struck by inequalities inside the same class than those observable between different classes. Slavery is understood but how can one allow several million citizens to live beneath the burden of eternal shame and exposed to hereditary wretchedness? In the North, a population of freed Negroes is experiencing such ills and resents these injustices but it is weak and its numbers are small; in the South, it would be strong and numerous.

As soon as it is agreed that whites and emancipated Negroes are placed upon the same land like two alien nations, it will not be difficult to understand that only two possibilities exist for the future: either Negroes and whites must blend together completely or they must part.

I have already expressed my conviction on the former.[46] I do

46. This opinion, moreover, is endorsed by authorities far weightier than mine. Amongst other things one can read in Jefferson's *Memoirs*: "Nothing is more clearly written in the book of destiny than the emancipation of the blacks, and it is equally certain that the two races, once equally

not think that the white and black races will ever manage to live in any country on an equal footing.

But I believe that the difficulty will be much greater still in the United States than anywhere else. A man may stand outside the prejudices of religion, country, and race; if such a man be king, he is able to achieve surprising revolutions in society. A whole nation could not possibly rise, as it were, above itself.

Some tyrant, who happened to link the Americans and their former slaves beneath the same yoke, might succeed in mixing the races together. As long as American democracy stays at the head of public business, no one will dare to try such an undertaking and one may anticipate that the more the whites in the United States are free, the more they will strive to remain in isolation.[47]

I have said elsewhere that the genuine link between the European and the Indian was the half-caste; similarly, the mulatto forms the bridge between white and black: wherever a very great number of mulattos exists, the fusion of these two races is not impossible.

There are areas of America where the European and Negro are so interbred that it is difficult to meet any man who is totally white or totally black. Once this state is reached, it can be said that the races are really mixed, or rather, that a third race has arisen, derived from the other two without belonging to either.

Of all the Europeans, the English have least mingled their blood with that of the Negroes. More mulattos are to be seen in the South than in the North but infinitely fewer than in any other European colony. Mulattos are not very numerous in the United States and have no strength on their own. In racial disputes they normally make common cause with the whites. So it is in Europe: you often see the servants of great lords cut a dash with the lower classes.

---

free, will not be able to live under the same government. Nature, habit, and opinion have established insurmountable barriers between them." (See extracts from Jefferson's *Memoirs*, by M. Conseil.)

47. If the English in the West Indies had governed themselves, one can be sure that they would not have passed the Emancipation Bill which the mother country has lately imposed upon them.

This pride in one's origin, so engrained in the English, is still more remarkably increased in the American by the personal pride derived from democratic freedom. The white man in the United States is proud of his race and of himself.

Moreover, if the whites and the Negroes do not mix in the North of the Union, how would they do so in the South? Might it be imagined for a single moment that the southern American, positioned as he always will be between the white man with all his physical and moral superiority and the Negro, can ever dream of joining forces with the latter? The southern American has two active passions which will always lead him to remain in isolation: he will dread both resembling his former Negro slave and drifting below the level of his white neighbor.

If I absolutely had to predict the future, I would say that, in the likely course of events, the abolition of slavery in the South will increase the repulsion the white population feels for the blacks. I base this view upon the parallels I have already noticed with the North where I have said that the white northerners shun the Negroes all the more carefully because the legislator has lessened the legal separation between them.

Why would the same not happen in the South? In the North, the white man, afraid of mixing with the blacks, is dreading a danger only in his imagination. In the South, where this danger would be real, I cannot think that the dread would be less.

If, on the one hand it is acknowledged (a fact which is beyond doubt) that Negroes in the deep South are constantly increasing more rapidly than the whites and if, on the other hand, it is granted that it is impossible to foresee the time when blacks and whites will manage to mix together and gain the same benefits from society, must we not conclude that, in the southern states, blacks and whites will sooner or later come to blows?

What will be the final result of this struggle?

It will easily be grasped that, in this respect, we are forced back into vague guesses. The human mind has difficulty enough in drawing some sort of great circle around the future within which the vagaries of chance slip past our efforts of understanding. In any portrait of the future, chance always forms a blind spot which the mind's eye can never fathom. The following can be said: in the West Indies, the white race seems destined to suffer defeat; on the continent, the black race.

In the West Indies, the whites are isolated within a vast black population; on the continent, the blacks are situated between the sea and a countless population which already extends above them like a solid mass from the icy boundaries of Canada to the frontiers of Virginia, from the banks of the Missouri to the shores of the Atlantic Ocean. If the whites of North America remain united, it is difficult to believe that the Negroes will escape the destruction threatening them; they will be defeated by the sword or misery. But the black population gathered along the Gulf of Mexico has some chance of salvation, if the conflict between the two races happens to take place at a time when the American confederation has been dissolved. Once the federal link has been broken, southerners would be wrong to count on any lasting support from their northern brothers who know that the threat can never reach them. Unless a decisive obligation compelled them to march to the assistance of the South, one may anticipate that racial sympathy will be powerless.

Moreover, whenever the conflict starts, the southern whites, even if they were abandoned to their own initiative, would enter the lists with a huge superiority of knowledge and resources; but the blacks would have numerical strength and the energy of despair on their side. These are powerful resources to men who have taken up arms. Perhaps then the southern whites will suffer the same fate as the Moors[e] in Spain. After occupying the region for centuries, they will end up by withdrawing gradually to the country which their ancestors left previously and will abandon to the Negroes the ownership of a land which Providence appears to have destined for them since they live and work there without difficulty and more easily than the whites.

The threat of a struggle, more or less distant yet inevitable, between the whites and the blacks in the South of the Union, constantly haunts the imaginations of Americans like a nightmare. Every day, northerners talk of these dangers even though they have nothing directly to fear from them. They seek in vain for some means of averting the calamity they foresee.

In the southern states, everyone is silent; no one talks about the future to strangers; they avoid discussing it with their friends; each man virtually conceals it from himself. This silence in the South has something more frightening about it than the noisy fears of the North.

This concern, shared by everybody, has prompted an enterprise which is almost unknown yet which might change the destiny of a section of the human race.

Fearing the dangers just described, a certain number of American citizens have found a society for the purpose of transporting to the Guinea Coast at their own expense those free Negroes who wished to escape from the tyranny oppressing them.[48]

In 1820, this society succeeded in founding a settlement in Africa, which it called Liberia, on the seventh degree of latitude north. The latest information is that two thousand five hundred Negroes have already gathered there. Transported to their former homeland, the blacks have introduced American institutions. Liberia has a representative system, Negro juries, magistrates and priests; churches have been built and newspapers established; by a strange reversal of fortune in this society, whites are forbidden to settle within its walls.[49]

Assuredly we see there a bizarre whim of fortune! Two centuries have elapsed since the European undertook to wrench the Negroes from their families and country to transport them to the shores of North America. Today, Europeans are busy carting the descendants of these same Negroes once again across the Atlantic Ocean to settle them on the land from which they had once snatched their fathers. Primitive Africans have acquired in slavery the enlightenment of a civilized country and have learned the art of freedom.

Until the present day, Africa was closed to the arts and sciences

48. This society took the name of the Society for the Colonization of the Blacks. See its annual reports, and in particular the fifteenth. See also the pamphlet already mentioned entitled: *Letters on the Colonization Society and on Its Probable Results*, by Mr Carey, Philadelphia, April 1833.

49. This last regulation can be traced to the founders of the settlement. They feared that something similar to that which had happened on the frontiers of the United States would happen in Africa and that the Negroes, like the Indians, coming into contact with a more enlightened race than their own, would be destroyed before they civilized themselves.

of the whites. Perhaps European enlightenment, if transported by the Africans, will penetrate into those regions. The founding of Liberia is, therefore, a fine and lofty idea which, although it may become creative for the Old World, is sterile for the New.

In twelve years, the Colonization Society has transported two thousand five hundred Negroes to Africa. Over the same period, about seven hundred thousand were born in the United States.

Even if the colony of Liberia were in a position to receive annually thousands of new inhabitants who could usefully be sent there, and if the Union took over from the Society, earmarking an annual sum[50] and using its own ships to export Negroes to Africa, it still could not counterbalance the natural increase of the black population. Since the Union cannot take away each year as many men as are born, it would not even manage to prevent the growth of this evil which daily increases within its boundaries.[51]

The Negro race will never again leave the shores of the American continent to which it has been brought by the passions and vices of Europe; it will vanish from the New World only by ceasing to exist. The inhabitants of the United States may push away the calamities they dread but they cannot today destroy what is causing them.

I must confess that I do not consider the abolition of slavery as a way to delay the conflict of the two races in the southern states.

The Negroes may remain slaves without complaining but once they join the ranks of free men they will soon be indignant

50. There would also be many other difficulties in such an enterprise. If the Union undertook to buy the blacks from the slave owners, in order to transport Negroes from America to Africa, the price of the Negroes, increasing with their rarity, would soon reach enormous sums and it is inconceivable that the northern states would ever consent to a similar outlay which they had no chance of recovering. If the Union took the southern slaves by force or at a low rate determined by itself, it would create an overwhelming resistance among the states in that part of the Union. Both courses of action are equally impossible.

51. In the United States, in 1830, there were 2,010,327 slaves and 319,439 freed blacks; 2,329,766 Negroes in all; this made up a little more than a fifth of the total population of the United States at that time.

at being deprived of almost all the rights of citizens and, not being able to become the equals of the whites, they will soon declare themselves their enemies.

In the North, there was every advantage in freeing slaves because in that way they were rid of slavery without having anything to fear from the free Negroes, who were too few ever to claim their rights. The same does not apply to the South.

The question of slavery was for northern masters one of commerce and industry; in the South, it is one of life and death. One must not muddle slavery in the North and in the South.

May God keep me from seeking to justify, as some American writers have done, the principle of Negro slavery; I simply say that all those who previously have accepted this awful principle are not now equally free to abandon it.

I admit that when I observe the South I see only two ways to act for the white race in these regions: freeing the Negroes and integrating with them or remaining apart from them and keeping them in a state of slavery for as long as possible. Interim measures seem to me likely to end shortly in the most horrific of all civil wars and possibly in the ruin of one or other of the two races.

Southern Americans conceive the issue in this light and behave accordingly. Since they have no desire to mix with the Negroes, they do not wish to set them free.

Not that all southerners consider slavery vital to the master's wealth; in this regard, many of them agree with northerners and readily acknowledge, along with them, that slavery is an evil which, in their opinion, has to be preserved in order to guarantee their own existence.

Increasing education in the South has revealed to the inhabitants of this part of the world that slavery harms the master and this same education demonstrates to them, more clearly than hitherto, the virtual impossibility of destroying it. From that arises a bizarre contrast: slavery becomes increasingly bedded down in the law just when its usefulness is the most challenged; and while the principle is gradually abolished in the North, that self-same principle gives rise to increasingly harsh consequences in the South.

The legislation of the southern states in relation to slaves displays nowadays a kind of unprecedented atrocity and one which, by itself, is evidence of a deep disturbance in the laws of humanity. It is enough to read the legislation of the southern states to judge the desperate situation of the two races living there.

The Americans of this part of the Union have not, in fact, increased the hardships of slavery; on the contrary, they have eased the physical conditions of the slaves. Ancient nations knew only shackles and death to maintain slavery; Americans in the South of the Union have found more intellectual justifications to assure the permanence of their power. They have, if I may put it in this way, psychologized tyranny and violence. The ancients sought to prevent the slave from breaking his chains; today we have attempted to take away from him the wish to do so.

The ancients chained the slave's body but left his mind alone and allowed him to be educated. In this, they were acting consistently. There was, therefore, a way out of enslavement: on any given day, the slave could be free and equal to his master.

Southern Americans, who have no thought of ever mixing with Negroes, have forbidden teaching them to read or write under severe penalties. Unwilling to raise them to their level, they keep them as close to the animals as possible.

Throughout history, the hope of freedom has been at the heart of slavery to soften its harshness.

The southern Americans have realized that freeing slaves always runs the risk that the freed slaves can never succeed in having the same status as their master. To give a man freedom and to leave him miserable and humiliated, what is that but to prepare a leader for some future slave revolt? Besides, it had long since been noted that the presence of the free Negro cast a vague anxiety into the hearts of those who were not free and introduced the glimmering notion of their rights. Southern Americans have, in the majority of cases, removed from slave owners the possibility of freeing their slaves.[52]

52. Emancipation is not forbidden but it is subjected to formalities which make it difficult.

In the South of the Union, I met an old man who had once lived in illegal circumstances with one of his Negro women. Several children had been born who had become their father's slaves from birth. He had several times contemplated giving them their freedom at the very least but years had passed and he was still unable to remove the obstacles placed by the legislator in the way of emancipation. Meanwhile he had reached old age and faced death. He then imagined his sons dragged from market to market exchanging the authority of a parent for the rod of a stranger. These horrific images threw the dying man's imagination into delirium. I saw him prey to the anguish of despair and I then understood how nature had a way of wreaking revenge for the wounds inflicted on her by human laws.

These evils may well be awful but are they not the anticipated and inevitable result of the very principle of slavery in modern times?

As soon as Europeans took their slaves from a race of men different from their own, which many of them considered as inferior to the other human races and an assimilation with whom they regarded with horror, they assumed that slavery would last forever. For there is no intervening state that can last between the excessive inequality created by slavery and the complete equality naturally promoted by independence. Europeans have dimly felt this truth but have not admitted it. Whenever it was a question of Negroes, they sometimes followed their self-interest or pride, sometimes their pity. In their treatment of the blacks, they violated all the rights due to human beings. After that, they taught the blacks that those rights were precious and inviolable. They have opened their ranks to their slaves and then, when they tried to come in, they drove them shamefully away. While they preferred to have slaves, they drifted toward liberty against their will or unconsciously, yet had not the courage to be completely wicked or wholly fairminded.

If it is impossible to foresee a time when Americans of the South will mingle their blood with that of the Negroes, are they going to be able to grant freedom to their slaves, without exposing themselves to peril? And if, in order to save their own race, they are forced to keep them in chains, should they not be forgiven for taking the most effective measures to achieve that?

What is happening in the South of the Union seems to me both the most horrible and the most natural consequence of slavery. When I see the natural order upturned and hear humanity crying out in its vain struggle against these laws, I confess that my sense of outrage is not at all directed against the men of our day who are the authors of these outrages; but I do concentrate all my hatred against those who introduced slavery once again into the world after more than a thousand years of equality.

Moreover, whatever efforts southern Americans make to preserve slavery, they will not succeed forever. Slavery, which is limited to one area of the globe, which is attacked by Christianity as unjust and by political economy as pernicious and which is placed next to the democratic freedom and enlightenment of our times, is not an institution which can last. It will end through the actions of the slave or of the master. In either case, great misfortunes are to be expected.

If freedom is refused the Negroes of the South, they will end up by seizing it themselves, using violent means; if it is granted them, they will soon abuse it.

WHAT ARE THE CHANCES THAT THE AMERICAN UNION WILL LAST? WHAT DANGERS THREATEN IT?

The predominant power resides in the states rather than the Union—The confederation will last only as long as the states composing it wish to belong to it—Reasons which tend to keep them united—Usefulness of being united in order to stand against foreigners and to prevent the presence of foreigners in America—Providence has not erected any natural barriers between the different states— No material interests divide them—The North's interest in the prosperity and unity of the South and West; the South's in those of the North and West: the West's in that of the other two—The spiritual concerns which unite Americans—Uniformity of opinions—The dangers of the confederation arising from the different characters and passions of its inhabitants—Characters of southerners and northerners—The rapid growth of the Union is one of its greatest dangers—Movement of the population toward the Northwest—Power gravitates in that direction—The passions aroused by these sudden surges of fortune—If the Union prevails, does its government gain or lose strength?—Different signs of weakness—Internal improvements—Wastelands—Indians—The Bank question—The tariff question—General Jackson

The maintenance of existing conditions in the various component states depends in part upon the existence of the Union. So we must first examine the likely outcome of the Union. But, above all, it is as well to clarify one point: if the present confederation happened to break up, it is beyond dispute that the constituent states would not revert to their original separateness. In the place of one single Union, there would be several. I do not intend to inquire into the possible bases upon which new unions might be formed; what I wish to demonstrate are causes which might lead to the dismemberment of the present confederation.

To do this, I shall have to return along a few of the paths I have already traveled. I must call attention to several matters already known. I realize that such a method risks arousing the reader's objections but the importance of the subject under scrutiny is my excuse. I prefer an occasional repetition to risking misunderstandings and I would rather the author suffered than the subject.

The legislators of the 1789 Constitution strove to give a separate existence to federal power and a predominant strength.

But they were constrained by the very conditions of the problem they had to resolve. They had not been given the task of forming the government of a single nation but to organize the association of several nations; whatever their own wishes, they always had to end up by sharing the exercise of sovereignty.

Some things are national by nature, that is to say they are connected to the whole body of the nation and can only be entrusted to the man or assembly which represents the whole nation as completely as possible. War and diplomacy come into this category.

Others are regional in nature, that is to say they concern certain localities and can only be suitably dealt with in that locality. An example would be the budget of the townships.

Lastly are those matters which might be either: they are national insofar as they involve all the individuals composing the nation; they are regional insofar as the nation itself has no need to provide for them. For example, there are rights which regulate the civil and political status of citizens. Every social state must have civil and political rights. Therefore, these rights involve all citizens equally but it is not always vital to the existence and welfare of the nation for these rights to be the same everywhere, nor, consequently, do they need to be regulated by central government.

Among the matters under the control of the sovereign power are two inevitable categories; they are found in all well-constituted societies whatever the basis upon which the social contract has been established.

Between these two extremes a mass of general matters drift to and fro; they are not of national concern and I have called them mixed. These matters, which are not exclusively national, nor wholly regional, may look to national or regional government for regulation, according to the agreement of the various parties involved, without prejudicing the contracts of these parties.

Frequently, ordinary individuals join forces to form a sovereign authority and their union constitutes a nation. Beneath this general level of government which they have adopted, there is nothing but individual forces or collective powers, each of which represents a very small fraction of the sovereign power. Thus it is most natural to call upon the general government to regulate not only those matters which are essentially of national importance but most of those regional issues I have already mentioned. Local government is restricted to that share of sovereign power which is vital to its prosperity.

Sometimes the sovereign power is composed of political

bodies already in place by virtue of circumstances which happened before the association; then it happens that the regional government takes responsibility not only for matters exclusively regional by nature but also for part of all those mixed matters which come into question. Consequently, confederated nations, which were sovereign governments themselves before their union and which continue to represent a very substantial share of that sovereign authority even after unification, never intended to cede to the central government anything but the exercise of those rights which are vital to the Union.

Whenever the national government is endowed with the right to regulate matters of mixed sovereignty outside the powers which properly belong to its own functions, then it has the predominant authority. Not only does it possess many rights but all those rights that it does not possess are at its mercy and the fear is that it will deprive regional government of the natural and necessary powers.

On the other hand, when the regional government is endowed with the right to regulate mixed questions, then the opposite tendency prevails in society. Then the predominant power rests with the regions and not with the nation and it is to be feared that the national government will ultimately be stripped of the privileges vital to its existence.

Single nations are, therefore, led naturally toward a centralized government and confederations to dismemberment.

It only remains for us to apply these generalizations to the American Union.

The individual states were bound to claim the right to regulate purely regional matters.

Moreover, these same states retained the right to determine the civil and political competence of their citizens, to regulate the relations of men to each other, and to dispense justice, all of which are rights of a general nature but do not necessarily belong to the government at national level.

We have seen how the power to give orders in the name of the whole nation was delegated to the government of the Union in those cases where the nation might have to act as a single undivided authority in foreign affairs and in directing common forces against a common enemy. To sum up, it deals with those matters which I have called exclusively national.

In this division of sovereign rights, at first sight the Union's share still seems greater than that of the states; deeper scrutiny proves that in actuality it is less so.

The undertakings of the Union government are on a grand scale but such actions rarely take place. Regional government performs smaller tasks but is constantly at work and continuously shows that it is active.

The government of the Union watches over the general concerns of the country but these general national concerns have a questionable influence on individual happiness.

However, regional affairs affect the welfare of the inhabitants in a tangible way.

The Union guarantees the independence and greatness of the nation, things which do not impinge immediately on private individuals. The state preserves the freedom, regulates rights, safeguards property, protects the life and entire future of each citizen.

The federal government stands at a great distance from its subjects; the regional government is within the reach of all. All you need to do for it to hear you is to raise your voice. Central government has on its side the passions of a few outstanding men who are ambitious to direct it; regional government is supported by the self-interest of men of lower rank who hope to achieve power only in their own state. These are the men who, being close to the people, exercise the most power over them.

Americans have, therefore, much more to expect and fear from the state than from the Union and, according to the natural emotions of the human mind, they are bound to feel a closer attachment to the former than to the latter.

In this respect, habits and feelings are in harmony with self-interest.

When a compact nation splits its sovereignty and reaches a state of confederation, memories, practices, customs struggle for a long time against laws and give the central government a force refused by these laws. When confederated nations join together under a single sovereign government, these same causes act in an opposite direction. If France were to become a confederated republic like the United States, I doubt whether it would prove at first to be more energetic than the Union and, if the Union turned into a monarchy like France, I think that the American government would stay weaker than ours for a long while. When the Anglo-Americans created their national life, life at a regional level was already long established and the necessary links between the townships and private individuals of the same states had been settled; people were used to viewing certain matters from a communal standpoint and to conduct other undertakings as exclusively relating to their own special concerns.

The Union is a vast body which presents only a dimly perceived image to inspire patriotic feelings. The state has a distinct shape and clearly drawn boundaries; it represents a certain number of familiar things cherished by its inhabitants. It is identified with the very soil itself, with property, family, past memories, present activities, future dreams. Patriotism, frequently only the extension of private egoism, has, therefore, remained attached to the state and has not yet, so to speak, passed on to the Union.

Thus, concerns, customs, opinions combine to centralize real political life in the state and not in the Union.

The difference in the strength of these two governments can easily be estimated by seeing them both in action in their own sphere of influence.

Whenever a state government addresses a man or an association of men, its language is clear and imperative, as is the language of the federal government toward individuals, but as soon as it confronts a state it begins to parley, to explain its motives, to justify its conduct; it argues, advises, and hardly ever issues orders.

If doubts arise over the degree to which the constitutional powers of the two governments are limited, the regional government claims its rights boldly and takes swift and energetic measures to support them. Meanwhile, the Union government reasons its case, appealing to the common sense, the interests, and the reputation of the nation; it plays for time and negotiates; only when driven to the final extreme does it decide to act. At first sight, one might suppose that it is the regional government which was armed with the strength of the whole nation and that Congress represented a state.

The federal government, despite the efforts of those who founded it, is, therefore, as I have already said elsewhere, a weak government by its very nature and one which, more than any other, needs the free support of its citizens to survive.

It is simple to see that its objective is to facilitate the states' desire to remain united. Once this preliminary condition has been fulfilled, it is wise, strong, and flexible. It has been organized in such a way as to limit the usual confrontation to individuals and to overcome with ease the obstacles raised against the common will, but the federal government has not been established in anticipation that the states, or several of them, would withdraw their wish to be part of the Union.

If the sovereignty of the Union were to come into conflict with that of the states, one can readily foresee that it would be defeated; I doubt whether the fight would ever be undertaken in any serious fashion. Whenever determined resistance is offered to the federal government, it will be found to yield. Experience has shown so far that whenever a state has been stubbornly determined on anything and was resolute in its demands, it never failed to obtain it and when it has flatly refused to act[53] it was left to do what it wanted.

Even if the government of the Union had power of its own, the physical condition of the country would make the use of it very difficult.[54]

53. See the conduct of the northern states in the war of 1812. "During that war," said Jefferson, in a letter of 17 March 1817 to General La Fayette, "four of the eastern states were only attached to the Union like corpses to living men." (*Jefferson's Correspondence*, published by M. Conseil.)

54. The state of peace in which the Union finds itself affords no reason for a permanent army. Without a permanent army, a government has nothing prepared in advance to take advantage of a favorable moment, overcome resistance, and seize the sovereign power by surprise.

The states of the Union cover an immense territory with long distances between them and the population is scattered throughout a country still half-wilderness. If the Union were to undertake to enforce the allegiance of the confederated states by force, it would find itself in a position similar to that of England in the War of Independence.

Besides, however strong a government, it cannot escape the consequences of a principle once it has been established as the foundation of its public constitution. The confederation was formed by the free will of the states which, by uniting together, did not forfeit their nationality nor became fused into one and the same nation. If, today, one of these same states wished to withdraw its name from the contract, it would be difficult to prove that it could not do so. The federal government would not be able in any obvious way to rely upon either force or law to overcome it.

To enable the federal government to conquer easily any resistance from any one of its subject states, the particular interest of one or several of them would have to be closely linked to the existence of the Union, as has often been observed in the history of confederations.

Suppose that, among those states bound together by the federal tie, some exclusively enjoy the major advantages of union and their prosperity depends wholly upon the existence of the fact of that union, it is obvious that the central government will have their considerable support to ensure the obedience of the others. But in that case, it will draw its strength not from itself but will derive it from a principle that is contrary to its nature. People join confederations only to gain equivalent advantages from the union and, in the case quoted above, the existence of inequalities among the confederated peoples guarantees the power of the federal government.

Again, suppose that one of the confederated states has gained enough of a predominance to be able to monopolize central power, it will regard the other states as subordinate and will enforce respect for its own sovereignty under the guise of the sovereignty of the Union. Great matters will be achieved in the name of the federal government but, in reality, the Union would have ceased to exist.[55]

In both these instances, the power which acts in the name of the confederation becomes stronger the more it deviates from the natural state and acknowledged principle of confederations.

In America, the present-day Union is useful to all the states but is not essential to any of them. Several states might break the federal ties without compromising the fortune of the others although the sum total of their happiness might be reduced. Since neither the existence nor the prosperity of any single state is entirely linked to the present confederation, neither is there a single state which is inclined to make very great personal sacrifices to preserve it.

On the other hand, I cannot see any state which has yet had its ambition much involved in upholding the confederation as we see it today. Of course, they do not all wield the same influence in federal councils but not a single one imagines that it is dominant there or can treat its other members as inferiors or subordinates.

Thus, it seems to me beyond doubt that, if one section of the Union seriously decided to split off from the rest, not only could no one prevent its happening but that no one would attempt to do so. The present Union will, therefore, last only as long as all the constituent states continue to wish to belong.

With that point decided, we can become less anxious: it is now not a matter of inquiring whether the present confederate states will separate but whether they will want to remain in the Union.

Among all the reasons which cause the present Union to be useful to Americans, two main ones stand out as strikingly obvious to any observer.

Although Americans are, in a sense, alone on their continent, commerce makes neighbors of all their trading nations. Despite

---

55. Thus it is that the province of Holland in the republic of the Netherlands and the Emperor in the German Confederation have sometimes put themselves in the place of the Union and have exploited the federal authority for their own advantage.

their seeming isolation, Americans need, therefore, to be strong, which they cannot achieve except by staying in the Union.

If the states were to split up, they would not only reduce their power in relation to foreign nations but they would create foreigners on their very own soil. From then on, a system of internal customs barriers would be set up, the valleys would be divided by imaginary lines, rivers would be closed and, in every possible way, the exploitation of this God-given domain would be hindered throughout this immense continent.

Today, they have no invasion to dread; thus, no armies to support; no taxes to levy. If the Union happened to break up, the need for all those things would, perhaps, soon be felt.

Americans have, therefore, an enormous incentive to remain united.

On the other hand, at the present time it is almost impossible to discover what kind of material advantage one section of the Union might have in splitting off from the rest.

A glance over a map of the United States reveals the Allegheny mountain chain, running north-east to south-west and crossing through the country for a thousand miles. It is tempting to think that Providence was aiming to erect, between the Mississippi basin and the Atlantic shores, one of those natural barriers which obstruct those mutual connections, always a feature of men's lives, and set necessary boundaries between different peoples.

But the average height of the Alleghenies does not exceed 800 metres.[56] Their rounded summits and the wide valleys enclosed within them offer easy access in a thousand places. What is more, the main rivers pouring their waters into the Atlantic Ocean, the Hudson, Susquehanna, and the Potomac, have their sources on the far side of the Alleghenies in the wide plain bordering the Mississippi basin. Starting from this region,[57] they make their way through the barrier which apparently should

56. The average height of the Alleghenies, according to Volney (*Tableau des Etats-Unis*, p. 33), is 700 to 800 metres; 5,000 to 6,000 feet, according to Darby; the highest point of the Vosges is 1,400 metres above sea level.
57. See *View of the United States*, by Darby, pp. 64 and 79.

force them west and clear natural and ever-open passages through the mountains.

Thus, no barrier stands between the different parts of the country now occupied by the Anglo-Americans. The Alleghenies, far from setting boundaries to nations, are not even the frontiers of states. New York, Pennsylvania, and Virginia include them within their land and extend as much to the west of these mountains as they do to the east.[58]

The territory now occupied by the twenty-four states of the Union and the three great districts not yet included in the ranks of the states, even though they are already inhabited, cover an area of 1,002,600 square miles,[59] which is about the same as five times that of France. Within these boundaries there is a variety of soil, a range of temperature, and very different produce.

This wide stretch of territory occupied by the Anglo-American republics has given rise to doubts about the continuation of the Union. A distinction has to be made at this point: opposed interests developing at times in different regions of a vast empire end up by coming into collision; then it happens that the size of the state is the greatest threat to its continued existence. But if the inhabitants of this vast territory have no interests dividing them, its very size is bound to encourage their prosperity, for a unified government especially supports the movement of the various agricultural products and increases their value by making the flow of trade easier.

Now I can see clearly that various areas of the Union have different interests but I cannot discover any which are hostile to each other.

The southern states are almost exclusively agricultural; the northern states are more especially commercial and manufacturing; the western states are both at the same time.

58. The chain of the Alleghenies is not so high as the Vosges, nor does it offer as many obstacles as the latter to the efforts of human industry. The countries situated on the eastern side of the Alleghenies are as naturally attached to the valley of the Mississippi as Franche-Compté, Upper Burgundy, and Alsace are to France.

59. See *View of the United States*, by Darby, p. 435.

In the South, tobacco, rice, cotton, and sugar are harvested; in the North and West, maize and corn. These represent varied sources of wealth but to draw advantage from these sources, one common means is equally favorable to everyone and that is the Union.

The North, which transports this Anglo-American wealth to all parts of the globe and the wealth of the whole world back to the Union, is clearly committed to the continuation of the confederation as it presently exists so that the number of American producers and consumers which it is called upon to serve may remain as large as possible. The North is the most natural intermediary both between the South and the West of the Union and between them and the rest of the world. The North is bound to want the South and West to remain in the Union and prosperous so that they can provide its factories with raw materials and its vessels with freight.

On their side, the South and West have an even more direct interest in the preservation of the Union and the prosperity of the North. Southern produce is exported in the main overseas; thus, the South and West need the commercial resources of the North. They are bound to want to see a very powerful Union fleet to provide effective protection. The South and West have to be ready to contribute to the fleet's costs even though they possess no ships of their own, for, if European fleets blockaded southern harbors and the Mississippi delta, what would happen to the rice from the Carolinas, the tobacco from Virginia, and the sugar and cotton growing in the Mississippi valleys? There is, therefore, no part of the federal budget which is not applied to safeguard a material interest common to all the confederated states.

Apart from this commercial benefit, the South and West of the Union derive a great political advantage from remaining united both with themselves and with the North.

The South includes within its boundaries an immense population of slaves which is currently a menace and potentially even more so.

The western states have settled the bottom of a single valley. The rivers irrigating the territory held by these states flow from the Rockies or the Alleghenies and all join the waters of the Mississippi down toward the Gulf of Mexico. These western states are entirely cut off by their location from the traditions of Europe and from the civilization of the Old World.

Thus, the southerners are bound to want the preservation of the Union so that they do not stand alone against the blacks and the westerners so that they do not become isolated in this central part of America, cut off from free communication with the outside world.

On its side, the North cannot but wish to avoid any division of the Union so that it can act as the connecting link between this great body and the rest of the world.

There is, therefore, a close tie between the material interests of all parts of the Union.

I would say the same thing for opinions and feelings which may be called man's spiritual interests.

The inhabitants of the United States speak much about their love for their country; I confess to having little faith in this calculated patriotism which is founded on self-interest and may be destroyed, if that changes direction.

Nor do I attach very great importance to the words of Americans when they display their daily intention to preserve the federal system of their fathers.

The thing which keeps a majority of citizens under the same government is much less the rational decision to remain united than the instinctive and, in a sense, unconscious agreement resulting from like feelings and similar opinions.

I shall never agree that men form an association simply because they acknowledge the same leader and obey the same laws. An association comes into being only when certain men look at a large number of subjects in the same way, when they have the same opinions on a large number of topics and when the same events give rise to the same thoughts and impressions.

Anyone viewing this question from this point of view and studying the events in the United States, will readily discover that the inhabitants, though divided as they are into twenty-four distinct sovereign authorities, are nonetheless one single nation and he might even come to think that the Anglo-American

Union represents more truly a state of society than that of certain nations of Europe which live under a single body of laws and are subservient to one man.

Although the Anglo-Americans have several religions, they all have the same way of viewing religion.

They do not always see eye to eye on the measures they must take for good government and differ over some of the forms of government they must adopt, but they do agree upon the general principles which should direct human societies. From Maine to the Floridas, from the Missouri to the Atlantic Ocean, the origin of all legitimate power is believed to reside in the people. Men have the same ideas about freedom and equality; they profess the same opinions on the press, the right of association, the jury system, and the responsibilities of political agents.

Moving from political and religious ideas to philosophic and moral opinions which direct the daily behavior of life and control the conduct of society, we find the same agreement.

The Anglo-Americans[60] see moral authority residing in universal reason as political power resides in the universality of citizens and they think that one must refer to the understanding of the public in order to discover what is allowed or forbidden, true or false. Most of them believe that an awareness of his self-interest properly understood is sufficient to lead a man toward fairness and honesty. They believe that at birth each person has received the capacity for self-government and that no one has the right to force his fellows to be happy. They all have a lively faith in human perfectibility; they judge that the spread of education is bound necessarily to achieve useful results just as ignorance must bring fatal consequences. They all consider society as a body making progress, humanity as a changing picture in which nothing is or has to be permanently fixed and they acknowledge that what they hold as good today may be replaced tomorrow by something better that is as yet hidden.

60. I'm sure I don't need to say that by the expression *Anglo-Americans* I am referring only to the vast majority of the people. There are always a few individuals who keep themselves apart from this majority.

I am not saying that all opinions are correct but that they are American.

While the Anglo-Americans are thus united by commonly held ideas, they are separated from all other nations by one feeling, which is pride.

For fifty years the inhabitants of the United States have been repeatedly told that they form the only religious, enlightened, and free nation. They see that the democratic institutions of their country are prospering whereas they are failing in the rest of the world. They possess, therefore, an inordinate opinion of themselves and are not far from believing that they form a species apart from the rest of humanity.

Hence the dangers faced by the American Union do not spring any more from diversity of opinions than from diversity of interests. They must be sought in the variety of American characteristics and passions.

Almost all the inhabitants of the immense territory of the United States come from a common stock but, as time goes by, the climate and especially slavery have introduced marked differences between the character of the English in the southern states and the English in the North.

It is generally believed among us that slavery gives one area of the Union interests quite opposed to those of another area. I have not observed this to be the case. Slavery has not created in the South interests opposed to those in the North but it has altered the character of southerners, giving them different customs.

I have revealed elsewhere the influence of slavery upon the commercial capacity of southern Americans and this same influence extends equally to their way of life.

The slave is a servant who does not argue and submits to everything without a murmur. Sometimes he murders his master but he never resists him. In the South, no family is so poor as not to have slaves. From birth, the southern American is invested with a kind of domestic dictatorship; his first conception of life teaches him that he is born to give orders and the first habit he learns is that of effortless domination. Education, therefore, has a powerful tendency to turn the southern American into a haughty, hasty, irascible, violent man, passionate in his desires and irritated by obstacles. But he is easily discouraged if he fails to succeed at his first attempt.

The northern American does not see slaves scurrying around his cradle. He does not even meet freed slaves, for mostly he is reduced to providing for his own needs. No sooner is he born than the idea of necessity assails his mind on all sides and thus he learns early on to know by himself the exact limitations of his natural power; he does not expect to force the will of his opponents to bow to his and he realizes that he has to win the favor of his fellows, if he wants their support. Therefore, he is patient, circumspect, tolerant, slow to react, but perseveres in his plans.

In the southern states, a man's most urgent needs are always satisfied. Hence, the southerner is not preoccupied with the material cares of life; someone else takes care to think of them for him. Free in that respect, his imagination is directed toward other greater and less well-defined objectives. The southerner loves grandeur, luxury, reputation, excitement, pleasure, and, above all, idleness; nothing constrains him to work hard for his livelihood and, as he has no work which he has to do, he sleeps his time away, not even attempting anything useful.

Since, in the North, wealth is equal and slavery non-existent, a man is absorbed by just those material cares which the southerner looks down upon. From his childhood, he is busy fighting poverty and he learns to place comfort above all other pleasures of mind or heart. Concentration on the trivialities of life snuffs out his imagination, reduces the number of his ideas which become less general but more practical, clear-cut, and precise. As he directs all his mental efforts toward his sole concern for prosperity, he quickly excels in that aim; he has a wonderful skill in exploiting nature and men in order to gain wealth; he marvelously understands the art of harnessing society to the advance of every man's prosperity and of extracting the happiness of all from the selfishness of each.

The northerner possesses not merely experience but knowledge;

however, he values science, not as a pleasure but as a means to an end and greedily seizes upon it for its useful applications.

The southerner is more spontaneous, witty, open, generous, intellectual, and brilliant.

The northerner is more active, reasonable, educated, and skilled.

The southerner has the tastes, prejudices, weaknesses, and greatness of all aristocrats.

The northerner has the qualities and failings which characterize the middle classes.

If two men belonging to the same society have the same interests and to some extent the same opinions but their characters, education, and style of living are different, it is highly likely that they will not see eye to eye. The same observation applies to a society of nations.

Slavery does not, therefore, attack the American confederation directly through interests but indirectly through customs.

Thirteen states belonged to the federal pact of 1790; today, the confederation numbers twenty-four. The population which was nearly four million in 1790 has quadrupled in the space of forty years; in 1830, it had risen to almost thirteen million.[61]

Such developments cannot come about without danger.

For a society of nations, as of individuals, three main ingredients give them the power to last: the wisdom of its members, their individual weakness, and their small numbers.

Americans who move away from the Atlantic Ocean to plunge into the West are adventurers irritated by any kind of yoke, greedy for wealth, often outcasts in the state of their birth. They arrive in the wilds without knowing one another. They have no traditions or family spirit nor examples of exercising restraint. In their midst, the power of law is weak and that of custom still more so. The men daily occupying the Mississippi valleys are inferior in every respect to the Americans who inhabit the former boundaries of the Union. And yet they are already having a great influence in its councils and they undertake the government

61.   Census of 1790, 3,929,328; census of 1830, 12,856,163.

of public affairs before they have learned to govern themselves.[62]

The weaker the members of a society are individually, the more likely are that society's chances of lasting for, in such a position, their only security depends upon remaining united. In 1790, when the most populous American republics had not reached five hundred thousand,[63] each state felt its insignificance as an independent nation and this thought made obedience to the federal authority easier. But when one of the confederate states has two million inhabitants, as the state of New York has, and covers an area equal to a quarter of France,[64] it feels strong in its own right and, if it continues to support union as useful to its wellbeing, it no longer reckons it vital to its existence; it can do without it and, although agreeing to remain within the Union, it rapidly seeks to hold a dominant position.

The increase of the members of the Union by itself would already represent a powerful threat to the federal bond. All men see the same things in a different way even when coming from the same point of view but this is all the more so when the point of view is different too. Thus, as the number of republics increases, the less there will be the chance of reaching unanimity about the same laws.

Today, the interests of the different parts of the Union are not opposed to one another but who can foresee the various changes which the near future will bring in a country where each day sees new towns and every five years new nations?

Since the time of the English settlements, the number of inhabitants doubles, broadly, every twenty-two years; I see no reason why over the next hundred years this rate of increase of the Anglo-American population should be halted.

Before the passing of that hundred years, I believe that the land inhabited or claimed by the United States will have a

---

62. It is true that this is only a temporary danger. I have no doubt that, with time, society in the West will settle down and become as stable as that on the Atlantic seaboard.

63. Pennsylvania had 431,373 inhabitants in 1790.

64. The state of New York covers an area of 6,213 square leagues (500 square miles). See *View of the United States*, by Darby, p. 435. [Translator's note: this is not an accurate equivalent.]

population of more than one hundred million and be divided into forty states.[65]

I acknowledge that this hundred million men will have no opposing interests. On the contrary, I see them all as having an equal interest in maintaining the Union and I am supposing that the very fact that they are one hundred million divided into forty distinct and unequally powerful states makes the continuance of federal government no more than a fortunate accident.

I would like to have faith in human perfectibility but, until men's nature has changed and men have been entirely transformed, I shall refuse to believe in the permanence of a government which has to unite forty different nations spread over an area equal to half Europe[66] to avoid inter-state rivalries, ambition, or conflicts and to unite all their independent wills in the achievement of common plans.

But the greatest danger to an expanding Union comes from the constant shift of its internal forces.

From the shores of Lake Superior to the Gulf of Mexico, it is, as the crow flies, about four hundred French leagues. The United States frontier winds along the whole of this immense line, sometimes retreating within its boundary, but more often extending well beyond it into the wilds. It has been calculated that over this huge front the whites advance on average seven leagues annually.[67] From time to time, there comes an obstacle,

65. If the population continues to double every twenty-two years for another century, as it has done for the last two hundred years, in 1852 the United States will have twenty-four million inhabitants, forty-eight million in 1874 and ninety-six million in 1896. This will still be the case even if the land on the eastern side of the Rocky Mountains is found to be unfit for cultivation. The lands which are already occupied can easily accommodate this number of inhabitants. One hundred million men spread across the land occupied by the twenty-four states and the three territories which make up the Union means that there are only 762 individuals per square league; this would be far below the average population of France, which is 1,006; below that of England, which is 1,457, and would even be below that of Switzerland. Switzerland, despite its lakes and mountains, has 783 inhabitants per square league. See Malte-Brun, vol. 6, p. 92.

66. The United States has an area of 295,000 square leagues; Europe, according to Malte-Brun, vol. 6, p. 4, has 500,000.

67. See *Legislative Documents*, 20th Congress, no. 117, p. 105.

maybe a barren area, a lake, an Indian nation encountered unexpectedly on the way. For a moment, the column comes to a halt, allowing its two ends to join together, and then renews its progress. This gradual and unending advance of the European race toward the Rocky Mountains has something providential about it: it resembles a flood of men rising constantly, uplifted daily by the hand of God.

Within this front line of conquering settlers, towns are built and vast states are founded. In 1790, scarcely a few thousand pioneers spread over the Mississippi valleys; today, these same valleys contain as many men as did the entire Union in 1790. The population now stands at almost four million.[68] The city of Washington was founded in 1800 at the very center of the American confederation; now it is situated at one of its extremities. The Deputies from the most distant states of the West,[69] in order to take their seat in Congress, are already forced to make a journey as far as that from Vienna to Paris.

All the states of the Union are simultaneously attracted to the gaining of wealth but cannot grow and prosper at the same rate.

In the North of the Union, detached offshoots of the Alleghenies stretch down to the Atlantic Ocean to form spacious harbors and ports always open to the largest ships. From the Potomac, however, along the American coast to the mouth of the Mississippi, there is nothing but a flat, sandy terrain. In this part of the Union, the mouths of almost all the rivers are blocked and the few ports available in these lagoons offer much shallower water for shipping and afford much less satisfactory facilities for trade than those in the North.

This initial inferiority, which stems from nature, is united to another, which results from the laws.

We have seen that slavery, which has been abolished in the North, still exists in the South and I have demonstrated the disastrous influence it exerts on the prosperity of the slavemaster himself.

68. 3,672,371, according to the census of 1830.
69. From Jefferson, the capital of the state of Missouri, to Washington, is 1,019 miles, or 420 leagues. (*American Almanac*, 1831, p. 48.)

The North is forced, therefore, to develop trade and industry[70] to a greater extent than the South. It is natural that population and wealth should increase more rapidly there.

The states on the Atlantic Coast are already half-populated. Most of the land has an owner; thus they cannot accept the same number of immigrants as the states in the West which still offer unbounded scope for industry. The Mississippi basin is infinitely more fertile than the Atlantic coastline. This, added to all the other reasons, drives Europeans westward. Statistics emphatically show this to be so.

If we concentrate on the United States as a whole, the population has almost tripled over forty years. But if we view only the Mississippi basin, over the same period of time, the population[71] has multiplied thirty-one times.[72]

70. To judge the difference between the commercial activity in the South and the commercial activity in the North, it is simply necessary to glance at the following facts:

In 1829, merchant shipping, on a grand or small scale, which belonged to Virginia, the two Carolinas, and to Georgia (the four great southern states), amounted to only 5,243 tons.

In the same year, ships belonging to the single state of Massachusetts amounted to 17,322 tons. (*Legislative Documents*, 21st Congress, 2nd session, no.140, p. 244.)

Thus the single state of Massachusetts had three times as many ships as the four above-mentioned states.

However, the state of Massachusetts covers an area of only 959 square leagues (7,335 square miles) and has 610,014 inhabitants, while the four states of which I spoke have 27,204 square leagues (210,000 square miles) and 3,047,767 inhabitants. Thus, the area covered by the state of Massachusetts equals just a thirtieth part of the area covered by the four states and its population is five times smaller than theirs (*View of the United States*, by Darby). In several ways, slavery harms the commercial prosperity of the South. It diminishes the spirit of enterprise amongst the whites and it prevents their finding the sailors that they need. Sailors are usually recruited from the lowest ranks of society. In the South it is the slaves who form this class and it is difficult to make use of them at sea: their service is inferior to that of the whites and their mutiny on the high seas is always to be feared, as is the fact that they might escape when reaching foreign shores.

71. *View of the United States*, by Darby, p. 444.

72. Note that, when I speak of the Mississippi basin, I am not referring to those parts of the states of New York, Pennsylvania, and Virginia which are west of the Alleghenies and which, however, should be considered as part of it.

The center of the federal authority is constantly shifting. Forty years ago, the majority of citizens in the Union lived near the coast, in the neighborhood of the place where Washington now stands. These days, the majority is centered further inland and more to the North. It is beyond doubt that within twenty years the majority will live on the other side of the Alleghenies. Should the Union last, the extent and fertility of the Mississippi basin will make it become, inevitably, the permanent center of the federal government. In thirty or forty years time, the Mississippi basin will have assumed its natural ranking. It is easy to calculate that, by that time, its population compared with that of the Atlantic Coast states will be in a ratio of forty to eleven, or thereabouts. In a few years time, control of the Union will have slipped entirely from the grasp of the founding states and the peoples of the Mississippi valleys will dominate the federal assemblies.

This constant shift of federal power and influence toward the Northwest becomes clear every ten years, when the general census of the population is completed and the number of representatives sent by each state to Congress is fixed.[73]

In 1790, Virginia had nineteen representatives in Congress. This number went on growing until in 1813 the figure reached twenty-three. Since that time, it has started to decline. In 1833, it was only twenty-one.[74] During this same period, the state

73. One will notice that, during the last ten years, the population of some states, such as Delaware, has increased by 5 per cent, while others, like the territory of Michigan, have increased by 250 per cent. Virginia finds that, during the same period, it has increased the number of its inhabitants by 13 per cent while the border state of Ohio has extended its numbers by 61 per cent. Looking at the general table given in the *National Calendar*, one will be struck by the unequal fortunes of the different states.

74. Further on one will see that, during the last period, the population of Virginia has grown by 13 per cent. It is necessary to explain how the number of representatives of a state can decrease while the population of that state, far from falling, is actually on the increase.

I take as the basis of my comparison the state of Virginia which I have already mentioned. The number of representatives from Virginia in 1823 was proportionate to the total number of representatives of the Union; the number of representatives in 1833 is likewise in proportion to the total number of representatives to the Union for that year and in proportion to

of New York followed an opposite path: in 1790, it had ten representatives in Congress; in 1813, twenty-seven; in 1823, thirty-four; in 1833, forty. Ohio had only one representative in 1803; in 1833, the total was nineteen.

It is difficult to imagine a lasting union between two nations, one of whom is poor and weak and the other rich and strong, even if it is proved that the strength and wealth of the one are in no way the cause of the weakness and poverty of the other. The union is even harder to maintain at a time when one party is losing strength and the other is acquiring it.

This rapid and uneven increase of certain states threatens the independence of the others. If New York, with its two million inhabitants and its forty representatives, tries to lay down the law in Congress, perhaps it might succeed. But even when the most powerful states did not seek to oppress the weaker ones, the danger would still exist for it lies as much in the possibility of such an event as in the event itself.

The weak rarely trust the justice and reasonableness of the strong. States growing at a slower pace than the others look upon those favored by fortune, therefore, with envy and distrust. That is the source of this profound disquiet and vague anxiety one can observe in one part of the Union in contrast to the prosperity and confidence which prevails in the other. In my opinion, the hostile attitude of the South has no other reason for it.

Of all Americans, those in the South ought to be the most attached to the Union for they would suffer most from being abandoned to themselves; yet, they are the only people threaten-

---

the numbers of its population as it has grown over these ten years. The ratio of the new number of representatives of Virginia to the old will, therefore, be in proportion, on the one hand, to the total number of new representatives compared with the old and, on the other hand, to the growth of population in Virginia, compared with that of the Union. Thus, for the number of representatives from Virginia to remain static, all that needs happen is that the relationship between the proportion of growth of the small region to that of the large be in inverse proportion to the ratio of the total new number of representatives to the old. If the increase of the population of Virginia be to that of the whole Union in a smaller ratio than the new number of Union representatives to the old, the number of representatives for Virginia will be smaller.

ing to break the federal tie. How is that so? The answer is easy: the South, which has supplied four Presidents,[75] which realizes today that federal power is slipping away, which sees an annual decrease in the number of its representatives in Congress and an increase in those from the North and West, is peopled by ardent and angry men whose frustration and restlessness are evident. It turns its despondent gaze upon itself and questions the past, constantly wondering whether it is being oppressed.

If it happens to notice that a Union law is clearly not in its favor, it cries out against this abuse of power; it vigorously remonstrates and, if its voice is not heard, it becomes indignant and threatens to withdraw from an association whose burdens it bears without enjoying the profits.

In 1832, the inhabitants of Carolina declared: "The tariff laws enrich the North and ruin the South for, without them, how could it be imagined that the North, with its inhospitable climate and arid soil, could constantly increase its wealth and power while the South, which is like the garden of America, rapidly falls into decline?"[76]

If the changes I have mentioned came about gradually, allowing each generation at least the time to pass away with the order of things it had witnessed, the danger would be reduced but there is something precipitous, one might almost say revolutionary, in the progress of American society. The same citizen may have seen his state striding out at the head of the Union only to see it lose its power in the federal assemblies. An Anglo-American republic may grow up as fast as a man, passing from birth to infancy to maturity in the space of thirty years.

However, one should not fancy that those states whose power diminishes are also losing population or fading away; their prosperity does not halt; they grow even faster than any European kingdom.[77] But they entertain the impression that they are

75. Washington, Jefferson, Madison, and Monroe.
76. See the report of its committee to the convention which proclaimed nullification in South Carolina.
77. The population of a region indubitably comprises the first element of its wealth. During the same period of 1820 to 1832, when Virginia lost two representatives in Congress, its population grew by 13.7 per cent; that of

growing poor since they are not getting as rich as their neighbors and thus believe that their power is declining because they suddenly come into collision with a power greater than their own.[78] Thus, their feelings and passions are wounded more than their interests. But is that not enough to place the confederation under threat? If, from the beginning of the world, nations and kings had had only their true interests in view, war between men would scarcely be known.

Thus, the greatest danger threatening the United States stems from this very prosperity, which tends to create in several of the confederate states the overexcitement that goes with a rapid increase in wealth and, in other states, the envy, distrust, and sorrow which frequently follow the loss of wealth.

Americans delight at the sight of this extraordinary change; it is my opinion that they should regard it with sorrow and dread. Whatever they do, the Americans of the United States will turn into one of the greatest nations of the world; their offshoots will cover almost all North America; the continent they inhabit is their kingdom and will not slip away from their grasp. Who, then, is forcing them to take possession of it this very day? One day wealth, power, and glory cannot fail to be theirs and they rush headlong toward this immense fortune as if only one moment remained for them to lay hands on it.

I think I have proved that the existence of the present-day confederation depends entirely upon the agreement of all the confederate states in wishing to remain in the Union. Starting from that premise, I have investigated the reasons which might lead different states to the desire to separate. But the Union has two ways of perishing: one of the confederated states might

---

the Carolinas by 15 per cent, and that of Georgia by 51.5 per cent. (See *American Almanac*, 1832, p. 162.) Now Russia, which has the fastest growing population of the European countries, has a population increase of only 9.5 per cent in ten years, France at the rate of 7 per cent, and Europe all together at a rate of 4.7 per cent (see Malte-Brun, vol. 6, p. 95).

78. It must be admitted, however, that the depreciation in tobacco prices which has taken place over the last fifty years has considerably reduced the affluence of the southern planters; but this fact is independent of what the men from the North would have wished, just as it is of their own wishes.

wish to withdraw from the contract and thus smash the common tie; most of the observations I have made previously apply to this eventuality. The federal government might gradually lose its power as a result of a coordinated policy on the part of the united republics to reclaim the use of their independence. The central authority, stripped of all its powers one by one and reduced to impotence through an unspoken agreement, would become incompetent to fulfill its purpose and the second Union, like the first, would die of a sort of senile debility.

Furthermore, the gradual weakening of the federal ties, leading to the final annulment of the Union, is a distinct event which may introduce many other less extreme consequences before that final result. The confederation would still exist although the weakness of its government might already be reducing the nation to powerlessness, causing internal anarchy and the slowing down of the country's general prosperity.

After researching what may lead Anglo-Americans to split up, it is, therefore, important to examine, if the Union remains intact, whether their government broadens or narrows its sphere of action and whether it becomes more energetic or more enfeebled.

Americans are clearly preoccupied by a considerable fear. They have realized that in most nations of the world the exercise of the rights of sovereignty tends to be concentrated in the hands of a few people and they are apprehensive at the prospect of such a thing eventually happening with them. Politicians themselves experience these terrors or at least pretend to do so, for, in America, centralization is not at all popular and there is no better way of flattering the majority than by rising up against the so-called encroachments of central government. Americans refuse to see that, in countries where this alarming centralizing tendency appears, there is one single nation, whereas the Union is one confederation of different peoples, a fact which is enough to upset all prophecies based upon this parallel.

I confess I regard as wholly imaginary these fears entertained by a great number of Americans. Far from joining in their fears that sovereignty will be consolidated in the hands of the Union, I think that the federal government is quite clearly weakening.

To prove my point, I shall not refer back to distant events but to those I have myself witnessed or which have occurred in our time.

On examining closely what is happening in the United States, we soon discover two opposing tendencies, like two currents, flowing in the same channel in opposite directions.

During the forty-five years of the Union's existence, time has disproved a host of regional prejudices which at the beginning were hostile to its authority. The feeling of patriotism which bound every American to his state has become less exclusive. The various parts of the Union have drawn closer through better acquaintanceship. The postal service, that great link between minds, now penetrates to the very heart of the backwoods[79] and steamboats forge daily connections between all points along the coast. Trade flows up and down the rivers of the interior with unparalleled speed.[80] To these facilities of nature and human skill are joined the restlessness of desires, mental anxiety, the craving for wealth which constantly drive Americans from their homes and put them in touch with a great number of their fellow citizens. They cross the country in every direction to call on all populations of the land. There is no region of France where the inhabitants know each other as well as the thirteen million men spread over the territory of the United States.

As they mingle together, Americans become more integrated; differences between them of climate, origins, and institutions grow fewer. They all increasingly resemble a common type. Every year, thousands of men emigrating from the North spread into every region of the Union, carrying with them beliefs, opinions, customs, and, since their education is superior to that

79. In 1832, the district of Michigan, which had only 31,639 inhabitants and was still a wilderness which had barely been cleared, developed more than 940 miles of mail routes. The almost entirely untamed territory of Arkansas had already been covered by 1,938 miles of mail routes. See *The Report of the Postmaster General*, 30 November 1833. The carriage of newspapers alone throughout the Union brought in $254,796 annually.

80. Over the course of ten years, from 1821 to 1831, 271 steamboats were launched on the rivers which flow through the valley of the Mississippi.

    In 1829, there were 256 steamboats in the United States. See *Legislative Documents*, no. 140, p. 274.

of the people they will live among, they soon take over public affairs and modify society to their advantage. This constant emigration from the North to the South is peculiarly favorable to the fusion of all regional characters into a single national character. So, civilization in the North seems destined to become the norm by which all the rest must one day be governed.

With the progress of American industry comes the tightening of commercial ties binding the confederated states and the Union, which started as only a concept of their minds, becomes part of their habits. The march of time has blown away a host of imagined terrors which tormented men's minds in 1789. Federal authority has not become oppressive; it has not destroyed state independence; it does not lead the confederate states toward monarchy; the inception of the Union has not caused small states to become dependent upon larger ones. The confederation has continued to expand its population, its wealth, and its power.

I am, therefore, convinced that, at present, Americans experience fewer natural difficulties in remaining united than they encountered in 1789; the Union has fewer enemies than at that time.

Nevertheless, a careful study of United States history over the last forty-five years readily convinces us that federal power is diminishing.

The reasons for this phenomenon are not difficult to explain.

When the constitution of 1789 was promulgated, anarchy was wreaking havoc; the Union which followed this disorderly time aroused much hatred and fear but had enthusiastic supporters because it answered a deeply felt need. Although under greater threat in those days than now, federal authority rapidly reached the height of its powers, as usually happens to a government which triumphs after bracing its strength for the struggle. At that time, the interpretation of the constitution seemed to broaden rather than restrict federal sovereignty and the Union appeared in several respects as one single undivided nation, controlled in both home and foreign policy by one single government.

But to reach this position the nation had in a sense risen above itself.

The constitution had not destroyed the separate identity of the states yet all bodies of every sort harbor a secret instinct which leads them to independence. This instinct is still more pronounced in a country like America in which every village is a kind of republic, used to self-government.

The states, therefore, had to make a special effort to submit to federal dominance from their side and all their efforts, crowned or not with great success, necessarily fade along with the original reason for them.

As the federal government strengthened its authority, America took its place among nations, peace reappeared along its frontiers, and public credit was restored; a settled order followed a period of confusion, one which allowed individual enterprise to pursue its natural course and to develop in freedom.

This very prosperity began to obscure the reasons which produced it; once the danger had passed, Americans no longer summoned up the energy and patriotism which had helped to ward it off. No sooner were they freed from the fears which preoccupied them than they made an easy return to their usual habits and did not resist a retreat into their accustomed inclinations. As soon as strong government no longer appeared vital, they began to see it as troublesome. Everything prospered under the Union and no one tried to break free of it but people wished to reduce the effect of the government which represented them. In general, their desire to be in the Union remained but in each particular case the tendency to independence asserted itself. As the days went by the principle of confederation was readily acknowledged and more rarely applied; thus the federal government, by creating order and peace, brought about its own decline.

As soon as this attitude of mind began to be obvious, the party machine, which feeds off the people's passions, started to exploit it to its advantage.

From then on, the position of the federal government became very critical; its opponents had the public on their side and, by promising to weaken its influence, they gained the right to control it.

From this period, whenever the Union government went into

the ring against the states, it almost always had to retreat. Whenever the terms of the federal constitution have needed interpreting, this interpretation has more often than not emerged as unfavorable to the Union and supportive of the states.

The Constitution invested the federal government with the duty of looking after national interests. It was thought that the Constitution was responsible for carrying out or encouraging those great "internal improvements," such as canals, whose purpose was to increase the wealth of the whole Union.

The states were scared by the idea that an authority other than their own should have such jurisdiction over an area of their territory. They feared lest the central power should acquire by this means a formidable patronage in their midst and exercise an influence which they wished to reserve exclusively for their own agents.

The Democratic Party, which has always opposed any extension to federal power, raised its voice to accuse Congress of overstepping its rights and the head of state of ambition. The central government, intimidated by this outcry, in the end acknowledged its mistake and confined its activity precisely to the area prescribed.

The Constitution grants the Union the privilege of treating with foreign nations. The Union had, generally speaking, regarded the Indian tribes living along the borders of its territory in this light. As long as these savages consented to withdraw before the encroachments of civilization, the federal law was not challenged; but as soon as an Indian tribe attempted to settle on a particular spot, the surrounding states claimed a right of ownership over this land and a right of sovereignty over the men living there. The central government hastily recognized both rights and delivered the Indians as subjects to the legislative tyranny of the states, after treating with them previously as independent peoples.[81]

Several of the states along the Atlantic seaboard spread

81. See in the *Legislative Documents* which I have already quoted, in the chapter on Indians, the letter of the President of the United States to the Cherokees, his correspondence on this subject with his agents and his messages to Congress.

endlessly westwards into the wild regions where Europeans had not before made their way. Those whose boundaries were irrevocably settled viewed with an envious eye the unbounded future open to their neighbors who, in a spirit of conciliation and to help the Union function smoothly, agreed to set limits to their own territory and gave all the land beyond that up to the Union.[82]

Since that time, the federal government has become the owner of all the uncultivated land outside the thirteen states of the original confederation. It takes charge of dividing it up for sale and the revenue reverts exclusively to the Union treasury. Helped by this income, the federal government purchases land from the Indians, opens up roads through these new districts and does all within its power to facilitate the rapid development of society.

Now, it has happened in the course of time that new states have been formed in those same wild areas formerly ceded by the Atlantic states. Congress still sells, on behalf of the nation as a whole, the uncultivated land which these states still have within their boundaries. But, at the present time, the latter are claiming that, once they have their own constitution, they should have the exclusive right to convert the produce of these sales to their own use. As these claims became increasingly threatening, Congress felt it ought to remove from the Union some of the privileges it had enjoyed up to that point and, at the end of 1832, it passed a law by the terms of which, without giving the new republics of the West ownership of their uncultivated lands, nevertheless converted the greater part of the revenue derived from the sale to their sole benefit.[83]

A journey through the United States is enough for anyone to appreciate the advantages which the country derives from the bank. These advantages are of several kinds but one above all

82. The first act of cession was made by the state of New York in 1780; Virginia, Massachusetts, Connecticut, South Carolina, and North Carolina followed this example at different times; Georgia came after that; its act of cession was not wound up until 1802.

83. It is true that the President refused to sanction this law but he did accept the principle. See *Message of December 8 1833*.

impresses the foreign observer: the notes of the United States Bank are of the same value on the furthest frontiers as they are in Philadelphia, where the seat of operations resides.[84]

The United States Bank is, however, the object of considerable loathing. Its directors have declared their opposition to the President and are accused, not improbably, of abusing their influence to thwart his election. Thus, the President attacks, with all the fire of a personal animosity, the institution represented by these people. What has encouraged the President to pursue his revenge in this way is the feeling he has that he is supported by the secret instincts of the majority.

The Bank constitutes the major financial link of the Union as Congress is the major legislative link; the passions which tend to make the states independent of central government also contribute to the downfall of the Bank.

The United States Bank always holds in its hands a great number of notes belonging to the regional banks; any day it could force the latter to repay these notes in cash whereas the Union Bank does not need to fear a similar danger. The size of its available resources allows it to face any demands. The regional banks, whose very existence is threatened in this way, are obliged to exercise restraint and to keep the number of notes in circulation proportionate to their capital assets. Regional banks tolerate this cautious control with impatience. The newspapers they have bought and the President, prompted to be their spokesman through his self-interest, attack the Bank, therefore, with a kind of frenzy. They rouse local passions and the blind democratic instinct of the country against the Bank. According to them, the directors of the Bank form a permanent aristocratic body whose influence cannot fail to be felt in government and is bound sooner or later to alter the principles of equality upon which American society rests.

The Bank's struggle against its opponents is merely one

84. The current Bank of the United States was established in 1816 with a
     capital of $35,000,000 (185,500,000 francs): its franchise expires in 1836.
     Last year, Congress passed a law to renew it but the President refused to
     sanction this. The struggle is being fought with extreme violence on either
     side and it is easy to foresee the imminent fall of the Bank.

incident in the greater struggle the regions of America are waging against the central government or the spirit of independence and democracy is waging against that of hierarchy and subordination. I do not claim that the opponents of the United States Bank are exactly the same individuals who attack the federal government in other matters, but I do say that these attacks against the United States Bank are the result of the same instincts which militate against the federal government and that the large number of enemies of the former is a vexing symptom of the weakening of the latter.

But the Union never showed its weakness more clearly than in the celebrated tariff question.[85]

The French revolutionary wars and the war of 1812 had brought into being factories in the North of the Union, by blocking the free communication between America and Europe. When peace had reopened the route to the New World for European products, the Americans thought fit to create a customs system, both to protect their burgeoning industry and to pay the amount of debt inflicted on them by the war.

The southern states, having no factories to foster and having no skills outside agriculture, soon complained about this measure.

I do not intend examining at this juncture the real or imaginary elements in their complaints, I simply point up the facts.

From 1820, South Carolina declared a petition to Congress that the tariff law was *unconstitutional*, *oppressive*, and *unjust*. Since then, Georgia, Virginia, North Carolina, Alabama, and Mississippi protested more or less vigorously on the same theme.

Far from taking note of these mutterings, Congress, in 1824 and 1828, again raised the tariff duties and asserted the principle afresh.

Then a famous doctrine was proclaimed or rather revived in the South, which took the name of *nullification*.

I have shown in its proper place that the aim of the federal constitution was not to create a league but a national govern-

85. See principally, for the details of this affair, the *Legislative Documents*, 22nd Congress, 2nd session, no. 30.

ment. In all instances anticipated by their Constitution, the Americans of the United States form one and the same nation. In all these issues the will of the nation is expressed, as in all constitutional nations, through a majority. Once this majority has pronounced, the duty of the minority lies in obedience.

Such is the legal doctrine and the only one in agreement with the text of the Constitution and the known intention of its founders.

The *nullifiers* of the South claimed, on the contrary, that the Americans did not intend to meld into one and the same nation when they united but that they simply aimed at forming a league of independent peoples. It ensues that each state has preserved its entire sovereignty, if not in fact at least in principle and has the right to interpret the laws of Congress as well as to suspend the implementation of those which seem hostile to its constitution or to justice within its borders.

The whole doctrine of nullification is summed up in a sentence uttered in 1833 before the United States Senate by Mr Calhoun,[f] the acknowledged leader of the southern nullifiers, who said: "The Constitution is a contract in which the states appear as sovereigns. Now, every time a contract is drawn up between parties with no common arbitrator, each of them retains the right to judge the scope of its obligation by itself."

It is clear that such a doctrine destroys the federal tie in principle and restores anarchy in fact, from which the 1789 Constitution had delivered Americans.

When South Carolina realized that Congress turned a deaf ear to its complaints, it threatened to apply the doctrine of nullification to the federal tariff law. Congress persisted in its system and finally the storm broke.

In the course of 1832, the people of South Carolina[86] appointed a national convention to advise on the extraordinary measures to be taken; on 24 November of the same year, this convention published, in the form of a decree, an act that

86. That is to say, a majority of the people; for the opposing party, called the *Union Party*, always could count on the support of a very strong and very active minority. Carolina may have about 47,000 voters—30,000 were in favor of nullification and 17,000 were opposed to it.

nullified the federal tariff law, prohibited the payment of dues contained in it and forbade the recognition of any appeal which might be made to the federal courts.[87] This decree was not to come into force until the following February and South Carolina indicated that, if Congress modified the tariff before that date, it might agree not to pursue its threats further. Later, a vague and indefinite desire was expressed to submit the question to an extraordinary assembly of all the confederated states.

Meanwhile, South Carolina armed its militia and prepared for war.

What did Congress do? Congress, which had not heeded the requests of its subjects, paid attention to the complaints the moment it saw weapons in their hands.[88] It passed a law[89] by which the tariff dues were to be reduced in stages over ten years until they had been brought down, in line with government requirements. Thus, Congress completely abandoned the principle of the tariff. It substituted a purely fiscal measure in place of a law designed to protect industry.[90] To conceal its defeat,

87. This decree was preceded by a report from a committee charged with its preparation: this report contained the explanation and the aim of the law. On page 34 we read: "When the rights reserved to the several states are deliberately invaded, it is their right and their duty to 'interpose for the purpose of arresting the progress of the evil of usurpation, and to maintain, within their respective limits, the authorities and privileges belonging to them as *independent sovereignties*.' If the several states do not possess this right, it is vain that they claim to be sovereign [. . .]. South Carolina claims to be a sovereign state. She recognizes no tribunal upon earth as above her authority. It is true, she has entered into a solemn compact of Union with other sovereign states, but she claims, and will exercise the right to determine the extent of her obligations under that compact, nor will she consent that any other power shall exercise the right of judgment for her. And when that compact is violated by her co-states, or by the government which they have created, she asserts her unquestionable right to judge by the infractions, as well as of the mode and measure of redress."

88. What finally determined Congress to take this step was a proposal from the powerful state of Virginia whose legislature offered to act as a mediator between the Union and South Carolina. Up until then the latter state had seemed entirely abandoned, even by those states who had made the same demands as she had.

89. Law of 2 March 1833.

90. This law was proposed by Mr Clay and passed in four days through both houses of Congress and with a huge majority.

the federal government had recourse to an expedient much employed by weak governments: having yielded on substance, it remained inflexible on principles. As Congress was altering the tariff legislation, it passed another law by which the President was endowed with an extraordinary power to overcome by force a resistance which was no longer to be feared.

South Carolina did not even leave the Union this feeble appearance of victory; the same national convention which had nullified the federal tariff law met once more and accepted the concession offered but simultaneously it declared its intention to persevere even more forcefully in the nullification doctrine. To prove this, it annulled the law which conferred extraordinary powers on the President, even though certainly no use would be made of it.

Almost all the events I have just mentioned took place during General Jackson's presidency. It cannot be denied that the latter, in this tariff affair, handled the Union rights with skill and energy. However, I believe that the very conduct of the man representing the federal authority must be counted among the dangers now facing that authority.

Some Europeans have formed an opinion of General Jackson's possible influence over his country's affairs which appears much exaggerated to those who have seen events at close hand.

I have heard that General Jackson has won battles, that he was a man of energy, prone to the use of force by character and habit, covetous of power, and tyrannical by inclination. All that may be true but the inferences to be drawn from these truths are very wide of the mark.

General Jackson is supposed to be working for the institution of a dictatorship in the United States, the introduction of a military regime and the extension of central power, which would be such a threat to regional liberties. In America, the time for such undertakings and the age of such men have not yet come: if General Jackson had wished for such domination, he would undoubtedly have forfeited his political position and jeopardized his life. So, he has not been rash enough to attempt it.

Far from wishing to extend federal power, the present President belongs to the opposite party which aims to restrict this

power to the clearest and most precise letter of the Constitution
and which will never allow any interpretation to be favorable
to the Union government. Far from appearing as the champion
of centralization, General Jackson is the spokesman of regional
jealousies; people's passion for *decentralization* (if I may put it
so) carried him to sovereign power. By constantly flattering
these passions, he maintains his position and his popularity.
General Jackson is the slave of the majority: he follows its every
wish, desire, half-revealed instincts, or rather he guesses what it
wants and takes a lead himself.

Whenever there is a dispute between state and Union government, it is rare for the President not to be the first to cast doubts
upon his rights; he almost always anticipates the legislature and
when it is a case of interpreting the scope of federal power, he
stands as it were against himself; he tries to shrink, to hide away,
and melt into the background. It is not that he is naturally weak
or hostile to the Union; once the majority had pronounced
against the claims of the southern nullifiers, he took a lead,
clearly and energetically formulating the Union's doctrines and
was the first to call for force. General Jackson, if I may use a
comparison borrowed from the vocabulary of American parties,
seems to me *federal* by inclination and *republican* by calculation.

After bowing thus before the majority in order to win its
support, General Jackson rises up; he then strides out to achieve
the objectives pursued by the majority or those that do not
arouse its jealousy and overturns all the obstacles in its path.
Sustained by a strength of support not enjoyed by his predecessors, he tramples his personal enemies underfoot, wherever
he comes across them, with an ease impossible for any previous
President to have contemplated. He assumes responsibility for
measures that no one before him would have ventured to take;
sometimes he even treats national representatives with an almost
insulting disdain. He refuses to sanction laws of Congress and
often fails to answer that important body. He is a favorite
who sometimes treats his master roughly. So General Jackson's
power is constantly increasing but that of the President is growing less. In his hands, the federal government is strong but he
will hand it over to his successor in a weakened state.

Either I am mistaken or the federal government of the United States is daily losing its power; it is gradually withdrawing from public affairs and is increasingly narrowing its sphere of action. Being naturally weak, it is giving up even the appearance of strength. On the other hand, I think I have seen a more lively feeling of independence and a more evident affection for regional government developing in the individual states of the Union.

People want the Union, but one reduced to a shadow; they want it to be strong in certain instances and weak in all others; they intend it to be able to unite in its hands the forces of the nation and all the country's resources in time of war while ceasing to exist, so to speak, in times of peace, as if this alternation between enfeeblement and vigor were a natural possibility.

At present, I see nothing to stop this general impulse of public opinion; the reasons for its appearance still operate in the same direction. It will, therefore, continue and predictably the government of the Union will weaken daily, barring some extraordinary circumstance.

However, it is my belief that the day is still far off when the federal authority somehow loses power of its own accord, because it has become incapable of protecting its own existence or of bringing peace to the country. The Union is part of custom and has people's affection; its achievements are obvious and its advantages evident. If people perceive that the weakness of the federal government is damaging the existence of the Union, I am quite convinced that a reaction in favor of strengthening it will take place.

The United States government, of all federal governments established up to the present time, is the one most naturally fitted to act. Provided that it is not attacked in some indirect way by the interpretation of its laws and provided that there is no alteration of its basic structure, a shift of opinion, some internal crisis or a war could suddenly restore the strength it requires.

The point I wish to make is simply this: many people in our midst think that there is a tide of American opinion which favors the centralization of power in the hands of the President and of Congress. I am claiming that a contrary tendency may be observed. Far from thinking that a maturing federal government is gaining strength and is threatening the sovereignty of the states, I hold that it is growing weaker by the day and that only Union sovereignty is under threat. Such is the current situation. What will the ultimate result of this tendency be and what events might halt, slow down, or accelerate the impulse I have described? The answer is hidden in the future and I do not claim the ability to lift the veil.

REPUBLICAN INSTITUTIONS IN THE UNITED STATES AND THEIR CHANCES OF SURVIVAL

The Union is only an accident—Republican institutions have more chance of lasting—A republic is at present the natural state for Anglo-Americans—Why this is so—To destroy it would require a simultaneous alteration of all laws and customs—Difficulties for Americans to create an aristocracy.

The dismemberment of the Union, bringing with it war between the present-day confederated states, standing armies, dictatorship, and taxes, might in the long run damage the fate of republican institutions.

However, the fate of the republic should not be confused with that of the Union.

The Union is an accident which will last only as long as circumstances support it but a republic seems to me the natural state for Americans; only the unremitting influence of hostile causes acting constantly in the same direction might replace it with a monarchy.

The Union's principal guarantee of existence is the law which created it. A single revolution, a change in public opinion, might shatter it forever. The republic has deeper roots.

What is meant by a republic in the United States is the slow and quiet action of society upon itself. It is an orderly state founded in reality upon the enlightened will of the nation. It is a conciliatory government where resolutions ripen over time, are discussed slowly and executed only when fully matured.

Republicans in the United States value customs, respect beliefs, recognize rights. They hold the view that a nation must be moral, religious, and moderate in proportion as it is free. What is called a republic in the United States is the quiet rule of the majority, which is the communal source of power once it has had the time to acknowledge and confirm its existence. But the majority is not itself all-powerful. Above it, in the world of moral issues, lie humanity, justice, and reason; in the world of politics lie rights acquired. The majority acknowledges both these limits and, if it ever does exceed them, it is because, like any individual, it has its passions and, like any person, it can act badly even though it knows what is good.

But we Europeans have made some odd discoveries.

According to some of us, a republic is not the reign of the majority as has been supposed up until now; it is the reign of those who are the strenuous supporters of the majority. In governments of this type, it is not the people who are in control but those who know what is best for the people—a fortunate distinction which allows rulers to act in the name of the nation without consulting them and to claim its gratitude while trampling it underfoot. Republican government is, moreover, the only one whose right to do everything has to be acknowledged and which is able to scorn everything which men have hitherto respected from the loftiest of moral laws down to the commonplace rules of accepted opinion.

It had been thought, until our time, that tyranny was a hateful thing in whatever shape or form. But at the present time, we have discovered that there are legitimate tyrannies and holy injustices as long as they are exercised in the people's name.

The Americans' conception of a republic remarkably eases their adoption of this form of government and guarantees its permanence. In America, although the practice of republican government is often defective, at least the theory is good and in the end the nation's acts always conform to it.

At the outset, it was impossible to establish a centralized administration in America and that still remains the case. Men are scattered over too large an area and separated by too many natural obstacles for a single man to attempt to control the details of their lives. America is, therefore, pre-eminently the land of regional and township government.

To this cause, whose influence was felt equally by all the Europeans of the New World, the Anglo-Americans added several more which were peculiar to themselves.

When the American colonies in the North were established, municipal freedom had already permeated the laws as well as the customs of the English and the immigrants adopted it, not only as a necessity but as an advantage they knew how to value.

Moreover, we have seen how the colonies were founded. Each province and, so to speak, every district was inhabited by men either unknown to each other or who had associated with others for very different purposes.

From the beginning, the English in the United States found themselves, therefore, divided into a large number of small distinct social groups, which were not attached to a common center and each of these small social groups had to take charge of their own business since there was no obvious central authority which was naturally or easily bound and able to provide for them.

Thus, the nature of the country, the very manner of the founding of the colonies and the habits of the first immigrants all combined to develop township and provincial liberties to an extraordinary degree.

In the United States, the main body of the country's institutions is essentially republican; in order to destroy permanently those laws which form the basis of the republic, all the laws together would somehow have to be abolished.

If a party, at the present time, were to undertake to found a monarchy in the United States, it would be in an even more difficult position than a French party wishing to proclaim a republic. The Crown would not find a system of legislation prepared in advance for it and then it would be abundantly clear that it would be a monarchy surrounded by republican institutions.

It would be equally difficult for the principle of monarchy to sink into American customs.

In the United States, the doctrine of the sovereignty of the people is no isolated concept unconnected either to people's habits or to the mass of prevailing ideas; on the contrary, it can be viewed as the final link in a chain of opinions which binds the whole Anglo-American world. Providence has granted to all conditions of men a measure of reason necessary for them to have autonomy in the things which concern them alone. Such is the grand maxim upon which rests civil and political society in the United States: the father of a family applies it to his children, the master to his servants, the township to its citizens, a province to its townships, the state to its provinces, the Union to the states. When extended to the nation, it becomes the doctrine of the sovereignty of the people.

Thus, in the United States, the principle underlying the republic is the same rule which governs most human actions. Therefore, the republic, if I may put it so, permeates ideas, opinions, and all American customs at the same time as it underpins their laws; and Americans would have to change themselves almost entirely in order to change these laws. In the United States, even the religion of most people is republican too; it subjects the truths of the next world to the rationality of the individual, just as politics cedes to everyone the care of this world's concerns and religion grants each man the free choice of which path he might take to heaven, just as the law recognizes each citizen's right to choose his own government.

Clearly, only a lengthy series of events in the same direction could substitute for this mass of laws, opinions, and customs an opposite mass of customs, opinions and laws.

If republican principles have to perish in America, they will concede defeat only after a long laborious social process, frequently halted and as often resumed; they will apparently revive several times and will vanish beyond recall only when an entirely new people has replaced the one which currently exists. Now, nothing at all would have us forecast such a revolution, nor is there any sign of its approach.

What most strikes the visitor to the United States is the kind of tumultuous agitation at the heart of which we find political society. Laws constantly change and, at first sight, it seems inevitable that a nation so uncertain about its intentions will soon replace its present form of government by an entirely new one. Such fears are hasty. When it comes to political institutions, one should not confuse two kinds of instability: one concerns changes in secondary laws and this can prevail for a long time in a settled society; the other constantly undermines the very foundations of the constitution and attacks the principles which uphold the laws. This latter is always a prelude to upheavals and revolutions and a nation suffering from it is in a state of violent transition. Experience reveals that both these kinds of legislative instability have no necessary connection for they have been seen occurring together and separately according to times and places. The first is present in the United States but not the second. Americans frequently change their laws but the basis of the constitution is respected.

Nowadays, the republican principle reigns in America as did the principle of monarchy in the France of Louis XIV. The French of that time were not merely friends of the monarchy but neither could they imagine anything in its place; their acceptance of it resembled their acknowledgement of the sun's course and the changes of the seasons. With them, royal power had neither advocates nor opponents.

Thus it is that a republic exists in America without a contest, without opposition, without argument, tacitly accepted like a *consensus universalis*.

However, I think that with these frequent changes to administrative procedures, the inhabitants of the United States are compromising the future of republican government.

There is a fear that men, endlessly frustrated in their plans by the continuous changes in the law, will end up by regarding the republic as an inconvenient way of living in society; the ill effects of this instability of secondary laws would then put into question laws more fundamental and would indirectly lead to a revolution; but such a time is still a good way off.

What can be foreseen now is that, if Americans were to deviate from a republic, they would speedily arrive at despotism without pausing for very long in monarchy. Montesquieu stated that nothing was more absolute than the authority of a prince who follows a republic, since those ill-defined powers which had been fearlessly allocated to an elected magistrate then pass into the hands of an hereditary head of state. This is true in general but applies more particularly to a democratic republic. In the United States, magistrates are not elected by a special group of citizens but by the majority of the nation; they immediately represent the passions of the crowd and depend entirely upon its wishes; as a result, they inspire neither dislike nor fear: thus, I have pointed out how little care has been taken to restrict their power of action and how great a share of power has been left to their discretion. This state of affairs has forged habits which will survive it. The American magistrate would retain his undefined power while ceasing to be accountable and it is impossible to say where tyranny would then end.

Some among us expect to see an aristocracy appear in America and predict already the exact period when it must seize power.

I have said once before and I say again that the current trend in American society seems to me increasingly toward democracy.

However, I do not deny that one day the Americans may restrict the sphere of political rights, but I cannot believe that they will ever entrust exclusive control to one particular class of citizens or, in other words, found an aristocracy.

An aristocratic body is composed of a certain number of citizens who, while being at a level quite close to the crowd, nevertheless rise permanently above it—a body within reach, yet beyond attack; one with which people are in daily contact and yet with which they can never combine.

It is impossible to imagine anything more contrary to nature or to the inner feelings of the human heart than subjection of this kind: left to themselves, men will always prefer the arbitrary power of a king to the well-ordered administration of a nobility.

An aristocracy needs, if it is to last, to enshrine the principle of inequality, legalized in advance and introduced into the family as well as into society—things which are all so violently repellent to natural equality that men are forced to give them up only by compulsion.

Since the first human societies, I do not think that one single example can be cited of a nation which, left to its own devices and by its own exertions, has ever created an aristocracy within its boundaries: all the aristocracies of the Middle Ages are born of conquest. The conqueror was a nobleman, the conquered was a serf. Then, force imposed a state of inequality which, once introduced into customs, established itself and passed naturally into law.

Societies have existed which, as a result of events preceding their beginnings, were, so to speak, aristocratic from birth and which, therefore, drifted toward democracy with the passing of each century. Such was the fate of the Romans and that of the barbarian regimes which followed them. But a nation which started from a civilized and democratic state, gradually veering toward an inequality of social conditions, ending up by establishing inviolable privileges and exclusive groups, that would be a novelty in the world.

Nothing indicates that America is destined to be the first to provide such a sight.

A FEW REFLECTIONS ON THE REASONS FOR THE COMMERCIAL GREATNESS OF THE UNITED STATES

Nature calls the Americans to be a great seagoing nation— Extent of their coasts—Depth of their harbors—Size of their rivers—However, the commercial superiority of Anglo-Americans must be accounted for by intellectual and moral reasons much more than by physical ones—Reason for this opinion—Future of Anglo-Americans as a trading nation—The downfall of the Union would not arrest the surge of maritime trade of the people composing it— Why—Anglo-Americans are naturally called to serve the needs of the inhabitants of South America—They will become, like the English, the agents for a great area of the world.

From the Bay of Fundy to the Sabine River in the Gulf of Mexico, the coast of the United States stretches along a length of about two thousand miles.

These shores form a single uninterrupted line, all subject to the same government.

No nation in the world can offer deeper, more extensive, or secure harbors for shipping than America.

The inhabitants of the United States form a great, civilized nation situated by good fortune amid wildernesses, three thousand miles from the main focus of civilization. Hence, America stands in daily need of Europe. In time, Americans will doubtless succeed in manufacturing or growing at home most of the things they need but never will the two continents manage to live entirely independently of each other: too many natural links exist between their needs, ideas, habits, and customs.

The Union produces things which have become vital to us and which our soil absolutely refuses to cultivate or provides only at great expense. The Americans consume only a very small part of these products; they sell us the rest.

Europe is, therefore, America's marketplace, as America is Europe's marketplace, and sea trade is as vital to the inhabitants of the United States to bring their raw materials to our ports as to bring our manufactured goods to them.

The United States had either to furnish a great deal of business to the other seafaring nations, if they chose to abandon trade themselves, as the Spanish of Mexico have done so far, or they had to become one of the foremost maritime powers on earth: this choice was unavoidable.

Anglo-Americans have, throughout history, shown a definite liking for the sea. When they broke commercial ties binding them to England, their independence gave a new and powerful stimulus to their seafaring genius. Since that time, the number of Union ships has increased at almost as swift a rate as the number of its inhabitants. Today, it is the Americans themselves who carry nine-tenths of European produce to their shores.[91] It is the Americans too who transport three quarters of the exports from the New World[92] to European consumers.

91. The total value of imports for the year ending 30 September 1832 was $101,129,266. Imports carried in foreign ships amounted to only $10,731,039, around a tenth.
92. The total value of exports during the same year was $87,176,943; the value exported in foreign vessels was $21,036,183, or about one quarter. (William's *Register*, 1833, p. 398.)

American ships crowd the docks of Le Havre and Liverpool. Only a small number of English or French vessels is found in New York harbor.[93]

Thus, not only does the American trader face competition on his own patch but he can even compete to advantage with foreigners on theirs.

The explanation for this is simple: of all the vessels of the world, those ships from the United States traverse the seas at the cheapest rate. As long as the merchant shipping of the United States retains this advantage over all the others, not only will it keep what it has gained but it will increase its conquests by the day.

It is a difficult problem to know why Americans can navigate more cheaply than other nations; the first temptation is to attribute this superiority to certain physical advantages placed within their grasp by nature but that is not the case.

American ships cost almost as much to build as our own;[94] they are no better built and generally do not last as long.

All American sailors earn more than their European counterparts; the proof lies in the large number of Europeans in the United States merchant navy.

How, then, do Americans sail more cheaply than we do?

I think it would be a mistake to seek the reasons for this superiority in physical advantages; it stems from purely intellectual and moral qualities.

The following comparison will illustrate my meaning.

During the wars of the Revolution, the French introduced

93. During the years 1829, 1830, 1831, ships of a collective tonnage of 3,307,719 entered the ports of the Union. Foreign ships accounted for just 544,571 tons of this total. They were, then, in the ratio of 16 to 100 approximately. (*National Calendar*, 1833, p. 304.)

During the years 1820, 1826 and 1831, English vessels using the ports of London, Liverpool, and Hull had a tonnage of 443,800. Foreign vessels using the same ports during the same years had a tonnage of 159,431. The ratio between them is, therefore, 36 to 100 approximately. (*Companion to the Almanac*, 1834, p. 169.)

In 1832, the ratio of foreign to English ships using the ports of Great Britain was 20 to 100.

94. Raw materials, in general, cost less in America than in Europe, but the cost of labor is much higher.

new tactics into the art of warfare which disturbed the older generals and almost destroyed the most ancient monarchies of Europe. They undertook for the first time to do without a lot of things previously considered indispensable in warfare; they demanded new efforts from their soldiers, which civilized nations had never before asked of theirs; they did everything at the double and had no hesitation in risking men's lives to attain the aim in view.

The French had fewer men and less money than their opponents; they had considerably fewer resources. However, they were constantly victorious until their opponents decided to imitate them.

The Americans have introduced something similar into trade. What the French did for the sake of victory, they are doing for cheaper prices.

The European sailor ventures upon the open seas with caution, setting sail only in suitable weather; if any unexpected accident occurs, he returns to port; at night he furls some of his sails and when he sees the whitening crests of the waves on the approach of land, he slows his speed and takes an observation of the sun.

The American disregards these precautions and braves these dangers. He sets sail even as the storm is still rumbling; by night as by day, he spreads all his sails to the wind; he repairs any storm damage sustained by his ship as he goes along and, when at last he nears the end of his journey, he continues to fly toward the coast as if he could already see the harbor.

The American is often shipwrecked but no other sailor crosses the seas as swiftly as he does. By achieving the same things as any one else in less time, he does so at less expense.

Before reaching the end of a long voyage, the European sailor feels he has to drop anchor at several ports. He loses valuable time looking out for ports of call or waiting for an opportunity of leaving and he pays the daily charge for the right to stay.

The American sailor sets sail from Boston to buy tea in China. He reaches Canton, stays a few days, and then returns. He has circumnavigated the globe in less than two years and has seen land only once. Throughout a voyage of eight or ten months, he has drunk brackish water and lived off salt beef; he has struggled constantly against the sea, illness, and boredom but on his return he is able to sell a pound of tea for a penny less than the English merchant and thus his aim has been achieved.

I cannot better express my thoughts than by saying that Americans endow their way of trading with a kind of heroism.

It will always be very difficult for a European businessman to pursue the same career as his American rival, who, by acting as I have described above, is pursuing not merely a calculation but also is obeying his very nature.

The inhabitants of the United States experience all the needs and desires born of an advanced civilization but they do not come across, as you do in Europe, a social system cleverly organized to satisfy that state of affairs. So they are often forced to obtain the varied objects which their education and personal habits have made necessary by their own efforts. In America, it often happens that the same man plows his field, builds his dwelling, makes his tools, cobbles his shoes, and, with his own hands, weaves the coarse cloth to cover himself. This is bad for the development of craftsmanship but is a powerful influence upon the intelligence of the workman. Nothing tends more to turn a man into a machine or to take any trace of soul from his work than the extreme division of labor. In a country like America, where specialist craftsmen are so rare, it is impossible to insist that anyone taking up a profession should embark upon a long apprenticeship. Consequently, Americans find it very easy to change trades and they tailor their efforts to the needs of the moment. One comes across men who have been by turn lawyers, farmers, businessmen, ministers of the Gospel, doctors. If the American has less skill than the European in each particular craft, there is almost no skill which is entirely foreign to him. His competence is more general and his intelligence operates on a wider front. The inhabitants of the United States are, therefore, never hampered by any axioms of their profession; they avoid all the prejudices of a professional body; they are no more attached to one way of working than to any other; they do not feel more tied to an old than a new method; they have not formed any fixed habits and they can easily evade the influence of foreign habits upon their minds because they are confident that their country is like no other and that their situation is something new in the world.

The Americans dwell in a land of wonders in which everything is in a constant state of motion and every movement seems a step forward. The concept of newness is, therefore, intimately bound up in their minds with that of improvement. Nowhere do they see any limit placed by nature upon man's efforts; in their eyes, whatever does not exist has simply not yet been tried.

This universal activity which prevails in the United States, these frequent reversals of fortune, these unforeseen shifts of public and private wealth, all combine to entrench in men's minds a kind of feverish agitation, which predisposes them to make every possible effort and keeps them, so to speak, above the common level of humanity. For Americans, their whole lives are spent as if in a game of chance, in a time of revolution or a day of battle.

The same causes operate simultaneously on every individual and thus, in the end, give an irresistible impulse to the national character. Choose any American at random and he should be a man of burning desires, full of initiative, enterprising, and, above all, an innovator. In fact, this outlook permeates all his works, enters his political laws, his religious doctrines, his theories of social economy, and his domestic occupations; he carries it everywhere with him, deep in the woods as in the heart of his cities. It is this same outlook which, once applied to maritime trade, allows the American to sail faster and more cheaply than the rest of the world's merchants.

As long as sailors from the United States retain these intellectual advantages and the resulting practical superiority, not only will they continue to provide for the needs of producers and consumers in their own country but they will increasingly tend to become, like the English,[95] the agents for other nations.

95. It must not be thought that English vessels are exclusively used to import foreign products into England or to export English produce to foreign countries; today, the merchant navy of England constitutes a huge enterprise of public transport, ready to serve all the producers of the world and to facilitate communication between all nations. The maritime genius of

This is starting to become a reality before our very eyes. Already we can see American sailors involved as intermediaries in the trade of several European nations;[96] America offers them an even greater future.

The Spanish and Portuguese have founded huge colonies in South America which subsequently have grown into empires. Civil war and despotism are today bringing wholesale destruction to these vast countries. Population expansion is at a standstill and the small number of inhabitants are so absorbed by the cares of self-defense that they hardly feel any need to improve their fortunes.

But it cannot always be like that. Left to its own efforts, Europe managed to pierce the gloom of the Middle Ages; South America is Christian like ourselves, with our laws and customs; it contains all the seeds of civilization which have developed within European nations and their offshoots; South America also had the benefit of our example. Why should it always remain uncivilized?

Clearly this is simply a matter of time: at some more or less distant period, the South Americans will doubtless come to form flourishing and educated nations.

But when the Spanish and Portuguese of South America begin to experience the needs of civilized nations, they will still be a long way from being able to satisfy these wants for themselves; as the youngest children of civilization, they will have to accept the superiority already attained by their elders. They will be farmers long before they are manufacturers and traders; they will need the mediation of foreigners to sell their produce overseas and to obtain in exchange those goods newly felt to be necessities.

One cannot doubt that the North Americans will one day be called upon to supply the needs of South Americans. Nature has positioned them close to each other and has supplied the North Americans with important means of knowing and judging these

---

the Americans allows them to set up an enterprise in competition with that of the English.

96. Part of the trade in the Mediterranean is already carried out by American vessels.

needs in order to forge permanent relations with these countries and gradually to gain control of that market. American merchants could only lose these natural advantages if they were substantially inferior to European traders, whereas in fact they are superior in several respects. The Americans of the United States are already exerting a great moral influence on all the New World nations. Enlightenment emanates from them. All the nations from the same continent are already accustomed to look upon them as the most enlightened, powerful, and rich members of the great American family. Consequently, they constantly turn their gaze toward the Union and seek to copy the peoples dwelling there as far as is within their power. Each day, they draw political doctrines from the United States and borrow their laws.

The Americans of the United States stand in relation to the peoples of South America in precisely the same way as their English forefathers did in relation to the Italians, Spaniards, Portuguese, and all those European nations who receive most consumables from their hands because they are less civilized and less industrialized.

England is now the natural commercial home of almost all the nations who are close by; the American Union is called upon to fulfill the same role in the other hemisphere. Every newly founded or developing nation of the New World comes into being or grows to some degree for the benefit of the Anglo-Americans.

If the Union should ever be dissolved, the surge of trade in the confederated states would doubtless be checked for some time, though less than might be thought. Whatever happens, it is clear that the trading states will stay united. They all share boundaries, exactly the same opinions, interests, and customs; they alone are capable of forming a very great maritime power. Even if the southern states of the Union became independent of the North, they still could not necessarily do without it. I have stated that the South is not a commercial region; there is still no evidence that it must become one. The Americans of the south of the United States will, for a long time, therefore, be forced to rely upon foreigners to export their produce and to carry the things they see as necessary to their needs. Now, of all the go-betweens they might adopt, their northern neighbors are undoubtedly the ones who can offer them the cheapest service. Consequently, they will serve them because cheapness of price is the supreme rule of trade. No sovereign will or national prejudice can struggle for long against cheap prices. No more poisonous hatred can be observed than that which exists between the Americans of the United States and the English. Yet, despite these hostile feelings, the English supply the Americans with most of their manufactured commodities simply because they charge less than other nations. Thus, the growing prosperity of America turns, against Americans' wishes, to the profit of English manufacturing.

Reason suggests and experience proves that no commercial greatness can last unless it is linked to a military power whenever the need arises. The truth of this is as fully understood in the United States as everywhere else. The Americans are already able to inspire respect for their flag; soon they will be able to make it feared.

I am convinced that the fragmentation of the Union, far from reducing American naval strength, would tend strongly to increase it. At present, the trading states of the Union are linked with others who do not trade and the latter are often reluctant to support an increase of naval power which benefits them only indirectly.

On the other hand, if all the trading states of the Union formed one and the same nation, trade, for them, would become a national concern of the first importance; then they would be inclined to make great sacrifices to protect their shipping and nothing would stop their following what they wanted in this respect.

I think that nations, like individuals, almost always reveal the main features of their future destiny from an early age. When I observe the commercial energy of Anglo-Americans, their ease of effort, the successes they achieve, I cannot help believing that they will one day turn into the leading naval power in the world. They are driven to take over the seas as the Romans were to conquer the world.

CONCLUSION

Now I am nearing the end. Until now, in speaking of the future destiny of the United States, I have tried hard to divide my subject into various topic areas so as to study each one more carefully.

It is time to gather them all together into a single point of view. What I am about to say will lack detail but gain in certainty. I shall observe each object less closely but I shall tackle generalizations with greater clarity. I shall resemble the traveler who leaves the walls of a great city to climb the nearby hill. As he moves away, the men he has just left vanish before his gaze; their dwellings become a blur; public squares move out of sight; he has difficulty distinguishing the streets but his eye follows the contours of the city with greater ease and, for the first time, he grasps its overall shape. Similarly, I seem to be viewing the whole future of the English race in the New World. The details of this huge picture remain in shadow but my eyes can grasp the general outline and I have a clear idea of the whole.

The territory now occupied or owned by the United States of America forms almost a twentieth of the inhabitable globe.

However broad these boundaries are, we would be wrong to believe that the Anglo-American race will be contained within them forever; it is already spreading far beyond.

There was a time when we too might have established a great French nation in the American wilderness, to share with the English the destinies of the New World. France used to own a territory in North America covering an area almost as vast as the whole of Europe. Then the three longest rivers of the continent flowed their full length within our dominions. The Indian nations dwelling between the mouth of the St Lawrence and the Mississippi delta heard no language but ours; all the established European settlements scattered over that immense area recalled memories of our homeland: Louisburg, Montmorency, Duquesne, St Louis, Vincennes, New Orleans, all names cherished by France and familiar to our ears.

But a combination of circumstances too long to enumerate[1] robbed us of this magnificent inheritance. Wherever the French were few in number and poorly settled, they disappeared. The remainder crowded into a narrow area and are now subject to other laws. The four hundred thousand Frenchmen of lower Canada now form the virtual remnants of a former nation displaced in the midst of a new one. Around them the foreign population is constantly growing, stretching out in every direction; it even forces its way into the ranks of the former owners of the soil, dominating their towns, and disfiguring their language. This population is identical with that of the United States. So I am right in saying that the English race does not stop at the boundaries of the Union but spreads far beyond them toward the Northeast.

To the Northwest stand only a few Russian settlements of no importance; but to the Southwest, Mexico presents a barrier to the Anglo-American advance.

In truth, therefore, only two rival races share the New World at present, the Spanish and the English.

The boundaries to separate these two races have been settled by treaty. Yet, however favorable this treaty is to the Anglo-Americans, I am quite convinced that they will soon infringe it.

Beyond the frontiers of the Union in the direction of Mexico lie vast uninhabited regions. The people of the United States will force their way into these solitary areas even sooner than those very peoples who have the right to occupy them. They will snatch ownership of the land, settle there in social communi-

---

1.   At the forefront is this: peoples who are free and used to municipal government manage to create flourishing colonies more easily than others. The practice of thinking for oneself and of governing oneself is indispensable in a new country, where success to a very large degree depends necessarily upon the individual efforts of the settlers.

ties and, when the lawful owner finally turns up, he will find the desert cultivated and foreigners quietly settled on his inheritance.

The land of the New World belongs to the first to settle there and dominion over it is reward for winning the race.

Those lands already populated will have some difficulty in protecting themselves from invasions.

I have previously spoken of events in Texas. The inhabitants of the United States are day by day gradually infiltrating into Texas where they acquire land and, although obeying the laws of the country, establish the dominion of their language and way of life. The province of Texas is still under Mexican rule; but soon you will not find any more Mexicans there. The same sort of thing takes place on all fronts when Anglo-Americans come into contact with peoples of a different origin.

It is impossible to pretend that the English have not won a huge dominance over all the other European races in the New World. They are much superior in civilization, industry, and power. Provided that they see in front of them only empty or sparsely inhabited land, provided that they do not come across massed populations in their way, through whose ranks they would find it hopeless to force a passage, they will expand endlessly. They will not come to a halt at boundaries drawn up by treaty but will overflow such imaginary dikes in every direction.

What helps this rapid progress of the English race even more wonderfully is its geographical position in the New World.

As you rise above the northern boundaries, you meet polar ice; as you move a few degrees below the southern boundaries, you enter the fiery heat of the equator. The English in America are, therefore, positioned in the most temperate zone and the most habitable section of the continent.

It is supposed that the prodigious increase observed in the population of the United States dates only from the time of independence: that would be wrong. The population was growing just as rapidly under the colonial system as in our day; there was almost the same doubling of numbers every twenty-two years. Then the numbers were in the thousands; now they are in the millions. The same phenomenon which passed unnoticed a century ago strikes everyone's attention these days.

The Canadian English, who obey a king, are increasing in numbers and are spreading as quickly as the American English who live in a republican administration.

During the eight years of the War of Independence, the population went on increasing at the same rate as mentioned above.

Although there existed along the boundaries to the west mighty Indian nations allied to the English, emigration to the west never slackened, so to speak. While the enemy was laying waste to the Atlantic coasts, Kentucky, the western districts of Pennsylvania, the states of Vermont and Maine were filling up with inhabitants. The disorder following that war did not prevent the population from growing and did not arrest its forward advance into the wilderness. Thus different laws, whether peace or war prevailed, order or anarchy, have had no perceptible influence upon the gradual development of the Anglo-Americans.

The reason is easily understood: no cause is sufficiently widespread to exert a simultaneous effect at every point over such a vast territory. Consequently, one large area of the country offers a secure shelter against the catastrophes that strike some other area and, however great such calamities might be, the remedy available is always greater still.

One should not, therefore, believe that it is possible to halt the rise of the English in the New World. The fragmentation of the Union and the ensuing war in this continent, the abolition of the republic and the resulting tyranny, may hold back their expansion, without being able to prevent the attainment of their inevitable destiny. No power on earth can block the advance of these immigrants to those fertile spaces which stand open everywhere to industry and which offer a refuge from every disaster. Future events of whatever kind will remove from Americans neither their climate, their inland waters, their great rivers, nor their fertile soil. Bad laws, revolutions, and anarchy cannot destroy their taste for prosperity or that spirit of enterprise which seems the particular character of their race, nor can they snuff out completely the knowledge which lights their way.

Thus, amidst the uncertainty of the future, at least one event is sure. Over a period which we can call imminent, since we are dealing here with the life of nations, Anglo-Americans alone will cover the whole of the extensive area between the polar ice and the tropics; they will spread from the Atlantic shores to the coasts of the Southern Seas.

I believe that the territory over which the Anglo-American race will one day spread equals three quarters of the size of Europe.[2] The Union's climate is, generally speaking, better than that of Europe; its natural advantages are as great and clearly its population will one day be proportionate to our own.

Europe, divided among so many different peoples, suffering from an endless series of wars and the barbarities of the Middle Ages, has managed to reach a population of sixty-eight inhabitants to the square mile.[3] What powerful cause is strong enough to stop the United States from having as many in the future?

Many centuries will pass before the diverse offshoots of the English race in America cease to present a common appearance. It is impossible to foresee a time when men will be able to establish permanent inequality of social conditions in the New World.

Consequently, whatever differences peace or war, freedom or tyranny, wealth or poverty may some time bring to the destiny of the various branches of the great Anglo-American family, they will at least preserve a similar social state and will share the customs and ideas which derive from this social state.

In the Middle Ages, religion offered the only sufficiently powerful bond to unite the diverse populations of Europe into one civilization. The English of the New World have a thousand other reciprocal links and they live in a century when everything conspires to establish equality amongst men.

The Middle Ages was a time of divisions. Each nation, each region, each city, each family had a strong urge to assert its individuality. At the present time, the opposite tendency is

2. The United States on their own cover an area equal to half that of Europe. Europe's landmass is 500,000 square leagues; its population is 205,000,000 inhabitants. Malte-Brun, vol. 6, bk 114, p. 4.
3. See Malte-Brun, vol. 6, bk 116, p. 92.

evident; nations appear to be moving toward unification. Intellectual links join the most remote areas of the earth together and men cannot remain strangers to each other for a single day, nor ignorant of what is happening in any corner of the globe. Thus we observe today less difference between Europeans and their descendants in the New World, despite the ocean separating them, than there was between certain towns in the thirteenth century, divided as they were by only a river.

If this process of assimilation draws foreign peoples closer together, it is all the more true that the branches of the same people cannot stay strangers to each other.

Therefore, a time will come when we shall be able to see in North America one hundred and fifty million people[4] all equal to one another, all belonging to the same family, sharing the same beginnings, the same civilization, the same language, the same religion, the same ways, the same customs and among whom thought will circulate in similar forms, depicted in the same colors. All else is uncertain but this is certain. And this is something wholly novel in the world, the significance of which the imagination itself cannot even grasp.

Today, two great nations of the earth seem to be advancing toward the same destination from different starting points: the Russians and the Anglo-Americans.

Both have grown unobserved and, while men's attention has been preoccupied elsewhere, they have climbed up into the leading rank of nations and the world has learned of both their birth and their greatness at almost the same moment.

All other nations appear to have reached almost the upper limits of their natural development and have nothing left to do except preserve what they have, whereas these two nations are growing:[5] all the others have either halted or are advancing by a great exertion of effort, whereas these two progress rapidly and comfortably on a seemingly unending course as far as we can see.

4.   This is a population equivalent to that of Europe, taking the mean to be 410 people per square league.
5.   Of all the nations of the Old World, Russia is the one whose population increases proportionately the most rapidly.

Americans struggle against obstacles placed there by nature; Russians are in conflict with men. The former fight the wilderness and barbarity; the latter, civilization with all its weaponry: thus, American victories are achieved with the plowshare, Russia's with the soldier's sword.

To achieve their aim, the former rely upon self-interest and allow free scope to the unguided strength and common sense of individuals.

The latter focus the whole power of society upon a single man.

The former deploy freedom as their main mode of action; the latter, slavish obedience.

The point of departure is different, their paths are diverse but each of them seems destined by some secret providential design to hold in their hands the fate of half the world at some date in the future.

VOLUME 2

VOLUME 3

THE AUTHOR'S NOTE TO
THE SECOND VOLUME

The Americans have a democratic state of society which has naturally suggested to them certain laws and political customs.

This very state of society has, moreover, engendered among them a multitude of feelings and opinions unknown in the old aristocratic societies of Europe. It has destroyed or modified the links which once existed and has established new ones. The appearance of civil society has undergone as much change as the outward face of the political world.

I dealt with the former subject in the work I published on American democracy five years ago. The latter subject is the object of the present volume. These two parts complete one another and form one work.

I must warn the reader right away against an error which would be very harmful to me. He might come to the conclusion, on seeing me attribute so many different effects to equality, that I view equality as the only cause of everything which happens at the present time. That would be to suppose that I had a very narrow view.

There is a host of opinions, feelings, instincts which in our time have owed their birth to factors alien to, or even opposed to, equality.

So if I took the United States as an example, I would easily prove that the nature of the country, the origin of its inhabitants, the religion of its first founders, the education they had acquired, their previous ways of life have exerted and do still exert, independently of democracy, an extensive influence over their manner of thinking and feeling. Different causes, equally distinct from the principle of democracy, would be found in Europe and would explain much of what is happening there.

I acknowledge the existence of all these different causes and their power, but my subject is not to speak about them. I have not set out to point out the reason for all our inclinations and ideas; I have simply attempted to show in what way both have been changed by equality.

Since I am firmly of the opinion that the democratic revolution which we are witnessing is an irresistible fact against which it would be neither desirable nor prudent to struggle, people may be surprised that I often come to address such strong words to the democratic societies which have been created by this revolution.

I shall merely reply that it is because I was not an opponent of democracy that I wanted to be sincere toward it.

Men do not receive the truth from their enemies and their friends scarcely offer it to them; that is why I have uttered it.

I believed that many would take it upon themselves to herald the new benefits which equality promises to men but that few would dare to highlight from afar the dangers with which it threatens them. Thus it is principally toward these dangers that I have directed my gaze and, thinking that I had revealed what they are, I have not been such a coward as to pass them by in silence.

I hope the impartiality which people seemed to observe in the first work will be found in this second. Placed in the midst of contradictory opinions which divide us, I have tried for the moment to remove from my heart both those sympathies in favor and those feelings against which exert any influence on me. If readers of my book come across a single sentence which sets out to flatter any one of those great parties creating agitation in our country, or any one of those minor factions presently harassing or weakening it, let them raise their voices and accuse me.

The subject I wished to encompass is huge, for it includes most of the opinions and ideas produced by the new state of the world. Such a subject surely exceeds my strength. I have not managed to satisfy myself in the treatment of it.

But if I have failed to reach the goal I strove for, readers will at least do me this justice—that I have conceived and pursued my enterprise in the spirit which could make me worthy of success.

PART 1
THE INFLUENCE OF DEMOCRACY UPON THE INTELLECTUAL MOVEMENT IN THE UNITED STATES

CHAPTER I

THE AMERICANS' PHILOSOPHIC METHOD

I think that in the civilized world there is no country less interested in philosophy than the United States.

The Americans have no philosophic school of their own and are very little bothered by all those which divide Europe; they hardly know their names.

However, it is easy to see that the minds of almost all the inhabitants of the United States move in the same direction and are guided according to the same rules; that is to say, they possess, without ever having gone to the trouble of defining the rules, a certain philosophic methodology common to all of them.

To escape the spirit of systems, the yoke of habit, the precepts of family, the opinions of class, and, to a certain extent, the prejudices of nation; to adopt tradition simply as information and present facts simply as a useful study in order to act differently and better; to search by oneself and in oneself alone for the reason of things; to strive for the ends without being enslaved by the means and to aim for the essence via the form: such are the main features which characterize what I shall call the American philosophic method.

If I venture still further and if, amid these different features, I seek the main one, the one which may sum up all the others, I discover that, in the majority of mental processes, each American has but recourse to the individual effort of his own reason.

America is thus one of the countries in the world where the precepts of Descartes[a] are least studied and most widely applied. We need not be surprised by that.

Americans do not read the works of Descartes because the state of their society diverts them from speculative study and they follow his maxims because it is this very social state which naturally disposes their minds to adopt them.

Amid the continuous shifts which prevail in the heart of a democratic society, the bond which unites generations to each other becomes slack or breaks down; each person easily loses the trail of ideas coming from his forbears or hardly bothers himself about it.

Men who live in a such a society could not possibly draw their beliefs from the opinions of the class they belong to, for there are not, so to speak, class divisions any more and those that still exist are composed of such shifting elements that the body could not ever exercise a real control over its limbs.

As for the effect which one man's intelligence can have upon another's, it is of necessity much curtailed in a country where its citizens, having become almost like each other, scrutinize each other carefully and, perceiving in not a single person in their midst any signs of undeniable greatness or superiority, constantly return to their own rationality as to the most obvious and immediate source of truth. So, it is not merely trust in any particular individual which is destroyed, but also the predilection to take the word of any man at all.

Each man thus retreats into himself from where he claims to judge the world.

The practice Americans follow of assuming control independently for their own judgment leads them to adopt other habits.

As they realize that, without help, they successfully resolve all the small problems they meet in their practical lives, they easily reach the conclusion that there is an explanation for everything in the world and that nothing is beyond the limits of intelligence.

So it is that they willingly deny what they cannot understand; that gives them little faith in the extraordinary and an almost invincible distaste for the supernatural.

As they are used to relying upon their own evidence, they like to observe very clearly the object they are dealing with; they remove it, therefore, as far as possible from its envelope, brush aside everything which keeps them apart from it, and remove everything which hides it from view, so as to see it close to and in full light. This proclivity of mind soon leads them to despise outer forms which they consider as a useless and inconvenient veil positioned between them and the truth.

Americans have, therefore, never felt the need to draw their philosophic method from books; they have discovered it within themselves. I shall make the same comment upon what has happened in Europe.

The very same method was established and popularized in Europe only as conditions became more equal and men more alike.

Let us for a moment consider the sequence of history:

In the sixteenth century, the reformers used the reason of the individual to put a certain number of the beliefs of the religion of their forbears to the test, while withholding from that very reason examination of all the others. In the seventeenth century, Bacon,[b] in the natural sciences, and Descartes, in philosophy proper, abolished accepted formulae, destroyed the influence of tradition, and overturned the authority of the teacher.

The philosophers of the eighteenth century, applying this principle more generally, undertook to expose to the personal scrutiny of each man the substance of all his beliefs.

Who cannot see that Luther,[c] Descartes, and Voltaire[d] used the same method and that they differed from each other only in the greater and lesser use they claimed to make of it?

How is it that the reformers have been locked so tightly in the circle of religious ideas? Why did Descartes, wishing to use his method only in certain areas, although he had shaped it to apply it to everything, declare that one ought to judge for oneself only the concepts of philosophy and not those of politics? How did it come about that in the eighteenth century they employed all of a sudden a general application of this very method which Descartes and his predecessors had not perceived or had been reluctant to uncover? In fine, how is it that at this time the method we are speaking of has suddenly emerged from the schools to make its way into society, becoming the common rule of intelligence and, after being popular with the French, has been conspicuously adopted or secretly pursued by all the peoples of Europe?

The philosophic method in question may have been born in the sixteenth century, become more sharply defined and generalized in the seventeenth; but it could not be adopted on a common basis in either. Political laws, social conditions, and ways of thinking which derive from these first ideals were against them.

It was discovered in an era when men were beginning to become more equal and more compatible. Generally, it could not be followed except in centuries when social conditions had become more or less the same and men more or less alike.

Therefore, the philosophic method of the eighteenth century is not only French but democratic, which explains why it has easily been adopted throughout the whole of Europe where it has contributed so much to the change in outlook. It is not because the French have changed their former beliefs and modified their former practices that they have shaken the world, it is because they were the first to generalize and illuminate a philosophic method with whose help one could readily challenge the things of the past and open the way to all things modern.

So that now, if I am asked why this same method is more rigorously followed and more frequently adopted these days by the French than the Americans, in whose hearts equality is nevertheless just as established and even older, I shall respond that, in part, it depends upon two sets of circumstances which I must first explain.

It is religion which has given birth to Anglo-American societies: one must never lose sight of that; in the United States, religion is thus intimately linked to all national habits and all the emotions which one's native country arouses; that gives it a particular strength.

To this powerful reason add yet another which is no less important: in America, religion has, so to speak, set its own limits; the realm of religion has remained entirely distinct from the realm of politics, so that it has been possible to alter the ancient laws easily without shaking previously held beliefs.

Christianity has therefore maintained a strong sway over the American mind and—something I wish to note above all—it rules not only like a philosophy taken up after evaluation but like a religion believed without discussion.

In the United States, Christian sects are infinitely varied and are endlessly modified, while Christianity itself is an established and unassailable fact which no one undertakes either to attack or defend.

The Americans, having accepted without question the main teachings of the Christian religion, are obliged to accept in the same way a great number of moral truths which derive from it and hold it together. That restricts within narrow limits the process of individual analysis and removes several of the most important human opinions from this analysis.

The other feature I spoke of is this:

The Americans have a democratic society and constitution but have not had a democratic revolution. They reached the land they now occupy in practically the same state as we see them now. That is a very significant fact.

All revolutions shake former beliefs, weaken authority, and obscure commonly held ideas. Every revolution thus has more or less the effect of releasing men to their own devices and of opening up an empty and almost boundless space before the mind of each person.

When social conditions become equal in the wake of a prolonged struggle between the different classes from which the former society was made up, envy, hatred, and scorn of one's neighbor, pride and an inflated self-confidence invade, so to speak, the human heart and for some time make it their domain. This, leaving aside equality, contributes forcefully to divide men, bringing about a distrust of each other's opinions and a search for illumination only within themselves.

Thus, each man strives for self-sufficiency and stakes his

reputation upon formulating beliefs which are his own. Men are no longer bound together except through self-interest and not through ideology and one might assert that human opinions form only a sort of intellectual dust which swirls in every direction, unable to settle or find stability.

Thus, the independence of mind assumed by equality is never so great nor appears so excessive as at the moment when equality begins to establish itself and during the painful effort of its foundation. So we must make a careful distinction between the kind of intellectual freedom which equality can offer and the anarchy which revolution brings in its train. We must consider each of these two things separately so as not to develop exaggerated hopes and fears for the future.

I believe that the men who will exist in the new social groupings will often employ their own individual reason; however, I am far from believing that they will often misuse it.

This stems from a cause more generally applicable to all democratic countries and which, in the long run, has to hold individual freedom of thought within fixed and sometimes narrow confines.

I shall expound this in the following chapter.

CHAPTER 2

THE PRINCIPAL SOURCE OF BELIEFS AMONG DEMOCRATIC NATIONS

Depending on the times, beliefs of a dogmatic character are more or less common. They arise in different ways and can change their shape and object; but it is not possible for such dogmatic opinions not to exist—that is to say, opinions which men take on trust and without discussion. If every man chose to form for himself all his opinions in an isolated pursuit for truth along paths followed by himself alone, it is unlikely that a great number of men would ever come together in any commonly shared belief.

But it is easy to see that no social grouping can prosper without shared beliefs or rather there are none which exist in that way; for, without commonly accepted ideas, there is no common action, and without common action, men exist separately but not as a social unit. For society to exist and all the more so, for such a society to prosper, all the citizens' minds must be united and held together by a few principal ideas. This could not possibly exist unless each of them occasionally draws his opinions from the same source and agrees to accept a certain number of ready-formed beliefs.

If I now consider men as individuals, I find that dogmatic beliefs are no less vital for a man on his own than for when he acts in common with his fellows.

If man was forced to prove for himself all the truths he employs each day, he would never reach an end; he would drain his energies in initial experiment without advancing at all. Since there is not the time, because of the short span of our lives, nor the ability, because of the limitations of our minds, to act in that way, he is reduced to the taking on trust a host of facts and opinions which he has neither the time nor the power to examine and verify by his own efforts but which have been discovered by abler minds than his or which have been adopted by the populace. Upon this primary foundation he erects the structure of his own thought. He is not brought to this manner of advancing by his own will but is limited by the unbending laws of his own condition.

Every great philosopher in the world believes a million things upon the authority of someone else and supposes many more truths than he can prove.

This is not merely necessary but desirable. A man who might attempt everything by himself could grant only scant time and attention to each thing. This would keep his mind in a state of constant agitation, preventing him from arriving at a deep understanding of any truth or from reaching a conviction with any certainty. His intelligence would be simultaneously independent and weakened. Therefore, he must, amid all the diverse human opinions, make a choice and accept many beliefs without any argument so as to deepen his understanding of a small number of them which he has examined carefully.

It is true enough that any man, accepting an opinion upon someone else's say-so, enslaves his own mind; but it is a salutary enslavement which allows him to make sound use of his freedom.

Whatever happens, authority for these opinions has always to have a place somewhere in the intellectual and moral world. Its place is variable but of necessity it has a place. The independence of an individual can be more or less extensive but it could not possibly be boundless. So, the question is not knowing whether such an intellectual authority exists during periods of democratic rule but simply where it is to be found and how extensive it is.

In the preceding chapter, I showed how equality of conditions persuaded men to conceive an instinctive disbelief in the supernatural and a very lofty, often very exaggerated, conception of human reason.

It is only, therefore, with great difficulty that men who live in times of equality are led to place outside and above human bounds the intellectual authority to which they submit. Normally they seek the source of truth in themselves or in their fellow men. That fact would be enough to prove that, at such times, a new religion could not be founded and that all attempts to bring it into being would be not only blasphemous but absurd and contrary to reason. One can foresee that peoples under democratic rule will not easily believe in messages from a divine source and will willingly laugh at new prophets since they will wish to choose the main arbiter for their beliefs within, and not beyond, the bounds of human understanding.

When conditions are unequal and men have dissimilar outlooks, there are a few very enlightened, learned, powerfully intelligent individuals while the masses are very ignorant and extremely limited. People who live under this aristocratic rule are naturally inclined to take as a guide for their opinions the superior reason of one man or one class, whereas they are not persuaded to recognize the infallibility of the masses.

In times of equality, the opposite prevails.

Gradually, as citizens become more equal and similar, the inclination for each man to have a blind belief in one particular man or class lessens. The predisposition to believe in mass opinion increases and becomes progressively the opinion which commands the world.

Not only is commonly held opinion the only guide to the reason of the individual in democracies but this opinion has, in these nations, an infinitely greater power than in any other. In times of equality, men have no confidence in each other because of their similarities but this very similarity gives them an almost limitless trust in the judgement of the public as a whole. For it appears likely, in their view, that, since they all have similar ideas, truth will reside with the greatest number.

When the man living in a democratic country compares himself individually with all those around him, he sees with pride that he is equal to each of them; but when he happens to contemplate the huge gathering of his fellow men and to take his place beside this great body, he is straightway overwhelmed by his own insignificance and weakness.

This very equality which makes him independent of each of his fellow men delivers him alone and defenseless into the hands of the majority.

In democratic nations, the general public possesses an unusual power which aristocracies could not imagine. It does not impose its beliefs by persuasion but inserts them in men's souls by the immense pressure of corporate thinking upon the intelligence of each single man.

In the United States, the majority takes upon itself the task of supplying to the individual a mass of ready-made opinions, thus relieving him of the necessity to take the proper responsibility of arriving at his own. Thus, he accepts without scrutiny a great number of philosophic, moral, or political theories on the word of the general masses. Looking very closely, it can be seen that religion itself dominates less a revealed doctrine than a commonly held opinion.

I do, therefore, realize that, among Americans, political laws are such that the majority exercises sovereign power over society, a fact which significantly increases the sway it has in the nature of things over intelligence. For it is the most unusual thing in the world for a man to perceive a superior wisdom in anyone who oppresses him.

This absolute political power, exercised by the majority in the United States, increases in effect the influence which the opinions of the general public would have over the mind of each citizen; however, it does not produce the influence. The sources for that must be sought in equality itself not in the more or less popular institutions which equal men impose on themselves. We can believe that the intellectual power of the majority would be less complete in a democratic nation ruled by a king than in a pure democracy. Yet, it will always be complete and, whatever the political laws governing men in times of equality, we can predict that the trust in commonly held opinions will devolve into a sort of religion with the majority acting as prophet.

The intellectual authority will be different but no less in extent. Far from believing in its disappearance, I prophesy that it will easily assume greater proportions and that it could come about that, in the end, it might restrict the reason of the individual within narrower limits than is appropriate to the grandeur and happiness of humankind. In equality, I see two tendencies: one which leads every man's thought into new paths and another which would force him willingly to cease thinking at all. I observe how, beneath the power of certain laws, democracy would blot out that intellectual liberty supported by the social, democratic state in such a way that, having broken the shackles formerly imposed upon it by class systems or men, the human spirit would be closely confined by the general will of the majority.

If, instead of all the diverse powers which excessively hindered or slowed down the flight of reason of the individual, democratic nations substituted the absolute power of a majority, only the character of this social ill would have been changed. Men would not have achieved the means of living independently; they would simply have lighted upon—a difficult enough task in itself—a new face of enslavement. I cannot repeat too often that therein is the source of profound reflection for those who see in the freedom of the intellect a sacred idea and who hate not only despots but despotism. As far as I am concerned, when I feel the hand of power weighing down upon my brow, I take no interest in knowing who oppresses me and I am not more inclined to put my head under the yoke simply because a million arms offer it to me.

CHAPTER 3

WHY THE AMERICANS SHOW MORE APTITUDE AND TASTE FOR GENERAL IDEAS THAN THEIR FOREFATHERS THE ENGLISH

God gives no thought at all to human kind in general. He casts a single and separate glance upon all the beings that form the human race, observing in each of them similarities which link him to them and differences which separate him from them.

So God has no need for general ideas; that is to say, he never experiences the necessity of grouping a great number of similar objects under one heading so as to think more comfortably.

Man does not share this attitude. If the human mind were to attempt an examination and judgement of all the individual cases that come to its notice, it would soon lose itself amid the complexity of detail and would lose sight of everything. In this extreme predicament, man follows an imperfect yet necessary method which assists his weakness while underlining it.

After a superficial consideration of a certain number of ideas and noticing that they are similar, he places them in one category, puts them to one side, and moves on.

General ideas do not bear witness to the strength of human intelligence but rather to its inadequacy for, in nature, beings are not exactly alike; there are no identical facts, no rules which can be applied loosely and in a similar manner to several objects at the same time.

General ideas have the wondrous attribute of allowing the human mind to reach swift judgments on a great number of ideas at the same time. On the other hand, they only ever provide the mind with half-baked notions which lose as much in accuracy as they gain in range.

As societies mature, they acquire knowledge of new facts and grasp, almost unknowingly, a few individual truths everyday.

As man grasps more truths of this kind, he is naturally led to imagine a greater number of general ideas. One could not perceive in separation a mass of individual facts without reaching a final discovery of the common bond which links them. Several individuals persuade us to the notion of the species; several species, of necessity, lead to that of genus. The habit and taste for generalizing will, therefore, always be all the greater in a nation of more ancient culture and greater knowledge.

But there are other reasons still which push men either toward or away from generalizing.

The Americans have greater use for, and take greater pleasure in, generalizations than the English, which seems strange at first sight, considering that the two nations have the same origins and have lived for centuries under the same laws and that they still ceaselessly share their opinions and customs. The contrast appears much more striking still when one looks closely at this Europe of ours and compares the two most enlightened nations dwelling there, the one with the other.

It could be said that, with the English, it is only reluctantly and painfully that the human mind tears itself away from the observation of individual facts in order to reach the sources of those facts and that if they do make generalizations, it is only in spite of themselves.

By contrast, in our case, it appears that the taste for general ideas has become such a frenetic passion that we must satisfy it with little or no provocation. As I wake each morning, I learn that a certain general and eternal law, of which I had never heard before, has just been unearthed. No writer, even a modest one, is satisfied with his attempt to discover truths applicable to a great kingdom; he remains dissatisfied if he has not encapsulated the whole human race into the subject matter of his treatise.

Such a difference between two enlightened nations surprises me. If I move my attention to England and take note of what has been happening at its heart for nearly half a century, I can with some confidence assert that the taste for generalizing has developed in proportion as the ancient constitution has grown weaker.

However great or small the state of knowledge might be, that is not alone enough to explain this attraction for generalizations in the human mind nor the repulsion from them.

When conditions are very unequal and these inequalities are permanent, individuals become gradually so dissimilar that one might say there are as many separate human groups as there are classes of men. Only one of these is observed at any one time and, losing sight of that bond which generally binds all men into the huge heart of mankind itself, one only ever considers certain individuals and not mankind as a whole.

Those who dwell in aristocratic societies never, therefore, adopt very general ideas in relation to themselves and that is enough to account for their customary distrust for these ideas and an intuitive distaste for them.

The man dwelling in a democracy, on the other hand, is aware of beings about him who are virtually similar; he cannot, therefore, think of any part of the human species without his thought expanding and widening to embrace the whole. Any truth which applies to himself seems to apply equally and similarly to all his fellow citizens and those like him. Having caught the habit of generalizing from that branch of education which he spends most time studying and which attracts him more, he transfers this very habit to all the other areas of study. Thus it is that the need to discover common rules which apply to everything, to include a great number of objects in one category and to explain a collection of facts by one single reason, becomes a burning and often blinding passion of the human mind.

The opinions of the ancients concerning slavery are the best example of the truth of the above argument.

The deepest and most eclectic minds in Rome and Greece were unable to reach this most general and yet most simple of generalizations, that men were alike and that all of them had equal rights to freedom at birth. They expended great effort to prove that slavery was a feature of nature which would always exist. Furthermore, everything goes to show that those ancients who were slaves before becoming free, several of whom have bequeathed us fine writings, themselves regarded slavery in the same light.

All the great writers of antiquity belonged to the noble elite of teachers or at least they saw this noble elite come into being uncontested before their very eyes. Their minds, although broadened in several directions, were limited in this one and Jesus Christ had to come into the world to reveal that all members of the human race were similar and equal by nature.

In ages of equality, all men are mutually independent, isolated, and weak; no one man's will controls the movements of the crowd in any permanent way. In such times, the human race seems to walk under its own power. To explain what happens in the world, we are, therefore, reduced to examining a few main reasons which act in a similar manner upon each of our fellows to persuade them to pursue the same path. That naturally leads the human mind to arrive at generalizations and gives it the taste for them.

I have already demonstrated how conditions of equality led every man to seek out the truth by himself. It is easy to see that a similar method must imperceptibly draw the human mind toward general ideas. Whenever I reject the traditional views of class, profession, or family and escape from the power of precedent so as to seek, by the sole efforts of my reason, the way to follow, I am disposed to draw the main features of my opinions from the very nature of man and this leads me, of necessity and almost unawares, toward a great number of general thoughts.

All the above manages to explain why the English display much less skill or taste for the generalizations of their sons the Americans, and especially of their neighbors the French, and why the English of the present time display this more than their fathers' generation.

The English have long been a very enlightened as well as a very aristocratic nation; their intelligence drew them ceaselessly toward general ideas while their aristocratic turn of mind restricted them to very individual ideas. Out of that came this philosophy, both daring yet modest, broad yet narrow, which has dominated England up until now and which still restricts and paralyzes so many minds.

Independently of those reasons I have demonstrated above, still more reasons, less apparent yet no less influential, account for the taste and often the passion for generalization among almost all democratic nations.

We have to distinguish between these categories of ideas. Some result from a slow, detailed, conscientious effort of intelligence, and those broaden the scope of human knowledge. Others emerge easily from a first swift effort of the mind, leading to very superficial and unstable notions.

Men who live in times of equality have much curiosity and little leisure time. Their lives are so workaday, complex, busy, active, that only a little time remains for thinking. Men in democratic times like general ideas because they free them from studying particulars. They embody, if I may thus express myself, many things in a small vessel and produce much in a short space of time. Thus when they think, they perceive, after a brief and casual scrutiny, a common link between certain objects; they do not pursue their researches further and, without a detailed examination of the similarities or differences of these various objects, they hasten to categorize them in the same formula so as to make further strides forward.

One of the distinctive features of democratic ages is the taste shared by every man for easy success and immediate enjoyment—a trait evident as much in the pursuits of the intellect as in any other. The majority of those who live in times of equality are filled with ambition both vigorous and mild. They wish for immediate success without expending great effort. These contradictory elements lead them to search for general ideas with whose help they congratulate themselves on being able to depict huge objects at little expense and drawing the public's attention with no effort.

I do not know whether they are mistaken in thinking like that, for their readers fear deep analysis as much as autonomous thought and usually seek in the efforts of the mind, only easily acquired pleasures and effortless work.

If aristocratic nations make insufficient use of generalizations and show a thoughtless disparagement of them, it happens conversely that democratic nations are always ready to misuse these kinds of ideas and to have an ill-advised and fervent passion for them.

CHAPTER 4

WHY THE AMERICANS HAVE NEVER BEEN AS ENTHUSIASTIC AS THE FRENCH FOR GENERAL IDEAS IN POLITICAL MATTERS

I have said above that the Americans displayed a less active taste than the French for generalizations. That is above all true for political generalizations.

Although the Americans insert in their legislation many more general ideas than the English and take many more pains than the latter to marry up theory and practice in human affairs, in the United States political bodies have never been so fond of generalizations as the Constituent Assembly and Convention in France[a] have been. Never has the American nation as a whole been fanatical about these kinds of ideas in the same way as the French people of the eighteenth century, nor manifested as blind a faith in the absolute truth of any theory.

This difference between the Americans and us has its source in several causes but the main one is as follows:

The Americans are a democratic nation which has always governed its public affairs independently while we are a democratic nation which long has only been able to dream of the best way to direct them.

The condition of our society was already leading us to generalizations in matters of government while our political constitution still prevented us from modifying these ideas by experiment, thus revealing gradually their inadequacy, while the Americans balance these two things endlessly and correct them naturally.

At first sight, this seems directly contrary to what I have said before namely that democratic nations derived from the very disturbances of their practical lives the affection they show for theory. Closer scrutiny reveals nothing contradictory in that.

Men who live in democratic countries avidly seek out generalizations because they have little leisure and such ideas free them from wasting their time on the examination of individual cases. While that is true, it must be understood as true only in matters which are not the normal and essential object of their thoughts. Men involved in trade will eagerly latch on to all generalizations presented to them in philosophy, politics, science, or the arts without looking at them closely, but will accept those pertaining to commerce only after close scrutiny and then with reservations.

The same thing happens with politicians when it is a question of general ideas relating to politics.

Therefore, when there is a subject where it is especially dangerous for democratic nations to enslave themselves to general ideas blindly and in excess, the best antidote you can use is for them to be forced to have daily practical dealings with them. They will then be obliged to enter into details which will reveal to them the weak aspects of the theory.

Such a remedy is often painful but it results in certainty.

Thus, those democratic institutions which encourage every citizen to have a practical involvement in government moderate the exaggerated liking for the general political theories which are prompted by equality.

CHAPTER 5

HOW RELIGION IN THE UNITED STATES MAKES FULL USE OF DEMOCRATIC TENDENCIES

I have established in one of the preceding chapters that men cannot do without dogmatic beliefs and that it was even desirable that they possessed such ideas. I now add that among all the dogmatic beliefs, the most desirable seem to me to be in matters of religion, a very obvious deduction even though one would wish to draw attention only to the concerns of this world.

There is almost no human action, however individual one supposes it to be, which does not originate in a very general idea men have about God, his connections with the human race, the nature of their souls, and their duties toward their fellows. We have to accept that these ideas are the shared source from which all others flow.

Men have, therefore, a huge interest in creating fixed ideas about God, their soul, their general duties toward their creator and fellow men; for any doubt about these first concerns would put all their actions at risk and would condemn them in some way to confusion and impotence.

This is, therefore, the most important matter upon which each of us should have settled ideas. Unfortunately, it is most difficult for each of us, if we are alone, to arrive at such settled ideas using only our own reason.

Only minds freed completely from the ordinary preoccupations of life, minds of great depth and astuteness can, with the help of ample time and attention, penetrate such vital truths.

Even then, we see that philosophers themselves are almost always hedged around with doubts, that, at every step, the natural light which illuminates them grows dim and threatens to be blotted out and that, in spite of all their efforts, they have as yet managed to uncover only a small number of contradictory notions upon which the human mind has floated endlessly for thousands of years without managing a firm hold upon the truths or even finding new errors. Such studies are quite beyond the average human capacity and, even when the majority of men were capable of such pursuits, they clearly would not have the free time.

Fixed ideas about God and human nature are vital to the daily practice of their lives but the practice of their lives prevents their acquiring such ideas.

That appears to me to be unique. There are in science ideas which are useful to the masses and within their understanding. Others are available to only a few people and are not fostered by the majority who require nothing beyond their distant application. Yet, the daily practice of science is vital for all, even though the study of science is out of reach of the majority.

General ideas relating to God and human nature are thus among all ideas those most fitted to be withdrawn from the usual practices of individual reason and which have the most to gain and the least to lose by recognizing an authority.

The first object, and one of the main advantages, of religions is to provide for each of these essential questions a tidy solution which is accurate, understood by people in general and lasting.

There are some very false and absurd religions; however, it can be said that any religion which stays within the circle I have just drawn and which has no intention of leaving it, as several religions have tried to do for the purpose of restraining the free flight of the human mind in every respect, imposes a healthy restraint upon the intelligence. We have to recognize that if religion does not save men in the other world, it is at least very useful for their happiness and importance in this.

That is above all true of men who live in free countries.

When a nation's religion is destroyed, doubt takes a grip upon the highest areas of intelligence, partially paralyzing all the others. Each man gets used to having only confused and vacillating ideas on matters which have the greatest interest for himself and his fellows. He puts up a poor defense of his opinions or abandons them and, as he despairs of ever resolving by himself the greatest problems presented by human destiny, he beats a cowardly retreat into not thinking at all.

Such a state cannot fail to weaken the soul, strains the forces of the will, and shapes citizens for slavery. Not only do the latter allow their freedom to be taken from them, they often give it up.

When authority in religious matters no longer exists any more than in political matters, men soon take fright at the sight of this boundless independence. This constant upheaval in everything brings disquiet and exhaustion. As everything in the domain of their intelligence is shifting, they crave at least for a firm and stable state in their material world. Being unable to recover their ancient beliefs, they find a ruler.

In my opinion, I doubt whether man can ever support at the same time complete religious independence and entire political freedom and am drawn to the thought that if a man is without faith, he must serve someone and if he is free, he must believe.

Yet I do not know whether this great advantage granted by religions is not more obvious still in nations where conditions are equal than in all the others.

It must be acknowledged that equality, which brings great benefits into the world, arouses in men, as I shall demonstrate, very dangerous instincts. It tends to their isolation from each other in order to persuade them to have concern only for their individual selves. It exposes their souls to an excessive love of material enjoyment.

The greatest advantage religions bring is to inspire quite contrary instincts. Every single religion places the object of man's desire beyond and above possessions of this earth, and by its nature lifts his soul toward those regions which are much above the senses. In addition, they all impose upon each man certain obligations toward the human race or encourage a shared endeavor, sometimes drawing him away from a contemplation of himself. This is found in the most false and most dangerous religions.

Religious nations, therefore, reveal their natural strength at the precise point where democratic nations show their vulnerability, which shows how important it is for men to retain their religion even on achieving equality.

I do not possess the right nor the will to examine the supernatural means God uses to bring about a religious belief in the heart of man. I cast my eye upon religions at this time only from a purely human standpoint, seeking to show how they can most readily maintain their power in the democratic times we are approaching.

I have demonstrated how, in times of enlightenment and equality, the human spirit had difficulty in accepting dogmatic beliefs and felt the need in religious matters only. This shows first of all that in such times religions must, more discreetly than in any other times, remain within the proper bounds, without attempting to escape from them. In wishing to stretch their powers beyond matters religious, they risk losing their credibility in all other spheres as well. So they must, with care, draw the circle within which they intend to contain the human spirit, while outside the circle the mind should be left entirely free to guide itself.

Mohammed drew down from heaven into the writings of the Koran not only religious teachings but political thoughts, civil and criminal laws and scientific theories. The Gospel, in contrast, refers only to general links of man to God and man to man. Beyond that, it teaches nothing and imposes no belief in anything. That fact alone, leaving aside a thousand other reasons, suffices to show that the first of these two religions could not possibly prevail for long in times of enlightenment and democracy, while the second is destined to have dominance in these times as much as in any other.

If I pursue this same investigation further, I discover that to enable religions, humanly speaking, to thrive in democratic periods, not only must they carefully remain within a circle of religious matters but also their power depends even more upon the nature of their beliefs, their external structures, and the duties they impose.

What I have previously said about equality driving man to broad generalities, must obtain mainly in religious matters. Men who are similar and equal find it easy to formulate the notion of a single God who imposes upon each of them the same rules, while granting them future happiness at the same cost. The idea of the oneness of the human race leads them constantly back to the oneness of the Creator, whereas men separated from each other and very dissimilar, willingly invent as many godheads as there are nations, races, classes, or families and trace out a thousand individual paths to reach heaven.

It cannot be denied that Christianity itself has felt, to some extent, the influence that social and political conditions exercise on religious beliefs.

At the time when the Christian religion appeared on the earth, Providence, which doubtless was preparing the world for its arrival, had gathered huge numbers of the human race like a great flock, under the rule of the Caesars. The men who formed this crowd revealed many individual differences but had this one feature in common: they all obeyed the same laws. Each of them, in relation to the power of the emperor, was so weak and small that all appeared equal when it came to comparison with him.

We have to acknowledge that this fresh and peculiar state in human affairs was bound to predispose men to accept the general truths inculcated by Christianity, and serves to explain the ease and speed with which Christianity entered the human mind at that time.

The counter-proof became obvious after the destruction of the Empire. When the Roman world shattered, so to speak, into a thousand pieces, each nation reverted to its own individuality. The social classes soon asserted their rankings; races became more distinct and groups broke each single nation into several nations. In this widespread effort, which seemed to lead human societies to break up into as many fragments as it is possible to imagine, Christianity never lost sight of the main generalities it had brought to light. Nevertheless, it appeared to subscribe, as best it could, to the new tendencies engendered by this fragmentation of human races. Men continued to worship only one single God as Creator and Protector of all things. Each nation, each town and, so to speak, each man believed they could gain a privilege for themselves and could achieve individual safeguards in relation to their Sovereign Master. Since they were unable to subdivide God, at least they increased and excessively multiplied the number of his servants. The homage rendered to angels and saints became for most Christians an almost idolatrous cult so that it might be feared for a moment that the Christian religion was regressing to religions which it had overcome.

It is clearly evident that, within the ranks of humanity, the more those barriers which separate one nation from another and, in the heart of each nation, one citizen from another, tend to disappear, the more the human spirit directs itself unilaterally toward the idea of a unique and omnipotent being which dispenses equally and in the same way the same laws to each man. It is, therefore, especially in democratic times that the important distinction is made between the homage paid to subordinate agents and the worship due only to the Creator.

One further truth seems very clear to me: religions must have less concern for external practices in democratic times than in any other.

In the philosophic methodology of America, I have revealed that, in times of equality, nothing disgusts the human spirit more than the idea of submitting to categories. Men who live in such times are frustrated by figures; symbols look like puerile devices used to veil or shield from their gaze truths it would be more normal to show in the full light of day. They remain coolly disposed to ceremonial and are naturally inclined to attach only secondary importance to the trappings of the cult.

Those charged with the direction of the external forms of religions in democratic times must pay close attention to these natural instincts of the human mind so as not to run up against them unnecessarily.

I have a firm belief in the necessity of forms. I know that they anchor the human spirit in the contemplation of abstract truths and, as they help man to take firm hold upon them, they invite him to adopt them fervently. I cannot imagine that religion can be maintained without external observances; yet, on the other hand, I think that, in the approaching times, it would be especially dangerous to increase their number without restraint; they ought rather to be restricted to what is absolutely necessary for the perpetuation of the doctrine, for that is the essence of religion, of which ritual is only the external form.[1] A religion which became more insistent upon detail, more burdened with minute observances at a time when men were becoming more equal, would soon find itself reduced to a pack of fanatic zealots in the midst of a crowd of unbelievers.

Readers will, I am sure, not fail to raise the objection that religions, each one of them having as their objective general and external truths, cannot yield in this way to the changing instincts of each century without sacrificing in men's eyes the character of certainty. Once again, I shall reply that we must make a careful distinction between the main opinions which constitute a belief and which theologians call an article of faith, and peripheral ideas. Religions must maintain close links with the former whatever the peculiar spirit of the time might be; but they must take good care not to become wedded in the same way to the latter at a time when everything is on shifting ground and when the mind, accustomed to changes in human affairs, tolerates being restricted, albeit regretfully. The permanence of external and peripheral things seems to me to have a chance of enduring only when civic society is itself static. Everywhere else, I am persuaded it is a danger.

We shall see that among all the passions conceived and fostered by equality, one in particular is sharply appreciated and set deep in the heart of man, namely the love of comfort which forms the prominent and indelible feature of democratic ages.

One may believe that a religion which set out to destroy this passion of all passions would in the end be destroyed by it. If religion wished to wrench men entirely from the contemplation of the things of this world solely to those of the other, in all likelihood souls would slip from its hands and would plunge headlong into the material and immediate pleasures well outside the range of religion.

The main concern of religions is to purify, govern, and restrain

1.   In all religions, there are some ceremonies which are inherent in the very substance of belief and which one must be careful not to change. This is especially true as far as Catholicism is concerned, where form and doctrine are often so closely united as to be one and the same thing.

the overly fervent and exclusive taste for comfort which men experience in times of equality. Yet I believe that they would be wrong to try to tame or destroy it entirely. They will never succeed in turning men away from wealth but can still persuade them to grow wealthy by honorable means alone.

This brings me to a final consideration which includes to some extent all the others. As men grow to be more like each other and equal to each other, it is all the more important that religions, by staying carefully away from the conduct of day-to-day affairs, avoid colliding unnecessarily with generally accepted ideas and the permanent interests which exist in the mass of people. For public opinion increasingly assumes the role of the primary and least resistible of powers, outside which there is no foothold strong enough to resist its attacks. That is no less true in the case of a democratic nation under the rule of a despot, than in a republic. In times of equality, kings command obedience but always the majority commands belief so that it is necessary to curry favor with the majority in whatever is not contrary to belief.

In my first work, I have demonstrated how American priests kept away from public affairs. This is the most striking but not the only example of their self-restraint. In America, religion is a world apart where the priest is sovereign but whose bounds he takes care never to leave. Within its limits, he guides intelligence; outside, he leaves men to their own devices and abandons them to the independence and instability which are features of the nature and the times they live in. I have not seen any country where Christianity has hedged itself round with fewer systems, rituals, or figures or laid before the human mind ideas which were sharper, simpler or more general. Although American Christians are divided into a mass of sects, they all view their religion in this same light, which applies to Catholicism as much as to other beliefs.

No Catholic priests show less taste for the minor rituals, the unusual and peculiar ways of achieving personal salvation, nor follow more the spirit and less the letter of the law than American Catholic priests. Nowhere is the doctrine of the Church which forbids the paying of that homage to the saints which is reserved for God alone more clearly or more closely followed. Yet American Catholics are very obedient and sincere.

One further observation applies to the clergy of all communions: American priests do not endeavor to draw and fix man's gaze upon the future life; they are willing to relinquish a part of his heart to the cares of the present and appear to treat the possessions of this world as important although of secondary moment. While having no direct association themselves with labor, at least they take an interest in its progress and applaud its efforts. While constantly revealing the other world to the believer as the great object of his hopes and fears, they do not forbid him from an honest pursuit of his wellbeing in this one. Far from teaching how these two things are separate and in opposition, they devote themselves rather to discovering points of close contact.

All American priests are aware of the intellectual power exercised by the majority and respect it. They never struggle against it unnecessarily. They stay outside factional disputes but are willing to adopt the general opinions of the country and times, flowing without resistance with the stream of feelings and ideas which carries everything along with it. They make efforts to correct their fellow citizens but do not assume a separate stance from them. Thus public opinion is never their enemy; rather it sustains and protects them while simultaneously their beliefs hold sway, based upon the powers which are their own and those they derive from the majority.

So it is that by respecting all democratic instincts which are not in opposition to it, and by using the support of several of these instincts, religion succeeds in gaining advantage in the struggle against the spirit of personal independence which is the most dangerous foe of all.

CHAPTER 6

THE PROGRESS OF CATHOLICISM IN THE UNITED STATES

America is the most democratic country on earth while, at the same time, the country where, according to reputable reports, the Catholic religion makes the most progress. At first sight this is surprising.

Two distinctions must be made: equality persuades men to judge for themselves. On the other hand, it gives them the taste for and the conception of a single, simple social power which is the same for everyone. Men who live in democratic times are, therefore, predisposed to slide away from all religious authority. But, if they agree to obey such an authority, they insist at least that it is unique and of one character for their intelligence has a natural abhorrence of religious powers which do not emanate from the same center and they find it almost as easy to imagine that there is no religion as several.

Nowadays, more than in previous times, we see Catholics losing their faith and Protestants converting to Catholicism. Looking at it from the inside, Catholicism seems to be losing; from an external standpoint, it makes a gain. Here is the reason.

Present-day men are, by nature, little inclined to belief but, as soon as they take up religion, they immediately encounter within themselves a hidden instinct which drives them unknowingly toward Catholicism. Several of the doctrines and customs of the Roman Church astonish them but they conceive a secret admiration for its organization and are drawn to its unity.

If Catholicism, in the end, managed to elude the political hatred it engenders, I have almost no doubt that this same spirit of the age which seems so opposed to it would become supportive and that it would suddenly achieve extensive conquests.

One of the commonest weaknesses of human intelligence is the wish to reconcile opposing principles and to purchase harmony at the expense of logic. Therefore, there have always

been and there always will be men who, after submitting a
certain number of their religious beliefs to a single authority,
will seek to exempt several others and will let their minds hover
at random between obedience and freedom. But I am drawn to
the belief that the number of those people will be smaller in
democratic times than in others and that our descendants will
tend increasingly to divide into only two parts, some leaving
Christianity entirely and the others embracing the Church of
Rome.

CHAPTER 7

WHAT CAUSES THE MINDS OF
DEMOCRATIC NATIONS TO INCLINE
TOWARD PANTHEISM

I shall later show how the prevailing taste democratic nations
have for general ideas has a parallel in politics; but I wish, for
the present, to mark its main effect in philosophy.

It would be impossible to deny that pantheism[a] has made
great progress at the current time. The writings of a proportion
of Europe bear the obvious imprint of it. The Germans introduce
it into philosophy, the French into literature. Among the works
of imagination published in France, the majority contain some
opinions and pictures borrowed from pantheist doctrines or
suggest some tendency toward these doctrines in their authors.
This does not appear to me to result simply from a chance
happening but to derive from a cause of substance.

As conditions become more equal and each individual man
resembles more and more all his fellows, weaker and smaller,
the habit grows up of giving attention to the nation at the
expense of the citizen and of thinking of the race while forgetting
the individual.

At such times, the human mind enjoys embracing a host of
different objects at the same time and constantly aims to associate a multitude of effects with a single cause.

Man is obsessed with the idea of unity. He seeks it in every direction; when he believes he has found it, he willingly rests in its arms. Not content with discovering that there is but one creation and one Creator in the world, he is still irritated by this primary division of things and he seeks to expand and simplify his thought by enclosing God and the universe in a single entity. If there is a philosophic system according to which things material and immaterial, visible and invisible within the world are to be considered only as the separate parts of an immense being who alone remains eternal in the continuous shift and constant change of everything which is within it, I shall have no difficulty reaching the conclusion that a similar system, although it destroys human individuality, or rather because it destroys it, will have secret attractions for men who live in a democracy. Their whole turn of mind prepares them to think like that and leads them to adopt this idea, which naturally attracts and arrests their imagination and nourishes their arrogance, while cosseting their laziness.

Within the different systems which help philosophy in its attempts to explain the universe, pantheism seems to me one of the most likely to entice the human mind in democratic ages. All those who are smitten with the nobility of man must join forces and fight against this idea.

CHAPTER 8

HOW EQUALITY SUGGESTS TO AMERICANS THE IDEA OF THE INDEFINITE PERFECTIBILITY OF MAN

Equality suggests to the human mind several ideas which without it would not have occurred; it also transforms almost all those ideas already in the mind. For an example I take the idea of man's perfectibility because it is one of the main ideas conceived by the intelligence and formulates an important philosophic theory whose consequences are ever obvious in the conduct of human affairs.

Although man resembles the animals in several respects, one characteristic is unique to him alone: he improves, they do not. The human race did not fail to notice this difference from the beginning. The idea of perfectibility is as old as the world itself. Equality did not invent it but gave it a new quality.

When citizens are categorized according to position, profession, or birth and are all forced to follow the path chance has placed before them, each man thinks that he can see in his own vicinity the utmost limits of human power and no longer seeks to struggle against an inevitable fate. While not absolutely denying man the faculty of improvement, aristocratic nations do not consider it as lasting indefinitely. They entertain progress not total change. They conceive that the condition of future societies is better but not different and while admitting the great steps made by human kind and the possibility of more to come, they restrict its progress within certain barriers which cannot be crossed.

Thus they do not believe they have reached the supreme heights of goodness or absolute truth (what man or nation has been mad enough ever to imagine that?), but they like to be persuaded that they have almost attained the nobility and knowledge which makes up our imperfect nature. Since nothing shifts around them, they are drawn to imagine everything is in its proper place. Then it is that the legislator sets out to formulate eternal laws, namely that nations and kings wish to raise only secular monuments and that the current generation takes it upon itself to spare future generations the bother of controlling their own destiny.

As classes disappear and grow closer, as the tumultuous mass of mankind, its practices, customs, and laws alter, as new facts emerge, as new truths come to light, as old opinions disappear and are replaced by others, the image of perfection in an idealized and fleeting form is offered to the human mind.

Continuous changes stream past the gaze of every man. Some worsen his predicament and he understands only too well that a nation or an individual, however enlightened, is not infallible.

Some changes improve his lot and he comes to the conclusion that, in general, man is endowed with the faculty of indefinite improvement. His setbacks reveal that no one can flatter himself that he has discovered absolute goodness; his successes stimulate him to a relentless pursuit of such a goal. Thus constantly seeking, falling, rising up, often disappointed, never giving up hope, he strives without ceasing toward this mighty achievement, glimpsed indistinctly at the end of the long path human beings have to tread.

We cannot credit how many facts flow naturally from the philosophic theory of the indefinite perfectibility of man, according to which man can improve throughout all time, nor how wondrous an influence it exerts even on those people who, only ever bothering to act and not to think, seem unknowingly to match their actions to it.

I meet an American sailor and ask him why his country's vessels are constructed to last for so short a time; he answers with no hesitation that the art of navigation is making such rapid progress that the finest ship would soon outlive its usefulness if it extended its life more than a few years.

Behind these words, spoken casually by a crude man about a particular fact, I glimpse the general and systematic idea by which a great nation directs its every action.

Aristocratic nations are by nature liable to restrict too much the bounds of human perfectibility while democratic nations stretch them sometimes to excess.

CHAPTER 9

HOW THE EXAMPLE OF THE AMERICANS DOES NOT PROVE THAT A DEMOCRATIC PEOPLE COULD HAVE NEITHER THE APTITUDE NOR THE TASTE FOR THE SCIENCES, LITERATURE, AND THE ARTS

We must acknowledge that in few of the civilized nations of our day have the higher sciences made less progress than in the United States and that in few have great artists, distinguished poets, or famous writers been more rarely found.

Several Europeans, struck by this phenomenon, have looked upon it as the natural and inevitable result of equality and have surmised that if democratic societies and institutions were to take over the whole earth, the human mind would see the gradual dimming of its guiding lights and the relapse of men into darkness.

Those who reason in this manner muddle together, I feel, several ideas which it is important to divide and examine separately. Without wishing to do so, they confuse what is democratic with what is solely American.

The religion professed by the first immigrants and bequeathed by them to their descendants, simple in its rituals, austere and almost primitive in its principles, hostile to external symbols and to ceremonial pomp, by its nature gives little support to fine art and only reluctantly allows the pleasures of literature.

The Americans are a very old and enlightened people who have encountered a huge new country where they spread out at will and cultivate with ease. That is unprecedented in this world. In America each man finds opportunities unknown elsewhere for making or for increasing his fortune. Greed is always in a breathless hurry; the human mind, constantly diverted from the pleasures of imaginative thought and the labors of the intellect, is swayed only by the pursuit of wealth. Not only do we see in the United States, as in all other countries, manufacturing and commercial classes, but also we see something which had never occurred previously, the whole community of men simultaneously engaged in production and commerce.

However, I remain convinced that, had the Americans been alone in the universe with the freedoms and the knowledge acquired by their forefathers, with passions which were their own, they would have been swift to discover that progress in the practice of science cannot be achieved for long without study of the theory and that all the arts reach perfection from contact with each other. For, however absorbed they might have been in the pursuit of the main object of their desires, they would soon have realized that occasional diversions from such ambitions are a better means of achieving them.

A taste for the pleasures of the mind is, moreover, so natural to civilized man that, in sophisticated nations which are least enthusiastic about such pleasures, we always find a certain number of citizens who pursue them. This intellectual craving would have been quickly satisfied once it was felt.

But at the very time when Americans were naturally inclined to require from science only specific applications to the arts and the means of making life comfortable, learned and literary Europe was engaged in researching the sources of truth and in improving at the same time all that serves the pleasures of life as much as everything which satisfies man's needs.

At the head of the enlightened nations of the Old World, the inhabitants of the United States picked out one particular nation with which they closely shared a common origin and similar habits. They found among this people famous scientists, skillful artists, great writers, and could collect the treasures of the intellect without having to work for it.

I cannot agree to separate America from Europe, despite the ocean that divides them. I consider the people of the United States as a sample of the English people responsible for developing the forests of the New World while the rest of the nation, enjoying more leisure time and less taken up with the material cares of life, can devote itself to thought and the enlargement in every direction of the human mind.

The American position is, therefore, entirely exceptional and it is quite possible that no democratic nation will ever be similarly placed. Their strictly Puritan origin, their exclusively commercial habits, the country they inhabit, which appears to divert their minds from the study of science, literature, and the arts, the nearness of Europe which allows them to neglect such study without relapsing into barbarism, a thousand such reasons of which I have been able to signal only the main ones, must have focussed the American mind, in this unusual manner, upon purely practical concerns. Everything—his passions, needs, education, circumstances—seems to unite in inclining the native of the United States earthward. Only religion persuades him to raise an occasional and absent-minded glance toward heaven.

Let us, therefore, stop viewing all democratic nations under the example of the American people and let us try to view them with their own characteristics.

One can imagine a nation with neither castes nor ranks nor class, where the law admits no privileges and divides inherited property into equal shares, yet which is devoid of knowledge or freedom. This is no empty hypothesis. A despot may find it in his interest to maintain the equal status of his subjects and to leave them in ignorance in order more easily to keep them in bondage.

Not only will such a democratic nation show no aptitude or taste for science, literature, and the arts but it is likely never to show any.

The law of descent would itself be responsible for the destruction of wealth and no one would create any new fortunes. The poor man, deprived of knowledge and freedom, would not even imagine the idea of achieving wealth, while the rich man would drift toward poverty, not able to defend himself. Soon, complete and unassailable equality would be established between these two citizens. Then, no one would have the time or the inclination to devote himself to the pleasures of the intellect. All would stay stolidly buried in a similar state of ignorance and an equal enslavement.

When I imagine a democratic society of this kind, I fancy myself in one of those dark, low, close places where light is brought in from outside soon to grow dim and die. A sudden heaviness appears to overwhelm me and I stumble about in the surrounding darkness looking for an escape route into air and daylight. But that cannot possibly happen to men who are already enlightened and remain free after having abolished those special hereditary rights which perpetuated property in the hands of certain individuals or bodies.

When men who dwell in a democratic society are enlightened, they have no difficulty in realizing that nothing restricts or pins them down, nothing forces them to limit themselves to their present state of wealth.

Then it is that they all have the idea of increasing it and, if they are free, they all try to do so but do not succeed in the same manner. The legislature grants no privileges, it is true, but nature does. Natural inequality being very great, fortunes become unequal from the moment each man uses all his talents to get rich.

The law of descent still stands in the way of wealthy families but does not prevent the existence of wealthy individuals. It constantly levels men to a common point, from which they constantly escape. Their inequality in possessions increases as their knowledge and liberty expand.

A famous sect[a] emerged in our time, famous for its unusual talent and extravagance, which proposed the concentration of all property in the hands of a central power whose function would be to distribute it to individuals according to merit. In that way, that complete and everlasting equality which seems to threaten democratic societies would have been avoided.

Another simpler and less risky solution is to grant privileges to no one, allowing all equal education and equal independence and leaving each man to establish his own place in the world for himself. Natural inequality will soon come to light and wealth pass automatically to the most able.

Democratic and free societies will, therefore, always contain a great number of the wealthy and comfortably off. These rich people will not be so closely linked to each other as the aristocracy which existed formerly; they will have different instincts and will almost never enjoy as secure or as complete a leisure time, although their numbers will be infinitely greater than the aristocracy could ever be. These men will not be so strictly confined to the preoccupations of practicalities and will be able, albeit at different levels of attainment, to give time to the pursuits and pleasures of the intellect. And they will in fact do so, for although it is true that the human mind inclines on one side toward what is limited, material, and utilitarian, it naturally rises on the other to the infinite, spiritual, and beautiful. Physical needs keep it pinned to the earth but as soon as the tie is loosened, it will rise again of its own accord.

Not only will the number of those interested in the works of the mind be greater, but the taste for intellectual enjoyment will move down ever further to those very people who seem in aristocratic societies to have neither the time nor the skills to devote to such enjoyment.

When inherited wealth, class privilege, and advantages of birth have ceased to exert influence and when each man derives his strength from himself alone, what produces the main disparity in the acquisition of wealth is intelligence. Whatever strengthens, stretches, and embellishes intelligence immediately acquires great value.

The usefulness of knowledge unfolds with special clarity even in the eyes of the masses. Those who are not attracted to its charms, value its results and make some effort to achieve it.

In times of democracy, enlightenment, and freedom, nothing exists to keep men apart or to keep them in their particular sphere; they rise or fall with unusual speed. All classes of men are constantly in touch with each other because of their close proximity. Every day, they contact, meet, imitate, and rival each other. Thus the people conceive a host of ideas, notions, and desires which they would not have entertained if the class barriers had been settled and society static.

In such nations, the servant never feels entirely alien to the pleasures and work of his master, nor the poor man to those of the rich; the man in the countryside makes efforts to imitate the town dweller and the provinces ape the capital city.

As a result, no one easily allows himself to be limited solely to the practical concerns of life and the humblest craftsman casts occasionally a furtive and eager glance at the superior world of the intellect. People do not read with the same attitude or in the same manner as they do in aristocratic circles; but the range of readers increases continuously and, in the end, includes all citizens.

From the time when the masses begin to take an interest in the work of the mind, they realize that through excellence in this field they have a good route to fame, power, and fortune. Restless ambition born of equality straightway takes this direction, as it does any others. The number of those who cultivate science, literature, and the arts becomes immense. The intellectual world bursts into tremendous activity; everyone endeavors to forge a path toward it, and to attract the eyes of the public after him. Something similar happens to what occurs in the political life of the United States. The achievements are often defective but are countless in number; although the results from single individuals are normally very slight, the general outcome is always huge.

Therefore, it is not true to say that men of democratic times are normally indifferent toward science, literature, and the arts; simply we have to acknowledge that they cultivate them after their own fashion and bring to them their own peculiar qualities and deficiencies.

CHAPTER 10

WHY AMERICANS ARE MORE ATTRACTED TO PRACTICAL RATHER THAN THEORETICAL ASPECTS OF THE SCIENCES

If a democratic society and its institutions do not impede the free flight of the human mind, it is at least beyond dispute that they impel it in one direction rather than another. Their efforts, although limited, are still very powerful and I trust I shall be forgiven if I pause for a while to consider them.

We have made several observations on the philosophic methods of the American people which may be useful here.

Equality encourages every man to be his own judge of everything, giving him, in all things, a taste for the tangible and concrete, along with a disdain for traditions and forms. These general instincts are mainly evident in the particular aims of this chapter.

Those who cultivate science in democratic nations are always fearful of losing their way in utopian speculation. They distrust systems, they enjoy adhering to facts which they themselves study. As they do not easily defer to the reputation of their fellow men, they are never inclined to swear by the authority of an expert. On the contrary, they always concentrate on finding the weak aspects of his theory. Scientific traditions hold little sway and they do not hang around for long in the subtleties of a particular school of thought. They are not impressed by high-sounding phrases, but explore as far as they can the main areas of the subject they are studying and enjoy describing them in everyday language. Then science has a freer and safer, though more modest, appearance.

It seems to me that the mind may divide science into three parts:

The first comprises the most theoretical principles, the most abstract theories whose application is either unknown or very remote.

The second is composed of general truths which, while still stemming from pure theory, nevertheless lead directly and immediately to practical results.

Methods of application and means of execution make up the third.

Each of these different areas of science can be studied separately although reason and experience show that not one of them can prosper long, if cut off completely from the remaining two.

In America, the purely practical aspect of science is studied admirably and careful attention is devoted to that theoretical area which is closely related to its application. Americans display, in this respect, an attitude which is always sharp, free, original, and productive, but hardly anyone in the United States devotes himself to the essentially theoretical and abstract aspects of human knowledge. In this, Americans carry to excess a tendency which is found to a lesser degree in all democratic nations.

Nothing is more vital to the study of the higher reaches of science than meditation; nothing is less suited to meditation than the internal constitution of democratic nations where you do not encounter, as in aristocracies, one class which sits back in its own comfort and another which will not stir itself because it despairs of ever improving its status. Everyone is in a state of agitation: some to attain power; others to grab wealth.

Amid this widespread upheaval, this repeated grating of opposed interests, men's unremitting progress toward wealth, where could we find the tranquillity needed for deep intellectual investigations? How could the mind dwell upon one point, if everything around it was in constant movement and every day man himself is dragged along like flotsam in the raging torrent which carries all before it?

The type of deep-seated agitation which lies at the heart of a quiet and well-established democracy has to be distinguished from those tumultuous and revolutionary movements which are almost always present at the birth and growth of a democratic society.

When a violent revolution takes place in a very civilized nation, it cannot fail to give an impetus to feelings and ideas. This is above all true of democratic revolutions which stir up all the classes in a nation and, at the same time, create inordinate ambitions in the hearts of all citizens.

If the French have achieved such swift and admirable progress in the exact sciences to coincide with their final destruction of the remnants of an ancient feudal society, we must account for this sudden creativity not by the arrival of democracy but by the unprecedented revolution which accompanied its growth. What transpired then was a particular event which it would be unwise to regard as the sign of a general law.

Great revolutions are not more common amongst democratic nations than others; I am even inclined to believe that they are less so. But at the heart of these nations resides a small, awkward movement, where incessant rumblings put men against each other; this disturbs and distracts their minds without stimulating or improving them.

Men living in democratic societies not only have difficulty with meditation but they entertain a naturally low regard for it. The state of society and the democratic institutions incline the majority of men to a constantly active life; now, the mental habits which suit action do not always promote thought. The man of action is frequently forced to accept compromise because he would never reach the fruition of his plans if he wished to achieve perfection in every detail. He has to rely endlessly upon ideas which he has not had the time to test thoroughly, for he is aided much more by the opportunity of an idea he is adopting than its strict accuracy. All in all, using a few false principles involves him in less risk than wasting his time guaranteeing the truth of all his principles. The world is not directed by long and learned proofs. All its affairs are decided by the swift glance at a particular fact, the daily examination of the changing moods of the crowd, occasional moments of chance, and the skill to exploit them.

In ages when almost every man is engaged in action, an excessive value is generally placed upon those rapid flights and superficial ideas of the intellect while its slower and deeper efforts are considerably undervalued.

This opinion of the public affects the judgment of men who study science, either persuading them that they can succeed in those pursuits without meditation or carrying them away from the sciences that require it.

Science is studied in several ways. Many men exhibit a selfish, mercenary, and practical liking for the discoveries of the mind which must not be confused with that disinterested passion which is kindled in the heart of the few. The desire to use knowledge is not the same as the desire to know. I am quite sure that, here and there, some men possess a burning and inexhaustible passion for the truth which is self-supported and a constant source of joy, without ever reaching any final satisfaction. This is the burning, proud, and disinterested passion for what is true which leads man to the abstract springs of truth from where they draw their basic knowledge.

If Pascal had had in mind only some great source of profit or had been motivated only by self-glory, I cannot think he would have been able, as he was, to gather, as he did, all the powers of his intellect for a deeper discovery of the most hidden secrets of the Creator. When I observe him tearing his soul away, so to speak, from the concerns of life to devote it entirely to this research and severing prematurely the ties which bind his soul to his body, to die of old age before his fortieth year, I stand aghast and realize that no ordinary cause can produce such extraordinary efforts.

The future will demonstrate whether such rare, creative passions are born and develop as readily in democratic as in aristocratic societies. My own opinion is that I can hardly believe it.

In aristocratic societies, the class which controls public opinion and takes the lead in public affairs naturally conceives a proud image of itself and of man because it feels itself permanently above the masses through its inherited position. It easily imagines glorious delights for man and sets splendid goals for his desires. Aristocrats commit actions which are tyrannical and very cruel but rarely entertain ignoble thoughts and they demonstrate a certain proud scorn for petty pleasures, even when they indulge in them. The effect is to raise the tone of society in general to a very high level. In aristocratic times, the ideas commonly held about the dignity, power, and nobility of man are very lofty indeed. These opinions affect scientists as much as everyone else and encourage the natural impulse of the mind toward the highest regions of thought which then has a natural inclination to raise the love of truth to a sublime, almost divine level.

Scientists at such times are, therefore, drawn toward theory and they often hold the practical in ill-considered contempt. "Archimedes,"[a] says Plutarch,[b] "had such an elevated spirit that he never stooped to leave a written treatise, to show how all these engines of war might be built. As he considered the entire science of inventing and constructing machines and all the skills that contribute to practical ends as cheap, shoddy, and mercenary, he devoted his mind and study to writing only those things whose beauty and refinement had no connection with necessity." There you have the aristocratic aims of science which cannot be the same in democracies.

Most men in these nations are very eager for immediate material pleasures and, as they are always dissatisfied with the position they occupy and always free to leave it, they dream only of the methods of changing or enhancing their lot. For men with such a frame of mind, any novel method which leads by the shortest route to wealth, any machine which lessens work, any means that diminishes the cost of production, any discovery which smoothes the way to increased pleasure, seems the most magnificent work of the human intellect. It is primarily from this direction that democratic nations approach the sciences in their understanding and reverence. In aristocratic times, people seek especially the pleasures of the mind from science; in democratic times, it is those of the body.

You may be sure that the more a nation is democratic, enlightened, and free, the greater the number of those self-interested champions of scientific genius and the more profit will result from discoveries immediately applicable to industry, bringing fame and even power to their inventors. For, in democracies, the working class takes its part in public affairs and those who serve its interests can expect honors as well as money.

In a society organized along these lines, it is easy to see how the human mind is unconsciously drawn to neglect theory and must, on the contrary, feel itself driven with unparalleled energy toward the practical applications or, at the very least, those aspects of theory which are vital to those who are involved in such applications.

That instinctive drive which draws the mind to the highest realms of the intellect fights a vain battle against self-interest which drags it down to the average. There it displays its strength and restless activity; there it produces its wonders. Those same Americans who have not laid eyes upon a single general law of mechanics have changed the face of the world with a new machine for navigation.[c]

Of course, I am far from claiming that democratic nations at the present time are fated to witness the snuffing out of the sublime lights of the human mind or that new ones will not blaze in their midst. In the present age of the world and in so many educated nations, constantly agitated by the fever of industrial activity, the ties which unite their different elements of science cannot fail to strike the observer. The very taste for practicality, once enlightened, ought to lead men not to neglect theory. Amongst the many investigations in applied science, and in the daily repeated experiments, it is almost impossible for general laws not to come to light. In this way, great discoveries are bound to be frequent, although great discoverers may be rare.

Besides, I believe in the high calling of science. Democracy may well not encourage men to study science for its own sake, but it considerably increases the number of those that do.

It is inconceivable that in such a large crowd some speculative genius does not appear from time to time who is fired by the love of truth alone. Such a man will surely strive to penetrate the deepest mysteries of nature whatever the spirit of the country or times he lives in. His flights of fancy need no help; it is enough to free him from obstacles. This is my meaning: a permanent condition of inequality locks men away in the arrogant and sterile search for abstract truths, while democratic societies and institutions prepare them to seek the immediate and useful practical results of the sciences.

Such a tendency is both natural and unavoidable. Such an observation is strange but it may be vital to point it out.

If those who are summoned to direct the affairs of present-day nations were to recognize clearly and in good time these new attitudes, which will soon be irresistible, they would understand that, with enlightenment and freedom, men living in democratic times cannot fail to perfect the industrial side of science and that, henceforth, all the effort of social authorities should concentrate on supporting the higher branches of learning and fostering the noble passion for science.

Nowadays, we need to force the human mind to study theory; it will rush automatically toward practical applications. Instead of perpetually concentrating man's mind on the minute analysis of secondary effects, it is salutary to distract him from that to inspire him occasionally to contemplate first causes.

Because Roman civilization disappeared as a consequence of the barbarian invasions, we may well be too ready to believe that civilization cannot die in any other way.

If our guiding lights are ever extinguished, they would grow dim gradually and, as it were, of their own accord. By confining ourselves to practical application, we would lose sight of basic principles and, when these had been entirely forgotten, we would find it difficult to pursue the methods which derive from them. We would stop inventing new ones and would use unintelligently and clumsily scientific processes we would no longer understand.

When Europeans landed in China three hundred years ago, they found there that almost all the arts had reached a certain degree of perfection and were surprised that they had not improved beyond that point. Later, they came across traces of some higher branches of knowledge which had been lost. It was an industrial nation where most scientific processes had been preserved, while science itself was dead. That explained the unusually static quality of mind of this nation. The Chinese, in following the path of their ancestors, had mislaid the reasons for the direction the latter had chosen. They still used the formula without asking why; they kept the tool but they had lost the skills to adapt or replace it. The Chinese were, therefore, not able to change anything and had to abandon any notion of improvement. They were forced to imitate their fathers in everything the whole time, for fear of falling into impenetrable darkness if they ever strayed from the tracks laid down for them. The well of human knowledge had almost dried up and although the flow still ran, it could neither increase its volume nor change its course.

Meanwhile, China had existed in peace for centuries; its invaders had adopted its ways and order prevailed. A sort of material prosperity was visible everywhere one looked. Revolutions were infrequent and wars were virtually unknown.

We should not, therefore, complacently think that the barbarians are still far away for, if some nations allow the torch to be snatched from their hands, others stamp it out themselves.

CHAPTER 11

IN WHAT SPIRIT THE AMERICANS CULTIVATE THE ARTS

It could well be a waste of readers' time, and my own, if I strove to demonstrate how the modest level of wealth, the absence of abundant riches, the universal desire for comfort, and the constant efforts of everyone to achieve such comfort, establish in men's hearts the dominance of their taste for the useful over the love of the beautiful. Democratic nations, where we encounter all these things, will, therefore, foster those arts which help to make life comfortable in preference to those which aim to adorn it. The useful will have preference over the beautiful and it is best for the beautiful to be useful.

But I intend to go further: having highlighted the first feature, I wish to sketch out several others.

It usually comes about in times of privilege that the practice of almost all the arts is a privilege itself and that each profession is a world apart into which there is no freedom of entry. Even where industry is free, that immobility which is natural to aristocratic nations separates off all those engaged in the same skill into a distinct class, always comprising the same families, whose members all know each other and soon develop a public reputation and corporate pride. In such an industrial class, each craftsman has both his fortune to make and his professional standing to protect. He is not ruled only by his self-interest nor by that of his customer but by the corporate body to which he belongs and the concern of that body is that each craftsman produces masterpieces. In aristocratic times, the ambition of the arts is, therefore, to produce the most beautiful work that is possible, not at the greatest speed nor at the lowest cost.

On the other hand, when every profession is open to all, with all the masses taking it up or dropping it all the time and when its different members do not know or see each other and treat each other with indifference because the numbers are so large, the social ties are broken; every workman retreats into himself and seeks to earn as much money as he can at the least cost. His only restraints are the wishes of the customer but he too is embroiled at the same time in an equally radical transformation.

In countries where wealth and power are permanently concentrated in the grasp of a few people, the enjoyment of most of the good things of this world belongs to a small number of individuals, who never change. Necessity, public opinion, and their moderate desires keep the rest away from this enjoyment.

As this aristocratic elite holds its high position without contraction or expansion, it always experiences the same needs and in the same manner. From their superior and inherited position, the men who make up this class naturally possess a liking for well-crafted things which will last.

This affects the general thinking of the nation toward the arts.

Among such nations, it often transpires that the peasant farmer will prefer to do entirely without objects he covets rather that acquire ones of inferior quality.

In aristocracies, workmen work, therefore, for only a limited number of fastidious customers. The profit they expect depends mainly on the perfection of their workmanship.

Things are very different when all privilege is dead, all classes intermingle, and all men move constantly up and down the social scale.

At the center of a democratic nation, one always encounters plenty of citizens whose inheritance is being divided up and reduced. They have retained from better times certain needs which linger after the means of satisfying them have gone, and they anxiously seek some roundabout way of providing for them.

On the other hand, in democracies a great number of men exist whose wealth increases but whose desires increase much more quickly, leaving them to ogle the goods this wealth promises long before they have the means to afford them. Such men are always on the lookout for shortcuts to these delights which lie so close. The inevitable consequence of the combination of these two causes is that one encounters in democracies a host of citizens whose needs are beyond their means and who would be all too ready to make do with an imperfect replacement rather than do without the object of their desire altogether.

The worker easily understands these feelings because he shares them; in aristocracies, he sought to sell his goods to a few at high prices; now he sees that a more effective way of becoming wealthy would be to sell cheaply to all.

Now, only two ways of lowering the price of goods exist.

The first is to find better, shorter, and cleverer ways of producing them. The second is to manufacture in greater quantities objects which are more or less the same but not so expensive. In democratic nations, all the intellectual faculties of the craftsman are directed to these two objectives. He sets out to find methods which enable him to work not only more effectively but also more quickly and at lower cost. If he cannot manage that, he reduces the intrinsic qualities of the object he is making without making it entirely unsuited to its intended use. When only the rich had watches, they were almost all of excellent quality; now, mostly mediocre specimens are produced but everyone possesses one. Thus, democracy not only directs the human mind to the useful arts but also persuades craftsmen to produce many second-rate goods and consumers to put up with them.

Not that art in democracies cannot produce marvelous artefacts when needs be. This happens sometimes when buyers agree to pay for the time spent and the trouble taken. In the struggle experienced by all industries, amid the widespread competition and countless experiments, some workmen are excellent and reach the utmost limits of their craft but have few opportunities to display what they can do. They carefully monitor their efforts; they maintain a clever and self-critical mediocrity which, although capable of reaching beyond the goal set for themselves, aims only at attainable goals. In aristocracies, on the other hand, craftsmen always achieve their potential and come to a halt only when they reach the limits of their skill.

To arrive in a country and see the arts producing wonderful objects teaches me nothing about the state of society or the political constitution of that country. Whereas, if I observed that the objects produced are generally of poor quality, very numerous and at low prices, I am convinced that in a nation where this happens privilege is on the decline and classes are beginning to mix to the point of disappearing altogether.

Craftsmen living in democratic times seek not only to bring their useful products within the reach of all citizens but strive also to give to these products a look of brilliance which they do not possess.

In this uniformity of classes, every man hopes to appear as something he is not and takes the trouble to achieve this. Democracy does not engender this feeling, which all too naturally resides in the heart of man, but it does apply it to material objects. Hypocrisy in matters of virtue belongs to all ages; hypocrisy in matters of luxury belongs more especially to democratic ages.

To satisfy these new cravings of human vanity, the arts will employ any deception and industry sometimes follows this path so excessively that it manages to harm itself. It has already succeeded in imitating diamonds so perfectly that it is easy to confuse them with the real thing. The instant that the art of manufacturing false diamonds is possible so that they are indistinguishable from real stones, both will probably be disregarded and will revert to their status as pebbles.

This leads me on to mentioning those of the arts which are called, exceptionally, the fine arts.

I do not accept that it is inevitable that democratic society and its institutions reduce the number of men who are engaged in fine art; but they do have a powerful influence on the way such fine art is cultivated. Since most of those who had already conceived a taste for fine art are impoverished and, on the other hand, many of those not yet wealthy are beginning to imitate a taste for fine art, the number of consumers in general increases while very wealthy and discriminating consumers become more scarce. Thus, something happens in the world of fine art to parallel what I have already highlighted in the useful arts. Works multiply while their merit declines. No longer capable of greatness, men seek elegance and prettiness; they aim for appearance rather than reality.

In aristocracies, men produce a few great pictures; in

democracies, a mass of insignificant paintings. The former erects statues in bronze, the latter statues cast in plaster.

When I reached New York for the first time, by that part of the Atlantic Ocean called the East River, I was surprised to observe along the bank some distance from the town a certain number of small palaces in white marble, several of which imitated a classical architectural style. The next day, on examining more closely the one which had especially drawn my attention, I discovered that its walls were of whitewashed brick and its columns of painted wood. The same went for all the monuments I had admired the day before.

Furthermore, democratic society and its institutions create in all the imitative arts certain and peculiar tendencies which it is easy to point out. They turn aside from the painting of the soul in order to concentrate on the body; movement and sensation replace the depiction of feelings and ideas. In the end, the real ousts the ideal.

I doubt whether Raphael[a] made a profounder study of the smallest details of the human body than today's artists. He did not attach in this matter the same importance as they do to rigorous precision since he claimed to surpass nature. He sought to make of man something superior to man and to enhance beauty itself.

David[b] and his pupils were, on the other hand, as good anatomists as they were painters. They depicted marvelously well the models before their eyes but rarely did they imagine anything beyond that. They faithfully followed nature, whereas Raphael aimed for something better than nature. The former have bequeathed us an exact painting of man, while the latter shows us a glimpse of the Divine in his works.

The same applies to the choice of subject as to what I have said about the method of treating it. Renaissance painters[c] sought usually great subjects above their heads or away from their own time which allowed ample scope to their imaginations. Our painters often devote their talents to the exact reproduction of details of the private life which they constantly see before them and they copy from all around them small objects which can all too frequently be seen in nature itself.

CHAPTER 12

WHY THE AMERICANS ERECT BOTH INSIGNIFICANT MONUMENTS AND OTHERS WHICH ARE VERY GRAND

I have just stated that in democratic times monuments produced by the arts tended to become more numerous and smaller. I now hasten to point out the exception to this rule.

In democratic nations, individuals are very weak but the state which represents them and holds them all in the palm of its hand is very powerful. Nowhere do citizens appear so insignificant as in a democratic nation; nowhere does the nation itself seem greater or the mind draw a greater picture of it. In democratic societies, the imagination shrinks when men think of themselves; at the thought of the state, it expands beyond all limits. Hence, men who live in the constricted condition of small houses often aspire to gigantic splendor in their public monuments.

The Americans have marked out the boundaries of a huge city on the place where they wished to make their capital and even today it has a smaller population than Pontoise.[a] According to them it is to contain one day a million inhabitants. They have already uprooted trees for ten miles around lest they should inconvenience future citizens of this imaginary metropolis. In the center of the city, they have erected a magnificent palace to serve as a seat for the Congress and given it the name of the Capitol.

Every day individual states plan and execute tremendous projects which would astonish the engineers of the great European nations.

Thus, democracy leads men to make not only many minor works but also to erect a small number of very considerable monuments. Between these two extremes there is nothing. Some scattered remains of huge edifices give no indication, therefore, of the social state and the institutions of the people who erected them. Nor, I may add, although this is beyond my subject, are they any better at revealing to us their greatness, knowledge, or actual prosperity.

Whenever any power has the means to bring a whole nation together upon one single project, it will succeed with little skill and a great deal of time, in drawing something huge from their combined efforts. Yet this does not have to lead to the conclusion that the people are very happy, enlightened or even very strong. The Spanish found Mexico City full of fine temples and vast palaces which did not prevent Cortez[b] from conquering the Mexican Empire with six hundred infantry and sixteen horses.

If the Romans had better understood the laws of hydraulics, they would not have erected those aqueducts which surround the ruins of their cities and would have made better use of their power and wealth. If they had invented the steam engine, perhaps they would not have extended to the far ends of their empire those long artificial rock formations which we call Roman roads. Such things are simultaneously mighty evidence of their ignorance and of their greatness.

The nation which left us no other trace of its presence than a few lead pipes in the ground and a few iron rods on the surface might have been more in control of nature than the Romans.

CHAPTER 13

HOW LITERATURE APPEARS IN DEMOCRATIC TIMES

When one visits a bookshop in the United States and looks at the American books ranged upon the shelves, the number of books seems very great while the number of well-known authors seems, on the contrary, to be very small.

First of all, there is a mass of elementary treatises intended to teach the rudiments of human knowledge. Most of these works have been written in Europe. The Americans reprint them and adapt them to their own uses. Then comes an enormous quantity of religious books: Bibles, sermons, holy stories, religious quarrels, reports of charitable trusts. Finally, there appears the long catalogue of political pamphlets for, in America, political parties do not publish books to conduct their disputes but pamphlets which, after an unbelievably swift circulation, last a day and die.

Amid these ranks of dim productions of the human mind appear the more remarkable works of only a small number of authors who are or who ought to be known to Europeans.

Although America is nowadays the one civilized country where literature is fostered the least, nevertheless a great number of individuals take an interest in things of the mind which become for them, if not a life study, at least a leisure entertainment. But it is England which supplies them with most of the books they call for. Almost all the great English works are republished in the United States. The literary genius of Great Britain still darts its beams into the depths of the New World forests. Scarcely a single pioneer's cabin is without a few odd volumes of Shakespeare. I remember reading the feudal drama of *Henry V* for the first time in a log house.

Not only will America draw each day upon the treasures of English literature, but one can truly say they find English literature growing in their own soil. Among the small number of men who are engaged in literary works in the United States, the majority are English in origin and above all in style. Thus, they transplant into the heart of a democracy ideas and literary uses which are current in the aristocratic nation they take as their model. They paint with colors borrowed from foreign customs and are rarely popular in the country of their birth because they almost never represent it in its proper light.

The citizens of the United States themselves seem so convinced that books are not published for their benefit that before settling on the merits of one of their own writers they normally wait for England to approve his work. Thus we are quite willing to let the painter of an original picture judge the copy.

Therefore, strictly speaking, the inhabitants of the United States have not yet gained a literature. The only authors I recognize as American are journalists, who are not great writers but speak the language of the country and make themselves understood. I consider the others to be aliens. They are for America what the imitators of the Greeks and Romans were at the time of the Renaissance, namely an object of curiosity not of general sympathy. They amuse the mind but have no effect upon the customs of the country.

I have already said that this state of affairs was far from stemming from democracy alone and that the causes of it had to be sought in several peculiar circumstances, unconnected with democracy.

If Americans, while still maintaining their social state and laws, had come from quite different beginnings and had been transplanted into another country, I do not doubt that they would have had a literature. Given who they are, I am convinced that they will have one in the end; but it will have a character different from the American writings of today and one which will be peculiarly its own. Nor is it impossible to forecast in advance what that character will be.

Let us suppose an aristocratic nation which fosters literature; the efforts of intelligence as well as the business of government are controlled by a ruling class. Literature, along with politics, is almost entirely concentrated within this class or those most closely connected with it. That is enough to give me the key to all the rest.

When a small number of the same men are concerned with the same objectives at the same time, they easily agree to settle in common certain fundamental rules which are to govern their own behavior. If the object of their attention is literature, the productions of their minds will soon be subjected to a few specific rules from which they will not be allowed to deviate.

If these men fill an hereditary position in the country, they will be inclined not only to adopt for themselves a number of fixed rules but also to follow those prescribed by their ancestors; their code will be both strict and traditional.

As they are not, nor ever have been, preoccupied with material things any more than their fathers before them, several generations of them have been interested in the works of the mind.

They have understood the art of literature; in the end, they love it for itself and feel a scholarly pleasure in seeing that the rules are kept.

Nor is this all: the men I speak of begin and end their lives in ease and wealth; they have naturally conceived a taste for exquisite enjoyment and an affection for subtle and refined pleasures. Moreover, a long and untroubled use of so many possessions often induces a certain flabbiness of spirit and feeling and will lead them to remove from these very same pleasures anything too unexpected or lively. They prefer amusement to deep emotion; they wish to be interested not carried away.

Now, imagine a great number of literary works produced by or for the men I have just described and you will have a good idea of a literature which will be entirely regular and mapped out in advance. The slightest work will be polished in its smallest detail; everything will bear witness to skill and effort; each genre of writing will have rules of its own which must not be bypassed and which will distinguish it from every other genre.

Style will appear almost as important as thought, form as content; the tone of the writing will be polished, measured, and sustained. The mind will always move in a dignified manner, rarely at a frenetic pace; writers will concentrate their attention more on perfecting their works than simply writing for the sake of it.

Sometimes the lettered classes, living as they do solely amongst themselves and writing for themselves alone, will lose sight of the rest of the world; this will project them into the abstruse and the false. They will lay down minor literary rules for their own use which will imperceptibly drive them from common sense and cause them to lose touch with nature.

In their desire to avoid speaking like the common people, they will eventually adopt a sort of aristocratic jargon which is scarcely less removed from fine language than popular dialect.

Those are the natural pitfalls of literature in aristocratic cultures. Any aristocracy wholly adrift from the people becomes powerless, a fact which is as true in literature as in politics.[1]

Let us now examine the other side of the picture.

Imagine a democracy sensitive to the pleasures of the mind through its ancient traditions and its present knowledge. Classes intermingle and coalesce; knowledge and power are divided up infinitely so as to become, if I may express it so, scattered in every direction.

We have a motley crowd whose intellectual needs crave satisfaction. These new enthusiasts for the pleasures of the mind have not all received the same education; they do not possess the same knowledge; they are unlike their fathers and they are in a constant state of transformation among themselves for they live in a state of incessant change of place, feelings, and wealth. The citizens have no shared intellectual links, traditions, or culture with each other and they have never had either the power or the will or the time to find a common understanding.

Authors emerge from the heart of this disparate and turbulent crowd which then dispenses profit and reputation to them.

I find it easy to understand that, things being as they are, I must expect to find in the literature of such a nation only a small number of the rigorous rules of style acknowledged by the readers and writers of aristocratic times. If the men of one period happened to agree about a few of these rules, that would still prove nothing for the following period, for in a democracy each new generation forms a new nation. Among such nations, literature would, therefore, have difficulty in submitting to rules which were restrictive, while permanent rules would always be an impossibility.

In democracies, men involved in literature are far from

---

1. All this is especially true of aristocratic countries which have been for a long time peacefully subjected to the rule of a king.

When liberty prevails in an aristocracy, the upper classes are constantly obliged to use the lower classes and, by using them, they draw closer to them. That often infects their hearts with something of the democratic spirit. Moreover, a privileged ruling class develops the habit of energetic enterprise and a taste for bustle and excitement which cannot fail to influence all its literary efforts.

receiving a literary education and among those who have some smattering of serious literature, most are engaged in politics or pursue a profession from which they are diverted only for brief moments to taste secretly the pleasures of the mind. These pleasures are not, therefore, the main attraction of their lives; rather, they are a needed passing relaxation amid the serious business of life. Such men would never be able to achieve a deep enough knowledge of literature to experience its refinements; its subtleties will pass them by.

Since they have only a brief time to devote to literature, they want to make the best use of it. They like books which are easily available, quick to read, and which demand no learned research for their understanding. They seek superficial beauties, immediately available and enjoyed; above all, they want the unexpected and the novel. Accustomed to the struggles and monotony of practical life, they crave lively and rapid emotions, sudden revelations, brilliantly depicted stories of truth or wrongdoing which offer immediate escapism and plunge them directly and almost violently straight into the subject.

Need I say more? All will understand what is coming before I express it.

Considered in its entirety, literature of democratic times could not possibly present, as it does in aristocratic times, a picture of order, regularity, science, and art; its formal qualities will normally be disregarded and sometimes despised. Style will often appear quirky, incorrect, inflated, flabby, and almost always extreme and violent. Authors will aim more at speed of execution than perfection of detail. Writing on a small scale will occur more often than weightier books, wit more often than scholarship, imagination more often than profundity.

An untutored and almost barbaric power will govern thought, accompanied by great variety and an unusual richness of writing. Writers will strive to startle rather than please and to rouse passions rather than charm the reader's taste.

Doubtless, a few writers will appear occasionally wishing to travel a different path and these will, if they possess a superior ability, gain, in spite of their faults and qualities, a readership. But these exceptions will be rare and those very few people who have escaped common practice in general will always relapse when it comes to details.

I have just described two extremes. However, nations do not proceed from one to the other in one sudden leap; rather the transition is gradual and marked by myriad subtle changes. In the process that a cultivated nation follows from one to the other, there almost always occurs a moment when the literary genius of democratic nations will vie with that of aristocratic nations, both wishing to establish their joint sway over the human mind.

Such are brief but brilliant periods, when creativity avoids ebullience and liveliness avoids confusion. That was the character of eighteenth-century French literature.

I would say more than I intend were I to state that a country's literature is always subservient to its social state and political constitution. I am aware that, aside from the above reasons, there are several others which confer certain characteristics upon literary works but these appear to me the main ones.

The connections between the social and political conditions of a nation and the genius of its writers are always very numerous; whoever knows one is never completely unaware of the other.

CHAPTER 14

THE LITERATURE INDUSTRY

Democracy not only introduces the taste for literature to the working classes, it brings the working spirit into the heart of literature.

In aristocracies, readers are fastidious and few in number; in democracies, they are immensely more numerous and more easily satisfied. The result is that among aristocratic nations no one can hope to succeed without huge efforts and such efforts, while gaining a great deal of fame, never earn much money, whereas with democratic nations a writer may flatter himself that he can gain cheaply a modest reputation and great wealth.

To achieve that, he does not have to be admired; it is enough for his works to be popular.

The ever-growing crowd of readers and the continuous need they have for something new ensures the sale of books no one much esteems.

In democratic times, the public often treats its authors as kings usually do their courtiers: it enriches and despises them. What more is merited by those mercenary souls who are born in courts or are worthy of living there?

Democratic literature always teems with authors who see in letters a mere trade, and for each of the few great writers, peddlers of ideas can be counted in their thousands.

CHAPTER 15

WHY THE STUDY OF GREEK AND LATIN LITERATURE IS PARTICULARLY USEFUL IN DEMOCRATIC COMMUNITIES

What men called the people in the most democratic republics of the ancient world had scant comparison with what we mean by the term. In Athens, all the citizens took part in public affairs, but there were only twenty thousand citizens in a population of three hundred and fifty thousand. All the others were slaves and fulfilled most of the functions which nowadays working and even middle classes perform.

Athens, with its universal suffrage, was, therefore, after all only an aristocratic republic where all the nobility had an equal right to the government.

The struggle between the patricians and the plebeians in Rome has to be seen in the same light; it was simply an internal quarrel between the younger and older members of the same family. They all belonged in fact to the aristocracy and exhibited its spirit.

Further, one has to observe that throughout the ancient world, books were scarce and expensive and that they were laborious to copy and circulate. Since those circumstances happened to concentrate the taste and habit of literature in the hands of a small number of men, they brought into being, as it were, a small literary aristocracy from the elite of a wider political aristocracy. In addition, in the case of the Greeks and the Romans, nothing indicates that literature was ever treated like an industry.

These nations, who were not only aristocracies but were also well regulated and enjoyed wide freedoms, must therefore have imparted to their literary efforts those peculiar defects and special qualities which characterize the literature of aristocratic times.

In fact, you have only to glance at the writings bequeathed to us by antiquity to realize that, if those writers sometimes lacked variety and imagination in their choice of subject, or boldness, energy, and the power of generalization in their ideas, they always exhibited admirable skill and care in the details. Nothing in their works seems hastily or haphazardly written, but is always aimed at the connoisseur and constantly seeks out an ideal of beauty. No other literature highlights more boldly than that of the ancients those qualities which are naturally missing from democratic writers.

Therefore, no other literature is better suited for study in democratic times. Such study is the most appropriate of all to combat the deficiencies inherent in such times, whereas the natural qualities will appear of their own accord, without the need to acquire them through study.

This is a point which must be clearly understood; such a study may be useful to the literature of a nation without having a bearing upon its social and political needs.

A persistent education in the classics alone, in a society where everyone was always struggling to increase or preserve their wealth, would produce very sophisticated but very dangerous citizens; for their needs would be prompted every day by their social and political state, which their education would never satisfy, and they would disrupt the state in the name of the Greeks and Romans, instead of enriching it with their industriousness.

It is clear that in democratic times, individual interest, as well as the security of the state, insists that the education of the masses should be scientific, commercial, and industrial rather than literary.

Greek and Latin should not be taught in all schools; but it is important that those destined by natural endowment or wealth to cultivate or appreciate literature should find schools where they can achieve complete proficiency in classical literature and deeply imbibe its spirit. A few first-rate universities would be more effective in reaching this goal than numerous poor colleges where badly taught and superfluous studies obstruct the establishment of necessary ones.

All those with the ambition to excel in literature in democratic nations should take frequent nourishment from the classics. That is a healthy regime.

Not that I hold classical literature to be without faults; simply that it has special qualities which can admirably counteract our own peculiar deficiencies. It supports us just where we are likely to fall down.

CHAPTER 16

HOW AMERICAN DEMOCRACY HAS MODIFIED THE ENGLISH LANGUAGE

If the reader has fully understood what I have already said about literature in general, he will have no difficulty in observing the kind of influence democratic society and its institutions can exert on language itself, which is the primary instrument of thought.

In truth, American authors live more frequently in England than in their own country, since they are immersed in their study of English writers, whom they take every day for their models. That is not the case with the population itself, which is more immediately subject to the influences peculiar to the United States. Therefore, we must pay attention to the spoken language, not the written, if we wish to note how the idiom of an aristocratic nation can change in becoming the language of a democracy.

Learned English scholars more skilled in discerning the subtle nuances than I am have often assured me that the well-educated classes in the United States speak a markedly different language from that of the educated classes in Great Britain.

They complain not only that the Americans have employed many new words (this could be explained by the difference of the two countries and their distance apart), but that these new words are more especially borrowed from political jargon, the mechanical arts, or the language of trade. They add that former English words are often given a fresh interpretation by Americans. Finally, they say that the population of the United States frequently muddle their styles in a bizarre fashion and occasionally juxtapose words which, in the mother language, are usually kept apart.

These remarks, repeated on several occasions by people who appeared worth believing, led me to reflect upon the subject and my thoughts brought me via theory to the same point my informants had reached by practical observation.

In aristocracies, language must naturally share the state of calm enjoyed by everything else. Few new words are forged because few new objects are made. In the case of any such new objects, efforts were made to describe them with known vocabulary whose meaning had been set by tradition.

If at last the human mind happens to stir itself of its own accord, or the light from outside rouses it, the new expressions coined have an educated, intellectual, and philosophical ring which shows that they do not owe their creation to democratic influences. When the fall of Constantinople[a] had turned the tide of science and literature toward the West, the French language was quite suddenly invaded by a mass of new words, all of which had their roots in Greek and Latin. A learned neologism sprang up in the France of that time, which was the peculiar preserve of the educated classes and whose effects were never felt by the common people or reached them only after a very long time.

All the European nations, one by one, mirrored this same picture. Milton[b] alone introduced more than six hundred words into the English language, almost all derived from Latin, Greek, or Hebrew.

The constant restlessness at the center of a democracy leads, on the contrary, to endless developments in the language, just as in business. Amid this general agitation and universal rivalry of minds, a great many new ideas are formed; old ideas disappear or reappear or are split off into minute shades of meaning. Thus some words are forced out of use while others must be brought in.

Besides, democratic nations like change for its own sake, which is as obvious in language as in politics. Even when they do not need to change words, they sometimes feel the desire to do so.

The character of democracies reveals itself not only in the great number of new words brought into use, but also in the kinds of ideas represented by these new words.

Among such nations, the majority lays down the law in matters of language as in everything else; its spirit prevails there as everywhere else. Now the majority is more engaged in business than in scholarship, in political and commercial concerns than in philosophic speculation or literature. Most of the words invented or adopted will bear the imprint of these preoccupations and will serve mainly to express the needs of industry, the passions of political parties, or the details of public administration. Language will expand in this direction, while gradually metaphysics and theology will lose ground.

It is easy to describe from where democracies draw their new words and how they set about giving shape to them.

Men living in democratic countries have scant knowledge of the language spoken in Rome or Athens and do not bother to revert to the classics to find the expressions they need. If occasionally they refer to learned etymologies, it is normally vanity which inspires their researches into dead languages and not learning which offers them naturally to their minds. Sometimes it can even happen that the most ignorant make the most use of them. The entirely democratic desire to rise above their station often leads them to enhance a very vulgar occupation by a Greek or Latin word. The more a job is lowly and remote from science, the more the name is pompous and learned. Thus our rope dancers have been transformed into acrobats and funambulists.

In the absence of dead languages, democratic nations are willing to borrow words from other modern languages, since they are in constant contact with each other and men from different countries are quite happy to copy each other since their points of similarity increase daily.

But it is primarily in their own language that democratic nations seek innovation. From time to time they restore forgotten expressions to their vocabulary or borrow a term belonging to a particular class of citizens, which they will introduce into normal usage with a figurative meaning; thus a huge number of expressions which had their first associations with the technical language of a group or occupation are drawn into general circulation.

The most frequent strategy used by democratic nations to create innovations of language is to give an unusual meaning to an expression already in current usage. This is a very simple, quick, and convenient method. No learning is needed to use it and ignorance even helps its practice. Yet, it is a practice which has dangers for the language; for democratic nations, in giving double meanings to a word, render the original meaning as ambiguous as the newly acquired meaning.

A writer starts by giving a slight twist to the original meaning of a well-known expression and, after this change, adapts it as best he is able to his purpose. A second turns the meaning in another direction; a third drags it down another track. Since there is no one to arbitrate, no permanent court to give a definitive meaning to the word, it wanders about freely. The result is that writers never appear to adhere to a single thought but seem to aim at a knot of ideas, leaving the reader to judge which of them they intend to hit.

This is a vexing consequence of democracy. I would prefer to see a language bristling with Chinese, Tartar, or Huron words than to confuse the meaning of French words. Harmony and uniformity are but secondary decorations of a language. General convention counts for a lot in these matters and can, at a pinch, be dispensed with. But good language has to have clear terms.

Of necessity, equality entails several other changes in language.

In aristocratic times, when each nation tends to stand aloof from all the others and likes to reflect its own character, several nations with a shared origin often become alienated from each other; the upshot of which is that they cease to speak in the same way, although they continue to understand each other.

In these same times each nation is divided into a number of classes who see but little of each other and make no social contact. Each class, without exception, assumes and preserves habits of mind peculiar to itself and prefers to use certain words and terms which pass down the generations like an inheritance. Then it is that the same idiom comprises one language for the poor and one for the rich, one for the commoner and one for the nobleman, an educated language and a colloquial one. The deeper the divisions and the more impassable the barriers, the more must this be the case. I would be willing to wager that among the castes of India the spoken language varies widely and that there exists as much difference between the language of an untouchable and that of a Brahmin as between their clothing.

On the other hand, when men are no longer fixed in one social position, seeing each other and communicating together, when the class systems are destroyed to assume a changed and uniform character, all the words of the language are mingled. Those words which do not suit the majority die out; the rest form a common store of expressions used by everyone almost at random. Almost all the different dialects which kept the European languages separate tend to disappear before our eyes; regional dialects do not exist in the New World and are daily disappearing from the Old.

This revolution in social conditions has as much effect upon style as upon language. Not only does everyone use the same words but people are accustomed to apply the same meaning to them without discrimination. The rules of style almost disappear. Hardly any expressions appear by their nature to be vulgar or refined. Individuals emerging from various social levels bring to their new social position expressions and terms to which they were accustomed; thus the origins of these words have been lost like the origin of individuals and language is in as much of a muddle as society.

I realize that some rules for the classification of words do not depend upon one particular form of society or another but derive from the very nature of things. Expressions and turns of phrase are vulgar because the feelings they have to convey are actually low, while others are refined because the objects they wish to portray are naturally elevated.

These differences never disappear through the intermingling of social classes. But equality is bound to destroy what is purely conventional and arbitrary in forms of thought. I am not even sure whether the inevitable classification I pointed out above will not always be less respected in a democratic nation than in any other because in such a nation there are no men inclined by their education, culture, or leisure to give sustained study to the natural laws of language or to cause these laws to be respected by their observation of them.

I will not quit this topic without describing one last characteristic which typifies democratic languages perhaps more than all the others.

I have noted before that democratic nations had a taste and often a passion for general ideas, which arise from qualities and deficiencies peculiar to them. This liking for general ideas takes the form of a constant use of generic and abstract terms and a peculiar way of using them. That is the great merit and the great weakness of such languages.

Democratic nations have a passionate addiction to generic terms and abstract words because these expressions enhance thought and aid the efforts of the mind by condensing many objects into a few words.

A democratic writer is likely to use the abstract term *capabilities*, meaning capable men, without entering into details as to the exact nature of these capabilities. He will speak of *topicality* in order to describe in one word everything happening before his eyes at that moment and he will include in the word *eventual-ities* all the possible events of the universe from the moment he starts speaking.

Democratic writers coin an endless stream of such abstract words or they use them in an increasingly abstract manner.

Furthermore, to speed up their speech, they personify these abstractions and make them act like a real person. They will say *the force of things insists upon capabilities to govern.*

No example can better illustrate my meaning than one of my own. I have often employed the word *equality* in an absolute sense and, what is more, in several places I have personified it so that I have said that equality did certain things or refrained from others. It can be stated that men from the century of Louis XIV would never have used such language; none of them would ever have thought of using the word *equality* without applying it to one particular thing and they would sooner have abandoned its use than turn it into a living person.

These abstract words which abound in democratic languages, and which are used on every occasion without reference to any particular fact, widen thought while obscuring it; they speed up modes of speech while reducing the clarity of the ideas expressed. But in matters of language, democracies prefer obscurity to hard work.

Besides, I wonder whether the imprecise may have a secret fascination for both those who speak and those who write in these nations.

As these people often rely upon the individual efforts of their own intelligence, they are almost always plagued by doubt. In addition, in their ever-shifting circumstances, the fickleness of their fortunes persuades them never to hold firm to any of their opinions.

Democratic citizens, therefore, will have unstable thoughts which require very flexible expressions to convey. As they never know whether today's idea will be appropriate for tomorrow's fresh event, they naturally acquire a liking for abstract expressions. One abstract word is like a box with a false bottom: you put into it the ideas you want and take them out again unobserved.

Among all these nations, generic and abstract terms form the basis of the language. I do not claim that such words are encountered only in democratic languages; I simply state that, in times of equality, men have a particular tendency to increase the number of such words, to assume their most abstract meaning without reference to other words, and to use them at every turn, even when what is being said does not require their use.

CHAPTER 17

A FEW SOURCES OF POETRY IN DEMOCRATIC NATIONS

Several very diverse meanings have been given to the word "poetry."

It would be tiresome to investigate with readers which of the different meanings it would be better to choose; I prefer to say outright which I have chosen.

Poetry, in my view, is the search for and depiction of the ideal.

The poet is the one who, by suppressing a part of what exists, by adding some imaginary features to the picture and by juxtaposing certain actual events which do not in fact happen at the same time, completes and elaborates the work of nature. Thus, poetry will not aim at the representation of reality but its adornment, by offering a loftier image to men's minds.

Verse appears to me the ideal beauty of language and in that sense will be eminently poetic but it does not in itself constitute poetry.

I would like to find out whether in the activities, opinions, or ideologies of democratic nations there are any which lead to a conception of ideal beauty or which may, for this reason, be considered as natural sources of poetry.

Firstly, we must acknowledge that the taste for ideal beauty and the pleasure of seeing it depicted are never as intense or widespread among a democratic as among an aristocratic people.

In aristocracies, it can sometimes happen that the needs of the body are automatically met whereas the soul is burdened with an abundance of leisure. In such nations, the people will display a taste for poetry and their spirit will sometimes rise above and beyond their surroundings.

But in democracies, the love of physical pleasure, the idea of self-improvement, competition, the lure of anticipated success spur all good men on to make progress in their chosen careers and prohibit them from deviating one single instant from the main path. The soul's major effort goes in that direction. The imagination has not been snuffed out but it devotes itself almost entirely to its idea of what is useful and to the portrayal of reality.

Equality not merely turns men away from the description of ideal beauty but also reduces the number of objects worth describing.

Aristocracy's control over social mobility preserves the stability and endurance of positive religions as well as political institutions. It not only keeps the human spirit within the realm of belief but also persuades it to espouse one belief rather than any other. An aristocratic nation will always be prone to place intermediate powers between God and man.

In this respect, aristocracy may be said to favor poetry. Whenever the universe is peopled with supernatural beings not perceived by the senses but revealed to the mind, the imagination feels unrestricted, poets discover a thousand different subjects to depict and countless audiences ready to appreciate their images.

In democratic ages, on the other hand, men's beliefs are sometimes as much in a state of flux as their laws. A time of skepticism brings poets' imaginations back to earth and shuts them away in the actual, visible world.

Even when equality does not disturb religions, it does simplify them; it diverts attention away from secondary beings to direct it chiefly to the supreme being.

Aristocracy naturally leads the human mind to contemplate the past and fixes it there. Democracy, on the contrary, gives men a sort of instinctive distaste for all that is old. In that respect, aristocracy is much more favorable to poetry for things commonly seem grander and more mysterious as they recede. This double characteristic makes them a better vehicle for the representation of ideal beauty. Once equality has removed the past from poetry, it partly deprives it of the present.

In aristocracies, a certain number of privileged individuals exist whose life is, so to speak, outside and beyond the usual human condition; in every respect, they appear to enjoy power, wealth, reputation, wit, refinement, and distinction as a natural right. The crowd never observes them at close quarters nor follows the details of their lives. It takes little to make the description of these people poetic.

On the other hand, in the same society there exist classes whose ignorance, modesty, and subjugation contribute to poetry from the very excess of their crudity and wretchedness, just as the others did for their refinement and greatness. Moreover, since the different classes in an aristocracy are very distant and have very little knowledge of each other, the imagination is always able to add something to or subtract something from the representation of them.

In democracies where men are insignificant and very much alike, everyone sees in himself a portrait of all the others. In such societies, poets can never, therefore, take one particular individual as the subject of their poetry because an object of mediocrity with obvious outlines will never contribute to the portrayal of ideal beauty.

Thus the establishment of equality on the earth dries up most of the traditional springs of poetry. Let me attempt to reveal what new sources it may disclose.

When skepticism had caused the heavens to empty and the progress of equality had reduced each of us to small and more familiar proportions, poets, unaware as yet what they might substitute for the great themes which disappeared with aristocracy, turned their attention toward inanimate nature. As gods and heroes disappeared from sight, they first of all undertook the description of rivers and mountains.

This gave rise in the last century to what is called, preeminently, descriptive poetry.

Some considered this enhanced portrait of the physical and inanimate objects which cover the earth's surface to be the poetry appropriate to democratic ages but that is, in my opinion, an error. I think that this is simply a period of transition.

In the long term, I am sure that democracy diverts the imagination from all that is external to man and fixes it on man himself

Democratic nations may take momentary pleasure in contemplating nature but they really become excited by the portrayal of themselves. That is the only natural source of poetry in such nations and it may be believed that any poets unwilling to draw inspiration from such a source will lose any sway they have over the minds they seek to enchant; in the end they will be left with nothing more than indifferent spectators of their raptures.

I have shown how the idea of progress and endless perfectibility of the human race was attuned to democratic times.

Democratic nations scarcely concern themselves with the past but readily dream of the future; in this direction, their unbounded imaginations spread and grow without limits.

This offers broad vistas to poets who have the chance of painting distant scenes. Democracy, which shuts the past to poetry, opens up the future.

Since citizens in a democratic society share a similar equality, the poet cannot treat any single one of them but the whole nation itself becomes a subject for his pen. The similarity of individuals taken separately rules them out as poetic subjects but does permit poets to group them into one image and depict the nation as a whole. Democracies have a clearer perception of themselves than any other nations and this noble conception admirably fosters the portrayal of the ideal.

I readily admit that Americans have no poets; I could not possibly allow that they have no poetic ideas.

Europeans pay much attention to the wilds of America but Americans themselves scarcely ever think about them. The wonders of inanimate nature leave them cold and they may be said to ignore the marvelous forests around them until they fall to the axe. Another sight catches their gaze. The American people views its progress across these wilds, draining marshes, diverting rivers, peopling the open spaces, and taming nature. It is not just occasionally that this magnificent image of themselves captures the American imagination; it haunts every one of them in the slightest, as in the most important, of their actions and ever floats before their minds.

It would be hard to imagine anything more insignificant, dull, more crowded with paltry interests, in one word, antipoetic, than the life of a man in the United States. But amid the thoughts which direct his life, there is always one which is full of poetry and is the hidden nerve giving strength to all the rest.

In aristocratic ages, each nation as well as each individual is prone to stay in the same place, divided from all the others.

In democratic ages, men are always moving and their frustrations cause them to travel from place to place; the inhabitants of various countries intermingle, see, hear, and borrow from one another. Thus, not only do the members of the same nation grow more alike; the nations themselves resemble each other and combine to represent to the observer simply one vast democracy where each citizen is a nation. For the first time in broad daylight the features of human kind are revealed.

The existence of the entire human race in all its aspects, from its changing fortunes to its future, becomes a very fertile source for poetry.

Poets living in aristocratic times have produced wonderful portraits by taking as subjects certain incidents in the life of a single nation or individual; yet not a single poet has ever ventured to include in his picture the destiny of the whole human race, whereas poets writing in democratic times can undertake such a task.

At the very time when each man raises his eyes beyond his own country and at last begins to perceive humanity itself, God reveals himself more and more to the human mind in his full and complete majesty.

If faith in positive religions is frequently unsteady in democratic ages and belief in intermediate agencies, by whatever name they are called, begins to decline, men are prone to imagine a far greater idea of the Godhead itself and they see its intervention in human affairs in a fresh and greater light.

Observing the human race as a single entity, men find it easy to imagine that the same plan rules its destiny and they are inclined to perceive, in the actions of any individual, the trace of that universal and consistent design by which God guides our race.

Again this may be judged a very rich source of poetry in such ages.

Democratic poets will always appear puny and cold when they attempt to give bodily shape to gods, demons, or angels and when they strive to bring them down from heaven to fight for the supremacy of the earth.

But when they desire to associate the great events they commemorate with God's universal plans and wish to reveal the thoughts of the supreme being without showing his hand, they will be admired and understood, for their contemporaries take this artistic direction of their own accord.

Equally, we may anticipate that poets living in democratic times will depict emotions and ideas rather than people and achievements.

The language, dress, and daily actions of men in democracies resist the concept of ideal beauty. Such things are not intrinsically poetic and anyway would cease to be so because they are too familiar to all who might be addressed by the poet. This drives poets to dive beneath the outer surface perceived by the senses in order to glimpse the soul itself. Now nothing fosters more readily the portrayal of ideal beauty than the hidden depths of man's spiritual nature.

I have no need to traverse heaven and earth to uncover a wondrous object full of contrast, of infinite greatness and smallness, of intense gloom and astounding light, capable at the same time of exciting piety, admiration, scorn, and terror. I need only contemplate myself: man emerges from nothing, passes through time and disappears forever into the bosom of God. He is seen wandering for a brief time along the edge of these two chasms and then is lost.

If man were wholly unaware of himself, he would have no poetry in him since what we cannot perceive cannot be portrayed. If he clearly discerned his own nature, his imagination would remain idle and would find nothing to add to the picture.

However, man is sufficiently revealed for him to perceive something of himself but sufficiently obscure for the rest to be buried in impenetrable darkness, into which he gropes again and again without success in order to complete his self-knowledge.

In democratic nations, we should not expect poetry to live on legends or traditions or ancient memories, or to attempt the colonization of the universe with supernatural beings in whom readers and poets no longer believe, or to portray, beneath a cold personification, virtues and vices which can be seen as they are in reality. Poetry lacks all these resources but man remains and is sufficient. Human destinies and man himself, considered outside his own age or country, confronted by nature and God, endowed with his passions, doubts, astonishing wealth, and incomprehensible wretchedness, will for these peoples become the principal if not virtually the sole theme for poetry.

This can already be confirmed, if we observe the writings of the greatest poets who have appeared on the scene since the world turned to democracy.

The writers who in our age have so admirably portrayed the features of Childe Harold,[a] René,[b] and Jocelyn[c] did not seek to relate the actions of a single man but wished to illustrate and enlarge certain dark recesses of the human heart.

Such are the poems of democracy.

Equality, therefore, does not destroy all poetic themes; it simply reduces their number but increases their scope.

CHAPTER 18

WHY AMERICAN WRITERS AND SPEAKERS ARE OFTEN BOMBASTIC

I have often observed that Americans who deal in general with their business in clear, crisp, and unadorned language, whose excessive simplicity is often coarse, easily turn to bombast as soon as they approach a poetic style. From one end to the other of their speech, they indulge in relentless pomposity and you would think, seeing them lavish imagery at every opportunity, that they had never said anything in simple language.

More rarely do the English fall into such an error, the reason for which can be demonstrated quite easily.

In democratic societies, every citizen is habitually busy considering one very small subject, namely himself. If he happens to look up, he sees nothing but the immense image of society or the even bigger picture of the human race. His ideas are either self-orientated and clear or his thoughts are very general and vague; the space between them is empty.

Whenever he has been drawn away from himself, he always expects to be presented with some wondrous object to look at and that is the only reason why he might agree to wrench himself away from the minor complications which excite and charm his life.

This is sufficient to explain why men in democracies who generally have such flimsy concerns require their poets to provide such vast conceptions and such disproportionate descriptions.

From their standpoint, writers rarely fail to respond to these instincts, because they share them. They perpetually inflate their imaginations, expanding them beyond all bounds; they aim at the gigantic, to reach which they often abandon real grandeur.

In this way, they hope to draw the immediate attention of the crowd upon themselves and this they often succeed in doing; for the crowd seeks from poetry only subjects of vast dimensions and has not sufficient time for an exact assessment of all the subjects offered to it nor a confident enough discernment to perceive with ease their distortions. The author and his public are engaged in a mutual exercise of corruption.

Moreover, we have seen that in democratic nations the springs of poetry were fine but few in number. They are soon exhausted. Poets, no longer discovering material to express ideal beauty in what is real and true, abandon entirely and create monsters.

I am not fearful that the poetry of democratic nations will prove weak or that it will stick too close to the ground. I am apprehensive rather that it will forever lose its way in the clouds, that it will end up by depicting entirely imaginary regions. I fear that the work of democratic poets may often present huge and jumbled images, bloated pictures, strange compositions, and that these fantastic creations of their minds will cause us sometimes to yearn for the world of reality.

CHAPTER 19

A FEW REMARKS ON THE THEATER OF DEMOCRATIC NATIONS

When the revolution which has altered the social and political state of an aristocratic nation begins to become evident in the literature, generally the theater is the first to show its effects and its influence is always to be seen there.

The audience of a dramatic performance is, to some degree, taken unawares by the impression conveyed. They have no time to refer to their memory nor to consult expert critics; they do not think of resisting the new literary instincts which begin to appear in them; they submit before knowing what they are.

Authors soon discover the secret inclinations of public taste. They direct their productions accordingly. After plays have served to herald the approaching literary revolution, they soon hasten to complete the task. If you should want advance knowledge of the literature of a nation which is turning toward democracy, just study its theater.

Plays, moreover, represent, even among aristocratic nations, the most democratic element of their literature. No literary pleasures are more within the grasp of the crowd than those which take place on the stage. Neither preparation nor study is needed to enjoy them. They seize hold of you, however preoccupied or ignorant you may be. When the yet undeveloped love for pleasures of the mind begins to affect a class of the community, it immediately draws these people to the theater. The theaters of aristocratic nations have always been filled with spectators not belonging to the aristocracy. Only in the theater have the upper classes mingled with the middle or lower classes and, if they have not consented to accept the opinions of the latter, they have at least allowed them to be expressed. In the theater, learned and educated scholars have always experienced the greatest difficulty in promoting their own tastes over those of the populace and in stopping themselves from being carried away by the latter's views. The pit has often made laws for the boxes.

If it is difficult for an aristocracy to prevent the people from invading the theater, it will easily be understood that the people will hold the upper hand when democratic principles permeate laws and customs, when classes mix together, when intelligence and wealth become equal and when the upper class loses its power, traditions, and leisure, along with its wealth.

The tastes and natural predispositions of democratic nations will, therefore, find their first literary form in the theater, where you can guarantee they will make a violent entry. In written works, aristocratic rules will become gradually modified in what we might call a legal manner. In the theater, they will be over-turned by riots.

The theater highlights most of the qualities and almost all the defects of democratic literature.

Democratic nations have only a lukewarm regard for learning and hardly spare a thought for the happenings of Rome or Athens. They insist on hearing about themselves and they require a portrayal of the present.

So, when the heroes and customs of antiquity are frequently represented on the stage and care is taken to remain very faithful to ancient traditions, it is proof enough that the democratic classes have not gained the upper hand in the theater.

Racine[a] is very apologetic in the preface to *Britannicus* for having introduced Junie into the ranks of the vestal virgins when, following Aulus Gellius, he says that "no one under the age of six and above twelve was accepted." It is probable that he would not have dreamed of accusing or defending himself for a crime like that had he been writing today.

A fact of this kind illustrates not only the state of literature of that time but also the state of society itself. A democratic theater is no proof that a nation is democratic for, as we have just seen, democratic tastes may influence the theater even in aristocracies. But when the ethos of aristocracy reigns alone on the stage, that is irrefutable proof that the whole society is aristocratic and the confident conclusion can be drawn that this same learned and educated class which lays down the rules for authors also controls the people and their affairs.

Rare it is for the refined tastes and arrogant bearing of the aristocracy, when it manages the theater, not to exercise some selection, so to speak, in human nature. Certain social conditions have a special interest for aristocrats and they like to see them reflected on the stage. Certain virtues and even certain defects appear to deserve particular portrayal. These they approve, while casting aside all the others from their sight. In the theater, as elsewhere, they wish to meet only the nobility and their emotions are stirred only by kings. The same applies to style. An aristocracy is quite willing to impose certain ways of speaking on dramatic authors and wish everything to reflect these canons of taste.

Thus the theater often succeeds in portraying only one side of a man's nature or even sometimes in depicting what is never found in human nature because it rises above and beyond nature.

In democratic societies, the audience does not have such preferences and they rarely display any such dislikes; they enjoy seeing on the stage that muddle of social conditions, opinions, and ideas that occurs before their eyes everyday. The theater becomes more striking, more common, and more truthful.

However, sometimes those who write for the stage in democracies also move outside the bounds of human nature but along a different route from their predecessors. Because of their desire to portray in detail the small peculiarities of the present and the individual features of certain men, they forget to represent the universal characteristics of mankind.

When democratic classes rule the stage, they support as much flexibility in the way of treating subjects as in the choice of them.

Since the love of drama is the most natural thing of all literary tastes among democratic nations, the number of writers and spectators, as well as theatrical shows, increases constantly in such nations.

Such a crowd, made up of such diverse components and scattered in so many different locations, could not accept the same rules nor submit to the same guidelines. No possible agreement exists among so many judges who will not meet again, each therefore pronouncing his own opinion. The general result is that democracy casts doubt upon the canons of taste and literary conventions; when it comes to the theater, democracy abolishes all the rules and replaces them by the whim of each author and each public.

Equally, the theater displays above all what I have demonstrated elsewhere, in talking more generally of style and art in dramatic literature. On reading the criticisms occasioned by the democratic productions of the century of Louis XIV, one is surprised at the great respect the public had for plausibility of plot and the importance placed upon consistency in characterization, which meant that no one did anything which could not be easily explained or understood. It is also surprising how much store was placed upon forms of language and how many petty squabbles about words landed at the door of theatrical writers.

Men of the age of Louis XIV seemed to attach a much exaggerated value to these details which loomed large in the study but passed unnoticed on the stage. For, after all, the prime objective of a play is to be performed and its greatest merit is to move people's emotions. The reason for this stemmed from the fact that the spectators in that age were readers too. On leaving the performance, they awaited the author at their homes in order to complete their assessment of him.

In democracies, plays are for the ear not for reading. Most of those who attend the amusements of the stage do not seek out the pleasure of the mind but the keener emotions of the heart. They are not anticipating a work of literature but want to see a play. Provided the writer speaks his native language correctly enough to be understood, that his characters stimulate their curiosity and awaken sympathy, they are satisfied. They ask no more of fiction and return immediately to the real world. Style is thus less necessary, for breaches of these rules pass unnoticed on the stage.

If you are slavish in your regard for plausibility of plot, it is often impossible to achieve novelty, surprise, and speed of action. Scant notice is therefore paid to it and this lapse is forgiven by the public.

It can be guaranteed that if, in the end, you introduce the audience to a subject which moves them, they will not concern themselves about the route you have taken. They will never reproach you for breaking the rules if you have aroused their emotions.

Americans display all these different instincts which I have just described when they go to the theater; but it must be acknowledged that as yet only a small number of them go. Although audiences and performances have grown enormously this last forty years in the United States, the population still shows the greatest reluctance to indulge in this kind of amusement.

The reader is already aware of the particular reasons for this and a couple of words will be enough to remind him of them.

The Puritan founders of the American republics were not only opposed to pleasure; even more so, they proclaimed a special abhorrence for the theater, considering it a devilish pastime. As long as their opinions held undivided sway, theatrical performances were totally unknown amongst them. These views belonging to the founding fathers of the colonies have left very deep marks in the minds of their descendants.

The entrenched regularity of habit and the great strictness of custom observable in the United States have, moreover, been until now unfavorable obstacles to the growth of dramatic art.

A country has no real dramatic subjects if it has not witnessed great political catastrophes and if love always follows a direct and simple road to marriage. People who spend every day of the week making money and Sundays praying to God give no scope to the comic muse.

A single fact is enough to demonstrate that the theater is unpopular in the United States.

Americans whose laws underline freedom and even license in their overall approach to language have nevertheless imposed a kind of censorship upon their dramatic writers. Performances

may take place only when the municipal administrators allow
them, which fully serves to show how communities resemble
individuals; they surrender themselves imprudently to their
main passions and then are careful not to yield to the impulses
of tastes they do not possess.

No form of literature has closer and more numerous links
with the current condition of society than the theater.

The theater of one period could never suit the next if, between
the two ages, an important revolution has affected customs
and laws.

Great writers of another century are still studied but plays
written for another public do not attract an audience. Drama-
tists of the past live only in books.

The taste for tradition fostered by a few men, by vanity,
fashion, and the genius of a particular actor may support or
revive an aristocratic style of drama in the heart of a democracy
but it soon falls away of itself, not overthrown but abandoned.

CHAPTER 20

CHARACTERISTICS PECULIAR TO
HISTORIANS IN DEMOCRATIC AGES

Historians writing in aristocratic times usually attribute all
events to the individual will and character of particular men
and are quite willing to link the most significant revolutions to
slight accidents. They shrewdly highlight the smallest causes
with no awareness of the greatest.

Historians of democratic periods exhibit quite the opposite
tendencies. Most of them attribute hardly any influence on the
destinies of mankind to individuals nor upon the fate of the
nation to its citizens; but they see great general causes behind
the slightest particular events. These opposing tendencies can
be explained.

When the historians of aristocratic times cast their gaze upon
the world stage, they observe, in the first instance, a very small

number of principal players who control the whole drama. These lofty characters holding the front of the stage block and hold their view; while they take pains to decipher the secret motivations which prompt these men to speak and act, they forget the rest.

The importance of the things some men are seen to do causes them to exaggerate the influence one man can exercise and leads them naturally to the opinion that one must always explain the activities of the crowd by reference to the particular behavior of one individual.

On the other hand, when all citizens are independent of one another and each of them is weak, no one is seen to exert a very great or very lasting power over the mass of the citizens. At first sight, single individuals seem quite powerless to influence them and society might be said to progress on its own, propelled by the free and spontaneous agreement of all its members.

Such an insight naturally inspires the human brain to seek out the general reason which may thus have struck so many minds and simultaneously directed them along the same path.

I am firmly convinced that even in democratic nations the genius, defects, and virtues of certain individuals delay or accelerate the natural progress of a nation's destiny. But causes of this accidental and secondary nature are infinitely more diverse, more concealed, more complex, less powerful, and thus less easy to unravel or trace in periods of equality than in aristocratic times when the individual behavior of one single man or of a few men is all that needs analyzing in the mass of general events.

The historian soon tires of such a labor; his mind loses its bearings inside this labyrinth and denies the existence of individual influences which he is unable to sight clearly or to illuminate satisfactorily. He prefers to speak to us of the characteristics of race, the physical constitution of the country, or the genius of its civilization. His work is reduced and he satisfies his readers better at less cost.

Lafayette says somewhere in his *Memoirs* that the inflated belief in general causes supplied wonderful consolations for second-rate statesmen. I should add that second-rate historians are similarly consoled. They are always provided with a few expansive reasons which extricate them from the most difficult part of their book; these allow them to indulge their incompetence or laziness while giving them a reputation for profundity.

My opinion is that in every age without exception, some of the events of this world must be explained by very general causes and some by very special influences. These two always coincide; only their proportion varies. General facts explain more in democratic times than they do in aristocratic ones and individual influences explain less. In aristocratic times, the opposite is the case; individual influences are stronger and general causes weaker, unless one considers as a general cause the very inequality of condition which allows a few individuals to counteract the natural tendencies of all the rest.

Historians seeking to describe what is happening in democratic societies are therefore right to assign much to general causes and to busy themselves in the principal aim of discovering them; but they are wrong to offer a complete denial of the special actions of individuals simply because of the difficulty of finding and tracing them out.

Not only are historians in democratic times prone to assign an important cause to every incident, they are also inclined to link such incidents together so as to elicit a system from them.

In aristocratic times, since the attention of historians is constantly diverted toward individuals, the interconnection of events passes them by, or rather they have no faith in such connections. The thread of history appears continuously broken by the course of one man's life.

In democratic times, in contrast, the historian sees many fewer players and many more events and, therefore, may easily establish a relationship and a methodical order in these latter.

Ancient literature, which has bequeathed to us such fine writings, does not offer a single great historical system whereas the most insignificant of modern literatures abound in them. Apparently, classical historians somewhat neglected these general theories which our own are always ready to exploit to excess.

Those writing in democratic times have yet another more dangerous tendency. Once the trace of the influence of individuals upon nations disappears, one often sees the world in motion without any sign of an engine. As it becomes very difficult to perceive and analyze the reasons which, acting separately upon the will of each citizen, end up by creating movement in the whole nation, one is tempted to suppose that this movement is involuntary and that societies are acting unconsciously in obedience to some superior dominating force.

Even when we discover that the general law which governs the private will of each individual may be discovered on the earth, that does not save human freedom. A reason vast enough to affect millions of men at the same time and powerful enough to incline them all together in the same direction, may well appear irresistible. Once everyone is seen to yield to it, we are close to believing that it is indeed irresistible.

Thus historians in democratic times not only deny that a few citizens have the power to influence the destiny of the nation, they also remove from the nation itself the capability of altering its own destiny and they subject it either to an inflexible Providence or to a sort of blind fatalism. According to them, every nation is inexorably bound by its position, its origin, its antecedents, its character, to a fixed destiny which resists all efforts to change. One generation is bound to the preceding one and thus, from epoch to epoch, from necessity to necessity, back to the beginnings of this world, they forge a close and boundless chain which girds and binds the whole of mankind.

It is not enough for them to demonstrate how events have come to pass; they take a delight in proving that they could not have happened otherwise.

They contemplate a nation which has reached a certain point in its history and they state that it has been forced to follow a path which has led it there. Such an assertion is easier than demonstrating what it could have done to take a better course.

Reading historians of aristocratic times, and especially those of antiquity, it seems that man has only to learn self-discipline in order to become master of his own destiny and to rule his fellows. In perusing the histories written nowadays, one would suppose that man can have no power over himself nor over his surroundings. Historians of antiquity taught the rules of command; those writing today give only a pale lesson on how to obey. In their writings, the author often appears great, while mankind is always tiny.

If this doctrine of fatality, so attractive to historians of democratic times, passes from author to reader and thus enters and seizes the minds of the entire body of citizens, one can anticipate that it would soon paralyze the activities of new societies and would bring Christians down to the level of Turks.

I would, moreover, say that such a doctrine is especially pernicious at the present time. Our contemporaries are only too inclined to doubt free will because each of them feels restricted on all sides by his own weakness, but they still freely admit the strength and independence of men when united in social groups. We must be careful not to obscure this idea, for we need to raise men's spirits not to complete their collapse.

CHAPTER 21

PARLIAMENTARY ELOQUENCE IN THE UNITED STATES

In aristocratic nations all men have a close dependency upon each other; all share a hierarchical connection which helps to keep everyone in his place and the entire body of society in subordination. Something similar always occurs in the political assemblies of these nations. Parties naturally gather under certain leaders whom they obey by a sort of instinct which is simply the result of habits acquired elsewhere. They transfer the customs of the wider social world to this smaller society.

In democratic countries it often happens that a large number of citizens tend toward the same point, but each one advances, or flatters himself that he advances, under his own steam. Accustomed to control his movements following his own impulses, he is reluctant to take orders from outside. This taste and habit of independence follow him into the councils of the nation. If he agrees to be associated with others in the pursuit of a common aim, at least he wishes to remain free to cooperate in the common success in his own way.

Consequently, in democratic countries parties are so impatient of control and submit to orders only when the danger is very great. Even then the authority of the leaders, which in such circumstances may be able to make men act and speak, hardly ever manages to keep them silent.

Among aristocratic nations members of political assemblies are members of the aristocracy at the same time. Each one of them enjoys high established rank in his own right so that the position he holds in the assembly is often less important in his view than the one he occupies in the country. This consoles him for playing no part in the discussion of affairs and persuades him not to seek too enthusiastically to play a modest one.

In America, the deputy is generally somebody only because of his position in the assembly. Thus he is constantly tormented by the need to achieve importance there and experiences a testy desire to air his ideas in and out of season.

He is pushed in this direction not only by his vanity but by his constituents and the continuous need to satisfy them. In aristocratic nations, a member of the legislature is rarely closely dependent upon his constituents for whom he is often their only possible representative. Sometimes he maintains in them a close dependency, and when they finally refuse to vote for him, he easily gets himself elected elsewhere, or, abandoning his public career, he retires to a life of splendid indolence.

In a democratic nation like the United States, the deputy almost never has a lasting hold on his constituents' minds. However small an electoral body may be, the instability of democracies causes it to change shape endlessly; it must, therefore, be courted daily. He is never sure of his supporters and if they abandon him, he is left without resource; for his natural position is not high enough for him to be easily known by those afar off. In the complete independence enjoyed by all citizens, he cannot hope that his friends or the government will find it easy to impose him on an electorate which does not know him.

It is therefore in the neighborhood that he represents that the seeds of his fortune are sown; it is from this corner of the country that he will set out to raise himself to command the nation and influence the destinies of the world.

Thus it is natural that, in democratic countries, the members of political assemblies think of their constituents more than of their party, whereas, in aristocracies, they concern themselves with their party rather than their constituents.

Now, what you have to say to please your constituents is not always what ought to be said in order to serve the political opinions they profess.

The general interest of a party often demands that the deputy belonging to it should never speak about important matters which he half understands, that he should speak little about small matters which might interfere with the important ones, and finally that he should generally keep his mouth shut entirely. To remain silent is the most useful service that a modest speaker can render to public affairs.

But that is not how constituents understand things.

The population of a neighborhood chooses one citizen to take part in the government of the state because they entertain a very lofty opinion of his merits. As men appear greater when surrounded by small objects, one may suppose that the opinions they have of the delegate will be all the higher as the talents of those he represents are slighter. The constituents will, therefore, often hope for all the more from their deputy, the less they have to expect from him; and whatever his defects, they have to demand from him significant efforts appropriate to the high position they have conferred upon him.

Apart from his role as legislator for the state, constituents still see their representative as the natural protector of the neighborhood in the legislature; they are even tempted to think that he has power of proxy to represent each constituent and they flatter themselves that he will be as enthusiastic in defending their interests as he is those of the country.

Thus the constituents are convinced beforehand that their chosen deputy will be an orator, that he will speak often if he can and that, whenever he has to hold back, he will strive at least to include in his infrequent speeches an examination of all the important matters of state as well as a statement of all the minor grievances which they themselves complain about. Thus, since he is unable to take the stage often, he should display at each opportunity what he can do and instead of constantly indulging his powers he should from time to time condense into a small compass a kind of brilliantly comprehensive résumé of what he and his constituents stand for. On those terms they promise to re-elect him.

This brings honorable men of mediocre ability to the point of despair, who, knowing their own qualities, would not have stepped forward willingly. The deputy, thus goaded on, begins to speak, to the considerable distress of his friends and, flinging himself unwisely into the midst of the most famous orators, he muddles the discussion and wearies the assembly.

All those laws which aim to make the deputy more dependent upon his constituents alter not only the conduct of the legislators, as I have noted elsewhere, but also their language. These laws influence both the matters under discussion and the manner in which they are discussed.

Hardly a single member of Congress will agree to return home without dispatching at least one speech back to his electorate, nor will he tolerate any interruption before he has succeeded in including within the scope of his harangue all the useful things he can say about the twenty-four states of the Union and especially about the district he represents. He, therefore, presents to the minds of his listeners a succession of great generalizations (which often he alone comprehends and expresses but confusedly) as well as very minor subtleties which he does not find easy to reveal clearly.

Very frequently the discussions in this important assembly become vague and confused; they appear to drag along toward their intended goal rather than advancing directly.

I think that something similar will always be seen in the public assemblies of democracies.

Fortunate circumstances and good laws might succeed in attracting into the legislature of a democratic nation men much more talented than those sent by Americans to Congress; but mediocre men who get there will never be prevented from complacently airing their many points of view.

This defect does not appear to me to be entirely curable because it does not simply stem from the rules of the assembly but from its constitution and that of the country.

The inhabitants of the United States themselves appear to consider the matter from this point of view and they bear witness to their long experience of parliamentary life, not by abandoning poor speeches but by courageously putting up with listening to them. They are resigned to them as to an evil which experience teaches them to acknowledge as unavoidable.

We have shown the trivial side of political discussions in democracies; let us now consider the more impressive.

The happenings over the last one hundred and fifty years in the English Parliament have never caused much of a stir in the outside world; the ideas and opinions expressed by orators have never evoked much sympathy even in those nations nearest to that great theater of British freedom, whereas Europe was excited by the very first debates in the small colonial assemblies of America at the time of the Revolution.

That was due not simply to particular and accidental circumstances but to general and long-lasting reasons.

I view nothing more wonderful or imposing than a great orator discussing great affairs in a democratic assembly. As the deputies there never represent the interests of one particular class, they always speak to the whole nation and for the whole nation. That ennobles their thought and exalts their language.

As precedent carries little weight, as there are no privileges associated with property nor rights belonging inherently to certain bodies or to certain men, the mind has to appeal to general truths drawn from human nature to deal with the particular matter in hand. That gives rise in the political discussions of a democratic nation, however small, to a general character which often attracts the attention of the whole human race. All men become involved because man, who is the same everywhere, himself is the focus.

Among the greatest aristocratic nations, by contrast, the most general questions are almost always treated by a few special arguments based upon the practice of a particular age or upon the rights of one class. Such matters involve only the class in question or at most the nation which contains this class.

It is as much due to this reason as to the greatness of France and the favorable support of those nations listening, that our political discussions sometimes produce so much effect in the world.

French orators often address all men at the very time they are speaking to their fellow citizens only.

PART 2
INFLUENCE OF DEMOCRACY ON THE OPINIONS OF AMERICANS

CHAPTER I

WHY DEMOCRATIC NATIONS DISPLAY A MORE PASSIONATE AND LASTING LOVE FOR EQUALITY THAN FOR FREEDOM

The first and liveliest of the passions inspired by equality of status, I need not say, is the love of equality itself. No one will be surprised, therefore, if I speak of that before all others.

Everybody has noticed that in our time, and above all in France, this passion for equality has occupied a greater place in the human heart every day. It has been said a hundred times that our contemporaries felt a much warmer and more persistent affection for equality than for freedom; but I feel that no one has adequately analyzed the reasons for this fact. I shall try to do so.

It is possible to imagine an extreme point at which freedom and equality meet and blend together.

I am assuming that all citizens work together in government and that each one has an equal right to do so.

Then, with no man different from his fellows, nobody will be able to wield tyrannical power; men will be completely free because they will be entirely equal; they will all be completely equal because they will be entirely free. Democratic nations aim for this ideal.

That is the most complete form of equality on the earth; but there are a thousand others which lack as perfect a form but are no less cherished by such nations.

Equality can take root in civil society without having any sway in the world of politics. A man may have the right to enjoy the same pleasures, enter the same professions, meet in the same places; in a word, to live in the same way and to seek wealth by the same means, without all men taking the same part in the government.

A sort of equality may even take root in the world of politics, although political freedom is lacking. A man is the equal of all but one of his fellow men and that one man is, without distinction, the master of all and appoints his agents of power equally from all.

It would be easy to invent several other hypotheses in which a very considerable measure of equality might be united to more or less free institutions or even to institutions which are not at all free.

Although men may not become absolutely equal without being wholly free and as a result equality, in its most extreme form, may be confounded with freedom, yet we are justified in distinguishing one from the other.

Men's taste for freedom and equality are, in effect, two different things and I am not afraid to add that in democratic nations they are also unequal.

Upon close inspection, it will be seen that in every century one unusual and predominant fact appears to which all the others are connected. This fact almost always produces a seminal thought or an overriding passion which in the end draws to itself all other feelings and ideas in its wake. It resembles the main river into which each of the surrounding streams seems to flow.

Freedom has revealed itself to men at different times and beneath different forms; it has not been exclusively bound to one social state and it makes its appearance elsewhere than in democracies. Thus it cannot possibly be taken as the distinctive characteristic of democracies.

The special and predominant fact which particularizes these centuries is the equality of social conditions; the main passion which stirs the men of such ages is the love of this equality.

Do not inquire what unusual attraction men of democratic

ages possess toward living as equals nor the particular reasons they may have for clinging so tenaciously on to equality rather than the advantages society offers. Equality forms the distinctive characteristic of the era in which they live and that alone is enough to explain why they prefer it to all the rest.

But, apart from this reason, several others will usually incline men of all ages to prefer equality to freedom.

If a nation could ever succeed in destroying or simply diminishing the equality at its heart, it would manage it only by long and laborious efforts. It would have to modify the state of society, abolish its laws, renew its ideas, change its customs, and debase its ways. But destroying political freedom is easy, for just loosening one's grip is enough for it to slip away.

Men, therefore, are attached to equality not simply because it is dear to them but also because they believe that it must last forever.

One does not come across men so unintelligent or superficial that they do not realize that political freedom can, if carried to excess, damage peace, property, and the lives of individuals. On the contrary, only people of perception and foresight see the dangers with which equality threatens us and usually they avoid pointing them out. They know that the troubles they fear are remote and they flatter themselves that only future generations will be affected; this scarcely worries the present generation. The evils brought occasionally by freedom have an immediate effect; they are obvious to everyone and are more or less experienced by everyone. The evils produced by extreme equality become apparent only gradually; little by little they creep into the heart of society; they are noticed every now and again so that, when they are at their most disturbing, habit has already nullified their effect.

The advantages of liberty become visible only in the long term and it is always easy to mistake the cause which brought them about.

The advantages of equality are felt immediately and you can observe where they come from daily.

Political freedom from time to time grants exalted pleasures to a certain number of citizens.

Equality offers daily an abundance of modest pleasures to every single man. The charms of equality are felt the whole time and are within the reach of all; the noblest hearts appreciate them and the commonest souls delight in them. The passion engendered by equality must, therefore, be both vigorous and widespread.

Men cannot enjoy political freedom without some sacrifice and they only ever acquire it after much effort. But the pleasures of equality are freely on offer; each small incident in private life seems to provide such pleasures so that to be alive is all that is necessary for their enjoyment.

Democratic nations are at all times fond of equality but during certain ages their passion for it verges on excess. This occurs when the old social class structure, long since threatened, at last collapses after a final internal struggle and when the barriers dividing citizens are at length overturned. At such a moment, men pounce on equality as their spoils of war and cling on to it like a priceless possession which somebody is threatening to snatch away. The passion for equality sinks deeply into every corner of the human heart, expands, and fills it entirely. It is no use telling such men, as they blindly obey such an exclusive passion, that they are damaging their dearest interests; they are deaf. Do not bother to show them that freedom which is slipping through their fingers while their gaze is elsewhere; they are blind, or rather they can see only one advantage worth pursuing in the whole world.

The above applies to all democratic nations; the following concerns only the French.

Among the most modern nations, especially those of Europe, the taste for freedom and the conception of it began to appear and develop only when social conditions were tending toward equality and were a consequence of that very equality. Absolute monarchs worked hardest to level down ranks among their subjects. Among such nations equality preceded liberty; equality was thus an established fact when liberty was still a novelty; the former had already shaped opinions, customs, and laws of its own when the latter was emerging for the first time into the daylight. Thus this latter was still only a theoretical matter of opinion and taste, whereas the former had already crept into customs, had laid hold of social habits, and had given a particular coloring to the smallest of life's actions. Why is it surprising that our contemporaries prefer the first to the second?

I think that democratic nations have a natural taste for freedom; left to themselves, they seek it out, become attached to it, and view any departure from it with distress. But they have a burning, insatiable, constant, and invincible passion for equality; they want equality in freedom and, if they cannot have it, they want it in slavery. They will endure poverty, subjection, barbarism but they will not endure aristocracy.

This is eternally true and especially in our time. Any man and any power which would contest the irresistible force of equality will be overturned and destroyed by it. Nowadays, freedom cannot take hold without it and despotism itself cannot reign without its support.

CHAPTER 2

INDIVIDUALISM IN DEMOCRATIC COUNTRIES

I have indicated how, in ages of equality, every man sought his beliefs within himself; I wish to show how, in these same periods, he directs all his feelings on to himself alone.

Individualism is a recently coined expression prompted by a new idea, for our forefathers knew only of egoism.

Egoism is an ardent and excessive love of oneself which leads man to relate everything back to himself and to prefer himself above everything.

Individualism is a calm and considered feeling which persuades each citizen to cut himself off from his fellows and to withdraw into the circle of his family and friends in such a way that he thus creates a small group of his own and willingly abandons society at large to its own devices. Egoism springs from a blind instinct; individualism from wrong-headed thinking rather than from depraved feelings. It originates as much from defects of intelligence as from the mistakes of the heart.

Egoism blights the seeds of every virtue, individualism at first dries up only the source of public virtue. In the longer term it attacks and destroys all the others and will finally merge with egoism.

Egoism is a perversity as old as the world and is scarcely peculiar to one form of society more than another.

Individualism is democratic in origin and threatens to grow as conditions become equal.

Among aristocratic nations, families remain in the same situation for centuries and often in the same location. This turns all the generations into contemporaries, as it were. A man practically always knows his ancestors and has respect for them; he thinks he can already see his great-grandchildren and he loves them. He willingly assumes duties toward his ancestors and descendants, frequently sacrificing his personal pleasures for the sake of those beings who have gone before and who have yet to come.

In addition, aristocratic institutions achieve the effect of binding each man closely to several of his fellow citizens.

Since the class structure is distinct and static in an aristocratic nation, each class becomes a kind of homeland for the participant because it is more obvious and more cherished than the country at large.

All the citizens of aristocratic societies have fixed positions one above another; consequently each man perceives above him someone whose protection is necessary to him and below him someone else whose cooperation he may claim.

Men living in aristocratic times are, therefore, almost always closely bound to an external object and they are often inclined to forget about themselves. It is true that in these same periods the general concept of human fellowship is dimly felt and men seldom think of sacrificing themselves for mankind, whereas they often sacrifice themselves for certain other men.

In democratic times, on the other hand, when the obligations of every person toward the race are much clearer, devotion to one man in particular becomes much rarer. The bond of human affection is wide and relaxed.

Among democratic nations, new families constantly emerge from oblivion, while others fall away; all remaining families shift with time. The thread of time is ever ruptured and the track of generations is blotted out. Those who have gone before are easily forgotten and those who follow are still completely unknown. Only those nearest to us are of any concern to us.

As each class closes up to the others and merges with them, its members become indifferent to each other and treat each other as strangers. Aristocracy had created a long chain of citizens from the peasant to the king; democracy breaks down this chain and separates all the links.

As social equality spreads, a greater number of individuals are no longer rich or powerful enough to exercise great influence upon the fate of their fellows, but have acquired or have preserved sufficient understanding and wealth to be able to satisfy their own needs. Such people owe nothing to anyone and, as it were, expect nothing from anyone. They are used to considering themselves in isolation and quite willingly imagine their destiny as entirely in their own hands.

Thus, not only does democracy make men forget their ancestors but also hides their descendants and keeps them apart from their fellows. It constantly brings them back to themselves and threatens in the end to imprison them in the isolation of their own hearts.

CHAPTER 3

HOW INDIVIDUALISM IS GREATER AT THE END OF A DEMOCRATIC REVOLUTION THAN AT ANY OTHER PERIOD

It is just at the moment when a democratic society is in the final throes of establishing itself on the ruins of an aristocracy that this isolation of men from one another and the egoism which follows most forcibly strike the observer.

These societies include not only a great number of independent citizens but they are daily filled with men who, having achieved independence only yesterday, are drunk with their new power. Such men entertain an arrogant confidence in their own strength and do not suppose that they may ever again need to seek help from their fellows. They have no scruples about showing that they think only about themselves.

Normally, an aristocracy does not surrender until after a prolonged conflict in the course of which implacable hatreds are kindled between the various classes. These emotions last beyond the moment of victory and traces of them are visible in the succeeding democratic confusion.

Those citizens who were leaders in the ruined hierarchy are not immediately able to forget their former greatness; for a long time they feel themselves aliens in a new society. They regard those men society has made equal to them as oppressors whose fate evokes no sympathy from them; they have lost sight of their former equals and no longer feel tied by a shared interest in their own fate; each of them withdraws and feels reduced to taking care of himself alone. On the other hand, those who used to be at the bottom of the social scale and are now raised by this sudden revolution to a common level enjoy with a kind of secret anxiety this newly acquired independence; when they walk shoulder to shoulder with some of their former superiors, they look upon them with fear mixed with triumph and they avoid them.

Usually, therefore, citizens are most inclined to isolate themselves when democratic societies are taking root.

Democracy persuades men not to have close links with their fellows; but democratic revolutions incline them to turn their backs and continue to foster in a state of equality those hatreds that were born in a state of inequality.

The great advantage enjoyed by Americans is to have reached democracy without the sufferings of a democratic revolution and to have been born equal instead of becoming so.

CHAPTER 4

HOW AMERICANS COMBAT THE EFFECTS OF INDIVIDUALISM BY FREE INSTITUTIONS

Despotism, suspicious by its very nature, views the separation of men as the best guarantee of its own permanence and usually does all it can to keep them in isolation. No defect of the human heart suits it better than egoism; a tyrant is relaxed enough to forgive his subjects for failing to love him, provided that they do not love one another. He does not ask them to help him to govern the state; it is enough that they have no intention of managing it themselves. He calls those who claim to unite their efforts to create general prosperity "turbulent and restless spirits" and, twisting the normally accepted meaning of the words, he gives the name of "good citizens" to those who retreat into themselves.

Thus the vices fostered by tyranny are exactly those supported by equality. These two things are complementary and mutually supportive, with fatal results.

Equality places men shoulder to shoulder, unconnected by any common tie. Tyranny erects barriers between them and keeps them separate. The former persuades them not to think of their fellows while the latter turns their indifference into a sort of public virtue.

Tyranny, dangerous at all times, is particularly to be feared in democratic periods, when it is easy to see that men have a special need for freedom.

Citizens who are forced to take a part in public affairs must turn from the circle of their private interests and occasionally tear themselves away from self-absorption.

As soon as communal affairs are treated as belonging to all, every man realizes that he is not as separate from his fellows as he first imagined and that it is often vital to help them in order to gain their support.

When the public is in charge, every single man feels the value of public goodwill and seeks to court it by attracting the regard and affection of those amongst whom he is to live.

Many of the emotions which freeze and shatter men's hearts are then forced to withdraw and hide away in the depths of their souls. Pride conceals itself; scorn dares not show its face. Egoism is afraid of itself.

Under a free government, as most public offices are elective, men whose elevated spirit and agitated aspirations feel cramped in the sphere of their private life realize each day that they cannot do without the people around them.

Then they think of their fellows out of ambition and they often find it is somewhat in their interest to forget themselves. I accept that in opposition to this view I may here have to account for all the intrigues born of an election, the shameful methods often used by candidates, and the personal abuse spread by their enemies. These are opportunities for hatred which occur all the more often as elections become more frequent.

These evils are doubtless great, but they do not last long, whereas the accompanying advantages remain.

The desire to be elected may bring certain men for a time to fight each other, but this same eagerness in the longer term brings all men to support each other. If an election accidentally divides two friends, the electoral system draws together in a lasting way a crowd of citizens who would have remained strangers to one another. Freedom evokes individual hatreds but tyranny gives birth to general indifference.

The Americans have exploited liberty in order to combat

that individualism which equality produced and have overcome it.

American legislators did not believe that a general representation of the whole nation would be enough to cure a disease so natural to the frame of democratic society and so fatal. They also thought it appropriate to give each area of the territory its own political life so as to multiply without limit the opportunities for citizens to act in concert and to let them realize every day their mutual dependence.

This was a wise plan.

The general business of a country takes up the time of the leading citizens only, who meet together from time to time in the same locations. Since they often lose contact with each other, no lasting ties form between them. But when control of the particular affairs of a district is placed in the hands of the people who live there, the same men are always in contact and are, to some extent, forced to become acquainted and to adapt to each other.

It is difficult to drag a man away from his own affairs to involve him in the destiny of the whole state because he fails to grasp what influence the destiny of the state might have on his own fate. But if it becomes necessary to make a road across the end of his own estate, he sees at once the connection between this minor public affair and his greatest private interests and will discover, without being shown, the close link between individual and general interests.

It is therefore by entrusting citizens with the management of minor affairs, much more than handing over the control of great matters, that their involvement in the public welfare is aroused and their constant need of each other to provide for it is brought to their attention.

The favor of the people may be won by some brilliant action but the love and respect of your neighbors must be gained by a long series of small services, hidden deeds of goodness, a persistent habit of kindness, and an established reputation of selflessness.

Local freedoms, then, which induce a great number of citizens to value the affection of their neighbors and kinsfolk, bring men constantly into contact with each other and force them to help one another, in spite of the instincts which separate them.

In the United States, the wealthiest citizens take good care not to become isolated from the people; on the contrary, they maintain constant contact with them, listening to them gladly and talking to them every day. They realize that the rich in democracies always need the poor and that, in democratic times, you attach a poor man to you more by your manner than by benefits conferred, the very size of which highlights the differences of status and irritates those who profit from them. But the charm of simple good manners cannot ever be resisted; their ease of approach wins men over and even their roughness does not always seem unpleasant.

The truth does not immediately penetrate the minds of the rich. Normally they resist as long as the democratic revolution lasts and they even refuse to accept it when the revolution is over. They are willing to do good to the people but they wish to continue to keep them carefully at a distance. They believe that to be enough; they are mistaken. They might spend their entire fortunes thus without gaining the hearts of their neighbors who do not require the sacrifice of their money but of their pride.

It might be said that, in the United States, there is no limit to the inventiveness of man to discover ways of increasing wealth and to satisfy the public's needs. The most enlightened inhabitants of each district constantly use their knowledge to make new discoveries to increase the general prosperity, which, when made, they pass eagerly to the mass of the people.

On close scrutiny of the defects and weaknesses of those who govern in America, the growing prosperity of the people is astonishing; but it should not be so. It is not the elected official who produces the prosperity of American democracy but the fact that the official is elected,

It would be unfair to think that the patriotism and enthusiasm shown by each American for the welfare of his fellow citizens are not truly felt. Although, in the United States as elsewhere, private interest governs most human actions, it does not control them all.

I must say that I have seen Americans making great and

sincere sacrifices for the common good and a hundred times I have noticed that, when needs be, they almost always gave each other faithful support.

The free institutions belonging to the inhabitants of the United States and the political rights they employ so much, provide a thousand reminders to each citizen that he lives in society. They constantly impress this idea upon his mind, that it is duty as well as self-interest to be useful to one's fellows and, as he sees no particular reason to hate others, being neither their slave nor their master, his heart easily inclines toward kindness. Attention is paid, in the first instance, to the common interest out of necessity and later out of choice; what started out as calculation becomes instinct; and by working for the advantage of one's fellow citizens, finally the habit and taste for serving them takes root.

Many French people consider equality of social conditions as the first of all evils and political freedom as the next. Once forced into suffering the former, they at least attempt to avoid the latter. But, for my part, I affirm that, to combat the evils produced by equality, there is but one effective remedy, namely political freedom.

CHAPTER 5

THE USE AMERICANS MAKE OF PUBLIC ASSOCIATIONS IN CIVIL LIFE

I do not propose to speak of those political associations by means of which men seek to defend themselves against the tyrannical action of a majority or against the encroachments of royal power. I have already dealt with that subject elsewhere. It is evident that unless each citizen learned the skills of uniting with his fellows to defend his freedom at a time when he is becoming individually weaker and consequently less capable of preserving his freedom in isolation, tyranny would be bound to increase together with equality. We are dealing here with associations created in civil life whose objectives have no political significance.

The political associations which exist in the United States represent only one single feature in the general picture of the total number of associations found there.

Americans of all ages, conditions, and all dispositions constantly unite together. Not only do they have commercial and industrial associations to which all belong but also a thousand other kinds, religious, moral, serious, futile, very general and very specialized, large and small. Americans group together to hold fêtes, found seminaries, build inns, construct churches, distribute books, dispatch missionaries to the antipodes. They establish hospitals, prisons, schools by the same method. Finally, if they wish to highlight a truth or develop an opinion by the encouragement of a great example, they form an association. Where you see in France the government and in England a noble lord at the head of a great new initiative, in the United States you can count on finding an association.

In America I have encountered several types of association of which I confess I had no notion and I have frequently admired the endless skill with which the inhabitants of the United States manage to set a common aim to the efforts of a great number of men and to persuade them to pursue it voluntarily.

Since then, I have traveled widely in England from where Americans have borrowed some of their laws and many of their practices; it appeared to me that the use of associations was far from being so consistently or skillfully employed in that country.

The English often perform great things as single individuals, whereas scarcely any minor initiative exists where Americans do not form associations. Clearly the former regard the association as one powerful means of action but the latter see it as the only way of acting.

Thus the most democratic country in the world is that in which men have in our time perfected the art of pursuing in concert the aim of their common desires and have applied this new technique to the greatest number of objectives. Has this just resulted from an accident or is there in reality a necessary connection between associations and equality?

Aristocratic societies always contain, at the very heart of a multitude of individuals unable to achieve anything on their own, a small number of very powerful and wealthy citizens each of whom has the ability to perform great enterprises single-handed.

In aristocratic societies men feel no need to act in groups because they are strongly held together.

Each rich and powerful citizen is virtually the leader of a permanent and compulsory association composed of all those dependent upon him and whose help he enlists in his projects.

But among democratic nations all citizens are independent and weak; they can achieve almost nothing by themselves and none of them could force his fellows to help him. Therefore they all sink into a state of impotence, if they do not learn to help each other voluntarily.

If men living in democratic countries had neither the right nor the inclination to join together in their political ambitions, their independence would run great risks but they would manage to preserve their wealth and knowledge for a long time. On the other hand, if they failed to acquire the practice of association in their day-to-day lives, civilization itself would be in danger. A nation in which individuals lost the capacity to achieve great things single-handed without acquiring the means of doing them in a shared enterprise would quickly revert to barbarism.

Unfortunately, the very same social conditions which make associations so vital for democratic nations also make them more difficult to achieve there than elsewhere.

When several members of an aristocracy wish to form an association, they easily manage to do so. Since each of them carries with him a considerable force in society, the number of members can be very small and when those members are small in number it is very easy for them to know and understand each other and to lay down settled rules.

The same efficiency does not happen in democratic nations where the number of associates has to be high for the associations to have any power.

I realize that many of my contemporaries are not the least embarrassed by this. They claim that as citizens become weaker and more incompetent, government has to be more able and active, so that society may accomplish what individuals find impossible. They are convinced that answers the whole problem but I think they are mistaken. A government could take the place of some of the largest American associations and several individual states in the Union have already tried to do so. But what political power could ever substitute for the countless small enterprises which American citizens carry out daily with the help of associations?

It is simple to see the time approaching when man will be decreasingly able to produce alone the commonest necessities of life. The tasks of government will therefore constantly increase and its very exertions must daily extend its scope. The more it replaces associations, the more individuals will need government to help as they lose the idea of association. This is the endless vicious circle of cause and effect. Will the public administration ever end up by controlling all those industries that no single citizen can cope with any longer? And if ultimately, as a result of the minute subdivision of landed property, the land itself is so split into an infinite number of plots that it can no longer be worked except by associations of laborers, must the head of government leave the helm of the state to guide the plow?

The moral wellbeing and intelligence of a democratic nation would be in no less danger than its business and industry if ever the government wholly took over the place of associations.

The only way opinions and ideas can be renewed, hearts enlarged, and human minds developed is through the reciprocal influence of men upon each other.

I have shown how these influences are practically non-existent in democratic countries. Thus, they have to be created artificially, which is what associations alone can achieve.

When the members of an aristocracy take up a new idea or espouse a new opinion, they give them something of a parallel status to their own and, by advertising them in this way to the public gaze, they introduce them with ease into the hearts and minds of all around.

In democratic countries only the power of society is by its

nature capable of acting thus but it can easily be seen that its influence is always inadequate and often dangerous.

A government could not by itself any more manage to maintain and renew the circulation of opinions and ideas in a great nation than it could control every industrial undertaking. The moment it tries to escape from the political arena to plunge on to this new track it will, even without intending to, exercise an intolerable tyranny. For a government can only dictate precise rules; it imposes the opinions and ideas which it supports and it is always difficult to distinguish its advice from its commands.

Things will be worse still if the government thinks that its real interest is to prevent anything from circulating at all. Then it will remain motionless and will allow itself to be weighed down by a deliberate torpor.

It is, therefore, vital for it not to act alone. In democratic nations, associations must take the place of those powerful individuals who have been swept away by the equality of social conditions.

In the United States, as soon as several inhabitants have taken up an opinion or an idea they wish to promote in society, they seek each other out and unite together once they have made contact. From that moment, they are no longer isolated but have become a power seen from afar whose activities serve as an example and whose words are heeded.

The first time I heard that one hundred thousand men in the United States had committed themselves publicly to give up strong drink, I thought this was more of a joke than a serious proposition and, at first, I did not see very clearly why these overly sober citizens did not content themselves merely with drinking water in the privacy of their own homes.

In the end, I realized that these one hundred thousand Americans, alarmed by the spread of drunkenness around them, had wished to give their support to temperance. They had acted exactly like a nobleman who dresses very plainly in order to inspire a contempt for luxury in ordinary citizens. It is probably true that if these one hundred thousand men had lived in France, each one of them would have made individual representations to the government asking it to keep a close eye on all the taverns throughout the realm.

In my view, nothing deserves to attract our attention more than the intellectual and moral associations of America. American political and industrial associations easily impinge upon our senses but others escape us. If we do come across them, we hardly understand them because we have almost never seen anything like them. However, we must acknowledge that the latter are as necessary as the former to the American people and possibly more so.

In democratic countries, the knowledge of how to form associations is the mother of all knowledge since the success of all the others depends upon it.

Among the laws governing human societies, one in particular seems more precise and clearer than all the others. In order to ensure that men remain or become civilized, the skill of association must develop and improve among them at the same speed as the spread of the equality of social conditions.

CHAPTER 6

CONNECTION BETWEEN ASSOCIATIONS AND NEWSPAPERS

When men are no longer united in any firm or lasting way, it is impossible to persuade any great number of them to act in cooperation unless you convince each of those whose help is vital that his private interests are served by voluntarily joining his efforts to those of all the others.

This cannot be achieved usually or conveniently except with the help of a newspaper, which is the only way of being able to place the same thought at the same moment into a thousand minds.

A newspaper is an adviser one need not seek out because it appears voluntarily every day to comment briefly upon community business without deflecting your attention from your own.

So, as men become more equal and individualism more of a menace, newspapers are more necessary. The belief that they just guarantee freedom would diminish their importance; they sustain civilization.

I shall not deny that, in democratic countries, newspapers often lead citizens to engage in very ill-considered enterprises together; but, without newspapers, there would be hardly any communal action. The evils they promote are, therefore, many fewer than those they cure.

The effect of a newspaper is not only to suggest a general plan to a great number of men; it provides them with the means of carrying through in a common effort the plans that they have thought of for themselves.

The principal citizens in an aristocracy see each other from a distance and, if they wish to join forces, they walk toward each other, drawing a crowd of men behind them.

On the other hand, it often happens that, in democratic countries, a large number of men who want or need to form an association cannot do so because they fail to see or find each other because they are all very puny and lost in the crowd. Then a newspaper appears to publish the opinion or idea which had occurred simultaneously but separately to each of them. Immediately, everyone turns towards this light and those wandering spirits, having sought each other for a long time in the darkness, at last meet and unite.

The newspaper has brought them together and continues to be necessary to keep them together.

For an association within a democratic nation to have power, it has to be numerous. Its members are, therefore, spread over a wide area and each of them is restricted to the place where he lives by the modesty of his wealth and by the mass of small necessary concerns. A means of daily communication has to be found which does not require contact and of common action which does not require meeting. Thus hardly any democratic association can do without a newspaper.

There is, therefore, a vital connection between associations and newspapers; the latter create associations which, in their turn, create newspapers. If it is a truism that associations must multiply as social conditions become more equal, it is no less certain that the number of newspapers increases as associations proliferate.

America, therefore, is, of all countries on this earth, where we come across the greatest number both of associations and of newspapers.

This connection between the number of newspapers and that of associations leads us to discover another between the state of periodicals and the form of government in the country and informs us that the number of newspapers in a democratic nation must diminish or grow in proportion to the greater or smaller centralization of the administration. For, in democratic nations, the exercise of local powers cannot be entrusted to the leading citizens as is done in aristocracies. These powers have either to be abolished or placed in the hands of a very great number of men, who form an authentic association permanently established by the law for the administration of a part of the territory and they need the daily delivery of a newspaper in the midst of their minor concerns to inform them of the progress of public affairs. The more numerous local powers, the greater the number of people required by law to exercise them and the more insistently this necessity is felt, the more newspapers abound.

This bizarre multiplication of American newspapers has more to do with the extraordinary subdivision of administrative power than the extensive freedom of politics or the absolute independence of the press. If all the inhabitants of the Union were electors, but if the system allowed only the right to vote for state legislators, they would need only a small number of newspapers, because the occasions when they had to act together, though important, would be very rare. But inside the great national association, the law has set up in each province, each city, and one might almost say each village, small associations responsible for local administration. The lawmaker has thus compelled every American to join forces daily with a few of his fellow citizens on community projects and each of them needs a newspaper to inform him of what the others are doing.

My opinion is that a democratic nation[1] without representatives at national level but with a large number of small local powers would, in the end, have more newspapers than would another nation governed by a centralized administration alongside an elected legislature. The best explanation for the astounding expansion of the daily press in the United States is the obvious combination of the most extensive national liberty enjoyed by Americans and local freedoms of every kind.

It is generally agreed in France and England that all you need to increase the number of newspapers indefinitely is to abolish the burden of taxes upon the press. That greatly exaggerates the effect of such a reform. Newspapers do not increase simply because they are cheap but because of the more or less frequent need of a great number of men to communicate and act together.

Equally, I would attribute the growing influence of newspapers to more general reasons than those often forwarded to explain it.

A newspaper survives only if it echoes a doctrine or opinion common to a large number of men. Thus a newspaper always represents an association of which its regular readers make up the membership.

This association can be more or less strictly defined, more or less restricted, more or less numerous but at least the seed of such an association must exist in men's minds to ensure the survival of a newspaper.

This leads to the last reflection to end this chapter.

The more social conditions become equal and the less power individuals possess, the more easily men drift with the crowd and find it difficult to stand alone in an opinion abandoned by the rest.

The newspaper represents the associations and one may say

1.   I say a *democratic nation*. The administration of an aristocratic people may be very decentralized without the need for newspapers making itself felt because local power is in the hands of a very small number of men who act in isolation, or who know each other and who can easily meet and come to an understanding.

that it speaks to each of its readers in the name of all the others, sweeping them along all the more readily as they are individually powerless.

The power of newspapers must therefore increase as men become equal.

CHAPTER 7

CONNECTIONS BETWEEN CIVIL AND POLITICAL ASSOCIATIONS

Only one country in the world makes daily use of the unrestricted freedom of political association. The same nation is the only one in the world whose citizens think constantly of using the right of association in civil life and thus have managed to enjoy all the benefits which civilization offers.

In all those nations where political association is banned, civil association is rare.

It is hardly likely that this is the result of accident. Rather, the conclusion suggests itself that there is a natural and possibly necessary connection between these two types of association.

By chance men share an interest in a certain matter; maybe the management of a commercial enterprise or the conclusion of an industrial operation; they meet and join together, gradually familiarizing themselves thus with the idea of association.

The more the number of these minor communal matters increases, the more men acquire, even unknowingly, the capacity to pursue major ones in common.

Civil associations, therefore, pave the way for political associations; on the other hand, political associations develop and improve in some strange way civil associations.

In civil life, every man can, if needs be, fancy that he is self-sufficient. In politics, he can imagine no such thing. So when a nation has a public life, the idea of associations and the desire to form them are daily in the forefront of all citizens' minds; whatever natural distaste men may have for working in partnership, they will always be ready to do so in the interests of the party.

Thus politics promotes the love and practice of association at a general level; it introduces the desire to unite and teaches the skill to do so to a crowd of men who would always have lived in isolation.

Politics engenders associations which are not only numerous but spread very wide.

In civil life, seldom does the same interest attract a great number of men naturally toward common action. Only with a great deal of skill can such an interest be created.

In politics, such opportunities occur spontaneously all the time. Now, only large associations manifest the general value of joining together. Citizens who are weak at an individual level are not clearly aware in advance of the strength they can gain by combining; to understand that, they have to be shown. That is why it is often easier to assemble a crowd for a common purpose than a few men. Where a thousand citizens fail to perceive the advantage of uniting, ten thousand do. In politics, men associate for large enterprises and the benefit they derive from such associations in important matters teaches them the practical advantages of mutual help in lesser ones.

A political association draws a lot of individuals at the same time out of their small circle; however separate they may feel naturally through age, attitude, and wealth, association brings them together and puts them in touch. They meet once and forever know how to meet again.

One cannot join most civil associations without risking a part of one's possessions; such is true for all industrial and commercial companies. When men are still unversed in the skill of association and are unaware of the major rules, they are afraid that they may pay dearly for the experience of combining for the first time in this way. Therefore, they prefer doing without this powerful means of success to incurring the dangers involved. But they show less hesitation in taking part in political associations which do not appear dangerous because their money is not at risk.

Now, they cannot belong to these associations for long

without discovering how order is maintained in a large number of men and what procedures enable men to direct themselves harmoniously and methodically toward a common aim. They learn to surrender their wishes to others and to subordinate their individual efforts to the common endeavor, all of which knowledge is vital no less in civil than in political associations.

Political associations can therefore be considered as great free schools in which all citizens learn the general theory of associations.

Even if political associations do not directly support the progress of civil associations, to destroy the former would still damage the latter.

When citizens can combine only in certain restricted cases, they look upon associations as a rare and peculiar occurrence and scarcely give any thought to them.

When they have the freedom to combine for all purposes, they end up by seeing associations as the universal and, as it were, the unique means for men to attain their various aims. Every fresh need immediately revives that idea. Thus the skill of association becomes, as I have said before, the root of all skills, which everyone studies and applies.

When certain associations are prohibited and others allowed, it is difficult to tell in advance the difference between the former and the latter. Doubt persuades people to steer clear of both and, in a vague way, public opinion tends to consider any association at all as a rash and almost illegal enterprise.[1]

1.   This is especially true when the executive power, which has the responsibility to allow or prohibit associations, follows its own arbitrary will.

When the law limits itself to prohibiting certain associations and leaves the punishment of those who disobey to the courts, the evil is far less serious; each citizen knows in advance more or less what to expect; to a certain extent he judges himself before he gets to court and, distancing himself from forbidden associations, he devotes himself to those which are permitted. It is thus that all free peoples have always understood that it is possible to restrict the right of association. But, if it should happen that the legislature gives a man the authority to sort out in advance those associations which are dangerous and those which are useful and allows him to nip associations in the bud, or allow them to be formed, as nobody would be able to predict in advance under what circumstances they might be formed or under what circumstances they would not be allowed, the

It is, therefore, a delusion to think that the spirit of association which is suppressed in one respect will develop with the same energy in all the others and that if, quite simply, men are allowed to prosecute certain undertakings in common, this permission is all that is required for them eagerly to do so. When citizens have the capacity and the habit of combining in everything, they will be as willing to combine for small as for great undertakings. However, if they can associate only for minor purposes, they will show neither the desire nor the capacity to do so. It would be useless for you to allow them complete freedom to combine in matters of trade; they will use the rights granted them in an indifferent fashion and, when you have exhausted your strength in keeping them from forbidden associations, you will be surprised that you cannot persuade them to form those that are allowed.

I am not saying that civil associations cannot exist in a country where political associations are prohibited, for men cannot ever exist in society without engaging in some common projects. But I am maintaining that, in such a country, civil associations will always be small in number, feebly conceived, incompetently run, and will never engage in plans on a vast scale or will fail in attempting to execute them.

This naturally leads me to think that the political freedom to associate is not as dangerous to the public peace as is supposed and that it could strengthen a state which for some time it had shaken.

In democratic countries, political associations could be said to create the only powerful individuals aspiring to rule the state. Thus present governments look upon these types of associations with the same regard as medieval kings viewed the great vassals of the crown; they entertain a sort of instinctive abhorrence toward them and combat them whenever they meet.

---

spirit of association would be hit by inertia. The first of these two laws only attacks certain associations; the second applies to society itself and is harmful to it. I can conceive that a law-abiding government may have recourse to the former but I do not accept that any government has the right to pass the latter.

But they feel a natural goodwill toward civil associations because they have quickly discovered that these, far from directing citizens' minds toward public affairs, do in fact turn attention from them and, by increasingly occupying citizens in enterprises which cannot be accomplished without a time of public tranquillity, they divert them from revolutions. However, governments fail to notice that political associations help in an amazing way to multiply civil associations and that by avoiding one dangerous evil, they lose an effective remedy. When you see Americans combining in free associations every day to further the cause of a political opinion, helping some politician into the government or wresting power away from another, you find it difficult to understand that such independently minded men do not constantly succumb to the abuse of freedom.

If, on the other hand, you come to observe the countless industrial enterprises run by partnerships in the United States and note Americans on all sides working unceasingly on the execution of important and difficult projects which could be disturbed by the slightest revolution, you will readily see why such busy men are not tempted to upset the state or destroy public calm by which they all profit.

Is it enough to note these things separately or should we discover the hidden link which connects them? It is at the heart of political associations that Americans from all the states, of every shade of opinion and age, acquire a general taste for associations and grow accustomed to using them. In them, large numbers of people are in touch, communicate, agree together and enjoy a shared enthusiasm for all sorts of enterprises. Then they transfer the ideas they have acquired into civil life where they make a thousand uses of them.

Thus it is by enjoying a dangerous freedom that Americans learn the skill of reducing the risks of freedom.

If one chooses one particular moment in the history of a nation, it is easy to show that political associations disturb the state and paralyze industry; but if one surveys the whole life of a nation, it may be easy to demonstrate that the freedom of political association favors the wellbeing and even the tranquillity of citizens.

I have stated in the first part of this work: "But *unrestricted* freedom of association cannot be confused with the freedom to write: the former is both less necessary and more dangerous than the other. A nation may set bounds upon it without losing control over its own affairs; it must sometimes do so in order to maintain this control." And I added further on: "It cannot be concealed that unrestricted freedom of association in the political sphere is, of all freedoms, the last that a nation can tolerate. If such a freedom does not lead to actual anarchy, it does ever bring it, so to speak, close to that brink."

Thus I do not believe that a nation is always safe to allow its citizens the absolute right of political association and I even doubt whether it would be prudent in any country or in any period not to place restrictions upon the freedom of association.

It is said that such and such a nation could neither maintain internal peace and respect for the law, nor found a lasting government without strictly limiting the right of association. Of course, such blessings are beyond price and I can understand that, in order to obtain or preserve them, a nation should agree temporarily to impose upon itself such severe inconveniences but still a nation does well to know precisely the cost of those blessings.

I realize that a man's arm can be amputated to save his life; but I am unwilling to be convinced that he is going to display as much dexterity as with the arm intact.

CHAPTER 8

HOW AMERICANS COUNTERACT INDIVIDUALISM BY THE DOCTRINE OF SELF-INTEREST PROPERLY UNDERSTOOD

When the world was controlled by a small number of powerful and wealthy individuals, they enjoyed promoting a lofty ideal of man's duties; they liked to advertise how glorious it is to forget oneself and how fitting it is to do good without self-interest just like God himself. At that time, such was the official moral doctrine.

I doubt whether men were more virtuous in aristocratic times than in others, but they certainly referred constantly to the beauties of virtue; only secretly did they examine its usefulness. But as man's imagination indulges more modest flights of fancy and everyone is more self-centered, moralists fight shy of this notion of self-sacrifice and dare not promote it for man's consideration. They are, therefore, reduced to inquiring whether working for the happiness of all would be to the advantage of each citizen, and when they have discovered one of those points at which individual self-interest happens to coincide and merge with the interest of all, they eagerly highlight it. Gradually, similar views become more numerous. What was an isolated observation becomes a universal doctrine and in the end the belief is born that man helps himself by serving others and that doing good serves his own interest.

I have already shown in several places in this book how the inhabitants of the United States almost always knew how to combine their own wellbeing with that of their fellow citizens. What I would like to note here is the general theory which enables them to achieve that.

In the United States, the beauty of virtue is almost never promoted. It is considered useful and this is proved daily. American moralists do not claim that one must sacrifice oneself for one's fellows because it is a fine thing to do but they are bold enough to say that such sacrifices are as necessary to the man who makes them as to those gaining from them.

They have observed that in their country and during their lifetime the force which was driving men in on themselves was irresistible and, since they could not hope to stop its progress, they thought only about controlling it.

They do not, therefore, deny that every man can pursue his own self-interest but they turn themselves inside out to prove that it is in each man's interest to be virtuous.

I do not intend to elaborate their reasons for this, which

would divert me from my theme; let me merely say that they convinced their fellow citizens.

Montaigne[a] said long ago: "If I do not follow the straight road because it is straight, I follow it because experience has shown me that in the last analysis it is the happiest and most useful."

The doctrine of self-interest properly understood is, therefore, not new but for present-day Americans it has been universally accepted. It has become popular; it is to be found at the root of all actions; it is woven into everything they say. It is uttered by the poor no less than the wealthy.

In Europe, the doctrine of self-interest is much cruder than in America but it is at the same time less widespread and, above all, less obvious. People still profess every day great sacrifices they no longer perform.

Americans, on the other hand, are delighted to explain almost all the acts of their life in the light of self-interest properly understood. They are quite willing to show how enlightened self-love continually leads them to help one another and inclines them to devote freely a part of their time and wealth to the welfare of the state. My opinion is that in this they often do themselves an injustice because sometimes, in the United States as elsewhere, citizens yield to those disinterested and spontaneous impulses natural to man. But Americans rarely admit that they are giving way to such kinds of emotions; they prefer to attribute the credit to their philosophy than to themselves.

At this point I could stop and not attempt an assessment of what I have just described. I could use the extreme difficulty of the subject as my excuse but I decline to use that. I would rather that my readers, clearly seeing my aims, refuse to agree with me than that I should leave them in suspense.

Self-interest properly understood is not a sublime doctrine but it is clear and unambiguous. It makes no attempt at reaching great objectives but it does achieve all the aims it envisages without too much effort. Being within the scope of everyone's understanding, it is effortlessly grasped and retained. Being wondrously in tune with the weakness of men, it easily achieves a hold which it has no difficulty in maintaining because it turns individual self-interest against itself, using the same goad which arouses them to control their passions.

The doctrine of self-interest properly understood does not inspire great sacrifices but does prompt daily small ones; by itself it could not make a man virtuous but it does shape a host of law-abiding, sober, moderate, careful, and self-controlled citizens. If it does not lead the will directly to virtue, it moves it closer through the imperceptible influence of habit.

If the doctrine of self-interest properly understood happened to exercise complete domination over the world of morality, no doubt it would not be common to see unusual virtues. But I also think that gross depravity would be less common. The doctrine of self-interest properly understood possibly prevents some from rising much above the ordinary level of humanity but many others who were falling below that standard do grasp it and retain their hold upon it. The doctrine might debase a few individuals but it does raise the race as a whole.

I am not afraid to say that the doctrine of self-interest properly understood seems to me to represent, of all philosophical theories, the one best suited to the needs of contemporary men and the most powerful guarantee against their own nature. So, moralists of our time ought to turn mainly toward that doctrine. They might consider it imperfect; nonetheless they ought to adopt it as vital.

All in all, I do not believe there is more selfishness in America than in France; the only difference is that in the former it is enlightened, in the latter it is not. Every American has the sense to sacrifice some of his personal interests to save the rest. We wish to retain everything and often lose the lot.

I only see around me people who daily wish to teach their contemporaries in word and deed that what is useful is always right. Shall I never come across any who are trying to convey how what is right can be useful?

No power on earth can stop the increasing equality of social conditions from persuading the human mind to seek what is useful or from disposing each citizen to become wrapped up in himself.

We must, therefore, expect private self-interest to become more than ever the principal, if not the only motivation, for human actions but it remains to be seen how each individual will interpret this private self-interest.

If, on the achievement of equality, citizens were to remain ignorant and coarse, it would be difficult to predict what ridiculous excesses their selfishness might commit and one would not be able to foretell to what shameful depths of wretchedness they would plummet for fear of sacrificing something of their own wellbeing to the prosperity of their fellow men.

I do not believe that the doctrine of self-interest as it is preached in America is obvious in all its aspects but it contains a great number of truths so clear that all you have to do to convince men is to educate them. Hence, give them education at any price, for the century of blind sacrifice and instinctive virtues is already distant from us and I see the time drawing near when freedom, public peace, and social order itself will not be able to do without education.

CHAPTER 9

HOW AMERICANS APPLY THE DOCTRINE OF SELF-INTEREST PROPERLY UNDERSTOOD TO RELIGIOUS MATTERS

If the doctrine of self-interest properly understood were concerned with this world only, that would be far from sufficient, for a great number of sacrifices can only find their reward in the next, and whatever efforts of mind are devoted to proving the usefulness of virtue, it will always be difficult to force a man who has no thought of dying to behave well.

It is, therefore, vital to know whether the doctrine of self-interest properly understood can be reconciled with religious beliefs.

Philosophers teaching this doctrine tell men that, to be happy in this life, they must keep close watch upon their passions and keep control over their excesses, that they cannot obtain a lasting happiness unless they renounce a thousand ephemeral pleasures and that, finally, they must continually control themselves in order to promote their own interests.

The founders of almost all religions have used the same language. There is no difference in the route they recommend, they simply push the goal further away; instead of situating in this world the reward for sacrifices imposed, they have transposed it to the next.

However, I refuse to believe that all those practicing virtue from religious beliefs are acting only with a reward in mind.

I have come across zealous Christians who constantly forgot themselves in order to work with greater enthusiasm for the general happiness, and I have heard them claim that they acted thus in order to deserve the rewards in the next world. Yet, I cannot get it out of my head that they were deceiving themselves. I respect them too much to believe them.

It is true that Christianity teaches us to place others before ourselves in order to gain heaven; but Christianity also teaches us to do good to our fellow men for the love of God. What a magnificent expression; man uses his intelligence to penetrate the mind of God and sees that God's aim is order. He freely joins in this grand design and, sacrificing his private interests to this admirable order of all creation, he expects no other reward than the joy of contemplating it.

I, therefore, do not think that the only motive of religious men is self-interest but it is the major means used by religions themselves to guide men, and I am quite sure that is how they seize the minds of the crowd to court popularity.

I, therefore, do not see clearly why the doctrine of self-interest properly understood would drive men away from religious beliefs; on the contrary, it seems to me possible to show how the doctrine brings them closer.

Let us suppose that, in order to obtain happiness in this world, a man resists at every turn his instinctive impulses and brings cool rationality to bear on every action of his life; that, instead of a blind surrender to the first onrush of his desires, he has learned the art of counteracting them and that he habitually makes an effortless sacrifice of the pleasure of a moment for the lasting interest of his whole life.

If such a man believes in his professed religion, it will scarcely cost him anything to submit to the constrictions it imposes. Reason itself advises this course and habits have already prepared him to endure it.

Even when he entertains doubts upon the object of his hopes, he will not easily allow himself to be stopped by them and he will estimate that it is prudent to risk some of the good things of this world so as to save his claims to the immense inheritance in the next.

"To make a mistake by thinking the Christian religion true," Pascal has said, "is not a very great loss, but how unfortunate to make the mistake of believing it false!"

Americans do not display a crude indifference to the afterlife nor a childish pride in scorning perils they hope to avoid.

Therefore, they practice their religion without shame or weakness but one generally observes at the heart of their zeal something so calm, so methodical, and so calculated that the head rather than the heart leads them to the foot of the altar.

Not only does self-interest guide the religion of Americans but they often place their interest in following it in this world. In the Middle Ages priests spoke only of the afterlife, hardly bothering to prove that a sincere Christian might be happy here below.

But American preachers return constantly to this world and have some difficulty in detaching their gaze from it. So as to touch their listeners more profoundly, they show them every day how religious belief is beneficial to freedom and public order. It is often hard to know from listening to them whether the main intention of religion is to obtain everlasting joy in the next world or prosperity in this.

CHAPTER 10

THE TASTE FOR MATERIAL PROSPERITY IN AMERICA

In America, the passion for material prosperity is not always exclusive but it is general; if everyone's experience of it is different, nevertheless it is felt by all. All men are preoccupied with the need to satisfy the slightest of their bodily needs and to provide for the little conveniences of life.

Something akin to this is increasingly evident in Europe.

Among the causes which produce these parallel effects in both hemispheres there are several which are connected with my subject and which I must mention.

When wealth is fixed by heredity in the same families, a great number of men enjoy material prosperity without feeling an exclusive taste for it.

What most sharply stirs the human heart is not the quiet possession of a precious object but the as yet unsatisfied desire of owning it and the constant fear of losing it.

In aristocratic societies, the wealthy have never known any state other than their own; thus they do not dread change and can scarcely conceive of anything different. Material prosperity does not constitute their aim in life but just a way of living. They take it as a part of existence and enjoy it with no further thought.

The natural and instinctive taste for comfort being thus satisfied without trouble or anxiety, all men turn elsewhere and become involved in some greater and more taxing endeavor which inspires and absorbs their souls.

Thus it is in the midst of these physical enjoyments that aristocrats often manifest a haughty scorn for these same comforts and discover unusual powers of endurance when ultimately deprived of them. All those revolutions which have disturbed and destroyed aristocracies have shown how easily people, accustomed to plenty, were able to do without necessities, whereas men who attained a life of comfort through their own toil can hardly survive once they have lost it.

If I turn from the upper to the lower classes, I can see similar effects from different causes.

In nations where an aristocracy dominates and immobilizes society, the people end up by becoming accustomed to poverty as the wealthy do to their riches. The latter are not preoccupied with material prosperity because they already enjoy it without any effort, and the former give no thought to it either because they have given up hope of ever acquiring such a thing or have too little knowledge of it to wish to possess it.

In such types of society the mind of the poor man is cast forward to the next world; his imagination is cramped by the wretchedness of real life, yet it escapes to seek for joys beyond.

But when distinctions of class are blurred and privileges abolished, when patrimonies are divided up and education and freedom spread, then the poor man's imagination conceives the desire to obtain comfort and the rich man's mind is overtaken by the fear of losing it. A lot of modest fortunes spring up. Their owners have enough physical comforts to have a liking for them but not enough to be content. They never win them without effort or indulge in them without anxiety.

They are, therefore, constantly engaged in the pursuit or the preservation of these precious, imperfect, and fugitive delights.

If I seek out a passion which is characteristic of men both fired and restricted by the obscurity of their birth or the modesty of their fortunes, no better example can be found than their liking for comfort. The passion for material prosperity is fundamentally a middle-class affair; it expands and grows with that class and becomes important along with it. Starting there, it works upwards into the higher levels of society and downwards to the mass of the people.

In America, I have never met a citizen so poor that he did not cast a glance of hope and envy toward the pleasures of the rich or whose imagination did not anticipate the good things which fate stubbornly refused to him.

Alternatively, I have never observed among the wealthy of the United States that arrogant contempt for material prosperity which sometimes manifests itself in the most opulent and dissolute aristocracies.

Most of these wealthy men have been poor and felt the sharp sting of necessity. For many years they have battled against a hostile fate and, now that victory is won, the passions which accompanied the struggle stay with them. They remain almost drunk on the trivial delights they have pursued for forty years.

Not that in the United States, as elsewhere, you do not encounter quite a large number of wealthy people who have inherited their possessions and enjoy, without the need for effort, wealth they have not earned. But even these appear to be no less attached to the delights of the material world. The love of comfort has become the dominant taste of the nation. The main current of human passions runs in that channel and sweeps all before it in its course.

CHAPTER 11

PARTICULAR EFFECTS OF THE LOVE OF PHYSICAL PLEASURES IN DEMOCRATIC TIMES

It might be thought, according to what has just been said, that the love of physical pleasures must constantly sweep Americans toward moral disorder, disturb family life, and finally threaten the fate of society itself.

But that is not the case; the passion for physical pleasures evokes in democracies very different effects from those in aristocracies.

Sometimes boredom with public affairs, excessive wealth, the decay of belief, and national decadence gradually deflect an aristocracy toward physical pleasures alone. At other times, the power of the prince or the weakness of the people, while not depriving the nobility of their wealth, force them to stand clear of administrative power and, while closing the path to great undertakings, leave them abandoned to their restless desires. At that point they fall back on their own resources with a heavy heart and seek to forget their former glories in the pleasures of the body.

When the members of an aristocracy turn in this way exclusively toward physical pleasure, they usually concentrate in that direction all the energy the long experience of power has given them.

The search for comfort is not enough for such men; they crave sumptuous depravity and stunning corruption. They turn materialism into a magnificent cult and vie with each other in their desire to excel in the art of coarsening their natures.

The more an aristocracy has once been strong, glorious, and free, the more depraved it will appear and, however splendid its virtues may have been, I am bold enough to predict that its virtues will always be outstripped by the blaze of its vices.

The taste for physical pleasure does not lead democratic nations to such excesses. The love of comfort appears as a deep-rooted, exclusive, universal passion but one always contained within bounds. There is no question of building vast palaces, conquering or going against nature, or sucking the world dry, the better to satisfy one man's passions; all that is needed is to add a few yards to one's fields, to plant an orchard, to enlarge one's house, to increase life's comforts and conveniences, to anticipate irritations and to satisfy one's slightest needs without trouble and almost without expense. Such objectives are small but the soul clings to them and considers them daily at close quarters; they end up by obscuring the rest of reality from one's view and sometimes intervene between one's soul and God.

This, it may be said, can apply only to those citizens with a modest fortune; the wealthy will display tastes akin to those which flourished in aristocratic times. I challenge that suggestion.

Where physical pleasures are concerned, the most opulent citizens of a democracy will not reveal tastes very different from those of the people either because, having originated from the people, they really do share their tastes, or because they think they ought to accept them. In democratic societies, the sensual pleasures of the public have taken a moderate and tranquil course to which all are expected to conform. It is as difficult to depart from the general rule whether it concerns one's vices or one's virtues.

The wealthy living in democracies are, therefore, aiming at the satisfaction of their slightest needs rather than excessive pleasures; they gratify a host of small desires but do not wallow in any disorderly passion. Thus they sink into self-indulgence rather than outright debauchery.

This individual taste for physical pleasures which occurs in democratic times is in no way a natural threat to good order; on the contrary, it often requires good order for its satisfaction. Nor is it hostile to moral orderliness, for good morals are conducive to public tranquillity and encourage industry. Often enough it may combine with a type of religious morality, for people wish to do as well as possible in this world without giving up their chances in the next.

Some physical delights cannot be obtained without crime; you have to be careful to avoid them. Others are permitted by religion and morality; the heart, imagination, and life itself are devoted to them without reserve and, in their efforts to seize such delights, men lose sight of those much more valuable possessions which constitute the glory and greatness of the human race.

My complaint against equality is not that it leads men to pursue forbidden pleasures but that it absorbs them completely in the search for those which are allowed.

Thus a kind of honorable materialism could be founded in the world which would not corrupt men's souls but would soften them and silently loosen the springs of their action.

CHAPTER 12

WHY CERTAIN AMERICANS DISPLAY AN EXALTED FORM OF SPIRITUALITY

Although the desire to obtain the good things of this world is the dominant passion of Americans, there are moments of respite when their souls appear suddenly to break the physical ties which hold them back and to rush impetuously toward heaven.

In every state of the Union, but mainly in the sparsely peopled lands of the West, you sometimes meet preachers hawking around the word of God from place to place.

Whole families, old men, women, and children cross difficult terrain and force their way through untrodden deserts to come from great distances to hear them. When they do arrive and listen to them, they forget for several days and nights to look after their affairs and neglect even the most urgent of their bodily needs.

Here and there throughout American society, you find men obsessed with an exalted, almost wild form of spirituality scarcely encountered in Europe. Weird sects appear from time to time striving to open up extraordinary paths to eternal happiness. Religious insanity is very common in the United States.

We should not be surprised at this.

It is not man who has inspired in himself the taste for infinite things and the love of what is everlasting. These lofty instincts are not the offspring of some whimsical desire; they have their firm foundations in human nature and exist despite man's efforts. Man can impede and disfigure them but he cannot destroy them.

The soul has needs which must be satisfied. Whatever efforts are expended upon diverting it from itself, it soon grows weary, anxious, and restless amid the pleasures of the senses.

If the thoughts of the great majority of the human race ever concentrated solely upon the search for material blessings, a colossal reaction could be anticipated in the souls of a few people who frantically would plunge into the world of the spirit for fear of being too tightly shackled by the fetters which the body imposed upon them.

You should not be surprised to meet, in the very heart of a society that considers only earthly matters, a small number of individuals whose gaze is fixed only upon heaven. I would be astonished if mysticism did not soon make progress in a nation solely preoccupied with prosperity.

It is said that the deserts of the Thebaid[a] were populated by the persecutions of the emperors and the tortures in the amphitheaters but I should rather blame Roman pleasure-seeking and Greek Epicureanism.[b]

If the state of society, circumstances, and laws did not concentrate American minds so narrowly upon the search for physical comfort, it is likely that they would show more reserve and experience when they came to engage in spiritual matters and would have no difficulty in controlling themselves. But they feel imprisoned within limits from which they are apparently not allowed to escape. Once they have broken free of these limits, they fail to find a place to settle and often rush headlong beyond the boundaries of common sense.

CHAPTER 13

WHY AMERICANS ARE SO RESTLESS IN THE MIDST OF THEIR PROSPERITY

Sometimes you still come across, in certain remote districts of the Old World, small populations which have been almost forgotten in the general commotion and which have stayed stationary while everything moved around them. Most of these peoples are very ignorant and wretched. They take no part in government affairs and often governments oppress them. Yet they normally look calm and possess a playful disposition.

In America, I have seen the freest and the best educated men in the happiest circumstances the world can afford; yet, it seemed to me that a cloud usually darkened their features and they appeared serious and almost sad even when they were enjoying themselves.

The main reason for this is that the first group ignore the sufferings they endure while the second constantly muse on the good things they are missing.

It is a strange thing to see the feverish enthusiasm which accompanies the Americans' pursuit of prosperity and the way they are ceaselessly tormented by the vague fear that they have failed to choose the shortest route to achieve it.

The inhabitants of the United States cling to the good things of this world as if assured that they will never die, and they are so impatient to snatch any that come within their grasp that they might be supposed to spend every moment frightened that they will stop living before being able to enjoy them. They snatch at them all without holding them fast; they soon let them slip from their hands in order to chase new pleasures.

In the United States, a man will carefully construct a home in which to spend his old age and sell it before the roof is on; he will plant a garden and will rent it out just as he was about to enjoy its fruit; he will clear a field and leave others to reap the harvest. He will take up a profession and then give it up. He will settle in one place only to go off elsewhere shortly afterwards with a new set of desires. If his private business gives him some time for leisure he will immediately plunge into the whirlwind of politics. And, if toward the end of a year of unremitting work he has some time to spare, he will trail his restless curiosity up and down the endless territories of the United States. He will also cover 1,500 miles in a few days as a diversion from his happiness.

Death steps in at last and brings him to a halt before he has grown tired of this futile pursuit of that complete happiness which continues to elude him.

At first, there is astonishment at the sight of this peculiar restlessness in so many happy men in the midst of abundance. Yet this is a sight as old as the world; what is new is to see a whole nation involved.

The taste for physical pleasures must be acknowledged as

the prime source of this secret anxiety in the behavior of Americans and of this unreliability which they exemplify every day.

The man who has set his heart exclusively on the search for the good things of this world is always in a hurry for he has only a limited time to find, grasp, and enjoy them. The reminder that life is short constantly spurs him on. Apart from the possessions he already has, he continually thinks of the thousand others which death will stop him enjoying if he does not hasten. This thought floods his mind with agitation, fear, and regret; it holds his soul in a sort of ceaseless nervousness which leads him perpetually to change plans and location.

If you add to this taste for physical comfort a social state in which neither the laws nor custom hold anyone in his place, that is yet another stimulus for this mental agitation. Then you will see men constantly changing path for fear of missing the shortest route to happiness.

It is, moreover, simple to understand that, if those men passionately seeking physical pleasures desire them overeagerly, they are also easily discouraged. Since the ultimate objective is enjoyment, the means to it has to be swift and easy; otherwise the trouble to attain it would outweigh the enjoyment itself. Most souls are, therefore, both enthusiastic and slack, violent, and nervous. Often death is less feared than the persistent efforts needed to achieve the same ambition.

Equality leads by a still shorter route to the various effects just described.

When all the privileges of birth and wealth are destroyed, when all the professions are open to all, and when a man can climb to the top of any of them through his own merits, men's ambitions think they see before them a great and open career and readily imagine they are summoned to no common destiny. Such, however, is a mistaken view which experience corrects daily. This very equality which allows each citizen to imagine unlimited hopes makes all of them weak as individuals. It restricts their strength on every side while offering freer scope to their longings.

Not only are they powerless by themselves but at every step they encounter immense obstacles unnoticed at first sight.

They have abolished the troublesome privileges of a few of their fellow men only to meet the competition of all. The barrier has changed shape rather than place. Once men are more or less equal and pursue the same path, it is very difficult for any one of them to move forward quickly in order to cleave his way through the uniform crowd milling around him.

This permanent struggle between the instincts inspired by equality and the means it supplies to satisfy them harasses and wearies men's minds.

One can imagine men enjoying a certain degree of freedom which wholly satisfies them. Then they savor their independence free from anxiety or excitement. But men will never establish an entirely satisfying equality.

No matter what a nation does, it will never succeed in reaching perfectly equal conditions. If it did have the misfortune to achieve an absolute and complete leveling, there would still remain the inequalities of intelligence which come directly from God and will always elude the lawmakers.

However democratic the state of society and the nation's political constitution, you can guarantee that each citizen will always spot several oppressive points near to him and you may anticipate that he will direct his gaze doggedly in that direction. When inequality is the general law of society, the most blatant inequalities escape notice; when everything is virtually on a level, the slightest variations cause distress. That is why the desire for equality becomes more insatiable as equality extends to all.

In democratic nations, men will attain a certain degree of equality with ease without being able to reach the one they crave. This retreats daily before them without moving out of their sight; even as it recedes, it draws them after it. They never cease believing that they are about to grasp it, while it never ceases to elude their grasp. They see it from close enough quarters to know its charms without getting near enough to enjoy them and they die before fully relishing its delights.

Those are the reasons for that unusual melancholy often

experienced by the inhabitants of democratic countries in the midst of plenty and for that distaste for life they feel seizes them even as they live an easy and peaceful existence.

In France, we complain of the growing number of suicides; in America, suicide is rare but I am told that madness is more common than anywhere else.

Those are different symptoms of the same illness.

Americans do not kill themselves however distressed they may be because religion forbids it and because a materialist philosophy is virtually unknown to them, although their passion for prosperity is general.

Their will resists but often their reason gives way.

In democratic ages, pleasure is felt more sharply than in aristocratic times and above all the number of the participants is immeasurably greater. On the other hand, one must acknowledge that hopes and longings are more often disappointed, minds more agitated and perturbed and worries felt more keenly.

CHAPTER 14

HOW IN AMERICA THE TASTE FOR
PHYSICAL PLEASURES IS COMBINED
WITH LOVE OF FREEDOM AND
CONCERN FOR PUBLIC AFFAIRS

When a democratic state turns to absolute monarchy, the activity which was previously directed to public and private affairs is suddenly concentrated upon the latter. The result, for some time, is great material prosperity but soon the impetus slackens and the growth of production comes to a halt.

I do not know whether one can cite a single trading or manufacturing nation, from the Tyrians[a] to the Florentines or the English, which was not free. There is, therefore, a close link and inevitable relationship between these two things, freedom and industry.

While that is generally true for all nations, it is especially so for democratic countries.

I have pointed out already how men living in times of equality continuously needed to form associations to gain almost all the good things they covet, and I have also shown how great political liberty improved and diffused the technique of association. Freedom in such ages is, therefore, especially conducive to the production of wealth; yet one can also see that tyranny is particularly hostile to it.

The nature of absolute power in democratic times is not to be cruel or savage but minute and interfering. Despotism of this kind, although it does not trample humanity under foot, is directly opposed to trade and the aims of industry.

Thus men of democratic times need to be free so as to gain with some measure of ease those physical pleasures for which they are endlessly longing.

Sometimes, however, it happens that the excessive taste for these very pleasures delivers them up to the first master who appears on the scene. The passion for prosperity then turns against itself and unwittingly drives away the object of their desires.

In fact, there is a dangerous phase in the life of democratic nations.

When the taste for physical pleasures in such a nation grows more speedily than education or the habit of liberty, a time occurs when men are carried away and lose self-control at the sight of the new possessions they are ready to grasp. Intent only on getting rich, they fail to perceive the close link between their own private fortunes and general prosperity. There is no need to wrench their rights from such citizens; they let them slip voluntarily through their fingers. The exercise of their political duties seems to them a tiresome nuisance which diverts them from industry. When they are required to elect their representatives, to offer help to government, to share in the business of the community, they have no time; they could not possibly waste such valuable time on futile work which is the pastime for idlers and quite unsuitable for important men busy with the serious concerns of life. Such people think they are following the doctrine of self-interest but their conception of that theory is crude and, in their aim to look after what they call their business, they neglect the chief concern which is to retain self-control.

Whenever working citizens refuse to attend to public affairs and the class which might have devoted its leisure hours to such concerns no longer exists, there is a virtual void in the place of government.

If a clever and ambitious man happens to seize power at such a critical moment, he discovers an open path to any encroachment.

As long as he makes sure, for a certain amount of time, that everything prospers, he will easily get away with the rest. Above all he must guarantee good order. Men with a passion for physical pleasures are usually quicker to realize how the restless desire for freedom disturbs prosperity than to perceive how freedom itself serves to promote it. If the slightest rumor of public excitement threatens to intrude into the trivial pleasures of their private lives, they wake up and feel anxious. The fear of anarchy long holds them on tenterhooks and ever ready to jettison liberty at the slightest sign of disorder.

I readily agree that public tranquillity is a benefit; but I do not intend to forget, however, that all nations have reached tyranny through good order. Of course, it does not follow that nations should despise public tranquillity but it should not be all that matters to them. A nation whose only requirement of its government is the preservation of good order is already enslaved at heart. It is a slave of its own wellbeing and may expect the arrival of the man who is bound to cast it into chains.

The tyranny of a faction is no less to be feared than that of a single man.

When the mass of citizens is engrossed solely with its own private affairs, even the most minor of parties should not give up hope of becoming all-powerful in public affairs.

At such a time, it is not uncommon to see on the vast world stage, just as you do in the theater, a whole host of people represented by a few players who alone speak on behalf of an absent or blasé crowd, who are alone active in the midst of the general immobility, who manage everything according to their own whim, who change laws at will and exert a tyrannical influence over moral standards. It is a source of astonishment to see a great nation falling into the hands of such a small number of weak and unworthy people.

Up to now, the Americans have happily avoided all the reefs I have just charted and one must really admire them for that.

There is possibly no country on the earth with fewer idle men than America and where all those who work are so eager to seek out their own prosperity. The American passion for physical pleasures may well be of a violent nature, but at least it is not blind and reason, powerless to restrain it, does direct its course.

An American attends to his private concerns as if he were alone in the world; a moment later, he devotes himself to public affairs as if he had forgotten his own. At times, he appears fired by the most selfish greed and sometimes by the keenest patriotism. The human heart cannot be divided up in this way. Americans alternately display so strong and similar a passion for prosperity and freedom that one must suppose these impulses to be united and mingled in some part of their souls. Americans in fact do regard their freedom as the best tool and surest safeguard of their wellbeing. They love them both, the one as a vehicle for the other. Therefore, they do not consider their concern for public matters to be none of their business; on the contrary, they believe it to be their chief concern to secure for themselves a government which allows them to obtain the good things they want and will not stop them from peacefully enjoying those they already possess.

CHAPTER 15

HOW RELIGIOUS BELIEF SOME-
TIMES DIVERTS THE THOUGHTS
OF AMERICANS TOWARD
SPIRITUAL PLEASURES

In the United States on the seventh day of the week, trade and industry seem suspended throughout the nation; all noise ceases. A deep peace, or rather a sort of solemn contemplation, takes its place. The soul regains its own domain and devotes itself to meditation.

On this day, places of business are deserted; each citizen goes to church accompanied by his children and there he listens to strange speech apparently little suited to his ear. He is regaled with the countless evils caused by pride and covetousness. He hears of the need to control his desires, of the subtle pleasures of virtue alone, and the true happiness they bring.

Having returned home, he does not hurry back to his business ledgers. He opens the Holy Scriptures and discovers the sublime or touching depictions of the greatness and goodness of the Creator, the infinite magnificence of God's handiwork, the lofty destiny reserved for man, his duties, and his claims to everlasting life.

Thus it is that from time to time the American hides away to some degree from himself and, snatching a momentary respite from those trivial passions which agitate his life and the fleeting concerns which invade his thoughts, he suddenly bursts into an ideal world where all is great, pure, and eternal.

Elsewhere in this book I have pointed out the causes which buttress the maintenance of American political institutions, and religion appeared to be one of the most important. Treating the Americans in their individual capacity, religion again comes into the picture and I see that it is no less valuable to each citizen than to the whole state.

Americans show in practice that they feel it necessary to instil morality into democracy by means of religion. Their thoughts about themselves in this context contain a truth which must permeate every democratic nation.

I am quite convinced that the social and political constitution of a nation predisposes it to certain beliefs or tendencies which then flourish without hindrance. At the same time these very causes keep certain opinions and leanings at a distance, without anyone's need to strive for that end or anyone's suspecting, so to speak, that it is happening.

All the legislator's skill consists in carefully appreciating the natural inclinations of human societies in order to gauge where he ought to help citizens' efforts and where it would be necessary to slow them down. For different times need different duties. Only the goal to be reached by the human race remains stationary; the means of getting there changes constantly.

If I had been born in an aristocratic era, in a nation where the inherited wealth of some and the insoluble poverty of others had the general effect of turning men away from the idea of improvement and retaining their minds in a state of numb contemplation of another world, I would have appreciated the possibility of arousing the feeling of need in such a nation and I would seek to discover the fastest and easiest means of satisfying the new desires I might have awakened. Finally, I would direct the greatest efforts of the best brains toward the physical sciences and would attempt to enthuse them into the search for the wellbeing of man.

If a few men happened to be overzealous in their ill-considered pursuit of wealth and manifested an altogether exaggerated love for physical pleasures, I would not be at all alarmed; these traits at an individual level would soon evaporate in the general picture.

Democratic legislators have other concerns.

If democratic nations have education and liberty, they can be left alone. They will easily succeed in extracting all the good things this world has to offer; they will perfect all the useful techniques and will make daily life more comfortable, relaxed, and pleasant. Since their social conditions urge them in this direction, I do not fear that they will stop.

But while man takes delight in this worthy and legitimate

search for prosperity, the fear is that he will finally lose the use of his most sublime faculties and that, in his desire to improve his environment, he may debase himself. Therein lies the real danger, not elsewhere.

Legislators and all worthy and enlightened men living in democracies must therefore work tirelessly to lift men's minds toward heaven. It is vital that all who are involved in the future of democratic societies unite together and with one accord combine their efforts to diffuse throughout these societies the taste for the infinite, the appreciation of greatness, and the love of spiritual pleasures.

Whenever among the opinions of a democratic nation you come across some of those evil theories which promote the belief that everything perishes with the body, you may consider men with such views as natural enemies of the people.

I am offended by many views held by materialists. Their doctrines appear to me pernicious and their arrogance disgusts me. If their system could be of some use to man, it would be in giving him a modest opinion of himself. But they do not demonstrate such a truth and when they think they have done enough to prove that they are brutish, they seem as proud as if they had demonstrated that they were gods.

In all nations materialism is a dangerous illness of the mind but in a democracy it must be especially feared because it unites marvelously well with that defect of the heart most familiar to those peoples.

Democracy encourages the taste for physical pleasures which, if excessive, soon persuades men to believe that nothing but matter exists. Materialism in its turn gives them the final impetuous enthusiasm for these very pleasures. Such is the vicious circle into which democratic nations are driven. Thank goodness they see the danger and hold back.

Most religions are only general, simple, and practical channels for teaching men that the soul is immortal. That is the most considerable advantage a democratic nation derives from religious beliefs and one which makes them more necessary for such a nation than for all others.

When, therefore, any religion has put down deep roots in a

democracy, be careful not to shake them; rather, take care to preserve them as the most valuable bequest from aristocratic times. Do not seek to snatch from men their ancient religious opinions in order to replace them with new ones, lest at the point of exchange the soul finds itself momentarily void of beliefs and the love of physical pleasures spreads to fill it entirely.

Certainly transmigration of souls is no more rational a doctrine than materialism; however, if it was absolutely vital for a democracy to choose between the two, I would judge without hesitation that its citizens run less a risk of being brutalized by believing that their souls will pass into the body of a pig than by thinking that their soul is nothing at all.

The belief in a spiritual and immortal principle united for a time with matter is so indispensable to man's greatness that its effects are striking even when not linked to the idea of rewards and punishments or when it merely holds that after death the divine principle embodied in man is absorbed in God or transferred to bring life to some other creature.

Those beliefs maintain that the body is the secondary and lower part of our nature and they despise it even as they succumb to its influence, whereas they harbor a natural regard and a secret admiration for the spiritual element in man even though they sometimes refuse to submit to its sway. That is enough to give a somewhat elevated tone to their ideas and tastes and to direct them unselfishly and as if of their own accord toward pure feelings and lofty thoughts.

It is doubtful whether Socrates and his school had very definite opinions upon what was to happen to man in the afterlife, but the one belief of which they were convinced, namely, that the soul has nothing in common with the body and would survive it, has been enough to give to Platonic philosophy this sort of sublime impetus which is its distinctive feature.

On reading Plato, we see that many writers before and during his lifetime anticipated the doctrine of materialism. These writers have not survived to our day or have only partially survived. The same is true for almost all other centuries; most great literary reputations have been linked to spirituality.

Instinct and taste direct the human race to follow this doctrine and they often preserve it in spite of themselves, keeping afloat the names of its adherents. It should not then be supposed that, at any period or under any political system, the passion for physical pleasures and the opinions which accompany it will ever be enough to satisfy a whole nation. The heart of man is greater than is supposed; it can contain both the taste for the good things of this world and the love of those in heaven. Sometimes it appears frantically intent on the one but it soon turns to thinking of the other.

If it is easy to see that, in democratic times especially, it is important to support the ascendancy of spiritual views, it is not so easy to say how the leaders of democracies must act to achieve this ascendancy.

I have no greater belief in prosperity than I have in the durability of official philosophies and, as far as state religions are concerned, I have always felt that, although they could sometimes momentarily serve the interests of political power, they always became sooner or later fatal to the Church.

Nor am I one of those who think that, in order to enhance religion in the people's eyes and to do honor to the spirituality of religious teaching, it is good to grant to its ministers an indirect political influence denied by law.

I am so deeply convinced of the almost unavoidable dangers which face beliefs when their interpreters meddle in public affairs and I am so firmly persuaded that Christianity should at all costs be maintained in the new democracies that I would sooner chain up the priests in their sanctuaries than allow them to leave them.

What means remain therefore to government authorities to lead men back to spiritual views or to retain them in that religion which promotes such views?

What I am about to state will certainly harm me in the eyes of politicians. I believe that the only effective means available to governments to bring respect to the dogma of the immortality of the soul is to act every day as if they believed in it themselves. I think, too, that only by conforming scrupulously to religious morality in great matters can they congratulate themselves that they have taught their citizens to know, love, and respect it in small matters.

CHAPTER 16

HOW AN EXCESSIVE LOVE OF PROSPERITY CAN HARM THAT VERY PROSPERITY

There is more of a link than is thought between the improvement of the soul and the betterment of the welfare of the body. Man is able to keep these two things apart and consider each of them in turn but he would not know how to separate them entirely without losing sight of both of them in the end.

Animals possess the same senses and much the same appetites as ourselves; we share every physical passion with them and the seed of such passions can be discerned as much in a dog as in ourselves.

So how are animals able to satisfy only their primary and coarsest needs whereas we can infinitely vary and continuously increase our pleasures?

What makes us superior to the animals in this respect is that we use our souls to discover physical benefits which they pursue through their instincts alone. The angel in man teaches the brute how to satisfy its desires. It is because man is capable of rising above the things of the body and to despise life itself, a notion quite unknown to animals, that he can multiply those very blessings to a level quite beyond their conceptions.

Everything which elevates, enlarges, and broadens the soul makes it able to reach success even in those undertakings which have nothing to do with the soul.

On the other hand, everything which irritates and debases it, weakens it for every purpose, major as well as minor, and makes it equally powerless in relation to both. Thus the soul must remain mighty and strong, if only to be able from time to time to place this strength and might at the service of the body.

If men ever succeeded in being satisfied with their physical possessions alone, it seems likely that they would gradually lose the skill of producing them and would end up by enjoying them without discernment or improvement like the animals.

CHAPTER 17

HOW IN AGES OF EQUALITY AND DOUBT IT IS IMPORTANT TO MOVE THE GOAL OF HUMAN ENDEAVOR BEYOND IMMEDIATE CONCERNS

In ages of faith, the final aim of life is placed beyond life.

The men of such ages are, therefore, used naturally and, as it were, involuntarily, to fix their gaze for many years on a static object toward which their progress is ever directed, and they learn by imperceptible degrees to repress a thousand small passing desires so as to satisfy more effectively this one great permanent longing which torments them. When these same men wish to concentrate upon worldly affairs, these habits come into their own. They readily settle upon one general and sure goal as an object for their actions here below and direct all their efforts toward it. You do not see them indulging in new projects every day but they do have definite plans which they never tire of pursuing.

This explains why religious nations have often achieved such lasting results. They discovered the secret of success in this world by concentrating upon the next.

Religions instil into men the general habit of conducting themselves with the future in mind and are no less useful to happiness in this life than to bliss in the next. That is one of their most marked political aspects.

But as the light of faith gradually dims, men's range of vision grows narrow and you would say that every day the object of human endeavors is more within reach.

Once they have grown accustomed to no longer bothering

about what is to happen after this life, they readily fall back into that completely brutish indifference about the future which is all too suited to certain attitudes found in the human race. As soon as they have lost the way of taking a long-term view for their principal hopes, they naturally tend to seek the immediate gratification of their smallest wishes and it seems to me that from the instant they give up the hope of living for ever they are inclined to act as if they were to live for only one single day.

In skeptical times, therefore, there is always the danger that men will surrender themselves endlessly to the casual whims of daily desire and that they will abandon entirely anything which requires long-term effort, thus failing to establish anything noble or calm or lasting.

If, in a nation so disposed, social conditions become democratic, the danger I am highlighting is increased.

When each citizen is constantly seeking to change station, when open competition is pursued by all, when wealth is amassed or frittered away in the space of a few moments amidst the turmoil of democracy, visions of sudden fortunes and great possessions easily acquired or lost, and images of chance in every shape or form, haunt men's minds. Social instability fosters the natural instability of man's desires. When destiny is in a perpetual state of flux, the present looms large; it masks the future from his sight and his thoughts are unwilling to go beyond the next day.

In those countries where irreligion and democracy join together in an unfortunate combination, the main business for philosophers and rulers is to be striving constantly to set before men's eyes a distant aim for their endeavors.

The moral leader should adapt himself to the spirit of his country and his times in order to defend his position. He should daily endeavor to show his contemporaries how, in the very midst of the perpetual change around them, it is easier than they suppose to plan and execute lengthy projects. He must reveal that, despite the changing aspect of humanity, the methods men employ to gain prosperity in this world have stayed the same and that, in democracies, as elsewhere, it is only through resisting the thousand trivial urges that the universal and anguished longing for happiness can be assuaged.

The task of those in power is no less clearly marked out.

In all ages, it is important that the rulers of nations should act with the future in view. But in democratic and skeptical times, it is even more necessary than in any others. By acting in this way, democratic leaders not only foster prosperity in public affairs but also teach individuals by their example the art of managing their private business.

Above all, they must strive as much as possible to eliminate chance from political life.

The sudden and undeserved promotion of a courtier causes no more than a fleeting impression in an aristocratic country because the general tenor of institutions and beliefs usually obliges men to move slowly along paths from which they cannot escape.

But nothing could be more damaging than similar examples of promotion offered in a democratic nation, for it encourages that mad rush of the heart down a slope which beckons. It is, therefore, mainly in times of skepticism and equality that one must take care to prevent the favor of the people or of the prince, which comes and goes according to chance, from taking the place of a man's knowledge or services. It is desirable that all promotion should appear to be the reward for some effort, in order that high positions should not be too easily gained and that ambition should have to gaze long and hard upon a goal before attaining it.

Governments should strive to restore to men that taste for the future which religion and the state of society no longer inspire and they should, without exactly saying as much, teach daily in practical terms that wealth, reputation, and power are the payment for work, that great success should come at the end of a lengthy period of waiting, and that nothing lasting is ever gained without difficulties.

When men have been accustomed to foresee from afar what is to happen in this world and to feed themselves upon hopes, they find it difficult to restrict their thoughts to the exact boundaries of this life and they are always ready to break free of these limits to cast their gaze beyond.

I am, therefore, quite sure that, in training citizens to consider their future in this world, they gradually and unconsciously draw near to religious beliefs.

Thus the very means which, to some degree, enable men to do without religion are perhaps, after all, the only remaining means for leading mankind, by a long and roundabout path, to a state of faith.

CHAPTER 18

WHY AMERICANS CONSIDER ALL HONEST OCCUPATIONS AS HONORABLE

In democratic nations where hereditary wealth does not exist, every man works for his living, or has worked, or comes from parents who have worked. The concept of work as a necessary, natural, and honest condition of human beings is, therefore, a widespread assumption among men.

Not only is work not considered dishonorable in such nations, it is indeed held in high esteem; the prejudice is for, not against it. A wealthy American believes he owes it to public opinion to devote his leisure time to some industrial or commercial pursuit or some public duties. He would consider his good name in jeopardy if he just spent his life in living. It is to escape this obligation to work that so many rich Americans come to Europe, where they find remnants of aristocratic societies among whom idleness is still honorable.

Equality not only ennobles the idea of work itself but also enhances it, even if it is for money.

In aristocracies, it is not exactly work itself which is despised but work aimed at profit. Work is glorious when prompted by ambition or virtue alone. In an aristocracy, however, we constantly come across the man who works for honor while being aware of the attraction of profit. But these two desires meet only in the depths of his soul. He takes good care to conceal the place where they meet from prying eyes. He will gladly hide it from himself. In aristocratic countries, there are scarcely any civil servants who do not claim to serve the state without self-interest. Their salary is a mere detail to which sometimes they give little thought and to which they always pretend to give none.

Thus the idea of profit remains separate from that of work. It is no use knowing that they are in actual fact joined because tradition keeps them apart.

But in democratic societies, these two ideas are always visibly linked. Since the desire for prosperity is universal, since fortunes are modest and ephemeral, since each man needs to increase his resources or create fresh ones for his children, everyone sees very clearly that profit is, if not entirely, at least in part, what prompts them to work. Even those who act principally with fame in mind have to accept the thought that they are not acting solely for that reason and they realize, whatever they possess, that the desire to live merges with the desire to bring glory to their lives.

As soon as work seems to all citizens an honorable necessity for the human race and is always clearly performed, at least in part, for payment, then the wide gap which used to separate the different professions in aristocratic societies disappears. If they are not exactly similar, at least they share a common characteristic.

All professions work for payment and this commonly shared salary gives them all an air of family resemblance, which helps to explain the views of Americans about the different callings.

American servants do not believe that they are degraded for working since everyone around them is working. They do not feel humiliated by the idea of receiving a wage, for the President of the United States also works for a salary. He is paid for giving orders as much as they are for obeying them.

In the United States, professions are more or less laborious, more or less lucrative but never higher or lower. All honest occupations are honorable.

CHAPTER 19

WHAT GIVES ALMOST ALL AMERICANS A PREFERENCE FOR INDUSTRIAL OCCUPATIONS

Of all the useful skills, agriculture is perhaps the one which improves least quickly in democratic nations. Often one might almost say that it does not progress at all because several other skills seem to be making such rapid strides.

On the other hand, almost all the tastes and habits inspired by equality naturally lead men toward commerce and industry.

I imagine a man who is active, enlightened, free, comfortably off, full of desires. He is too poor to live in idleness but rich enough to feel himself above the immediate fear of need and thinks how he can improve his lot. This man has formed a taste for physical pleasures; he sees a thousand others enjoy them to the full; he himself has begun to indulge them and he is eager to increase the resources to enjoy them more. However, life flows by and time presses. What is he to do?

The cultivation of the ground promises an almost certain result for his efforts but a slow one. Gradual and laborious is the path to wealth. Agriculture suits only the wealthy who already have a lot of money to spare or the poor who ask only to live. His choice is made; he sells his field, leaves his house, and embarks upon some risky but profitable profession.

Now, democratic societies abound in people of this type and, as equality of social conditions becomes greater, their numbers increase.

Democracy, therefore, does not simply multiply the numbers of workers, it leads men into one type of work rather than another. While it gives them a distaste for agriculture, it does direct them toward commerce and industry.[1]

1. It has been noticed several times that manufacturers and businessmen were possessed of an immoderate taste for material pleasures and this has been blamed on trade and industry; I think this is to take the effect for the cause.

  It is not trade and industry which bestow the taste for material pleasures

This turn of mind is evident even among the most wealthy citizens.

In democratic countries, however rich a man is thought to be, he is almost always dissatisfied with his wealth, because he is less rich than his father was and fears that his sons will be less so than himself. The majority of the rich in democracies ceaselessly ponder, therefore, the ways to wealth and naturally turn their gaze toward trade and industry, which seem to them the quickest and the best way of obtaining it. In this respect, they share the instincts of the poor while avoiding the same necessities or, rather, they are prompted forward by the most demanding of all necessities, that of not sinking.

In aristocracies, the rich are also the rulers. Their constant attention upon the great affairs of state diverts them from the small concerns of trade and industry. Nonetheless, should one of their number wish to turn toward business, the will of that greater number immediately bars his way. Whatever you do to escape the rule of this numerous opposition, you cannot ever completely evade its yoke. At the very heart of those aristocratic groups whose opposition to the rights of the majority is at its most stubborn, a private majority is formed to govern the rest.[2]

In democratic countries, where money does not carry its owner to power but often keeps him away from it, the wealthy do not know what to do with their leisure time. The restlessness and extent of their longings, the greatness of their resources, that taste for the unusual felt by almost all those who rise by

---

on men, but rather this taste which encourages men to take up careers in industry and trade so as to satisfy these desires more rapidly and more completely.

If trade and industry increase the desire for wellbeing, that is because every passion grows stronger in proportion to its nurture and is increased by all the efforts made to satisfy it. All the causes which make the love of the good things of this world predominate in the human heart favor the development of industry and trade. Equality is one of these causes. It favors trade, not directly by giving men the taste for business, but indirectly, by strengthening and increasing in their minds the love of wellbeing.

2.   See the notes at the end of the volume (Appendix A, p. 852).

whatever means above the crowd urge them into action. The road to trade is the only one open to them. In democracies nothing is greater or more brilliant than commerce. It attracts the eyes of the public and fills the imagination of the crowd; all passion and energy are directed toward it. There is nothing to stop the rich from engaging in it, neither their own prejudices nor those of anyone else. The wealthy in democracies never form a body with its own customs and police; they are never held back by their own private ideas but are encouraged by the generally held ideas of their country. Moreover, the great fortunes found in a democracy always have a commercial origin and so several generations pass by before their owners entirely lose the habits of business.

Thus, the wealthy men of democracies, being constricted by the narrow field of political action left to them, throw themselves on all sides into commerce where they can extend themselves and employ their natural advantages. To some degree, the very boldness and extent of their industrial undertakings allow us to judge just how much they would have despised industry, if they had been born in an aristocracy.

A similar observation can also be applied to all men in democracies whether rich or poor.

Those living in the instability of a democracy have the constant image of chance before them and, in the end, they come to like all those projects in which chance plays a part.

They are, therefore, all led to commerce, not only because of the promise of profit but because they like the emotions evoked.

It is only fifty years since the United States emerged from the colonial dependence in which England held it. The number of great fortunes is very small and capital is still scarce. Yet no nation of the earth has made such swift progress in trade and industry as the Americans. Today they are the second maritime nation of the world and although their goods have to struggle against almost insurmountable obstacles, they still do not fail to make fresh advances daily.

In the United States, the greatest industrial projects are completed without trouble because the entire population is engaged in industry and because the poorest and the richest citizens are ready to unite their efforts for this purpose. It is thus a daily surprise to see the huge works achieved without difficulty by a nation which has, so to speak, no wealthy people. The Americans arrived but yesterday upon the ground they inhabit, but already have turned the natural order inside out, to their financial advantage. They have joined the Hudson and Mississippi rivers and linked the Atlantic to the Gulf of Mexico across a continent of more than twelve hundred miles separating the two seas. The longest railroads ever constructed up until the present are in America.

But what strikes me most in the United States is not the extraordinary size of a few projects; it is the countless numbers of small ones.

Almost all the farmers in the United States have incorporated some trade into agriculture; most of them have made their agricultural career into a business.

It is rare for an American farmer to settle forever on the land he occupies. In the new provinces of the West in particular, a field is cleared for its sale not its cultivation; a farmhouse is built in anticipation that as the state of the country will soon be changed by an increase in population, a good price may be obtained for it.

Every year, a swarm of inhabitants comes down from the North to the South to settle in the lands where cotton and sugar cane grow. These men cultivate the earth with the aim of producing wealth within only a few years and they are already looking forward to the time when they will be able to return home to their native land to enjoy the comfortable living they have earned. Thus, Americans transfer to agriculture the spirit of business and their industrial passion is displayed there as elsewhere.

Americans make great progress in industry because they are all engaged in it at once. For this same reason they are subject to very unexpected and formidable crises.

As they all follow commercial careers, trade is exposed to so many complex influences that the snags which may arise are impossible to foresee. Since every single one of them is more or less involved in industry, at the slightest shock experienced by business all private fortunes stumble at the same time and the state begins to totter.

I believe that the recurrence of industrial crises is an endemic sickness for all democracies in our day. It can be made less dangerous but not completely cured because it does not stem from an accident but from the very temperament of such nations.

CHAPTER 20

HOW AN ARISTOCRACY MAY EMERGE FROM INDUSTRY

I have shown how democracy fosters industrial development and multiplies without limit the number of industrialists. We shall see by what out of the way road industry could, in its turn, bring men back to aristocracy.

It is acknowledged that when a worker spends every day solely upon one process, general items are produced more easily, rapidly, and economically.

It is likewise acknowledged that the larger the scale on which an industrial undertaking is conducted with large amounts of capital and extensive credit, the cheaper its products will be.

These truths had long been perceived but they have been proved true in our day. They have already been applied to several very important industries and smaller ones have exploited them in their turn.

I see nothing in the political world which should be of closer concern to the legislator than these two axioms of industrial science.

When a craftsman is constantly and solely engaged upon the making of one single object, he ultimately performs this work with unusual dexterity; but at the same time, he loses the general capacity to apply his concentration on the way he is working. Day by day, he gains in skill but is less industrious; one may say that as he, the workman, improves, so does he, the man, lose his self-respect.

What can be expected of a man who has spent twenty years of his life making pinheads? To what might this powerful human intelligence, which has often stirred the world, apply itself except research into the best ways of making pinheads?

When a workman has spent a considerable part of his existence in such a manner, his thoughts are forever taken up by the object of his daily toil; his body has contracted certain fixed habits which it cannot discard. In short, he no longer belongs to himself but to the profession he has chosen. It is no use laws and customs striving to break down all the barriers around this man or opening up on every side a thousand different paths to wealth. An industrial theory more powerful than custom or law has tied him to a trade and often to a place, which he cannot abandon. It has assigned him a certain station in society which he cannot escape. It has brought him to a stop in the midst of universal movement.

As the principle of the division of labor is applied more completely, the worker becomes weaker, more limited and more dependent. The craft makes progress, the craftsman slips backwards. On the other hand, as it becomes clearer that industrial products are all the better and cheaper as production lines are more extensive and capital is greater, very wealthy and enlightened men appear on the scene to exploit industries which, up to that point, had been left in the hands of ignorant or restless craftsmen. They are attracted by the scale of the efforts required and the huge results to be obtained.

Thus at the very moment that industrial science constantly lowers the standing of workers, it raises that of the bosses.

While the worker, more and more, restricts his intelligence to the study of one single detail, the boss daily surveys an increasing field of operation and his mind expands as the former's narrows. Soon the one will need only physical strength without intelligence; the other needs knowledge and almost genius for success. The one increasingly looks like the administrator of a vast empire, the other, a brute.

So, the employer and the worker share nothing in common on this earth and their differences grow daily. They exist as two links at each end of a long chain. Each holds a place made for him from which he does not move. The one is dependent upon the other.

The dependency the one has upon the other is never-ending, narrow, and unavoidable; the one is born to obey as the other is to give orders.

What is this, if not aristocracy?

As conditions become more and more equal in the body of the nation, the need for manufactured products is universal and ever greater; the cheap prices which bring goods within the reach of modest fortunes become a great ingredient of success.

Richer and better educated men emerge daily to devote their wealth and knowledge to industry; by opening great workshops with a strict division of labor they seek to satisfy the new demands which are evident on all sides.

Thus, as the mass of the nation turns to democracy, the particular class which runs industry becomes more aristocratic. Men resemble each other more in one context and appear increasingly different in another; inequality grows in the smaller social group as it reduces in society at large.

Thus it is that, when we trace things back to their source, a natural impulse appears to be prompting the emergence of an aristocracy from the very heart of democracy.

But that aristocracy is not like any that preceded it.

In the first place, you will notice that it is an exception, a monstrosity in the general fabric of society, since it applies only to industry and a few industrial professions.

The small aristocratic societies formed by certain industries inside the immense democratic whole of our day contain, as they did in the great aristocracies of ancient times, some men who are very wealthy and a multitude who are wretchedly poor.

These poor men have few ways of escaping from their social conditions to become rich but the wealthy are constantly becoming poor or leave the world of business after realizing their profits. Thus, the elements which form the poorer classes are virtually fixed but those that produce the richer classes are not so. In fact, although there are rich men, richer classes do not exist, for the wealthy do not share a common spirit or objective or traditions or hopes; there are individual members, therefore, but no definite corporate body.

Not only are the rich not firmly united to each other, but you can also say that no true link exists between rich and poor.

They are not forever fixed, one close to the other; moment by moment, self-interest pulls them together, only to separate them later. The worker depends upon the employer in general but not on any particular employer. These two men see each other at the factory but do not know each other anywhere else; and while they have one point of contact, in all other respects they keep their distance. The industrialist only asks the worker for his labor and the latter only expects his wages. The one is not committed to protect, nor the other to defend; they are not linked in any permanent way, either by habit or duty.

This business aristocracy seldom lives among the industrial population it manages; it aims not to rule them but to use them.

An aristocracy so constituted cannot have a great hold over its employees and, even if it succeeded in grabbing them for a moment, they escape soon enough. It does not know what it wants and cannot act.

The landed aristocracy of past centuries was obliged by law, or believed itself obliged by custom, to help its servants and to relieve their distress. However, this present industrial aristocracy, having impoverished and brutalized the men it exploits, leaves public charity to feed them in times of crisis. This is a natural consequence of what has been said before. Between the worker and employer, there are many points of contact but no real relationship.

Generally speaking, I think that the industrial aristocracy which we see rising before our eyes is one of the most harsh ever to appear on the earth; but at the same time, it is one of the most restrained and least dangerous.

However, this is the direction in which the friends of democracy should constantly fix their anxious gaze; for if ever aristocracy and the permanent inequality of social conditions were to infiltrate the world once again, it is predictable that this is the door by which they would enter.

PART 3
THE INFLUENCE OF
DEMOCRACY ON
CUSTOMS AS SUCH

CHAPTER I

HOW CUSTOMS BECOME SOFTER
AS SOCIAL CONDITIONS BECOME
MORE EQUAL

We have seen for centuries that social conditions have been growing more equal and at the same time we have realized that customs have softened. Are these two things simply coincidental or is there some secret link between them which ensures that the one cannot make any headway without prompting the other into motion?

Several causes may combine to make the customs of a people less crude; but the most powerful of these seems to me to be the equality of social conditions which, along with the softening of manners, are not only, in my view, coincidental events but also connected.

When the writers of fables wish to interest us in the behavior of animals, they give them human ideas and emotions. The poets do the same when they speak of spirits and angels. There is no misery so profound, nor any happiness so pure, as to affect our minds or move our hearts, unless we are shown to ourselves under a different guise.

This is very relevant to the subject now under scrutiny.

When all the men of an aristocratic society take their irrevocable station according to profession, property, and birth, the members of each social class experience a constant and active mutual sympathy from thinking of themselves as all children of the same family, which can never be found to the same degree in the citizens of a democracy.

But the same feeling for one another does not exist between the different classes.

In an aristocratic nation each caste has its own separate opinions, feelings, rights, customs, and style of living. Thus, its members are not like the members of all the other castes; they do not share the same modes of thought or feeling; they scarcely believe that they belong to the same human race.

They could not, therefore, very well understand what the others experience nor judge them by themselves.

However, they are sometimes eager to lend each other mutual aid but that does not contradict what I have just said.

These very aristocratic institutions which had caused such differences between beings of the same race nevertheless had bound them to each other by a very close political connection.

Although the serf had no natural concern for the fate of the nobles, he, nonetheless, felt any less obliged to devote himself to the one who was his lord and, although the lord believed he had a nature quite different from that of his serfs, he nevertheless considered that his duty and honor obliged him to defend those who lived on his lands, at the risk of his own life.

These mutual obligations clearly did not originate in the law of nature but from the law of society and that society achieved more than humanity itself could have done. People did not believe that they were bound to render assistance to the man but to the vassal or the lord. Feudal institutions aroused a sensitivity to the sufferings of particular men not to the miseries of the whole human race. Their generosity was prompted by custom rather than compassion and, although they hinted at great devotion, they did not awaken real sympathy; for real sympathy exists only between those who are alike and in aristocratic ages only members of the same caste are seen as alike.

When the chroniclers of the Middle Ages, who were all members of the aristocracy by birth or habits, relate the tragic end of a nobleman, they feel an infinite grief, whereas they tell of the massacre and torture of the common people in one breath without batting an eyelid.

Not that these writers felt habitual hatred or organized scorn for the common people; the war between the various classes of the community had not yet been declared. They were obeying an instinct rather than a passion; since they had not formulated any clear idea of the sufferings of the poor, they took only a feeble interest in their fate.

The same feelings were exhibited in the common people once the feudal ties were broken. The same centuries which witnessed so many examples of heroic loyalty from vassals to lords also saw unheard-of cruelties inflicted from time to time by the lower classes upon the upper.

You should not suppose that this mutual insensitivity existed only because of the absence of public order and education, for traces of it were evident in the following centuries which, for all their good order and education, still remained aristocratic.

In 1675 the lower classes in Brittany were roused into opposition to a new tax. The disturbances were put down with unprecedented cruelty. This is how Madame de Sévigné,[a] a witness of these horrors, tells her daughter about them:

Aux Rochers, 30 October 1675

Good heavens, daughter, how amusing your letter from Aix! At least reread your letters before posting them. Let yourself be surprised at their charm and take consolation in this pleasure for the trouble of writing so many. So you have embraced the whole of Provence? There would be no satisfaction in embracing the whole of Brittany unless one liked the smell of wine. Would you like to know the news from Rennes? A tax of 100,000 crowns has been imposed upon the citizens and will be doubled and collected by soldiers unless the sum is found within twenty-four hours. A whole main street has been emptied and entry denied to the inhabitants who have been forbidden to give refuge to anyone on pain of death. As a result one could see all these wretched people, pregnant women, old men, children wandering in tears out of the town not knowing where to go, without food or bedding. The day before yesterday a violinist was put on the rack and quartered for starting up a dance and for stealing stamped paper; his quartered limbs were posted at the four corners of the town. Sixty townspeople have been taken into custody and hanging them will start tomorrow. The province is a good warning to others to respect the governors and their wives above all and not to throw stones into their garden.[1]

Madame de Tarente was here yesterday in the woods in delightful weather. No question of a room or meal for her. She comes in by the gate and goes back the same way . . .

In another letter she adds:

You speak to me very amusingly about our distress; we are no longer broken so much on the wheel. One in a week, to maintain justice. It is true that hanging now seems quite a treat. Since being in this part of the country I have quite a different idea of justice. Your galley slaves seem to me a group of worthy folk who have withdrawn from society to lead a peaceful life.

It would be wrong to think of Madame de Sévigné, who wrote these lines, as a selfish and insensitive person. She was passionately fond of her children and showed herself very aware of the sorrows of her friends. You can even see, in reading her letters, that she treated her vassals and servants with kindness and indulgence. But Madame de Sévigné had no clear conception of people's suffering when they were not of noble birth.

Nowadays, the hardest of men writing to the most insensitive of people would not dare to indulge so indifferently in such cruel jokes as I have just quoted and, even when his private morality allowed him to do so, the general morality of the nation would forbid it.

How does that come about? Are we more sensitive than our fathers? I do not know but, certainly, our sensitivity embraces a greater range of objects.

When all the members of a community are almost equal and

1.   To understand the relevance of this last pleasantry, one should remember that Mme de Grignan was married to the governor of Provence.

all men have almost the same way of thinking and feeling, each one of them can judge in a flash the feelings of all the others; all he needs to do is to cast a quick glance at himself. There is not, therefore, any distress that he cannot understand without difficulty and a secret instinct reveals to him its extent. Whether it be strangers or enemies will not matter to him as his imagination immediately puts him in their place, mingling something personal with his pity and making him suffer himself when the body of his fellow man is being torn apart.

In democratic ages, men scarcely ever sacrifice themselves for each other but they display a general compassion for all the members of the human race. One never sees them inflicting pointless cruelty and when they are able to relieve another's suffering without much trouble to themselves, they are glad to do so. They are not entirely altruistic but they are gentle.

Although Americans have, so to speak, reduced selfishness to a social and philosophic theory, nonetheless they show themselves just as open to pity.

No country administers its criminal law with more kindness than the United States. While the English seem bent on carefully preserving in their penal legislation the bloody traces of the Middle Ages, the Americans have almost eliminated the death penalty from their codes.

North America is, I think, the only country on earth where for fifty years no single citizen has lost his life for political offenses.

What clinches the proof that this unusual mildness among Americans comes mainly from their social state is the treatment of their slaves. It may be that, generally speaking, there is no European colony in the New World where the physical conditions of the blacks are less harsh than in the United States. However, slaves still undergo fearful distress and are constantly exposed to very cruel punishments.

It is easy to see that the lot of these wretched people evokes but little pity in their masters who look upon slavery not merely as a source of profit but also an evil which does not affect them. Thus, the same man who is full of human feeling for his fellow men when they are also his equals becomes insensitive to their afflictions the moment equality ceases. His mildness has, therefore, to be attributed to this state of equality much more than to the impact of civilization or education.

What I have just said of individuals applies to some extent to nations.

When each nation has its own opinions, beliefs, laws, and customs, it looks upon itself as representing the whole of humanity and feels moved only by its own sufferings. If war happens to break out between two nations possessing this outlook, it cannot fail to be conducted with great cruelty.

At the height of their cultural development, the Romans cut the enemy generals' throats after dragging them in triumph behind a chariot and offered their prisoners to wild beasts for the people's amusement. Cicero,[b] who utters such profound complaints at the notion of crucifying a Roman citizen, has nothing to say about this vicious abuse of victory. In his eyes, a foreigner clearly belongs to a different human species from a Roman.

But as people become more like one another they display a reciprocal compassion for their sufferings and the laws of nations become gentler.

CHAPTER 2

HOW DEMOCRACY MAKES THE NORMAL RELATIONS BETWEEN AMERICANS EASIER AND SIMPLER

Democracy does not create strong attachments between men but it does make their normal relations easier.

Two Englishmen meet by chance at the antipodes; they are surrounded by foreigners whose language and habits they hardly understand.

These two men at first look at each other with great curiosity and a sort of secret anxiety; then they turn away or, if they do accost each other, they take care to limit themselves to awkward and detached exchanges about unimportant topics.

However, no intimacy exists between them; they have never seen each other before and each of them believes the other to be a man of honor. Why do they take such pains to avoid each other?

To understand that, we need to return to England.

When it is birth alone and not wealth which governs a man's class, everyone knows precisely his place on the social ladder; he neither seeks to rise nor fears to fall. In a society so organized, men from the different castes have little contact with each other but, when chance contact does occur, they are ready to come together without wishing or dreading to lose their own position. Their relations are not based upon equality but they do not experience any restraint.

When an aristocracy based on money takes over from one based on birth, this ceases to be the case.

The privileges of some people are still extensive but the potential for acquiring them is open to all. The result of that is that those who possess them are constantly obsessed by the fear of losing them, or of seeing them shared, and those as yet without them long to possess them at any cost or at least to appear to possess them if they fail, which is not impossible to achieve. Since the social importance of men is no longer fixed by blood in any obvious and permanent manner and since wealth produces infinite variations, classes still exist but it is not easy to distinguish clearly their members at first glance.

Straightaway an unspoken war is declared between all citizens; some employ a thousand tricks to join, or to appear to join, those above them, while others constantly fight to repulse those who seek to usurp their rights, or rather the same person does both these things for, while he is attempting to infiltrate the level above him, he fights relentlessly against those working up from below.

Such is the present state of things in England and I believe that what I have said must be traced back to this state.

As aristocratic arrogance is still very pronounced with the English and as the boundaries of aristocracy are ill-defined, everyone is afraid lest at any moment his familiar advances may be taken wrongly. Being unable to judge at first glance the social position of those he meets, he wisely avoids making any contact with them. The fear is that by some slight service he might render, he might inadvertently form some unsuitable friendship. He fears civilities and withdraws as carefully from receiving any indiscreet expression of gratitude from a stranger as from his hatred.

Many people explain this strange unfriendliness and this reserved, morose disposition of the English by purely physical causes. I grant that blood may count for something in this matter but I believe that social conditions count for much more. The example of the Americans serves to prove this.

In America, where privileges of birth have never existed and where wealth grants no particular right to its owner, strangers readily congregate in the same places and find neither danger nor advantage in telling each other freely what they think. If they meet by chance, they neither seek each other out nor keep away from each other. Their manner is, therefore, natural, open, and unreserved; we see that there is practically nothing they expect or fear from each other and they make no more effort to reveal than to conceal their social position. They may often appear cold and serious but they are never haughty or restrained. When they fail to speak, it is because they do not feel like doing so, not because they think it to be to their advantage to keep silent.

In a foreign country, two Americans are immediately friends from the very fact that they are Americans. No prejudice drives them from each other; the country they have in common brings them together. Two Englishmen will not find the same blood sufficient; they must have the same rank to bring them together.

The Americans, as well as the French, notice the unfriendly disposition of the English to each other and are no less astonished by it. However, the Americans feel close to England through their origins, religion, language, and, to some extent, their customs; only their social condition is different. We may, therefore, say that English reserve proceeds from the constitution of the country much more than from the make-up of its citizens.

CHAPTER 3

WHY AMERICANS ARE SO DIFFICULT TO OFFEND AT HOME YET SO EASILY OFFENDED IN EUROPE

Americans share a vindictive temperament with all other serious and thoughtful nations. They hardly ever forget an offense but are not easily offended. Their resentment is as slow to kindle as it is to go out.

In aristocratic societies governed in everything by a few individuals, the outward relationships of men are subject to conventions that are virtually fixed. Then everyone believes he knows precisely how to show respect or goodwill and social niceties are assumed to be common knowledge.

The customs of the highest class then serve as models for all the others, each of which, in addition, creates a separate code of behavior to which all its members are expected to conform.

Rules of polite society thus constitute a complex set of rules which it is difficult to master completely, yet from which one is not allowed to deviate with impunity. As a result, men are daily in danger of inflicting or suffering bitter insults.

But as classes disappear and men of different educational attainment and birth meet and mingle in the same places, it is virtually impossible to agree over the rules of good manners. As the law is vague, it is no crime to contravene it, even in the eyes of those who know what it is.

People rely, therefore, upon the substance rather than the form of behavior and are both less polite and less quarrelsome.

There is a mass of trivial considerations which an American does not value; he thinks that they are not due to him or imagines that people do not know they are due to him. Therefore, either he does not notice the social gaffe or he forgives it. His behavior becomes less polite but his manners simpler and more masculine.

This shared tolerance displayed by Americans and this manly confidence with which they treat each other result from another profounder and more general cause, which I have already mentioned in the last chapter.

In the United States, there is very little difference of rank in civil society and none at all in political life. Thus, an American does not believe that he is obliged to show any particular considerations to any of his fellow citizens, nor does he ever dream of demanding any for himself. Since he fails to see that it is to his advantage eagerly to seek out the company of some of his fellow citizens, he has difficulty in imagining that his own company is unwelcome. Since he despises no one for their social status, he cannot imagine that anyone will despise him for the same reason and until he becomes aware of an insult, he does not believe that an insult was intended.

Social conditions naturally accustom Americans not to take offense over trivial matters. And, further, the democratic freedom they enjoy ends up by introducing this mildness into national manners.

American political institutions bring citizens of all classes into constant contact and force them to undertake great projects together. People busy in this way have scarcely any time to consider details of polite behavior and, besides, have too great an interest in living in harmony to let that stop them. They therefore easily acquire the habit of considering the feelings and ideas of those they meet more than their manners and do not allow themselves to be annoyed by trifles.

I have noticed many times that it is not an easy matter in the United States to convey to someone that his presence is unwelcome. To make that point, roundabout methods are not always enough.

If I contradict an American at every turn, in order to show him that his conversation bores me, at every moment I see him making renewed efforts to convince me. If I remain obstinately silent, he imagines that I am reflecting deeply on the truths he is putting to me.

When, at last, I escape his onslaught, he supposes that urgent business calls me elsewhere. This man will never grasp that he exasperates me unless I tell him so and I shall be unable to get rid of him except by becoming his mortal enemy.

At first sight, the surprising thing is that this same man, transported to Europe, becomes suddenly so sensitive and touchy that I often find it as difficult to avoid offending him as it once was to cause offense. Both these very different results are due to the same cause.

Democratic institutions in general give men a grandiose idea of their country and themselves.

The American leaves his country with a heart swollen with pride. He arrives in Europe and observes at once that we are not as concerned with the United States and the great people living there as he had supposed. This begins to annoy him.

He has heard that social conditions in our hemisphere are not equal. In fact, he observes that, among European nations, traces of class have not been entirely erased and that wealth and birth retain some doubtful privileges which are as difficult to ignore as to define. He is both surprised and disturbed by this state of affairs because it is completely new in his experience. Nothing that he has seen in his own country helps him to understand it. He, therefore, has not the faintest idea of the position he ought to occupy in this half-ruined hierarchy, among classes distinct enough to hate and despise each other, but sufficiently alike for him always to confuse them. He is afraid to take too high a position and even more to be ranked too low; this twin danger introduces a constant worry into his mind and an embarrassment to his every action and word.

Tradition has taught him that in Europe ceremonials of politeness show endless variations according to social conditions. This memory from another age ends up by disturbing him and he is all the more fearful at not receiving the respect due to him because he does not know exactly what governs that respect. So, he is always stepping forward like a man surrounded by pitfalls; social relations are no relaxation for him but a serious business. He weighs your slightest move, questions every look and carefully analyzes all your remarks, lest they contain some hidden allusions to affront him. I doubt whether one could find a country gentleman more scrupulous than he is about every detail of social politeness. He strives to observe the slightest rules of etiquette and will not tolerate any slight to himself. He is both extremely meticulous and very demanding; he would be anxious to do enough but fears to do too much and, as he does not know the limits of either of these aims, he maintains a self-conscious and haughty reserve.

That is still not the whole story; here is yet another twist of the human heart.

An American daily refers to the wonderful equality which prevails in the United States; he proclaims out loud his pride on behalf of his country but secretly on his own behalf he feels considerable distress and aims to show that he is an exception to the general rule he is advocating.

Almost every American wishes to claim some connection by birth to the first founders of the colonies and America is awash, as far as I can see, with offshoots of great English families.

When a wealthy American lands in Europe, his first concern is to surround himself with the luxuries of wealth; he has such a great fear of being taken for the unsophisticated citizen of a democracy that he seeks a hundred roundabout ways each day to advertise a fresh image of his opulence. He usually lodges in the most fashionable part of the town and has an endless stream of servants around him.

I have heard an American complain that, in the best Parisian drawing rooms, one encountered a very mixed group of people. The prevailing manners did not seem to him refined enough and he subtly suggested that, in his opinion, there was a lack of distinction in behavior found there. He could not get used to the sight of wit lying hidden in that way beneath a vulgar surface.

Such contrasts should not surprise us.

If traces of the old aristocratic distinctions had not so completely disappeared in the United States, Americans would behave less simply and with less tolerance in their country and be less demanding and less awkward in ours.

CHAPTER 4

CONSEQUENCES OF THE THREE PRECEDING CHAPTERS

When men feel a natural pity for the sufferings of others and when relaxed and frequent contacts bring them together undivided by any touchiness, it is easy to understand that they will give each other mutual support when the need arises. When an American seeks the cooperation of his fellows, they seldom refuse him and I have often noticed that their help is both spontaneous and enthusiastic.

Should some unforeseen accident occur on the public highway, people run from all sides to help the victim; should some family fall foul of an unexpected disaster, a thousand strangers willingly open their purses and a goodly number of modest gifts come to aid their distress.

Frequently among the most civilized nations of the world, a poor wretch happens to find himself as isolated at the heart of a crowd as a savage in his own woods; such a thing is almost never seen in the United States. Americans are always cool and often crude in their manner but are almost never insensitive; although they never rush to volunteer their services, they never refuse to render them.

All this does not contradict what I have said already about individualism and, far from being in conflict, these things actually agree with each other.

Equality of social conditions makes men feel their independence and at the same time reveals their weakness; they are free but exposed to a thousand accidents. Experience soon teaches them that, although they do not usually need another person's help, the moment will almost always arrive when they cannot do without it.

Daily, we see in Europe that men of the same profession readily help each other; they are all liable to the same disasters. That is reason enough for them to seek mutual safeguards against them, however self-centered and hard-hearted they may be in other respects. When, therefore, one of them is in danger and when others are able to save him by a small, brief sacrifice or by a sudden impulse, they never fail to make the attempt. Not that they have some deep concern for his fate, for if, by chance, their efforts to help him prove futile, they immediately forget him and return to their own affairs. But a kind of tacit agreement has grown up between them which provides that each of them owes temporary support, which he will be able to seek himself in his turn.

If you extend to a nation what I am saying about one single class, you will catch my meaning.

In fact, all citizens in a democracy accept an understanding similar to the one I have described; everyone feels subject to the same weakness and to the same dangers; their concern as well as their sympathy prompts them to lend one another assistance when the need arises.

The more social conditions become simpler, the more men display this shared obligation to help each other.

In democracies, no great benefits are granted but small kindnesses are constantly shown. A man rarely sacrifices himself but all men are willing to help.

CHAPTER 5

HOW DEMOCRACY ALTERS THE RELATIONS BETWEEN MASTER AND SERVANT

An American, who had traveled extensively in Europe, once said to me: "The English treat their servants with an arrogance and imperiousness which surprises us but the French, by contrast, sometimes employ a familiarity or politeness toward theirs which we cannot comprehend. They seem afraid to give orders. The position of superior and inferior is badly maintained."

The observation is fair and I have often made it myself.

I have always considered England as the country in the world where the bonds of domestic service are the most restricted and France as the country in the world where they are the most relaxed. Nowhere does the master appear to be higher or lower than in those two countries.

The Americans hold a place between these two extremes.

That is a fact both superficial and obvious. One must seek the causes much further back.

We have never seen societies with such equality of social conditions that neither rich nor poor exist and, consequently, neither masters or servants.

Democracy does not prevent the existence of these two classes of men but it changes their attitudes and modifies their relationships.

Among aristocratic nations, servants form a distinct class just as variable as that of the masters. A fixed order is soon established; in the latter, as in the former class, we soon observe the appearance of a hierarchy, countless distinctions, well-defined ranks, and generation follows generation with no change in the positions held. They represent two social groups, one lying above the other, always clearly defined by parallel principles.

This aristocratic constitution has no less an influence upon servants' ideas and habits than it does upon those of their masters and, although the effects are different, it is easy to recognize the same cause.

Both classes form small nations within the large nation in which, in the end, certain permanent concepts of what is fair and unfair are established. Different acts of human behavior are viewed in a peculiar and unchanging light. In the society of servants, as in that of masters, men exercise a great influence upon each other. They acknowledge fixed rules and, in the absence of the law, they are guided by public opinion; their customs are ordered and policed.

The men whose fate it is to obey doubtless have no understanding of fame, virtue, honesty, honor in the same way as their masters. But they have devised a servant's reputation, virtues, and honesty and they have conceived, if I may put it so, a sort of servile honor.[1]

Because a class is humble, one must not suppose that all its members are mean-hearted; that would be a serious mistake. However lowly a class may be, the leader of it, with no thought of leaving, occupies an aristocratic position which prompts elevated thoughts, a strong pride and a self-respect which fit him for high actions and virtues out of the ordinary.

In aristocratic nations, it was not uncommon to come across, in the service of the great lords, men of noble and energetic character who did not feel the status of servant they suffered and who obeyed their master's will with no fear of arousing his anger.

But this was almost never the case in the lower ranks of domestic servants. It may be imagined that the man occupying the lowest step in a hierarchy of valets is mean indeed.

The French have coined a word especially for this lowest of servants in an aristocracy: a lackey.

The word "lackey" served, when all other words failed, to express the meanest human condition; under the old monarchy, when they wished to depict at any time a worthless and debased fellow, he was said to have the soul of a lackey. That was enough; the meaning was complete and understood.

A permanent state of inequality does not simply give servants certain particular virtues and vices. It places them in a peculiar position in relation to their masters.

In aristocratic nations, the poor are trained from birth to the idea of obedience. In whatever direction they look, they immediately see the image of hierarchy and the spectacle of obedience.

In countries where a permanent state of inequality prevails, the master easily obtains from his servants an obedience which

---

1. If the main opinions which guide men are examined closely and in detail, the analogy appears even more striking and one is astonished to find amongst them, just as much as amongst the most snobbish members of feudal hierarchy, pride of birth, respect for their ancestors and descendants, disdain for their inferiors, fear of close contact, a taste for etiquette, traditions, and history.

is prompt, complete, respectful, and easy because they honor in his person not only the master but also the class of masters. He brings the whole weight of the aristocracy to bear upon their wills.

He controls their actions and, to a certain extent, he also directs their thoughts. In aristocracies, the master often exercises even unwittingly an inordinate sway over the opinions, customs, and habits of those who obey him and his influence extends much further still than his authority.

In aristocratic societies, there are not only hereditary families of valets alongside those of masters, but the same families of valets are attached to the same families of masters for several generations (like two parallel lines which never meet nor diverge). All this alters considerably the mutual connection of these two classes.

So, although in aristocracies masters and servants share no natural similarities and although wealth, education, opinions, and rights keep them a great distance apart on the scale of human beings, the passing of time winds up nevertheless by tying them closely together.

Long-shared memories keep them together and, despite their differences, they grow alike, while in democracies where they are similar by nature, they remain strangers to each other.

In aristocratic nations the master comes, therefore, to view his servants as an inferior and secondary part of himself. He often concerns himself with their fate through a final effort of selfishness.

From where they stand, servants are not so far from seeing themselves in the same light and sometimes adopt an identity from their master to such an extent that they end up as his appendage in their own eyes, as in his.

In aristocracies, the servant holds a subordinate position that he cannot escape; next to him is another man who occupies a superior rank he cannot shake off. On one side lie everlasting obscurity, poverty, and obedience; on the other, fame, wealth, and power to command forever. These conditions are always distinct and always close; the link between them is as durable as they are themselves.

Reduced to this extremity, the servant ends up by losing all interest in himself; he becomes detached and gives himself up somewhat or rather he transfers the whole of himself into his master's character where he creates for himself a fictitious personality. He takes pleasure in decking himself out with the wealth of those who give him orders; he revels in their fame, exalts himself in their nobility, and constantly feeds on borrowed grandeur which he often prizes more than do those who are the real and true owners of it.

There is something both touching and ridiculous in this bizarre muddling of two lives.

These passions of masters, when transposed into the souls of valets, assume dimensions appropriate to the place they occupy, shrinking and reduced in size. What was pride in the former becomes a childish vanity and mean pretentiousness in the latter. The servants of a great man usually display a punctiliousness about the respect due to him and they attach more importance to his slightest privileges than he does himself.

Among the French, one still sometimes comes across one of those ancient servants of the aristocracy who survives a race which will soon vanish.

In the United States, I have not seen his like. Not only are Americans ignorant of the type of man in question but one has a great deal of trouble explaining his existence to them. They experience just as much difficulty in forming an idea of him as we have in imagining what a Roman slave or medieval serf was like. All these men are in fact, though to different degrees, the result of the same cause. They recede together from our view and daily slip into the darkness of the past, together with the society which engendered them.

Equality of social conditions turns servants and masters into new beings and establishes a new relationship between them.

When conditions are almost equal, men constantly change their situations. There is still a class of valets and one of masters but they are not always composed of the same individuals nor, more especially, of the same families; there is no more permanency in those who give orders than in those who obey.

As servants do not form a separate race, they do not have

their own peculiar customs, prejudices, or manners; we do not see in them a particular turn of mind or way of feeling. They know nothing of the virtues or vices of their status but they share the education, ideas, opinions, virtues, and vices of their contemporaries; they are honest or scoundrels in the same way as their masters.

The same equality exists among servants as among masters.

Since in the class of servants neither fixed ranks nor permanent hierarchies are to be found, one must not expect to meet either the meanness or the nobility which characterize the aristocracy of valets as all other aristocracies.

I have never seen, in the United States, anything to put me in mind of the top-ranking servant, the memory of whom still haunts us in Europe, nor have I found the conception of the lackey either. Traces of both have equally disappeared.

In democracies, servants are not only equal to each other, they are, one may say, in some fashion equal to their masters.

This needs an explanation to be fully understood.

At any moment, the servant may become a master and he has the ambition to do so; the servant is, therefore, no different from the master.

Why, therefore, has the latter the right to give orders and what forces the former to obey? A temporary and freely made agreement. They are not inferior to one another by nature; they become so temporarily only by contract. Within the terms of this contract, one is servant, one is master; beyond that they are two citizens, two men.

What I ask the reader to understand clearly is that this is not only the view held by servants of their position. Masters consider domestic service in the same light and the exact limits of command and obedience are just as much fixed in the mind of the one as of the other.

When most citizens have long since reached a roughly similar condition and when equality is an accepted fact of long standing, public opinion, uninfluenced by exceptions, broadly speaking assigns certain limits to a man's worth and it is difficult for any man to move for long either above or below these limits.

It is no use for wealth and poverty, command and obedience

accidentally to place great distances between two men because public opinion, based upon the normal way of things, brings them back to a common level and creates between them a sort of imaginary equality in spite of the actual inequality of their social condition.

This all-powerful opinion finally infuses the very soul of those who might have the strength to resist it; it alters their judgement just as it subdues their willpower.

Deep inside their souls, master and servant no longer perceive any profound difference between them and they neither hope nor fear ever to encounter one. Thus, they are neither scornful nor angry and look at each other without humility or pride.

The master estimates that the sole source of his power lies in the contract and the servant thinks it the sole reason for his obedience. They do not quarrel with each other over their mutual relationship but each of them easily sees what is his and keeps to it.

In our army, the soldier is conscripted from roughly the same classes as the officers and may reach the same ranks; in civilian life he considers himself exactly equal to his commanders, as he is in fact; but under the flag, he does not hesitate to obey and his obedience is no less prompt, precise, and ready for being freely given and regulated.

This example shows what happens in democratic societies between servant and master.

It would be preposterous to suppose there could ever spring up between these two men any of those warm and deep emotions which are sometimes kindled in the domestic service of an aristocracy, nor should we expect to see the appearance of striking examples of self-sacrifice.

In aristocracies, servant and master observe each other only infrequently and often communicate only through a third party. And yet they usually stand firmly by each other.

In democracies, servant and master are very close; their bodies constantly touch but their souls do not mix; they share occupations but hardly ever have interests in common.

Among such nations, the servant always views himself as a visitor in his master's house. He has not known their ancestors and will not see their descendants; he has nothing lasting to expect from them. Why would he identify his life with theirs and what reason could he have for such a strange sacrifice of himself? The mutuality of their two positions has changed and the relationship must also be changed.

I would like to be able to rely upon the example of the Americans to underline what I have just stated but I cannot do so without carefully distinguishing people and places.

In the South of the Union slavery exists. So all I have just said cannot apply there.

In the North, most servants are freed slaves or the sons of these. These men hold a doubtful place in public esteem. The law brings them up to the same level as their master; custom obstinately pushes them back. They themselves have no clear conception of their place and almost always behave insolently or subserviently.

But in these same northern provinces, especially in New England, you meet quite a large number of whites who agree temporarily to obey their fellow men in return for wages. I have heard that these servants usually perform the duties of their position accurately and intelligently and that, since they have no natural belief in their inferiority to the man who gives them orders, they have no trouble in obeying him.

Such men seem to me to carry into domestic service some of those manly habits born of independence and equality. Once they have opted for this difficult occupation, they do not seek by indirect means to escape from it and they have sufficient self-respect not to refuse their masters the obedience they have freely promised.

On their side, masters ask from their servants only the loyal and energetic fulfillment of their contract; they do not seek respect nor do they claim their love or devotion. All they require is punctuality and honesty.

It would not, therefore, be true to say that in democracies the relations of servant and master are disorganized; they are simply organized in a different way; the rule is different but one does exist.

I have no need to inquire whether this new state of affairs just described is inferior to that which preceded it, or whether it is simply different. It is enough for me that it is organized and settled, for what is important to find among men is not any particular order but order itself.

But what shall I say of those sad and troubled times when equality is established amid the tumult of a revolution and when democracy, after its entry into the social system, still struggles with difficulty against prejudice and habit?

Already law and, in part, public opinion are declaring the end to any natural and permanent inferiority between servant and master. But this newly founded faith has not yet seeped into the latter's mind, or rather his heart rejects it. In the secret recesses of his mind, the master still considers that he belongs to a special and superior species but dares not say so; with a shudder, he allows himself to be drawn down to the same level. His commands become timid and, at the same time, harsh; already he has lost those protective and humane feelings for his servant which are always the result of a long and unchallenged authority and, changed himself, he is surprised to find his servant changed. His wish is that this man, who is, so to speak, only passing through domestic service, shall adopt regular and permanent habits; that he shall appear satisfied and proud of that servant status which he must sooner or later escape; that he shall sacrifice himself for a man who can neither protect nor ruin him and that, by an eternal bond, he shall be loyal to people who are just like him and will not last any longer than he does.

In aristocratic nations, domestic service often avoids any humiliation in those who submit to it because they neither know, nor imagine, any other state of affairs and because the amazing inequality evident between them and their masters appears to be the necessary and inevitable result of some abstruse law of providence.

In a democracy, the condition of domestic service is not degrading because it is freely and temporarily chosen; public opinion does not stigmatize it and it creates no permanent inequality between servant and master.

But in the transition between these two conditions almost always a turning point occurs when men's minds hesitate between the aristocratic notion of subjection and the democratic one of obedience.

At that point, obedience loses its moral basis in the eyes of the man who obeys; he stops treating it as some sort of divine obligation and he does not yet see it in its purely human light; it is in his view neither holy nor fair; he submits to it as he would to a degrading though useful condition.

At such a moment, the confused and imperfect image of equality haunts servants' minds; at first, they do not perceive whether this equality to which they have a right is to be found inside or outside the very condition of domestic service. In the recesses of their heart, they revolt against a state of inferiority to which they themselves have submitted and from which they draw a profit. They consent to serve and are ashamed to obey; they like the advantages of service but not the master; or rather, they are not sure that they should not be the masters themselves and are inclined to treat the man who gives them orders as the unjust usurper of their rights.

Then it is that we see in the house of each citizen something parallel to the sad sight seen in political society at large, where an unceasing war of unspoken and internal ferocity wages between permanently suspicious and rival power blocs: the master is ill-natured and soft; the servant is ill-natured and intractable. The one wishes by dishonest restrictive practices to evade his duty to protect and remunerate; the other his duty to obey. Between them hover the reins of domestic administration which each strives to grab. The lines dividing authority from tyranny, freedom from license and right from power, appear in their eyes jumbled and confused so that no one knows exactly what he is, what he may do or what his duties are.

Such a state of affairs is not democratic but smacks of revolution.

CHAPTER 6

HOW DEMOCRATIC INSTITUTIONS AND CUSTOMS TEND TO RAISE THE COST AND SHORTEN THE LENGTH OF LEASES

What I have said of servants and masters applies, to a certain degree, to landowners and tenant farmers, but the subject deserves a separate treatment.

In America there are no tenant farmers, properly speaking, as every man is the owner of the field he is cultivating.

One must acknowledge that democratic laws have a strong tendency to increase the number of landowners and to lessen the number of tenant farmers. However, what is happening in the United States has to be attributed much less to its institutions than to the country itself. The land in America costs little and every man readily becomes an owner, but the returns are low and its products could not easily be shared between a landowner and a tenant.

Thus, America is unique in this as in other respects, so that it would be a mistake to use it as a model.

I think that in democracies, just as in aristocracies, both landowners and tenant farmers will be found but they will not relate to each other in the same way.

In aristocracies, rents are not paid in money alone but in respect, affection, and service. In democracies, money is the only payment. When estates are divided to change ownership and the permanent ties between families and the land disappear, only chance puts landlord and tenant in contact. They meet briefly to settle the terms of the contract and then lose sight of each other. They are two strangers brought together by common interest, who keenly talk over a matter of business, which is only concerned with money.

As property is subdivided and wealth scattered here and there over the land, the state is populated with those whose former wealth is declining and with those whose wealth is newly won and whose wants are increasing faster than their resources. For both these types, the smallest profit matters and neither of them is inclined to let any of his advantages slip away nor to lose any part at all of his income.

As classes intermingle and very large as well as very small fortunes become rarer, as the days go by there is less distance between the status of landowner and that of tenant farmer; the former has no natural or undisputed superiority over the latter. Now, when you have two insecure men of equal status, what other basis than money could there be for tenancy agreements between them?

A man who owns a whole district with a hundred farms realizes that he has to win over the hearts of several thousand people; he thinks that such a task deserves a great deal of his effort. To achieve such a considerable goal, he is ready to make sacrifices.

The man who has a hundred acres does not bother with such concerns and hardly takes any interest in winning over the goodwill of an individual tenant.

An aristocracy does not die in one day like a man.

Its *raison d'être* slowly falls apart in men's minds before being challenged by law. Thus, a long while before this conflict breaks out, the link which ties the upper to the lower classes gradually loosens. Indifference and scorn are displayed by the one class, jealously and hatred by the other; the connections between poor and rich become less frequent and less kind; and rents rise. This is still not the result of the democratic revolution but it is certainly a warning sign. For an aristocracy which has once and for all let the people's affections slip through its hands resembles a tree dead at its roots which winds will overturn all the more easily the higher it is.

For fifty years rents have risen drastically, not simply in France but in most of Europe. The unusual progress made by agriculture and industry in the same period is not enough, in my view, to account for this happening. We must look for some other, more powerful and hidden reason. I think that this reason must be sought in the democratic institutions adopted by several

European nations and in the democratic passions which are stirring almost all the others.

I have often heard great English landlords congratulating themselves on deriving much more money these days from their estates than their fathers did.

Perhaps they are right to rejoice but for certain they do not know why they are glad. They believe they are making a clear profit whereas they are simply making an exchange. Influence is what they are surrendering for cash and any gain in monetary terms will soon be lost in terms of power.

There is yet another indication which clearly demonstrates the presence or approach of a great democratic revolution.

In the Middle Ages, almost all lands were leased in perpetuity or at least for very long terms. On studying the domestic economy of those times, we see that leases of ninety-nine years were much more frequent than the twelve-year leases of today.

Men then believed in the immortality of families, social conditions seemed fixed forever, and the whole of society appeared so stable that they imagined that nothing was ever going to change within it.

In times of equality, men think in quite a different way. They readily imagine that nothing lasts and are haunted by the idea of instability.

In this situation, the landowner and the tenant farmer himself feel a sort of instinctive terror of long-term commitments; they are afraid of being hemmed in tomorrow by the agreement from which they profit today. They vaguely expect some sudden and unforeseen change in their circumstances. They mistrust themselves and, if their taste were to change, they dread that they may have to suffer the distress of being unable to abandon what they once coveted. They are right to harbor such fears, for in democratic ages when everything is unstable, the most unstable of all is the human heart.

CHAPTER 7

INFLUENCE OF DEMOCRACY ON WAGES

Most of my observations above about servants and masters apply to masters and workmen.

As the rules of social hierarchy are less strictly observed, while the great sink and the humble rise, as poverty along with wealth ceases to be inherited, every day sees the lessening of the gap between workman and master both in actual fact and in men's minds.

The workman adopts a more lofty idea of his rights, his future, and himself; he is filled with new ambition, new desires; he is besieged by new wants. Constantly he casts covetous eyes upon the profits earned by his employer; in striving to share them he tries to put up the price of his labor and in the end usually manages to do so.

In democratic countries, as elsewhere, most industrial concerns are managed at small cost by men whose wealth and education do not raise them much above the level of those they employ. These industrialists are very numerous; they have different concerns; thus they could not possibly reach an easy agreement or unite their efforts.

On the other hand, workmen almost always have a few sure resources which allow them to withdraw their services when they are not awarded what they consider is the fair payment for their work.

In the unbroken struggle over wages between these two groups, power is thus divided and success alternates from one to the other.

It is even probable that in the long run the interests of workmen must prevail, for the high wages they have already obtained lessen the dependency on their masters as the days go by and, as they become more independent, they are able more easily to earn higher wages.

I shall take as my example the occupation which, in our times, is the one pursued by most people among the French as among almost all the nations of the world: agriculture.

In France, most of those who hire out their services to till the ground are themselves owners of a few plots of land which, at a pinch, will enable them to live without working for anyone else. When these people offer to work for a great landlord or a neighboring tenant farmer but are refused a certain wage, they withdraw to their smallholding and await another opportunity.

I think that, on the whole, it can be said that the slow and gradual rise in wages is one of the general laws of democratic societies. As conditions become more equal, wages rise; as wages increase, conditions become more equal.

But nowadays one great and unfortunate exception occurs.

I have demonstrated in a previous chapter how the aristocracy, once expelled from political life, had withdrawn into certain areas of industrial enterprise and had created its power there in a different form.

This has a strong influence on the rate of wages.

As one must already be very rich to take on the great industries of which I speak, the number of entrepreneurs is very small. Being few in number they can easily league together and fix the level of wages as they like.

Workmen, by comparison, are very numerous and their numbers are constantly on the increase for, from time to time, extraordinary periods of prosperity occur when wages rise wildly, attracting people in the locality into manufacturing industry. Now, once men have embarked upon this career, we have seen that they cannot escape from it because they soon pick up habits of body and mind which render them unsuited for any other work. These men usually lack education, energy, or resources. They are, therefore, at their master's mercy. When competition, or any other circumstances, reduce the master's profits, he can curb their wages almost at will and can easily recoup from them what the fortunes of business take from him.

Should they choose to strike, the master, who is wealthy, is easily able to wait, without risk of ruin, until necessity brings them back since they must work every day so as not to die, for they own almost nothing but the strength of their arms.

Oppression has long since reduced them to poverty and, as they become poorer, they are easier to oppress—a vicious circle from which they cannot escape.

Thus, one must not be surprised if wages, after occasional sudden rises, drop in this area permanently, whereas in other professions the reward of work, which generally grows gradually, does increase constantly.

This state of dependency and suffering in which a section of the industrial population lives at the present time is an exception to the rule and contrary to conditions all around. But for this very reason, it is all the more serious and deserves to attract the particular attention of the legislator for it is difficult to hold one class stationary when all the rest of society is on the move. Likewise, when the majority never cease to open up new roads to fortune, it is difficult to force the few to suffer in peace their needs and desires.

CHAPTER 8

INFLUENCE OF DEMOCRACY ON THE FAMILY

I have just examined how, in democratic nations and especially in America, equality of social conditions alters the relations between citizens.

I wish to pursue the matter further and inquire what happens within the heart of the family. My aim is not to seek new truths but to demonstrate how already known facts have a bearing on my theme.

Everybody has noticed that in our time new relations have evolved between different members of families, that the distance formerly separating father and son has diminished and that paternal authority has been, if not destroyed, at least modified.

Something similar to this but much more striking may be observed in the United States.

In America, the family in its Roman or aristocratic sense no longer exists. Only a few traces have been found in the first years of children's lives when the father exercises an unopposed domestic dictatorship made necessary by his sons' weakness and justified by both their weakness and his unquestionable superiority.

But from the moment the young American nears manhood, the ties of filial obedience slacken from day to day. Control of his own thoughts soon extends to his own behavior. In America, there is no real period of adolescence. At the close of boyhood, the man appears and begins to trace out his own path.

It would be wrong to suppose that this happens after some internal struggle in which the son wins the freedom his father was refusing through a sort of moral violence. Those very habits and principles which incite the former to seize independence incline the latter to consider its enjoyment as an indisputable right.

So in the former, one sees none of those hateful and disorderly passions which torment men a considerable time after they have shaken off a longstanding yoke. The latter does not experience those bitter and angry regrets which normally remain after his power has fallen. The father has kept his eyes upon the distant end of his authority and, when the moment arrives, he surrenders it without difficulty. The son has anticipated the exact time when his own will rules and he takes hold of his freedom without haste or struggle as a possession which is his due and which no one seeks to snatch from him.[1]

---

1.   It has not yet occurred to the Americans to do as we have done in France, that is to deprive the parent of one of the foremost elements of his power by removing from him the freedom to dispose of his property after his death. In the United States, there are no restrictions placed on those who make a will.

In this regard, as in almost everything else, it is easy to see that, if the political legislation of the Americans is much more democratic than ours, our civil legislation is infinitely more democratic than theirs. This can be understood without difficulty.

Our civil legislation was the work of a man who saw that it was in his interest to satisfy the democratic passions of his contemporaries in all that was not directly and immediately hostile to his power. He was willing to allow property and the government of families to be managed by a few popularly claimed principles, provided that these were not to be

Maybe it is of some use to reveal how these changes which have taken place in the family are closely connected to the social and political revolution which is coming to completion as we watch.

There are certain great social principles which a nation either introduces everywhere or tolerates nowhere.

In countries governed on aristocratic and hierarchical lines, power never makes a direct appeal to the mass of the governed. As men are closely connected to each other, only the leaders need controlling; the rest will follow. This applies to the family as to all other groups with a leader.

Amongst aristocratic nations, society recognizes, if truth be told, only the father and retains its hold upon the sons through the father; society rules the father who rules his sons. So the father not only has a natural right, he is granted a political right to hold authority. He is the author and support of his family as he is its magistrate.

In democracies, where the long arm of government seeks out each individual citizen in the crowd to bend him separately to the community's laws, no such intermediary is needed; in the eyes of the law, the father is simply an older and richer citizen than his son.

When most social conditions are very unequal and inequality is permanent, the concept of superiority looms large in men's minds. If parental prerogatives were not granted by law, they would be conceded by custom and public opinion. When, on the other hand, the differences between men are slight and are not permanent, the general concept of superiority becomes weaker and indistinct. It is useless for the legislator to strive to subordinate the person receiving orders to the one giving them.

---

introduced into state administration. While the democratic torrent overflowed into civil law, he hoped he could easily shelter behind political law. This view is both extremely clever and selfish; but such a compromise could not last. For, in the long run, political institutions cannot avoid becoming the expression and reflection of civil society; and it is in this sense that one can say that there is nothing more political in a nation than its civil legislation.

Custom forces the men nearer together and daily puts them on the same level.

So, if I fail to see any special privileges granted by the laws of an aristocratic nation to the head of the family, I shall certainly remain convinced that his authority is widely respected and more extensive than in a democracy, for I observe that, whatever the laws, the superior will always appear higher and the inferior lower in aristocracies than in democracies.

When men recall what has been, rather than concentrate upon what is, and worry much more about what their fore-fathers thought, rather than thinking for themselves, the father is the natural and necessary tie between the past and the present, the link where the ends of two chains meet. In aristoc-racies the father is, therefore, not only the political head of the family, he is the instrument of tradition, the interpreter of cus-tom and the judge of behavior. He is heard with deference; he is approached with respect; the love felt for him is always tempered by fear.

As the state of society becomes democratic and as men adopt the general principle that it is good and proper to judge every-thing for oneself by seeing former beliefs as information not precedent, the power of a father's opinions over his sons is reduced, as is his legal power over them.

Perhaps the division of estates which democracy brings along with it contributes more than anything else to alter the relations between fathers and children.

When the father owns little, his son and he live permanently in the same place and carry on the same work together. Habit and need bring them close together and make them communi-cate with each other all the time. A sort of intimate familiarity is bound, therefore, to exist between them, which makes power less absolute and which goes ill with external tokens of respect.

Now, in democratic nations, the class which possesses these small fortunes is precisely the one to give ideas their power and to set the direction of customs. It insists everywhere on its opinions at the same time as its wishes and the very people who are the most disposed to resist the dictates of democracy end up by allowing themselves to be persuaded by its example. I have seen fiery opponents of democracy being addressed with familiarity by their children.

Thus, at the same time as power slips away from aristocracies, the austere, the conventional, and the legal part of paternal authority is seen to disappear and a kind of equality to reign around the domestic fireside.

I do not know whether, all in all, society stands to lose by this change but I am inclined to think that individuals gain from it. I think that as customs and laws are more democratic, the relations of father and sons become more intimate and kinder. Rules and authority are less in evidence; trust and affection are often greater; it seems as though natural ties draw closer while social ties loosen.

In the democratic family, the father scarcely exercises any other power than that gladly given to the gentleness and experience of an old man. Perhaps his commands would be underrated but his advice is usually weighty. He might not be surrounded by ceremonial respect but at least his sons approach him with trust. No recognized formula of address exists but they are forever speaking to him and are ready to consult him daily. Master and magistrate have gone; the father remains.

All we need to judge the difference between the two social states in this respect is to peruse the family correspondence left to us by the aristocracy. Its style is always correct, ceremonious, strict, and so cold that the natural warmth of the heart can hardly be conveyed through the words.

On the contrary, in all the words addressed by a son to his father in democratic nations, something both free, familiar, and gentle prevails which reveals at first sight the fresh relationships now existing at the center of family life.

A parallel revolution is altering the relations between children.

In the aristocratic family, as in aristocratic society, all positions are defined. Not only does the father hold a rank apart and enjoy great privileges, the children, too, are not at all equal in relation to each other. Age and gender irrevocably fix each person's rank and confirm certain prerogatives. Democracy overturns or diminishes most of these barriers.

In the aristocratic family, the oldest son, by inheriting the greatest share of the property and almost all the rights, becomes the chief, and to some extent, the master of his brothers. He gains the greatness and the power; they have the mediocrity and dependence. However, it would be incorrect to suppose that, in aristocratic nations, the privileges of the eldest son were an advantage to him alone and aroused only envy and hatred around him.

Usually the eldest son strives to bring wealth and power for his brothers because the general splendor of the house reflects credit on its chief representative. The younger sons seek to help the eldest in all his undertakings because the greatness and power of the head of the family place him increasingly in a position to promote all the branches of the family.

The various members of the aristocratic family are, therefore, closely bonded together; their interests are connected, their minds agree but their hearts are seldom in harmony.

Democracy also binds brothers together but sets about doing it in quite a different manner.

Under democratic laws, children are completely equal and consequently independent; nothing forces them to be close nor does anything drive them apart. As they have a shared origin, as they grow up beneath the same roof, as they are treated with the same care and as no peculiar privilege either distinguishes or divides them, the kindly and youthful intimacy of their early years readily springs up between them. The ties thus formed at the start of life are scarcely ever broken, for brotherhood brings them into close daily contact without cause for friction.

Democracy, therefore, cements brothers' closeness not through self-interest but by shared memories and the unhampered harmony of their opinions and tastes. It divides their inheritance but allows their hearts the freedom to unite.

The gentleness of these democratic customs is so great that the supporters of aristocracy are attracted by it and, after experiencing it for some time, they are not at all tempted to return to the respectful and cold formalities of the aristocratic family.

They would gladly retain the domestic habits of democracy provided that they could reject its social and legal conditions. But these things are all of a piece and the former cannot be enjoyed without enduring the latter.

What I have just said about filial love and fraternal affection applies to all those spontaneous emotions which emanate from human nature itself.

When a certain way of thinking and feeling results from a particular human condition, nothing is left if ever that condition changes. Thus, the law can tie two citizens closely together only for them to be separated when the law is abolished. Nothing was tighter than the knot between the medieval vassal and his lord. Now these two men no longer know each other. The fear, gratitude, and affection which formerly bound them together have gone without a trace.

But such is not the case with the feelings natural to man. The law seldom avoids weakening such feelings by striving to mold them in a certain way and by wishing to add something, it almost always removes something from them, for they are always stronger when left alone.

Democracy, which destroys or obscures almost all former social conventions and prevents men from creating new ones easily, leads to the complete disappearance of most of the feelings originating in such conventions. But it merely modifies all the others, often imparting to them a vigor and gentleness that they had not possessed before.

I think that it is not impossible to encapsulate in a single sentence the main sense of this chapter and several others preceding it. Democracy loosens social ties but tightens natural ones; it draws families more closely together while separating citizens.

CHAPTER 9

EDUCATION OF GIRLS IN THE UNITED STATES

No free societies ever existed without morals and, as I have said in the first part of this work, morals are made by women. Therefore, everything connected with the status of women, their habits, and opinions, has great political interest, in my view.

In almost all Protestant nations, girls are much more in control of their behavior than in Catholic ones.

This independence is even greater in Protestant countries which, like England, have kept or gained the right of self-government. Then freedom filters down into the family through politics, habits, and religious beliefs.

In the United States, Protestant doctrines combine with a very free constitution and a very democratic social state; nowhere else is a girl left so soon or so entirely to look after herself.

Long before a young American woman has reached marriage-able age, her emancipation from her mother's supervision has gradually started. Hardly has she emerged from childhood than she is already thinking for herself, is speaking freely and acting independently; the great scene of society lies constantly exhibited for her to see; far from attempting to conceal this sight from her, she is daily shown more and more of it and is taught to contemplate it with a steady and calm gaze. Thus, the defects and dangers of society are soon revealed to her; she sees them clearly, assesses them without any illusions, and confronts them fearlessly for she is full of confidence in her own powers and that confidence is shared by all who surround her.

You should, therefore, hardly ever expect to come across, in a young American girl, that pure openness of heart which marks a wakening desire, any more than those naive and guileless charms which usually accompany, in a European girl, the trans-ition from child to adolescent. An American girl, whatever her age, rarely suffers from childish shyness or ignorance. Like her European counterpart, she seeks to be liked but knows exactly what that costs. If she does not succumb to evil, at least she knows about it; she has a purity of moral behavior more than a chaste mind.

I have often been taken aback and almost scared by the unusual skill and lucky boldness with which these American girls could steer their thoughts through the reefs of lively conversations; a philosopher would have stumbled a hundred times along the narrow path they negotiated with ease and without mishap.

In fact, it is easy to see that, even in the independence of early youth, the American girl never completely ceases to be in control of herself; she enjoys all the permitted pleasures without losing her head to any of them, and her reason does not lose the reins even though she often seems to hold them loosely.

In France, where we still maintain this odd mixture of opinions and tastes taken from the remnants of past ages, our women are often given a cautious, reserved, and almost cloistered education, as they would have received in aristocratic times, and then we suddenly abandon them without guidance or help, amid disorders inseparable from democratic society.

Americans have a greater inner confidence.

They have realized that in a democracy, individual independence cannot fail to be very great; youth will be impetuous, tastes ill-restrained, customs will change, public opinion will be vacillating or feeble, paternal authority will be weak, and a husband's power challenged.

In these circumstances, they have calculated that there was little chance of repressing the most tyrannical passions of a woman's heart and that the surer line was to teach her the art of controlling them herself.

As they could not prevent her virtue from being in danger, they wished her to know how to defend it, and they counted upon the free efforts of her own determination more than upon obstacles which could be shaken or overthrown. Instead, therefore, of teaching her to mistrust herself, they constantly seek to increase the confidence she has in her own strength. Since they could and would not keep a girl in perpetual and complete ignorance, they are impatient to give her a premature knowledge of everything. Far from concealing the corruption of society from her, they wanted her to see it in the first place and to take steps to evade it; they preferred to ensure her honesty than to overrespect her innocence.

Although Americans are a very religious people, they have not relied upon religion alone to protect a woman's virtue; they have tried to arm her reason. In this, they have pursued the same method as in many other circumstances. First of all, they make incredible efforts to make sure that individuals control their own freedom and it is only when human strength has reached its utmost limits that they finally call for religion to help.

I realize that such a method of education is not free from danger; I am fully aware as well that it will tend to develop judgement at the cost of imagination and to turn women into virtuous and cold companions to men, rather than tender and loving wives. Although society is more peaceful and better ordered as a consequence, private life has often fewer charms. But those are minor ills which must be braved for a greater good. At the point we have now reached, we no longer have a choice: we need a democratic education to safeguard women from the dangers with which democratic institutions and customs surround them.

CHAPTER 10

HOW THE GIRL CAN BE SEEN BENEATH THE FEATURES OF THE WIFE

In America, a woman's independence is irretrievably lost in the ties of marriage. If a young woman is less restricted there than anywhere else, as a wife she submits to narrower duties. The former enjoys a place of liberty and pleasure in her father's house, the latter, in her husband's home, lives in almost cloistered surroundings.

These two very different circumstances are perhaps not so

contradictory as might be supposed and Americans naturally pass from the one to reach the other.

Religious and industrial nations entertain a particularly serious conception of marriage. Some regard the ordered life of a woman as the finest guarantee and the the surest sign of her virtuous morals. Others see it as the most reliable safeguard of the order and prosperity of the house.

Americans are simultaneously a puritanical and a trading nation; their religious beliefs alongside their industrial practices lead them, therefore, to demand a self-sacrifice from women and a constant denial of pleasure for the sake of business which are seldom required of them in Europe. Thus, in the United States, an inflexible public opinion prevails to contain women within the restricted sphere of domestic business and duties and to forbid them to step beyond it.

Upon her entrance into society, the young American woman finds these ideas firmly established and sees the rules that spring from them; she is soon convinced that she cannot avoid for one moment the etiquette of her contemporaries without immediately endangering her own peace of mind, her honor, and even her social existence; she finds the energy required to submit to these rules in the firmness of her reason and in the virile habits bequeathed by her education.

It can be said that it is from the enjoyment of her independence that she has drawn the courage to tolerate the sacrifice of it, without struggle or complaint, when the time comes for that to happen.

The American woman, moreover, never falls into the bonds of marriage as into a trap laid for her simplicity or ignorance. She has been taught in advance what was expected of her and she herself freely bows beneath the yoke. She courageously endures her new state because she has chosen it.

Since in America paternal discipline is very lax and the marriage tie is very tight, a girl enters into it only with great caution and trepidation. Premature weddings scarcely occur. American women marry, therefore, only when their minds are mature enough to govern their decisions, whereas elsewhere most women usually begin to find enough maturity to govern their decisions only after marriage.

However, I am far from thinking that this great change in all the habits of American women, as soon as they are married, should be attributed to the restrictions imposed by public opinion. Often they impose this sacrifice upon themselves simply by the effort of their will.

When the moment has arrived to choose a husband, her cold and austere powers of reasoning, which have been educated and strengthened by a free view of the world, tell the American woman that a flippant and independent attitude is the everlasting cause of trouble, not of pleasure, within the ties of marriage; a girl's amusements cannot be the recreations of a wife and, for a married woman, the source of happiness lies in the marital home. Seeing clearly beforehand the only path to domestic happiness, she sets out in that direction with her first steps and follows it to the end without seeking to turn back.

This very strength of will exhibited by young American wives in their immediate and uncomplaining submission to the severe duties of their new estate is no less echoed in all the great tests of their lives.

In no country in the world are private fortunes more unstable than in the United States. It is quite common for the same man to climb up and down all the rungs from opulence to poverty in the course of his life.

American women tolerate these upheavals with a quiet and indomitable energy. Their desires seem to contract as easily as they expand as their fortunes alter.

Most of the adventurers who annually people the wastes of the West belong, as I said in my first volume, to the former Anglo-American stock of the North. Several of these men who rush so boldly in pursuit of wealth were already enjoying a comfortable life in their own part of the country. They take their wives with them upon whom they impose the countless dangers and sufferings which always attend such undertakings. In the furthest reaches of the wilderness, I have often come across young women who, brought up in the midst of the refinements of New England towns, had made the transition from the wealthy parental home to an insecure hut in the depths of a forest. Neither fever, nor loneliness, nor boredom had shattered the springs of their courage. Their features seemed changed and lined but their looks were firm. They appeared both saddened and resolute. (See Appendix A, p. 853.)

I am sure that these young American women had drawn this internal strength, which they now exploit, from their early education.

Thus, in the United States, the girl can still be seen beneath the features of the wife: the role has changed, her ways are different but the spirit remains the same.

CHAPTER 11

HOW THE EQUALITY OF SOCIAL CONDITIONS HELPS TO MAINTAIN GOOD MORALS IN AMERICA
(See Appendix B, p. 856.)

Some philosophers and historians have said, or hinted, that women's morals were more or less strict according to the distance they lived from the equator, which is a cheap way of getting out of the matter and, by that calculation, all you would need would be a globe and a compass to solve in an instant one of the most thorny problems of human behavior.

I do not find this materialist theory established by the facts.

The same nations have been virtuous or dissolute at various times of their history. The orderliness or disruption in their morality was therefore due to variable conditions and not simply to the unchanging nature of the country.

I shall not deny that, in certain climates, the passions that stem from mutual sexual attraction are peculiarly intense; but I feel that this natural intensity can always be aroused or dampened by social conditions and political institutions.

Although travelers to North America hold differences of

opinion on several issues, they are all agreed that morals in that country are much more strict than everywhere else.

It is clear that on this point Americans are much superior to their fathers, the English. A cursory glance at the two nations is enough to prove this fact.

In England, as in all European countries, public malice rails constantly against the weaknesses of women. Philosophers and statesmen are often heard complaining about the irregularity of moral behavior and literature suggests this every passing day.

All books in America, including novels, assume that women are virtuous and no one relates amorous affairs.

This great strictness of American morality is doubtless due in part to the country, the race, and the religion. But all these reasons, which can be found elsewhere, are not yet enough to account for it. To do that we must have recourse to some particular reason.

That reason appears to me to be the principle of equality and the institutions which derive from it.

Equality of social conditions does not lead of itself alone to strict moral behavior but without any doubt it helps and increases such a tendency.

Among aristocratic nations, birth and wealth often make a man and a woman such different creatures that they could never succeed in uniting with each other. Passion draws them together but social conditions and notions suggested by them prevent their forging a permanent and open union. That leads unavoidably to a great number of transient and clandestine liaisons. Nature secretly gets her own back for the restraint imposed by laws.

This does not occur in the same way when equality of social conditions has swept away all the real or imagined barriers between men and women. No girl then feels that she cannot become the wife of the man who likes her best, which makes the disruption of moral behavior before marriage very uncommon. For, however believable a passion may be, in no way will a woman be persuaded that she is loved when her lover is perfectly free to marry her and does not do so.

The same cause acts upon marriage though in a more indirect manner.

Nothing better serves to justify an illicit passion in the eyes of those experiencing it or of the watching crowd than forced marriages or ones embarked upon by chance.[1]

In a country where women are always free to make their own choice and where education has taught them to choose well, public opinion is unforgiving when they make any mistake.

The austerity of Americans stems in part from that cause. They regard marriage as a contract which, though onerous, must nevertheless be strictly honored in all its clauses because these have all been known beforehand and people have enjoyed the complete freedom not to bind themselves to anything at all.

The factors which make fidelity more obligatory also make it easier.

In aristocratic countries, marriage aims rather to unite property than individual persons; thus sometimes it happens that the husband is betrothed when he is at school and the wife when she is at the breast. It is not surprising that the marriage tie which binds the fortunes of the couple together leaves their hearts to wander where they will. Such flows naturally from the spirit of the contract.

When, on the other hand, each person always chooses his companion for himself without any external constrictions or control, normally only similarity of tastes and ideas brings a

1.   The study of the various European literatures will easily convince us of this truth.

     When a European wants to portray in his fiction some of those great catastrophes in marriage which are so common amongst us, he is careful first to arouse the compassion of the reader by depicting marriages which are either ill-matched or forced. Although a prolonged tolerance has, for some time, relaxed our customs, it would be difficult for the author to interest us in the misfortunes of these characters if he did not begin by finding an excuse for their faults. This device seldom fails. Our daily experiences prepare us in advance to be indulgent.

     American authors would not be able to make these same excuses credible to their readers; their customs and their laws are opposed to doing so and, finding the task of depicting disharmony as attractive a hopeless one, they do not depict it at all. In part, it is because of this that there are so few novels published in the United States.

man and a woman together and this similarity holds and keeps them by each other's side.

Our forefathers had a very strange idea of marriage.

As they had observed that the small number of love matches which took place in their day almost always ended in disaster, they came to the firm conclusion that in such matters it was very dangerous to listen to the dictates of the heart. They felt that chance saw things more clearly than choice.

It was not very hard to see, however, that the examples before them proved nothing.

In the first place, I suggest that, if democratic nations grant women the right of choosing their husbands freely, they are careful to educate their understanding in advance and to give their will the necessary strength for such a choice; whereas the girls in aristocratic nations who secretly escape from their father's authority to throw themselves into the arms of a man they have neither had the time to know nor the competence to judge, lack all these guarantees. One should not be surprised that they misuse their freedom of choice the first time they avail themselves of it nor that they make such cruel mistakes when, without the benefit of a democratic education, they decide to follow the customs of democracy in marriage.

But this is not all. When a man and a woman wish to come together despite the inequalities of an aristocratic society, they have mighty obstacles to overcome. After breaking down or loosening the ties of filial obedience, they must make a final effort to escape from the power of tradition and the tyranny of public opinion. When at last they reach the end of this arduous undertaking, they find themselves estranged from their natural friends and relatives: the prejudices which they have defied lead to their isolation. This predicament soon wears down their courage and embitters their hearts.

So, if it happens that couples united in this way are first unhappy and then guilty, one should not attribute this to their freedom of choice but rather to the fact that they live in a society which does not allow such a choice.

Besides, it must not be forgotten that the same effort which makes a man violently break out of a generally accepted error almost always drives him to lose his reason; that to dare to declare even a justified war upon the ideas of his century, a man must possess a certain violent and adventurous attitude of mind. Men of this disposition seldom achieve happiness or virtue whatever direction they take. And that, one may say in passing, explains why, in the most necessary and hallowed revolutions, one meets so few moderate or honest revolutionaries.

One should not therefore be surprised if, in an aristocratic age, a man who takes it upon himself to consult nothing but his own opinion and taste in his choice of wife soon finds moral breakdown and suffering invading his household.

But when this same course of action is part of the natural and normal order of things, when the social system favors it, when paternal authority supports it, and public opinion recommends it, it cannot be doubted that the inner peace of families will be increased and married confidence will be better protected.

Almost all the men in a democracy pursue a political career or practice a profession, whereas the women are forced, because of the limitations upon their common income, to stay every day inside their houses to preside in person very closely over the details of domestic affairs.

All these distinct and necessary occupations form so many natural barriers which, by keeping the sexes apart, make the entreaties of the one less common and less urgent while making the resistance of the other easier.

Equality of social conditions can never succeed in making men faithful but it does impart a less dangerous character to the breakdown of morality. Under those conditions, as no one has either the time or the opportunity to attack a virtue armed in self-defense, there are both a great number of prostitutes and a host of virtuous women.

Such a state of affairs fosters deplorable individual suffering but does not prevent society from being strong and alert, nor does it destroy family ties or weaken the morals of the nation. Society is endangered not by the great corruption of the few but by the laxity of all. In the legislator's view, prostitution is less to be feared than love affairs.

This disturbed and constantly harassed life which equality

imposes on men not only diverts them from the passion of love by depriving them of the time to devote to it, but also turns them away by a more secret but more certain path.

All men in democratic times adopt more or less the mental habits of the industrial and trading classes; their attitude takes a serious, calculating, and positive turn; they willingly veer away from the ideal to pursue some obvious and available goal, which seems to them to be the natural and essential object of their desires. Equality does not destroy the imagination but clips its wings and only lets it fly along the ground.

No one has fewer dreams than the citizen of a democracy; and few are ever known to indulge in those idle and solitary contemplations which normally anticipate and end up in great agitations of the heart.

They do, it is true, set great store on obtaining that sort of deep, reliable, and peaceful affection which adds charm and security to one's life. But they do not pursue those violent and capricious emotions which disturb and shorten one's life.

I realize that all I have just said is only relevant in its full extent to America and, up to now, cannot apply in any general way to Europe.

In the fifty years since laws and customs have been propelling with unprecedented force several European nations toward democracy, the relations between men and women have not been seen to become more orderly or more virtuous. In fact, the opposite may be detected in certain places. Some classes are more orderly; general morality appears more lax. I do not hesitate to make that observation for I feel as little inclined to flatter my contemporaries as to slander them.

This spectacle must sadden but not surprise the observer.

The fortunate influence which a democratic social system may exercise on orderly habits is one of those factors which only time can reveal over the long term. If equality of social conditions is favorable to good morals, the social upheaval which achieves this equality is very damaging to them.

In this last fifty years of France's transformation, we have seldom seen any freedom but always disorder. In the midst of this universal confusion of ideas, this general disturbance of opinion, this incoherent muddling of fairness and unfairness, truth and falsehood, right and might, public virtue has become unsure and private morality wavering.

But all revolutions, whatever their objectives or their means, have always led, in the first instance, to such results. Even those which, in the end, tightened moral standards, started by relaxing them.

The disordered times we have often witnessed do not, therefore, seem to last for very long. There is already some evidence pointing in that direction.

There is nothing more wretchedly corrupt than an aristocracy which preserves its wealth while losing its power and which still has endless leisure to devote to nothing but vulgar pastimes. Those energetic passions and important ideas which had once inspired it then disappear and scarcely anything remains but a mass of petty, gnawing vices which cling to it like worms to a corpse.

No one challenges that the French aristocracy of the last century was very dissolute. But at the same time, old habits and beliefs still maintained a respect for morality in the other classes.

Yet we shall all be able to agree that the remnants of this same aristocracy exhibit now a certain austerity of principles, whereas the breakdown of morality appears to have spread into the middle and lower classes of society. Thus, those very families which were the most lax fifty years ago now set the best example and democracy seems to have improved the moral standards only of the aristocratic classes.

While the Revolution divided up the wealth of the nobility, forced them to concentrate conscientiously upon their own business and families, restricted them to living under the same roof with their children, and finally gave a more rational and serious character to their thought, it also put into their hands, without their being conscious of this independently, a respect for religious beliefs, a love of order, of peaceful pleasures, of family joys and prosperity. Meanwhile, the rest of the nation, which naturally had the same tastes, was dragged down toward disorder because of the very effort needed to overturn political laws and practices.

The former French aristocracy has suffered the consequence of the Revolution without experiencing the revolutionary excitement and without sharing the often anarchic impulses which produced it. It is easy to imagine that it felt the salutary influence of this revolution before the very people who were responsible for it.

I may, therefore, be allowed to say, although at first sight this appears surprising, that currently the most antidemocratic elements in the nation exhibit best that kind of morality which may be reasonably expected from a democracy.

I cannot help thinking that, when we have seen all the results of the democratic revolution and have emerged from the upheaval it has caused, what is true today of the few will gradually become so for all.

CHAPTER 12

HOW THE AMERICANS VIEW THE EQUALITY OF MEN AND WOMEN

I have shown how democracy destroyed or altered the various inequalities which originate with society. But is that all? Will it not succeed ultimately in affecting that great inequality between men and women which has appeared, up to the present time, to be based on the timeless dictates of nature herself?

I think that the social change which places father and son, servant and master and, in general, lower and upper classes on the same level, will gradually raise women to make them the equals of men.

But in this matter, more than ever I need to make myself clearly understood, for no other subject in this century has given greater scope to crude and muddled imaginings.

There are Europeans who confuse the various characteristics of the sexes and would make of men and women beings not only equal but alike. To both, they attribute the same functions equally, impose on them the same duties and grant them the same rights. They would involve them both in everything—work, pleasure, business. It is easy to see that, in this ambition to make the one sex equal to the other, both are demeaned and that, from this crude mixing of nature's works, will emerge weak men and immodest women.

That is far from being the American view of the type of democratic equality which can be brought about between men and women. Their idea is that since nature has established such a great variation in the physical and moral make-up of men and women, and she clearly intended to give different employment to their different faculties. They have concluded that progress would not be achieved by having dissimilar creatures doing the same jobs but by enabling each of them to accomplish their respective tasks as effectively as possible. The Americans have applied to the sexes the great principle of political economy which currently dominates industry. They have carefully divided up the functions of men and women so that the great work of society might be better performed.

America is the one country where the most consistent care has been taken to trace clearly distant spheres of action for the two sexes and where both are required to walk at an equal pace but along paths that are never the same. You do not see American women directing concerns outside the range of the family, or handling business dealings, or entering politics. Neither do you see any women forced to face the rough work of plowing fields, nor any of those heavy tasks which demand the exertion of physical strength. No family is so poor that it forms the exception to this rule.

If the American woman is not allowed to escape the tranquil sphere of her domestic duties, neither is she forced to leave it.

Consequently, American women who display a quite manly intelligence and energy generally maintain very delicate features and always remain feminine in their ways even though they sometimes show they have the hearts and minds of men.

Nor have Americans ever imagined that the result of democratic principle would be to overturn a husband's authority or to introduce any ambiguity about who is in charge in the family. They have judged that any association must have a head to be effective and that the natural head of the marriage association is the man. Therefore, they do not deny him the right of directing his partner and they believe that, in the smaller association of husband and wife, just as in the greater political community, the objective of democracy is to regulate and authenticate the powers that are necessary, not to destroy all power.

This opinion is not in any way peculiar to one of the sexes and opposed by the other.

I have not noticed that American women considered the husband's authority as a lucky encroachment on their rights or that they believed that they degraded themselves by submitting to it. Rather, it appeared to me that they derived a sort of pride in the willing surrender of their wishes and that they felt their stature increased by their bending to this yoke and not seeking to escape from it. At least that is the feeling expressed by the most virtuous of them; the others remain silent and, in the United States, you do not hear any adulterous wife noisily claiming the rights of women even as she tramples under foot the most sacred of her duties.

It has often been observed that in Europe a certain scorn lies at the heart of the very compliments lavished on women by men: although the European often becomes a woman's slave, you realize that he never sincerely thinks her his equal.

In the United States, women are hardly ever praised but daily they are shown how much men value them.

Americans constantly display their complete confidence in the understanding of their wives and have a deep respect for their freedom. They estimate that her mind is as capable as a man's of discovering the plain truth and that her heart is just as resolute in following it. They have never sought to place her virtue, any more than his, under the protection of prejudice, ignorance, or fear.

It seems that in Europe, where men so easily submit to the tyrannical sway of women, the latter are nevertheless denied some of the greatest qualities of the human race and are regarded as attractive but incomplete beings. And what is more than astonishing is that women too end up by seeing themselves in the same light and that they are not a million miles from considering it a privilege that they are entitled to appear useless, weak, and timid. American women never claim rights of that sort.

Moreover, in matters of morals, it may be said that Europeans have granted a sort of strange immunity to men so that there is one virtue for them to use and another for their partners and that the same act can be seen by public opinion as either a crime or simply a fault.

Americans know nothing of this unfair distribution of duties and rights. For them the seducer is as much disgraced as his victim.

It is true that Americans seldom lavish upon women those eager attentions that Europeans like to pay them; but they always demonstrate by their behavior that they assume them to be virtuous and refined; and they have such a considerable respect for their moral freedom that they all keep, in their presence, a careful watch over the language they use lest women are forced to hear expressions which might offend them. In America a girl can set out on a long journey alone and without fear.

American legislators, who have softened almost all the articles of the penal code, still punish rape by death. And no other crime is prosecuted with the same relentless severity by public opinion. The explanation is this: since Americans have nothing they value or respect more than a woman's honor and independence, they consider no punishment too harsh for those who deprive her of both against her will.

In France, where this same offense is subject to much milder penalties, it is often difficult to find a jury to convict. Would that indicate scorn for a woman's modesty or her person? I cannot help believing that it is both.

Thus Americans do not believe that men and women have the duty or the right to perform the same things but they show the same regard for the role played by both and they consider them as equal in worth although their lot in life is different. They do not give to a woman's courage the same character or role as a man's but they never question its strength; and, while they do not think that a man and his partner should always use their intelligence and understanding in the same way, at least they consider that the one has as sound an understanding and as clear a mind as the other.

Americans, then, who have allowed the social inferiority of women to remain, have done their utmost to raise her intellectually and morally to man's level. In this way, they seem to me to have admirably understood the true concept of democratic progress.

For my part, I say this without hesitation: although the American woman rarely leaves her domestic sphere and in certain respects is very dependent within it, nowhere does she enjoy a higher status. And now, as I come near to the end of this book in which I have recorded so many considerable achievements of the Americans, if I am asked how we should account for the unusual prosperity and growing strength of this nation, I would reply that they must be attributed to the superiority of their women.

CHAPTER 13

HOW EQUALITY NATURALLY DIVIDES AMERICANS INTO A MULTITUDE OF SMALL PRIVATE SOCIETIES

One would be led to believe that the final outcome and necessary result of democratic institutions is to jumble together all the citizens in private as well as in public life and to force them all to live a similar lifestyle.

That is to understand the equality produced by democracy in a very coarse and oppressive way.

No social state and no laws can make men so much alike that education, wealth, and tastes cannot put any difference between them. If different men can sometimes find it to their advantage to cooperate in the same ventures, you should not think that they will ever derive any pleasure from so doing. They will, therefore, always escape the clutches of the legislator whatever he does; and they will depart in some respect from the sphere within which he wishes to constrict them in order to create, alongside the great political society, small private societies held together by similar conditions, habits, and customs.

In the United States, no one citizen exercises any dominance over any other; they owe each other neither obedience nor respect; together they administer justice and rule the state; in general, they all meet to manage those affairs which influence the destiny of the community; I have never heard it said that there was ever any intention of persuading them all to amuse themselves in the same way or to take their pleasures indiscriminately in the same locations.

Americans, who mix so comfortably in the confines of political meetings and courtrooms, by contrast are careful to break up into small, very distinct groups to enjoy the pleasures of private life. Each of them is very willing to acknowledge his equality with his fellow citizens but he only ever accepts a very small number as his friends or guests.

This appears very natural to me. As the circle of public associations increases, so we must expect the extent of private links to shrink; instead of supposing that the citizens of these new societies will eventually live all in one community, I am very much afraid that they will ultimately come together in very small groups.

In aristocratic nations, the various classes resemble vast enclosures which one can neither leave nor enter. There is no communication between these classes, but within each one men are necessarily in daily contact. Even though they would not naturally agree with each other, the general conveniences of their social conditions draw them close together.

But when neither law nor custom is responsible for establishing frequent and habitual contact between particular men, the chance similarities of opinions and inclinations decide the matter and that leads to an infinite variation of private societies.

In democracies where the differences between citizens are never very great and they naturally become so close that at any moment they can merge in the mass of the community, numerous artificial and arbitrary distinctions are invented to help individuals in their attempt to remain aloof for fear of being swept along with the crowd, despite all their efforts.

This can never fail to be the case, for human institutions may be altered but not man himself. Whatever the general efforts of society to keep citizens equal and similar, the personal pride of individuals will always strive to rise above the common level and will hope to achieve some inequality to their own advantage.

In aristocracies, insuperably high barriers keep men apart from one another; in democracies, they are divided by a lot of small and almost invisible threads which are continually broken and moved about from place to place.

Thus whatever progress equality makes in democratic nations, a great number of small private associations will always be formed within the general political society. But none of them will share the manners of that upper class which rules aristocracies.

CHAPTER 14

SOME REFLECTIONS ON AMERICAN MANNERS

Nothing at first sight seems less important than the external features of human actions and yet there is nothing upon which men set greater store. They can get used to anything except living in a society which does not share their manners. It is, therefore, well worthwhile examining the influence exercised by the social and political system on manners.

Manners are generally the product of moral behavior; they are also sometimes the result of an arbitrary convention between certain men. They are thus both natural and learned.

When certain men realize that they are indisputably and effortlessly the leading citizens of society, when daily they behold the great enterprises they undertake, leaving the details to others, and when they live amid wealth which they did not amass and are not afraid of losing, it may be supposed that they experience a kind of arrogance for the petty concerns and material cares of life and that they have a natural grandeur of thought revealed in their speech and manners.

In democratic countries, manners rarely display much dignity because private life is very trivial. They are often coarse because people have few opportunities to raise their thoughts above their preoccupation with domestic concerns.

True dignity of manners consists in always occupying one's proper station, neither too high nor too low—that is as much within the reach of a peasant as of a prince.

In democracies, everybody's status seems unsure; the result is that manners, though often full of arrogance, are rarely dignified. Moreover, they are never very well disciplined, nor very accomplished.

There is too much mobility in the population of a democracy for any particular group to be able to establish a code of behavior or to direct people to follow it. Each man acts, therefore, practically as he likes and there is always a certain dislocation of manners which follow the feelings and ideas of individuals rather than provide an ideal model for everyone to imitate.

In any case, this is much more obvious at the time when an aristocracy has just collapsed than when it has long been destroyed.

Then, new political institutions and new patterns of behavior bring men together in the same places and force them to live in common even though their education and customs have made them vastly different; all this highlights at every moment the motley composition of society. We still recall the existence of an exact code of polite manners but no one now knows what was in it, nor where it is to be found. Men have mislaid the common rules of manners and have not as yet made up their minds to do without them. But each individual strives to shape some sort of arbitrary and variable rule from the ruins of former customs, the result of which is that manners have neither the regularity and dignity frequently evident in aristocratic nations, nor the simplicity and freedom sometimes observed in democracies; they are constrained and unconstrained by turns.

But this is not the normal state of things.

When equality is complete and long-established, all men, having roughly the same ideas and doing roughly the same things, have no need of agreement or imitation to act and speak in the same way; one may constantly observe slight dissimilarities in their manners but no great differences. They are never perfectly alike because they do not copy from the same pattern; they are never very unlike because they have the same social condition. At first sight, the manners of all Americans might be seen as exactly alike. It is only on close scrutiny that the peculiarities of their differences become evident.

The English make much fun at the expense of American manners, and what is odd is that most of the people who have drawn such an amusing portrait of them belonged to the English middle classes, whom this same portrait fits very well too. So, these merciless critics normally represent just what they criticize in America; they do not realize that they are scoffing at themselves much to the great delight of their own aristocracy.

Nothing does more harm to democracy than its outer forms of behavior. Many people who would be willing to put up with its defects cannot tolerate its manners.

However, I cannot possibly admit that there is nothing praiseworthy in the manners of democratic nations.

In aristocracies, all within reach of the ruling class normally strive to imitate it, which prompts quite ridiculous and banal imitations. If democratic nations do not have before them models of high breeding, they at least escape the necessity of daily looking upon cheap copies.

In democracies, manners are never as refined as in aristocracies but neither are they ever as coarse. Neither the crude language of the crowd is heard, nor the elegant and choice expressions of the nobility. Often you find a triviality of manners but nothing brutal or mean.

I have said that in democracies an exact code of social etiquette cannot be established, which leads to inconveniences and advantages. In aristocracies, the rules of propriety impose the same outer appearance on each individual and make all the members of the same class seem alike in spite of their personal inclinations; they adorn and conceal what is natural. In democratic nations, manners are not as sophisticated nor as regular but they are often more sincere. They form, as it were, a thin and loosely woven veil through which every man's sincere feelings and personal opinions can easily be seen. Hence, a close connection often exists between the form and the substance of human actions and, if the greater tableau of human kind is less embellished, it is more true to life. Thus it is that the effect of democracy is not to impose certain manners on men but, in a sense, to stop them having any at all.

You can sometimes find, in a democracy, the opinions, passions, virtues, and vices of an aristocracy but not its manners which disappear and vanish never to return when the democratic revolution has been completed.

Apparently nothing is more lasting than the manners of an aristocratic class which preserves them for some time after the loss of its property and power; nor anything more fragile, for scarcely have they disappeared than all trace disappears and it is difficult to say what they were, once they have gone. A change in the state of society brings this marvel about; and only a few generations are needed to complete the process.

The main features of aristocracy remain etched in history whenever an aristocracy is destroyed, but the delicate and slight forms of its manners vanish from men's memories almost immediately after its downfall. Men would not be able to imagine them as soon as they are no longer seen. Their disappearance is unseen and unfelt. For, to appreciate this kind of refined pleasure afforded by distinguished and elegant manners, the heart must be prepared through education and custom, and the taste for such things is easily lost once the habit has gone.

Thus democratic nations not only cannot have aristocratic manners but they neither imagine nor desire them; as they cannot imagine them, it is as if for them such things had never existed.

Too much importance should not be attached to this loss but it may well be regretted.

I realize that it has happened more than once for the same men to have very elegant manners along with very vulgar opinions; the interiors of courts have revealed well enough that grandiose appearances may often conceal the meanest hearts. Yet, although aristocratic manners never created virtue, they did sometimes embellish it. It was no ordinary sight to see a numerous and powerful class whose every outward action seemed constantly to display the natural nobility of opinions and thoughts, the refinement and regularity of tastes and the urbanity of manners.

The manners of the aristocracy cast fine illusions over human nature and, although the picture often proved deceptive, looking at it gave the viewer a noble satisfaction.

CHAPTER 15

THE SERIOUS ATTITUDE OF AMERICANS AND WHY IT OFTEN DOES NOT PREVENT THEM FROM ILL-CONSIDERED ACTIONS

Men who live in democratic countries do not value those kinds of naive, rowdy, and coarse entertainments in which the people in aristocracies indulge; they find them childish or tasteless. Nor have they any more inclination for the refined intellectual amusements of the aristocratic classes; they look for something solid and productive from their pleasures and seek to add fulfillment to their enjoyments.

In aristocratic societies, the people readily indulge in bursts of wild and noisy gaiety which tears them away from the recollection of their wretchedness. Democratic peoples dislike that feeling of being violently shaken out of themselves and always feel sorry if they lose sight of themselves. These frivolous delights take second place to serious and quiet relaxations which have the air of business and which do not entirely drive business out of their minds.

A typical American, instead of spending his leisure hours dancing gaily in the public square like the fellow members of his class continue to do in the greater part of Europe, will withdraw to his own home to have a drink. Such a man enjoys two pleasures side by side; he goes on thinking about his business affairs and gets drunk decently with his family.

I used to think that the English were the most serious nation on the earth but, having seen the Americans, I have changed my mind.

I do not intend to suggest that temperament is not very important in the American character but I do think that their political institutions count for even more.

I believe that the seriousness of Americans stems partly from their pride. In democratic countries, even poor men entertain a high notion of personal worth. They look upon themselves with pleasure and readily assume that others are looking at them too. This disposes them to watch carefully over their words and deeds; they do not slacken their efforts lest they reveal their own deficiencies. They imagine that they have to retain their serious appearance in order to preserve their dignity.

But I detect another more deep-seated and powerful cause for this astonishing display of instinctive seriousness in Americans.

Under a despotism, people give way to occasional mad fits of gaiety but usually they are gloomy and constrained through fear.

Under absolute monarchies tempered by customs and manners, their spirits are often cheerful and even because, having a degree of freedom and a good deal of security, they are removed from the major cares of life. But all free peoples are serious because their minds are habitually preoccupied with some dangerous or difficult project.

This is especially true of those free nations with a democratic constitution. Then all classes have a countless number of people constantly involved in the serious business of government and those whose thoughts are not engaged in controlling public welfare devote themselves entirely to increasing their own personal wealth. Among such a people, seriousness is no longer peculiar to certain men, it becomes a national trait.

Mention is made of small ancient democracies where citizens gathered in public squares with garlands of roses and spent almost all their time in dancing and theatrical performances. I have no more belief in such republics than in that described by Plato; or, if things existed as we are told they did, these supposed democracies must assuredly have been formed of quite different elements from our own and indeed had nothing in common with the latter than the name.

However, one must not suppose that, in the midst of all their efforts, people living in democracies think of themselves as objects of pity; quite the contrary. No men are more attached to their social condition than they are. Life would lose its savor if they were freed of the anxieties which harass them and they appear more attached to their cares than aristocratic peoples to their pleasures.

I wonder why those very democratic nations, while being so serious, sometimes behave in such ill-considered ways.

Americans, who almost always retain a calm bearing and cool appearance, are nevertheless carried away well beyond boundaries of common sense by some sudden passion or rash opinion, so that they commit in all seriousness strangely absurd things.

One should not be surprised by this contrast.

There is one kind of ignorance that comes from extreme publicity. In despotic states, men do not know how to act because they are told nothing; in democratic nations they often act at random because there has been an attempt to tell them everything. The former lack knowledge; the latter simply forget. The principal features of each picture disappear in a mass of detail.

There is no surprise in the unwise remarks sometimes uttered by public figures in free states, and especially democratic states, without compromising themselves, whereas, in absolute monarchies, a few casually dropped words are enough to unmask them forever and ruin them with no hope of recovery.

What I said before explains this. When a man speaks to a large crowd, many of his words are not heard or are immediately blotted out from his hearers' memories but, in the quiet of a silent and unmoving multitude, the slightest whisper strikes the ear.

In democracies, men are never still; a thousand accidental circumstances move them constantly from place to place and almost always something unforeseen, something, so to speak, improvised, prevails in their lives. Hence, they are often forced to do what they have not properly learned to do, to talk about what they have hardly understood and to devote themselves to projects for which they are unprepared by a long apprenticeship.

In aristocracies, everyone has one aim which he constantly pursues; but in democracies, a man's life is more complicated. The mind of one man will almost always embrace several aims at the same time and these are frequently wholly foreign to each other. Since he cannot be expert in all of them, he easily becomes content with half-baked ideas.

When the democratic citizen is not urged on by necessity, he is so, at least, by his longings, for he sees none of the good things around him as completely beyond his reach. So, he does everything in a hurry, is content with approximations, and never stops for more than a moment to reflect upon each of his actions.

His curiosity is both insatiable and cheaply satisfied, for he is anxious to know a great deal quickly rather than to know anything well.

He has hardly any time, and soon loses the taste, for deepening his knowledge.

Thus, democratic nations are serious because their social and political circumstances constantly lead them to think about serious matters, and their actions are ill-considered because they devote but little time or attention to each of these matters.

The habit of inattention has to be regarded as the greatest defect of the democratic character.

CHAPTER 16

WHY THE NATIONAL VANITY OF THE AMERICANS IS MORE RESTLESS AND QUARRELSOME THAN THAT OF THE ENGLISH

All free nations are self-important but national pride does not have the same character in each case. (See Appendix C, p. 856.)

In their relations with foreigners, Americans seem irritated by the slightest criticism and appear greedy for praise. The flimsiest compliment pleases them and the most fulsome rarely manages to satisfy them; they plague you constantly to make you praise them and, if you show yourself reluctant, they praise themselves. Doubting their own worth, they could be said to need a constant illustration of it before their eyes. Their vanity is not only greedy, it is also restless and jealous. It grants nothing while making endless demands. It begs one moment and quarrels the next.

If I say to an American that the country he lives in is beautiful, he answers: "True enough. There is not its like in the world!" I admire the freedom enjoyed by its citizens and he answers: "Freedom is indeed a priceless gift, but very few nations are worthy of enjoying it." If I note the moral purity which prevails in the United States, he says: "I realize that a foreigner, struck by the corruption in all the other nations, will be surprised by this sight." Finally, I leave him to his self-contemplation; but he comes back at me and refuses to leave me until he has prevailed upon me to repeat what I have just said. A more intrusive and garrulous patriotism would be hard to imagine. It wearies even those who respect it.

The English are not at all like that. The Englishman quietly enjoys the real or supposed advantages which, in his view, his country possesses. If he concedes nothing to other nations, neither does he seek anything for his own. Foreigners' criticisms do not affect him at all and their compliments hardly flatter him. His attitude to the whole world is a scornful and contemptuous reserve. His pride needs no nourishment; it lives off itself.

What is remarkable is that two peoples, sprung so recently from the same stock, should feel and speak in ways so diametrically opposed.

In aristocratic countries, great men possess extensive privileges to sustain their pride without any need to rely upon those smaller advantages which accrue to them. Those privileges, having reached them through inheritance, are regarded to some extent as a part of themselves or, at least, as a natural and inherent right. They have, therefore, a quiet sense of their own superiority; they have no thought of boasting about privileges obvious to everyone and denied by no one. There is nothing in these things surprising enough to merit comment. They stand still in the midst of their solitary grandeur, convinced that they are on view to everyone without their needing to show themselves and that no one will attempt to remove them from that position.

When an aristocracy conducts public business, national pride naturally assumes this reserved, casual, and arrogant character which is imitated by all other social classes.

On the other hand, when class distinctions are not very great, the smallest advantages gain in importance. As each person observes around him a million others enjoying identical or similar advantages, pride becomes demanding and jealous; it latches on to wretched details and guards them stubbornly.

In democracies where social conditions are very fluid, men have almost always won only recently the advantages they possess, which causes them to feel an endless satisfaction from publicizing them, from displaying them to others and from testifying to themselves that they do in fact enjoy them. As it can happen at any moment that these advantages can slip away from them, they are constantly anxious and strive to show that they still have them. Men living in democracies love their country after the same manner as they love themselves and transfer the habits of their private vanity to their vanity as a nation.

This restless and insatiable vanity displayed by democratic nations is due both to the equality and to the precariousness of social conditions, to such an extent that the members of the proudest nobility display entirely the same passion in the minor aspects of their lives in which there is something unstable and challenged.

An aristocratic class is always profoundly different from the other classes of the nation due to the scope and permanence of its privileges; but sometimes it happens that several of its members are different only by small fleeting advantages which can be lost or gained any day.

The members of a powerful aristocracy meeting in a capital city or a court have been observed in violent dispute over those frivolous privileges which rely on the whim of fashion or the will of their sovereign. Then they showed exactly the same childish jealousies toward each other which stir men in democracies, the same enthusiasm to grasp the slightest advantages which their equals were disputing and the same need to advertise those they enjoyed, for everyone to see.

If courtiers ever took it into their heads to be proud of their nation, I am quite certain that their brand of pride would possess entirely the same character as is found in democratic nations.

CHAPTER 17

HOW AMERICAN SOCIETY APPEARS BOTH AGITATED AND MONOTONOUS

Nothing seems more likely to arouse and sustain people's curiosity than the appearance of life in the United States. Fortunes, ideas, and laws are constantly altering. Unchanging nature herself appears to change, so greatly is she transformed daily by the hand of man.

In the long run, however, the sight of this agitated community becomes monotonous and, after watching this moving pageant for some time, the spectator becomes bored.

In aristocratic nations, each man is virtually fixed in his own sphere of action; but men are wondrously different with passions, ideas, customs, and tastes basically diverse. Nothing alters, everything differs.

In democracies, on the contrary, all men are alike and perform almost the same tasks. It is true that they are constantly victim to great changes of circumstance but, since the same successes and reverses recur continually, only the names of the actors change because the play is the same. American society appears agitated because men and events are constantly changing; it is monotonous because all the changes are similar.

Men living in democratic ages are very passionate but most of their passions end in love of wealth or derive from it. That is not because their souls are narrower but because the importance of money is really greater at such times.

When every citizen is independent and indifferent to each other, the cooperation of each of them can be obtained only by payment of money, which infinitely multiplies the functions of wealth and increases its value.

When the prestige of what is old has vanished, birth, status, and profession no longer mark the differences between men or scarcely do so; there is thus hardly anything left but money to establish very obvious differences between them or to raise some of them above the common level. Distinction based on wealth increases as all other distinctions disappear or decrease.

In aristocracies, money leads to a few points only on the vast circle of men's desires; in democracies, it seems to lead to them all.

Therefore, usually love of wealth lies at the heart of Americans' actions, either as a principal or a secondary motive, which gives a family likeness to all their passions and soon makes the description of them tiresome.

This constant recurrence of the same passion is monotonous, as are the particular details of the methods used to satisfy it.

In a peaceful and well-ordered democracy like the United States, where neither war nor public office nor political confiscation open the door to wealth, love of money chiefly directs men toward industry. Now, although industry often brings great upheavals and great disasters, it cannot prosper without the support of very orderly habits and a long succession of small

regular acts. Such habits and acts are all the more orderly and
regular as the passion behind them is strong. It may be said that
it is the very violence of their desires which makes Americans
so methodical. It disturbs their minds but disciplines their lives.

What I am saying about America applies to almost all our
contemporaries. Variety is disappearing from the human race;
the same ways of acting, thinking, and feeling occur in every
corner of the globe. That is due not only to the increased contact
between nations and to their closer emulation, but also to the
fact that, in each country, men increasingly discard the ideas
and opinions of a particular class or profession or family and
draw nearer to what is the essence of man, which is everywhere
the same. Thus, they grow alike although they have not copied
one another. They resemble travelers dispersed throughout a
large forest where all the paths end at the same spot. If they all
perceive that central location at the same time and direct their
footsteps toward it, imperceptibly they draw closer together
without seeking or seeing or knowing each other and they will
in the end be surprised to find themselves assembled in the same
place. All nations which take not any particular man but man
himself as the object of their studies and imitations will end up
by adopting the same customs just as these travelers converge
on that central point in the forest.

CHAPTER 18

HONOR IN THE UNITED STATES AND
IN DEMOCRATIC SOCIETIES[1]

Men seem to use two very different methods in assessing the
actions of their fellow men: sometimes they judge them by the
simple notions of right and wrong which are common all over

---

1.   The word *honor* does not always mean the same thing in French.
        Firstly, it signifies the esteem, glory, or respect that one receives from
     one's fellow men: it is in this sense that one is said to *win honor*.
        Secondly, honor signifies the collection of those rules with the help of
     which one obtains this glory, this esteem, and this respect. Thus it is that

the world; sometimes they value them with the aid of very special notions peculiar to one age and one country. It often happens that these two standards differ; sometimes they are in conflict but they never completely coincide or cancel each other out.

Honor, in times when it is at its most powerful, controls men's wills more than their beliefs and even when they obey its commands without hesitation or complaint, they still feel, by some obscure but forceful instinct, the existence of a more general, ancient, and sacred rule which they transgress, although they never cease to acknowledge it. Some actions have been considered both honorable and demeaning. Refusing to fight a duel has often fallen into this category.

I think such happenings may be explained by reasons other than the whim of particular individuals or nations, which has been the reason given hitherto.

Mankind feels certain immutable and universal needs. These have given rise to moral laws which, if they are broken, have naturally carried the idea of guilt and shame in all men's minds everywhere and at all times. To disregard them is *to do wrong*; to obey them is *to do right*.

Within the vast community of mankind, narrower associations have been formed and called nations within which still smaller groups have assumed the name of classes or castes.

Each of these associations represents, as it were, a particular species of the human race and, although no different essentially from the mass of men, stands to some extent apart with needs of its own. These are special needs which alter, to some degree and in certain countries, the way of looking at human behavior and the value attached to it.

Mankind has the universal and permanent interest that men should not kill one another, yet a nation or class might, in special instances, adopt the peculiar and temporary interest of excusing or even honoring homicide.

---

it is said that *a man has always strictly conformed to the laws of honor* or that *he has betrayed his honor*. When writing this particular chapter I have always used the word *honor* in this second sense.

Honor is nothing but this particular rule founded on a particular state of affairs, by means of which a nation or class allots praise or blame.

Nothing is a greater waste of effort for the human mind than an abstraction. So, I hasten on to reveal the facts. An illustration will make my meaning clear.

I shall choose the most extraordinary example of honor that has ever been seen on this earth and the one we know best: that aristocratic honor residing at the heart of feudal society. I shall explain it by means of what I have stated elsewhere and will use this example for a further clarification.

I have no need to examine here when and how medieval aristocracy came into being, why it had become so profoundly separate from the rest of the nation and what had founded and strengthened its power. I take its existence as an established fact and I seek to understand why it regarded most human behavior in such an unusual light.

What strikes me in the first place is that in the feudal world actions were not always praised or condemned for their inherent value but were sometimes appreciated exclusively with reference to the person who performed them or suffered from them, which is repellent to the universal conscience of mankind. Certain acts thus carried no significance, if performed by a commoner, but would dishonor a nobleman; others altered character, if the person affected by them belonged or did not belong to the aristocracy.

When these distinct opinions arose, the nobility formed a separate body within the nation, which it dominated from the inaccessible heights to which it had withdrawn. To sustain this special position which constituted its strength, it not only required political privileges but needed rules of right and wrong tailored for its own use.

That some particular virtue or vice belonged to the nobility rather than to commoners, that such and such an action was neutral when it affected only a peasant and punishable when it had to do with a feudal lord, these were what were often arbitrary matters. But whether honor or shame should attach to a man's actions according to his social status, that was the result of the very constitution of an aristocratic society. In fact that appears the case in all countries which have had an aristocracy. As long as a single trace of this principle remains in force, such peculiarities will be found: to corrupt a colored girl scarcely harms an American's reputation; marrying her dishonors him.

In certain instances, feudal honor insisted on revenge and condemned any forgiveness of insults; in others, it loftily ordered men to rein themselves in and to forget their own desires. It did not make human kindness or gentleness its general rule but praised generosity; it valued liberality more than charity; it allowed men to grow rich from gambling or war but not from work; it preferred great crimes to small earnings. Greed was less a source of disgust than miserliness; it often sanctioned violence while it always viewed cunning and treachery as contemptible.

These strange ideas did not solely arise from the whim of those who invented them.

A single class which has managed to place itself above all the others and works hard constantly to maintain this dominant position should take especial care to respect those virtues which possess nobility and splendor and can easily be combined with pride and love of power. Such a class of men is not afraid to upset the natural order of conscience by placing those virtues before all others. It may even be easy to imagine that they will raise certain bold and brilliant vices above virtues which are quiet and unpretentious. To some extent such a class is hemmed in by its social condition to adopt such principles.

Noblemen of the Middle Ages reckoned military valor as the greatest of all virtues and one which pushed many of those virtues aside.

Feudal aristocracy was born of warfare and for warfare. Its power had been founded by arms and arms maintained it. Nothing, therefore, was more necessary than military courage; it was natural that such courage was glorified above all other virtues. Everything that showed it off, even at the expense of common sense and human kindness was, therefore, approved and often demanded. Only in the details of this system can we see the way men's imagination worked.

That a man should look upon a blow on the cheek as a great insult and should feel obliged to kill in single combat the person who has struck him so lightly is an arbitrary rule; but that a nobleman should not peacefully tolerate an insult and would be dishonored if he allowed himself to be struck without fighting back, that was the result of the very principles and needs of a military aristocracy.

It was, therefore, to some extent true to say that honor exhibited whimsical ways which, however, were always confined within certain necessary limits. These particular rules, called "honor" by our forefathers, appear to me so far from being arbitrary that I would gladly undertake to show that the most confused and bizarre of its injunctions were closely linked to a small number of fixed and immutable needs of feudal societies.

If I were to trace the notion of feudal honor in the political domain, it would be just as easy to explain its manifestations.

The social conditions and political institutions of the Middle Ages were such that power at a national level never governed its citizens directly. Indeed the latter did not exist as far as they could see; each person was aware only of the man he had to obey. Through that man, he was connected unwittingly to all other authorities. In feudal societies all public administration, therefore, moved forward upon the feeling of loyalty to the person of the lord. With the destruction of that, anarchy immediately ensued.

Loyalty to the political leader was, moreover, a feeling whose importance was in daily evidence for the aristocracy since each member of that class was both lord and vassal and had both to give and obey orders.

To remain faithful to one's lord, to sacrifice oneself for him, if needs be, to share his lot in good times and bad, to help him in whatever enterprises he undertook, such were the primary injunctions of feudal honor in political matters. A vassal's betrayal was condemned with extraordinary strictness by public opinion. An especially infamous name was invented for the offence, namely a *felony*.

On the other hand, the Middle Ages reveal few traces of that passion which had such a lively influence upon antiquity; I mean patriotism. The very name is far from ancient in our language.[2]

Feudal institutions concealed the homeland from view and reduced any necessity to love it. The nation was forgotten in the attachment to one man. Hence it was never a strict law of feudal honor to be loyal to one's country.

That does not mean that love of one's country did not exist in our ancestors' hearts but that it was only a kind of weak and hidden instinct, which became stronger and clearer as class distinction has been destroyed and power centralized.

This point is clearly illustrated by the contradictory assessments which European nations have made of different events of their history, according to the generation which made the judgement. The chief stain on the honor of the constable of Bourbon in the eyes of his contemporaries was that he bore arms against his king; what dishonors him most in our eyes is his waging war against his country. We brand such people just as severely as our ancestors but for different reasons.

To clarify my meaning, I have taken feudal honor as my example; its characteristics are more distinct and familiar than any other. I could have taken examples from elsewhere and arrived at the same destination by a different path.

Although we know the Romans less well than we do our own ancestors, nevertheless we know that, when it came to their reputation and dishonor, they held certain peculiar opinions which did not derive solely from their general ideas about right and wrong. Many human actions were regarded by them in a different light according to whether they were dealing with a Roman citizen or a foreigner, a freedman or a slave; certain vices were glorified and certain virtues were elevated above all the others.

"Now, in those times," said Plutarch, in his life of Coriolanus,

2.   The word *patrie* was not used by French authors until the sixteenth century.

"courage was honored and valued in Rome above all other virtues, which is proved by the fact that they named it 'virtus', using the very specific name of virtue as a term to denote a general category, so much so that virtue in Latin came to mean manly valor." Everyone can surely recognize in this the peculiar needs of that extraordinary community which was shaped to conquer the world.

Every nation will add similar observations for, as I have stated above, every time men come together to form a particular social grouping, a rule of honor is immediately set up among them, that is to say, a collection of opinions belonging only to them about what is worthy of praise or blame. The specific habits and interests of this social grouping always produce these particular rules.

This rule applies to some extent to democratic societies as to others. We shall find the proof of this among the Americans.[3]

Among American opinions, we still come across a few scattered notions that have come loose from the ancient European aristocratic idea of honor. These traditional opinions are few in number with no depth of root or strength of influence. They are a religion some of whose churches have been allowed to remain standing but in which one no longer believes.

Amidst these half-obliterated notions of some exotic honor, some new opinions appear on the scene to form what might be termed the American honor of our time.

I have shown how Americans were driven constantly into trade and industry. Their beginnings, their social condition, their political institutions, the very land they live in urge them irresistibly in this direction. They form, therefore, at this time, an almost exclusively industrial and trading community, placed at the heart of a new and boundless country which they are primarily aiming to exploit. That is the characteristic which most particularly distinguishes the American nation of today from all others.

All those quick virtues which tend to give the body of society

3.   Here, I am referring to Americans who live in regions where slavery does not exist. These are the only ones who can present the complete picture of a democratic society.

an orderly pace and to favor business are sure to be held in special honor in this nation. To neglect them is unavoidably to incur public contempt.

All those violent virtues which often dazzle but still more often bring disturbance to society will hold, by contrast, a subordinate position in the public opinion of this same people. These virtues could be disregarded without forfeiting the esteem of one's fellow citizens but if they were acquired one would perhaps risk losing that esteem.

Americans make an equally arbitrary classification of men's vices.

Certain tendencies which appear condemned by common sense and the universal conscience of mankind are in agreement with particular and temporary needs of the American community which blames them only feebly and sometimes praises them; I shall quote particularly the love of money and the secondary tendencies connected to it. To clear, cultivate, and transform the realm of this vast uninhabited continent of his, the American must have the daily support of some energetic passion which can only be the love of money. This love of money has, therefore, never been stigmatized in America and, provided that it does not exceed the limits set by public order, it is held in high esteem. The American calls noble and praiseworthy that ambition which our medieval ancestors used to describe as slavish greed, just as he considers as blind and barbarous frenzy that burning desire for conquest and that warlike spirit which hurled them daily into new battles.

In the United States, fortunes are easily lost and made again. Theirs is a boundless country, full of inexhaustible resources. The people have all the needs and appetites of a growing creature and, whatever their efforts, they are always surrounded by more good things than they can grasp. In a people so placed, the threat is not the ruin of a few individuals, which is soon remedied, but the sloth and apathy of the whole community. The primary reason for their rapid progress, their strength and greatness is their bold approach to industrial undertakings. There, industry is like a vast lottery in which there are a few daily losers but the state is a consistent winner; such a nation is, therefore, bound to view favorably and to respect industrial speculations. Now, any bold undertaking risks the fortune of the man who embarks upon it as well as the fortunes of all those who put their trust in him. Americans, who regard commercial rashness as a kind of virtue, would not be able to condemn any of those who practice it.

That is why, in the United States, a trader who goes bankrupt is viewed with such an unusual degree of indulgence; his honor is not impaired by such an accident. In that, Americans differ not only from European nations but from all contemporary trading nations. Thus, they are unlike any of them in their position or their needs.

In America, all those vices which tend to impair the purity of morals and damage the marriage bond are viewed with a severity quite unknown in the rest of the world. At first sight, this is in strange contrast to the tolerance they show in other areas. One is surprised to come across a moral system both so relaxed and so austere in one and the same nation.

These things are not quite so muddled as one might suppose. American public opinion only gently checks the love of money which promotes great industrial progress and national prosperity; but it is particularly hard on bad morals which divert men's minds from their search for material success and disturb the family harmony which is so vital for business success. To be respected by their fellows, Americans feel forced, therefore, to conform to orderly habits. In this sense, it can be said that living virtuously is with them a point of honor.

American codes of honor are in harmony with the ancient honor of Europe on one point: both rank courage first of all virtues and treat it as the greatest moral necessity for a man to pursue. But they do not conceive of courage in the same light.

In the United States, military courage is not highly prized; the best known and most favorably regarded courage is that which endures the raging ocean to reach port more quickly, which uncomplainingly faces the privations of life in the wilds and that isolation which is harsher than all sufferings; the courage which makes a man indifferent to the sudden loss of a fortune acquired with so much labor and which immediately prompts him to fresh endeavors to gain another. Courage of this kind is vital mainly to the maintenance and prosperity of the American community which holds it in particular esteem and honor. To reveal a lack of it would bring dishonor.

One last characteristic will serve to make the underlying theme of this chapter stand out more clearly.

In a democratic society such as that of the United States, where fortunes are small and insecure, everyone works and work opens all doors; this has turned honor inside out and set it against idleness.

In America, I have sometimes met some rich young men, temperamentally hostile to any difficult exertions, who were obliged to adopt a profession. Their nature and fortune allowed them to stay idle, public opinion forbade it and its imperious order had to be obeyed. On the other hand, among European nations where the aristocracy is still battling against the flood which is carrying it away, I have often seen men constantly goaded on by their needs and desires who yet remained idle so as not to forfeit the respect of their equals and who surrendered more readily to boredom and discomfort than to work.

Everyone can see that both these opposing obligations are two different rules of conduct which stem from the notion of honor.

What our forefathers have termed honor, par excellence, was none other in reality than one of its forms. They gave a generic name to what was only one species of it. Honor exists, therefore, in democratic, as much as in aristocratic, periods. But it will not be difficult to show that in the former it assumes a quite different appearance.

Not only are its demands different but we shall discover that these are smaller in number, less well defined, and more loosely obeyed.

A social grouping is always in a much more peculiar position than a nation. Nothing is more unusual on earth than a small social caste always composed of the same families, such as the aristocracies of the Middle Ages, whose ambition is to concentrate and keep all education, wealth, and power exclusively in their own hereditary hands.

Now, the more the situation of any society is extraordinary, the more numerous its special needs and the more its notions of honor, which correspond to those needs, will multiply.

The requirements of honor will, therefore, always be less numerous in a nation which is not divided into castes than in any other. If there ever come to be nations where it is difficult to discover any trace of class, honor will be limited to a few rules which will be more and more in accordance with the general moral laws of humanity.

Thus the laws of honor will be less odd and fewer in number in a democracy than in an aristocracy. They will also be less clearly defined, which is an inevitable consequence of what has just been said.

Since the characteristic features of honor are less odd and fewer in number, it is often bound to be difficult to discern them.

There are other reasons as well.

In the aristocratic nations of the Middle Ages, the passing of the generations seemed an empty event because each family was like a man who stood still forever and never died; ideas varied hardly any more than social conditions.

Every man in that society, therefore, saw the same objects before his eyes and viewed them in the same light. His eye gradually took in the smallest details and his vision could not fail in the long term to become sharp and accurate. Thus, not only had the men of feudal times very extraordinary opinions of what constituted their honor but each of these opinions assumed a definite and precise shape in their minds.

It could not ever be the same in a country like America where all the citizens are on the move and where society, itself subject to daily modification, changes its opinions according to its needs. In such a country, men have glimpses of the rule of honor but rarely have enough time to consider it attentively.

Were society to stand still, it would even then be difficult to settle the meaning of the word honor.

In the Middle Ages, each social class had its own code of honor so that exactly the same opinion was never accepted at the same time by a significant number of men; this made it possible for it to have a fixed and precise interpretation. This was all the easier as those who used the word, all having an exactly identical and exceptional position, were naturally disposed to agree on all the terms of a law which was tailored expressly for them.

Thus, honor became a detailed and complete code where everything was prescribed and ordered in advance and which always applied a fixed and obvious rule for human actions. In a democratic nation such as America where social classes are indistinct and where society as a whole appears as one single mass composed of elements which, though similar, are not exactly the same, there could never be precise agreement beforehand over what honor allows or prohibits.

Indeed, at the heart of this people, some national needs exist which promote commonly held opinions when it comes to honor; but such opinions never present themselves at the same time, in the same way or with equal force to all citizens; the law of honor exists but often lacks people to interpret it. The confusion is even greater in a democratic country such as France where the different classes which composed the former society come together without managing to mingle closely and introduce each other on a daily basis to diverse and often contradictory notions of honor, where each man, according to his own whim, gives up one set of opinions handed down by his ancestors and retains another. The result is that no common rule can ever be established amid so many arbitrary views. It is then almost impossible to say in advance which actions will be honored, which condemned. Such times are wretched but do not last long.

In democratic nations, when honor is poorly defined, it is, of necessity, less powerful, for a law which is imperfectly understood is difficult to apply with any certainty or firmness. Public opinion, which is the natural and supreme interpreter of the law of honor, if it has no definite guide as to how it should allocate praise or blame, always hesitates in pronouncing judgement. It often manages to contradict itself; often it stands paralyzed and lets things slide.

The relative weakness of honor in democracies is due to several other causes besides.

In aristocratic countries, identical codes of honor are only ever accepted by a few men who are often limited in number and always separated from the rest of their fellow citizens. Honor, in the minds of such men, is associated and identified with the very conception of their own distinctiveness. It is, in their eyes, the peculiar trait of the face they present to the world. They apply its various rules with the enthusiasm of personal involvement and, if I may be permitted the expression, they are passionate about complying with its dictates.

The truth of this becomes clear on reading the medieval law books dealing with trial by combat. There we find that the nobles were bound to use lance and sword in their quarrels, whereas peasants used sticks, "seeing as," state the old law books, "peasants have no honor." That did not mean, as may be imagined today, that these men were to be despised but simply that their actions were not judged by the same rules as the aristocracy.

The first and astonishing fact is that, when honor has so powerful a place, its rules are generally very peculiar, so that men appeared to be the more prepared to obey these rules, the further they appear to depart from common sense. From this, some people have drawn the conclusion that honor derived its strength precisely because it was extravagant.

Both these things in fact come from the same source but one is not derived from the other.

Honor assumes this odd appearance in proportion to the peculiarity of the needs it satisfies and the very few men who feel them and, just because it stands for needs of this kind, it is powerful. Honor is not, therefore, powerful because it is odd, rather it is odd and powerful for the same reason.

I add a further observation. In aristocratic nations, all ranks are different but fixed; each man in his own sphere occupies a place which he cannot leave and where he lives among other men around him tied in the same way. In such nations no one, therefore, can hope or fear that he is not on view; no man is so lowly placed that he has not a stage of his own and no one can avoid praise or blame by living in obscurity.

In democracies, on the other hand, where all citizens are jumbled together in the same constantly fluctuating crowd, public opinion cannot find a toehold; what it latches on to is always vanishing from sight or slipping away. There, honor will thus always be less demanding and less intrusive, for it only operates when seen by everyone. That makes it different from pure virtue which feeds upon itself and is content with its own approval.

If the reader has fully grasped the above, he must have understood that between inequality of social conditions and what we have termed honor, there exists a close and inevitable connection which, if I am not mistaken, has not been clearly pointed out before. I must, therefore, make a final effort to illustrate this properly.

Suppose a nation stands apart from the human race. Aside from certain general needs felt by the whole of humanity, it has concerns and needs peculiar to itself. Immediately, certain opinions of its own will arise to judge what is worthy of praise or blame and these are what its citizens call honor.

Within this same nation, a caste comes to be established, which in its turn separates itself from all other classes and adopts individual needs which, once again, give rise to special opinions. The code of honor belonging to this caste, an odd mixture of the peculiar notions of the nation and the even more peculiar notions of the caste, will be as far removed as can possibly be imagined from the simple and general opinions of men. We have arrived at the furthest point of the argument; let us now return.

With the mingling of ranks, privileges are abolished. The men who make up the nation become alike and equal; thus their concerns and needs become identical and, one by one, all the unusual notions of honor in each caste will vanish. Honor flows entirely from the peculiar needs of the nation itself and stands for its individual personality among other nations.

Finally, if one may suppose that all races will blend into one and all nations of the world reach the point of having the same concerns and needs, with no longer a single characteristic trait to distinguish one from another, then we would entirely cease to attach one conventional value to men's actions which would be seen in the same light by everyone; the common needs of mankind, which each man realizes through his own conscience, would be the yardstick for everyone. Then one would encounter in this world only simple and general notions of good and evil to which the ideas of praise and blame would be associated by a natural and inevitable bond.

Thus, to sum up finally my ideas in one single sentence, it is men's dissimilarities and inequalities which have given rise to honor; as these differences disappear, honor grows feeble and vanishes along with them.

CHAPTER 19

WHY SO MANY AMBITIOUS MEN EXIST IN THE UNITED STATES BUT SO FEW LOFTY AMBITIONS

The first striking thing about the United States is the countless numbers of those seeking to escape from their original social condition and the second is the rarity of lofty ambitions evident in this land where all are actively ambitious. There is not a single American who is not eaten up with the desire to better himself but you meet almost no one who appears to cherish very great hopes or to aim very high. All constantly wish to acquire material possessions, reputation and power; few have a lofty conception of all these things. At first sight that is surprising since nothing in American customs or laws suggests any limit to people's desires or anything to prevent their taking flight in whatever direction they choose.

It seems difficult to attribute this state of affairs to the equality of social conditions for, as soon as this same equality was first established in France, it immediately inspired almost boundless ambition. Yet, I believe that one must seek the cause for this fact mainly in the state of society and the democratic customs of the Americans.

All revolutions increase men's ambitions. Above all, that is true of a revolution which overthrows an aristocracy.

When the former barriers separating the mob from fame and power happen to fall down quite suddenly, there is a violent and universal surge toward these long-envied heights of power which can at last be enjoyed. In this initial triumphant burst, nothing seems impossible to anyone. Not only do desires have no limits, the power to gratify them certainly has almost none either. Amid this general and sudden change of custom and law, in this widespread muddle of men and rules of all kinds, citizens rise and fall with unprecedented speed and the power passes so quickly from hand to hand that no one should give up the hope of seizing it when his turn comes.

Moreover, it must be remembered that those who destroy an aristocracy have once lived under its laws, they have glimpsed its splendors and have been unconsciously influenced by the ideas and opinions it has invented. Therefore, when an aristocracy melts away, its ethos still hovers above the crowd and its instincts are preserved long after its defeat.

Ambitions still remain, therefore, on a grand scale as long as the democratic revolution lasts and it will remain so for some time after it is over.

The recollection of extraordinary events which men have witnessed is not blotted out from their minds in one day. Passions roused by the revolution do not disappear when it has gone. The feeling of instability is perpetuated when order has been established. The notion of easy success outlives the strange changes in fortune which gave it birth. Longings stay on a vast scale when the means of satisfying them are daily less. The liking for large fortunes persists although such fortunes rarely occur and on every side we see the kindling of ungainly and unfortunate ambitions burning secretly and fruitlessly in the hearts of those harboring them.

Gradually, however, the final traces of the struggle fade away and the remnants of aristocracy finally disappear. The mighty events which accompanied its fall are forgotten; peace follows war; the sway of order rises again in the new world; longings match the means of satisfying them; needs, ideas, and opinions are in harmony; men end up at the same level and democratic society is finally settled.

If we observe a democratic nation which has reached this state of permanence and normality, we shall see a sight quite different from the one we have just been contemplating and we shall have no difficulty in judging that, if ambition is magnified while social conditions are becoming equal, it loses that characteristic when equality has been achieved.

As great wealth is divided up and learning has expanded, no person is entirely deprived of education or material possessions. Since the privileges and the disqualifications of class have been abolished and men have broken forever the bonds which once held them fixed, the idea of progress settles in everyone's mind, the desire to better oneself takes root at once in everyone's heart, and every man wishes to quit his station. Ambition is the universal feeling.

But if equality of social conditions gives all citizens a few resources, it stands in the way of any one of them having very extensive resources and for this reason desires are necessarily confined within fairly narrow limits.

In democracies, ambition is, therefore, passionate and sustained but usually it cannot aim very high and life is normally spent eagerly coveting small prizes which are within reach.

What chiefly diverts men in democracies from lofty ambitions is not their scanty wealth but the strenuous daily efforts required to increase it. They strain their faculties to the utmost to achieve paltry results, which soon cannot fail to narrow their vision and restrict their powers. They could be a lot poorer and yet be greater.

The small number of very wealthy citizens in a democracy does not invalidate this rule. A man who rises gradually to wealth and power contracts in the course of all this effort habits of prudence and restraint which he cannot afterwards shake off. One cannot enlarge one's mind as one does a house.

Much the same observation applies to the sons of this same man who indeed are born into a high social position although their parents were humble; they have grown up amid opinions and ideas which it is difficult later for them to avoid. It is likely that they will inherit both their father's instincts and his property.

On the other hand, it may happen that the poorest offshoot of a powerful aristocratic family displays a vast ambition because the traditional attitudes of his race and the general spirit of his caste will for some time still maintain him in a position which exceeds his fortune.

The other impediment men of democratic ages encounter, which makes it far from easy to launch into large-scale ambitions, is the time that must elapse before they are in a position to undertake them. "It is a great advantage to be a man of quality," said Pascal, "since that allows a man of eighteen or twenty to be on his way to success whereas another man could have to wait until he is fifty, which is a clear gain of thirty years." Those thirty years are not normally available to ambitious men in a democracy. Equality, which allows each of us to reach any height, prevents our doing it at any speed.

In a democratic society, as elsewhere, there is only a certain number of huge fortunes to be made and, since the careers which lead to them are open without distinction to every citizen, everyone's progress is bound to be slow. As candidates seem virtually alike and it is difficult to choose from them without violating the principle of equality, which is the supreme law of democratic societies, the prime idea is to make them all walk at the same pace and to inflict the same tests upon them.

Therefore, as men become more alike and the principle of equality has permeated more quietly and deeply the institutions and customs of the country, the rules of personal advancement become more inflexible and advancement itself slower. The difficulties of reaching an eminent position increase.

Out of hatred for privilege and there being too many aspirants to choose from, all men, whatever their capacities, must finally climb up the same rungs to the top and must submit without distinction to a mass of petty preliminary tests, in the process of which their youth disappears and their imagination is snuffed out. The result is that they despair of ever being able to enjoy fully the good things on offer and, on reaching at last the point where they could achieve something extraordinary, they have lost the taste for it.

In China, where equality of social conditions is a deep-rooted and ancient tradition, no man moves from one public office to another without taking an examination. Such a test takes place at every step of his career and this idea is so fixed in the customs of the people that I recall having read a Chinese novel in which the hero, after many ups and downs, at last reaches his loved one's heart by taking a difficult examination. Lofty ambitions breathe uncomfortably in such an atmosphere.

What I am stating about politics extends to everything; equality everywhere produces the same results; even where no law regulates and impedes men's progress, competition achieves the same end.

In a well-established democratic society, great and rapid promotions are therefore rare and represent exceptions to the rule. Their very rarity allows men to forget how few of them there are.

Men living in democracies end up by realizing all these truths; in the long run, they perceive that the legislator opens up a boundless field of action in which everyone may take a few easy steps but no one can delude himself that progress will be rapid. Between them and the great object of their final desires, they see a mass of minor intermediate obstacles which they must slowly negotiate; such a prospect lying before their eyes tires and discourages their ambition. So they give up these distant and ambiguous hopes in order to seek less lofty delights which are easier to reach and are closer to home. The law sets no limits to their horizons but they do so for themselves.

I have said that great ambitions were rarer in democratic times than in aristocracies; I must add that when, despite these natural obstacles, they do arise, they have a quite different appearance.

In aristocracies the progress of ambition is often extensive but it does have fixed limits. In democratic countries its field of action is usually very narrow but, once those narrow bounds are exceeded, there are no apparent limitations to hold it back. As men are weak, isolated, and constantly on the move and as precedent has little sway and laws last for so short a time, resistance to novelty is feeble and the body of society never stands very straight or firm. The result is that, when ambitious men once have power in their grasp, they believe they can dare to do anything and, when it slips from their grip, they immediately contemplate overthrowing the state in order to recover their loss.

That gives great political ambitions a violent and revolutionary character, which it seldom exhibits to the same extent in aristocratic societies.

A mass of modest and very reasoned ambitions from the midst of which burst from time to time a few ill-controlled desires on a grand scale: such is the usual state of affairs in democratic nations. Hardly ever does one encounter a well-balanced and moderate ambition which is at the same time vast.

Elsewhere I have demonstrated by what hidden means equality exalts in the human heart a passion for material pleasures and a love of the present moment, to the exclusion of all else; these various instincts mingle with the sentiment of ambition and stain it, so to speak, with their colors.

It is my opinion that the ambitious men in democracies busy themselves less than those in other countries with concerns and judgements about what is to come; the present alone engages and absorbs their attention. They rapidly complete a great number of projects rather than erect a few lasting monuments; they much prefer success to fame. What they require from men above all is obedience; what they long for above all is power. Their manners almost always fall below the social position they reach, which means that very often they carry some very coarse tastes over into their extraordinary wealth and that their rise to supreme power was seemingly to guarantee easier access to trivial and vulgar pleasures.

I believe it necessary nowadays to purge ambition, to control it, and keep it in proportion but it would be very dangerous to seek to starve it or restrict it overmuch. One must attempt to hedge it round with severe limits which it will never be allowed to exceed but to be careful not to hamper too much its flight within those permitted boundaries.

In my view, democratic societies have much less to fear from the boldness than from the meanness of desires. What seems more frightening to me is that ambition might lose its energy and greatness amid the constant trivial preoccupations of private life and that human passions might abate, at the same time lowering their sights; the result is that the progress of society lacks energy and aspiration from day to day.

I, therefore, think that the leaders of these new societies would be wrong to seek to lull their citizens to sleep with too flat and quiet a happiness and that it is good occasionally to give them difficult and dangerous tasks, so as to rouse their ambition and give it a stage upon which to perform.

Moralists are constantly complaining that the favorite failing of our age is arrogance.

In a certain sense that is true: in fact everyone believes himself better than his neighbor and no one agrees to obey his superior. But in another that is quite false: for this same man who tolerates neither subordination nor equality, nonetheless has so low an opinion of himself that he thinks he is born only to indulge in vulgar pleasures. He readily wallows in mediocre longings without daring to tackle any lofty projects; indeed, he can scarcely conceive of them.

Far, therefore, from believing that one should recommend humility to our contemporaries, I should like us to strive to give them an enlarged idea of themselves and their kind. Humility is far from healthy for them. What they most lack, in my view, is pride. For that failing I would readily relinquish several of our trivial virtues.

CHAPTER 20

THE TRADE OF SEEKING OFFICIAL POSITIONS IN CERTAIN DEMOCRATIC NATIONS

In the United States, as soon as a citizen has some measure of education and some financial resources, he seeks to grow rich in commerce or industry, or he buys a stretch of forest and turns into a pioneer. All he asks of the state is not to trouble him while he is working and to guarantee the fruit of his labor.

Among most European nations, when a man begins to feel his strength and increase his desires, his first idea is to get an official appointment. These contrasting results, springing from the same cause, deserve a moment's consideration.

When public appointments are few in number, poorly paid, and insecure, whereas careers in industry are many and lucrative, men's fresh and impatient ambitions, created by the principle of equality, turn from every side toward industry and not administration.

But if, while classes are moving toward equality, men's education stays incomplete, or their minds diffident, or commerce and industry are hampered in their upward growth so that they offer only a slow and difficult path to wealth, citizens, in despair at improving their lot by themselves, rush to the head of state clamoring for his help. To increase their comfort at the expense of public funds seems to them, if not the only available path, at least the easiest and the most open for all of them to escape from a situation which they find unsatisfactory: the hunt for official positions is taken up by more men than any other trade.

Such is bound to be the case especially in the great centralized monarchies where the number of paid posts is extensive and the livelihood of public servants is relatively secure, so that everyone entertains the hope of obtaining a job which they may enjoy in peace as if it were an inheritance.

I shall not suggest that this universal and excessive desire for official appointments is a great social ill, that it destroys the spirit of independence in every citizen and spreads a mercenary and slavish mood throughout the body of the nation; nor shall I make the observation that a trade such as this creates only unproductive activity which unsettles the country without adding to its wealth: all that is readily understood.

But I do want to note that the government which supports such a tendency risks its own peace and puts its very existence in great jeopardy.

I realize that, in a time like ours, when we see the gradual decline of the love and respect which used to be associated with power, it may seem necessary to governments to bind a man to them by closer ties of self-interest and that it may appear convenient to use his very passions to keep him in order and silent; but that arrangement cannot last long and what may look for a certain time a source of strength is bound, in the long term, to prove a great cause of upset and weakness.

In democratic countries, as in all others, the number of public appointments ends up by being limited but, in these same nations, the number of ambitious men is not limited; this number constantly increases with a regular and irresistible progress as social conditions grow equal. The only check is the shortage of men.

So when administration is the only outlet for public ambition, the government ends up, inevitably, facing a permanent opposition for its task is to satisfy ever limitless desires with limited means. One must be quite certain that the most difficult of all nations to control and govern is one full of supplicants. Whatever the efforts of its leaders, they could never satisfy such a people and the fear always exists that the constitution of the country might finally be overturned, changing the shape of the state, simply for the purpose of making official positions vacant.

The sovereigns of our day who strive to attract to themselves all those new desires aroused by equality and to satisfy them, will, therefore, end up, if I am not mistaken, by regretting having ever embarked upon such an enterprise; they will one day realize that they have risked their own power by making it so necessary and that it would have been a safer and more honest course to teach every one of their subjects the skill of providing for themselves.

CHAPTER 21

WHY GREAT REVOLUTIONS WILL HAPPEN LESS OFTEN

A nation which has lived for centuries under a class and caste system does not reach a democratic state of society other than through a long series of more or less painful transformations, involving violent efforts and accompanied by many changes of fortune in the course of which property, opinions, and power are subject to rapid changes.

Even after this great revolution has come to an end, those revolutionary habits of mind created by its upheaval can still be seen for a long time, followed by profound disturbances.

As all this is taking place at a time when social conditions are becoming more equal, the conclusion is that a hidden connection and secret tie exists between equality itself and revolutions so that the former cannot occur without the latter.

On this point reason seems in agreement with experience.

In a nation where classes are virtually equal, no obvious tie unites men or holds them firmly in place. No one of them has the permanent right or the power to issue orders, nor is anyone bound to obey. But each person endowed with some education and a few resources may choose his own path to follow separately from all his fellows.

The very reasons which lead to the independence of citizens from each other daily prompt them to new and restless longings and constantly goad them on.

So it seems normal to believe that, in a democratic society, ideas, things, and men are for ever bound to change shape and position and that democratic ages will witness times of swift and unceasing transformations.

Is that in fact so? Does equality of social conditions usually and permanently drive men toward revolution? Does it possess some disturbing principle which prevents society from settling down and persuades citizens endlessly to alter their laws, beliefs, and morals? I believe not. The subject is important; I beg the reader to follow my argument closely.

Almost all the revolutions which have changed the shape of nations have been undertaken to reinforce or destroy inequality. Pushing aside subsidiary reasons which have instigated great upheavals among men, you will almost always come across inequality. Either the poor have aimed to snatch the property of the rich or the rich have attempted to enslave the poor. Thus, if you could found a state of society in which everyone had something to keep and little to take from others, you would have done much for the peace of the world.

I am well aware that among a great democratic people, you always come across very rich and very poor citizens; but the poor, instead of forming the huge majority of the nation as always happens in aristocracies, are few in number and the law has not bound them together by the ties of a wretchedness which has no remedy and passes from generation to generation.

The rich, on their side, are thinly scattered and powerless; they have no conspicuous privileges; their very wealth, no longer bound up synonymously with land, is imperceptible and, as it were, invisible. Just as the race of poor men has gone, so has that of the wealthy; the latter daily emerge from the crowd and constantly return to it. Thus, they do not form a separate class easily identified and plundered. Moreover, since they are attached to the mass of their fellow citizens by a thousand hidden threads, the people can scarcely attack them without harming themselves. Between these two extremes in democratic societies lives a countless multitude of almost identical men who, neither exactly rich nor poor, own sufficient property to desire order but not enough to rouse the envy of others.

Such men are the natural opponents of violent upheavals; their stability keeps everything above and below them in peaceful equilibrium and maintains a settled social state.

It is not that they are content with their current fortune or that they feel a natural horror of a revolution whose spoils they might share without suffering the disasters; on the contrary, they desire to get rich with unparalleled eagerness but their problem is to know whom to plunder. Exactly the same state of society which endlessly prompts their desires contains those desires within necessary boundaries, for it gives men more freedom to change and less interest in doing so.

Not only do men in democracies feel no natural inclination for revolutions, they are afraid of them.

Any revolution threatens, to a lesser or greater degree, the tenure of property. Most men in democratic countries are property owners; not only do they own property but they live in social conditions in which men attach the greatest value to that property.

On scrutinizing each of the classes making up society, one can see without difficulty that none feels the passions aroused by property more keenly or tenaciously than the middle class.

The poor often do not trouble much about their possessions because their suffering from what they lack is greater than their enjoyment of the little they have. The rich have many other passions to satisfy than their pursuit of wealth; besides, the lengthy and burdensome management of a great fortune sometimes ends up by diminishing their feeling for its charms.

But men living comfortably off at an equal distance from wealth or impoverishment set great store by their possessions. Since they are still never far from poverty, they observe its severities at close quarters and fear them; they are separated from poverty by nothing but a scanty inheritance which immediately attracts their hopes and fears. At every moment their interest in it grows because of the constant anxieties it involves and their daily efforts to increase it keep them attached to it. The idea of surrendering the smallest portion of it is unbearable and they regard the loss of the whole inheritance as the worst of misfortunes. Now, equality of social conditions constantly increases the number of these enthusiastic and anxious small property owners.

Thus in democratic societies, the majority of citizens fail to see what they might gain from a revolution but are keenly aware, all the time and in a thousand ways, of what they might lose.

I have said in another part of this work how the equality of social conditions naturally drove men toward industrial and commercial careers and how it increased and expanded the ownership of property. I have indicated how it inspired in each man a burning and sustained desire to increase his material wealth. Nothing opposes revolutionary passions more effectively than both these things.

The final outcome of a revolution may serve industry and commerce but its first effect will almost always be to destroy industrialists and traders because it cannot fail to alter, in the first instance, the general habits of consumption and to overturn, for a brief time, the balance between supply and demand.

Moreover, I know of nothing more hostile to revolutionary conditions than commercial ones. Commerce is a natural opponent of all violent passions. It likes moderation, delights in compromise, carefully avoids angry outbursts. It is patient, flexible, subtle, and has recourse to extreme measures only when absolute necessity obliges it to do so. Commerce makes men independent of each other, gives them quite another idea of their personal value, persuades them to manage their own affairs, and teaches them to be successful. Hence it inclines them to liberty but draws them away from revolutions.

In a revolution, those who own personal property have more to fear than everyone else for, on the one hand, their property is easy to seize and, on the other, it may completely disappear at any moment. Owners of land have less to fear because, while they lose the income from their estates, they at least hope to retain the land itself as circumstances change about them. Thus, some are much more frightened than others at the spectacle of revolutionary upheavals.

Nations are, therefore, less inclined to revolution as personal property increases and becomes more widespread amongst them and as the number of owners multiplies.

Moreover, whatever a man's profession and the type of property he owns, one characteristic is common to all.

No one is entirely satisfied with his present fortune and all men strive daily to increase it in a thousand different ways. Consider any one of them at any time of his life and you will see him absorbed in some new plan tailored to increase his personal comfort. Do not talk to him about the concerns or rights of mankind; this minor domestic project preoccupies all his thoughts for the moment and persuades him to postpone political disquiet to some other time.

This not only prevents men from causing revolutions but also deters them from wishing to do so. Violent political passions have but little hold over men who have devoted their entire lives to the pursuit of comfort. The enthusiasm they display in small matters brings a calm in momentous undertakings.

Occasionally, it is true, in democratic societies enterprising and ambitious citizens do appear whose deep longings cannot be satisfied by following the conventional path. These men love and demand revolutions but find it difficult to instigate them unless extraordinary events come to their aid.

There is no advantage in struggling against the spirit of one's century or country and, however powerful a man may be, it is hard for him to persuade his fellow men to share opinions and ideas which run counter to the generally accepted desires and beliefs. One should not suppose, therefore, that, once equality of social conditions has become a long-established and undisputed fact, molding customs to its dictates, men will easily allow themselves to rush into perilous risks, through following some rash leader or bold innovator.

Not that they oppose him openly with the help of well-contrived schemes or even by means of a premeditated plan of resistance. They fight him without great energy, sometimes even applaud him, but do not become his followers. Secretly, their apathy is opposed to his fire, their conservative concerns to his revolutionary instincts, their homely tastes to his passion for adventure, their common sense to the flights of his genius, their prose to his poetry. For one brief moment, after a thousand efforts, he manages to rouse them, only for them soon to escape him and fall back under the drag of their own weight, as it were. He wears himself down in his efforts to stir this indifferent and preoccupied crowd and is soon reduced to helplessness, not because he is conquered but because he is isolated.

I do not claim that men living in democratic societies are by nature stationary; on the contrary, I think that continuous activity lies at the heart of such societies and that none of its members knows what rest is. But I believe that men's activities are governed by certain boundaries which they hardly ever exceed. Daily, they alter, change, and renew things of secondary importance; they take great care not to touch fundamentals. They like change but fear revolutions.

Although Americans are constantly modifying or repealing some of their laws, they are far from displaying any revolutionary passions.

From the promptness with which they check themselves or calm down just when public agitation starts to become threatening and passions seem most excited, it is easy to see that they fear a revolution as the greatest of misfortunes and that every one of them is secretly determined to make great sacrifices to avoid one. No country in the world has a more lively or concerned feeling for property than the United States and nowhere else does the majority display less inclination toward those doctrines which threaten to impair in any way at all the manner in which property is owned.

I have often noticed that theories which are by their nature revolutionary, in that they can be realized only by a complete and sometimes sudden upheaval in the rights of property or the status of persons, are infinitely less to people's liking in the United States than in the great monarchies of Europe. If they are promoted by a few men, they are rejected with an instinctive horror by the mass of the population.

I have no fear of stating that most of the maxims customarily called democratic by the French would be banned by American democracy. That is easily understood. In America, their ideas and passions are democratic; in Europe we still have passions and ideas which are revolutionary.

If America ever experiences great revolutions, they will be instigated by the presence of blacks on American soil: that is to say, it will not be the equality of social conditions but rather their inequality which will give rise to them.

When social conditions are equal, each man readily lives a life independent of others and forgets the crowd. If legislators of democratic nations did not seek to correct this fatal tendency or indeed encouraged it, thinking that it diverts citizens from political passions, thus distancing them from revolutions, they could well end up by bringing about the evil which they wish to avoid and a time might come when the disorderly passions of a few men, with the help of the stupid selfishness and small-mindedness of the majority, would ultimately force the main body of society to suffer strange social changes.

In democratic societies, only small minorities look for revolutions but even they may sometimes succeed.

I am not saying that democratic nations are sheltered from revolutions; I say simply that the social state of such nations does not carry them in that direction, but rather keeps such happenings at a distance. Democratic nations, when left to themselves, do not become involved in grand adventures; they are drawn toward revolutions only when their attention flags; occasionally they suffer from them but they never instigate them. I would add that, once they have been allowed to gain education and experience, they never let them happen.

I know full well that, in this context, public institutions may themselves have great influence; they can encourage or restrain the instincts bred by the social state. I do not, therefore, maintain, I repeat, that a nation is sheltered from revolution simply because social conditions are equal in the community. But I do believe that, whatever the institutions of such a nation, revolutions on the grand scale will always be infinitely less violent and less common than is supposed, and I can easily discern a political state which, when joined to a principle of equality, would create a society more stationary than we have ever known in the Western world.

What I have just said about events applies in part to ideas.

Two things are surprising in the United States: the great flexibility of most human behavior and the unusual stability of certain principles. Men are constantly on the move while the human mind appears almost to stand still.

Once an opinion has spread abroad on American soil and taken root, it would seem that no power on earth is strong enough to eradicate it. In the United States, universal doctrines in religion, philosophy, morality, and even politics show no variation or, at least, are only modified by a hidden and often imperceptible process; even the crudest of prejudices take an incredibly slow time to remove, as men and events endlessly wear them away.

I hear it said that democracies are, by nature and custom, ever changing their opinions and ideas. That may be true of small democracies as we saw in the ancient world when whole communities met together in a public square to be carried away by an orator's eloquence. I have seen nothing similar in the great democracy which dwells on the other shore of the Atlantic Ocean. What has struck me in the United States is the difficulty experienced in getting an established idea out of the heads of the majority and stopping them from following a leader they have chosen. Neither writings nor speeches can have much effect; experience alone can do it and even there it has sometimes to be repeated.

At first sight that is surprising but closer scrutiny provides an explanation.

I do not consider it as easy as is supposed to eradicate the prejudices of a democratic nation, or to change its beliefs, or to substitute new religious, philosophic, political, or moral principles for those already established; in a word, to bring about great or frequent shifts in men's minds. Not that the human mind is idle there, for it is constantly active; but it is much more involved in the infinite variations that flow from well-known principles and in the discovery of new variations than in seeking new principles themselves. It shows great agility at turning on the spot, rather than plunging forward in any swift and direct movement; a gradual and sustained extension of its orbit of power is preferred to a sudden change of position.

Men with equal rights, education, and wealth, who, in a word, enjoy the same social status, must have needs, customs, and tastes which are hardly dissimilar. As they look at objects from the same viewpoint, their minds naturally incline toward similar ideas and, although each of them may differ from his fellows and have his own beliefs, they all end up, unconsciously and unintentionally, holding a certain number of common opinions.

The more closely I observe the effects of equality upon intelligence, the more I am convinced that the intellectual anarchy we see around us is not, as several people suppose, the natural condition of democratic nations. I think that one should rather regard it as an accident peculiar to their youthfulness and something which is evident only during a transitional period when men have already broken the ancient ties which held them together and are still amazingly different in origin, education, and manners. The result is that, having preserved quite different ideas, instincts, and tastes, nothing prevents them from airing them. Men's principal opinions become similar as social conditions grow more alike. That seems to be the general and permanent law; the rest is accidental and temporary.

I think that it will rarely happen that, inside a democratic society, a man suddenly comes up with a system of ideas far removed from the one adopted by his contemporaries. If such an innovator were to appear, I suppose that he would experience at first considerable difficulty in making himself heard and still more in persuading people to believe him.

When social conditions are almost the same, one man is not easily to be persuaded by another. As all are closely in touch with each other and have absorbed the same things together and lead the same lifestyle, they are not naturally inclined to take one of their number as a guide or to follow him blindly. People scarcely ever take on trust the opinion of anyone equal to themselves.

Not only is confidence in the knowledge of certain individuals weakened in democratic nations, as I have stated elsewhere, but the general notion of the intellectual superiority achieved by some man or other soon dims.

As men increasingly grow alike, the doctrine of intellectual equality gradually creeps into their beliefs and it becomes harder for any innovator to gain and exercise great power over the mind of a nation. In such societies sudden intellectual revolutions will, therefore, occur less frequently for, casting a glance over the history of the world, it is much less the strength of an argument than the authority of a name which has produced the mighty and swift changes in men's opinions.

Note also that, as men living in democratic societies are not bound in any way to each other, each man has to be convinced

individually, whereas, in aristocratic societies, it is sufficient to
be able to influence a few individuals for the rest to follow. If
Luther had lived in an age of equality and had not been heard
by lords and princes, he would perhaps have found it more
difficult to change the face of Europe.

Not that men living in democracies are completely convinced
by nature of the certainty of their opinions or are unwavering
in their beliefs; they often entertain doubts which, in their view,
no one can resolve. During such an era, the human mind may
sometimes be quite willing to change its position but with nothing to give it any powerful impetus or direction, it wavers and
does not move on.[1]

When one has won the trust of a democratic nation, it is still
a difficult achievement to gain its attention. It is very hard to
make the men of democracies listen when one is not talking
about them. They fail to listen to what is said to them because
they are always very busy with the things they are doing.

In fact, few men are idle in democratic nations. Life passes
surrounded by noise and excitement; men are so busy acting
that little time remains for them to think. What I especially wish
to stress is that not only are they busy but also that they are
passionately interested in their business. They are constantly on

1.   If I look for what state of society is the most favorable to the great
     revolutions of the mind, I find it somewhere between the total equality of
     all citizens and the total separation of the different classes.

        Under a caste system, generations follow one another without men ever
     changing their position; some expect nothing more and others expect
     nothing better. The imagination falls asleep in the middle of this silence
     and universal stillness. The idea of change no longer suggests itself to the
     human mind.

        When the class system has been abolished and conditions become almost
     equal, all men are constantly on the move but each of them is isolated,
     independent, and weak. This is very different from the previous state of
     affairs; however, it is similar in one respect—great revolutions of the
     human mind are extremely rare.

        But between these two extremes in the history of nations, there is an
     intermediary period, a glorious and restless period where conditions are
     not so fixed that intelligence stultifies or so unequal that some men exercise
     great power over the minds of others and where a few can modify the
     beliefs of all. It is then that powerful reformers appear and, at a stroke,
     new ideas change the face of the world.

the move and every one of their actions engrosses their minds; the burning zeal they devote to their work extinguishes the flame of enthusiasm for ideas.

It is, in my view, very arduous to arouse the enthusiasm of a democratic nation for any theory which has no obvious, direct, and immediate connection to the daily occupations of life. Such a nation does not, therefore, give up its ancient beliefs, for it is enthusiasm which heaves the human mind out of the beaten track and instigates great intellectual as well as political revolutions.

Thus, democratic nations have neither the time nor the inclination to seek out new opinions. Even when they happen to doubt the ones they hold, they nevertheless hold on to them because they would need too much time and inquiry to change them. They keep them, not because they are certainly true, but because they are accepted.

There are also other and even more powerful reasons which stand in the way of any easy change coming about in the principles of a democratic nation. I have already mentioned them at the beginning of this book.

If, at the heart of such a nation, the influence of each individual is weak and almost non-existent, the power of the mass over each individual mind is very extensive. I have given the reasons for this elsewhere. What I wish to say here is that it would be wrong to suppose that this depends solely upon the type of government and that the majority is bound to lose its intellectual power if it loses its political power.

In aristocracies, men often possess a greatness and strength of their own. Whenever they find themselves at variance with the majority of their fellows, they withdraw into themselves to find support and consolation. Such is not the case with democratic nations; there, public approval seems as vital as the air they breathe and being at odds with the population as a whole is, so to speak, no life at all. The masses have no need to use the law to bend those who think differently from them. Disapproval is enough. The feeling of isolation and powerlessness immediately overwhelms them and drives them to despair.

Whenever social conditions are equal, the opinion of all bears down with a great weight upon the mind of each individual, enfolding, controlling, and oppressing him. This is due much more to the constitution of society than to its political laws. As all men grow more alike, each individual feels increasingly weak in relation to the rest. Since he can find nothing to elevate himself above their level or to distinguish himself from them, he loses confidence in himself the moment they attack him; not only does he mistrust his own strength but he even comes to doubt that he should have rights and is close to accepting that he is in the wrong, since the greater number of his fellows assert this fact. The majority has no need to compel him; he is convinced by them.

However the powers of a democratic society are organized and weighted, it will always, therefore, be very difficult for a man to believe what the mass of the people reject or to profess what they condemn.

All this grants a marvelous stability to beliefs.

Whenever an opinion has taken hold in a democracy and has become established in the minds of the majority, it thereafter exists in its own right and persists without effort because no one attacks it. Those who had initially rejected it as false eventually acknowledge its general acceptance and those who continue to fight against it within their own hearts conceal their dissent, taking great care not to involve themselves in a dangerous and purposeless contest.

It is true that, when the majority in a democracy changes its mind, it may choose to bring about sudden and strange revolutions in men's minds. However, it is very hard for it to change its mind and almost as difficult to say for sure that such a change has taken place.

It happens sometimes that time, circumstances, or the isolated efforts of individuals ultimately shake or destroy a belief little by little, without any outward sign of change. Opposition has not come out into the open; no conspiracy has been formed to wage war against it. One by one, its supporters silently abandon the field; each day a few of them drift away until in the end only a small group of believers still remains.

In that event, the belief still prevails.

As its opponents continue to say nothing or only stealthily exchange their opinions with others, they are unable to ascertain that a great revolution has taken place and in this state of uncertainty they make no moves. They observe and remain silent. Most people have ceased to believe but still look as if they did and this empty ghost's publicly held opinion is enough to freeze innovation to the spot and to keep opponents silent and respectful.

We live at a time which has witnessed the most rapid changes in the minds of men; however, it might happen that the leading opinions of society will soon be more stable than at any previous time in our history. Such a time has not arrived but perhaps it is near.

As I examine more closely the needs and natural feelings of democratic nations, I am persuaded that, if ever equality is established universally and permanently in society, intellectual and political revolutions on a grand scale will become more difficult and less frequent than is supposed.

Because men in democracies always appear nervous, uncertain, out of breath, ready to change their minds and situation, it is supposed that they are suddenly about to change their laws, take up new beliefs, and adopt new customs. The thought does not occur that, if equality leads men toward change, it promotes interests and tastes which need stability for their fulfillment. It pushes men on while holding them back; it goads them forward while rooting them to the ground; it inflames their longings while limiting their strength.

This is not obvious at first sight: the passions which keep the citizens of democracies apart from each other are clear enough but the hidden force which restrains and unites them is not visible at first glance.

Can I be bold enough to say this amid the ruins which I see about me? What I fear above all for succeeding generations is not revolutions.

If citizens continue to shut themselves more and more narrowly within the sphere of small domestic concerns in a state of restless agitation, there is the fear that they will, in the end, become practically removed from those great and powerful public emotions which, while disturbing nations, do develop and renew them. When I see property changing hands so quickly and love of property becoming so restless and passionate, I cannot help fearing that men will reach the point of regarding every new theory as a threat, every innovation as a vexatious disturbance, all social progress as the first step toward a revolution and that they will refuse absolutely to move at all lest they are swept away. I confess to the dread that they will ultimately allow themselves to be so overtaken by a craven love of immediate pleasures that concern for their own future and that of their descendants may vanish, and that they will prefer to follow tamely the course of their own destiny rather than make a sudden and energetic effort to set things right when the need arises.

It is generally believed that new societies will change shape day by day but my fear is that they will end up by being too unalterably fixed in the same institutions, the same prejudices, the same customs, with the result that the human race may stop moving forward and grind to a halt, that the mind of man may forever swing backwards and forwards without fostering new ideas, that man will wear himself out in lonely, futile triviality and that humanity will cease to progress despite its ceaseless motion.

CHAPTER 22

WHY DEMOCRATIC NATIONS HAVE A NATURAL DESIRE FOR PEACE AND WHY DEMOCRATIC ARMIES NATURALLY SEEK WAR

The same concerns, fears, and passions which distance democratic nations from revolutions also alienate them from war; the military and revolutionary spirit weakens at the same time and for the same reasons. The ever-increasing number of landowners devoted to peace, the development of personal wealth which is so swiftly swallowed up by war, that kindness of manners, that gentleness of heart, that inclination to pity which is inspired by equality, that cool rationality which leaves little room for sensitivity to the violent and poetic excitements which accompany arms, all these reasons combine to quench the military spirit.

I think one can accept it as a general and constant rule that, in civilized nations, warlike passions will become less frequent and less intense, as social conditions approach a level of equality.

However, war is an accident to which all nations are subject, democracies as well as others. Whatever the devotion of these nations to peace, they must be ready to repel aggression or, in other words, they must have an army.

Fortune, which has conferred such special favors upon the inhabitants of the United States, has placed them in the middle of a desert where, one can almost say, they have no neighbors. A few thousand soldiers are enough but that is something entirely American and not typical of democracies.

The equality of social conditions, along with the resulting customs and institutions, do not exempt a democratic nation from the obligation of maintaining an army, which always exerts a very considerable influence on the destiny of the country. It is, therefore, of unusual importance to discover the natural instincts of the men who join an army.

In aristocratic nations, especially those in which birth is the only source of rank, inequality is as established in the army as in the nation; the officer is of noble birth; the soldier is a serf. The former is necessarily called upon to give orders, the latter to obey them. In aristocratic armies, therefore, a soldier's horizons are much restricted. Those of the officers are no less limited.

An aristocratic body is not only part of a hierarchy, it always contains a hierarchy within itself where the people composing it are ranked one above the other in a particular and unchanging arrangement. One man is naturally called by birth to command a regiment, another a company. Once they have reached these ultimate goals of their hopes, they come to a halt of their own accord and feel satisfied with their lot.

First of all, in aristocracies there is one strong reason which weakens an officer's desire for promotion.

In aristocratic nations, an officer, apart from his rank in the army, also occupies a high position in society; he views the former as almost always secondary to the latter; the nobleman, in adopting a career in the army, is less devoted to ambition than to a kind of duty imposed upon him by birth. He enters the army in order to spend the idle years of his youth in the service of honor and to be able to bring back to his family and fellows a few creditable recollections of military life. But his major objective is not to acquire property, reputation, or power from this career since he already enjoys these advantages in his own right without leaving home.

In the armies of a democracy every soldier may become an officer, which extends the desire for promotion to everyone and which opens up the bounds of military ambition immeasurably.

From his point of view, the officer sees nothing that naturally and necessarily limits him to one rank rather than another and each rank has immense importance in his eyes because his position in society almost always depends upon his rank in the army.

In democratic nations, an officer may have nothing but his pay and cannot expect any other claim to distinction than his military honors. Each time he changes his duties, his fortune changes and, in some sense, he becomes a different man. What was a secondary consideration in the armies of an aristocracy has thus become the chief element, the be-all and end-all of life itself.

Under the old French monarchy, officers were always addressed by their titles of nobility. These days only their military titles are used. This small change in the use of language is enough to illustrate that a great revolution has taken place in the make-up of society as well as in the army.

Within democratic armies, the desire for promotion is almost universal; it is keen, persistent, and constant; it is fed by all other desires and is only quenched with life itself. Now, it is easy to see that promotion in times of peace must be slower in democratic armies than any other armies in the world. Since the number of commissions is naturally limited and competitors unlimited, since the inflexible rule of equality bears down on everyone, no one can make rapid progress and many are unable to move at all. Thus, the need for promotion is greater and the opportunities less than elsewhere.

All the ambitious men within a democratic army are, therefore, vehemently keen on war because war clears out the ranks to allow an attack on the rule of seniority which is the sole privilege natural to democracies.

Thus, we reach this bizarre conclusion that of all armies, the ones most keen upon war are those in democracies and that, of all the nations, the ones with the greatest attachment to peace are democracies. What finally makes this extraordinary is that equality produces both these conflicting results.

Being equal, citizens constantly cherish the desire and harbor the possibility of altering their social condition and increasing their prosperity: this inclines them to love peace, which allows industry to prosper and enables each man to bring his little undertakings to a quiet conclusion. On the other hand, this same equality, because it values military honors for those pursuing a career in the army and makes these honors available to all, inspires soldiers to dream of battlefields. In either case, the fluttering of the heart is the same, the taste for enjoyment is as insatiable, the ambition is equal; only the means of gaining satisfaction is different.

These conflicting positions of nation and army expose democratic societies to great dangers.

When a nation loses its military spirit, a military career immediately ceases to be respected and warriors sink to the bottom rank of public servants. They are not greatly esteemed and are no longer understood. The reverse of what takes place in aristocratic ages then occurs. It is no longer the leading citizens but the lowliest who enter the army. Men surrender to military ambitions only when no others are allowed. This sets up a vicious circle from which it is difficult to escape. The top people in a nation avoid a military career because it carries no prestige and it carries no prestige because the top people of the nation no longer take it up.

One must not, therefore, be surprised if democratic armies are often seen to be restless, prone to complaint, and dissatisfied with their lot, although their physical condition is normally much more comfortable and discipline less strict than in all other armies. The soldier feels that he occupies an inferior position and his wounded pride ends up by giving him a taste for war which will make him needed, or a liking for revolutions during which he hopes to win by force of arms political influence and that personal respect now denied him.

The make-up of democratic armies increases the fear of this last-mentioned danger.

In democratic society, almost all citizens have property to safeguard but democratic armies are generally led by men of the people. Most of these have little to lose when civil disturbances break out. The mass of the nation is naturally much more frightened by revolutions than in aristocratic times but the leaders of the army are much less fearful of them.

Moreover, as I have said before, since in democracies the wealthiest, best educated, and ablest citizens hardly ever take up a career in the military, the army collectively ends up by forming a small nation apart with a lower level of intelligence and cruder manners than the nation at large. Now, this small, uncivilized nation possesses the weapons and it alone knows how to use them.

The danger in democracies from the turbulent spirit of the army is indeed increased by the peaceful temper of the citizens; nothing is as dangerous as an army amid a nation with no taste for war; the citizens' excessive liking for quiet daily exposes the constitution to the mercy of soldiers.

It can thus be said in general terms that, if democratic nations are naturally inclined toward peace through their interests and feelings, they are constantly pulled toward war and revolutions because of their armies.

Military revolutions, which are hardly ever a threat in aristocracies, are always to be feared in democracies. Such perils should be reckoned among the most threatening of all those which their future existence faces; politicians should relentlessly direct their attention to finding a remedy for this evil.

When a nation feels its internal peace disturbed by the restless ambitions of its armed forces, its first thought is to provide a goal for this inconvenient ambition by going to war.

I have no desire to speak ill of war which almost always broadens a nation's mental horizons and lifts its heart. In some instances it is the only factor which can prevent the excessive development of certain tendencies which equality naturally produces and one must regard it as the necessary cure of certain deep-seated illnesses to which democratic societies are liable.

War has considerable advantages but one must not delude oneself that it can lessen the danger I have just mentioned. It simply keeps it at a distance for it to return in a more terrible form when war is over, for the army tolerates the frustrations of peacetime even less once it has experienced war. War would only be a remedy for a people always seeking glory.

I anticipate that any warlike prince who might arise in the great democratic nations will find it easier to pursue conquests with his army than to make his army live in peace after its victories. There are two things which will always be difficult for a democratic nation to do: beginning and ending a war.

Besides, if war has some particular advantages for democracies, it entails, by contrast, certain dangers for them which aristocracies have no need to fear to the same extent. I shall quote only two examples.

If war pleases the army, it annoys and often depresses the countless numbers of citizens whose trivial passions daily require peace for their satisfaction. Thus it runs the risk of causing, in another form, the very upheaval which it should anticipate.

Any lengthy war in a democratic country places freedom under threat. Not that we need entertain the precise fear that, after each conquest, the victorious generals will seize sovereign power by force after the manner of Sulla or Caesar;[a] the danger is of another kind. War does not always surrender democratic nations to military rule but it invariably and immeasurably increases the powers of civil government, into whose hands it almost unavoidably concentrates the control over all men and all things. If it does not lead to tyranny by sudden violence, it leads men gently there by habituation.

All those who wish to destroy freedom within a democratic nation should realize that the most reliable and the most rapid means of achieving it is war. That is the first principle of knowledge.

One remedy obviously at hand, when the ambitions of officers and soldiers become threatening, is to increase the number of commissions on offer by increasing the size of the army. Such a move relieves the immediate problem but makes the future all the more difficult.

Increasing the size of the army may well produce a lasting effect in an aristocracy because, there, military ambition is restricted to one class of men and every man has well-defined limitations. The result is that almost all those who harbor such ambitions may well satisfy them.

But in a democracy, no gain is achieved by increasing army numbers because the number of ambitious men grows in exact proportion to that of the army itself. Those whose wishes have been granted in the formation of new ranks are immediately replaced by a crowd of new recruits who cannot be so satisfied; the first group soon renew their complaints, for the same restless spirit which prevails among the citizens of a democracy emerges in the army where it is not the reaching of a particular rank that a soldier wants but constant promotion. Although desires are not overly strong, they persist. A democratic nation which enlarges its army achieves only a temporary weakening of military ambition, which soon returns more threatening than ever because the number of those harboring such feelings has increased.

My own opinion remains that a restless and disturbed spirit is a fundamental flaw in the very constitution of democratic armies and that cure is beyond hope. Democratic legislators should not delude themselves that they have found a way of organizing the army which will, of itself, have the power to calm and restrain the military; their efforts would wear them down to no effect with no hope of reaching their goal.

Not that the remedies for these defects of the army are to be found in the army itself but in the country.

Democratic nations have a natural dread of disturbance and tyranny. The important aim is to turn these feelings into considered, intelligent, and stable tastes. When citizens have finally learned to use freedom peacefully and productively and have perceived its blessings, when they have conceived a manly love of order and have freely bowed to discipline, these very citizens will embark upon a military career, taking with them unconsciously and, almost in spite of themselves, these same attitudes and customs The general spirit of the nation, infiltrating the particular spirit of the army, tempers the opinions and desires aroused by military life, or, by the all-powerful influence of public opinion, totally represses them. Once citizens are educated, disciplined, decisive, and free, you will have orderly and obedient soldiers.

Any law which, by repressing the turbulent spirit of the army, tended to lessen the spirit of freedom at the heart of the nation and to obscure the concept of law and rights, would defeat its object. It would do much more to foster the establishment of military tyranny than to damage it.

After all, whatever measures are taken, a large army within a democracy will always constitute a great threat; the most effective way of lessening this threat will be to reduce the army; but that is a remedy not available for all nations to use.

CHAPTER 23

WHICH IS THE MOST WARLIKE AND REVOLUTIONARY CLASS IN DEMOCRATIC ARMIES

The essential feature of a democratic army is how numerous it is in proportion to the number of people who provide its manpower; I shall say more on the reasons for that later.

On the one hand, men living in times of democracy seldom choose a career in the army.

Democratic nations are, therefore, soon led to give up

voluntary recruitment, in order to fall back on conscription. The needs of their social condition force them to adopt the latter method and one may readily predict that all nations will do so.

Military service being compulsory, the responsibility is shared equally and indiscriminately by all citizens. That also is a necessary result of the social condition and ideas of these nations. Their government may do more or less what it likes provided that its orders apply simultaneously to everyone. Resistance usually results from the unfairness of a burden and not from the burden itself.

Now, since military service is shared by all citizens, the obvious consequence is that each of them remains on active service for only a few years.

Thus, it is in the nature of things that the soldiers spend only a brief time with the army whereas, in most aristocratic nations, soldiering is a profession the soldier adopts or has imposed upon him for life.

This has important consequences. Among the soldiers of a democratic army, some acquire a taste for the military life but the majority, being forced reluctantly into service, are ever ready to return home and do not consider themselves as seriously committed to the life of a soldier and think only of quitting. These men do not acquire the wants and only ever half-heartedly share the passions which that career inspires. They submit to their military duties but their hearts remain tied to the concerns and longings which engaged them in civilian life. Thus, they never adopt the ethos of the army; rather they carry the spirit of their social life over into the army and preserve it there. In democratic nations, it is the ordinary soldiers who remain most like civilians and it is upon them that national customs have the firmest hold and public opinion the strongest influence. It is through the ordinary soldiers above all that one may hope to inspire an army with the love of freedom and respect for the law which have been so successfully introduced into the nation itself. The opposite is true of aristocratic nations where eventually soldiers have nothing in common with their fellow citizens among whom they live as aliens and often as enemies.

In aristocratic armies, the officers represent the conservative element because they alone have retained close ties with civilian society and never abandon their desire to take up their place in it again sooner or later; in democratic armies that is true of the soldiers for exactly the same reasons.

On the other hand, it often happens in these same democratic armies that officers acquire tastes and desires quite different from those of the rest of the nation, all of which is understandable.

In democracies, the man who becomes an officer breaks all his ties with civilian life; he leaves it forever and has no interest in returning. His real country is the army since his rank represents all that he possesses; as a result, he follows the fortunes of the army, rising and falling with it and henceforth setting all his hopes upon the army alone. Since the officer has needs very distinct from those of his country, it may happen that he longs for war or works for revolution at just the time when the nation most desires stability and peace.

However, some factors do modify his warlike and restless spirit. Although ambition is universal and constant in democratic nations, we have seen that it rarely occurs on a grand scale. The man who emerges from the second class of the nation and has succeeded in rising through the lower ranks of the army to the position of officer, has made an immense advance. He has a foothold in a sphere superior to the one he occupied within civilian society and he has achieved rights which most nations will always regard as belonging to him permanently.[1] He is quite ready to pause after this great effort and to think of enjoying his victory. The fear of risking what he possesses is already weakening his heart's desire to gain what he still has not got. Having crossed the first and greatest barrier to his advancement, he resigns himself more patiently to the slowness of further progress. This cooling of ambition will intensify as he rises further up the ranks and realizes he has more to lose. If I am not

---

1.   The position of officers is, in effect, much more secure in democratic nations than in others. The less an officer feels he is worth in himself, the greater the comparative importance of his rank and it is necessary and just that the law guarantees his enjoyment of this.

mistaken, the least warlike and least revolutionary section of a democratic army will always be its leaders.

What I have just said of the officers and soldiers does not apply at all to the numerous class which in all armies comes between these two, that of non-commissioned officers.

This class of non-commissioned officers which, before this century, had not acted a part in history, is, in my opinion, destined from now on to play a role.

Like the officer, the non-commissioned officer has in his own mind broken all his ties with civilian society; like him, he has made the military his career and, possibly to even a greater degree, he centers all his hopes on it. But, unlike the officer, he has not yet reached a secure and high enough position in which he has the leisure to pause and breathe freely while he waits for his next advancement.

By the very nature of his functions which cannot alter, the non-commissioned officer is condemned to an obscure, narrow, and precarious existence. As yet, all he sees in the military life is its dangers; all he knows are the privations and obedience which are harder to tolerate than its dangers. He suffers all the more from his current discomforts because he knows that the constitution of both society and army allows him to break free of them; in fact, he may become an officer any day. Then he will give orders, receive honors, freedom, rights, pleasures; not only does the object of his aspirations loom large but he is never sure of reaching it until it is in his grasp. His rank possesses nothing irrevocable; he is daily subject entirely to the decisions of his commanding officers; the necessity of discipline imperiously requires him to act thus. One slight mistake or whim can always deprive him of the fruit of several years' hard work in a flash. His achievements are as nothing until he reaches his coveted rank. Only then does he feel he has started his career. A man spurred on without respite by his youth, needs, passions, the spirit of the time, and his hopes and fears cannot fail to be aflame with a desperate ambition.

So, the non-commissioned officer longs for war; he longs for it all the time and at any price; if he does not get his wish, he looks to revolutions which would suspend the authority of rules and would give him the hope, amid the confusion of political passions, of removing his officers and taking their place. It is not impossible for him to bring about such events for their common origin and way of life enable him to exercise great influence over the soldiers, although his passions and desires are very different from theirs.

It would be wrong to think that the different attitudes of officer, non-commissioned officer and soldier are peculiar to a particular time or country. They manifest themselves in all eras and in all democratic nations.

In every democratic army, the non-commissioned officer will always least represent the peaceful and orderly spirit of the country and the soldier will best represent it. The soldier will bring the strengths and weaknesses of national attitudes into military life; he will reflect a faithful image of the nation. If the nation is ignorant and weak, he will let himself be drawn by his leaders into disorderly behavior either unconsciously or even against his will; if it is enlightened and energetic, the soldier himself will restrain his officers.

CHAPTER 24

WHAT MAKES DEMOCRATIC ARMIES WEAKER THAN OTHER ARMIES AT THE OUTSET OF A CAMPAIGN AND MORE DANGEROUS IN PROLONGED WARFARE

Any army runs the risk of defeat at the beginning of a campaign which follows a long period of peace; any army engaged in a lengthy war has a good chance of victory: this truth applies especially to democratic armies.

The military profession in aristocracies, being a privileged career, is honored even in peacetime. Men of great talent, education, and ambition take it up; the army is, in every respect, on a level with the nation or often even above it.

On the other hand, we have seen among democratic countries how a nation's elite gradually moves away from a military career in order to seek respect, power, and, above all, wealth by other routes. After a long period of peace (and in democratic ages peace lasts for a long time), the army is often inferior to the nation itself. War catches it in this state and, until war has wrought a change, this is a perilous time for both country and army.

I have shown how seniority is the supreme and unbending rule for democratic armies in peacetime. As I have said, that does not stem simply from the constitution of armies but from that of the nation itself and it will always happen.

Moreover, the officer gains his reputation in such nations from his rank in the army, which procures him all the social respect and comfort he enjoys; he does not withdraw from the army nor is he superannuated until near the end of his life.

The result of these two reasons is that, when a democratic nation finally goes to war after a long period of peace, all the leading officers are found to be old men. I am not simply singling out the generals but also the subordinate officers, most of whom have stood still or have managed to advance step by step. On taking a close look at a democratic army after a long period of peace, one is surprised to find that all the soldiers are barely out of childhood and all the leaders are in their declining years, which results in the former's lack of experience and the latter's lack of energy.

This is an important cause of defeats, for the primary condition of successful leadership in war is youth. I would never have dared to say so had not the greatest captain of modern times not said as much.

Those two causes do not have a similar effect on aristocratic armies.

As promotion is governed more by right of birth than by seniority, a certain number of young men always feature in all levels of the army and they bring to warfare all the early vigor of body and mind.

In addition, since men seeking military honors in an aristocratic nation have a guaranteed place in civilian society, it rarely happens that they wait for the onset of old age before leaving the army. Having devoted the most vigorous years of their youth to an army career, they retire of their own accord and wear away their remaining maturer years at home.

A lengthy period of peace not only fills democratic armies with elderly officers but it also instils in all officers habits of body and mind which render them ill-suited to warfare. The man who has lived long in the peaceful and lukewarm atmosphere of democratic manners at first has great difficulty in adapting himself to the rough work and stern duties imposed by war. If he does not lose completely his taste for arms, at least he assumes a way of life which stops him from being victorious.

In aristocratic nations, the ease of civilian life exerts less of an influence upon military manners because, in such nations, the aristocracy leads the army. Now, an aristocracy, however deeply it is involved in luxurious pleasures, always pursues several other passions than those of personal comfort and is willing to make a temporary sacrifice of that comfort the better to satisfy those passions.

I have pointed out the extreme slowness of promotion in democratic armies in times of peace. At first, officers tolerate this state of things with impatience; they become agitated, anxious, and desperate but in the longer term most of them resign themselves to it. The most ambitious and resourceful of them leave the army; the others, levelling down their tastes and wishes to the mediocrity of their lot, end up by looking upon the life as a soldier from a civilian point of view. What they value most are the comfort and stability that go with it; they build the entire prospect of their future upon the guarantee of this small provision and all they ask is the ability to enjoy it in peace.

Thus, not only does a lengthy peace fill democratic armies with elderly officers but it often also instils the instincts of old men into those who are still in the full flush of youth.

Equally, I have pointed out how a military career is held in low esteem and attracts few recruits in democracies in peacetime.

This public disapproval is a very heavy burden on the morale of the army. Their spirits are weighed down by it and, when war breaks out, they cannot recover their spring and energy immediately.

Aristocratic armies do not reflect such a reason for moral weakness. Their officers never lose their self-esteem nor the respect of their fellow countrymen because, apart from their importance as soldiers, they are aware of their own personal importance.

Even if the influence of peace were felt upon both armies in a similar way, the results would still be different.

When aristocratic army officers have lost the spirit of warfare and the desire for promotion in their military career, they still command a certain respect for the honor of their class and retain an ingrained habit of being leaders and of setting an example. But when democratic army officers no longer have a liking for war and military ambition, they have nothing left.

I think, therefore, that a democratic nation undertaking a war after a long peace runs more risk of defeat than any other nation but it should not allow itself to be downcast by its setbacks, for its army's prospects of success increase with the very prolongation of the war.

When war has lasted long enough finally to have wrenched every citizen from his peacetime activities and has brought disaster to his small-scale enterprises, those very passions which made him attach so much value to peace will turn toward war. When war has destroyed the whole of industry, it becomes itself the great and only industry and those enthusiastic and ambitious desires spawned by equality direct all their various efforts toward its demands. That is why those very democratic nations which are so hard to drag on to the battlefield often perform such marvelous feats once weapons have successfully been placed in their hands.

As war increasingly draws attention to the army and great reputations and huge fortunes are seen to be made in so short a time, the nation's elite adopts a career in arms; every naturally enterprising, proud, and warlike man, not only from the aristocracy but from the entire nation, is drawn in this direction.

Since the number of rivals for military honors is large and war propels every man into his intended place, great generals always emerge in the end. A long war has the same effect upon a democratic army as a revolution has upon the nation itself. It shatters the rules and fosters the rise of unusual men. Those officers, whose body and soul have grown old in times of peace, are pushed aside to withdraw or die. In their stead a crowd of young men already hardened by war push forward with inflated and ambitious desires. These men look to continual promotion at any price; others come after them with the same passions and desires; then still more follow in numbers restricted only by the size of the army. Equality allows all to be ambitious while death makes sure that there are continuing opportunities to satisfy that ambition. Death constantly levers open the ranks to create vacancies, closing and opening career prospects.

Moreover, there is a hidden connection between military procedures and democratic manners which is revealed by war.

The men of democracies have a natural and passionate desire to obtain quickly what they long for and to enjoy it without effort. Most of them love risk and fear death much less than obstacles. This is the attitude they bring to their conduct of trade and industry and this same attitude, when transferred to the battlefield, leads them to be willing to expose their lives to danger in order to secure in a moment the rewards of victory. No achievement satisfies the imagination of a democratic nation more than the brilliant and sudden greatness of war, won without effort by risking only one's life.

Consequently, while the self-interest and tastes of the citizens in a democracy keep war at a distance, their habits of mind prepare them for success in it; they easily become good soldiers as soon as they have been torn away from their own concerns and comfort.

If peace is particularly damaging to democratic armies, war does secure advantages totally denied to other armies. These advantages, at first barely perceptible, cannot fail to procure them victory in the end.

If an aristocratic nation in conflict with a democracy does not destroy it in the opening campaigns, it always runs the considerable risk of being defeated. (See Appendix D, p. 857.)

CHAPTER 25

DISCIPLINE IN DEMOCRATIC ARMIES

It is a very widespread opinion, especially among aristocratic nations, that the great social equality prevailing in democracies ends up by making soldiers independent of officers, which thus destroys the bond of discipline.

That is a mistake for, in fact, there are two kinds of discipline which should not be confused.

When the officer is a nobleman and the soldier a serf, the one rich and the other poor, the one educated and strong, the other ignorant and weak, the tightest bond of obedience can easily be established between these two men. The soldier is broken in to military discipline, even, so to speak, before entering the army, or rather, military discipline is merely the completion of social enslavement. In aristocratic armies, soldiers quite easily become virtually insensitive to everything except the orders of their leaders. They act without thought, they triumph without passion, and die without complaint. In this condition, they are no longer men but still very fearsome animals trained for war.

Democratic nations are bound to despair of ever obtaining such blind, detailed, resigned, and unvarying obedience from their soldiers as aristocratic nations can impose upon them with no effort at all. The state of society does not prepare men for this and they would run the risk of losing their natural advantages by wishing artificially to acquire it. In democracies, military discipline should not attempt to obliterate men's creative freedom; it can only hope to control it so that the resulting obedience, though less ordered, is more eager and more intelligent. It is rooted in the very will of the man who obeys it; it relies not only upon instinct but also upon reason and, consequently, will automatically grow stricter as danger makes this necessary. The discipline of an aristocratic army is apt to relax in wartime because it is founded upon habit which is upset by war. But the discipline of a democratic army is strengthened in the face of the enemy because soldiers see very clearly the need to be silent and to obey to achieve victory.

These nations which have achieved the most considerable things in war have known no other discipline than that of which I speak. Among ancient peoples, only free men and citizens were accepted in the army; these men were little different from one another and were used to treating each other as equals. In that sense, the armies of antiquity can be called democratic even though they sprang from an aristocracy; consequently, a kind of familiar brotherhood existed between officer and soldier. A reading of Plutarch's *Life of Great Commanders* convinces us of this. There the soldiers speak constantly and very freely to their generals who are ready to listen and reply to whatever their soldiers have said. They were led much more by word and example than by any constraint or punishments. Their leaders were considered as companions as much as superiors.

I do not know whether Greek and Roman soldiers ever perfected the small details of military discipline to the same degree as the Russians but that did not prevent Alexander[a] from conquering Asia, or Rome the world.

CHAPTER 26

A FEW REMARKS ON WAR IN DEMOCRACIES

When the principle of equality develops, not simply in one single nation but simultaneously in several neighboring peoples, as in Europe at the present time, the inhabitants of those different countries, despite the dissimilarity of language, customs, or laws, are still agreed on this one point, that equally they dread war and long for peace.[1] It is to no avail that ambitious or angry

---

1. I think it unnecessary to draw the attention of the reader to the fact that the fear European peoples have of war should not be attributed simply to the progress made by equality among them. Independently of this constant cause, there are several other accidental causes which are very influential.

princes take up arms, for a kind of universal apathy and goodwill calms them down in spite of themselves and makes them drop their swords; wars become less frequent.

As equality develops to the same degree in a good number of countries and impels their inhabitants toward industry and trade, not only do their tastes grow alike but their interests become so mixed and entangled that no nation can inflict evils upon others which do not rebound upon itself and they all end up by regarding war as a disaster almost always as serious for victor as for vanquished.

Thus, on the one hand, it is difficult in democratic times to draw nations into conflict but, on the other, it is almost impossible for two of them to wage war in isolation. The interests of all of them are so intertwined, their views and needs so similar, that no single country could rest in peace while the others are so disturbed. Wars, therefore, become less frequent but spread over a larger area once they break out.

Democratic neighbors not only grow alike in certain respects, as I have just stated; they end up by resembling each other in almost all respects.[2]

Above all, I shall mention the extreme lethargy which the wars of the Revolution and the Empire have left behind them.

2.   This is not just because these nations have the same social condition but because this same social condition is such that it encourages men to imitate each other and share each other's identity.

When citizens are divided into castes and classes, not only do they differ the one from the other, but they have neither the taste nor the desire to resemble each other; on the contrary, everyone seeks more and more to keep his opinions intact and his habits his own, to remain himself. The spirit of one's separate individuality is very strong.

When a state of social democracy exists in a nation, that is to say that there no longer exist at its heart either castes or classes, and all citizens are more or less equal in education and possessions, the human spirit takes a contrary path. Men resemble each other and they become annoyed in some way when they do not resemble each other. Far from wanting to preserve their own individual distinguishing features, they seek to abandon these so as to blend in with the masses which alone represent, in their view, what is right and what is strong. The spirit of one's separate individuality is almost destroyed.

In aristocratic times, even those who are naturally similar aspire to

Now, this similarity between nations has very important consequences as far as war is concerned.

When I ponder why the Swiss Confederation of the fifteenth century inspired fear in the greatest and most powerful European nations, whereas, at the present time, its power is exactly proportionate to the size of its population, I realize that the Swiss have become similar to all their surrounding neighbors who now resemble the Swiss. The result is that numbers alone form the difference between them and victory is bound to go to the biggest battalions. One of the consequences of the democratic revolution in Europe is, therefore, to make numerical strength matter most on the field of battle and to force all the smaller nations to join themselves to bigger states, or at least to adopt the political principles of the latter.

Since numerical strength is the determining factor in victory, each nation should, as a result, direct all its efforts toward bringing as many men as possible on to the battlefield.

When one was able to enlist a category of soldier superior to all others, such as the Swiss infantry or the French cavalry of the sixteenth century, one never considered it necessary to raise very large armies, but such is no longer the case when all soldiers are as effective as each other.

The same cause which prompts this new need also provides the means of satisfying it, for, as I have said, when all men are alike, they are all weak. The power of society is naturally much stronger in democracies than anywhere else. These nations, just as they feel the need to enroll the whole male population into the army, also have the power to do so. The result is that, in

---

create imaginary differences between themselves. In democratic times, even those who are not similar ask only to become so and copy each other, so much is the mind of every man always drawn along with the general momentum of humanity.

Something similar may also be observed between nations. Two nations having the same aristocratic social condition may remain utterly distinct and very different, because the spirit of aristocracy promotes individuality. But two neighboring nations could not share the same democratic social condition without also adopting similar opinions and manners, because the spirit of democracy encourages men to become alike.

ages of equality, armies seem to grow in size as the military spirit disappears.

In the same periods, the methods of waging war are also changed by the same causes.

Machiavelli[a] observes in *The Prince*: "It is much more difficult to subdue a nation with a prince and barons for leaders than a nation led by a prince with slaves." To avoid giving offense, let us say "public officials" instead of "slaves" and we shall then be able to apply an important truth to the matter in question.

It is very difficult for a great aristocratic nation to conquer its neighbors or to be conquered by them. It cannot conquer them because it is never able to assemble all its forces or keep them together for long; and it cannot be conquered because the enemy comes across small pockets of resistance everywhere which halt its progress. I may compare war in an aristocratic country to war in a mountainous region: the defeated can find abundant opportunities to rally their forces and to make a stand in new positions.

Exactly the opposite occurs in democratic nations which are readily able to gather their available forces on the battlefield and, when the nation has wealth and a large population, it finds victory easy to achieve. But once it has suffered defeat and its territory is invaded, it has few resources left; if its capital has been seized, the nation is lost. The explanation for this is obvious. Since each citizen on his own is very isolated and very weak, no one can either defend himself or offer a rallying point to others. Nothing is strong in a democracy except the state; as the military power of the state is shattered by the destruction of its army and its civil power is paralyzed by the capture of its capital, what is left is simply a disorderly and impotent crowd unable to struggle against the well-organized power which is attacking it. I realize that the danger can be reduced by creating regional freedoms and, consequently, regional authorities but such a remedy is never enough.

Not only will the population then be unable to continue fighting but the fear is that they will not even want to try.

According to the law of nations adopted by civilized peoples, the purpose of wars is not to seize the property of private individuals but to get possession of political power. Private property is destroyed only by accident and to achieve the latter objective.

When an aristocratic nation is invaded after its army has been defeated, the nobles, even though they are also the wealthy, prefer to go on defending themselves individually rather than submit, for, if the conqueror were to remain master of the country, he would snatch their political power, which they value even more than their worldly goods. So, they would rather fight than be conquered, for that is the greatest of disasters, and they easily carry the people with them because the people have long been used to follow and obey them and, besides, they have almost nothing to lose in the war.

But in a nation where equality of social conditions is the order of things, each citizen enjoys only a small share of political power and often no share at all; on the other hand, all are independent and have property to lose; as a result, they are much less afraid of conquest and much more afraid of war than an aristocratic nation. It will always be very difficult to persuade a democratic population to take up arms when hostilities have reached its own territory. That is why it is necessary to provide such peoples with the rights and political drive which will instil into each citizen some of those concerns which inspire the nobles in aristocratic countries.

The princes and other leaders of democracies would do well to remember this. Only a passion for freedom which has become ingrained can carry the day against a deep-set passion for personal comfort. I can imagine no better preparation for conquest after a defeat than a democratic nation without free institutions.

In times gone by, men embarked upon campaigns with few soldiers, to fight minor skirmishes and to conduct lengthy sieges. Now men engage in great battles and, as soon as they have a free path before them, they rush upon the capital so as to end the war with a single blow.

Napoleon is said to have discovered this new tactic but it did not depend upon one man, whoever he might be, to create this idea. Napoleon's method of conducting a war was suggested to him by the social conditions of his day and succeeded because it was wonderfully suited to those conditions and he was the first man to put it into practice. Napoleon is the first man to have traveled at the head of an army from capital to capital along a route opened before him by the ruins of feudal society. It is permissible to believe that, if this remarkable man had been born three hundred years earlier, he would not have derived the same fruits from his method, or rather, he would have employed a quite different one.

I shall add no more than a few words about civil wars, for I am afraid I shall tire the reader's patience.

Most of my remarks concerning foreign wars apply with even greater force to civil wars. Men living in democratic countries have no natural inclination for military ways; sometimes they adopt them when they have been reluctantly dragged on to the battlefield, but to rise in a spontaneous body and to confront willingly the wretched conditions of war and especially those of a civil war is a course of action democratic men are not likely to take. Only the most adventurous of citizens would agree to rush into such risks; the bulk of the population would stay quiet.

Even if the population were willing to act, it would not be easy to do so, for men would not find in their hearts those ancient and well-established influences which they would agree to obey, nor any leaders well enough known to rally, discipline, or lead the discontented, nor any political authorities below the level of national government which might exercise an effective resistance against their opponents.

In democratic countries the moral power of the majority is immense and the physical forces at its disposal are out of all proportion to those which can at first be united against it. Therefore, the party which occupies the seats of the majority, speaks in its name, and deploys its power, will immediately and without difficulty triumph over all private resistance. It does not allow it even the time to spring into life; it nips it in the bud.

Those who, in such nations, wish to instigate an armed rebellion have no other recourse than to seize by surprise the whole machine of government as it stands, which can be achieved by a single raid rather than by a war. For, once a regular war has been declared, the party representing the state is almost always sure to win.

The only case where a civil war might spring up would be when the army separates into two parts, one raising the standard of rebellion and the other remaining loyal. An army constitutes a small, tightly knit society which is very vigorous and able to supply its own needs for a certain time. The war might be bloody but not lengthy for the rebel army would draw the government over to its side either by a simple demonstration of its power or by its first victory, which would end the war. Otherwise a struggle would ensue when that part of the army which did not have the support of the organized power of the state would soon disperse of its own accord or be destroyed.

We can, therefore, accept as a general truth that, in ages of equality, civil wars will become much less frequent and less protracted.[3]

3. It should be understood that I am speaking here about *sovereign* democratic nations and not confederated democratic nations. In confederations, as the predominant power always resides, despite any pretense, with the state governments and not the federal governments, civil wars are but foreign wars in disguise.

PART 4
THE INFLUENCE EXERCISED
BY DEMOCRATIC IDEAS
AND OPINIONS ON
POLITICAL SOCIETY

I would not be fulfilling the object of this book if, after demonstrating the ideas and opinions prompted by equality, I did not, in conclusion, indicate the general influence these very opinions and ideas may exert upon the government of human societies.

To achieve this, I shall be forced to go over old ground but I hope that the reader will not refuse to follow me when well-known paths lead him toward some new truth.

CHAPTER I

EQUALITY NATURALLY GIVES MEN A LIKING FOR FREE INSTITUTIONS

Equality, which makes men independent of each other, persuades them to adopt the habit and liking for following their own persuasion when it comes to their private affairs. This complete independence, which they enjoy in relation to their equals and in their private lives, inclines them to view all authority with a jaundiced eye and soon promotes the idea and love of political liberty. Men living in such times advance, therefore, upon an incline which naturally leads them toward free institutions. Choose any man among them at random and delve down, if possible, to his basic instincts; you will discover that, of all the different forms of government, the one he first entertains and values the most is that whose leader he has elected and whose actions he controls.

Love of independence is the first and most striking feature of all the political effects caused by equality of social conditions and the one which frightens timid spirits most. Nor can it be said that they are completely mistaken in such a fear because anarchy does have a more fearful appearance in democratic countries than elsewhere. As soon as citizens cease to influence each other and the national authority holding them in their place begins to falter, it would seem that disorder must instantly reach its climax and that, as each citizen moves aside, the fabric of society must immediately crumble away.

However, I remain convinced that anarchy is not the greatest disaster which democratic ages should fear but the least.

In fact, equality prompts two tendencies: one leads men directly to independence and could suddenly push them as far as anarchy; the other directs men by a longer, more covert but surer route toward slavery.

Nations easily see the former and stand against it; they drift along with the latter without seeing it; it is particularly important to make them aware of it.

For my part, far from blaming equality for the intractability it inspires, I am praising it mainly for that very reason. I admire the way it deposits in the depths of the mind and heart of every man this secret concept and instinctive inclination toward political independence, which consequently prepares the remedy for the ill it has produced. I am attached to equality because of this very aspect.

CHAPTER 2

THE IDEAS DEMOCRATIC NATIONS HAVE ON GOVERNMENT NATURALLY FAVOR THE CONCENTRATION OF POLITICAL POWERS

The idea of intermediary powers between sovereign and subjects was natural to the imagination of aristocratic peoples because these powers belonged to individuals or families whose birth, education, or wealth singled them out or who seemed destined to command. This same idea is naturally absent from the minds of men in times of equality for opposite reasons; it cannot be introduced, except artificially, nor retained except with considerable effort, whereas the thought of a single central authority which governs all citizens directly occurs, so to speak, effortlessly in men's consciousness.

Moreover, in politics as in philosophy or religion, democratic nations welcome with pleasure simple and general ideas. Complex systems put them off and they like to picture a great nation whose citizens resemble one set type and are controlled by a single authority.

Following the idea of a single, central authority, the one that occurs most spontaneously to men's minds in times of equality is that of a uniform legislation. Since each man sees little difference between him and his neighbor, he has difficulty in understanding why a rule applying to one person should not equally apply to all the others. Privileges of the smallest kind are, therefore, repellent to him. The slightest differences in the political institutions of the same nation pain him and legislative uniformity seems the foremost condition of a good government.

On the other hand, this same idea of a uniform rule, equally imposed on every member of society, is virtually foreign to the human mind in aristocratic ages. Either it did not occur to them, or they rejected it.

These opposed mental tendencies end up, in one way or another, by becoming blind instincts or insuperable habits to such a degree that they continue to direct men's behavior despite a few individual cases. Occasionally, for all the variety of medieval life, you come across a few individuals who are entirely alike but that did not prevent the legislator from assigning different duties and rights to each of them. And, by contrast, present governments wear themselves out imposing the same customs and laws on populations which have as yet nothing in common.

As a nation's social conditions grow more equal, individuals seem smaller and society bigger or rather, each citizen, having grown like the rest, melts into the crowd and only a vast and imposing image of the whole nation now stands before the observer.

This naturally gives men of democratic times a very elevated opinion of society's privileges and a very low opinion of an individual's rights. They readily acknowledge that the interest of the former is all-important, whereas that of the latter is not so at all. They are quite willing to grant that the authority representing society is endowed with more enlightenment and wisdom than any of the men composing it and that its duty and its right are to guide each citizen by the hand.

If we look closely at our contemporaries and seek out the very roots of their political opinions, we shall find a few of the ideas I have just traced out and, perhaps, we shall be surprised that so much agreement exists among people so often at war.

Americans believe that the social authority of any state should emanate directly from the people but that, once this authority has been established, they hardly conceive any limits for it; they freely recognize that it has the right to do everything.

As for special privileges granted to towns, families, or individuals, this idea has entirely disappeared. It has never entered their heads that the same law cannot be applied uniformly to all parts of one state and all the men living in it.

These same opinions are increasingly spreading throughout Europe; they are making their way into those very nations which have the most violent objections to the doctrine of the sovereignty of the people and which disagree with the Americans about the origins of power but see power in the same light. In all these nations the concept of an intermediary authority is obscured and blotted out. The idea of a right belonging to certain individuals is rapidly disappearing from men's minds to be replaced by the all-powerful and, so to speak, unique right of society itself. These ideas take root and grow as social conditions become more equal and men more alike; equality engenders such ideas and they, in their turn, hasten the progress of equality. (See Appendix A, p. 858.)

In France, where the revolution to which I refer is more advanced than in any other European country, these very opinions have completely seized hold of men's minds. Listening carefully to the voice of the different parties in France, it will be obvious that everyone is adopting them. Most consider that the government is acting badly but everyone thinks that the government should keep acting and interfering in everything. Those same people who wage the most fearsome wars nevertheless agree on this point. The unity, the universality, the omnipotence of society's power, and the uniformity of its rules represent the outstanding feature of all the political systems invented in our day. They recur at the heart of the strangest utopias. The human mind still pursues these images even in its dreams.

If such ideas arise spontaneously in the minds of individuals, they strike the imaginations of princes even more readily.

While the old state of European society undergoes these changes and collapses, sovereigns invent new beliefs in relation to their competence and duties; they are realizing for the first time that the central government which they represent can and should, solely and in a uniform manner, administer all state business and all citizens. Such an opinion, which I hazard to say no European monarch had ever thought of before our time, reaches the deepest realms of these princes' minds and it stands firm amid the disturbance of all other thoughts.

Our contemporaries are, therefore, much less divided than is supposed; they quarrel endlessly about who should administer sovereign power but find it easy to agree over its duties and rights. Everyone portrays government as a unique, simple, caring, and creative force.

All subsidiary political ideas are unstable but that one remains fixed, unchangeable, and consistent. Publicists and politicians adopt it; the crowd greedily snatches it up; those governed and those governing agree to pursue it with equal enthusiasm: it is the primary idea to be adopted and appears to be innate.

It is not, therefore, the result of some whim of men's minds but the natural condition of men's present state.

CHAPTER 3

THE OPINIONS OF DEMOCRATIC NATIONS ARE IN ACCORD WITH THEIR IDEAS, LEADING THEM TO CENTRALIZE POLITICAL POWER

If men, in times of equality, readily entertain the idea of a great central power, it is quite certain that their habits and opinions incline them to acknowledge such a power and to foster its progress. A few words are sufficient to make this point clear since I have already outlined most of the reasons for it elsewhere.

Men living in democracies, having neither superiors nor inferiors, nor habitual and indispensable partners, readily fall back upon themselves and think of themselves as individuals. I had the chance of illustrating that at some length when dealing with individualism.

It is, therefore, only with some effort that these men wrench themselves from their private business to turn their attention to communal affairs; their natural inclination is to leave responsibility for them to the single, public, and permanent representative which is the state.

Not only do they have no natural liking for public business but often they lack the time for it. In democratic times, private life is so active, so frantic, so full of desires and work that each man has almost no energy or leisure left for political life.

I am certainly not the one to say that such inclinations are invincible since my main aim in writing this book has been to challenge them. It is simply that I am asserting that, in these times, a hidden power is constantly at work developing them in the human heart and that, by leaving them unhindered, they will come to fill it entirely.

Equally, I have had the chance to show how the growing love of prosperity and the shifting nature of property lead democratic nations to dread all material upheavals. The love of public peace is often the only political passion these nations retain and it becomes more active and powerful with them as all the others wither and die out. This naturally inclines citizens to grant or surrender endless new rights to central government, which alone appears to them, in the exercise of its own defense, to be possessed of both the interest and the means to defend them from anarchy.

Since in times of equality no one is obliged to lend his assistance to his fellow men and no one has the right to expect any great support from them, each man is both independent and weak. These two conditions which one must not view either separately or connected together give the citizen of democracies very contradictory urges. Independence fills him with confidence and pride amongst his equals while his vulnerability occasionally makes him feel the need for outside support, which he cannot expect from one of his own people since they are all powerless and unsympathetic. In such extreme circumstances he naturally turns his gaze toward this huge authority rising above the general impotence. His needs and, above all, his desires constantly bring him back to that authority which he ends up by regarding as the sole and necessary support for his weakness as an individual.[1]

---

1. In democratic societies, it is only the central power which has any stability in its position and any permanence in its undertakings. All the citizens are in a state of ceaseless movement and change. Thus, it is in the nature of every government to seek constantly to enlarge its sphere of influence. It is, therefore, impossible for this not to be successful in the long run, since it acts with a fixed design in mind and a constant will imposed upon men whose position, ideas, and desires change from day to day.

    It often happens that citizens work for the central power without meaning to.

    Democratic periods are times of experiment, innovation, and adventure. There is always a host of men who are engaged upon some difficult or

That may more completely explain what often happens in democracies in which men, who feel so uncomfortable submitting to superiors, patiently tolerate one master, proving themselves both proud and servile.

The loathing men feel for privilege increases as these privileges become rarer and less important, so that democratic passions would seem to burn the brighter in those very times when they have the least fuel. I have already accounted for this phenomenon. No inequality, however great, strikes the eye in a time of general social inequality, whereas the slightest disparity appears shocking amid universal uniformity; the more complete this uniformity, the more intolerable it looks. Therefore, it is natural that love of equality should thrive constantly with equality itself: to foster it is to see it grow.

This ever-burning and endless loathing which democratic nations feel for the slightest privilege has an unusual effect upon the gradual concentration of every political right in the hands of a single representative of the state. Since the sovereign authority stands necessarily and indubitably above all the citizens, it does not arouse their envy and each citizen thinks that he is depriving all his fellow men of those powers that he grants to the crown.

The man living in democratic ages is always extremely reluctant to obey his neighbor who is his equal; he refuses to acknowledge that the latter has any ability superior to his own; he distrusts his form of justice and looks enviously upon his power;

---

new enterprise that they pursue by themselves without disturbing their peers. These people are the first to admit that, as a general principle, the public authority should not interfere in private affairs; but, as an exception to that, each one of them wants its assistance with the particular affair which concerns him and seeks to attract the government to act on his behalf, all the time seeking to restrict it in every other sphere.

With a whole host of people taking this particular view on a range of different issues at one and the same time, the sphere of the central power extends imperceptibly in all directions although everyone wants to restrain it. A democratic government, therefore, increases its powers simply because of its permanence. Time is on its side; it profits from every chance event; individual passions unconsciously help it along and it could be said that the older a democratic society is the more centralized its government becomes.

he both fears and despises him; he likes to bring home to him the whole time that they are both equally dependent upon the same master.

Any central power which pursues these natural feelings loves and promotes equality, for equality eases, extends, and guarantees the actions of such a power to an unusual degree.

Equally it can be said that all central governments worship equality because that saves them the trouble of inquiring into the endless details they ought to consider if they had to adapt rules to individuals instead of subjecting them all indiscriminately to the same rules. So the government likes what the citizens like and naturally hates what they hate. This shared feeling which, in democratic nations, constantly unites each individual and the sovereign power in a common thought, establishes between them a hidden and permanent bond of sympathy. The government's faults are forgiven for the sake of its inclinations, the public is reluctant to withdraw its trust, whatever excesses or errors occur, and restores this trust whenever it is called upon to do so. Democratic nations often hate those in whose hands central power is placed but they always retain their affection for the power itself.

Thus I have reached the same goal along two contrasting paths. I have demonstrated that equality directs men to think of a single, uniform, and strong government. I have just shown that it gives men a taste for it, so that present-day nations lean toward this type of government, directed by the natural inclination of heart and mind. All they have to do to reach such a goal is not to hold back.

I think that, in the democratic times opening before us, individual independence and local freedoms will always be artificially contrived whereas centralization will be the natural form of government. (See Appendix B, p. 858.)

CHAPTER 4

A FEW SPECIAL AND ACCIDENTAL REASONS WHY A DEMOCRATIC NATION ADOPTS CENTRALIZATION OF GOVERNMENT OR TURNS AWAY FROM IT

If all democratic nations are instinctively drawn toward the centralization of power, this attraction is uneven. It depends on special circumstances which may further develop or restrain the natural effects of the state of society. Such circumstances are many in number and I shall mention only a few.

In the case of men who have long enjoyed freedom before achieving equality, the feelings engendered by freedom conflict to some degree with the inclinations prompted by equality and, although central government increases its privileges, individuals never quite lose their feeling of independence.

But, whenever equality happens to appear in a nation which has never known, or has ceased for a long time to know what freedom is, as we see on the European continent, the nation's former habits, by some sort of natural attraction, suddenly join forces with the new habits and doctrines engendered by the state of society so that all powers appear to rush spontaneously toward the center; they gather there with astonishing speed and the state suddenly reaches the furthest limits of its power, whereas individuals drift down to the lowest level of weakness after only a short time.

The English arriving three centuries ago to establish a democratic society in the wilds of the New World had all grown accustomed to taking part in the public affairs of their homeland; they knew the jury system; they had freedom of speech and of the press, personal liberty, the concept of rights and the practice of making use of them. They imported these free institutions and manly customs to America and these in their turn protected them from any encroachments of the state.

Thus, in America, it is freedom which is old and equality is comparatively young. The opposite is happening in Europe, where equality was introduced by the absolute power of kings and had already sunk deep into the people's habits long before freedom had entered their minds.

Among democratic nations I have said that the only form of government which occurs to men's minds most naturally is a single centralized authority and that the concept of secondary powers has not been familiar to them. That is especially true for those democratic nations which have seen the triumph of the principle of equality through violent revolution. As the classes that managed local affairs disappeared suddenly in the storm, and as the confused mass remaining behind had as yet neither the organization nor the habit which would allow it to take hold of the administration of these very affairs, only the state itself was seen capable of taking charge of all the details of government. Centralization becomes a fact and, in a sense, a necessity.

Napoleon should be neither praised nor blamed for having concentrated almost the whole administrative power in his own hands for, after the sudden disappearance of the nobility and the upper levels of the middle class, these powers devolved upon him automatically; it would have been almost as difficult to reject as to accept them. Such a necessity has never happened to Americans who, since they had not suffered a revolution and had governed themselves from the first, have never had to call upon the state to act temporarily as their guardian.

Consequently, centralization does not grow in a democracy simply in step with the progress of equality but depends also upon the way this equality has been established.

At the beginning of a great democratic revolution, when the conflict between the various classes is just starting, the people strive to centralize public administration in the hands of the government so as to wrench control of local affairs from the aristocracy. But, toward the end of this very revolution, it is normally the defeated aristocracy which attempts to deliver control of everything to the state because it dreads the petty tyranny of the people who have become its equal and often its master. Thus, it is not always the same class of citizens which strives to increase the powers of the government but, as long as the democratic revolution lasts, you always come across one numerically or financially powerful class whose particular passions and interests lead them to centralize public administration, notwithstanding that hatred of being governed by one's neighbor—a universal and permanent feeling among democratic nations. It may be observed that, in our day, it is the English lower classes who are making every possible effort to destroy local independence and to transfer administration from the circumference to the center, whereas the upper classes are struggling to keep it within its former boundaries. I venture to predict that one day we shall see quite the opposite picture.

These observations show clearly why the power of society at large should always be stronger and the individual weaker in a democracy which has reached equality after a long and painful social struggle than in a democratic society in which the citizens have always been equal from the outset. The American example gives the final proof of that.

The inhabitants of the United States have never been divided by any form of privilege, nor have they known the mutual relationship between servant and master and, since they do not fear or hate each other, they have never known the need to call in the supreme power to manage the details of their affairs. The American experience is unusual: they borrowed the idea of individual rights and the taste for freedom at local level from the aristocracy and managed to preserve both these because they have had no aristocracy to fight.

In all periods of history, education helps to defend men's independence but this is especially true in times of democracy. When all men are alike, it is easy to establish a single, all-powerful government, for men's instinctive feelings are enough to achieve it. But men need great intelligence, knowledge, and skill to manage and sustain subsidiary powers in such circumstances and to create, within the body of independent but individually weak citizens, free associations capable of resisting tyranny without destroying public order.

The concentration of powers along with individual subjection will, therefore, increase in democracies not only in the same proportion as their equality but because of their ignorance.

It is true that, in unenlightened times, the government often lacks the knowledge to impose complete tyranny just as citizens are too ignorant to escape it. But the effect is not the same on both sides.

However crude a democratic nation may be, the central government which rules it is never entirely without knowledge because it finds it easy to attract whatever little skill is to be found in the country and because, if necessary, it will seek assistance from outside. So, in a nation which is ignorant as well as democratic, there is soon bound to be a gigantic difference between the intellectual capacity of the sovereign power and that of each of its subjects. This completes the easy concentration of all power in its hands. The administrative function of the state constantly increases because the state alone is capable of administration.

Aristocratic nations, however unenlightened they may be, never perform in this way because education is almost equally shared between the ruler and the leading citizens.

The pasha who now rules in Egypt discovered the country's inhabitants both very ignorant and very equal and he exploited the knowledge and intelligence of Europe to govern them. As the individual education of the ruler thus came to join with the ignorance and democratic weakness of his subjects, the final phase of centralization was completed without effort and the ruler managed to turn his country into a factory and his citizens into workmen.

I believe that an extreme form of centralization of political power ultimately weakens society and enfeebles the government itself in the longer term. But I am not denying that a centralized social power may be quite easily capable of achieving great projects at a particular time and for a specific purpose. That is especially true in wartime when success depends much more upon the efficient and speedy transfer of all one's resources to one location than upon the actual extent of those resources. It is, therefore, chiefly in time of war that nations feel the desire and often the need to increase the powers of central government. All brilliant military men like centralization because it concentrates their powers and all brilliant centralizers like war because it forces a nation to gather all its powers into the hands of the state. Thus the democratic tendency which leads men to augment constantly the powers of the state and to restrict the rights of individuals is much more swift and sustained among those democratic nations which are exposed by their position to great and frequent wars and whose existence may often be placed in danger than in all other nations.

I have said how the fear of disorder and the love of comfort imperceptibly led democratic nations to increase the functions of central government which seemed to them to be the only authority strong, intelligent, and stable enough of itself to protect them from anarchy. I hardly need to add that all the special circumstances which increase the trouble and instability of a democratic society enhance this general feeling and lead individuals increasingly to sacrifice their rights for the sake of their tranquillity.

A nation, therefore, is never more prone to increase the function of the central government than at the close of a long and bloody revolution which, after wrenching the possessions from the hands of their former owners, has shaken all belief, filled the nation with fierce hatreds, opposed interests and hostile political groups. The taste for public tranquillity then grows into a blind passion and citizens are liable to develop an inordinate devotion to good order.

I have just examined several chance events, all of which may help to promote the centralization of power. I have not yet spoken of the principal cause.

The most important of all chance events which, in democracies, may concentrate the management of all political affairs in the hands of the sovereign power, is where that power itself comes from and its inclinations.

Men who live in times of equality naturally prefer a central government and widen its powers but if this very government happens to reflect faithfully their own interests and is an exact mirror of their basic feelings, their trust in it has almost no limits and they think that they are granting to themselves all they give to it.

This attraction of administrative powers to the center will always be less easy and less swift under the reign of kings who are still in some way connected to the former aristocratic order than under new princes who, being children of their own achievements, seem indissolubly tied to the cause of equality by birth, prejudice, and instincts. I do not mean that rulers of aristocratic origins living in democracies do not seek to centralize. I believe that they are as diligent as all the others in such a pursuit. For them that is the advantage of equality; but their opportunities are not so great because citizens, instead of anticipating the ruler's desires, are often reluctant to fall in with them. In democratic societies, centralization will always be greater the less aristocratic the ruler is: that is the rule.

When an old race of kings governs an aristocracy, the natural prejudices of the ruler are in perfect harmony with those of the nobility and the inherent defects of aristocratic societies grow without hindrance and with no hope of a corrective. The opposite occurs when the son of a feudal family is placed at the head of a democratic nation. The ruler is constantly disposed by his education, customs, and memories to adopt opinions prompted by the inequality of social conditions, while the social conditions of the people incline them endlessly toward habits which spring from equality. Then it often happens that citizens strive to limit central government not so much because it is tyrannical as because it is aristocratic. They firmly assert their independence, not simply because they wish to be free, but especially because they intend to remain equal.

A revolution which overturns an ancient royal family in order to place new men at the head of a democratic nation may temporarily weaken central authority but, however anarchic it may at first appear, we need not hesitate to predict that its final and inevitable consequence will be to widen and reinforce the powers of this same authority.

The chief and, in a sense, the only condition one needs in order to reach a centralized public power in a democratic society is to love equality or to make men believe you do. Thus, the art of despotism, which was formerly so complicated, is now quite simple: it is reduced, as it were, to a single principle.

CHAPTER 5

AMONG CONTEMPORARY EUROPEAN NATIONS THE SOVEREIGN POWER IS INCREASING ALTHOUGH THE RULERS ARE LESS STABLE

Reflecting upon what has been said, we shall be surprised and dismayed to see how, in Europe, everything seems to conspire to increase infinitely the powers of central government and to make the lives of individuals constantly more insecure, subordinate, and precarious.

The democratic nations of Europe possess all the general and permanent tendencies which urge Americans to adopt the centralization of powers and they are, in addition, exposed to a mass of subsidiary and accidental causes unknown to them. It would seem as if every step made toward equality draws them nearer to despotism.

We need only to glance around us and at ourselves to be convinced of it.

In the aristocratic ages before our own, the rulers of Europe had been deprived of, or had given up, several of the inborn rights of their power. Less than a hundred years ago, in most European countries there were private individuals or almost independent bodies which administered justice, enlisted and maintained troops, levied taxes and often even enacted or interpreted laws. The state has everywhere reclaimed for itself alone those features which naturally belong to the sovereign power; in everything connected with government, the state does not tolerate anything standing between citizens and itself and it controls all matters of general concern itself. Far from criticizing this concentration of powers, I merely point it out.

In Europe, at the same time, there were a great number of

secondary powers representing local interests and administering local affairs. Most of these local authorities have already vanished; they all tend rapidly to disappear or to fall into a state of complete subordination. From one end of Europe to another the privileges of the nobility, the freedom of cities, regional administrations have been or soon will be destroyed.

Europe has been through the last fifty years of numerous revolutions and counter-revolutions which have buffeted it in opposite directions. But all these commotions have one element in common: they have all either shaken or destroyed these secondary powers. Local privileges which the French nation had not abolished in countries it had conquered finally collapsed beneath the efforts of the rulers who defeated the French. These rulers rejected all the new ideas of the French Revolution except centralization: that was the only thing they agreed to accept from it.

What I wish to note is that all these various rights, wrested one by one in our time from classes, corporations, and individual men, have not helped to raise new secondary powers upon a more democratic footing, but have everywhere been concentrated into the hands of the ruling power. On all sides, the state moves increasingly toward sole control over the humblest citizens and exclusive direction of their affairs down to the smallest detail.[1]

Years ago, almost all the charitable institutions were in the

---

1.   This gradual weakening of the individual in relation to society manifests itself in thousands of ways. I will quote, amongst others, an example which pertains to the making of wills.

   In aristocratic countries, one usually professes a profound respect for a man's last wishes. This even turned into a superstition amongst the ancient peoples of Europe: the power of the state, far from hampering the whims of dying men, lent its strength to the very least of them and guaranteed them a perpetual power.

   When all the living are weak, the wishes of the dead are less respected. There is a narrow circle within which to operate and, if this is exceeded, the sovereign annuls or controls these wishes. In the Middle Ages, testamentary power had, as it were, no limits. In France today, one cannot distribute one's inheritance amongst one's children without intervention from the state. Having regulated a man's whole life, it even wants to control his final act.

hands of individuals or corporations; they have almost all become dependent on the government and, in several countries, are administered by that power. The state has undertaken almost exclusively to provide the hungry with bread, the sick with help and shelter, and the idle with work; it has become almost the sole relief against every misery.

Education, alongside charity, has turned into a national concern in most contemporary nations. The state welcomes and often takes the child from its mother's arms to entrust it to its official agents; it assumes responsibility for forming the feelings and shaping the ideas of each generation. Uniformity prevails in the classroom as in everything else; diversity is daily vanishing along with freedom.

Nor am I afraid to affirm that in almost all present-day Christian nations, Catholic as well as Protestant, religion is threatened with falling into the hands of the government. Not that rulers are overjealous to settle dogma themselves but they increasingly assert a hold over the will of those who interpret it. They remove the clergy's property, pay them a salary, divert for their own use the influence of the priesthood; they turn priests into their own public officials or often their servants with whose help they may reach into the depths of each man's soul.[2]

But that is still only one side of the picture.

Not only has the power of the authority of the government broadened, as we have just seen, over the whole spectrum of previously existing powers which are no longer able to contain it; it also floods over into everything, even spreading into an area reserved up until now to individual independence. Many actions which formerly lay entirely outside the control of society have in our age been brought under its direction and the number of them is constantly increasing.

2.   As the functions of the central power increase, the number of officials which represent it also increases in proportion. They form a nation within a nation and, as government lends them its own stability, each one of them becomes more and more like an aristocracy.

 Almost everywhere in Europe, the sovereign government rules in two ways: it controls some of the inhabitants through the fear they have of its agents and the others with the hope they have of becoming its agents.

The social power in aristocracies was normally restricted to the management and supervision of citizens in everything which had a direct and obvious connection with the national interest; it was willing to leave decisions over everything else to their own wishes. Among such peoples the government often seemed to forget that there comes a moment when the mistakes and disasters of individual citizens may damage the wellbeing of all and that preventing the downfall of a private citizen has sometimes to be a matter of public concern.

The democratic nations of our time lean excessively in the opposite direction.

It is clear that most of our rulers are not content simply to control the nation as a whole. They seem to hold themselves responsible for the actions and personal fate of their subjects; they seem to have undertaken to guide and enlighten each one of them in the different acts of their lives and, when necessary, to force happiness upon them.

From their side, private citizens increasingly regard the power of society in the same light; they call upon its help whenever they are in need and always look upon it as a teacher or a guide.

I assert that there is no European country in which public administration has become not only more centralized but also more intrusive and more detailed; everywhere it meddles further than before in private affairs; it regulates more activities in its own fashion and in greater detail; day by day it gains a firmer footing alongside, around, and above each individual in order to help, advise, and constrict him.

Formerly the ruler lived off the revenue from his estates and the income from taxes. Things are quite different today as his needs have increased along with his power. In those circumstances which used to cause a ruler to impose a new tax, nowadays one has recourse to a loan. Gradually the state comes to owe money to most of its wealthy subjects and centralizes the bulk of capital in its own hands.

It attracts smaller holdings of capital in a different manner.

As men make closer contact and social conditions grow more equal, the poor have greater resources, education, and aspirations. They imagine that they can improve their lot and seek to do so through saving money, daily producing countless small accumulations of capital which slowly and gradually accrue from their work; these savings are always increasing. But the greater part of this money would remain unprofitable if it stayed in scattered accounts. All this has given rise to a philanthropic institution which will soon become, if I am not mistaken, one of our most important political institutions. Charitable men thought of the idea of collecting the savings of the poor and using the interest from them. In a few countries, these benevolent associations have remained entirely separate from the state but, in almost all countries, patently they tend to identify themselves with the government which, in some countries, has even replaced them and there they have attempted the enormous task of centralizing in one place, and investing profitably, the daily savings of several million workers.

Thus the state attracts the money of the wealthy by loans and exploits the poor man's mite through the savings banks. The wealth of the country is constantly making its way into the hands of the government. This wealth accumulates all the faster as equality of social conditions increases for, in a democracy, only the state inspires confidence in private citizens because the state alone appears to possess some force and permanence.[3]

Thus, the ruling power does not restrict itself to controlling the public income; it enters the realm of private fortunes as well; it is the leader and often the master of every citizen and, in addition, becomes his steward and banker.

Not only does the central power alone fill, enlarge, and exceed the whole sphere of former authorities, it conducts its activities with greater speed, force, and freedom of action than ever before.

3.   On the one hand, the taste for wellbeing is constantly increasing and the government gains possession of more and more of all the sources of that wellbeing.
      Men, therefore, take two different paths toward servitude. The taste for wellbeing turns them away from getting involved in government, and their love of wellbeing makes them more and more closely dependent upon those who govern.

All European governments have in our time introduced tremendous improvements in the science of administration; they perform every task with greater order, greater speed, and smaller costs; they appear to grow constantly in wealth from all the ideas they have stolen from individuals. European rulers daily assert control over their delegated officials, inventing new ways of keeping a closer hold over them and supervising them more easily. It is not enough for them to regulate all business through their agents; they attempt to control the behavior of their agents in all matters. The result is that public administration not only depends upon the same power but it is concentrated increasingly in one place and resides in ever fewer hands. The government centralizes its activities at the same time that it increases its powers—a twin source of strength.

On examining the former constitution of judicial power in most European countries, two features stand out: the independence of this power and the extent of its functions.

Not only did the courts decide almost all the disputes between private individuals but, in many cases, they acted as judges between the individual and the state.

I do not intend here to refer to the political and administrative functions which the courts had usurped in some countries but the judicial functions which they possessed everywhere. In all European nations, there were and still are many private rights, mostly connected with the universal right of property, placed under the judge's protection and which the state could not violate without his permission.

This is the semi-political power which principally distinguishes European lawcourts from all others. For all nations have had judges but not all have granted judges the same privileges.

If we now look at what is happening in the democratic nations of Europe which are called free, as well as in all the others, we see that everywhere alongside these old courts others have been established which are more dependent and whose particular purpose is to arbitrate in those exceptional legal questions arising between the public administration and citizens. The older judiciary is left with its independence but with a restricted sphere of action and the tendency is increasingly to turn it into merely an arbiter in private disputes.

These tribunals are constantly increasing in number, as are their functions. Thus, daily, the government slides further away from its obligation to have its will and rights sanctioned by another authority. Being unable to do without judges, it at least wishes to choose those judges itself and to keep them under its thumb; that is to say, it still places the appearance of justice, rather than justice itself, between itself and private individuals.

Thus, the state is not satisfied with drawing all concerns to itself; it is still increasingly likely to decide everything by itself without check or appeal.[4]

Among modern European nations, there is one important reason which, apart from all those I have just pointed out, ever helps to extend the government's activity and powers and one to which not enough attention has been paid. I refer to the development of industry which is favored by the progress of social equality.

Industry normally causes a multitude of men to congregate in one place, establishing new and complex relationships between them. It exposes them to sudden and great alternations of plenty and poverty, during which public peace is threatened. Finally, this type of work can come to damage the health and even the lives of those who make money out of it or those who engage in it. Thus, the manufacturing classes have a greater need of regulation, supervision, and restraint than all other classes and it is to be expected that the functions of government will multiply as they do.

This truth applies to everything but here are a few points which especially concern European countries.

In the centuries preceding our own, the aristocracy owned

4.   A strangely spurious argument has been made of this in France. When a court case arises between the government and an individual, it is not heard before an ordinary judge, in order, so it is said, not to confuse governmental and judicial powers; as if investing the government at one and the same time with the right to judge as well as to govern was not to confuse these two powers and to muddle them in the most dangerous and despotic fashion.

the land and was capable of protecting it. Therefore, landed property was surrounded by guarantees and its owners enjoyed a great independence. That created laws and customs which have lasted despite the break-up of estates and the overthrow of the nobility. In our day, landowners and farmers are still better able to escape the control of social power than other citizens.

During those same aristocratic ages, where we find the sources of all our history, personal property was of little importance and its owners were despised and weak; industrialists formed a class apart in an aristocratic world and, since they had no guaranteed supporters, they had no outward protection and often could not protect themselves.

Hence the habit arose of looking upon industrial property as something of a private nature which did not warrant the same deference and was not worthy of the same guarantees as property in general, and of considering industrialists as an exception in the social order whose independence was not worth very much and which it was perfectly in order to abandon to the ruler's passion for regulation. In fact, if we consult the medieval codes, it is amazing to find how, at a time of individual independence, industry was constantly regulated by kings even down to the most trivial details. In this respect centralization was as vigorous and as minute as it ever could be.

Since that time, a great revolution has taken place in the world; industrial property, then no more than a seed, has spread throughout Europe; the industrial class has extended and grown wealthy on the remnants of all the other classes. It has grown in numbers, importance, and wealth; it is still growing; almost all those people not belonging to it have some connection, at least at some point; it threatens to become the leading and, one might say, the only class. Meanwhile, the political ideas and habits which it had engendered long ago have remained. These ideas and habits have not changed because they are of long standing and also because they are in perfect harmony with the new ideas and general habits supported by the men of today.

Consequently, industrial property does not increase its rights as it becomes more important. The industrial class does not gain in independence as its numbers grow; on the contrary, it might be said that it carries despotism within its ranks and this naturally spreads as the class grows.[5]

As the nation becomes more industrialized, it feels a greater need for roads, canals, ports, and other semi-public works which aid the growth of wealth and as it becomes more democratic, individuals experience greater difficulty in executing such enterprises while the state finds it easier to do so. I can assert with confidence that the clear tendency of all present rulers is to assume responsibility for the execution of such undertakings, by which they daily hold their populations in an ever-tighter dependence.

On the other hand, as the power of the state increases and its needs grow, it consumes itself an ever-growing quantity of industrial products which it normally manufactures in its own arsenals and factories. Thus, in each kingdom, the ruling power becomes the leading industrialist; it attracts and retains in its service a vast number of engineers, architects, mechanics, and craftsmen.

Not only is the ruling power the leading industrialist, it

5.   I shall quote a few facts in support of this. The mines are the natural sources of industrial wealth. As industry has developed in Europe, as the production of the mines becomes of more general interest and their profitability is made more difficult because of the division of ownership which is brought about by equality, most governments have claimed the right to possess the ground which contains the mines and to supervise the work; this has never been the case with any other kind of property.

Mines, which were private property, subject to the same obligations and provided with the same guarantees as other real estate, have thus fallen into the public domain. It is the state which works them or leases them out; the owners are transformed into tenants, obtaining their rights from the state, and, furthermore, the state claims practically everywhere the power to direct them; it lays down rules, imposes methods, subjects them to constant inspection, and, if they resist, an administrative court will dispossess them and the public administration transfers their rights to others. Thus the government possesses not only the mines but has all the miners under its thumb.

However, as industry develops, the working of the old mines increases. New ones are opened up. The mining population expands and grows. Each day, the sovereign governments expand their domain beneath our feet and people them with their agents.

increasingly tends to become the chief, or rather the master, of all the others.

As citizens have grown weaker through greater equality, they can achieve little in industry without forming associations. Now, public authority naturally wishes to place such associations under its control.

We have to acknowledge that these collective bodies known as associations are stronger and more formidable than a single individual could ever be and that they feel less responsibility for their own actions. Consequently, it seems sensible to leave them with less freedom from the power of society than would be allowed in the case of an individual.

Rulers are all the more disposed to act thus as it suits their tastes. Among democratic nations, associations offer the only possible resistance citizens have against government power; hence, the latter never looks with approval upon associations it does not have under its thumb. It is worth noting that in democracies citizens often regard these associations, which they need so much, with a concealed attitude of fear and jealousy and this feeling prevents their defending them. The power and duration of these small individual societies, amid the weakness and instability of the general community, astonish and alarm them so that they are not far removed from looking upon the free use each society makes of its natural attributes as dangerous privileges.

All these associations, presently springing into being, are, moreover, equivalent to new corporate bodies whose rights have not been sanctified by time; they enter the world just when the idea of the rights of individuals is weak and social power knows no limits. It is not surprising that they lose their freedom at the moment of their birth.

Among all European peoples certain associations cannot be formed until the state has scrutinized their statutes and sanctioned their existence. In several countries, efforts are made to extend this rule to all associations. It is easy to see where such an enterprise would lead, if successful.

Once the ruling body had the general right to sanction all kinds of association under prescribed conditions, it would soon claim the right to supervise and control them in order to prevent their departure from the rule it had imposed upon them. In this way, once the state had made dependent all those wishing to form an association, it would also push all those already in associations into the same position, that is to say almost all the men alive today.

Sovereign governments increasingly appropriate for themselves and exploit for their own purposes the greater share of the new industrial power created in today's world. Industry leads us along and they lead industry.

I attach so much importance to all I have just said that I am tormented by the fear of having spoiled my meaning by seeking to make myself clearer.

If, then, the reader finds the examples quoted in support of my observations are not enough or poorly chosen, if he thinks that I have exaggerated at some point the encroachments of society's power or that, by contrast, I have excessively underrated the context in which individual independence operates, I beg him to put down the book for a moment and to consider for himself the subjects that I have attempted to explain to him. Let him carefully examine what is happening every day around us and beyond our boundaries; let him question his neighbors; finally, let him take a look at himself. Unless I am much mistaken, he will reach, unguided and by other routes, the point to which I wished to lead him.

He will perceive that, over the last fifty years, centralization has increased everywhere and in a thousand different ways. Wars, revolutions, and conquests have promoted its progress; every person has worked to increase it. In this same period, when men, at a tremendous rate, have followed each other at the head of affairs, their ideas, interests, and passions have shown infinite variety; yet all have wished to centralize in one way or another. The instinct to centralize has been virtually the only stable feature amid the general instability of their lives and thoughts.

And when the reader has examined these details of human affairs and turns to take in the whole picture in its entirety, he will be astonished.

On the one hand, the most stable of regimes have been shaken or overthrown; on every side, peoples have violently shaken free from the constraint of their laws; they destroy or limit the power of their lords or princes; all those nations not yet in the throes of revolution appear at least restless and disturbed; all of them are enlivened by the same spirit of revolt. And, on the other hand, in this very same period of anarchy and among these same unruly peoples, the power of society endlessly increases its authority; it becomes more centralized, more adventurous, more absolute, and more widespread. Citizens are perpetually falling under the control of this public administration; imperceptibly and virtually unknowingly, they are drawn to sacrifice each day a few new facets of their personal independence to this government and these very same men, who have from time to time overturned a throne or trampled kings underfoot, increasingly bow to the slightest wishes of some clerk without showing any resistance.

Thus, in our time, two contrary revolutions seem to be at work: the one continually weakens supreme power, the other endlessly reinforces it. At no other time in our history has such power ever appeared to be either so weak or so strong.

But when we finally examine more closely the state of the world, we realize that those two revolutions are intimately linked to each other, that they stem from the same root and that they lead men in the end to the same spot even though along different courses.

I am not afraid to repeat one last time what I have already said or implied in several places in this book: one must take good care not to confuse the fact of equality itself with the revolution which successfully introduces it into the condition of society and into the laws. Therein lies the reason for almost all the events which astonish us.

All the old political powers of Europe, the greatest as well as the least, were founded in aristocratic times and represented, or more or less supported, the principle of inequality and privilege. In order to give priority in government to the new needs and interests proposed by a growing equality, men in the present age had, therefore, to overturn or restrict these old powers. That led them to make revolutions and inspired in a great number of them this barbaric love of disorder and independence which all revolutions, whatever their aim, always engender.

I do not think that there is a single European country where the progress of equality has not been preceded or followed by some violent changes in the status of property and of persons, and almost all these changes have been accompanied by much anarchy and license because they were brought about by the least civilized section of the nation against the most civilized.

That resulted in two opposed tendencies which I have previously portrayed. As long as the democratic revolution was at its height, the men involved in destroying the old aristocratic powers which opposed it displayed a strong spirit of independence; but, as the triumph of equality moved to completion, they gradually gave way to those feelings natural to that condition of equality and they strengthened and centralized the power of society. They had wished to be free in order to become equal but, as equality took greater hold with the help of this freedom, it put freedom further from their grasp.

These two conditions have not always followed each other. Our ancestors have manifested how a nation was able to organize a vast internal tyranny at the very time that it was escaping from the authority of the nobility and was confronting the power of every king, thus teaching the world how to win independence and to lose it at the same time.

Nowadays, men can see that the old powers are crumbling all around them; they observe all the old influences dying away and all the ancient barriers falling down; this disturbs the judgment of even the wisest men who pay attention only to the amazing revolution seething before their eyes and believe that the human race is about to collapse forever into anarchy. Were they to conceive the final consequences of this revolution, they would perhaps entertain quite different fears.

For my part, I own that I do not trust this spirit of freedom which seems to fire my contemporaries; I see plainly enough that the nations of this age are in a turbulent state but it is not so clear to me that they have a liberal attitude. And I am afraid that at the end of these agitated times, sovereigns may be more powerful than ever before.

CHAPTER 6

WHAT SORT OF DESPOTISM DEMOCRATIC NATIONS HAVE TO FEAR

I had noted in my stay in the United States that a democratic state of society similar to the American model could lay itself open to the establishment of despotism with unusual ease, and I had seen on my return to Europe to what extent most of its rulers had already exploited the ideas, opinions, and needs engendered by such a state of society to enlarge the range of their power.

That led me to think that the nations of Christendom would perhaps end up by suffering some similar oppression to the one which once burdened several of the peoples of the ancient world.

A study of the subject in more detail and five years of further meditation have not lessened my fears but they have redirected them.

Centuries past never witnessed any ruler so absolute or powerful as to undertake the administration, on his own and without the support of secondary powers, of every part of a great empire; nor did anyone try to subject all his people indiscriminately to the details of a uniform code of conduct; nor did anyone descend to the level of every common citizen in order to rule and direct him. The idea of such an enterprise never occurred to the mind of man and, had it done so, the lack of education, the defects of administrative machinery, and, above all, the natural obstacles aroused by the inequality of social conditions would soon have stopped his attempts at so grandiose a design.

When the Roman emperors were at the height of their powers, the various nations inhabiting the Roman world still preserved their different customs and manners: although they obeyed the same monarch, most of the provinces were administered separately: they abounded in powerful and energetic townships and, although the whole government of the empire was concentrated in the emperor's hands and he remained the arbiter of everything when the need arose, the small details of social life and private everyday existence normally eluded his control.

The emperors, it is true, wielded immense and unchecked power which allowed them to indulge freely any strange whims they might have and to use the entire power of the state to satisfy them; they often abused this power to deprive a citizen arbitrarily of his property or his life: their tyranny was an excessive burden on a few people but never spread over a great number; it latched on to a few main objects, leaving the rest alone; it was violent but its extent was limited.

If despotism were to be established in present-day democracies, it would probably assume a different character; it would be more widespread and kinder; it would debase men without tormenting them.

Doubtless in an age of enlightenment and equality such as our own, rulers could more easily manage to gather all public powers into their own hands and to intrude further and more regularly into the realm of private interests than was ever possible for any ancient sovereign. But this same equality which fosters despotism also tempers it. We have seen how public customs become more humane and gentler as men grow more alike and equal; when no single citizen has great power or wealth, tyranny is to some extent deprived of opportunity and field of action. Since all fortunes are modest, passions are naturally limited, imagination restricted, and pleasures simple. This universal moderation controls the ruler's excesses and constrains the disorderly surge of his desires within certain limits.

Aside from these reasons borrowed from the nature of the state of society itself, I could add many others which I would be taking from areas beyond the range of my subject but I intend to stay within the boundaries I have set myself.

Democratic governments might become violent and cruel at certain times of great excitement and danger but these crises will not happen often or last long. (See Appendix C, p. 859.)

When I consider the trivial nature of men's passions, the mildness of their manners, the extent of their education, the purity of their religion, the gentleness of their morality, their industrious and tidy habits, the restraint they almost all display in their vices as in their virtues, I have no fear that their leaders will be considered as tyrants but rather as guardians.

Thus, I think that the type of oppression threatening democracies will not be like anything there has been in the world before; our contemporaries would not be able to find any example of it in their memories. I, too, am having difficulty finding a word which will exactly convey the whole idea I have formed; the old words despotism and tyranny are not suitable. This is a new phenomenon which I must, therefore, attempt to define since I can find no name for it.

I wish to imagine under what new features despotism might appear in the world: I see an innumerable crowd of men, all alike and equal, turned in upon themselves in a restless search for those petty, vulgar pleasures with which they fill their souls. Each of them, living apart, is almost unaware of the destiny of all the rest. His children and personal friends are for him the whole of the human race; as for the remainder of his fellow citizens, he stands alongside them but does not see them; he touches them without feeling them; he exists only in himself and for himself; if he still retains his family circle, at any rate he may be said to have lost his country.

Above these men stands an immense and protective power which alone is responsible for looking after their enjoyments and watching over their destiny. It is absolute, meticulous, ordered, provident, and kindly disposed. It would be like a fatherly authority, if, fatherlike, its aim were to prepare men for manhood, but it seeks only to keep them in perpetual childhood; it prefers its citizens to enjoy themselves provided they have only enjoyment in mind. It works readily for their happiness but it wishes to be the only provider and judge of it. It provides their security, anticipates and guarantees their needs, supplies their pleasures, directs their principal concerns, manages their industry, regulates their estates, divides their inheritances. Why can it not remove from them entirely the bother of thinking and the troubles of life?

Thus, it reduces daily the value and frequency of the exercise of free choice; it restricts the activity of free will within a narrower range and gradually removes autonomy itself from each citizen. Equality has prepared men for all this, inclining them to tolerate all these things and often even to see them as a blessing.

Thus, the ruling power, having taken each citizen one by one into its powerful grasp and having molded him to its own liking, spreads its arms over the whole of society, covering the surface of social life with a network of petty, complicated, detailed, and uniform rules through which even the most original minds and the most energetic of spirits cannot reach the light in order to rise above the crowd. It does not break men's wills but it does soften, bend, and control them; rarely does it force men to act but it constantly opposes what actions they perform; it does not destroy the start of anything but it stands in its way; it does not tyrannize but it inhibits, represses, drains, snuffs out, dulls so much effort that finally it reduces each nation to nothing more than a flock of timid and hardworking animals with the government as shepherd.

I have always believed that this type of organized, gentle, and peaceful enslavement just described could link up more easily than imagined with some of the external forms of freedom and that it would not be impossible for it to take hold in the very shadow of the sovereignty of the people.

Our contemporaries are ceaselessly agitated by two conflicting passions: they feel the need to be directed as well as the desire to remain free. Since they are unable to blot out either of these hostile feelings, they strive to satisfy both of them together. They conceive a single, protective, and all-powerful government but one elected by the citizens. They combine centralization with the sovereignty of the people. That gives them some respite. They derive consolation from being supervised by thinking that they have chosen their supervisors. Every individual tolerates being tied down because he sees that it is not another man nor a class of people holding the end of the chain but society itself.

Under this system citizens leave their state of dependence just long enough to choose their masters and then they return to it.

At the present time, many people very easily fall in with this type of compromise between a despotic administration and the sovereignty of the people and they think they have sufficiently safeguarded individual freedom when they surrendered it to a national authority. That is not good enough for me. The character of the master is much less important to me than the fact of obedience.

However, I shall not say that such a constitution is not infinitely preferable to one which brings all powers together and then places them in the hands of one man or one irresponsible body of men. Of all the various forms of democratic despotism, that would be the worst.

When the ruling power is elected or closely supervised by a genuinely elected and independent legislature, the oppression it imposes on individuals is sometimes greater but is always less degrading because each citizen, faced with these restrictions and his own impotence, can still imagine that his obedience is only to himself and that he is sacrificing to one of his desires all his others.

Equally, I realize that, when the ruling power represents and is dependent upon the nation, the powers and rights taken from each citizen do not simply serve the head of state but the state itself and that private individuals derive some advantage from the sacrifice of their independence to the public good.

Creating a national representative system in a very centralized country is thus to lessen the damage extreme centralization can produce but it does not entirely destroy it.

I see quite clearly that, in this way, individual intervention in the most important affairs is preserved but it is just as much suppressed in small and private ones. We forget that it is, above all, in the details that we run the risk of enslaving men. For my part, I would be tempted to believe that freedom in the big things of life is less important than in the slightest, if I thought that we could always be guaranteed the latter when we did not possess the former.

Subjection in the minor things of life is obvious every day and is experienced indiscriminately by all citizens. It does not cause them to lose hope but it constantly irks them until they give up the exercise of their will. It gradually blots out their mind and enfeebles their spirit, whereas obedience demanded only in a small number of very serious circumstances involves enslavement on rare occasions and then burdens only a certain number of people. It will be useless to call upon those very citizens, who have become so dependent upon central government, to choose from time to time the representative of this government; this very important but brief and rare exercise of their free choice will not prevent their gradual loss of the faculty of autonomous thought, feeling, and action so that they will slowly fall below the level of humanity.

I may add that they will soon lose the capacity to exercise the great and only privilege open to them. The democratic nations which introduced freedom into politics at the same time that they were increasing despotism in the administrative sphere have been led into the strangest paradoxes. Faced with the need to manage small affairs where common sense can be enough, they reckon citizens are incompetent; when it comes to governing the whole state, they give these citizens immense prerogatives. They turn them by degrees into playthings of the ruler or his masters, higher than kings or lower than men. Having exhausted all the various electoral systems without finding one which suited them, they look surprised and continue to search, as if the defects they see had far more to do with the country's constitution than with that of the electorate.

It is, indeed, difficult to imagine how men who have completely given up the habit of self-government could successfully choose those who should do it for them, and no one will be convinced that a liberal, energetic, and prudent government can ever emerge from the voting of a nation of servants.

A constitution, republican in its head and ultra-monarchist in all its other parts, has always struck me as a short-lived monstrosity. The vices of those who govern and the ineptitude of those governed would soon bring it to ruin and the people, tired of its representatives and of itself, would create freer institutions or would soon revert to its abasement to one single master. (See Appendix D, p. 859.)

CHAPTER 7

CONTINUATION OF THE PRECEDING CHAPTERS

I believe it to be easier to establish an absolute and despotic government among a people whose social conditions are equal than in any other and I think that such a government, once established in such a nation, would not only oppress men but would, in the end, strip each man there of several of the principal attributes of his humanity.

Despotism, therefore, strikes me as particularly threatening in democratic ages.

I think that at all times I should have loved freedom, but in the times in which we live I feel inclined to worship it.

On the other hand, I am convinced that all those who will be alive in the coming centuries and might try to base their authority on privilege and aristocracy will fail. All those who might wish to attract and retain authority within one single class will also fail. At the present time there is no ruler so skillful or so strong that he could establish despotism by restoring permanent distinctions of rank between his subjects; nor is there a legislator so wise or so powerful that he is capable of maintaining free institutions without adopting equality as his first principle and emblem. Thus, all those who now wish to found or guarantee the independence and dignity of their fellows should show themselves friends of equality, and the only worthy means of appearing such is to be so: upon this depends the success of their sacred enterprise.

Hence it is not a matter of reconstructing an aristocratic society but of drawing freedom from within the democracy in which God has placed us.

Both these basic truths appear simple, clear, and fertile to me and they bring me naturally to consider what kind of free government may be founded in a nation where social conditions are equal.

The very constitutions and needs of democracies make it inevitable that their sovereign authority has to be more uniform, centralized, widespread, searching, and powerful than in any other nation. There, society is naturally more active and stronger while the individual is more subordinate and weaker; the former does more, the latter, less; that is unavoidable.

We should not, therefore, expect the sphere of personal independence in democracies ever to be as broad as in aristocracies. But that is not something to be desired for, in aristocracies, society is often sacrificed to the individual and the prosperity of the majority to the greatness of the few.

It is both necessary and desirable that the central government which controls a democratic nation should be active and powerful. It is not a question of making it weak or indolent but simply of preventing it from abusing its agility and strength.

What helped most to guarantee the independence of private individuals in aristocratic ages was that the ruler did not assume total responsibility for the governing and administration of his citizens but was forced to delegate part of this task to members of the aristocracy, so that the power of society was always divided and never fell with its whole weight or in the same manner upon any one individual.

Not only did the ruler avoid managing everything by himself but most of his civil servants, deputizing for him and deriving their power from their birth and not from him, were not permanently under his thumb. He was not able either to appoint or destroy them whenever the whim struck him nor could he bend them all together to his slightest wishes. That still guaranteed the independence of private individuals.

I fully understand that nowadays we could not use the same methods but I observe democratic processes which may take their place.

Instead of entrusting to the ruler alone all the administrative powers removed from corporations or from the nobility, some of them could be handed over to secondary bodies temporarily formed of ordinary citizens; in that way the freedom of private individuals will be more secure without diminishing their equality.

Americans, who attach less importance to words than we do, have preserved the name of country for the largest of their administrative districts but they have partly replaced the country by a regional assembly.

I readily agree that, in a time of equality such as our own, it would be unfair and unreasonable to institute hereditary officials but there is nothing to stop us, to some extent, substituting elected officials for them. Election is a democratic expedient which guarantees the independence of the official from central government to quite the same degree, if not more so, as could be secured by the hereditary principle in aristocracies.

Aristocratic countries are full of wealthy and influential individuals who know how to look after themselves and cannot easily or secretly be oppressed; these people restrain those in power within general habits of moderation and self-control.

I am aware that democratic countries do not contain such people in the natural course of things but something similar can be created by artificial means.

I firmly believe that an aristocracy could not be founded again in this world but I do think that associations of ordinary citizens may produce very wealthy, influential, strong people who resemble, in a phrase, aristocratic bodies.

In this way, several of the greatest political advantages of aristocracy would be obtained without any of its injustices or dangers. A political, industrial, commercial, or even scientific and literary association equals an educated and powerful citizen who cannot be persuaded at will nor suppressed in some shadowy corner and who saves the liberties of all by defending its own rights against the demands of the government.

In aristocratic times, each man is always tied very closely to several of his fellow citizens in such a way that he cannot be attacked without the others coming to his aid. In ages of equality, each individual is naturally isolated with no hereditary friends whose help he can demand, no class whose sympathetic support he can rely on; he is thrust easily aside and trampled underfoot without redress. At the present time, a citizen who is oppressed has only one means of defense which is to appeal to the whole nation and then to the human race, if the former is deaf to his complaints. The only means of achieving this is through the press. Consequently, the freedom of the press is infinitely more valuable in democratic nations than in all the others; it alone can cure most of the ills which equality may produce. Equality sets men apart and weakens them but the press brings to their side a very powerful weapon available to the weakest as well as the most isolated. Equality removes from each individual the support of his neighbors but the press enables him to summon all his fellow citizens to his assistance. Printing has accelerated the progress of equality and it is one of its best correctives.

I think that men living in aristocracies may, if they have to, do without the freedom of the press but those living in democratic countries cannot do so. To guarantee the personal independence of these people, I would not trust great political assemblies, parliamentary powers, or the trumpeting of the sovereignty of the people.

All these things may, to a certain extent, involve the enslavement of the individual but this loss of liberty cannot be complete, if there is a free press. The press is by far the most effective democratic instrument of freedom.

Something similar may be said of judicial power.

The essential function of judicial power is concern for private interests and a ready supervision of all those small things that come before its scrutiny; another essential quality of this power is never to volunteer its assistance to those who are oppressed but to be constantly at the disposal of the humblest of them. However weak we assume such a man to be, he can always force the judge to listen and reply to his complaint, for that is at the heart of the very constitution of judicial power.

Such a power is, therefore, particularly adapted to the needs of liberty at a time when the eye and finger of the ruling authority are constantly interfering with the slightest details of human behavior and when private individuals are too weak to protect themselves and too isolated to be able to rely on help from their fellow men. The strength of the courts has ever been the greatest guarantee available to individual independence but that is true above all in democratic ages; rights and private interests are always threatened at such times, if the power of the courts does not increase or expand in proportion to the growth of social equality.

Equality introduces into men's minds several tendencies which are a danger to liberty and toward which the legislator should always pay close attention. I will refer only to the most important.

Men who live in democratic times do not find it easy to understand the usefulness of social conventions for which they feel an instinctive contempt. I have stated the reasons for this elsewhere. Conventions arouse their disdain and often their loathing. Since they are usually aiming at easy and available gratification, they rush thoughtlessly toward the object of their every desire, driven to desperation by the slightest delay. This attitude, which they carry over into political life, causes them to be hostile to conventions which hinder or retard some of the daily plans.

Yet, this drawback which democratic men see in conventions is the very feature which makes them so useful to liberty, for their chief merit is to be a barrier between strong and weak, government and people, and to hold the former back while giving the other time to look about. Conventions are more necessary when the ruling power is more energetic and powerful and when private individuals are more lethargic and enfeebled. Thus, democratic nations naturally need conventions more than other nations yet, just as naturally, pay them less respect. That deserves serious attention.

Nothing is more dispiriting than the arrogant disdain displayed by most of our contemporaries for questions of convention, for the minutest of such questions have assumed, in our time, an importance which they did not have before. Several of the greatest human problems are tied up with them.

If politicians in aristocratic ages could occasionally look down upon conventions with impunity and could often rise above them, I think that those men who are the leaders of present-day nations should regard the least of them with respect and should not neglect them unless something urgent or necessary demands it. In aristocracies, conventions were held with superstitious belief; we need to have an enlightened and considered deference for them.

Another very natural, yet very dangerous feeling with democratic peoples is the one which leads them to despise and undervalue the rights of private individuals.

In general, men cling to a right and show it consideration in proportion to its importance and the length of time it has been enjoyed. Individual rights amongst democratic peoples are normally of little importance, of recent vintage, and extremely unstable, which often results in their being readily sacrificed and almost always violated without regret.

But it happens that at the same period and amongst the same nations in which men conceive a natural contempt for the rights of individual citizens, the rights accorded to society as a whole show a natural tendency to extend and strengthen; in other words, men become less attached to private rights at the very moment that it would be most necessary to retain and defend the few that remain.

It is, therefore, in democratic times, above all, that the true friends of the liberty and greatness of humanity should be constantly ready to make a stand to prevent the power of society from carelessly sacrificing the private rights of a few individuals to the general execution of its own plans. At such moments, no citizen is so obscure that it is not very dangerous to allow him to be oppressed, nor any individual rights so unimportant that they can with impunity be surrendered to capricious government decisions. The reason for this is simple: to violate the right of a private individual in an age when the human mind is imbued with the importance and sanctity of such rights is to damage only the person who loses them; but to violate such a right these days is deeply to corrupt the manners of the nation and to endanger the whole of society because the very idea of these kinds of rights tends endlessly to deteriorate and disappear amongst us.

There are certain customs, ideas, and defects which are peculiar to a period of revolution and which cannot fail to appear and grow in a protracted revolution whatever its character or objectives may be and whatever the stage on which it conducts its affairs.

When any nation has, within a short space of time, repeatedly changed its leaders, opinions, and laws, the men of whom it is composed eventually catch the taste for change and become used to associating all these changes with the swift involvement of violence. They then naturally adopt a contempt for conventions whose powerlessness they observe daily and they tolerate impatiently the power of rules which they see people trying so often to avoid.

As common notions of justice and morality are no longer capable of explaining and justifying all the innovations daily inspired by revolution, people latch on to the principle of public usefulness, creating the doctrine of political necessity as they grow used to sacrificing willingly and without qualms the interests of private individuals and to trampling underfoot personal rights so as to attain more speedily the general aim before them.

These customs and ideas, which I shall call "revolutionary" because all revolutions bring them into being, appear in aristocracies just as much as in democracies, but with the former they are often less powerful and last for less time as they run up against customs, ideas, defects, and impediments which oppose them. They vanish automatically, therefore, as soon as the revolution is over and the nation reverts to its former political ways. This does not always happen in democratic countries where the fear always exists that revolutionary tendencies, becoming gentler and more orderly without entirely disappearing, will be gradually transformed into the methods and customs of administrative government.

To my knowledge, therefore, there are no countries where revolutions are more threatening than democratic ones because, apart from chance and shortlived disasters which they could manage to avoid, they always risk the creation of some evils which are permanent and, so to speak, unending.

I believe that there are some honorable types of opposition

and some rebellions which are legitimate. I am not, therefore, making an absolute statement that men living in democratic times should never make revolutions but I do think that they rightly hesitate more than any other peoples before embarking upon one and that it is preferable for them to suffer many discomforts in their present conditions than to resort to such a perilous solution.

I shall conclude with one general idea which comprises not only all the individual ideas expressed in this present chapter but also most of those which this whole book has aimed to highlight.

In the aristocratic ages before our own, there were very powerful individuals and very weak public authorities. The very picture of society was dimly drawn and constantly disappeared in all the various powers which ruled the populace. The major efforts of men in such periods were required to strengthen and support the central authority by increasing and guaranteeing its powers, by restricting, on the other hand, individual independence within stricter limits and by subordinating private interests to those of the community.

Other dangers and other concerns await men of the present age.

Among most modern nations, the government, whatever its origin, constitution, and name, has become almost omnipotent and private individuals are increasingly sinking into the lowest levels of weakness and dependency.

All was different in ancient societies. Unity and uniform conditions were nowhere to be seen. Everything in modern society threatens to become so similar that the individual character of each person will soon vanish entirely into the common features of humanity. Our ancestors were always ready to take advantage of the idea that the rights of private individuals should be respected, and we are naturally prone to exaggerate this other idea that the interest of one person should always bend to that of the greater number.

The political world is changing; henceforth we must seek out new solutions to new disorders.

To lay down extensive but transparent and settled boundaries for governmental power, to grant private individuals certain rights as well as guaranteeing undisputed enjoyment of those rights, to preserve what remains of an individual's modicum of independence, strength, and authenticity, to raise him up to the level of society as a whole and support him in that position, such appears to me to be the objective of the legislator for the era we are about to enter.

Today's rulers appear to be seeking to use men to achieve great things. I should like them to think a little more of creating great men, to attach less value to the work and more to the workman and never to fail to remember that a nation cannot remain strong for long when each individual man is weak, and that we have still not discovered a social formula, nor any political ruse, which can turn a nation of small-minded and flabby citizens into one that is full of energy.

Among our contemporaries I can see two ideas which are as incompatible as they are disastrous.

Some people can see in equality only the anarchical tendencies which it engenders. They are frightened by their freedom of choice and are frightened of themselves.

Others, fewer in number but more enlightened, maintain a different viewpoint. Alongside the road which starts with equality and leads to anarchy, they have at last discovered the path which seems to lead men to inevitable enslavement. They incline their souls in advance to this unavoidable slavery and, abandoning any hope of remaining free, they are already prepared to worship in their hearts the master who is bound to make an imminent appearance.

The former give up freedom because they regard it as dangerous; the latter because they judge it to be impossible.

If I had entertained this latter conviction, I would not have written this work; I would merely have groaned quietly by myself over the destiny of my fellows.

My wish has been to highlight the dangers imposed by the principle of equality upon human independence because I am of the firm belief that these dangers are the most daunting as well as the least foreseen of all that the future holds in store, but not, I believe, insurmountable.

Men living in the democratic ages we are entering have a natural liking for independence although just as naturally they find regulations frustrating. They are wearied by the fact that the very state they prefer is so permanent; they love power but are prone to despise and loathe those who wield it and they find it all too easy to slip from under their ruler's thumb because of their very insignificance and mobility.

These tendencies will always occur because they originate in the fabric of society which will not change. They will prevent for a long time the establishment of any despotism and they will provide new weapons for every new generation which wishes to fight for men's freedom.

Let us, therefore, look to the future with that precautionary fear which keeps men ready to fight rather than with that feeble and indolent terror which depresses and weakens men's hearts.

CHAPTER 8

GENERAL SURVEY OF THE SUBJECT

Before leaving for ever the theme I have just pursued, I should like to manage a final all-embracing survey of all the various characteristics of the modern world and to make a final assessment of the general influence which equality is bound to exert on the destiny of men; but the difficulty of such an undertaking brings me to a halt and, faced with such a great objective, I feel my eyes blurring and my reason stumbling.

This new society which I have sought to portray and which I wish to judge has only just been born. Time has not yet fixed its shape; the great revolution which created it still creeps on and in the events of our time it is almost impossible to make out what must disappear along with the revolution itself and what is bound to survive its end.

The world which is rising into being is still half-involved in the remnants of the world that is disappearing and, in the immense confusion of human affairs, no one can say what will be left standing from the old institutions and ancient customs or what will vanish in the end.

Although the revolution which is taking place in social conditions, the law, ideas, and men's opinions is still far removed from completion, already no one can compare its influence with anything seen previously in this world. I survey century after century back to remotest antiquity and I can see nothing resembling what I perceive before my very eyes. The past no longer casts light upon the future; our minds advance in darkness.

Nevertheless, amid the breadth, novelty, and confusion of this description, I already glimpse, emerging from the picture, a few prominent characteristics which I can point out:

I see that advantages and evils are nearly equally balanced in the world. Great wealth is disappearing; the number of small fortunes is on the increase; men's desires and pleasures are multiplied; there are no longer cases of extraordinary prosperity or of insoluble catastrophes. Ambition is a universal sentiment but ambition on a large scale is rarely encountered. Each individual is isolated and weak; society is active, provident, and strong; private persons act on a small scale, the state on a broad front.

Men's characters are not energetic but manners are gentle and systems of law are humane. If we encounter few instances of great dedication or very lofty, dazzling, pure courage, nevertheless customs are orderly, violence rare, and cruelty almost unknown. Human existence becomes longer and ownership of property more secure. Life is not very elaborate but is very relaxed and peaceful. Few pleasures are very refined or very brutish; elegant manners are as rare as coarse tastes. Learned men are as scarce as unlearned populations. Genius becomes a rare occurrence while education is more widespread. The human mind achieves improvements through the modest efforts of men combined together rather than by the powerful drive of a few. There is less perfection but more abundance in work achieved. All the ties of race, class, and country slacken while the great bond of humanity tightens.

If I attempt to highlight the most widespread and striking of all these different features, I light upon the fact that what is evident in the case of men's fortunes appears under a thousand different guises. Almost all extremes become softer and blunter in outline; almost every prominent excess is rubbed smooth to make way for something average, both less high and less low, less glittering and less obscure than what existed in the world before.

I cast my eye over the countless crowd of similar beings among whom no one stands above or below the rest. The sight of this universal uniformity saddens and chills me and I am tempted to regret the state of society which no longer exists.

When the world was filled with men of great importance and extreme insignificance, of great wealth and extreme poverty, of great learning and extreme ignorance, I would turn away from the latter so as to concentrate solely upon the former who delighted my gaze; but I realize that this pleasure sprang from my weakness. Simply because I am not capable of seeing everything around me at one and the same time, I am allowed to select and to separate off from so many others the things which I enjoy contemplating. The almighty and everlasting being has no such luxury, for his eye necessarily includes the whole of creation and can see the whole of mankind and each man in detail even though simultaneously.

It is a natural belief that this creator and preserver of men derives the greatest satisfaction not from the unusual prosperity of the few but the widespread wellbeing of all. What seems to me to be a decline is, therefore, progress in his eyes; what bruises me is a pleasure to him. Equality persists at a lower level perhaps but is fairer and this fairness constitutes its greatness and its beauty.

I struggle to penetrate God's point of view, from which vantage point I try to observe and judge human affairs.

No one on the earth is yet able to state in any absolute or universal manner that this new condition of society is superior to the old one but it is already simple to see that it is quite different.

Certain defects and certain qualities associated with the constitutions of aristocracies are so hostile to the spirit of our new nations that they could not possibly be introduced into them. Some beneficial tendencies and some bad attitudes were foreign to the former but quite normal for the latter; some ideas automatically register in the imagination of one which the other rejects. They resemble two distinct human types, each one of which has its advantages and individual drawbacks, its typical good and bad points.

Care must, therefore, be taken not to judge up and coming societies by ideas borrowed from those which have ceased to exist. That would be unfair, for such societies are exceedingly different from each other and not eligible to be compared.

It is almost as unreasonable to expect our contemporaries to display virtues which were peculiar to the social conditions of their ancestors, since this very society has collapsed and has dragged the confused collection of all its good and bad features down with it.

Our present grasp of these things is still poorly developed.

I observe a large number of my contemporaries attempting to choose from the institutions, opinions, and ideas which sprang from the aristocratic constitution of society as it was; they would readily abandon some features but would want to retain others which they would transport to their new world.

I believe such men are wasting their time and efforts in an honorable yet sterile task.

No longer is it a matter of retaining the particular advantages which equality of social conditions provides for men but of guaranteeing the new benefits offered by equality. We should not strive to resemble our fathers but should strain to achieve a type of greatness and happiness which belongs to us alone. Now that I have reached the last stage of my course and have discovered from afar, yet all at once, all the various objects which I have examined on my way, I feel full of foreboding and hopes. As I see great dangers which can be warded off and great evils which can be evaded or minimized, I am strengthened increasingly in the conviction that, to be honest and prosperous, democratic nations still only have to wish to be so.

I am quite aware that several of my contemporaries have thought that nations are never masters of themselves on this earth and that of necessity they obey some kind of insurmountable and senseless force which stems from past events, or from race, or from the soil, or from climate.

Those are false and craven doctrines which can only be the product of feeble men or small-minded nations. Providence has created a human being neither wholly independent nor totally slavish. It has, true enough, drawn around each man a circle of fate from which he has no means of escaping but, within its broad boundaries, man is powerful and free, just like nations.

Present-day nations cannot stop social conditions from becoming equal within their land but they can determine whether equality can lead to slavery or freedom, to enlightenment or barbarism, to prosperity or wretchedness.

APPENDICES

VOLUME 1

PART 1

A. (p. 30)   For all the countries of the West which have not yet been explored by Europeans, consult the two journeys undertaken at the expense of Congress by Major Long.

Mr Long states in particular, on the subject of the great American desert, that a line should be drawn more or less parallel to the 20th degree of longitude,[1] beginning at the Red River and ending at the Plate River. From this imaginary line as far as the Rocky Mountains which encircle the Mississippi Valley in the west, lie vast plains, which are, in general, covered with sand, resistant to cultivation or scattered with granite boulders. There is no water in the summer. All that can be found there are immense herds of buffalo and wild horses. Some Indian tribes can also be found there but they are few in number.

Major Long has heard it said that if you climb above the Plate River in the same direction, you still find the same desert on your left, but he has not been able to confirm the accuracy of this report himself. Long's *Expedition*, vol. 2, p. 361.

Whatever credence one may wish to bestow upon Major Long's account, do not forget, however, that he merely crossed the country of which he speaks following this line and without deviating from it widely.

---

1.   The 20th degree of longitude, the Washington meridian, corresponds to about the 99th degree of the Paris meridian.

B. (p. 31)   South America produces in its inter-tropical
regions an incredible profusion of climbing plants known by
the generic name of lianas. The flora of the West Indies accounts
on its own for more than forty different species.

Among the most graceful of these shrubs is a form of passion
flower. This pretty plant, says Descourtiz in his description of
the plant kingdom of the West Indies, attaches itself to trees by
means of its characteristic tendrils to create rippling archways,
and rich, elegant swathes decorated with beautiful purple and
blue flowers which overwhelm the senses with their perfume;
vol. 1, p. 265.

The large-podded acacia is an enormous liana which grows
rapidly and, climbing from tree to tree, sometimes covers more
than half a league; vol. 3, p. 227.

C. (p. 33)   Upon American languages. The languages which
the American Indians speak, from the North Pole to Cape Horn,
are, it is said, all based on the same model and subject to the
same grammatical rules. From this it is possible to conclude
that, in all likelihood, the Indian nations all came from the same
stock.

Each tribe of the American continent speaks a different dialect; but specific languages are small in number. This would
seem equally to prove that the nations of the New World are
not very old.

Additionally, the languages of America have a great degree
of regularity; it is probable that the people who speak them have
not been through great revolutions, neither have they been
forced either willingly or otherwise to mix with foreign nations.
It is usually the amalgamation of several languages into one
which produces irregularities in grammar.

It is only recently that the languages of America and, in
particular the languages of North America, have attracted the
serious attention of philologists. It was then discovered for the
first time that this idiom of a primitive people was the product
of a system of very complicated ideas and extremely well-
thought out constructions. It was noticed that the languages

were very rich and that, in their formation, great care had been taken to make them easy on the ear.

The grammatical system of the native Americans differs in several ways from all other systems but principally in this:

Some European peoples, the Germans for example, are able to combine different expressions if the need arises and to give a complex meaning to certain words. The Indians have extended this in a most surprising way and have managed to fix, as it were, on to one term a great number of ideas. This will be easily understood with the help of an example quoted by M. Duponceau in his *Memoirs of the American Philosophical Society*.

When a Delaware woman plays with a cat or a young dog, he says, you will sometimes hear her say the word *kuligatschis*. This word is made up as follows: *K* is the sign of the second person and represents the familiar form of address; *uli*, which is pronounced *ouli*, is part of the word *wulit* which means "beautiful" or "pretty"; *gat* is part of the word *wichgat* which means "paw"; finally there is *schis*, which is pronounced *chise*, and this is a diminutive ending which gives the idea of "tiny." Thus, in one single word, the Indian woman has said: "Your pretty little paw."

Here is another example of the effectiveness with which the American Indians have formed their words.

A Delaware youth is called *pilapé*. This word is formed from *pilsit* meaning "chaste," "innocent," and from *leénapé* meaning "man"; thus it is a man who is still pure and innocent.

This facility for combining words is especially remarkable in the strange manner with which they form their verbs. The most complicated action can often be rendered by a single verb which conveys all shades of meaning by modifying its construction.

Those who would like to examine in greater detail this subject which I have been only able to touch on in a superficial way should read:

1. The correspondence of M. Duponceau and the Reverend Mr Hecwelder about the Indian languages. This correspondence can be found in volume 1 of *Memoirs of the American*

Philosophical Society, published in Philadelphia, in 1819, by Abraham Small, pp. 356–464.

2. The grammar of the Delaware or Lenape language, by Geilberger with M. Duponceau's preface to it. This is found in the same collection, vol. 3.

3. An excellent résumé of these works is contained at the end of volume 6 of the *American Encyclopaedia*.

D. (p. 35)   In Charlevoix, vol. 1, p. 235, will be found a history of the first war which the French inhabitants of Canada undertook against the Iroquois in 1610. The Indians, although they were armed with bows and arrows, offered desperate resistance to the French and their allies. Charlevoix, who is not a great commentator, is, however, able to show in this extract the contrast between the European manner and that of the Indians as well as the different idea which the two races had of honor.

"The French," he said, "seized hold of the beaver skins with which the fallen Iroquois were covered. The Hurons, their allies, were scandalized by the sight of this. The latter, for their part, began to exercise their usual cruelties upon the prisoners, devouring one of those who had been killed, which horrified the French. Thus, these barbarous men prided themselves on a detachment which they were surprised at not finding in our nation and did not understand that it is less heinous to strip the bodies of the dead than to feed upon their flesh like wild animals."

Charlevoix again, in another extract, vol. 1, p. 230, describes thus the first torture which Champlain witnessed and the return of the Hurons to their own village:

After having covered eight leagues our allies halted and, taking one of their captives, reproached him for all the cruelty which the braves from their nation who had fallen into his hands had suffered and told him that he should expect to be treated similarly, adding that if he had any courage he would prove it by singing. He immediately intoned his battle song and all the songs that he knew but in a very mournful way, said Champlain, who had not yet had the time to get to know that all primitive music contains a lugubrious element. His torture, accompanied by all the horrors which will be described later, terrified the French who made every effort to put a stop to it, but in vain. The following night, when a Huron dreamed that they were being followed, the retreat changed to real flight and the Indians did not stop anywhere until they were out of all danger.

From the moment that they spied the huts of their village, they cut long sticks to which they attached the scalps that they had shared between them and they carried them in triumph. Seeing them, the women ran toward them, flung themselves into the water and, having swum out to the canoes, took the bloody scalps from the hands of their husbands and tied them around their necks.

The braves offered one of these horrible trophies to Champlain and also made him a present of some bows and arrows, the only spoils which they had been willing to seize from the Iroquois, begging him to show them to the King of France.

Champlain lived alone all one winter surrounded by these barbarous people without either his person or his property being compromised for a single moment.

E. (p. 51)   Although the puritanical rigor which presided over the birth of the English colonies in America is now much less intractable, singular traces of it are still to be found in their habits and laws.

In 1792, at the same time as the anti-Christian republic of France began its temporary existence, the legislative body of Massachusetts promulgated the following law to force the observance of the Sabbath upon the citizens. Here are the preamble and the principal clauses of this law which merit the attention of the reader:

"Whereas," says the legislator, "the observance of the Lord's Day is highly promotive of the welfare of a community, by affording necessary seasons for relaxation from labor and the cares of business; for moral reflections and conversation on the duties of life, and the frequent errors of human conduct; for public and private worship of the maker, Governor and Judge of the world; and for those acts of charity which support and adorn a Christian society: And whereas some thoughtless and irreligious persons, inattentive to the duties and benefits of the Lord's Day, profane the same, by unnecessarily pursuing their worldly business and recreation on that day, to their own great damage, as members of a Christian society; to the great disturbance of well-disposed persons, and to the great damage of the community, by producing dissipation of manners and immoralities of life:

"Be it therefore enacted by the Senate and House of Representatives,

"That no person or persons shall open his shop, ware-house or work-house, nor shall do any manner of labor, business or work nor be present at any concert of music, dancing, or any public diversion, show or entertainment, nor use any sport, game, play or recreation, on the Lord's Day upon penalty of a sum not exceeding twenty shillings, nor less than ten shillings, for every offense.

"That no traveler, drover, waggoner, teamster shall travel on the Lord's Day (except from necessity or charity) upon the penalty of a sum not exceeding twenty shillings, nor less than ten shillings.

"That no vintner, retailer of strong liquors, innholder shall entertain or suffer any of the inhabitants of the respective towns where they dwell to abide and remain in their houses drinking or spending their time, either idly or at play, or doing any secular business on the Lord's Day on penalty of ten shillings, payable by such vintner, retailer or innholder; and every person drinking or abiding: and every such licensed person having been three times convicted, shall be debarred from renewing his license forever after.

"That any person, being able of body and not otherwise necessarily prevented, who shall, for the space of three months together, absent him or herself from the public worship of God, on the Lord's day shall pay a fine of ten shillings.

"That if any person shall, on the Lord's Day, within the walls of any house of public worship, behave rudely or indecently, he or she shall pay a fine of not more than forty shillings, nor less than five shillings.

"That the tythingmen in the several towns and districts, within this Commonwealth, shall be held and obliged to inquire into, and inform of all offenses against this Act;

"And every tythingman is hereby authorized and empowered, to enter into any of the rooms and other parts of an inn, or public house or entertainment, on the Lord's Day, to examine all persons whom they shall have good cause to suspect of unnecessarily traveling as aforesaid, on the Lord's Day, and to demand of all such persons the cause thereof; and if any person shall refuse to give answer, he shall pay a fine not exceeding five pounds; and if the reason given for such traveling shall not be satisfactory to such tythingman, he shall enter a complaint against the person traveling, before a Justice of the Peace in the county where the offense is committed." *Law of 8 March 1792. General Laws of Massachusetts*, vol. 1, p. 410.

On 11 March 1797, a new law increased the amount of fines, half of which was to be given to the person who had denounced the offender. Same collection, vol. 1, p. 525.

On 16 February 1816, a new law confirmed these same measures. Same collection, vol. 2, p. 405.

Comparable arrangements exist in the laws of the state of New York, revised in 1827 and 1828. (See *Revised Statutes*, pt 1, ch. 20, p. 675.) In these it is stated that no one can go hunting, fish, play games, or frequent places where alcohol is available on the Sabbath. No one may travel unless it is unavoidable.

And this is not the only trace which the religious spirit and austere ways of the first immigrants have left in the laws.

In the revised statutes of the state of New York, vol. 1, p. 662, the following article can be found:

"Every person who shall win or lose at play, or by betting at any time, the sum or value of twenty-five dollars" (about 132 francs) "or upwards, within the space of twenty-four hours, shall be deemed guilty of a misdemeanor, and on conviction shall be fined not less than five times the sum so lost or won; which shall be paid to the overseers of the poor of the town.

"Every person who shall lose at any time or sitting, the sum or value of twenty-five dollars or upwards may sue for and recover the money. In case the person losing such sum or value shall not sue for the sum or value so by him lost, the overseers of the poor of the town where the offense was committed, may sue for and recover the sum or value so lost and paid, together with treble the said sum or value, from the winner thereof, for the benefit of the poor."

The laws which we have just quoted are very recent; but who could understand them without recourse to the origins of the colonies? I have no doubt that, currently, the penal part of this legislation is rarely enforced; laws preserve their inflexibility whereas customs have succumbed to the passage of time. However, the observance of the Sabbath in America is still something that strikes the visitor forcibly.

There is, in particular, a large American town in which, from Saturday evening onwards, social activity is suspended. You pass through it at a time when it would seem ideal for the middle-aged to be engaged upon business and the young upon pleasure, and you will find yourself surrounded by a profound silence. Not only does no one work but there seems to be no living soul there. You can hear neither the movement of industry nor the sounds of joy, not even the muffled murmuring which constantly arises from the heart of a great city. Chains are hung across the streets near to the churches; half-closed shutters grudgingly admit a ray of sunshine into the houses of the inhabitants. Now and then you notice an isolated man gliding silently through the deserted thoroughfares and along abandoned streets.

The next day at daybreak, the wheels of carriages, the noise of hammers, the shouts of the people start to make themselves heard; the city wakes up; an enthusiastic crowd rushes toward the places of business and industry; everything is buzzing, moving, pushing around you. A kind of feverish activity replaces the lethargic stupor of the day before; you might suppose that each man had but one day at his disposal to acquire wealth and to enjoy it.

F. (p. 56)   I don't need to say that, in the chapter which has just been read, I have not tried to give a history of America. My sole aim has been to enable the reader to appreciate the influence which the opinions and customs of the first immigrants had exercised upon the fate of the different colonies and of the Union in general. I limited myself, therefore, to quoting just a few isolated fragments.

I don't know whether I am mistaken, but it seems to me that, by taking the path which I have merely touched on here, one could represent the early days of the American republics in a way that would not be unworthy of attracting the attention of the public and that would, without question, give those in government matters upon which to reflect. Not being able to devote myself to this task, I did at least want to make it easy for others. Thus, I had it in mind to present a short catalogue and brief analysis of the works which it would seem to me to be the most useful to consult.

At the top of the list of the general documents which it would be fruitful to consult, I place the work entitled *Historical Collection of State Papers and other authentic documents, intended as materials for an history of the United States of America*, by Ebenezer Hazard.

The first volume of this collection, which was published in Philadelphia in 1792, contains an exact copy of all the charters granted by the Crown of England to the emigrants, as well as the principal acts of the colonial governments at the very beginning of their existence. Amongst others, a great number of authentic documents relating to the affairs of New England and Virginia during this period can be found.

The second volume is almost entirely devoted to the acts of the confederation of 1643. This federal pact, which the colonies of New England set up with a view of resisting the Indians, was the first example of union demonstrated by the Anglo-Americans. There were several other confederations of the same type, up to the one of 1776, which led to the independence of the colonies.

The Philadelphia historical collection is housed in the Bibliothèque Royale.

Each colony has, besides, its historical monuments, several of
which are very useful. Let me begin with Virginia, which is the
state that was inhabited the earliest.

The first of all the historians of Virginia was its founder, John
Smith. Captain Smith has left us a volume entitled: *The General
History of Virginia and New England by Captain John Smith,
sometime Governor in those Countries and Admiral of New
England*, printed in London in 1627. (This volume can be found
in the Bibliothèque Royale.) Smith's work is enhanced by very
curious maps and engravings, which date from the time when it
was printed. The historian's account runs from 1584 until 1626.
Smith's book is highly thought of and deservedly so. The author
is one of the most celebrated adventurers to have appeared in a
century which was full of adventure, living at its end; the book
itself imparts that passion for discovery, that spirit of enterprise
which characterized men of that period; courtly manners are
seen to accompany negotiating skills which led to the acquisition
of wealth.

But what is especially remarkable about Captain Smith is that
he combines the virtues of his contemporaries with qualities
which remained alien to most of them; his style is simple and
clear, his accounts all have the ring of truth, his descriptions are
not elaborate.

This author throws valuable light on the state of the Indians
at the time of the discovery of North America.

The second historian who should be consulted is Beverley.
Beverley's work has been translated into French and was published in Amsterdam in 1707. The author begins his account
with the year 1585 and finishes it with the year 1700. The
first part of the book contains what should properly be called
historical documents, relative to the infancy of the colony. The
second contains a curious picture of the state of the Indians at
that distant time. The third provides very clear ideas about the
manners, social state, laws, and political habits of the Virginians
who were the author's contemporaries.

Beverley was a Virginian, which leads him to say at the
beginning, "that he begs his readers not to examine his work
too critically, given that he was born in the Indies and cannot

aspire to purity of language." Despite this colonist's modesty, the author shows, throughout the whole book, that he vehemently supports the supremacy of the mother country. Also to be found in Beverley's work are numerous examples of that spirit of civil liberty which has, since then, inspired the English colonists of America. Examples of the divisions which have so long existed among them and which have often delayed their independence can equally be found there. Beverley detests his Catholic neighbors in Maryland even more than the English government. The author's style is simple; his accounts are often full of interest and inspire confidence. The French translation of Beverley's work can be found in the Bibliothèque Royale.

I saw, in America, but have not been able to find in France, a work which also deserves to be consulted. It is entitled *History of Virginia*, by William Stith. This book provides curious details but it seemed to me to be long and diffuse.

The oldest and the best document to be consulted on the history of the Carolinas is a little book entitled *The History of Carolina*, by John Lawson, printed in London in 1718.

Lawson's work begins with a journey of discoveries in the west of Carolina. This journey is written in the form of a journal; the author's accounts are confused; his observations are very superficial; but you will find there a quite striking description of the ravages caused by both smallpox and brandy among the Indians of that period, as well as a curious picture of the corruption of manners prevalent among them which were fostered by the presence of the Europeans.

The second part of Lawson's work is devoted to giving the physical condition of Carolina and its products.

In the third part, the author gives an interesting description of the way of life, habits, and government of the Indians at that time.

There is often a degree of wit and originality in this part of the book.

Lawson's history ends with the charter granted to Carolina in the time of Charles II.

The overall tone of the book is light, often licentious, and presents a perfect contrast to the deeply serious works published at the same period in New England.

Lawson's history is an extremely rare document in America and cannot be obtained in Europe. There is, however, a copy in the Bibliothèque Royale.

From the deep south of the United States, I move immediately on to the northern extremity. The area between was not populated until much later.

Firstly, I must mention a very curious collection entitled; *Collection of the Massachusetts Historical Society*, printed initially in Boston in 1792, reprinted in 1806. This work is not in the Bibliothèque Royale, nor, I believe, in any other library.

This collection, which still continues, contains a great number of very valuable documents relating to the history of the different states of New England. Unpublished correspondence and authentic items which have been buried in provincial archives can be found there. Gookin's entire work about the Indians has been included therein.

I have mentioned several times, in the course of the chapter to which this appendix refers, the work of Nathaniel Morton entitled: *New England's Memorial*. What I said about it is sufficient proof that it is worthy of the attention of those who would wish to know the history of New England. Nathaniel Morton's book was reprinted in Boston in 1826. It cannot be found in the Bibliothèque Royale.

The most highly thought of and most important document on the history of New England that exists is the work of R. Cotton Mather, entitled: *Magnalia Christi Americana, or the Ecclesiastical History of New England, 1620–1698*, 2 volumes, reprinted in Hartford in 1820. I do not believe there to be a copy in the Bibliothèque Royale.

The author divided his work into seven books.

The first presents the history of the preparations for the foundation of New England and what led up to it.

The second contains the lives of the first governors and the principal magistrates who ran the region.

The third is devoted to the lives and works of the evangelical ministers who, during the same period, had the care of souls.

In the fourth, the author explains about the foundation and development of the university of Cambridge in Massachusetts.

In the fifth, he lays out the principles and disciplines of the Church of New England.

The sixth is devoted to retracing certain facts which show, according to Mather, the beneficial acts of Providence on behalf of the people of New England.

And finally, in the seventh, the author tells us about the heresies and problems to which the Church of New England was exposed.

Cotton Mather was an evangelical minister who spent his life in Boston where he had been born.

His accounts are enlivened and fired by all the zeal and religious passions which led to the foundation of New England. Frequently traces of poor taste in his manner of writing can be found; but he is compelling because he is full of an enthusiasm which communicates itself to the reader. He is often intolerant, still more often credulous; but he does not ever give the impression of seeking to deceive; sometimes you can even find fine passages and true and profound reflections such as the following:

"Before the arrival of the Puritans," he says, vol. 1, ch. 4, p. 61, "there were more than a few attempts of the *English*, to people and improve the parts of *New England*; but the designs of those attempts being aimed no higher than the advancement of some *worldly interests*, a constant series of disasters has confounded them, until there was a plantation erected upon the nobler designs of *christianity*; and that plantation, though it has had more adversaries than perhaps any one upon earth; yet, *having obtained help from God, it continues to this day*."

Mather sometimes adds soft and tenderhearted images to the harshness of his descriptions: having spoken with an English woman whose religious zeal had taken her to America with her husband and who shortly afterwards died as a result of the fatigue and misery of exile, he adds this:

"As for her virtuous spouse, Isaac Johnson, he tried to live without her, lik'd it not, and dy'd" (vol. 1, p. 71).

Mather's book portrays in an admirable way the times and the country which he sets out to describe.

Wishing to show us what motives led the Puritans to seek a refuge overseas, he says:

> The God of Heaven served as it were, a summons upon the *spirits* of his people in the English nation; stirring up the spirits of thousands which never saw the *faces* of each other, with a most unanimous inclination to leave all the pleasant accommodations of their native country; and go over a terrible *ocean*, into a more terrible desert, for the *pure enjoyment of all his ordinances*. It is now reasonable that before we pass any further, the *reasons* of this undertaking should be more exactly made known unto *posterity*, especially unto the *posterity* of those that were the undertakers, lest they come at length to forget and neglect *the true interest* of New England. Wherefore I shall now transcribe some of *them* from a manuscript, wherein they were then tendered unto consideration.
>
> *First*, It will be a service unto the *Church* of great consequence, to carry the *Gospel* into *those* parts of the world (North America), and raise a bulwark against the kingdom of *antichrist*, which the *Jesuits* labor to rear up in all parts of the world.
>
> *Secondly*, All other Churches of *Europe* have been brought under *desolations*; and it may be feared that the like judgments are coming upon *us*; and who knows but God hath provided this place (New England) to be a *refuge* for many, whom he means to save out of the *General Destruction*.
>
> *Thirdly*, The land grows weary of her *inhabitants*, insomuch that *man*, which is the most precious of all creatures, is here more vile and base than the earth he treads upon: *children*, *neighbors*, and *friends*, especially the *poor*, are counted the greatest burdens, which if things were right would be the chiefest earthly *blessings*.
>
> *Fourthly*, We are grown to that intemperance in all *excess of riot*, as no mean estate almost will suffice a man to keep sail with his *equals*, and he that fails in it, must live in scorn and contempt: hence it comes to pass, that all *arts* and *trades* are carried in that deceitful manner, and unrighteous course, as it is almost

impossible for a good upright man to maintain his constant charge, and live comfortably in them.

Fifthly, The *schools* of learning and religion are so corrupted, as most children, even the best, wittiest, and of the fairest hopes, are perverted, corrupted, and utterly overthrown, by the multitude of evil examples and licentious behaviors in these *seminaries*.

Sixthly, The *whole earth* is the *Lord's garden*, and he hath given it to the sons of *Adam*, to be tilled and improved by them; why then should we stand starving here for places of habitation, and in the mean time suffer whole countries, as profitable for the use of man, to lie waste without any improvement?

Seventhly, What can be a better or nobler work, and more worthy of a *christian*, than to erect and support a *reformed particular Church* in its infancy, and unite our forces with such a company of faithful people, as by a timely assistance may grow stronger and prosper; but for want of it, may be put to great hazard, if not be wholly ruined.

Eighthly, If any such are known to be godly, and live in wealth and prosperity here (in England), shall forsake all this to join with this *reformed church*, and with it run the hazard of an hard and mean condition, it will be an example of great use, both for the removing of *scandal*, and to give more *life* unto the *faith* of God's people in their prayers for the plantation, and also to encourage others to join the more willingly in it.

Further on, while describing the moral principles of the Church of New England, Mather comes out violently against the custom of drinking people's health at the table, which he calls a pagan and abominable practice.

He censures with the same rigor all the decorations that women might put in their hair and condemns, without pity, the fashion which he says has grown up among them of uncovering their necks and arms.

In another part of his work, he gives a detailed account of some incidents of witchcraft which had alarmed New England. One can see that visible deeds of the devil in the affairs of the world seemed to him to be an incontestable and proven fact.

In a great number of places this book reveals the spirit of civil liberty and political independence which characterized the author's contemporaries. Their principles in matters of government are evident throughout. Thus, for example, we find that, in 1630, ten years after the establishment of Plymouth, the inhabitants of Massachusetts contributed £400 toward the foundation of the university of Cambridge.

Moving from those general documents relating to New England's history to those which refer to the separate states within its boundary, I must first mention the work entitled: *The History of the Colony of Massachusetts*, by Hutchinson, the lieutenant-governor of the Massachusetts province, in two volumes. A copy of this book can be found in the Bibliothèque Royale; it is a second edition, printed in London in 1765.

Hutchinson's history, which I have quoted several times during the chapter to which this note refers, began with the year 1628 and finished with the year 1750. Throughout the work there runs an impressive strand of truth; the style is simple and unaffected. The account is full of detail.

The best document to consult, as far as Connecticut is concerned, is the history by Benjamin Trumbull, entitled: *A Complete History of Connecticut, Civil and Ecclesiastical, 1630–1764*, in two volumes, printed in New Haven in 1818. I do not believe that Trumbull's work is in the Bibliothèque Royale.

This account contains a clear and dispassionate description of all the events which took place in Connecticut during the period given in the title. The author has consulted the best sources and his narrative has the ring of truth. Everything that he says about the early days in Connecticut is extremely interesting. In his work, see particularly *The Constitution of 1639*, vol. 1, p. 100, and also *The Penal Laws of Connecticut*, vol. 1, ch. 7, p. 123.

Jeremy Belknap's work entitled *The History of New Hampshire*, printed in two volumes in Boston in 1792, is quite rightly very highly thought of. In particular, in Belknap's work, see chapter 3 of the first volume. In this chapter, the author gives very important facts about the political and religious principles of the Puritans. In this work can be found this curious quotation from a sermon given in 1663: "New England should remember at all times that it was founded for religious not commercial reasons. You can tell from its face that it has made purity of doctrine and discipline an article of faith. Let tradesmen and all those who are engaged in piling up their money remember that it was religion and not profit which was the aim in founding these colonies. If there is anyone among us who, in his valuation of the world and of religion, regards the first as thirteen and the second as twelve, he is not inspired by the feelings of a true son of New England." Readers will find more general ideas and more considered opinion in Belknap than in any other work of American historians at present.

I do not know whether this book can be found in the Bibliothèque Royale.

At the forefront of the central states which are long established and which are worthy of our attention, are the states of New York and of Pennsylvania. The best history which we have on the history of New York is entitled: *History of New York*, by William Smith, printed in London in 1757. There is a French translation of this which was also printed in London, in 1767, in one volume. Smith provides us with facts about the wars between the French and the English in America. Of all American historians, it is he who gives the best description of the famous confederation of the Iroquois.

As for Pennsylvania. I could not do better than recommend the work of Proud entitled: *The History of Pennsylvania, from the Original Institution and Settlement of the Province, under the First Proprietor and Governor, William Penn, in 1681 till after the Year 1742*, by Robert Proud, in two volumes, printed in Philadelphia in 1797.

This book is especially worthy of the reader's attention; it contains a whole host of interesting documents about Penn, the doctrine of the Quakers, the character, customs, and habits of the first inhabitants of Pennsylvania. As far as I know, there is no copy of this in the Bibliothèque Royale.

I do not need to add that among the most important documents relating to Pennsylvania are the works of Penn himself and those of Franklin. Many readers are familiar with these works.

During my stay in America, I consulted most of the books which I have just mentioned. The Bibliothèque Royale made some available to me; others were lent to me by Mr Warden, former Consul General of the United States in Paris and author of an excellent work on America. I would not wish to end this note without expressing my gratitude to Mr Warden.

G. (p. 64)   We read the following in Jefferson's *Memoirs*: "In the early times of the colony, when lands were to be obtained for little or nothing, some provident individuals procured large grants; and, desirous of founding great families for themselves, settled them on their descendants in fee tail. The transmission of this property from generation to generation, in the same name, raised up a distinct set of families, who being privileged by law in the perpetuation of their wealth, were thus formed into a Patrician order, distinguished by the splendor and luxury of their establishments. From this order, too, the king habitually selected his consellors of State."

In the United States, the principal provisions of English law relating to inheritance have been universally rejected.

"The first rule of inheritance," says Mr Kent, "is, that if a person owning real estate, *dies seised*, or as owner, without devising the same, the estate shall descend to his lawful descendants in the direct line of lineal descent, and if there be but one person, then to him or her alone, and if more than one person, and all of equal degree of consanguinity to the ancester, then the inheritance shall descend to the several persons as tenants in common in equal parts without distinction of sex."

This rule was laid down for the first time in the state of New York by a statute of 23 February 1786 (see *Revised Statutes*, vol. 3; Appendix, p. 48); it has been adopted in all revised statutes in this state. At present it prevails throughout the United States, with the sole exception of the state of Vermont where the male heir inherits a double share. Kent's *Commentaries*, vol. 4, p. 370.

In the same work, vol. 4, pp. 1–22, Kent gives us the history of American legislation relating to entailment. We learn from this that, before the American Revolution, English law on entailment was the accepted law in all the colonies. Actual entailments (Estates' tail) were abolished in Virginia from 1776 (this abolition was a motion presented by Jefferson; see Jefferson's *Memoirs*), and in the state of New York in 1786. This same abolition took place subsequently in North Carolina, Kentucky, Tennessee, Georgia, and Missouri. In Vermont, the states of Indiana, Illinois, South Carolina, and Louisiana, entailment was never in force. States which set out to preserve English law relating to entailment modified it so as to remove the main aristocratic characteristics. "The general policy of this country does not encourage restraints upon the power of alienation of land," said Kent.

What will particularly strike the French reader who studies American inheritance law is that our laws on the same subject are infinitely more democratic even than theirs.

American laws share the father's possessions out equally, but only in instances where his wishes are not known: "for each man," says the law in the state of New York (*Revised Statutes*, vol. 3; Appendix, p. 51), "shall have full and free liberty, power and authority, to give, dispose, will or devise, to any person or persons (except bodies politic and corporate) by his last will and testament."

French law makes equal division or nearly equal division the legal responsibility of the testator.

Most American republics still accept entailment and limit themselves to trying to curtail its effects.

French law does not allow entailment under any circumstances.

If the social condition of the Americans is even more democratic than ours, our laws are more democratic than theirs. This is more easily explained than one might think: in France, democracy is still preoccupied with the work of destruction; in America, it reigns quietly over the ruins it has already made.

H. (p. 71)   SUMMARY OF VOTING RIGHTS IN THE UNITED STATES

All states grant the privilege of voting at the age of twenty-one.

In all states, one must have been resident for a certain length of time in the district where one is to vote. This period varies between three months and two years.

As for financial qualification: in the state of Massachusetts, to be allowed to vote one must have an income of £3 or capital of £60.

In Rhode Island, one must have real estate worth $133 (704 francs).

In Connecticut, one must have property which gives an income of $17 (about 90 francs). A year's service in the militia also gives one the right to vote.

In New Jersey, a voter must have assets of £50.

In South Carolina and Maryland, the voter must possess 50 acres of land.

In Tennessee, he must have some kind of property.

In the states of Mississippi, Ohio, Georgia, Virginia, Pennsylvania, Delaware, and New York, to be granted voting rights one must merely have paid one's taxes: in most of these states, service in the militia equates with paying taxes.

In Maine and New Hampshire, as long as one does not appear on the list of the destitute, one may vote.

Finally, in the states of Missouri, Alabama, Illinois, Louisiana, Indiana, Kentucky, and Vermont, none of the conditions relate to wealth.

Only North Carolina, I believe, imposes different conditions for electing senators and for electing to the House of Representatives. To vote in the first, one must have 50 acres of land but to elect a representative, it is sufficient merely to pay one's taxes.

J. (p. 113)   A prohibitive system exists in the United States. The small number of customs officers and the great extent of coastline make smuggling very easy; however, it is much less widespread than elsewhere because every one works to prevent it.

In America, as there is no fire-prevention service, there are more fires than in Europe; but in general they are put out more quickly because the surrounding population congregate rapidly at the place of danger.

K. (p. 115)   It is not right to say that centralization was
a product of the French Revolution; the French Revolution
perfected it but did not create it. The taste for centralization and
the mania for governmental regulation in France goes back to
the time when jurists entered government; this goes back to the
time of Philippe the Fair. Since then, these have both been on
the increase. This is what M. de Malesherbes, speaking in the
name of the *Cour des Aides*, said to Louis XVI in 1775 (see
*Mémoires pour servir à l'histoire du droit public de la France en
matière d'impôts*, p. 654, printed in Brussels in 1779):

> . . . Every corporation and every community of citizens retained
> the right to administer its own affairs; a right which was not just
> part of the early constitution of the kingdom but had a higher
> origin: it is the right of nature, it is the right of reason. Yet it has
> been taken away from your subjects, Sire, and we have no fear in
> stating that from this point of view your administration has fallen
> into what we might describe as childish extremes.
>
> From the time when powerful ministers made it a political
> principle not to allow the convocation of a national assembly,
> one consequence has followed another until the deliberations of
> the inhabitants of a village are declared invalid if they have not
> been authorized by an intendant; so, if a community has an
> expensive undertaking, it must suffer the control of the intend-
> ant's sub-delegate and, thus, follow the plan he proposes, employ
> the workers he prefers and pay them as he decides; and if the
> community is to take a legal action, it must also be authorized by
> the intendant. The cause must be pleaded before this first tribunal
> before being brought to justice. And if the opinion of the intendant
> is contrary to that of the people, or if their adversary is favored
> by the intendant, the community is deprived of the power of
> exercising its rights. These, Sire, are the means by which all
> municipal spirit has been stifled in France and by which all the
> opinions of the citizens have been smothered, as far as it was
> possible; the entire nation has been as it were *silenced* and given
> over to guardians.

How could one express it better today, than that the French Revolution has achieved what one might call *conquests* in the matter of centralization?

In 1789, Jefferson wrote to one of his friends from Paris: "Never was there a country where the practice of governing too much had taken deeper root and done more mischief." *Letters to Madison*, 28 August 1789.

The truth is that in France, for several centuries, the central power has always done all that it could to extend central administration; in this aim, it has had no other limits than its own strength.

The central power created by the French Revolution has gone further than any created by its forbears because it has been stronger and more knowledgeable than they: Louis XIV committed the minutiae of community living to the whims of an intendant; Napoleon left them to that of a minister. It is still the same principle but the effects were more or less far-reaching.

L. (p. 118)   The immutability of the constitution in France is an inevitable consequence of our laws.

And, to begin with the most important of all the laws—the one which decides the order of succession to the throne—what can be more constant in its principle than a political order founded upon the natural succession of father to son? In 1814, Louis XVIII had declared the perpetuity of the law of political succession in favor of his own family; those who controlled the consequences of the Revolution of 1830 followed his example: only they established the perpetuity of the law in favor of another family; in this, they imitated Chancellor Maupeou, who, by setting up the new parliament upon the ruins of the old, took care to declare in the same ordinance that the new magistrates should be as permanent as their predecessors had been.

The laws of 1830, like those of 1814, give no indication of any way of changing the constitution. Moreover, it is obvious that ordinary legislation would not be sufficient for such a thing.

From whom does the king draw his powers?—From the constitution. And the peers?—From the constitution. How then could the king, the peers, and the deputies, collectively, change any part of a law by virtue alone of which they govern? Without the constitution they are nothing: where then should they position themselves so as to change the constitution? There are two possibilities: either their efforts are powerless against the charter, which continues to exist despite them, and thus they continue to reign in its name; or they manage to change the charter and thus, as the law which caused their existence no longer exists, they no longer exist either. By destroying the charter, they themselves are destroyed.

This is even more evident in the laws of 1830 than in those of 1814. In 1814, the royal prerogative placed it somehow outside and above the constitution; but in 1830, it was, by its own admission, created by the constitution and was absolutely nothing without it.

So it is then that a part of our constitution is immutable, because it has been bound to the destiny of one family; and the body of the constitution is equally immutable, because there appears to be no legal method of changing it.

None of this is applicable to England. Who can say if England changes its constitution since it is nowhere written down?

M. (p. 118)   The most respected authors who have written about the English constitution confirm at every possible opportunity the omnipotence of Parliament.

Delolme says, ch. 10, p. 77: "*It is a fundamental principle with the English lawyers, that Parliament can do everything, except making a woman a man or a man a woman.*"

Blackstone expresses himself even more explicitly, if not more energetically than Delolme as follows:

The power and jurisdiction of parliament, says Sir Edward Coke (4 Hist. 36), is so transcendent and absolute, that it cannot be confined, either for causes or persons, within any bounds. And of this high court, he adds, it may be truly said, *si antiquitatem spectes, est vetustissima; si dignitatem, est honoratissima; si jurisdictionem, est capacissima*. It hath sovereign and uncontrolable authority in the making, confirming, enlarging, restraining, abrogating, repealing, reviving, and expounding of laws, concerning matters of all possible denominations, ecclesiastical, or temporal, civil, military, maritime, or criminal; this being the place where that absolute despotic power, which must in all governments reside somewhere, is intrusted by the constitution of these kingdoms. All mischiefs and grievances, operations and remedies, that transcend the ordinary course of the laws, are within the reach of this extraordinary tribunal. It can regulate or new-model the succession to the crown; as was done in the reign of Henry VIII and William III. It can alter the established religion of the land; as was done in a variety of instances, in the reigns of king Henry VIII and his three children. *It can change and create afresh even the constitution of the kingdom* and of parliaments themselves; as was done by the act of union, and the several statutes for triennial and septennial elections. It can, in short, do everything that is not naturally impossible; and therefore some have not scrupled to call its power, by a figure rather too bold, the *omnipotence* of parliament.

N. (p. 130)   There is no question on which the American constitutions agree better than on that of political judgments.

All the constitutions which are concerned with this give the House of Representatives the exclusive right of impeachment, all that is except North Carolina, which grants the same right to grand juries (article 23).

Almost all the constitutions grant the Senate, or the assembly which takes its place, the exclusive right of pronouncing judgment.

The only punishments which the political tribunals can impose are: removal from office or debarment from public duties in the future. The constitution of Virginia alone is able to impose all types of punishment.

The crimes which are subject to political judgments are: in the federal constitution (section 4, article 1), in that of Indiana (article 3, p. 23, 24), of New York (article 5), of Delaware (article 5), high treason, bribery, and other serious crimes or offenses.

In the constitution of Massachusetts (Ch. 1, section 2), of

North Carolina (article 23), and of Virginia (p. 252), misconduct and maladministration.

In Vermont (ch. 2, article 24), maladministration.

In South Carolina (article 5), Kentucky (article 5), Tennessee (article 4), Ohio (article 1, sections 23, 24), Louisiana (article 5), Mississippi (article 5), Alabama (article 6), Pennsylvania (article 4), offenses committed while carrying out official duties.

In the states of Illinois, Georgia, Maine, and Connecticut, no particular crimes are specified.

O. (p. 199)   It is true that European powers can wage great maritime wars against the Union but it is always easier and less dangerous to undertake a maritime war than a land war. Maritime war requires only one kind of effort. A trading nation which agrees to give the government the necessary money will always have a fleet. Now, it is much easier to conceal from a nation the sacrifice of money than that of men and personal effort. Besides, defeats at sea rarely compromise the existence or independence of the peoples who suffer them.

As for land wars, it is clear that the European people offer no threat to the American Union.

It is extremely difficult to transport and sustain more than 25,000 soldiers in America, which would be the army for a nation of about 2,000,000 men. The largest European nation fighting thus against the Union would be in the same position as a nation of 2,000,000 inhabitants at war with one of 12,000,000. Add to this the fact that the American is within reach of all his supplies and the European is 4,000 miles from his and the fact that the vastness of the territory of the United States would present an insurmountable obstacle to conquest.

PART 2

A. (p. 217)   It was in April 1704 that the first American newspaper appeared. It was published in Boston. See *Collections of the Historical Society of Massachusetts*, vol. 6, p. 66.

One would be wrong to think that the periodical press has

always been entirely free in America; an attempt was made to establish something akin to preliminary censorship and warranty. This is what can be found in the legislative documents of Massachusetts, 14 January 1722.

The committee appointed by the General Assembly (the legislative body of the province) to examine the affair relating to the newspaper called *The New England Courant*, "thinks that the tendency of said newspaper is to greet religion derisively and to make it fall into contempt; that the holy authors are treated in a profane and irreverant manner in it; that the conduct of the ministers of the Gospel is interpreted with malice; that the government of His Majesty is insulted, and that the peace and tranquillity of this province are troubled by said newspaper; consequently, the committee is of the opinion that James Franklin, printer and editor, should be forbidden to print and publish said journal or any other writing any more in the future before having submitted them to the secretary of the province. Justices of the peace of the district of Suffolk shall be charged with obtaining from Mr Franklin a surety that vouches for his good conduct for the coming year."

The suggestion of the committee was accepted and became law but the effect was nil. The newspaper avoided the constraint by putting the name of *Benjamin* Franklin instead of *James* Franklin at the bottom of its columns and this measure was supported by public opinion.

B. (p. 318)   To be a voter in the counties (those who represent landed property) before the Reform Bill passed in 1832, it was necessary to have, either through ownership or on lease for life, land bringing in an income of 40 shillings net. This law was passed under Henry VI around 1450. It has been calculated that 40 shillings in the time of Henry VI is equivalent to £30 today. However, this prerequisite adopted in the fifteenth century has been allowed to survive up to 1832, which proves how democratic the English Constitution became over time, while appearing to remain static. See Delolme; see also Blackstone, bk 1, ch. 4.

English juries are chosen by the sheriff of the county (Delolme, vol. 1, ch. 12). The sheriff is generally speaking a man of standing in the county; he carries out judicial and administrative duties; he represents the king and is appointed by him every year (Blackstone, bk 1, ch. 9). His position places him above the suspicion of corruption in relation to the parties involved; moreover, if his impartiality is in doubt, one can object to the entire jury which he has appointed and then another official is charged with choosing new jurors. See Blackstone, bk 3, ch. 23.

In order to have the right to be sworn in as a juror, one must possess land which brings in an income of at least 10 shillings (Blackstone, bk 3, ch. 23). It will be noted that this condition was imposed during the reign of William and Mary, that is to say around 1700, a time when the value of money was infinitely greater than it is today. It can be seen that the English based their jury system not on ability but on landed property, just like all their other political institutions.

Farmers were finally permitted to become jurors, but they were required to have very long leases and a net income of 20 shillings, independent of rents. (Blackstone, idem.)

C. (p. 318)   The federal constitution has introduced the jury into the tribunals of the Union just as the states had themselves introduced it into their own individual courts; but it has not made any particular rules for the choice of jurors. The federal courts draw their jurors from the ordinary list which each state has produced for its own use. It is, therefore, amongst state laws that one should search in order to understand the theory behind the composition of the jury in America. See Story's *Commentaries on the Constitution*, bk 3, ch. 38, pp. 654–659, and Sergeant's *Constitutional Law*, p. 165. See also the federal laws of 1789, 1800, and 1802 on this subject.

In order to be able to understand thoroughly American principles as far as the composition of juries is concerned, I have investigated the laws of widely separated states. Here are the general conclusions which can be drawn from such an examination.

In America, all citizens who are eligible to vote have the right to become a juror. The great state of New York, however, has made a slight difference between these two functions, but it is contrary to the spirit of our laws; that is to say that there are fewer people who can serve on juries in New York than there are voters. In general, in the United States, it can be said that the right to serve on a jury, just like the right to elect representatives, is extended to everyone; but the exercise of this right does not fall into everyone's hands.

Each year a body of town or county magistrates, called *selectmen* in New England, *supervisors* in the state of New York, *trustees* in Ohio and *sheriffs* in the parish of Louisiana, choose a certain number of citizens for each county who are to have the right to be elected to serve on a jury and who are supposed capable of so doing. These magistrates, being themselves elective, cause no distrust; their powers are very extensive and very arbitrary, like those, in general, of the republican magistrates, and they frequently make use of them, it is said, especially in New England, to set aside unworthy or incompetent jurors.

The names of jurors thus chosen are transmitted to the county court and from this list of names a jury which is to decide a case is drawn by lot.

Moreover, the Americans have tried in every way to make jury service open to the people and to make it as little onerous as they can. As there are many jurors, each person's turn comes round only every three years. The sessions are held in the main town of each county—the county being roughly equivalent to our *arrondissement*. Thus, the court comes to the jury, rather than the jury having to go to the court, as happens in France; and finally, jurors are remunerated, either by the state or by the parties concerned. In general, they receive one dollar (5 francs 42 centimes) per day, in addition to their traveling expenses. In America, jury service is often seen as a burden but it is a burden which is easy to bear and one to which one submits without difficulty.

See Brevard's *Digest of the Public Statute Law of South Carolina*, vol. 2, p. 338; idem, vol. 1, pp. 454–6; idem, vol. 2, p. 218.

See *The General Laws of Massachusetts, revised and published by authority of the legislature*, vol. 2, pp. 331, 187.

See *The Revised Statutes of the State of New York*, vol. 2, pp. 720, 411, 717, 643.

See *The Statute Law of the State of Tennessee*, vol. 1, p. 209.

See *Acts of the State of Ohio*, pp. 95 and 210.

See *Digeste général des actes de la législature de la Louisiane*, vol. 2, p. 55.

D. (p. 322)   When one closely examines the constitution of civil juries in England, one readily discovers that jurors cannot escape being under the control of the judge.

It is true that the jury's verdict, in civil and criminal cases, generally speaking takes the form of a simple pronouncement which encompasses both the facts and the law. Example: a house is claimed by Peter as having been bought by him; this is the fact. His adversary claims the vendor was disqualified from selling; this is the legal question. The jury restricts itself to deciding that the house should be handed over to Peter; this decides both the factual and legal questions. As far as juries in civil matters are concerned, the English have not accorded them the same infallibility as in criminal cases, if they decide to acquit.

If the judge thinks that the verdict is the result of the law being wrongly applied, he can refuse to accept it and can send the jury back to reconsider.

If the judge allows the verdict to pass without observation, the trial is not finally decided: there are several avenues open to delaying judgment. The principal one consists in asking the law to set aside the verdict and to assemble a new jury. It is true to say that such a request is rarely allowed and never more than twice; nevertheless, I have myself witnessed such an event. See Blackstone, bk 3, ch. 24; idem, bk 3, ch. 25.

VOLUME 2

PART 2

A. (p. 642)   There are, however, some aristocracies which have taken up commercial activity with enthusiasm and have cultivated industry with success. World history offers striking examples of this. But, in general, it must be said that the aristocracy is not at all favorable to the development of industry and trade. Moneyed aristocracies are the only exception to this rule.

Among these there are hardly any desires which do not need wealth to satisfy them. The love of wealth becomes, so to speak, the main pathway for human passions. All others lead to it or cross it.

The taste for money and the thirst for recognition and power become so intermingled in the same souls that it becomes difficult to discern whether it is because of ambition that men become avaricious or whether it is because of avarice that they become ambitious. This is what happens in England where one seeks to become rich in order to obtain preferment and where one seeks preferment as a manifestation of wealth. The human mind is thus gripped by both ends and swept into trade and industry, these being the quickest routes that lead to affluence.

This, however, seems to me to be an exceptional and transitory condition. When wealth has become the only symbol of aristocracy, it is very difficult for the wealthy to keep power for themselves and to exclude all others.

The aristocracy of birth and pure democracy are at the two extremes of the social and political state of nations; in the middle there is the moneyed aristocracy which tries to match the aristocracy of birth by conferring great privileges upon a small number of citizens; it is democratic enough in that these privileges can be acquired by each successive generation. It frequently forms a natural transition between these two conditions and one could not say if it is bringing the reign of aristocratic institutions to an end or if it is opening up a new era of democracy.

PART 3

A. (p. 689)   In my travel diary I find the following passage, which will enable the reader to understand the trials that American women who consent to accompany their husbands into the wilderness frequently suffer. The only thing which recommends this description to the reader is its absolute truth.

. . . From time to time we come upon new clearings. All these settlements are alike. I shall describe the one where we have stopped this evening as it will provide me with a picture of all the others.

The bells which the pioneers hang round the necks of their cattle so that they can find them in the woods indicated to us from some way off that we were nearing a clearing; soon we could hear the noise of the axe cutting down the trees in the forest. As we came nearer, signs of destruction indicated the presence of civilized man. Cut branches covered the path; trunks half-charred by fire or mutilated by the axe still stood in our way. We carried on and came to a wood in which all the trees seemed suddenly to have perished; in the middle of summer, they looked as they do in winter; examining them more closely, we saw that a deep circle had been scored into their bark which, by stopping the flow of the sap, had caused them to die rapidly. We learned that this is what the pioneer generally begins by doing. Not being able, during his first year, to cut down all the trees which grow on his property, he sows corn under their branches and then, by killing them, he prevents them from shading his crop. Beyond this field, we see, not yet completed, the first steps of civilization in the desert— the owner's cabin. It is positioned in the middle of a plot of land more carefully cultivated than the rest but where man still wages his unequal struggle against the forest. There the trees are cut, but not uprooted, their trunks still stand and encumber the land which formerly they shaded. Around these dried-out remains, wheat, oak seedlings, plants, and grasses of all kinds grow chaotically together on this intractable and semi-wild land. It is in the middle of this vigorous and varied vegetation that stands the pioneer's house, or *log house* as it is called here. Like the field which surrounds it, this rustic property shows evidence of recent and hurried work; its length seems not to exceed thirty feet, its height, fifteen; its walls, like the roof, are made from rough-hewn tree trunks, between which moss and earth have been inserted, to prevent the cold and rain from penetrating the interior.

As night was approaching, we decided to go and ask the owner of the log house for shelter.

At the sound of our steps, the children who had been rolling around amongst the debris of the forest, got up rapidly and fled toward the house as if frightened by the sight of men, while two large, half-wild dogs, ears pricked and muzzles outstretched, came out of their hut and, growling, covered the retreat of their young masters. The pioneer himself came to the door of his house; he threw us a rapid and inquiring glance and indicated to his dogs that they should go into the house and he himself hurried to set them the example, without giving any sign that our arrival had excited his curiosity or his concern.

We went into the log house: the inside is not at all like the cottages of peasants in Europe; it contains more of what is not necessary and less of what is.

There is only one window over which a muslin curtain hangs; in the hearth of beaten earth crackles a huge fire which lights everything within the building; above the hearth there is a fine rifle, a deerskin, and some eagle feathers; to the right of the mantelpiece a map of the United States is spread out which the wind catches and ruffles through the gaps in the wall; nearby, on a shelf made from a roughly hewn plank, there are a few volumes of books: I notice the Bible, Milton's first six books and two plays of Shakespeare; along the walls there are trunks instead of cupboards; in the center there is a crudely made table, the feet of which, being made from green wood which has not been stripped of its bark, look as though they are growing out of the soil upon which they stand; on this table I can see an English porcelain teapot, some silver spoons, chipped teacups, and some newspapers.

The master of this house has the angular features and slender limbs which are peculiar to the native of New England; it is clear that this man was not born in the solitude in which we find him: his physical constitution suffices to show that his early years were spent in the bosom of an intellectual society and that he belongs to that restive, questioning, and adventurous race who coolly do those things which can only be explained by the fervor of passion and who endure for a time the life of the savage so as better to conquer and civilize the wilderness.

When the pioneer noticed that we were crossing his threshold, he came to meet us and held out his hand, according to custom; but his face remained expressionless; he spoke first to ask us about what was going on in the world and when he had satisfied his curiosity, he was silent, as if tired of harassment and noise. We questioned him in our turn and he gave us all the information we needed; next, diligently but with little enthusiasm, he busied himself with our needs. Watching him tending kindly to our wants, why did we feel, despite ourselves, our gratitude freeze on our lips? It is because, while dispensing his hospitality, he gave the impression of submitting to the painful necessity of his lot: he saw it as a duty which his position had imposed upon him and not as a pleasure.

At the other side of the hearth sat his wife, cradling a small child on her lap; she nodded to us without stopping what she was doing. Like the pioneer, this woman was in the prime of life, her appearance seemed superior to her condition, her outfit was evidence of a still burning taste for fashion; but her delicate limbs seemed weakened, her features tired, her eyes mild but serious; her whole bearing was imbued with a religious resignation, a deep repose of passions and some kind of natural, calm determination ready to confront all the vicissitudes of life without fear and with acceptance.

Her children pressed around her; full of health, vitality, and energy; they were true children of the wilderness; from time to time, their mother looked at them with both melancholy and joy; to see their strength and her weakness, you could imagine that she had exhausted herself giving them life and she did not regret the cost.

The house that these emigrants lived in had no internal walls or loft. The whole family takes shelter for the night in its one room. This house is a little world in itself; it is the ark of civilization lost in an ocean of greenery. A hundred paces away, the eternal forest spreads its shadows at the edges where the uninhabited solitudes begin again.

B. (p. 689)   It is not equality of social conditions which makes men immoral and irreligious; but when men, who are also equal, are immoral and irreligious the effects of this immorality and ungodliness are more easily apparent since men have little influence upon one another and no one class exists which can undertake to keep society in order. Equality of social conditions never creates moral corruption but sometimes it allows this corruption to emerge.

C. (p. 710)   If one puts to one side all those who do not think at all and those who do not dare say what they think, one will still find that the vast majority of Americans seem satisfied with the political institutions which govern them and, in fact, I think that this is indeed so. I look upon this inclination of public opinion as an indication of the excellence of American laws but not as proof of this. National pride, the gratification of certain dominant passions accorded by the legislation, fortuitous circumstances, unnoticed failings, and, more than all of this, the interest of the majority which shuts the mouth of all opponents, can delude a whole people as well as a single man for a long time.

Look at England in the course of the eighteenth century. Never has a nation showered itself with so much praise; no nation has ever been more perfectly self-satisfied; all was well with the constitution, everything, even including its most visible defects, was beyond reproach. Today a whole host of Englishmen seem only to be occupied with proving that this constitution was defective in thousands of ways. Who was right, the English people of the last century or those of the present day?

The same thing happened in France. It is certain that, under Louis XIV, the vast majority of the nation was extremely attached to the form of government which governed society at the time. Those who think that there was a debasement in the character of the French at that time are making a serious mistake. There might have been a certain degree of servitude in France in that century but there was most certainly no servile spirit. The writers of the time felt a genuine enthusiasm for the elevation of royal power above all other and there was no peasant in his hovel so obscure as not to take pride in the glory of his sovereign and who would not cheerfully die with the cry of "Long live the King!" upon his lips. These same practices have become hateful to us. Who were wrong, the French people of Louis XIV's time or those of today?

We must not then base our judgment of the laws of a people merely upon their inclinations, because these can change from one century to the next, but we must base them on higher principles and a wider experience.

The love which a people have for their laws proves just one thing: one should not be in a rush to change them.

D. (p. 765)   In the chapter to which this note refers, I have pointed out one danger; I want to mention another less frequent but one which, should it ever occur, is much more to be feared.

If the love of material pleasure and the taste for wellbeing which the state of equality suggests naturally to men gains possession of the minds of a democratic people in such a way as to take them over completely, the national character would become so opposed to the military ethos that perhaps even the armies would finish up by loving peace despite that particular interest which leads them to desire war. Placed in the midst of this general softness, soldiers would come to think it better to gain promotion gradually, in comfort and with minimum effort during a period of peace rather than to purchase a rapid advancement at the price of the toils and miseries of life in the field. Feeling like this, the army would take up arms without enthusiasm and would use them without energy; it would allow itself to be led to the enemy rather than marching to meet it.

It should not be thought that this peaceful inclination of the army would distance it from revolutions, for revolutions, and especially military revolutions, which are usually very swift, carry great danger but do not require a lengthy commitment; they satisfy ambition at less cost than war; one risks only one's life and men in democracies care less for their lives than their comforts.

There is nothing more dangerous for the freedom and tranquillity of a people than an army which fears war since, no longer gaining glory and influence on the battlefield, it will seek to find them elsewhere. It might happen, then, that men who make up a democratic army lose the concerns of the citizen without acquiring the virtues of the soldier and that the army ceases to be capable of waging war without ceasing to be a disturbing influence.

I shall repeat here what I have said above. The remedy for such dangers is not found in the army but in the country. A democratic people which preserves a manly character will always be able to find a military aptitude in its soldiers, when the need arises.

PART 4

A. (p. 779)   Men put the greatness of the idea of unity in the means, God in the end; hence this idea of greatness leads us to much pettiness. Forcing all men to follow the same path toward the same goal, that is a human concept. Introducing an infinite variety of action, but combining them so that all these acts lead in a thousand different ways to the accomplishment of one great design, that is a divine concept.

The human concept of unity is almost always sterile, that of God enormously fertile. Men think they attest to their greatness by simplifying the means: it is God's purpose which is simple, his means are infinitely varied.

B. (p. 783)   A democratic people is led not only by its own inclinations to centralize power; the passions of all those who govern it push it constantly in that direction.

One can easily predict that almost all the ambitious and capable citizens of a democratic country will work ceaselessly to extend the powers of government because they hope one day to be in charge themselves. It is a waste of time to seek to prove to these people that extreme centralization can be harmful to the state, since they are centralizing it for their own benefit.

Amongst the public figures of a democracy, there are scarcely any other than very uninvolved or mediocre people who would like to decentralize power. The former are few in number, the latter powerless.

C. (p. 805)   I have often wondered what would happen if, amid the easy-going life in a democracy and as a consequence of the restless spirit of the army, a military government were ever to be founded in any of the nations of our times.

I think that such a government would not differ from the picture which I have drawn in the chapter to which this note refers and that it would not reproduce the savage traits of a military oligarchy.

I am convinced that in this case there would be a kind of amalgamation of the clerical turn of mind with that of the soldier's. The administration would take on some military characteristics and the military would assume some civil practices. The result of this would be a regulated, clear, exact, and absolute chain of command; the people would be a reflection of the army and society would be run like a barracks.

D. (p. 809)   It could not be said in any absolute or general way whether the greatest danger of our time is freedom or tyranny, anarchy or despotism. Both are equally to be feared and can result just as easily from one and the same cause, namely *general apathy*, which is the fruit of individualism; it is this apathy which makes it possible for the executive government, having assembled a few troops, to be able to commit acts of oppression and the next day, when a party can muster thirty men, it also can commit acts of oppression. Neither one nor the other can establish anything durable; the cause of their success easily stops that success from lasting long. They rise to the top because there is nothing to resist them and they fall because there is nothing to support them.

It is, therefore, far more important to resist apathy than anarchy or despotism for apathy can give rise, almost indifferently, to either one.

NOTES

VOLUME 1

AUTHOR'S INTRODUCTION

a. *Louis XI, Louis XIV,* and *Louis XV* each reigned as kings of France (1461–83), (1643–1715), (1715–74) respectively.

b. *Crusades* Series of wars beginning in 1095 and ending in the mid to late thirteenth century, fought by European Christians, against those they considered religious enemies, including pagan Slavs in north-eastern Europe, Mongols in eastern Europe, Moors in Spain, and, most notably, Muslims in the Middle East. The idea of a religious crusade would later become a symbol of religious intolerance and fanaticism.

c. *English wars* Tocqueville refers to the "Hundred Years' War," a territorial struggle between England and France that lasted (despite its name) from 1337 to 1453.

PART 1

CHAPTER 2

a. *Tudor monarchy* Began with the reign of Henry VII in 1485 and ended with the reign of Elizabeth I in 1603. The Tudor monarchy was noted for its commanding stature and authority and is often regarded as the peak of monarchical rule in Great Britain.

b. *immigrants* The immigrants who arrived in Virginia in 1607 and founded Jamestown, the first permanent British settlement in North America.

c. *Charles I* King of England and Great Britain who reigned from 1625 to 1649. His pro-Catholic and anti-Parliamentarian views led to civil war in 1640 and culminated in his execution in 1649 by the republican regime that emerged victorious from the civil war.

d.   *Charles II* The son of Charles I who returned from exile in France to assume the English throne in 1660, ending the twenty-year Commonwealth. His "Restoration" reign ended with his death in 1685.

CHAPTER 3

a.   *American Revolution* The eight-year armed conflict between the thirteen American colonies, self-declared as independent and united states in 1776, and the British crown.

CHAPTER 5

a.   *Franklin* Benjamin Franklin (1706–90) was an American author, philosopher, diplomat, and scientist, widely regarded as one of America's "founding fathers."

b.   *French Convention* The Convention was assembled in 1792 after the overthrow of Louis XVI to draft a republican constitution for France. It came to an end in 1795 after intense and often violent conflict between rival factions.

c.   *Mohammed* Mohammed (570?–632), the founder and chief prophet of Islam, whose revelations from God form the core of the Koran, the sacred text of the Muslims. He also founded a federation of Arab states unified by the precepts of Islam, that eventually conquered the Byzantine and Persian empires.

d.   *Montesquieu* Charles Louis de Secondat, baron de Montesquieu (1689–1755) was a French Enlightenment author, historian, and political philosopher. His novel *Persian Letters* (1721) was acclaimed for its satirical critique of institutions such as the Church and the French monarchy. He is, however, best remembered today for his political treatise, *The Spirit of Laws* (1748), a work which expounded on balanced government and the separation of powers and had a seminal influence on the debates which took place in the American constitutional convention.

e.   *French Revolution* The French Revolution of 1789 erupted after a period of severe economic hardship and financial crisis, exacerbated, in part, by the cost of France's military support for the revolutionaries in North America. French liberals and radicals of the time seized this opportunity to destabilize the *ancien régime* and put in place a republican form of government that would protect property and individual rights, and end the unequal conditions of the feudal past.

CHAPTER 6

a.   *council of state* The chief governing body instituted under Napoleon Bonaparte's constitution of the year VIII (1799).

CHAPTER 8

a.   *thirteen colonies* Delaware, New York, New Jersey, Pennsylvania, Maryland, Virginia, North Carolina, South Carolina, Georgia, Connecticut, Rhode Island, New Hampshire, and Massachusetts, all of whom in 1776 declared themselves independent and united states.

b.   *union* The Articles of Confederation, signed in 1781, was the first American constitution. It remained in effect until 1788. It was believed to be ineffectual and in need of replacement because it did not vest enough authority in a central government.

c.   *George Washington* George Washington was the Commander of the Continental Army during the American Revolution (1775–83) and would later become the first President of the United States (1789–97).

d.   *President Jefferson* Thomas Jefferson was the author of the Declaration of Independence (1776) and also served as the third President of the United States (1801–9).

e.   *Normandy and Brittany Regions* (or provinces) located in northern France along the English Channel, and on the north-west tip of France, west of Normandy respectively.

f.   *Canton of Vaud and . . . Uri* Cantons are political subdivisions that comprise the Swiss Confederation. The Canton de Vaud is located on the western border of Switzerland. The canton of Uri is located in Central Switzerland.

g.   *war of 1812* Conflict between the United States and Great Britain over territories in Canada, the British blockade of France during the Napoleonic Wars, the pressing of American sailors, and the seizure of US ships by the Royal Navy. This military conflict, which ended in 1815 with the Treaty of Ghent, would be the last to occur between these two nations.

PART 2

CHAPTER 2

a.   *Federalists* The Federalist Party was a party that favored a strong
     national government and large manufacturing interests. It suf-
     fered a devastating defeat in the presidential election of 1800 and
     had ceased to be a national political force by 1817.

b.   *Republicans* The original Republic Party formed in the 1790s
     was the party led by Thomas Jefferson that was against centralized
     authority and favored agrarian interests and states' rights. It later
     became the Democratic Party under the leadership of Andrew
     Jackson.

c.   *General Jackson* Andrew Jackson was a military general and hero
     from the war of 1812 who later became the seventh President of
     the United States (1829–37). He was the first person from west
     of the Appalachian Mountains to be elected President.

b.   *the President attacked the Bank* On 10 July 1832, President
     Jackson vetoed a bill to extend the Bank's charter which was
     due to expire in 1836. This action was celebrated by Jackson's
     agrarian populist supporters who viewed the Bank as an insti-
     tution that privileged wealthy classes and monopoly capitalists.

CHAPTER 3

a.   *a great man* Blaise Pascal (1623–62) was a mathematician, physi-
     cist, and religious philosopher known for his *Lettres Provinciales*
     (1656–7) in which he engaged the ongoing debates between the
     Jansenists, a Catholic religious movement, and the Jesuits. The
     publication of *Pensées* (1670), where he addressed fundamental
     epistemological and theological questions, brought Pascal great
     repute within philosophical circles.

CHAPTER 5

a.   *Chancellor Kent* James Kent (1763–1847) was a widely known
     jurist who served as the chancellor of the New York Court of
     Chancery (1814–23) and was appointed the first professor of
     law at Columbia University. He is best known for his work
     Commentaries on American Law, originally a series of lectures
     that addressed topics ranging from international law to the US
     Constitution.

b.   *Hamilton* Alexander Hamilton (1755/7–1804) was a leader of
     the Federalist Party and was appointed by President George

Washington to be the first Secretary of the Treasury of the United States. He was one of the principal authors of *The Federalist*, a collection of essays written with James Madison and John Jay in favor of the adoption of a new federal constitution to replace the Articles of Confederation.

c. *Madison* James Madison (1751–1836) was the fourth President of the United States (1809–17) and was also one of the principal authors of *The Federalist*.

d. *new states of the Southwest* Louisiana was admitted as a state in 1812, Mississippi in 1817, Alabama in 1819, Missouri in 1821, and Arkansas in 1836.

CHAPTER 6

a. *Homo puer robustus* (Latin) Man is a boy grown strong.

CHAPTER 7

a. *auto-da-fé* (Spanish) A public ceremony where criminal sentences are pronounced and executed, employed during the Spanish Inquisition.

b. *La Bruyère* Jean da La Bruyère (1645–96) was a French satirist known for his masterpiece *Characters* (1688), a translation of the vignettes drawn by fourth-century Greek moralist Theophrastus to which he appended his own sardonic commentary on the pretentious social mores of his time.

c. *Molière* Originally named Jean-Baptiste Poquelin, Molière (1622–73) is considered to be the greatest writer of French comedy. His innovative style contrasted binary oppositions such as the normal versus the abnormal and the moral versus the immoral.

d. *Inquisition* The Spanish Inquisition, which was initiated by Pope Sixtus IV in 1478 to persecute Jews, Muslims, and others the Catholic Church deemed heretics.

CHAPTER 8

a. *Napoleon* Napoleon Bonaparte (1769–1821) was France's most celebrated military leader at the time of the Revolution. He overthrew the republican government in a *coup d'état* in 1799, amassed dictatorial powers and declared himself emperor in 1804. His military adventurism helped him build a vast empire in Europe which crumbled, grossly overextended, after his unsuccessful invasion of Russia.

CHAPTER 9

a.   *New Orleans victory* The Battle of New Orleans, victory over the British on 8 January 1815 at the close of the war of 1812.

b.   *Spinoza* Benedict Spinoza (1632–77), Dutch–Jewish philosopher noted for his belief in rationalism: a belief that the universe, as well as the human good, are ordered according to principles knowable to the human mind. His philosophy also maintains that God and Nature are identical. This idea is considered particularly controversial because it does not grant God a separate existence from the natural world.

c.   *Cabanis* Pierre-Jean Cabanis (1757–1808) was a French physiologist and philosopher who associated with such notable figures as Diderot, D'Alembert and Condorcet, and knew Benjamin Franklin and Thomas Jefferson when they stayed in Paris. Cabanis believed that entities commonly believed to be immaterial, such as the soul and consciousness, were really products of physical, biological systems.

d.   *Fulton* Robert Fulton (1765–1815) was an American engineer and inventor responsible for the commercialization of the steamboat.

e.   *states bordering the Gulf of Mexico* Louisiana, Mississippi, and Alabama. Florida was ceded to the US in 1819 and admitted as a state in 1845.

f.   *Henry IV* King of France who reigned from 1589 to 1610.

CHAPTER 10

a.   *Indian tribes* The Creeks occupied the flatlands of Georgia and Alabama; the Cherokees, eastern Tennessee and the western Carolinas; the Narragansetts, Rhode Island; the Mohicans, the upper Hudson Valley; the Pequots, Connecticut; the Lenapes, Delaware and parts of Pennsylvania, New Jersey, and Long Island; the Iroquois, territory surrounding Lakes Ontario, Huron, and Erie.

b.   *Penn* William Penn (1644–1718) was an English Quaker leader and advocate of religious freedom who founded the Commonwealth of Pennsylvania.

c.   *Choctaws* Indian tribe which inhabited the land which is now south-eastern Mississippi.

d.   *Tacitus* Gaius Cornelius Tacitus (AD 55?–117?) was a Roman historian who authored the *Germania*, a work describing the virtues, vices, and primitive lifestyle of the Germanic tribes living on the Roman frontier. He is also noted for his *Historiae*, a history of the Roman Empire from AD 69 to 96.

e. *Moors* The Moors were the ethnic Muslim group living in the Iberian Peninsula. They were first conquered by the Christians in the late fifteenth century, and then persecuted again in the Spanish Inquisition as the Spanish tried to forge a nation-state unified through Christianity.

f. *Calhoun* John C. Calhoun (1782–1850) was the seventh vice-president of the United States (1825–32) and a vigorous advocate of slavery and states' rights.

VOLUME 2

PART 1

CHAPTER 1

a. *Descartes* René Descartes (1596–1650) was a French philosopher often regarded as the father of modern philosophy. His *Discourse on Method* (1637) and his *Meditations on the First Philosophy* (1641) set out a revolutionary approach to questions of knowledge and certainty.

b. *Bacon* Francis Bacon (1561–1626) was an English philosopher who revolutionized scientific method through his critique of Aristotelian and Platonic approaches and his emphasis on empirical investigation and inductive logic.

c. *Luther* Martin Luther (1483–1546) was a German Augustinian monk who questioned received Catholic tradition and provided the impetus that led to the Protestant Reformation.

d. *Voltaire* François-Marie Arouet (1694–1778) was an author, historian, and French Enlightenment *philosophe* who was influenced by the empiricism of Locke and Newton. He was an outspoken advocate for the important liberal causes of his time, such as the protection of individual liberties and religious tolerance.

CHAPTER 4

a. *the Constituent Assembly and Convention in France* The Assembly ruled revolutionary France from 1789 to 1791 and drew up the *Declaration of the Rights of Man and Citizen*. This document, inspired by the example set by the American Declaration of Independence, employed concepts of liberty, rationalism, and universalism that were popularized by Enlightenment political thought. The Convention met from 1792 to 1795 during the French Revolution to draft a republican constitution for France.

CHAPTER 7

a. *pantheism* Doctrine that stresses the identity between God and the natural universe, associated with the seventeenth-century Dutch rationalist Benedict Spinoza and later with the German idealist Georg Wilhelm Friedrich Hegel (1770–1831). Naturally, this doctrine has drawn criticism for its tendency to reduce God to Nature.

CHAPTER 9

a. *a famous sect* This is a reference to Claude Henri de Saint-Simon (1760–1825) and his followers. Saint-Simon was a utopian social theorist who argued that history was driven by the progress of the human mind leading up to a future "golden age" of industrialism and socio-political order. In the view of some scholars, his work has greatly influenced such notable philosophers as John Stuart Mill and Karl Marx.

CHAPTER 10

a. *Archimedes* Archimedes (?287–212 BC) was a famous Greek mathematician and inventor. His most noted discoveries include the mathematical relationship between the surface and volume of a sphere, as well as the invention of a device for raising water.

b. *Plutarch* Plutarch (AD 46–119) was a Greek biographer and author whose famous work, *Lives*, recounted the lives of notable Greeks and Romans and influenced the development of historical and biographical writing. Plutarch was also a widely read moralist, known for the *Moralia*, a series of essays dealing with ethical, political, and religious issues.

c. *new machine for navigation* The first successful trial of the steamboat was carried out by the American John Finch in 1787. Robert Fulton (1765–1815) is responsible for developing the paddle-wheel-propelled steamboat which was of significant commercial use.

CHAPTER 11

a. *Raphael* Raphael (1483–1520) was an Italian Renaissance painter and architect best known for his paintings of the Madonna.

b. *David* Jacques-Louis David (1748–1825) was the leading pro-
    ponent of neoclassical art, a form that embraced classical Roman
    themes and images of patriotic, heroic deeds. David contributed
    to the Revolution as a planner of public festivals and ceremonies
    which the *philosophes* believed would help inspire national spirit
    and foster republican virtues.

c. *Renaissance painters* Notable examples include Michelangelo
    (1475–1564), Leonardo da Vinci (1452–1519), and Raphael.
    Renaissance painting employs a style that idealizes nature.

CHAPTER 12

a. *Pontoise* A town in France north-west of Paris.

b. *Cortez* Hernan Cortez (1485–1547) was a Spanish military leader
    whose politically savvy maneuver to garner the support of Indian
    tribes resentful of Aztec rule led to his conquest of the Aztec
    empire in 1521. This success claimed Mexico for Spain and
    resulted in a dramatic expansion of the Spanish crown's colonial
    reach in the Americas.

CHAPTER 16

a. *Constantinople* The former capital of the Byzantine and Ottoman
    empires. Constantinople was renamed Istanbul by the Ottomans
    after its conquest in 1453.

b. *Milton* John Milton (1608–74) is considered the most notable
    English poet, next to Shakespeare. He is best remembered for his
    epic poem, *Paradise Lost*, which dealt with the tale in Genesis of
    the fall of mankind from divine grace.

CHAPTER 17

a. *Childe Harold Childe Harold's Pilgrimage* is an autobiographical
    poem written by the English poet Lord Byron (1788–1824)
    detailing the travels of a disillusioned young man in search of
    diversions throughout Europe.

b. *René René* (1805) is an autobiographical novel written by
    Chateaubriand (1768–1848) featuring a melancholy, disoriented
    hero. This work came to represent the *mal du siècle* (malady of
    the age), the sense of uneasiness and dissatisfaction that was a
    popular theme addressed by the Romantic movement in French
    literature.

c. *Jocelyn Jocelyn* (1836) is a poem written by Lamartine (1790–
    1869), about a fallen angel who had to choose between dedication
    to God and the love of a woman. Lamartine, like Chateaubriand,

was an important figure of the Romantic movement in French
literature.

CHAPTER 19

a. *Racine* ... Britannicus Jean Baptiste Racine (1639–99) was a
noted French dramatist. His tragedy *Britannicus* (1669) dealt
with the teenage Roman emperor Nero's attempt to rid himself
of his dictatorial mother's control.

CHAPTER 20

a. *Lafayette* Marquis de Lafayette (1757–1834) was a French general, deputy to the Assembly of Notables, the Estates General,
and the Constituent Assembly, as well as commander of the Paris
National Guard. He was famous in the United States for his
assistance to the Continental Army in the American Revolution.

PART 2

CHAPTER 8

a. *Montaigne* Michel Eyquem de Montaigne (1533–1592) was a
famous French writer whose work *Essais* (1580) introduced a
new literary form: a short, often personal and informal prose
composition that we now call the essay.

CHAPTER 12

a. *Thebaid* Relating to Thebes, an ancient Egyptian city.
b. *Greek Epicureanism* Epicureanism is a philosophy founded on
the teachings of Epicurus (341–270 BC), which conceives of
pleasure as the only true good and pain, conversely, as the only
true evil.

CHAPTER 14

a. *Tyrians* Tyre was an ancient Phoenician city.

PART 3

CHAPTER 1

a. *Madame de Sévigné* Marie de Rabutin-Chantal, Marquise de
Sévigné (1626–96) was a French writer born to nobility, whose
letters written to her daughter about current events and everyday
life within aristocratic society received much literary recognition.

b.   *Cicero* Marcus Tullius Cicero (106–43 BC) was a Roman states-
     man, lawyer, and philosopher whose classical republican treatises
     were the first expositions on political theory written in Latin.

CHAPTER 22

a.   *Sulla or Caesar* Lucius Cornelius Sulla (138–78 BC) was the victor
     in a civil war that took place within the Roman empire from 88
     to 82 BC. He ruled as a dictator for several years following his
     victory (82–79 BC). Julius Caesar (100?–44 BC) was the Roman
     empire's most famous leader. Like Sulla, Caesar also reigned as a
     dictator (46–44 BC) following his victory in a civil war (49–
     46 BC).

CHAPTER 25

a.   *Alexander* Alexander III, or Alexander the Great (356–323 BC),
     was king of Macedonia (336–323 BC) and conqueror of the
     Persian empire.

CHAPTER 26

a.   *Machiavelli* Niccolò Machiavelli (1469–1527) was an Italian
     statesman and political theorist whose work *The Prince* marked
     an important break with classical political theory in its amoral
     approach to princely leadership within government.

Two Essays on America

TWO WEEKS IN
THE WILDERNESS

One of the things which most sharply stung our curiosity upon our arrival in America was our journey to the furthest limits of European civilization and even, when the weather permitted, our contact with some of those Indian tribes which preferred to flee into the most brutal wastes rather than bow to what the whites call the delights of life in society. But it is more difficult than one might think these days to come across the wilderness. On setting out from New York and as we progressed toward the north-west, the destination of our journey seemed to disappear before us. We traveled through places famous in Indian history, made our way along valleys with Indian names, forded rivers which still carry the titles of their tribes, but everywhere the savage's hut had given way to the civilized man's house; the woods had fallen, the empty spaces were coming to life.

However, we appeared to be walking over the tracks of the native peoples. We were told that ten years before, they had existed in this place, five years before, in that place, two years before, in another. "On the spot where you can now see the finest of the village churches," one man related to us, "I felled the first of the forest trees." "In this place," another recounted, "the great council of the Iroquois confederation used to be held." "And what has become of the Indians?" I would say. "The Indians," our host continued, "went, I'm not too sure where, on the other side of the Great Lakes. Theirs is a race under threat of extinction; they are not suited to civilization; it kills them off."

Man gets used to everything—to death on the battlefield or in the hospitals, to slaughter and to suffering. He becomes inured to everything he sees—an ancient people, the original and rightful masters of the American continent melting away daily like snow in sunshine and disappearing before our eyes from the face of the earth. In the same areas another race rises in their stead at an even greater pace. This race instigates the clearing of the forests, the draining of the marshland; lakes as big as seas and huge rivers offer empty opposition to its triumphant progress. Every year wild areas become villages; villages become towns. The American, a daily witness of these wonders, sees nothing astonishing in any of that. This unbelievable destruction, this even more surprising growth, looks to him like the normal forward march of events. He grows accustomed to it as to the unchangeable order of the natural world.

This was how we traversed the three hundred and sixty miles separating New York from Buffalo, in our search for savages and wilderness.

The first thing that struck our gaze was a large number of Indians who had gathered that day in Buffalo to receive payment for the lands they had ceded to the United States.

I think I have never experienced a more profound disappointment than the sight of these Indians. I was full of the memories of Monsieur de Chateaubriand and of Cooper and I was expecting to see, in these native peoples of America, savages whose faces carried the traces, left by nature, of some of those proud virtues fostered by the spirit of freedom. I believed I would meet in them men whose bodies had been developed by hunting and war and who lost nothing from being seen naked. You may judge my astonishment by comparing this portrait with the one about to follow: the Indians I saw that evening were small in stature; their limbs, as far as one could assess beneath their clothes, were spindly and lacking in energy; their skin, instead of displaying the red shade of copper as is commonly supposed, were of a dark shade of bronze which suggested at first sight that these men appeared to have a strong resemblance to mulattos. Their black shiny hair fell unusually straight upon their necks and shoulders. Their mouths were generally inordinately large while the expression on their faces was base and vicious. Their facial features heralded that profound degradation which the lengthy abuse of the blessings of civilization alone can produce. One might have described these men as belonging to the lowest rabble of our great European cities. And yet they were still savages. To the vices they learned from us was linked something barbarous and uncivilized which made them a hundred times more repulsive still. These Indians carried no weapons; they were covered in European clothes which they did not use in the same way as ourselves. It was evident that they had not been made for them and that they found themselves yet imprisoned in their folds. To European ornaments, they had added articles of barbaric luxury such as feathers, huge earrings, and shell necklaces. These men's movements were fast and jerky, their voices shrill and discordant, their looks anxious and wild. At first glance, you might have been tempted to see in each of them simply an animal out of the forests to which education had succeeded in giving the look of a man but which had remained no less an animal. These weak and depraved beings belonged nevertheless to one of the most famous tribes of the old American world. We had in front of us, and I am sorry to say so, the final remnants of that renowned confederation of Iroquois whose virile wisdom was no less famous than their courage and who long maintained the balance between the two greatest European nations.

However, we would be wrong in wishing to judge the Indian race by this shapeless sample, this stray offshoot of a wild tree which has grown from the mud of our towns. That would be to repeat the mistake we committed ourselves and which we had the chance to realize later on.

In the evening we left the town and, not far from the last houses, we spotted an Indian lying at the edge of the road. It was a young man. He was not moving and we thought him dead. A few muffled groans were emitted from his chest and led us to believe that he was still alive and was fighting against one of those dangerous drunken stupors brought on by drinking brandy. The sun had already set and the ground was becoming increasingly damp. Everything indicated that this wretched fellow would breathe his last breath on that spot if he were not rescued. At that time of night the Indians were leaving Buffalo on their way back to their village; occasionally a group of them happened to pass by. They came closer, brutally turned the body of their fellow compatriot over to find out who he was and then continued on their way without even bothering to reply to our remarks. Most of these men were themselves drunk. In the end a young Indian woman came along. At first she drew nearer with a certain concern; I thought that she was the wife or sister of the dying man. She took a close look at him, called his name out loud, put her hand to his heart and, reassured that he was alive, attempted to shake him from his lethargic state. But as her efforts were in vain, we saw her furiously attack this inert body lying before her. She struck its head, twisted its face with her hands, trampled on it. While engaging in these ferocious acts, she uttered a series of wordless and savage cries which, even now, still seem to resonate in my ears. In the end, we thought we ought to intervene and peremptorily ordered her to withdraw. She did so but we heard her release a peal of barbaric laughter as she moved away.

On our return to the town, we talked to several of the young Indian's friends. We spoke of the imminent danger which threatened him; we even offered to pay the expense of an inn. All that proved useless. We were unable to persuade anyone to move. Some said to us: "These fellows are used to excessive drinking and collapsing on the ground. They don't die from such accidents." Others acknowledged that the Indian would probably die but you could read this half-expressed thought on their lips: "What's the life of an Indian worth?" That was the essential feeling of everyone. At the heart of this very civilized, prudish, pedantically moral and virtuous society, lay a completely insensitive attitude, a kind of cold and relentless selfishness when it came to the native races of America. The inhabitants of the United States do not hunt the Indians down with a great clamor, like the Spanish in Mexico. But here, as elsewhere, it is the same pitiless sentiment which drives the European race.

In the course of our travels, we have so often met upstanding citizens who told us, comfortably sitting by their fireside of an evening: "Every day the numbers of Indians decrease. It is not, however, that we very often wage war against them, but the brandy which we sell to them cheaply annually removes more of them than our weapons could manage. This world belongs to us," they added; "God, by his refusal to grant its first inhabitants the art of civilization, doomed them to an inevitable destruction. The true owners of this continent are those who are able to take advantage of its wealth."

Pleased with his argument, the American repairs to church where he listens to a minister of the Gospel repeat to him that men are brothers and that the everlasting Being, who has fashioned each of them upon the same model, has given them all the duty of helping one another.

At ten o'clock in the morning of 19 July, we embarked upon the steamship *Ohio*, in the direction of Detroit. A fierce breeze blew from the north-west and gave the waters of Lake Erie every appearance of an ocean. On the right, the horizon stretched out limitless; on the left, we hugged the southern shores of the lake which we frequently approached within shouting distance. These shores were entirely flat and contrasted in that respect with all the European lakes I had ever had the opportunity of visiting. Nor were they at all like seashores. Extensive forests cast their shade over them and formed around the lake a dense and almost uninterrupted belt. Occasionally, however, the countryside suddenly changed its appearance. Coming around the angle of a wood, we glimpsed the elegant spire of a bell tower, brilliantly white, and spruce houses and shops. A few steps more and the primitive and apparently impenetrable forest recovered its sway and once again cast the reflection of its foliage upon the waters of the lake.

Those who have traveled widely in the United States will find in this depiction a striking symbol of American society. In America everything jostles together, full of the unexpected. Everywhere, the furthest reaches of civilization and nature abandoned to its own devices, in some way confront each other. That is beyond our imagining in France. With my own preconceptions as a traveler—and what class of men is without such illusions?— I had imagined something quite different. I had noticed that in Europe, the more or less remote situation of any provincial region or town, its wealth or poverty, its size, big or small, would exercise great influence upon its inhabitants and would often establish the variations of several centuries between the different parts of the same area.

I imagined that this was all the more so in the New World and that a country like America, whose population was as yet incomplete and partly formed, was bound to exhibit all the conditions of life and to offer the portrait of society in all its stages of development. According to me, therefore, America was the only country in which one might follow the step-by-step changes which a state of society forces upon man and in which it would always be possible to perceive, as it were, a lengthy chain whose links stretched from the wealthy city patrician right down to the savage in the wilderness. In a word, that is how I reckoned on encountering the encapsulation of the history of the whole human race within a few degrees of longitude.

Nothing of that picture has any truth. Of all the countries of the world, America is the least suited to provide the sight which I had come there to seek. In America, much more than in Europe, only one society exists. It may be rich or poor, modest or brilliant, engaged in commerce or farming, nevertheless, it consists everywhere of the same elements. The level of an egalitarian civilization had been laid upon it. You will come across the man you left on the streets of New York in the middle of almost impenetrable solitudes—same clothes, same spirit, same language, same habits, same pleasures. He reflects nothing of the rustic, nothing of the unsophisticated, nothing which smacks of the wilds, not even anything you find in the villages of Europe. It is easy to understand the reason for this unusual state of affairs. Those territories which have been populated for the longest time and to the greatest extent have reached the highest degree of civilization; their schooling has been lavishly extensive and the spirit of equality and republicanism has spread an exceptionally uniform coloring over the personal habits of life. Now, pay especial attention to this—these are precisely the same men who will inhabit the wilderness every year. In Europe, each person lives and dies on the same plot of earth which witnessed his birth, but nowhere in America does one come across men who represent a race, grown in numbers in isolation, unknown to the world for a long period of time and occupied with its own labors. Those who dwell in isolated places arrived there only yesterday. They have come with the customs, ideas, habits, and needs of civilization. They grant to life in the wilds only what the demands of nature force them to do. That results in weird contrasts. You pass seamlessly from the wilderness to the city street, from the most savage of situations to the sunniest scenes of civilized life. If nightfall catches you in the countryside and does not force you to find shelter at the foot of a tree, you have every chance of reaching a village where you will find everything you need, even French fashions and boulevard cartoons. The shopkeepers of Buffalo and Detroit are as well stocked as those in New York. The factories of Lyons work equally for both. You leave the main roads, plunge along paths that are hardly cleared. At length, you glimpse a cleared field, a cabin made from half-hewn logs through which only a narrow window filters the daylight, and you believe you have at last reached the dwelling of an American farmer. Wrong. You enter this dwelling, which appears to be the refuge from every kind of poverty, but the owner of this place is clothed in the same way as you are, he speaks a town language and on his crude table lie books and newspapers. He speedily leads you aside to get an accurate picture of the happenings of old Europe and to ask you to tell him what has struck you most forcibly about his country. He will draw on a piece of paper a plan of campaign for the Belgians and will tell you seriously what further steps must be taken for France to be prosperous. You would believe him to be a wealthy landowner who has briefly come to take up residence for a few days' hunting. In actual fact, the wooden cabin is for the American only a brief refuge, a temporary concession to the necessity of circumstances. When the neighboring fields are completely profitable and the new owner has the spare time to busy himself with the pleasurable things of life, a roomier house, more suited to his way of life, will replace the log house and will act as the shelter for numerous children who also one day will build a dwelling in the wilderness.

But, to return to our travels, we steered a laborious course throughout the day within sight of the Pennsylvania coast and

later that of Ohio. We stopped for a time at Presqu'Ile, today
Lake Erie. That is where the Pittsburgh canal will end. By means
of this work, the entire construction of which, I am told, is easy
and, thus, guaranteed, the Mississippi will be linked with the
Northern River and the wealth of Europe will circulate freely
over the 1,200 miles of land separating the Gulf of Mexico from
the Atlantic Ocean.

In the evening, as the weather became more pleasant, we
made our way swiftly toward Detroit, crossing the center of the
lake. In the morning, we were in sight of the small island
called Middle Sister, near which Commodore Perry had gained
a famous naval victory over the English in 1814.

Shortly afterwards, the flat shores of Canada seemed to come
swiftly toward us and we saw the River Detroit opening up in
front of us and, appearing in the distance, the houses of Fort
Malden. This place, founded by the French, still bears many
traces of its origin. The houses retain the shape and the situation
of French farmers' dwellings. In the center of the hamlet stands
the Catholic bell tower topped by a cockerel. You would suppose
it to be a village in the outskirts of Caen or Evreux. While we
were contemplating, with some emotion, this picture of France,
our attention was drawn elsewhere by the sight of an unusual
scene: on our right, on the shoreline, a Scottish soldier was
standing guard in full uniform. He was wearing the outfit which
the fields of Waterloo have made so famous. The feathered
bonnet, the jacket—there was nothing missing. The sun made
his coat and arms sparkle. On our left, as though to provide us
with a parallel, two naked Indians, their bodies daubed with
paint, their noses pierced with a ring, came into view at that
very moment from the opposite bank. They stepped into a small
bark rowing boat with a blanket acting as a sail. Allowing this
flimsy boat to float with the impulse of the wind and current,
they shot like an arrow toward our vessel which they sailed
around in a brief moment. Then they moved quietly away to
fish near the English soldier who, still sparkling and motionless,
seemed planted there as the representative of the brilliant and
well-equipped European civilization.

We reached Detroit at three o'clock. Detroit is a small town of two or three thousand souls, which was founded by the Jesuits in woodland in 1710 and which still includes a very great number of French families.

We had traveled the length of the state of New York and sailed two hundred and twenty miles on Lake Erie. On this occasion, we were skirting the edges of civilization but were completely unaware of what destination we should aim for. Obtaining information was not as easy a task as one might think. Crossing almost impenetrable forests, fording deep rivers, confronting disease-ridden marshes, sleeping exposed to the dampness of the woods, were labors the American imagines without difficulty, if it is a matter of earning money; for therein lies the issue. But to undertake similar things through curiosity is something which does not quite enter his mind. In addition, as an inhabitant of a wilderness, he values only the work done by man. He will readily send you to see a road, a bridge, a fine village. But attaching value to lofty trees and the beauty of empty spaces is something which is absolutely beyond him.

There is, therefore, nothing more difficult than to come across someone prepared to understand you. "It is your wish to see woods," our hosts would say to us with a smile, "walk straight ahead, you will find enough to satisfy you. New roads and well-cleared paths are indeed in this neighborhood. As for the Indians, you'll see too many of them in our public squares and streets, you do not need to go very far to see that. Those, at least, are beginning to be civilized and look less savage." It did not take us long to realize that it was impossible to achieve truth from them by a frontal attack and that we had to be more subtle.

So we visited the officer empowered by the United States to sell land which was still uninhabited in the district of Michigan; we introduced ourselves as people who, without having a definite desire to establish a settlement in the area, might nevertheless have a distant interest in knowing the cost of plots of land and their position. Major Biddle—that was the officer's name— understood excellently on this occasion what we wished to do and embarked upon a good number of details to which we listened avidly. "This area," he told us, indicating on the map the St Joseph River which, after lengthy meanderings, is about to discharge its waters into Lake Michigan, "seems to me the most suitable to coincide with your plan; the soil is good; some fine villages have already been established there and the road to them has been so well maintained that public transport travels along it daily." "Good!" we said secretly to ourselves, "we already know where not to go unless we wish to visit the wilderness by horse and carriage." We thanked Mr Biddle for his information and asked him in an indifferent tone with a touch of scorn which was the section of the district which up until now had least experienced the inflow of immigrants. "In this direction," he said to us, attaching no more importance to his own words than we did to our question, "toward the northwest. As far as Pontiac and in the neighborhood of this village a few fine settlements have quite recently been established. But you shouldn't consider settling any further on; the area is covered with almost impenetrable forest stretching endlessly toward the northwest where only wild animals and Indians are to be found. The United States have in mind the project to open up a road soon; but this has as yet only just started and it stops at Pontiac. I repeat, that is a decision not worth considering." Once again, we thanked Mr Biddle for his sound advice and left determined to take precisely the opposite view. We were delighted to get to know, in fact, a place as yet untouched by the flood of European civilization.

On the next day, 23 July, we hastened to hire two horses. As we were reckoning on keeping them for ten or so days, we were anxious to deposit a certain sum with the owner but he refused to accept it, saying that we would pay on our return. He was quite unworried. Michigan is surrounded on all sides by lakes and wilderness. He was letting us loose within a confined space to which he held the key. So, after buying a compass as well as munitions, we set off, rifles on our shoulders, with as carefree a concern for the future and as unburdened a heart as two schoolboys leaving school, off to spend their holidays under their father's roof.

If in fact we had wanted to see only woods, our Detroit hosts would have been right in telling us that it was not necessary to travel very far, for a mile from the town the road enters the forest, never to emerge again. The land it occupies is entirely flat and often marshy. From time to time, along its length, we come across fresh clearings. As these settlements are exactly alike, whether situated in the depths of Michigan or at the gateway to New York, I shall try to describe them at this point once and for all.

The bells, which the pioneers are careful to hang round the necks of their cattle so that they can find them in the depths of the woods, indicate to us from some way off that we are nearing a clearing. Soon we can hear the echo of the axe cutting down the trees in the forest and, as we come nearer, signs of destruction indicate yet more clearly the presence of man. Cut branches cover the path, trunks, half-charred by fire or mutilated by the axe, still stand along our way. We carry on and come to a wood in which all the trees seem suddenly to have perished. In the middle of summer their dried branches appear like a picture of winter. Examining them more closely, we see that a deep circle has been scored into their bark which, stopping the flow of the sap, has caused them to die rapidly. Indeed that is where the pioneer usually begins. Not being able, during his first year, to cut down all the trees which grow on his property, he sows corn under their branches and then, by killing them, he prevents them from shading his crop. Beyond this field, we see, not yet completed, the first steps of civilization in the wilderness—the owner's cabin. It is generally positioned in the middle of a plot of land more carefully cultivated than the rest but where man still wages his unequal struggle against the forest. There the trees have been cut, but not uprooted; their trunks still stand and encumber the land which formerly they shaded. Around these dried-out remnants, wheat, oak seedlings, plants, and grasses of all kinds grow chaotically together on this intractable land, still in a half-wild state. It is in the middle of this vigorous and varied vegetation that the pioneer's house, or *log house* as it is called here, stands. Like the field which surrounds it, this rustic property shows evidence of recent and hurried work. Its length rarely exceeds thirty feet. It is twenty feet wide and fifteen high. Its walls, like the roof, are made from roughly hewn trunks, between which moss and earth have been inserted to prevent the cold and rain from penetrating the interior. As the traveler draws near, the scene takes on more life. Alerted by our footsteps, children who were rolling around among the surrounding debris get up rapidly and flee toward their father's safe haven as if frightened by the sight of men, while two large, half-wild dogs, ears pricked and muzzles outstretched, come out of the cabin and, growling, cover the retreat of their young masters.

Then it is that the pioneer himself comes to the door of his house; he throws an inquiring glance at the new arrival, indicating to his dogs that they should go into the house and he himself hurries to set them the example, without giving any sign of curiosity or concern.

Having set foot on the threshold of the *log house*, a European is unable to avoid casting a look of astonishment upon the sight before him.

There is generally only one window over which a muslin curtain sometimes hangs; for, in these places where it is not uncommon to see the absence of what is necessary, you frequently observe the presence of what is not. In the hearth of beaten earth crackles a resinous fire which illuminates the interior of the building better than daylight. Above this rustic hearth, you can see some trophies of war or hunting—a long, scratched carbine, a deerskin, some eagle feathers. To the right of the mantelpiece, continuously caught and ruffled by the wind as it blows through the gaps in the wall, is often spread out a map of the United States. Nearby, on a single shelf of roughly hewn planks, stand a few odd volumes: on this shelf are assembled a Bible whose cover and edges have already been worn away by the piety of two generations, a prayer book and, sometimes, a book of Milton's verse or a tragedy of Shakespeare. A few crude chairs—the results of the owner's enterprise— are placed along the walls, trunks instead of cupboards, farm implements, and some samples from his harvest. In the center of the room there is an unsteady table whose feet, still embellished with leaves, look as though they are growing out of the soil upon which they stand. That is where the whole family gathers every day to eat its meals. An English porcelain teapot, spoons, more often than not made from wood, a few chipped teacups, and some newspapers can still be seen.

The appearance of the master of this dwelling is no less remarkable than the place which serves as his shelter.

Well-defined muscles, slender limbs allow us to recognize an inhabitant of New England from the first glance. This man was not born in the solitude he occupies. His constitution by itself underlines this. His earliest years were spent in the bosom of an intellectual and rational society. It is his willpower which has thrust him into the labors of the wilderness for which he seems little suited. But if his physical strength does not seem adequate for the task he is undertaking, on his features etched by the cares of life reigns an air of practical intelligence, of cool and persistent energy, which strikes you on first meeting. He moves in a slow and controlled manner, his words are measured and his appearance austere. Habit and, even more, pride have given his face this stoic solidity belied by his actions: it is true that the pioneer despises what often violently disturbs men's hearts; his possessions and his life will never follow the throw of dice or the destiny of a woman; but, to obtain a comfortable life, he has braved exile, solitude, and the countless disasters of the primitive life; he has laid his head on the bare earth and he has been exposed to the fever of the woods and the Indian tomahawk. One day he started this work which he has been repeating for years and he will continue for perhaps another twenty, without being put off and without complaint. Is a man who is capable of such sacrifices a cold and insensitive being, therefore; should we not recognize in him, on the contrary, one of those burning, tenacious, relentless enthusiasms of the mind? Focussed upon this single aim of making his fortune, the immigrant has finally created a totally individual existence for himself; family feelings have fused into a bottomless egoism and it is doubtful whether he sees in his wife and children anything other than a detached part of himself. Deprived of the normal relations with his fellows, he has learned to derive pleasure from solitude. When we appear on the threshold of his isolated dwelling, the pioneer comes forward to meet us; he holds out his hand, according to custom, but his face expresses neither goodwill nor joy. He opens his mouth only to ask you questions; he is satisfying a rational not a heartfelt need and hardly has he extracted from you the news he wanted to learn than he falls silent again. You might think you are looking at a man who has withdrawn to his dwelling in the evening, tired of the harassments and the noise of the world. Ask him questions in your turn and he will furnish you intelligently with the information you ask; he will even provide for your needs and will look after your safety as long as you are beneath his roof. But in all his ways there prevail so much restraint and pride; you observe such a profound indifference for the outcome of his efforts that you can feel your gratitude freeze on your lips. Yet the pioneer is hospitable after his own manner but his hospitality has nothing to affect you because, while dispensing it, he gives the impression of submitting to the burdensome necessity of the wilderness; he sees it as a duty which his position imposes upon him, not a pleasure. This unknown man is the representative of a race to which the future of the New World belongs—a restless, rational, and adventurous race which coolly achieves what the heat of passion alone explains and which deals in everything, not even leaving out morality or religion.

This is a nation of conquerors who submit to leading a savage life without allowing themselves to be drawn by its sweetness, who like only the practical contribution to comfort which civilization and education have to offer, and who imprison themselves in the wilderness of America with an axe and newspapers. This is a people which, like all great peoples, have only one thought and which step out to acquire wealth, as the sole aim of their efforts, with a persistence and a scorn for life which we might call heroic, if this term were suitable for anything else besides the efforts due to virtue. It is these nomadic people who are not halted by rivers and lakes, before whom forests fall and prairies are covered by shadows and who, after reaching the Pacific Ocean, will retrace their steps to disturb and destroy those societies which they have formed behind them.

In speaking of the pioneer, we cannot forget the companion of his misfortunes and dangers. On the other side of the hearth, take a look at that young woman who cradles her youngest son on her lap while watching over the preparations for the meal. Like the immigrant, this woman is in the prime of life; like him, she can recall the comforts of her early years. Her attire is evidence of a still burning taste for fashion but time has weighed heavily upon her. In her features prematurely lined with age, from her weakened limbs, it is easy to see that life has been a heavy burden for her. In fact, this slight creature has already been exposed to unbelievable misfortunes. Hardly has she embarked upon life than she has had to endure being snatched away from her mother's tenderness and those gentle brotherly ties which a girl never gives up without shedding tears, even when she leaves them to go and share the luxurious home of a new husband. The pioneer's wife, plucked from this innocent cradle of her youth in an instant and with no hope of returning, has exchanged the attractions of society and the pleasures of her own home for the isolation of the forests. It is upon the bare earth of the wilderness that her marriage bed has been placed. Devotion to her austere duty, obedience to privation foreign to her, espousal of an existence not at all suited to her, that was how she employed the finest years of her life; for her, those have been the pleasures of marital union. Privation, suffering, and boredom have affected her vulnerable constitution but have not felled her courage. Amid the profound sadness depicted upon her delicate features, we easily discern a religious resignation, a deep peace and some kind of quiet and natural determination which confronts all the tribulations of life without fear and with acceptance.

Her children press around her, half-naked, shining with health, careless of the morrow, the true children of the wilderness. From time to time, their mother looks at them with eyes full of melancholy and pleasure; to see their strength and her weakness, you could imagine that she has exhausted herself giving them life and she does not regret the cost.

The house that these emigrants live in has no internal walls or loft. The whole family takes shelter for the night in its one room. This house is a little world in itself. It is the ark of civilization lost in an ocean of greenery, a sort of oasis in the desert. A hundred paces away, the eternal forest spreads its shadows all around and the uninhabited solitudes begin.

It was only in the evening and after the sun had set that we reached Pontiac. Twenty very clean and pretty houses, including as many well-stocked shops, a clear stream, a clearing about two square miles in area and the eternal forest all round—that is an accurate portrait of the village of Pontiac, which will perhaps be a town in twenty years' time. The sight of this place reminds me of what Monsieur Gallatin had said to me a month before in New York, that there are no villages in America, at least in the accepted meaning we give to this word in France. Here the farmers' houses are all scattered amid fields. The only reason to assemble in one place is to set up a sort of market for the use of the people in the neighborhood. Only lawyers, printers, or shopkeepers can be seen in these so-called villages.

We were directed to the finest inn in Pontiac (for there are two) and were, as usual, led into what is called the *bar room*, which is a room where drink is served and where the simplest of workmen as well as the richest of local tradesmen come to smoke, drink, and talk politics together on a footing of seeming perfect equality. The master of the place, or the *landlord*, was, I shall not call him a rough peasant—there are no peasants in America—but at least a very rough man who wore on his face that expression of frankness and simplicity which distinguishes horse traders from Normandy. He was a man who, out of fear that he might intimidate you, never looked directly at you when he spoke, but waited until you were busy conversing with someone else before scrutinizing you without embarrassment. Yet, he was deeply political and, following the American habit, a pitiless interrogator. This worthy citizen, just like the others gathered there, at first eyed us up and down with astonishment. Our traveling clothes and our rifles were hardly an indication that we were industrial entrepreneurs and travel for the sake of sightseeing was a most unusual thing. So as to curtail any explanations, in the first instance we made out that we wanted to buy land. Hardly had the word been uttered than we noticed that, in seeking to avoid one evil, we had hurtled into another even more dreadful.

It is true that they stopped treating us like extraordinary people but each of them wished to enter into negotiations with us. To rid ourselves of them and their farms, we told our host that, before concluding any deal, we were anxious to obtain from him useful information on the price of plots of land and on the manner of cultivation. He led us immediately into another room, spread out with suitable deliberation a map of Michigan on the oak table which stood in the middle of the chamber and, placing the candle between the three of us, waited impassively and in silence for us to communicate what we had to say to him. The reader, with no more intention than ourselves of settling in one of these American solitudes, may nevertheless be curious to know how each year so many thousand Europeans and Americans go about seeking refuge there. At this point, I shall, therefore, convey the information provided by our Pontiac host. Since that time we have often been in a position to verify exactly its accuracy.

"Things here are not as they are in France," our host told us, having listened calmly to all our questions and snuffed out the candle; "manpower is cheap in your country and land is expensive; here land purchase is nothing, a man's labor is beyond price. What I am saying is to help you understand that, in order to settle in America you need capital, just as in Europe, even though it is employed in a different manner. For my part, I would not advise anyone at all to seek their fortune in our wilderness unless they had at their disposal a sum of 150–200 dollars (800–1000 francs). An acre in Michigan never costs more than ten shillings (about 6 francs 50 centimes) when the land still remains uncultivated. That is about a day's pay. A workman can, therefore, earn in one day the price of the purchase of an acre but once the purchase has been made, then the difficult part begins. This is how one generally manages to overcome it. The pioneer makes his way to the land he has just acquired with a few cattle, some salt pork, two barrels of flour and some tea. If a cabin is to be found nearby, he repairs to it and obtains temporary accommodation. In the opposite eventuality, he puts up a tent in the middle of the wood which is to become his field. His first concern is to fell the nearest trees with which he hurries to build the crude house, the structure of which you have already been able to examine. Here, the upkeep of the cattle does not cost very much. The immigrant lets them loose into the forest having tied an iron bell on them. Only occasionally do these animals, let loose in this way, stray from the surroundings of their home. The greatest expense is in the clearing of the ground. If the pioneer arrives in the wilderness with a family able to help him with his initial labors, his task is quite easy. But rarely are things like that. Generally, the immigrant is young and, if he already has children, they are in their very early years. Then, alone, he has to provide for the first needs of his family, or hire the services of his neighbors. It costs from four to five dollars (from 20 to 25 francs) for the clearance of an acre. Once the land is prepared, the new owner plants one acre with potatoes, the rest with wheat and maize. A crop of maize is a salvation in this wilderness; it grows in the swampy water and flourishes beneath the foliage of the forest better than in the sunshine. Maize it is which saves the immigrant's family from inevitable destruction when poverty, illness, or negligence have prevented his clearing sufficient land in the first year. Nothing is a greater burden to endure than the first years spent after clearing the ground. Later comes a time of comfort, followed by wealth."

That is what our host said to us; we, in our turn, heeded these details with almost as much interest as if we had wished to take advantage of them ourselves and, when he had stopped speaking, we said to him:

"In all these woods, the ground, left to itself, is usually marshy and unhealthy; the immigrant who is exposed to the wretchedness of such isolation, does he at least have nothing to fear for his life?"

"Clearing land is always a dangerous undertaking," went on the American, "and there are almost no instances of a pioneer or his family having avoided forest fever during the first year. Often when people travel in the autumn, they find all the inhabitants of one cabin down with the fever, from the immigrant to his youngest son."

"And what becomes of these wretches when struck down by Providence in this way?"

"They are resigned to it, as they await a better future."

"But can they hope for any help from their fellow men?"

"Almost none."

"At least, can they obtain medical help?"

"The nearest doctor often lives sixty miles away from their home. They do as the Indians do; they die, or get better according to God's will."

We continued, "Does the word of religion sometimes reach them?"

"Very rarely; in our woods, we have still been unable to make provision to ensure the public observance of religion. It is true that almost every summer a few Methodist clergymen do their rounds of the new settlements. News of their arrival spreads with an unbelievable speed from cabin to cabin; it is the great news of the day. At the time specified, the immigrant, his wife, and children, make their way along the half-cleared paths of the forest toward the advertised meeting place. People come from fifty miles around. The believers gather not in a church but in the open air, beneath the foliage of the forest. A pulpit made from rough hewn trunks, tall upturned trees serving as seats— such are the ornaments of this rustic church. The pioneers and their families camp in the surrounding woods, where, for three days and nights, the crowd practices religious exercises with almost no interruption. You ought to see the zeal with which these men devote themselves to prayer and with what contemplation they listen to the solemn voice of the clergyman. In the wilderness they reveal how starved of religion they are."

"One last question: it is generally accepted in France that the American wilderness is populated with the help of European emigration. How is it then that, since we have been scouring your woods, we happen not to have met a single European?" A smile of superiority and complacent pride appeared outlined upon our host's features as he heard this question.

"Only Americans," he pompously replied, "are able to display the courage to submit to such wretchedness or know how to

purchase their comfort at such a price. The European emigrant
comes to rest in the big towns on the sea coast, or in the
neighboring districts, where he becomes a craftsman, farmhand,
or a servant. He leads an easier life than in Europe and appears
satisfied to leave the same inheritance to his children. On the
other hand, the American seizes possession of the earth and
seeks to create a great future with it."

After uttering these final words, our host stopped. He blew a
huge column of smoke from his mouth and appeared ready to
listen to what we had to tell him of our plans.

First of all, we thanked him for his valuable opinions and
wise advice which we assured him we would profit from some
day and we added: "Before settling in your district, my dear
host, we intend to go to Saginaw and we are keen to ask your
advice on this matter." On hearing the word Saginaw a strange
transformation came about on the American's face. We seemed
to have hauled him violently out of real life to thrust him into
the realm of the imagination. His eyes spread wide, his mouth
half-opened and the greatest astonishment showed on all his
features. "You wish to go to Saginaw," he cried, "to Saginaw
Bay! Two rational men, two well-bred foreigners wish to go to
Saginaw Bay? The idea is hardly credible."

"And why not, pray?" we replied.

"But do you not realize," continued our host, "what you are
involving yourselves with? Do you not realize that Saginaw is
the furthest inhabited point before the Pacific Ocean? That from
here to Saginaw almost all you encounter is a wilderness and
empty space untouched by clearing? Have you thought that the
woods are full of Indians and mosquitoes? That you will have
to sleep at least one night in their shady dampness? Have you
considered fever? Will you know how to manage in the wilderness and find your way through the impenetrable maze of the
forests?" After this outburst he paused, the better to judge the
impression he had produced. We continued: "All that may be
true but we shall set out tomorrow morning for Saginaw Bay."
Our host gave a few moments' reflection, shook his head, and
said in a slow and positive tone: "Only a very great matter can
drive two foreigners to such an undertaking; doubtless you have

thought, quite wrongly, that there was some advantage to settle in those places furthest away from any competition?" We made no reply. He went on: "Perhaps you have also been given the charge by the Canadian skin companies to establish contacts with the Indian tribes on the frontiers?" Same silence. Our host had run out of conjectures and became silent but continued to reflect deeply on the oddity of our plan.

"Have you never been to Saginaw?" we said. He replied: "I have been there five or six times for my sins but I had a good reason to do so and I can find none in your case."

"But, my worthy host, do not lose sight of the fact that we are not wondering whether to go to Saginaw but simply what means we need to employ to get there with ease." Brought back like this to the question, our American recovered all his calm and all the sharpness of his ideas; he explained to us briefly and with admirable good practical sense how we should set about crossing the wilderness; he went into the smallest details and anticipated the most unexpected circumstances. At the end of his instructions, he paused once again to observe whether we were at last realizing the mysterious nature of our trip and noticing that neither side had anything further to impart, he took the candle, led us to a bedroom, and, very democratically shaking us by the hand, went off to finish his evening in the public lounge.

We got up as day broke and prepared to leave. Our host was himself soon up. The night had not revealed to him what was persuading us to go on behaving in a way which was, in his view, so extraordinary. However, since we seemed absolutely determined to act in opposition to his advice, he dared not return to the attack but kept on walking around us. From time to time, he would repeat under his breath: "*I can hardly imagine what might drive two foreigners to go to Saginaw.*" He repeated this sentence several times until, at length, I told him as I put my foot in the stirrup: "There are many reasons driving us to it, my dear host." He pulled up short on hearing these words and, looking me in the face for the first time, he appeared to prepare himself for the revelation of a great mystery. But, as I quietly mounted my horse, I concluded the matter by waving him a

friendly goodbye and trotted off. When I turned round fifty
yards further on, I saw him still rooted to the spot in front of
his door like a haystack. Not long afterwards he went indoors
with a shake of his head. I imagine he was still muttering: "I
hardly know what two foreigners will do in Saginaw."

It had been recommended to us that we contact a Mr Williams
who could provide us with some useful information since he
had longstanding trade links with the Chippeway Indians and
had a son who had settled in Saginaw. After a journey of a few
miles in the woods, and already fearful of having missed our
man's house, we encountered an old man busy working in a
small garden. We approached him. It was Mr Williams himself.
He received us with great kindness and gave us a letter for his
son. We asked him whether we had anything to fear from
the Indian tribes whose territory we were about to cross. Mr
Williams rejected this idea somewhat indignantly: "No! No!"
he said. "You can walk without fear. For my own part, I would
sleep more calmly among Indians than among whites." I mention this as the first favorable impression I have received on the
Indians since my arrival in America. In the very populated areas,
people speak of them only with a blend of fear and scorn and I
believe that they do in fact deserve these two opinions in those
places. We have seen earlier what I thought of them myself when
I met the first of them in Buffalo. As you read on in this journal
and follow me among the European populations along the
frontiers and the Indian tribes themselves, you will entertain an
idea of the first inhabitants of America both more honorable
and more equitable.

Having left Mr Williams, we continued on our way through
the woods. From time to time, a small lake—the district is full
of them—came into view like a sheet of silver beneath the forest
foliage. It is difficult to imagine the charm surrounding these
pretty places where man has not erected his dwellings and where
a deep peace and an uninterrupted silence still reign. I have, in
the Alps, traveled through frightening and isolated places where
nature resists the work of man but where it displays, even in its
horrors, a grandeur which thrills and fascinates the soul. Here
the isolation is no less intense but does not evoke the same

impressions. The only feelings one has from passing through these deserts in flower where everything, as in Milton's *Paradise*, is ready to welcome man, is a quiet admiration, a gentle and melancholic emotion, a vague disgust for civilized life, a sort of savage instinct which inspires the painful thought that soon this delightful solitude will have assumed a different appearance. In fact, the white race is already marching through the woods which surround it and, in a short number of years, the European will have cut down the trees reflected in the clear waters of the lake and forced the animals inhabiting its banks to retreat toward new wildernesses.

Still making our way forward, we reached a region which looked quite different. The ground was no longer flat but intersected by hills and valleys. Several of these hills had the wildest of aspects. It was in one of these picturesque landscapes that, to our great surprise, we spotted just behind our horses, as we suddenly turned back to gaze at the imposing spectacle, an Indian who appeared to be following us step for step. He was a man about thirty years of age, tall and wonderfully proportioned, as almost all of them are. His black, shiny hair fell down to his shoulders except for two plaits tied to the top of his head. His face was daubed with black and red. He was wrapped in a kind of very short blue smock. He wore red *mittas*—a type of trouser reaching only as far as the thighs—and his feet were furnished with moccasins. A knife hung at his side. In his right hand he was holding a long carbine and in his left, two birds he had just killed. The first glance at this Indian exerted an unpleasant impression upon us. The place was badly chosen to resist an attack—on our right a pine forest rose to a dizzy height, on our left stretched a deep ravine in the bottom of which a stream flowed among the rocks obscured from our sight by the density of the foliage and toward which we were descending like blind men. It took only a moment to place our hands upon our rifles, to turn round and to stand on the path opposite the Indian. He similarly came to a halt. We stood in silence for half a minute. His face betrayed all the characteristic features which mark the Indian race from all others. In his completely black eyes shone that savage fire which still animates the look on a

half-caste's face and which disappears only with the second or
third generation of breeding with whites. The middle of his nose
was hooked while the end was slightly flattened; his cheekbones
were high and his strongly cleft mouth revealed two brilliantly
white rows of teeth which were ample proof that the savage had
cleaner habits than his American neighbor and did not spend
his days chewing tobacco. I said that the Indian had stopped the
moment we had turned round and placed our hands on our
weapons. He tolerated the swift scrutiny we made of his person
with complete passivity and a still, firm appearance. As he could
see that, on our side we had no hostile intent, he began to smile;
he probably realized that he had alarmed us. This was the first
time that I was able to note the extent to which the expression
of cheerfulness totally changes the features of these savage men.
Since then, I have had a hundred opportunities to make the same
observation. A serious and a smiling Indian are two entirely
different men. In the motionless look of the former reigns a
savage majesty which transmits an unwitting feeling of terror.
Should this same man happen to smile, his whole face assumes
an expression of simplicity and goodwill which bestows a real
charm upon him.

When we saw our fellow brighten up, we spoke to him in
English. He let us speak in a quite relaxed manner, then he
indicated that he could not understand. We offered him a little
brandy, which he accepted unhesitatingly with no sign of gratitude. Still speaking in sign language, we asked him for the birds
he was carrying and he gave them to us for the payment of a
small coin. Having thus made his acquaintance we waved to
him and galloped off. After a quarter of an hour of rapid
progress, I turned round once again to be astonished at seeing the
Indian still there behind my horse. He ran with the nimbleness of
a wild animal, without uttering a word or appearing to lengthen
his stride. We stopped; he stopped. We continued; he continued.
We hurtled forward at full speed. Our horses, reared in the
wilderness, easily cleared all obstacles. The Indian doubled his
pace; I could see him now to the right, now to the left of
my horse, leaping over bushes and landing noiselessly on the
ground. One might have thought of him as one of those wolves

from the north of Europe which follow after horsemen in the hope that they will fall from their horses and can be more easily devoured. The sight of this motionless face sometimes disappearing into the darkness of the forest, sometimes reappearing into the daylight and seemingly hovering at our side, became in the end an irritation. Unable to imagine what persuaded this man to pursue us at such a headlong pace—he had possibly been doing so for a long time before we first became aware of him—the idea occurred to us that he was leading us into an ambush. We were absorbed by these thoughts when we spotted another carbine in the wood ahead of us. We were soon standing by the side of the man carrying it; we took him at first for an Indian. He was clad in a kind of short frock coat which hugged his back and showed off a straight and very neat waist. His neck was bare and his feet shod in moccasins.

When we reached him and he looked up, we immediately recognized a European and we halted. He came up to us, shook us warmly by the hand and we began to talk: "Do you live in the wilderness?" "Yes, that's my house." He pointed to a hut in the middle of the leafy background more wretched than the normal log houses. "Alone?" "Alone." "And what do you do here, then?" "I scour these woods and kill the game I come across on both sides of the path but there aren't any good catches at the moment." "And do you like this kind of life?" "More than any other!" "But aren't you afraid of the Indians?" "Afraid of Indians! I prefer to live among them than in white society. No, no, I don't fear Indians. They are worth more than we are except when we have brutalized them with our liquor, the poor creatures!" We then revealed to our new acquaintance the man who was so obstinately pursuing us and who had now halted a few steps away as still as a statue. "He's a Chippeway," he said, "or as the French call him a *Sauteur* (jumper). I bet he's back from Canada where he has received the annual gifts from the English. His family cannot be far from here." Having said this, the American signaled to the Indian to draw near and began to talk to him in his own language with extreme fluency. It was a remarkable thing to behold the pleasure that these two men, so different by birth and manners, derived from sharing their ideas. The conversation clearly revolved around the respective merit of their weapons. The white man, having paid close attention to the native's rifle, said, "That's a fine carbine; the English probably gave it to him to use against us and he won't fail to do so in the next war. That's how the Indians draw upon their heads all the misfortunes which overwhelm them. But they haven't much idea, the poor people." "Do the Indians use these long and heavy guns with any skill?" "There are no marksmen like the Indians," our new friend went on sharply, in a tone of the greatest admiration. "Just look closely at the small birds he has sold you, Monsieur; they have been pierced with a single bullet and I'm sure he has only fired twice to get them." "Oh," he added, "there's no happier sight than an Indian in an area where we haven't yet driven the game away. But the large animals can smell our scent at more than three hundred miles and, as they withdraw, turn everything in front of us into a virtual wilderness where the Indians can no longer exist unless they plough the land."

As we were setting off again, our new friend called after us, "When you come back this way, knock at my door. I like to meet white faces in these parts."

I have recounted this conversation which, in itself, contains nothing unusual, in order to reveal a category of men we met very frequently after that along the borders of the colonized lands. They are Europeans who, in spite of the ways of their youth, have ended up by discovering an inexpressible charm in the freedom of the wilderness. Attached to the American wastes by preference and enthusiasm, to Europe by religion, principles, and opinions, they join love of life in the wild to their pride in civilization and they prefer Indians to their fellow countrymen, yet without acknowledging them as their equals.

So we set off again and, still advancing at the same speedy pace, we reached a pioneer's house after half an hour. In front of the door of this cabin an Indian family had established its temporary dwelling. An old woman, two girls and several children crouched around a fire in the heat of which lay exposed the remains of a whole roe deer. On the grass, a few steps away, a naked Indian warmed himself in the sun's rays while a small child was rolling about in the dust next to him. That was where our silent companion came to a halt; he left us with no word of farewell and went to sit seriously among his compatriots. Who could have persuaded this man to follow our horses' journey in this way for five miles? It was something we were never able to work out. After lunch in this spot, we remounted and continued our journey through an uncluttered group of high trees. The copse had been burned at one time since we could observe the fact from the scorched remains of a few trees lying on the grass. Today the ground is covered with ferns, which we could glimpse stretching out as far as the eye could see beneath the forest canopy.

A few miles further on my horse lost its shoe, which caused us considerable anxiety. Fortunately, we met a planter nearby who managed to reshoe it. Had we not met him, I doubt whether we could have gone any further, for at that time we were nearing the most distant of the clearances. This same man, who thus enabled us to continue our journey, invited us to move quickly as the day was beginning to fade and five good miles still separated us from Flint River where we wished to sleep.

In fact, a profound darkness soon began to surround us. We had to go on on foot. The night was calm but freezing cold. In the heart of these forests lay a silence so intense and a tranquillity so absolute that it appeared that all the forces of nature had become virtually paralyzed. Only the irksome buzzing of mosquitoes could be heard there, along with the noise of our horses' hooves. Occasionally we could see an Indian's fire in the distance, through the smoke of which was outlined the austere and motionless profile of a man. After an hour, we reached a place where the path divided. Two tracks opened up at this point. Which of the two should we take? The choice was a fine one: one of them ended at a stream whose depth we did not know, the other at a clearing. The moon, which was then rising, lighted a valley filled with debris in front of us. Further on we spotted two houses. It was so important not to get lost in such a place and at this hour that we decided to obtain information before going further. My companion stayed, holding the horses, while I threw my rifle over my shoulder and made my way down into the valley. I soon realized that I was entering an area quite recently cleared. Huge trees, with their branches not yet removed, covered the ground. By jumping from one to the other, I managed quite quickly to reach the vicinity of the houses but the same stream, which we had already encountered, stood between me and them. Fortunately its course was blocked at this point by tall oaks which the pioneer's axe had doubtless felled. I succeeded in sliding along these trees and finally reached the other side. Cautiously, I drew near to the two houses, fearing that they were Indian wigwams. They were not yet finished. I found the doors open and no one responded to my cries. I returned to the banks of the stream where I could not but admire for some minutes the sublime horror of the place. This valley appeared to form a huge arena, enveloped on all sides by the foliage of the wood like a black drapery and at the center of which the moon's rays splintered to create a thousand fantastic images which created a silent display amid the debris of the forest. Moreover no sound at all, no sign of life, rose from this emptiness. At last I thought of my friend and I called out to him at the top of my voice to tell him of the outcome of my investigations, to get him to cross over the stream and to come and join me. But I obtained no reply. Once more I shouted out and listened again. The same deathly silence reigned in the forest. I was seized by anxiety and I ran along the stream to find the path which crossed the water lower down. Once there I heard horses' hooves in the distance and soon afterwards I saw Beaumont himself appear. Surprised by my lengthy absence, he had taken the decision to advance toward the stream. He had already been stepping into the shallows when I had called to him. My voice could not have reached his ears at that moment. He told me that he too had made every effort to make himself heard and had, like me, been scared at receiving no reply. Without the ford which was our meeting place, we would have possibly been looking for each other most of the night. We set off again with the firm promise not to split up further. Three-quarters of an hour later, we finally spotted a clearing, two or three cabins and, a source of the greatest pleasure, a light. The river, strung out like a crimson thread at the end of the valley, finally proved that we had reached Flint River. In fact, the barking of dogs soon echoed through the woods and we stood in front of a *log house* separated from us by a single gate. As we were preparing to pass through, the moonlight allowed us to observe on the other side a tall black bear standing on its feet and pulling on its chain. It was demonstrating as clearly as it could its intention to bestow upon us an entirely fraternal embrace. "What sort of country is this," I said, "that they have bears as guard dogs?" "We must give a shout," my friend replied. "If we attempted to go through the gate, we would have some difficulty explaining ourselves to the gate-keeper." So we shouted out loud and so successfully that a man finally appeared at the window. After examining us by the light of the moon, he said to us, "Come in, gentlemen. Lie down, Trinc. To your kennel, I tell you. These are not thieves." The bear waddled back and we went in. We were half dead with tiredness. We asked our host if we could have some oats. "Of course," he replied. He began immediately to scythe the nearest field with an entirely American coolness, as he might have done in the middle of the day. Meanwhile, we unsaddled our horses and tied them, in the absence of a stable, to the fences through which we had just passed. Having thus thought of our traveling companions, we began to consider our own shelter. There was only one bed in the house. Since fate had awarded it to Beaumont, I wrapped myself in my overcoat and, lying down on the floor, I fell asleep as deeply as is appropriate to a man who has just traveled forty miles on horseback.

The next day, 25 July, our first concern was to ask about a guide. A hundred or so miles of wilderness lay between Flint River and Saginaw and the path there is a narrow track hardly recognizable to the eye. Our host gave our plan his approval and soon afterwards he led in two Indians, assuring us that we could trust them entirely. One was a child of thirteen or fourteen, the other a young man of eighteen whose physique, while not yet endowed with the vigorous shape maturity brings, nevertheless already displayed the image of agility linked to strength. He was of average height, his waist straight and slender, his limbs supple and well-proportioned. Long tresses fell from his bare head. In addition, he had taken pains to paint perfectly symmetrical black and red lines upon his face. A ring through his nose, a necklace, and earrings completed his finery. His war gear was no less noteworthy. On one side hung the battle axe, the famous tomahawk; from the other, a long and sharpened knife, by means of which the savages remove the hair from the vanquished. From his neck was suspended a bull's horn which served him as a powder pouch and, in his right hand, he was holding his carbine. As with most Indians, his look was wild while his smile was kindly. By his side, as if to finish the portrait, padded a dog with pricked ears and pointed jaw, more like a fox than any other type of animal, whose wild appearance matched perfectly the countenance of its master. After examining our new companion with a close scrutiny which he appeared not to notice for a single moment, we asked him what he wanted to receive as payment for the service which he was about to render us. The Indian replied with a few words in his own tongue and the American hurriedly started to speak and told us that what the savage was requesting could be valued at two dollars. "As these poor Indians," our host added charitably, "do not know the value of money, you can give me the dollars and I shall willingly look after supplying him with the equivalent." I was curious to see what this worthy man called the equivalent of two dollars and I followed him quietly to the place where he was settling the bargain. I saw him passing our guide a pair of moccasins and a pocket handkerchief, objects whose total worth certainly did not amount to half that sum. The Indian withdrew very pleased while I moved off silently, saying along with La Fontaine: "Ah! If only lions knew how to paint!"

Besides, it is not only Indians that the pioneers take for fools. We were daily victims ourselves of their inordinate greed for gain. It is very true that they do not steal. They have too much enlightenment to commit such an unwise act but I have never seen a big town innkeeper overcharge with more impudence than these inhabitants of the wilderness among whom I reckoned on finding the original honesty and simplicity of the ways of their fathers.

All was ready: we mounted, forded the stream which acted as

the furthest boundary between civilization and the wilderness and set off once and for all into the isolation.

Our two guides walked or rather leaped like wild cats over obstacles on the track. Whenever an upturned tree, a stream or marshy ground happened to greet us, they would point to the best path, going on without even turning round to see us extricate ourselves from the difficulty. Being accustomed to rely only upon himself, the Indian has trouble in imagining that anyone else might need help. He knows how to offer help when needs be but no one has yet taught him the art of turning consideration or caring to good effect. This way of acting would nonetheless have entailed some remarks from us but it was impossible for us to convey a single word to our companions. And there again, we felt entirely in their hands. Therein the social scale was in fact turned upside down; thrown into complete darkness, reduced to his own devices, the civilized man moved like a blind man, incapable not only of guiding himself through the maze he was crossing but even of discovering the means of sustaining life there. It was in the midst of these same difficulties that the savage could triumph; for him the forest had no veil. He was entirely at home there. He walked, head held high, under the guide of an instinct more reliable than a navigator's compass. In the tops of the tallest trees, beneath the thickest undergrowth, his eye could uncover prey close to which the European would have passed to and fro a hundred times to no avail.

Occasionally our Indians would stop; they would place their finger on their lips to indicate to us to move in silence and signal us to dismount. Guided by them, we would reach a place where game could be observed. It was an unusual sight to see the scornful smile with which they would lead us by the hand like children, finally bringing us near to the object which they had been able to see for a long time.

Meanwhile, as we moved forward, the final traces of man faded away. Soon everything ceased to indicate the presence even of the savage and we had before us the sight we had been pursuing for so long—the interior of an untouched forest.

In the heart of a thinnish copse through which we could see objects quite a long way away, a tall group of trees, composed almost wholly of pines and oaks, shot up into the sky. Forced to grow on a very circumscribed plot and almost entirely deprived of the sun's rays, each of these trees rises swiftly in its search for air and light. As straight as a ship's mast, it soon tops all its surroundings. Reaching an upper region, it then quietly spreads its branches and wraps itself round with their shade. Others soon follow it into this lofty area and they all intertwine their fronds, virtually forming a huge dais above the ground which supports them. Beneath this damp and still canopy, the appearance changes and the scene assumes a different character. Above one's head reigns a regal orderliness. Down near the ground, everything displays a contrary image of confusion and chaos. Trunks of trees, unable to bear their branches any longer, have been split at half their height and present only a sharp and torn point to the gaze. Others, long shaken by the wind, have been hurled entire to the earth; wrenched from the ground, their roots form a sort of natural rampart behind which several men could easily take cover. Huge trees, held steady by the branches around them, hang suspended in the air and fall into dust without touching the ground. In our part of the world, there is no countryside so free of people where a forest can be abandoned to itself so that the trees finally fall into decay after quietly living out their existence. Man it is who strikes them down in the strength of their maturity and who clears the forest of their remains. In the American solitudes, nature in its omnipotence is the only agent of destruction, as it is the only force for reproduction. Just as in those forests subjected to the sway of man, death strikes here without pause, but no one is responsible for removing the remains it produces. Each day adds to this quantity. They fall and pile upon each other. There is not time to reduce them quickly enough into dust or to prepare fresh spaces. Several generations of dead trees lie side by side. Some of them in the final throes of their decay appear to one's gaze as only a long trail of red dust marked upon the grass. Others are already half wasted away by the weather yet still preserve their shape. Finally, there are those, fallen only yesterday, which still spread their long branches over the earth and block the traveler's steps with an impediment he had not anticipated. In the midst of these various remains, the work of reproduction continues without ceasing. Saplings, climbing plants, grasses of all kinds seek the light through all obstacles. They crawl along fallen trunks and slip into their dust, raising and breaking the bark which still covers them. Here life and death come face to face; they seem to have wished to mingle and meld together their works.

On the ocean, we have often been brought to admire one of those serenely calm evenings when the sails flutter peacefully down the masts and leave the sailor in ignorance of the direction of the next breeze. This period of rest for the whole of nature is no less imposing in the solitudes of the New World than over the measureless expanses of the sea. In the middle of the day, when the sun shoots its rays over the forest, you often hear the echo of what sounds like a long groan in its depths, a piteous cry which floats into the distance. It is the final effort of a dying wind. Then everything around you reverts to a silence so profound, a stillness so perfect that the soul feels pierced with a sort of religious awe. The traveler comes to a halt and looks; the trees of the forest huddled together, their branches intertwined, seem simply to form an entire whole, a huge and indestructible building, beneath whose vaulting reigns an everlasting darkness. Whatever direction commands his gaze, he sees only a field of violence and destruction. Broken trees, shattered trunks, everything proclaims that the elements are here endlessly at war. But the struggle is interrupted. One might say that the activity has suddenly come to an end on the orders of a supernatural power. Half-broken branches still seem to be attached by a few secret ties to the trunk, which has stopped supplying any support; already uprooted trees have not had the time to drop down to the ground and have remained suspended in the air. He listens, fearfully holding his breath, all the better to grasp the slightest stirring of existence. No sound, no whisper reaches him.

More than once, in Europe, we have found ourselves lost in the depth of the woods but every time a few signs of life came to our ears—the distant striking of the nearest village bell, a traveler's footsteps, a woodcutter's axe, the report of a firearm, a dog's bark or simply that vague murmur rising from a civilized country. Here, not only does man not feature but even the calls of the animals cannot be heard. The smallest among them have left these places to move nearer human habitation; the largest to move even further away. The remaining animals keep themselves hidden from the sun's rays. Thus all is still in the woods; all is silent beneath their foliage. The Creator appears to have turned his face away for a moment and the forces of nature are in a state of paralysis.

Moreover, this is not the only case we have noted of the unusual analogy between the sight of the ocean and the appearance of a wild forest. In both scenes equally the concept of measureless space presses in upon you. The unbroken aspect of these same scenes and their uniformity surprise and overwhelm the imagination. Perhaps we found the feeling of loneliness and abandonment, which had seemed so heavy in the middle of the Atlantic, stronger and more poignant in the solitudes of the New World. At least, on the sea, the traveler contemplates a vast horizon toward which he always directs his gaze with a sense of hope. But in this ocean of foliage, who is able to point the way? Which objects draw his gaze? It would be no use rising to the tops of the tallest trees; others taller still surround you. There would be no purpose climbing the hills; everywhere the forest seems to march alongside you and this same forest stretches out in front of your steps as far as the North Pole and the Pacific Ocean. You can cover thousands of miles beneath its shade and are still walking without seeming to change position.

But it is time to return to the road to Saginaw. We had already been walking for five hours entirely unaware of the place in which we found ourselves, when our Indians stopped and the elder, whose name was Sagan-Cuisco, drew a line in the sand. He pointed to one end shouting: Miché-Couté-Ouinque (this is the Indian name for *Flint River*) and for the opposite end he said the name Saginaw. Marking a point in the middle of the line, he indicated to us that we had reached halfway along the route and that we should rest for a few moments. The sun was already high over the horizon and we would have been pleased to accept the invitation made to us, if we had been able to glimpse water within reach. But, not seeing any in the vicinity, we signaled to the Indian that we wished to eat and drink at the same time. He understood us immediately and set off again with the same speed as before. After an hour, he stopped once more and pointed to a place in the wood thirty yards away where he indicated the presence of water. Without waiting for our reply, nor helping us to unsaddle our horses, he made for the spot himself. We hurried after him. The wind had recently toppled a tall tree in this place. In the hole which the roots had filled lay a small amount of rainwater. This was the spring to which our guide had directed us without appearing to think that we might hesitate to partake of such a drink. We opened our bag; another misfortune! The heat had totally ruined our provisions and there we were reduced to a very small piece of bread as the only dinner available, the only food we had been able to find at *Flint River*. If you add to that a cloud of mosquitoes drawn by the proximity of the water, which we had to fight off with one hand while taking the piece of bread to our mouths with the other, you will realize what a country dinner was like in an untouched forest. All the time we ate, our Indians stayed seated, arms crossed, on the fallen trunk I have mentioned. When they saw that we had finished, they signaled that they too were hungry. We showed them our empty bag. They shook their heads without a word. The Indian has no idea about regular times for meals. He fills up with food when he can and goes without until he once again finds something to satisfy his appetite. Wolves act similarly in the same circumstances. Soon we thought about remounting but we were very frightened when we realized that our mounts had disappeared. Bitten by mosquitoes and goaded on by hunger, they had moved off from the path where we had left them and only with difficulty were we able to follow their tracks. If we had remained unaware for a further quarter of an hour, we would have awoken like Sancho with a saddle between our legs. We heartily blessed the mosquitoes which had made us think of leaving so quickly and we set off again. The path we were following soon became more and more difficult to make out. Our horses had to push their way continually through thick bushes or to leap over huge tree trunks which blocked our way.

After two hours along an extremely difficult route we at last reached the bank of a river which was shallow but very steep-sided. We forded it and, scaling to the top of the opposite bank, we saw a field of maize and two cabins resembling *log houses*. As we approached, we recognized that they were a small Indian settlement. The *log houses* were wigwams. Moreover, the deep sense of isolation prevailed there as in the surrounding forest. Arriving at the first of these abandoned dwellings, Sagan-Cuisco halted; he carefully examined all the things lying about, then laying down his carbine and coming up to us, he firstly drew a line in the sand, indicating, in the same way as before, that we had as yet completed only two-thirds of our way. Then standing up, he pointed to the sun and indicated that it was setting rapidly. Then he looked at the wigwam and closed his eyes. This language was very clear. He wanted to persuade us to bed down in this place. I admit that the proposal surprised us a lot and pleased us scarcely at all. We had not eaten since the morning and had only the slightest interest in going to bed without supper. Moreover, the gloomy and wild majesty of the scenes we had witnessed since the morning, the total isolation of our location, the fierce appearance of our guides with whom it was impossible to enter into communication, nothing of all that was destined to inspire us with confidence. In addition, in the Indians' behavior there was something peculiar which gave us no reassurance. The route we had just followed for two hours seemed even less used than the one we had traveled before. No one had ever told us that we would have to pass through an Indian village; on the contrary, everyone had assured us that one was able to go from Flint River to Saginaw in one day. We could not imagine, therefore, why our guides wished to detain us overnight in the wilderness. We insisted on proceeding. The Indians indicated that we would be caught by the darkness in the woods. To force our guides to continue their journey would have been a dangerous endeavor. We decided to try their greed. But the Indian is the most philosophic of men. He has few needs and, consequently, few desires. Civilization has no hold over him; he is unaware or scornful of its pleasures. However, I had perceived that Sagan-Cuisco had paid especial attention to a small wicker bottle which hung from my side—an unbreakable bottle. It was an object whose usefulness had come to his notice and had aroused a tangible admiration in him. My gun and bottle were the only items of my European equipment which might have stimulated his desire. I indicated to him that I would give him my bottle, if he took us straightaway to Saginaw. The Indian then appeared in a violent quandary. Once again, he looked at the sun and then the ground. Coming finally to a decision, he seized his carbine, twice uttered a cry of Ouh! Ouh! by placing his hand against his mouth and thrust his way ahead of us into the undergrowth. We galloped after him and, forcing a path before us, we soon lost sight of the Indian dwellings. Our guides ran like this for two hours at a greater speed than they had so far traveled. Meanwhile, night was overtaking us and the final rays of the sun had just disappeared behind the forest trees when Sagan-Cuisco was surprised by a severe nose bleed. However accustomed this young man appeared to be to bodily exercise, as was his brother, it was clear that fatigue and the lack of food were beginning to drain his strength. We were ourselves starting to fear that they would abandon this enterprise and would want to sleep at the foot of a tree. So we made a decision to have them mount our horses in turn. The Indians accepted our offer without surprise or humility. What a strange thing it was to see these half-naked men sitting seriously on an English saddle, carrying our game bags and rifles over their shoulders while we made our way laboriously on foot in front of them. Nightfall arrived at last and a freezing dampness began to settle beneath the foliage. The darkness then gave the forest a new and terrible appearance. There was nothing for the eye to see about us but a confusion of shapes, heaped up without order or symmetry, unusual and distorted forms, fantastic images seemingly borrowed from the diseased imagination of a man with a fever. Our steps had never produced more echoes; never had the silence of the forest appeared so frightening. You might have thought that the humming of the mosquitoes was the only breath from this slumbering world. As we advanced, the darkness became denser; only the occasional firefly crossing the wood traced a kind of luminous thread in its dark interior.

It was too late for us to recognize the rightness of the Indians' advice but it was no longer a question of going back. We continued, therefore, to walk on as swiftly as our strength and the night could allow us. After an hour, we left the wood and stood in a vast prairie. Three times our guides uttered a wild cry which echoed like the discordant notes of the tom-tom. A reply came back from the distance. Five minutes afterwards, we were on the bank of a river, prevented by the darkness from discerning the opposite side. The Indians halted at this spot; they wrapped themselves up in their blankets to avoid the mosquito bites and, lying on the grass, they soon rolled into a ball of wool which we could hardly make out and in which it would have been impossible to discern the shape of a man. We dismounted ourselves and patiently waited to see what would follow. After a few moments a slight noise could be heard and something was drawing near the bank. It was an Indian boat about ten feet long, cut out of a single tree. The man was crouched in the bottom of this fragile craft, wearing the outfit and with all the appearance of an Indian. He spoke to our guides who, on his command, hurried to remove the saddles from our horses to lay them in the canoe.

As I was getting ready to get in myself, the so-called Indian came toward me, placed two fingers on my shoulder and said to me in a Norman French accent which startled me: "Don't move too quickly, sometimes people drown." I would not have been more astonished if my horse had addressed me. I stared at the man who had spoken to me and whose face, bathed in the first rays of moonlight, was then gleaming like a copper ball: "So, who are you?" I said to him. "French seems to be your language and you look like an Indian." He replied that he was a half-breed Indian—that is, the son of a Canadian man and an Indian woman. I shall often have the chance to speak about this unusual race of half-castes which inhabit all the Canadian boundaries as well as part of the United States. For the moment I thought only of the pleasure of speaking my native language. Following the advice of our savage fellow countryman, I sat in the bottom of the boat, balancing as well as I could. The horse plunged into the river and began to swim while the Canadian paddled the craft forward while singing under his breath the following coup-let to an old French tune; I could not catch more than the first two lines:

> Between Paris and Saint-Denis,
> There was a girl.

In this way, we arrived without mishap on the other bank. The boat returned immediately to fetch my friend. All my life, I shall remember the moment when for the second time he approached the bank. The moon, at its full, was rising exactly over the prairie we had just crossed. Only half its circular shape appeared on the horizon; it was like a mysterious door through which the light of another sphere was reaching our gaze. The emerging ray of light came to be reflected in the waters of the river, sparkling as it reached me. The Indian canoe moved forward along the very line of this pale shimmering light; no oars could be discerned; no paddles could be heard; long, nar-row, and black, it slid swiftly and effortlessly like a Mississippi alligator which stretches toward the bank to seize its prey. Crouched at the prow of the boat, Sagan-Cuisco, his head leaning upon his knees, revealed only the gleaming locks of his hair. At the other end, the Canadian was rowing in silence, while, in his wake, the horse was churning up the water of the Saginaw through the effort of its powerful chest. The whole of this sight presented a savage grandeur, which produced, then and subsequently, a deep impression in our hearts. After landing on the bank, we hurried to find a house, which had just been revealed by the light of the moon, a hundred yards from the river and where the Canadian assured us we could find lodging. In fact, we managed to bed down decently and we would prob-ably have recovered our strength after a good night's sleep, if we had been able to rid ourselves of the swarms of mosquitoes which filled the house; but that was a goal we could never reach. The creature called *mosquito* in English and *maringouin* in French Canadian is a small insect similar to the French *midge* which differs from it only in size. It is generally bigger and its proboscis so strong and sharp that only woolen material can

protect against its bites. These small midges are the scourge of
the American wilderness. Their presence would be enough to
make a long stay intolerable. For myself, I can say that I have
never experienced torment similar to that I suffered from them
throughout the course of this journey and especially during our
stay in Saginaw. By day, they stopped us sketching, writing,
staying still for a moment; at night, they flew round us in their
thousands. Every part of the body left uncovered immediately
became a place for them to gather. Wakened by the pain of their
bite, we would cover our heads with our sheets; their bites
penetrated through. Thus harassed and pursued by them, we
would rise and go outside to breathe in the air until tiredness
allowed us a heavy and disturbed sleep.

We left very early and the first sight which greeted us on
leaving the house was the spectacle of our Indians, wrapped in
their blankets near the doorway, sleeping by the side of their
dogs.

Then we could see for the first time in full daylight the village
of Saginaw, which we had come so far to see.

A small cultivated plain, edged to the south by a beautiful
and calmly flowing river, to the east, west, and north by the
forest, comprises for the present all the territory occupied by
the growing township.

Near us stood a house whose construction suggested the
wealth of the owner. This was where we had just spent the night.
A dwelling of the same kind could be seen at the other end of
the clearing. In between, along the edge of the wood, two
or three *log houses* half-disappeared into the foliage. On the
opposite bank of the river, a prairie stretched away like a boundless ocean on a calm day. A column of smoke emerged from it
at that moment and rose peacefully heavenward. Following its
line down toward the ground, we could finally make out two or
three wigwams whose conical shapes and pointed tops melted
into the grasses of the prairie.

An upturned plow, oxen renewing their plowing, a few half-
wild horses completed the picture. Wherever our gaze wandered,
the eye would search in vain to see the spire of a gothic bell
tower, the wooden cross marking the path or the moss-covered

threshold of a presbytery. Those respected vestiges of our ancient Christian civilization have not been transported to the wilderness. There is nothing there yet to evoke any idea of the past or the future. You do not even come across sanctuaries dedicated to those who have gone before. Death has not had the time to claim its kingdom nor to mark out its grounds.

In this place man still seems to step into life like a thief. There is no meeting of several generations around his cradle to express their often deceptive hopes or to indulge in premature rejoicing, which the future will disappoint. His name is not inscribed in the registers of the city. Religion does not come to join its moving rituals to the concerns of the family. A woman's prayers and a few drops of water poured over the child's head by the hand of his father silently open his way to the doors of heaven.

The village of Saginaw is the furthest point inhabited by Europeans to the northwest of the vast peninsula of Michigan. It can be considered an outpost, a sort of sentry box positioned by the whites in the heart of the Indian nations.

Europe's revolutions and the clamorous upheavals which endlessly occur in the civilized universe reach this place only every now and again and resemble the echo of a sound of which the ear can no longer discern either the nature or the source.

Sometimes it will be an Indian who will casually relate in the poetic vein of the wilderness some of those sad realities of life in society, or a newspaper forgotten in a hunter's haversack, or simply that vague rumor spread by unknown voices, almost never failing to alert men to something extraordinary happening under the sun.

Once a year, a vessel, coming up the Saginaw River, reforges this link which has come loose from the great European chain which already envelops the world with its folds. It brings to the new settlement various industrial products and transports the fruits of the soil on its way back.

At the time of our visit, thirty people, men, women, old men, and children were the only components of this small society— an embryo in its earliest stages and a burgeoning seed entrusted to the wilderness, which the latter was to foster.

Accident, self-interest, or enthusiasms had assembled these

thirty people in this narrow area. Moreover, no common link existed between them and they were profoundly different from each other. You encountered there Canadians, Americans, Indians, and half-castes.

Philosophers have thought human nature to be the same everywhere, changing according to the institutions and laws of different societies. That is one of those opinions which every page of the history of the world seems to contradict. All nations, like individuals, display an appearance which is their own. The characteristic features of their faces keep occurring through all the transformations they undergo. Laws, customs, religions suffer changes; power and wealth move around; the external aspects vary, clothing alters, and prejudices disappear or change places with others. Amid these diverse shifts you can still discern the same nation. Something inflexible emerges at the heart of human flexibility.

The men who inhabit this small cultivated plain belong to two races who, for almost a century, have existed on American soil, obeying the same laws. But they have nothing in common. They are English and French just as they appear on the banks of the Seine and the Thames.

Make your way into this leafy cabin and you will encounter a man whose warm welcome and open face will from the outset herald the liking for the pleasures of human contact and the carefree side of life. In the first instance, you will perhaps take him for an Indian; in his submission to life in the wild, he has assumed his clothes, ways, and, to a degree, his customs. He wears moccasins, a hat of otter skin, and a woolen coat. He is a tireless hunter, sleeps on the alert, lives on wild honey and bison meat. Yet this man has no less remained a Frenchman, cheerful, enterprising, proud, glorying in his origins, a passionate enthusiast for military honors, more vain than self-interested, a man of instinct, obeying his first emotion more than his reason, preferring reputation to money. In order to come to the wilderness, he seems to have broken all ties which linked him to life; you do not see him with wife or children. This state is alien to his way of life but he submits to it easily, as he does to everything. Left to his own devices, he would naturally have a desire to stay at home—no one has a greater liking for the domestic fireside than he has; no one likes to rejoice at the sight of the paternal bell tower more than he does. But he has been wrenched from his peaceful habits despite himself; his imagination has been assailed by fresh scenes; he has been transplanted beneath another sky. This same man has suddenly felt invaded by the insatiable need for violent emotions, for sudden changes of fortune and for danger. The most civilized European has become the worshiper of life in the wilds. He will prefer savannahs to city streets, hunting to agriculture. He will make light of life and will live with no thought for the future.

The Canadian Indians used to say that the white men from France are as good hunters as themselves. Like them, they despise the conveniences of life and confront the terrors of death. God had created them to dwell in the wild man's cabin and to live in the wilderness.

A few yards away from this man lives another European who, enduring the same difficulties, has grown hardened against them.

This man is cold, stubborn, mercilessly argumentative. He clings to the land and rips from the life in the wilds everything he can snatch from it. He engages in a neverending struggle against it; everyday, he strips it of a few more of its spoils. Bit by bit, he transports his own laws, ways, customs, and, wherever possible, even the smallest benefits of advanced civilization into the wilderness.

The United States immigrant values only the results that stem from his victory; he maintains that honor is an empty rumor and that a man comes into the world only to obtain the comforts and conveniences of life. Nevertheless, he is courageous with a courage based on calculation and because he has discovered that there were several things more difficult to bear than death. He is an adventurer surrounded by his family; yet, he little values the pleasures of the mind or the attractions of life in society.

Settled on the other bank of the river, amid the reeds of the Saginaw, the Indian now and again casts a stoical glance at the dwellings of his European brothers. Do not give way to the idea that he admires their works or envies their lot. For nigh on three hundred years, the savage of America has struggled against this civilization which has been encroaching and surrounding him. He has not yet learned to know or value his opponent. Generations have come and gone in the two races without results. Like two parallel rivers, they have been flowing for three hundred years toward a common abyss. A narrow gap lies between them but they never join their waters. However, it is not that the native of the New World lacks any natural aptitude but that his nature appears stubborn in its rejection of our ideas and skills. Lying upon his coat, surrounded by the smoke of his hut, the Indian casts a scornful glance at the European's comfortable dwelling. For himself, he proudly derives pleasure from his wretchedness and his heart swells and is uplifted by the sight of his primitive independence. He smiles bitterly on seeing us tormenting our lives in the acquisition of useless wealth. What we call industry, he calls shameful servitude. He compares the plowman to the ox which plies its burdensome furrow. What we name the conveniences of life, he calls the playthings of children or the pursuits of women. He envies only our weapons. When a man can find shelter at night for his head beneath a leafy tent, when he manages to light a fire to keep mosquitoes away in summer and to protect himself from the cold in winter, when his dogs are good and the land is full of game, what more could he possibly ask for from the eternal Being?

On the other bank of the Saginaw, near the European clearings and at the confines, so to say, of the old and new worlds, stands a rustic cabin, more comfortable than the savage's wigwam and cruder than the house of the civilized man. This is the home of the half-caste. When we stood for the first time before the door of this half-civilized hut, we were taken aback to hear from inside a gentle voice intoning penitential psalms to an Indian melody. We paused for a moment to listen. The modulations of the notes were slow and profoundly sad. It was easy to recognize that plaintive harmony which characterizes all the songs of the man from the wilderness. We went in. The master of the house was not there. Sitting in the middle of the room, legs crossed on a mat, a young woman was working on a pair of moccasins. With her foot, she was rocking a child whose bronzed complexion and features displayed its twin origin. The woman was dressed like one of our peasant women except that her feet were bare and her hair fell freely upon her shoulders. On seeing us, she grew quiet with a kind of respectful silence. We asked her whether she was French. "No," came the reply with a smile. "English?" "Not that either," she said; she looked down and added: "I am only a savage." A child of two races, brought up in the tradition of two languages, nourished upon different beliefs and reared upon contradictory prejudices, the half-caste constitutes a mixture which is as inexplicable to others as it is to himself. When the images of the world come to be reflected upon his crude brain, they appear to him as a chaotic muddle from which his mind cannot extricate itself. Proud of his European beginnings, he despises the wilderness: yet, he loves the wild freedom which prevails there. He admires civilization and cannot entirely submit to its power. His tastes are at variance with his ideas, his opinions with his ways. Not knowing how to make his way in the ambiguous daylight around him, his spirit struggles painfully in the wrappings of a universal confusion. He adopts conflicting ways; he prays at two altars; he believes in the redeemer of the world and the juggler's amulet. He reaches the end of his career without being able to unravel the dark problem of his existence.

Thus, the hand of God had, therefore, already cast the seed of the different nations into this unknown corner of the world; here, already, several different races, several distinct peoples, had come face to face.

A few exiled members of the great human family came together in the endless tracts of these woods; they have common needs; they have to fight together against forest animals, hunger, and the unkindness of the seasons. There are scarcely thirty of them in the middle of the wilderness where everything resists their efforts and they all eye each other with hatred and suspicion. Skin color, poverty or comfort, ignorance or education have already laid down indestructible classifications between them. National prejudices, as well as those of education and birth, keep them apart and isolated from each other.

Where would one come across a more complete picture of the wretchedness of our natural state within a narrower frame? However, one feature is still missing.

The deep lines traced by birth and opinion upon the destiny of these men are not confined to life but stretch beyond the grave. Six religions or different sects claim for themselves a share of the beliefs of this growing society.

Catholicism with its frightening immutability, its absolute dogmas, its awful curses, and huge rewards, the religious anarchy of Reform, and the ancient paganism find their representatives in this place. Already, the sole and eternal Being, who has created all men in his own image, is worshipped in six different ways. The heaven which each one claims exclusively as his inheritance is a subject of zealous quarreling. Furthermore, in the midst of the wretchedness of present loneliness and suffering, the imagination of men still wears itself away in producing inexpressible pain for the future. The Lutheran condemns the Calvinist to eternal fire, the Calvinist condemns the Unitarian, and the Catholic enfolds them all in a common disapproval.

The Indian, who is more tolerant in his crude faith, does nothing more than keep his European brother away from the happy fields he claims as his own. Loyal to the muddled traditions bequeathed to him by his forefathers, he himself easily finds consolation from the evils of life and dies peacefully, dreaming of the evergreen forests which will never be shattered by the pioneer's axe and where the deer and the beaver will offer themselves to his blows during the countless days of eternity.

After lunch we went to see the richest property owner in the village, Mr Williams. We found him in his shop busy selling a mass of objects, worth very little, such as knives, glass necklaces, and earrings, to some Indians. It was pitiful to observe how these unhappy people were treated by their civilized European brothers. Moreover, all those we saw there meted out an astonishing justice to the savages. They were kind, harmless, a thousand times less inclined to steal than white people. It was simply a shame that they were beginning to have a clearer idea about the value of things. And why is that, if you please? Because the profits from the business conducted with them were becoming less substantial as the days passed. In this can you see the superiority of the civilized man? The Indian, in his coarse simplicity, would have said that he was finding it daily more difficult to fool his neighbor. But the white man discovers, in the perfecting of the language, a fortunate slant which gives expression to this matter and avoids any shame.

Returning from Mr Williams's house, we had the idea to row some way up the Saginaw to shoot the wild duck which abounded along its banks. As we were busy hunting, a canoe left the reeds in the river and some Indians came to meet us in order to scrutinize my rifle, which they had spotted from some way off. I have always noticed that this weapon, which is, however, in no way unusual, drew very special regard in my direction from the savages. A rifle which can kill two men in a second and disappears into the fog was, in their view, an inestimable wonder—a priceless masterpiece. The men who approached us gave evidence, according to their customs, of great admiration. They asked where I had got my rifle. Our young guide replied that it had been made on the other side of the Great Waters, where the fathers of the Canadians lived—a fact which did not reduce its value in their eyes, as you can imagine. They remarked meanwhile that, since the sights were not positioned in the middle of each barrel, one could not be as certain of one's aim—a remark to which I had no very clear idea of reply.

When evening had come, we rowed back in the boat and, trusting the experience we had acquired in the morning, we set off alone to go up a tributary of the Saginaw only half-glimpsed until then.

The sky was cloudless and the atmosphere was sharp and still. The water of the river flowed through an extensive forest, but so slowly that it would have been impossible to say which way the current was moving. In order to obtain an accurate idea of these New World forests, we always realized that we had to follow some of the rivers which flow beneath their overhanging shadows. Rivers resemble great tracks carefully provided by Providence, from the beginning of the world, to penetrate the wilderness, allowing man access. When one carves a way through the wood, one's vision is often very limited. Besides, the very path along which one is moving is the work of human hands. By contrast, rivers are routes free of debris and their banks freely reveal all the great and wonderful sights which a rampant vegetation, left to its own devices, can offer to one's gaze.

In that spot, the wilderness was probably just as it appeared six thousand years before to our first ancestors' eyes—a delightful and scented solitude festooned with flowers; a magnificent dwelling, a living palace constructed for man but into which the master had not yet made his way. The rowing boat slipped along effortlessly and silently. All around us reigned total serenity and peace. It was not long before we ourselves became, as it were, soothed at the sight of such a scene. Our conversation began to become more and more intermittent. Soon we were only whispering our thoughts. At length we fell silent altogether and, both putting up our oars, we descended into a quiet reverie filled with inexpressible magic.

How is it that human speech, which has the words for every suffering, encounters an invincible difficulty in conveying the gentlest and most natural emotions of the heart? Who will ever faithfully depict those exceptionally rare times in life when your physical wellbeing shapes you for a moral peacefulness and when your eyes perceive before them a perfect balance in the universe; a time when the soul, halfway toward sleep, hovers between the present and the future, the real and the possible; when man, surrounded by the beauty of nature, inhaling a calm, cool air, at peace with himself in the midst of a universal quiet, listens closely to the even throb of his arteries, each beat of which thus registers the passage of time, seemingly flowing drop by drop into eternity. Perhaps many men have seen the accumulating years of a long life without once experiencing anything to compare with what we have just described. Such people could not possibly understand us. But we are convinced that there are several men who will discover in their memories and deep down in their hearts the means of adding color to these images and, on reading our words, will sense the awakening of the memory of a few fleeting hours, which neither time nor the obvious troubles of life have been able to blot out.

We were disturbed in our reverie by a rifle shot suddenly echoing through the woods. At first, the noise seemed to ricochet from both banks of the river; then it rumbled into the distance until it was entirely lost in the depths of the surrounding forests. It resembled a long, frightening war cry uttered by an advancing civilization.

One evening in Sicily, we happened to lose our way in a vast marshland, which these days occupies the former site of the town of Hymera. The impression evoked by the sight of this famous city, now turned into a rough wilderness, was profound and deeply engraved on our minds. In our travels, we had never encountered a greater witness to the unstable state of human affairs and to the sorrows of our natural life. Here the isolation still prevailed but one's imagination, instead of moving backwards and seeking to recede into the past, by contrast launched itself forward, immersing itself in an endless future. We were wondering by what peculiar license of destiny we, the children of an ancient people, were led to be present at one of the settings of the primitive world and to see the yet empty cradle of a great nation when we had been able to look upon the ruins of empires already gone and to walk in the wilderness created by men. These are not the more or less rash forecasts of hindsight, they are facts as definite as if they were already achieved. After not many years, these impassible forests will be felled. The din of civilization and industry will break the silence of the Saginaw River. Its echo will be silent . . . Wharfs will enclose its banks. Its waters, which today flow unknown and quiet in the heart of a nameless wilderness, will be stemmed by the prows of ships. One hundred and twenty miles still separate this isolated area from the great European settlements and we are possibly the last travelers to be granted the chance of seeing it in its original splendor, so great is the drive which brings the white race to the total conquest of the New World.

It is this idea of destruction, this ulterior motive of an imminent and inevitable change which gives, in our view, the American wastes such an original appearance and such a touching beauty.

One looks upon them with a melancholic pleasure; somehow there is an urgency to wonder at them. The idea of this natural and wild grandeur, which will come to an end, blends with the imperious images evoked by the triumphant progress of civilization. One feels proud to be a man and one experiences at the same moment some kind of bitter regret for the power which God has granted us over nature. The soul is disturbed by ideas and opposing feelings, but all the impressions received are magnificent and leave a deep mark.

We wished to leave Saginaw on the next day, 27 July, but one of our horses had been chafed by its saddle. Thus, we decided to stay one day more. Lacking any other way of spending our time, we went hunting in the prairies alongside the Saginaw below the clearings. These prairies are not marshy, as one might suppose. They are flat areas, more or less extensive, where the woods have not reached, despite the excellent soil. The grass there is coarse and three or four feet high. We found only a small amount of game and returned early. The heat was stifling, as when a storm is near, and the mosquitoes even more irksome than usual. We never moved other than in a cloud of these insects around us and against which we had to wage a constant war. Woe betide the man who was obliged to stop. He would be delivered up to a pitiless enemy. I recall having been forced to load my rifle on the run because it was so difficult to stay still for a single moment.

As we were tracing our way back across the prairie, we noticed that our Canadian guide was following a small marked-out path and was watching the ground most carefully before stepping forward. "So, why do you take so many precautions?" I said to him, "Are you afraid of getting wet?" "No," he replied, "but when I cross the prairies, I have got used to looking where I put my feet all the time so as not to step on a rattlesnake." "What the devil," I resumed, with a jump on to the path, "are there rattlesnakes here?" "Indeed, yes," replied our French American with an unflappable calm, "the place is full of them." Then I reprimanded him for not warning us earlier. He claimed that, since we were wearing stout shoes and a rattlesnake never bit above the ankle, he had not considered that we ran a great risk.

I asked him if the wound from a rattlesnake was fatal. He replied that death always ensued in less than twenty-four hours unless one had recourse to the Indians. The latter knew a remedy which, he said, saved the patient, if administered in time.

Nevertheless, for the remainder of the journey, we imitated our guide and, like him, looked closely at our feet.

The night following this hot day was one of the most difficult I have ever spent in my life. The mosquitoes had become so irritating that it was impossible to close my eyes despite being overwhelmed by tiredness. About midnight, the storm which had been threatening for a long time finally burst. Having abandoned any hope of falling asleep, I rose and went to open the door of our cabin to breathe the fresh night air at least. It had not rained again and the atmosphere appeared calm but the forest was already swaying; it growled and moaned far into its depths. Occasionally lightning lit up the sky. The quiet flow of the Saginaw, the narrow strip along its banks, the roofs of five or six cabins, and the belt of surrounding foliage looked just then, for a moment, like an evocation of the future. Everything melted into the darkest obscurity and the frightening voice of the wilderness began again to be heard.

I was watching this great spectacle with warm feeling when I heard someone sigh nearby and, in the brightness of a lightning flash, I perceived an Indian leaning, as I was, against the wall of our dwelling. Almost certainly the storm had just interrupted his sleep for he was casting a troubled stare over everything around him.

Did this man fear the thunder? Or could he see, in this clash of the elements, something other than a fleeting upheaval of nature? Did these ephemeral images of civilization, springing as if automatically from the heart of the tumult of the wilderness, have a prophetic meaning for him? Did these cries of pain in the forest, which seemed locked in an unequal struggle, reach his ear like a hidden warning from God, a solemn revelation of the final destiny reserved for the savage races? I could not say. But his agitated lips appeared to be muttering prayers and all his features were marked with a superstitious terror.

At five o'clock in the morning, we thought about leaving. All the Indians from the Saginaw neighborhood had disappeared; they had left to go and receive the presents which the English gave them every year while the Europeans were occupied with the harvest. We had, therefore, to resolve to travel through the forest without a guide. The undertaking was not as difficult as one might suppose. There is generally only one path through these vast solitudes and it is only a matter of keeping to the track in order to reach one's destination.

So, at five o'clock in the morning we crossed the Saginaw once more. We received the farewells and final advice from our hosts and, turning our horses' heads, we were alone in the middle of the forest. I confess that it was not without a serious feeling that we began to push forward into these humid depths. This very forest around us stretched from there on toward the Pole and the Pacific Ocean. Only one inhabited spot lay between us and the limitless wilderness and we had just left it behind. Moreover, these thoughts simply served to spur our horses on and after three hours we reached an abandoned wigwam and the isolated banks of the River Cass. A green area jutting out into the river, shaded by tall trees, served as our table and we started lunch with a view over the river whose crystal clear waters wound through the wood.

On leaving this Cass River wigwam we came across several paths. We had been told which one to take but it is easy to forget a few details or to have misunderstood such explanations. That is what we certainly experienced that day. Two ways had been mentioned and there were three. It is true that of these three ways, two came together further on, as we have since learned, but we did not know that then and our confusion was serious.

After a long examination and discussion, we behaved like nearly all great men and acted in an almost random manner. We forded the river as best we could and plunged our way swiftly towards the southwest. More than once the path seemed about to disappear into a thicket; in other places, the way appeared so slightly trodden that we could scarcely believe that it led to anything other than an abandoned wigwam. It is true that our compass indicated that we were still walking in the right direction. However, we were not entirely reassured until we discovered the place where we had taken our dinner three days before. A gigantic fir, whose wind-torn trunk we had admired, enabled us to recognize it. Nevertheless, we did not continue our course with any less speed for the sun was beginning to set. Soon we reached an open space which usually anticipates clearings and, as night was starting to overtake us, we spotted the Flint River. Half an hour later, we stood before the door of our host. This time the bear greeted us like old friends and stood up only to celebrate his joy at our happy return.

Throughout this entire day, we saw no other human face. The animals had also disappeared; they had probably withdrawn into the undergrowth to escape the heat of the day. Simply, from time to time, we would come across a sparrowhawk which dozed quietly, standing on one leg in the sun's rays on the leafless top of some dead tree; it seemed sculpted out of the very wood it was using as a perch.

It was in the heart of this profound solitude that we suddenly thought of the 1830 Revolution whose first anniversary we had just reached. I cannot say how impetuously the memories of 29 July took hold on our minds. The shouts and smoke of the conflict, the noise of the cannon, the rumble of the muskets, the even more horrific ringing of the alarm bell, this whole day with its heated atmosphere seemed suddenly to emerge from the past and to be reproduced like a living tableau in front of me. It was only a sudden illumination, a fleeting dream. When I looked up and glanced around me, the apparition had already vanished but never had the silence of the forest seemed to me more glacial, its shades more gloomy, or its isolation more complete.

EXCURSION TO LAKE ONEIDA

We left the small village of Fort Brewerton on 8 July 1831 at sunrise and began to travel north-eastwards.

About a mile and a half from our host's house, a path led into the forest; we hurried along it. The heat was beginning to become irritating. A stuffy morning had followed a troubled night. We were soon sheltered from the sun's rays and deep into one of those dense forests of the New World whose dark and savage majesty takes hold on the imagination and invades the soul with a kind of religious awe.

How might I depict such a scene? Upon marshland where a thousand streams, as yet unencumbered by the hand of man, freely flow and vanish, nature has sown haphazardly and with unbelievable richness the seeds of almost every plant which creeps along the ground or stands above the earth.

Stretched out above our heads was a huge canopy of green foliage. Above this thick veil and within the damp heart of the wood, the eye could pick out a boundless confusion; a sort of chaos. Every age of tree, every color of leaf, grasses, fruits, a thousand species of flower, grew in profusion, woven together on the same spot.

For centuries, generations of trees have followed each other without break and the earth is strewn with their leftovers. Some seem felled just yesterday; others, already half buried in the earth, reveal only a hollow and spindly surface; yet others have been reduced to dust and serve as compost for their most recent saplings. Among them a thousand different plants hurriedly take their turn to seek the light. They slip between these motionless corpses, creep over the top of them, slither beneath their rotten bark, lifting and scattering the dust of their remains. This is a virtual struggle between life and death. Sometimes we happened upon a huge tree upended by the wind which, despite its weight, had often failed to find a path down to the ground because the rows of trees were so close together in the forest. Its dried branches still swayed in the breeze.

There reigned a solemn silence within this loneliness and little or no animal life could be seen. Man was nowhere to be found and yet this was in no way a wilderness. On the contrary, the whole natural scene displayed a vigor of growth unknown elsewhere. Here everything was alive; the atmosphere appeared imbued with the scent of vegetation. We seemed to hear a sort of noise from within, which revealed the work of creation, and we glimpsed the flow of sap and life along channels which were always open.

We had been walking for several hours amid these dominating solitudes and in a daylight that was not very bright, without hearing any other noise than that of our horses crushing beneath their hooves leaves heaped up by several winters or forcing their burdensome way through the dead branches covering the path. We stayed silent; our hearts were filled with the grandeur and novelty of the sight. At length we heard the echo of the first blows of an axe which heralded the presence of a European some way away. Fallen trees, burned and blackened, a few plants useful to man sown in a tangled muddle of different undergrowths, guided us to the dwelling of the pioneer. In the middle of quite a restricted circle outlined by fire and the axe arose the crude home of this forerunner of European civilization. It was, as it were, the oasis in the middle of the desert.

Having spent some moments in conversation with the man dwelling in this place, we resumed our ride and, half an hour later, reached a fisherman's cabin constructed on the very edge of the lake we had come to visit.

Lake Oneida is situated amid modestly tall hills and still intact forests. A band of dense foliage surrounds it in every direction and its waters bathe the roots of the trees which stand reflected in its transparent and silent surface. The isolated cabin of a fisherman rose by itself on its banks. Moreover, there was no sail to be seen across its expanse nor could we see any smoke rising above its woods, for the European, while not having taken complete possession of its banks, had achieved enough possession to drive out the populous and aggressive tribe which had formerly given it its name.

About a mile from the bank where we stood were positioned two oval-shaped islands of equal length. These islands are covered with such dense woodland that it entirely hides the land upon which it stands. You could say that they were two groves afloat upon the surface of the lake.

No highway passes near this place. No great industrial establishments, nor places renowned for their picturesque beauty, could be seen in these regions.

However, it was no accident which had led us to the vicinity of this solitary lake. It was, on the contrary, the aim and objective of our expedition.

It had been many years before that a book entitled *Expedition to Lake Oneida* had come into my hands. In it the author told the tale of a young Frenchman and his wife who were driven from their homeland by the turbulence of our first Revolution and had come to seek refuge on one of the islands surrounded by the waters of this lake. There, divided from the entire universe, far from the storms of Europe and rejected by the society which had given them birth, those two wretches lived for each other, in mutual consolation for their unhappiness.

This book had left a profound and lasting trace in my soul. That this effect was due to the skill of the author, to the actual charm of the events or to the influence of the times, I could not say but I have been unable to efface from my memory the recollection of the two French people from Lake Oneida. How often had I not envied the tranquil delights of their isolation. Domestic happiness, the attraction of married union, love itself were linked in my mind to the image of the solitary island where my imagination had created a new Eden. This story, once told to my traveling companion, had had a lively effect upon him in his turn. We frequently happened to speak of it and we always ended by repeating, either with a smile or with sadness: there is no happiness in this world except on the shores of Lake Oneida.

When events which we could not have predicted had driven us to America, this memory returned to us more forcefully. We promised each other that we would call upon our two French people, if they were still alive, or at least walk round their homestead. Simply wonder here at the strange power of the imagination over the mind of man: those wild places, that still and silent lake, those islands covered by greenery did not strike us as new objects. On the contrary, we seemed to be seeing again a place where we had spent some of our early years.

We hurried into the fisherman's cabin. The man was in the woods. An elderly woman was its sole occupant. She limped out to greet us on the stoop of her house. "What is the name of that green island, which stands a mile from here in the waters of the lake?" we said to her. "It's called Frenchman's island," she replied. "Do you know what caused this name to be given to it?" "I was told it had been called this name because of a Frenchman who came to settle there some years ago." "Was he by himself?" "No, he'd brought his wife with him." "Are they still living there?" "Twenty years ago, when I settled in this spot, the French people were no longer on the island. I recall being curious enough to go and visit it. At that time, the island, which appears so wild to you from here, was still a beautiful place: the interior was carefully cultivated, the Frenchman's house stood in the middle of an orchard surrounded by fruit and flowers. A grapevine covered its walls and grew all around it but it was already in ruins for want of an occupant." "What had become of the French people then?" "The woman had died, the man had abandoned the island and it is not known what became of him after that." "Can you lend us the boat moored against your door to cross the section of the lake which divides us from the island?" "Of course, but it is a long way to row and the effort is hard for anyone not used to it. Anyway, what can you see of interest in a place which has returned to the wild?"

As we hurried to push the boat into the water, without offering her a reply, she said, "I can see what this is about. You want to buy this island; the ground is good and the land in our district is not yet expensive." We replied to her that we were travelers. "Then," she continued, "you are doubtless relatives of the

Frenchman and he has asked you to visit his inheritance." "Still less than that," we replied. "We don't even know his name." The good woman shook her head in disbelief while we operated the oars and began to make rapid progress toward the island of this Frenchman.

We maintained a deep silence during this brief crossing; our hearts were filled with gentle and painful feelings. As we drew nearer, we had less understanding how this island could have been inhabited before, since its surroundings were so wild. We were almost ready to believe ourselves the playthings of a fictional tale. At last we reached its shoreline and, sliding beneath the great branches which the trees had cast out over the lake, we began to push further inland. First we crossed a ring of centuries-old trees which appeared to protect the approaches to the place. Beyond this rampart of foliage, we suddenly came across another sight. A scattering of trees and a young plantation had taken over the whole interior of the island. In the forests we had traveled through during the morning, we had often seen man engaged in a hand-to-hand struggle against nature and succeeding, although with difficulty, in removing its vibrant and wild character in order to shape it to his laws. Here, by contrast, we could see the forest regaining its power, once again striding on to conquer the wilderness, outfacing man and rapidly swallowing up the brief signs of his victory.

It was easy to recognize that a caring hand had previously cleared the place now taken over at the heart of the island by the young generation of trees I have mentioned. You did not come across aging trunks scattered on the undergrowth. Everything, by contrast, smacked of youthfulness. It was clear that the surrounding trees had sprouted from shoots in the midst of abandoned fields; grasses were growing more thickly in the place which once carried the harvests of this exiled man; brambles and parasitical plants had repossessed their former kingdom. Hardly anywhere could the trace of a fence or the sign of a field be found. For an hour we searched in vain for any signs of the abandoned dwelling through the foliage of the woods and in amongst the undergrowth which invaded the ground. The rustic richness which the fisherman's wife had just described to us, the

mown grass, the borders, the flowers, fruits, that production of
civilized living, which a talented and tender touch had introduced into the heart of the wilderness, all had gone, along with
the human beings who had lived here. We were about to give
up our enterprise when we spotted an apple tree, half dead with
age. This set us off on the track. Nearby, a plant which we first
thought was a creeper rose along the length of the tallest trees,
winding itself up their slender trunks or hanging down from
their branches like a garland of greenery. On closer scrutiny, we
recognized a vine. Then we could judge for sure that we were
on the very site chosen forty years before by our two unhappy
compatriots as their final refuge. But by barely digging beneath
the dense bed of leaves covering the ground, we managed to
come across a few remnants now turning to dust and which
after a short time will be no more. As for the remains themselves
of the woman who was not afraid to exchange the delights of
civilized life for a grave in a deserted isle of the New World, we
could not discover any sign of them. Did the exile leave this
precious deposit behind in his wilderness? Or did he carry it to
the place where he went to end his days? No one has been able
to tell us that.

Maybe the readers of these lines will not imagine the feelings
which they convey and will treat them as exaggerated or illu-
sory? However, I will accept that it was with a heart full of
emotion, troubled by fears and hopes, no less than fired by a
kind of religious feeling, that we devoted ourselves to these
detailed investigations and that we went in search of the traces of
these two people whose name, family, and, in part, story were
unknown to us and whose only claim to recognition was that
they had experienced in these very places pains and joys which
interest all hearts because they find their beginnings in all hearts.

Is there a greater wretchedness than that felt by this man?

This was an unhappy man bruised by human society: his
fellow men rejected him, banished him, forcing him to renounce
contact with them and to escape into the wilderness. Only one
person followed his footsteps into isolation and healed the
wounds of his soul. She substituted the deepest feelings of the
heart for the joys of society. There he was reconciled to his lot.

He forgot revolutions, political parties, towns, his family, his position in society, his wealth; at last he can breathe. His wife dies. Death comes to strike her down while sparing him, the wretch. What is to become of him? Will he stay by himself in the wilderness? Will he return to a society where he has so long been forgotten? He is no longer equipped for isolation or for the social round. He can live no longer with or without men. He is neither a wild nor a civilized man. He is nothing but a ruin like those trees of the American forests which the wind has had the power to uproot but not to fell. He stands but no longer lives.

Having scoured the island in every direction, visited its faintest remains, and listened to the frozen silence which now reigns beneath its shadows, we made our way back to the mainland.

Not without regret, I saw this vast mound of greenery retreat; it had been able to protect the two exiles for so many years against the bullets of Europeans and the arrows of savages but had failed to remove their cottage from the unseen blows of death.

MADISON, HAMILTON AND JAY

The Federalist Papers

'The establishment of a Constitution, in a time of profound peace, by the voluntary consent of a whole people, is a PRODIGY'

Written at a time when furious arguments were raging about the best way to govern America, *The Federalist Papers* had the immediate practical aim of persuading New Yorkers to accept the newly drafted constitution in 1787. In this they were supremely successful, but their influence also transcended contemporary debate to win them a lasting place in discussions of American political theory. Acclaimed by Thomas Jefferson as 'the best commentary on the principles of government which ever was written', *The Federalist Papers* make a powerful case for power-sharing between state and federal authorities and for a constitution that has endured largely unchanged for more than two hundred years.

In his brilliantly detailed introduction, Isaac Kramnick sets the *Papers* in their historical and political context. This edition also contains the American constitution as an appendix.

'The introduction is an outstanding piece of work ... I am strongly recommending its reading' WARREN BURGER, former Chief Justice, Supreme Court of the United States

Edited with an introduction by ISAAC KRAMNICK

THE STORY OF PENGUIN CLASSICS

Before 1946 ... 'Classics' are mainly the domain of academics and students; readable editions for everyone else are almost unheard of. This all changes when a little-known classicist, E. V. Rieu, presents Penguin founder Allen Lane with the translation of Homer's *Odyssey* that he has been working on in his spare time.

1946 Penguin Classics debuts with *The Odyssey*, which promptly sells three million copies. Suddenly, classics are no longer for the privileged few.

1950s Rieu, now series editor, turns to professional writers for the best modern, readable translations, including Dorothy L. Sayers's *Inferno* and Robert Graves's unexpurgated *Twelve Caesars*.

1960s The Classics are given the distinctive black covers that have remained a constant throughout the life of the series. Rieu retires in 1964, hailing the Penguin Classics list as 'the greatest educative force of the twentieth century.'

1970s A new generation of translators swells the Penguin Classics ranks, introducing readers of English to classics of world literature from more than twenty languages. The list grows to encompass more history, philosophy, science, religion and politics.

1980s The Penguin American Library launches with titles such as *Uncle Tom's Cabin*, and joins forces with Penguin Classics to provide the most comprehensive library of world literature available from any paperback publisher.

1990s The launch of Penguin Audiobooks brings the classics to a listening audience for the first time, and in 1999 the worldwide launch of the Penguin Classics website extends their reach to the global online community.

The 21st Century Penguin Classics are completely redesigned for the first time in nearly twenty years. This world-famous series now consists of more than 1300 titles, making the widest range of the best books ever written available to millions – and constantly redefining what makes a 'classic'.

The Odyssey continues ...

The best books ever written

PENGUIN CLASSICS

SINCE 1946

Find out more at www.penguinclassics.com